SEVENTH EDITION

STRATEGIC ORGANIZATIONAL COMMUNICATION IN A GLOBAL ECONOMY

CHARLES CONRAD AND MARSHALL SCOTT POOLE

WILEY-BLACKWELL
A John Wiley & Sons, Ltd., Publication

This seventh edition first published 2012

Blackwell Publishing was acquired by John Wiley & Sons in February 2007. Blackwell's publishing program has been merged with Wiley's global Scientific, Technical, and Medical business to form Wiley-Blackwell.

Edition History: Wadsworth (6e, 2005)

Registered Office
John Wiley & Sons Ltd, The Atrium, Southern Gate, Chichester, West Sussex, PO19 8SQ, UK

Editorial Offices
350 Main Street, Malden, MA 02148-5020, USA
9600 Garsington Road, Oxford, OX4 2DQ, UK
The Atrium, Southern Gate, Chichester, West Sussex, PO19 8SQ, UK

For details of our global editorial offices, for customer services, and for information about how to apply for permission to reuse the copyright material in this book please see our website at www.wiley.com/wiley-blackwell.

Library of Congress Cataloging-in-Publication Data

Conrad, Charles R.
Strategic organizational communication : in a global economy / Charles R. Conrad and Marshall Scott Poole. – 7th ed.
p. cm.
Includes bibliographical references and index.
ISBN 978-1-4443-3863-8 (pbk.)
1. Communication in organizations. 2. Communication in management. 3. Communication–Social aspects. I. Poole, Marshall Scott, 1951- II. Title.

HD30.3.C655 2012
658.4′5–dc23

2011042672

A catalogue record for this book is available from the British Library.

Set in 10/12 pt Minion by Toppan Best-set Premedia Limited
Printed and bound in Malaysia by Vivar Printing Sdn Bhd

1 2012

To:
Helen and Cecil,
who gave me a love of knowledge,
BJ,
who has given me knowledge of love,
and
Travis and Hannah,
our gifts of love.

To:
Ed, Helen, and Kim,
who are the foundation,
Lisa,
who built the home,
and
Sam,
who keeps it warm
with all my love.

CONTENTS

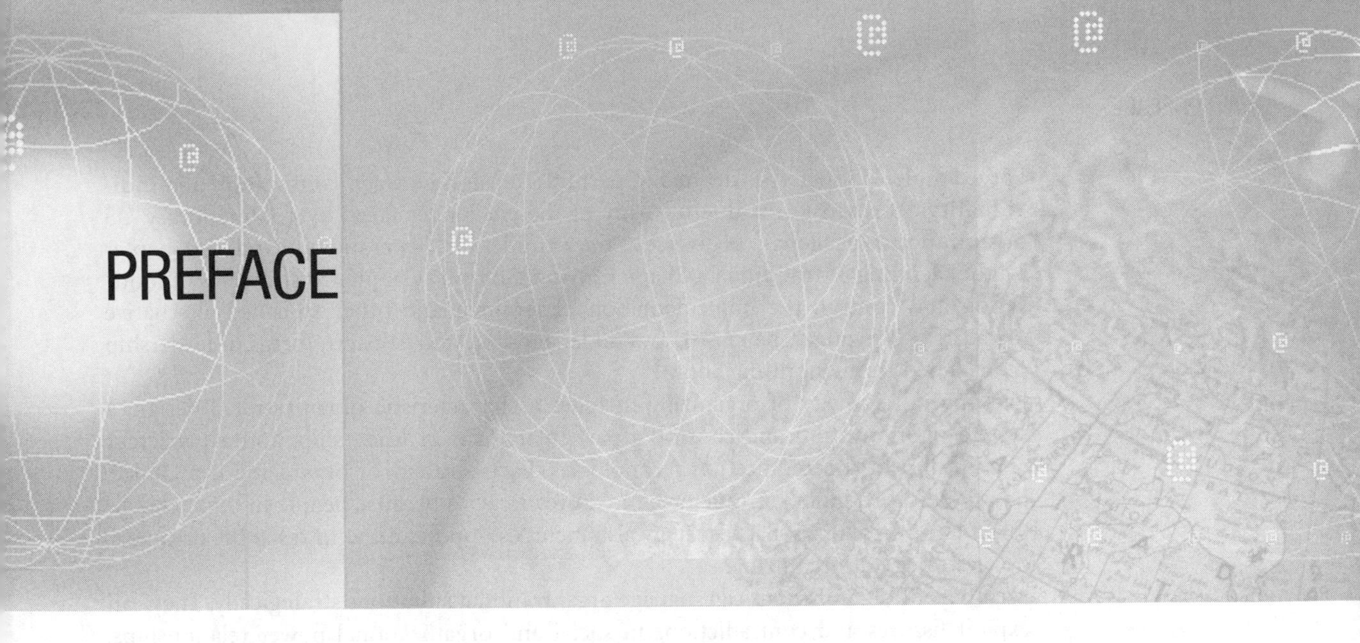

PREFACE

From its beginning more than 20 years ago, the goal of *Strategic Organizational Communication* has been to provide a unified description of the incredibly diverse array of ideas that make up our rapidly expanding field. Responses to the first six editions have been especially gratifying. Readers have been particularly complimentary about the level of sophistication of the book and its ability to integrate research from a number of academic disciplines. Responses to the later editions also have praised our efforts to place organizations and organizational communication within a broader social, economic, and cultural context and have appreciated our relaxed, engaging writing style. Of course, we have retained or expanded each of these characteristics.

We also have tried to maintain and strengthen the theoretical framework that has been central to the book since its inception. Each edition has focused on the two-level concept of *strategic choice making.* We believe that people make choices about the overall strategies that they will use to operate in the societies and organizations they will live within. Ironically, people tend to normalize and naturalize these choices, treating them as inviolable truths that need not be justified rather than as choices that are under their control. Eventually they institutionalize these taken-for-granted assumptions in social systems and organizational structures and practices that make some options *seem* to be the only "rational" choice and make others *seem* to be impossible. These overall choices, in turn, create the specific situations that people encounter every day– the challenges they face, the resources they have available to manage those challenges, and the guidelines and constraints that limit the options that are available to them. People adapt strategically to the situations that they create, but in adapting, they tend to reproduce those situations, creating a complicated cycle of acting, creating situations, and adapting.

Understanding this action–situation–adaptation cycle requires people to realize these things:

- Organizations are embedded in societies and cannot be understood outside of a society's beliefs, values, structures, practices, tensions, and ways of managing those tensions.

For example, US society is defined in part by a tension between **community** and **individuality**. This tension is due to many of the challenges faced by contemporary US organizations – challenges as diverse as the attitudes of "Generations X and Y" (Chapter 1), the blending of traditional (Chapter 3) and cultural (Chapter 5) strategies of motivation and control, the implementation of feminist and other so-called alternative forms of organizing (Chapter 6), and understanding non-Western forms of leadership (considered throughout the book).

- Each overall strategy of organizing includes a characteristic organizational design, a system of motivation and control, a particular form of leadership, and a particular relationship to communication technologies. Each strategy of organizing is a choice, however; for example, bureaucracies are bureaucracies because people in them choose to act like bureaucrats. Each strategy also includes opportunities to resist the organization's strategy of organizing.
- Members of organizations can manage organizational situations strategically. They can exploit fissures and contradictions in social and organizational power relationships. Even in the turbulent world created by the new, global economy, members of organizations can manage organizational situations in ways that achieve their personal goals and the goals of other members of their organizations.

RESPONDING TO READER SUGGESTIONS

Readers also have been very open about changes that they would like to see us make. As a result, each new edition really has been a *new* edition. This one is no exception.

The New and Improved

The most obvious change involves our efforts to locate organizational communication within the new, global economy. We started to focus on globalization in the fifth edition, and have increased that focus as the world economy has become progressively more interconnected. The same progression has been true of our treatment of communication technologies, and for the same reason – their importance continues to grow. Both concepts are woven through this edition because they are woven into the fabric of contemporary organizations. We also have added a chapter on "Organizational Change," since change is both the impetus and the outcome of strategic adaptation. We also have expanded the analysis of "Ethics and Organizational Rhetoric" (Chapter 12) that we introduced in the sixth edition, and have updated it to encompass the collapse of the world financial industry in 2007–2008, as well as subsequent taxpayer bailouts and the continuing Great Recession. We both have long been interested in ethical issues facing contemporary organizations, as evidenced in Charley's *The Ethical Nexus* (1993) and a special issue of *Communication Research* on "Communication in the Era of the Disposable Worker" that we coedited in 1997.

Other changes are more subtle, and each one reflects recent advances in organizational communication theory and research. Chapter 7 deals with dissent and employee resistance in more detail, and now includes an extended case study on bullying in organizations. Chapter 8 revises and reorganizes the discussion of decision making to reflect important new research related to bounded rationality as the "default mode" of decision making, and links it to processes of human evolution. Chapter 12 includes new case studies involving organizational ethics, and many of the cases that we have carried over from the sixth edition have been substantially revised. Eleven of the 24 case studies in this edition are new, and six of the ones we retained from the sixth edition have been revised. Copies of the cases we deleted from all previous editions will be available on the book's website (www.wiley.com/go/conradpoole).

Oldies but Goodies

There are two aspects of *Strategic Organizational Communication* that we never want to change. One is the extensive research base for the book. The bibliography for this edition is abbreviated in comparison to earlier editions, but as in earlier editions it identifies readings that are especially appropriate for graduate students. In general, we have focused on works published after 1990, and have cited earlier sources only if they are classics in organizational communication research and theory. As a result, the endnotes for each chapter provide a number of additional readings and web citations on virtually every facet of contemporary organizational communication research and theory.

The second aspect that we hope always to retain is the conceptual coherence of the analysis. Two beliefs underlie all that we say in this book. The first is that organizations (and societies) are *sites* in which various tensions and contradictions are negotiated through communication (this idea is explained at length in Chapter 1). The second belief is that understanding organizations and organizational communication requires an analysis of *both* symbolic *and* structural processes.

We realize that this both-and perspective is an anomalous position in a discipline that relishes either-or distinctions between functionalism and interpretivism, qualitative and quantitative research methods, and so on. We also realize that advocates of each of these polar terms often will feel that we are too sympathetic with the opposite pole and spend too little space examining their favored position. But we have consistently tried both to balance various perspectives and to indicate how each can be enriched by the key concepts of the others. Life is simply too complex for either-or thinking to capture its nuances; organizations are far too fluid and complicated for bimodal or trimodal paradigms to reveal much of importance.

ORGANIZATION OF THE BOOK

Like the earliest editions, this book is divided into three units. Unit I introduces the theoretical framework that unifies the book, develops the concept of *strategies of organizing*, and introduces the frame of reference for thinking about and analyzing organizations that will be utilized repeatedly in the remainder of the book. Unit II examines those strategies of organizing in more detail, discusses the communicative strategies that members of organizations might use to *strategically manage* the situations created by applications of those strategies of organizing, and offers a critical analysis of each. Unit II concludes with a discussion of contingency theories of organizing, and of the process of choosing among available strategies. Unit III examines key issues facing organizations during the early twenty-first century – organizational power and politics, organizational decision making and conflict, organizational change, issues related to workforce diversity, globalization, and ethics and organizational rhetoric.

THANKS

If they are to be effective, all communicative acts must be interactive. This dictum includes the writing of books. Consequently, our greatest vote of thanks goes to the many readers of the earlier editions who made thoughtful and valuable suggestions for improvement. Of the advice that we received on the different drafts of this edition, the comments of many colleagues were exceptionally helpful: Linda Putnam, George Cheney, Kathy Miller, Kevin Barge, Ted Zorn, Steve Corman, Bob McPhee, John Lammers, Peter Monge, Janet Fulk, Joe Folger, Michelle Shumate, and Trina Wright are constant sources of exciting new ideas. Our students are a constant source of insightful questions and valuable suggestions, and one, Elizabeth Odom, wrote much of the "On Death and Dying" case study in Chapter 7. A number of anonymous reviewers made many helpful comments for this new edition. The editorial staff at Wiley-Blackwell provided superb support at all stages of this project. We would like to express our deep appreciation to Elizabeth Swayze, Julia Kirk, Allison Kostka, and Margot Morse, and also to freelances Matthew Brown, Cheryl Adam, and Alta Bridges, for project management, copy-editing, and proofreading respectively. Private encouragement was provided by Betty Webber Conrad and Lisa O'Dell, and Travis, Hannah, and Sam helped us keep our priorities straight.

Charles Conrad
College Station, Texas
Marshall Scott Poole
Urbana, Illinois
June 2011

UNIT I

UNDERLYING CONCEPTS

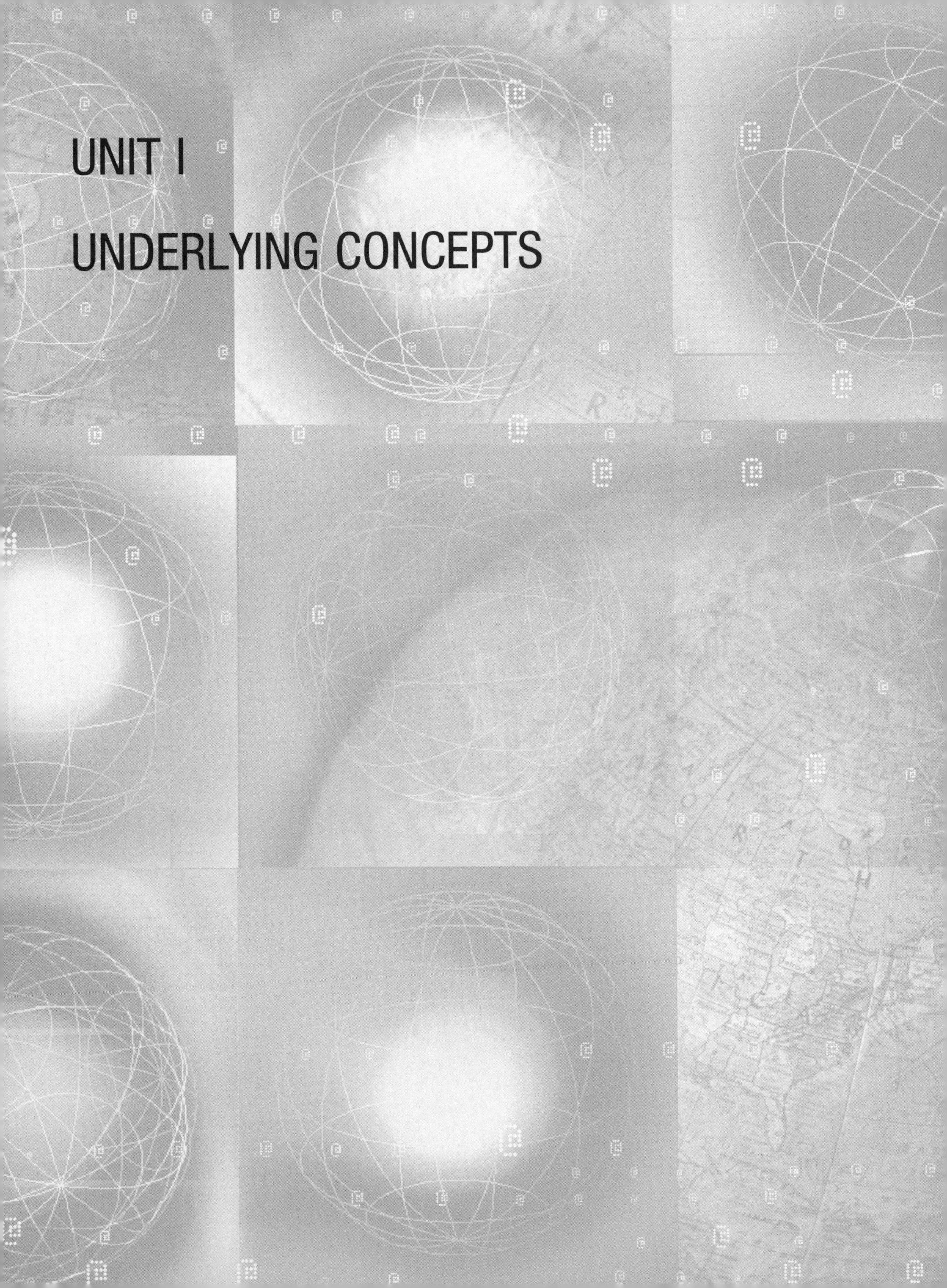

CHAPTER 1

STRATEGIC ORGANIZATIONAL COMMUNICATION

Don't ask me. I just work here.
Anonymous

We must hold a man [sic] amenable to reason for the choice of his daily craft or profession. It is not an excuse any longer for his deed that they are the custom of his trade. What business has he with an evil trade?

Ralph Waldo Emerson

[H]istory matters. . . . What comes first (even if it was in some sense "accidental") conditions what comes later. Individuals [policy makers] may "choose these institutions, but they do not choose them under circumstances of their own making, and their choices in turn influence the rules within which their successors choose.

Carolyn Tuohy

CENTRAL THEMES

- Organizational communication is strategic in two senses. Organizations emerge from strategic choices about how they will be designed and operated. These choices create the situations that employees encounter at work. Employees must then make their own strategic choices about how to manage those situations.
- Societies and organizations face a fundamental paradox. They must control and coordinate the activities of their members. But doing so frustrates their members' needs for autonomy, creativity, and sociability.

Strategic Organizational Communication: In a Global Economy, Seventh Edition.
Charles Conrad and Marshall Scott Poole.

- Organizations are designed through conscious choices among a number of strategies of organizing. Employees make their own choices about how to communicate within the guidelines and constraints created by those strategies of organizing. By doing so, they reproduce the strategies, the guidelines, and the constraints.

KEY TERMS

blended relationships
reification
autonomy needs
creativity needs
sociability needs
stability/predictability needs
specialization
deconstruct
legitimize
unintended consequences
coercive influence
social institution
normative influence
mimetic influence

At one time or another, almost everyone has responded to the question "How did this (disaster) happen?" with a statement like "Don't ask me. I just work here." In some cases the excuse is legitimate. The person giving the answer is not allowed by his or her organization to make even simple decisions or take any initiative. "I just work here" means that the person knows the answer or is aware of a solution to the problem but has too little power to make the necessary changes. In other cases, someone else failed to inform the person of the policy, problem, or procedure that is in question. "I just work here" means that the speaker simply does not have the information needed to answer the question. But sometimes the person did act in ways that caused the problem, and the response is merely an excuse. Although viable excuses are often available in organizations, in the final analysis it is an employee's own choices that create the situations she or he faces.[1]

This book is about the choices and choice-making behaviors of members of formal organizations. It concentrates on communication because it is through communication that employees obtain information, make sense of the situations they encounter, and decide how to act. And, it is by communicating that employees translate their choices into action. Organizations must maintain at least an adequate level of communication effectiveness to survive and prosper. People who have developed an understanding about how communication functions in an organization, who have developed a wide repertory of written and oral communication skills, and who have learned when and how to use those skills seem to have more successful careers and contribute more fully to their organizations than people who have not done so.

As a result, the number of college courses and professional training programs concerned with organizational communication has mushroomed. Of course, employees cannot function effectively unless they possess the technical skills that their positions require. But more and more it appears that being able to recognize, diagnose, and solve communication-related problems is vital to the success of people in even the most technical occupations. Accountants must be able to gain complete, accurate, and sometimes sensitive information from their clients. Supervisors of production lines must be able to obtain adequate and timely information on which to base their decisions. Managers of all divisions must be able to give their subordinates clear instructions, make sure those instructions are understood, create conditions in which their commands will be carried out, and obtain reliable feedback about the completion of the tasks that they have assigned.[2]

Understanding organizational communication has advantages above and beyond career advancement. At many times during their careers, people feel powerless because they simply do not understand the events taking place around them and/or do not know how to deal with those events. In the worst cases they are victimized by those events and do not understand how they became victims. As the title of a popular book says, bad things do happen to good people (and vice versa), both in our lives as a whole and in our organizations. People need to be able to take a critical perspective on organizational events, that is, they need to be able to examine the situations they find themselves in and understand the many pressures and constraints that make up those situations. People can learn from their experiences only if they understand the situations they face and the communicative strategies that they could have used to manage them more effectively. In short, understanding organizational communicative processes is itself empowering – it allows people to determine which events are their responsibility and which events are outside of their control and to discover new strategies that they could have used successfully.

The primary goal of the book is to give readers a sense of how organizational communication is used strategically, that is, how employees can analyze the organizational situations they face and choose appropriate communication strategies. It assumes that all employees are goal oriented and that if they understand how communication functions in their organizations they will be better able to achieve their objectives and those of their organizations. It explains when it is appropriate to use a variety of communication strategies, including the denial of responsibility and the claim of ignorance ("Don't ask me. I just work here"), and, as important, when not to use them. In this chapter, we will introduce the core concept that underlies the rest of the book. We will observe that organizational communication is *strategic* and explain the two dimensions of that concept. As the book progresses, this concept will become clearer and clearer.

ORGANIZATIONAL COMMUNICATION AS STRATEGIC DISCOURSE

One way to understand a complicated phenomenon is to begin with definitions of key terms. The simplest definition of organizational communication is that it is communication that occurs within organizations, but that definition is not very informative. Communication is generally defined as a process through which people, acting together, create, sustain, and manage meanings through the use of verbal and nonverbal signs and symbols within a particular context. Of course, the key terms in this definition are people, acting together, meaning, and context. In even a simple conversation, individuals bring a number of things with them. They each have histories of past conversations with one another or with people they perceive as similar to the other person. For example, conversations with one's boss are in some ways influenced by one's past conversations with bosses and other authority figures. They also bring expectations about future conversations with one another, goals for the conversation and for their relationship, assumptions about how people are supposed to communicate with one another, different kinds and levels of communicative skills, and so on.

During every conversation people create and exchange a complex set of messages with one another and in doing so create meanings for each message and for the interaction. Some of the meanings that are created during interactions are consistent with the communicators' intentions; others are not. People create systems of meaning together, and those meaning systems influence their impressions of one another, their interpretations of their relationship, and their selection of communication strategies in future interactions. As their conversations continue, their goals may change as they discover that the other person is more (or less) sympathetic to their position than they expected the person to be. Similarly, their understanding of the best ways to communicate with the people around them also emerges over time through successful (and unsuccessful) interactions.

For example, one of our graduate students studied a committee that was charged with designing guidelines for the sex education program of a city school district. To represent both sides of the issue, the committee was composed of some members who were "liberal" in the sense that they supported a fairly extensive sex education program and others who were "conservative" and were opposed to most types of current sex education programs. Both the liberal and conservative subgroups came to the first meeting of the committee with little direct knowledge of one another. But each thought they knew what the others would be like based on their interpretations of the public debate in the United States over teenage sexuality and abortion. Conservatives feared that the liberals would want a program that encouraged sexual promiscuity among teenagers and would advocate abortion as a primary method of birth control; liberals were convinced that the conservatives would want a program that gave students little information and a great deal of fear and guilt.

During an early meeting, the conservative group gave a number of long speeches arguing that the district's sex education program should persuade students to abstain from sexual activity. To both the liberal and conservative groups' surprise, everyone in the room agreed. Although it took a while for the two groups to recover from the shock of finding that they agreed on something important, the rest of the committee's deliberations were different than they otherwise would have been. They continued to be suspicious of one another, but at least they listened to one another. In doing so, they discovered many other areas of disagreement and some additional areas of agreement. By communicating with one another over a six-month period, the committee members created, sustained, and modified a system of meaning that was uniquely their own. Their discussions were always influenced by the context in which they took place, both the local situation faced by the school board and the national debate over sexual issues. But the messages they exchanged and the meanings that they attributed to those messages could only be understood within the communicative process that they created (Legg, 1992). In short, people with varying degrees of communicative skills acted together through the use of verbal and nonverbal cues to create, sustain, and modify systems of meaning. That is, they communicated.

Our definition of *organizational* communication differs from this general definition of communication primarily in terms of its complexity. Organizational relationships are both like and unlike "normal" interpersonal relationships. We communicate with people at work because our assigned tasks require us to do so. Sometimes we like them and would communicate with them even if our tasks did not require us to do so; sometimes we talk with them only because we have to. Our relationships at work have *both* an interpersonal and an organizational dimension. As later chapters will explain, we constantly have to negotiate an appropriate mix of these two dimensions. We may have a strong personal relationship with our supervisor, but have to maintain the kind of relational distance, detachment, and subservience that are appropriate to our organizational relationship. We may like one of our subordinates very much, but his or her inability to do the job well creates constant stresses in our interpersonal relationship. Work relationships are like "regular" interpersonal relationships, but they also are different.

Case Study 1.1

How to Handle the Scarlet Email?

In some ways, the interpersonal relationships that we form at work are like the other interpersonal relationships that we form throughout our lives. But in other ways they are different.[1] Natural relationships seem to be voluntary – we encounter people, discover that we are attracted to one another, and begin to develop a relationship. We learn about them, develop expectations about how they will act, and begin to trust them when those expectations are fulfilled. If they violate our expectations, we interpret their behavior as a negative comment on them or as a negative comment on our relationship. If the relationship continues, we develop psychological contracts about how we will act and communicate toward one another, and we try to ensure that those contracts are understood by both parties. The nature of our relationships is influenced by our relational histories and our anticipated future, and by our expectation that our relationships should be mutually fulfilling. We continue them because they fulfill what leadership expert Fredric Jablin called "psychological-individual" functions.

Being members of the same organization complicates the relationships in many ways. Since we spend so much of our time at work, we are likely to form close relationships with some of our coworkers. But, many organizational relationships are imposed on us, at least initially. We accept them because we have to do so in order to do our jobs well. Sometimes these involuntary relationships are with people we like, and would have voluntarily formed relationships with on our own. Others are with people we would avoid like the plague if we were able to do so (Hess, 2000). In addition, differences in power and status complicate our work relationships – buying lunch for someone in the next cubicle does not mean the same thing as buying lunch for the vice president of sales or one of a person's subordinates. We communicate differently with people of different power and status, and we expect to be treated differently by them. Third, organizational role relationships complicate work relationships. Friends usually provide comfort and support to one another. But supervisors are required to evaluate their subordinates' work (and in some organizations, subordinates also evaluate their supervisors), and doing so may involve uncomfortable assessments of one another's competence, performance, and personality. Working relationships are also complicated by a "fishbowl" effect; they are public in a way that natural relationships are not.

The work situation also complicates normal aspects of relationships. All friends have to balance autonomy and connectedness – too much autonomy and the friends feel emotionally distant from one another, or too little and one or more of them feels "smothered." If friends work together, their jobs may require them to spend *too much* time together or to work *too closely*. Friends in voluntary relationships also can be relatively open and honest with one another because of their mutual trust. But, organizational roles often require people to keep information secret, even from their closest friends. So, for a number of reasons, the **blended relationships** that people form at work are more complicated than natural relationships. As they develop, some work relationships become close friendships because the parties are attracted to one another, as well as because they help one another solve work-related problems. Some coworkers become trusted confidantes, and communication with them becomes more personal and less cautious. Eventually some coworkers become an important part of one another's personal life.

These complications are easiest to see in romantic relationships at work. Most experts on office etiquette still advise people to keep romance out of their careers. Nevertheless, about 40 percent of workers admit to dating a colleague, a figure that has remained relatively stable for the past few years, and attitudes about doing so have softened enough that today two thirds of employees involved in relationships with coworkers no longer feel a need to hide them. Curiously, the percentage has increased to more than 50 percent during the Great Recession. The risks are higher, since losing one's job due to a romance gone bad is a bigger problem with high levels of unemployment. But, alternative sources of connection are expensive, and when budgets are tight people forgo the expenses of clubbing – trendy clothes, transportation, and bar tabs. A veritable cottage industry of publications has popped up providing "how to" advice for dating coworkers – items in *Glamour* and *Cosmo*, of course, and on websites of AskMen.com, *Forbes*, and *Inc.*, as well as popular books with salacious titles such as *Office Romance: Love, Power and Sex in the Workplace* or *Officemate: Your Employee Handbook for Romance on the Job*.[2] With people working 50–60-hour weeks, they simply do not have the time or opportunity to look elsewhere for romantic partners. Perhaps more importantly, people can gather accurate information about a potential mate by working with him or her – much more than they can learn at a singles' bar, from a classified ad, or through an online dating service (all of which have their own complications).

Most office romances involve people at different levels of the organizational hierarchy (about 70 percent). The riskiest pairings involve married, male supervisors and single, female subordinates. Most workplace romances seem to be based on "true love" rather than on job- or advancement-related motives (about 80 percent). In general, research indicates that romances do not harm organizational performance, unless they generate such a high level of gossip that it interferes with task performance. But, obviously, perceptions of favoritism are more likely for employees involved in a romantic relationship with their supervisors. Gossip and discomfort among coworkers are extremely likely. If the parties terminate their relationship, it is awkward to see one's ex every day (Dillard and Miller, 1993; Dillard, Hale, and Segrin, 1993; deWine, Pearson, and Yost, 1993).

A few organizations have formal, written policies that forbid dating between supervisors and their subordinates, and more than 70 percent of employees say that people should never date their bosses or people who report to them, although about 15 percent do so anyway. However, 70 percent of organizations have no official policies, so the rules can be very ambiguous. The most common, unwritten rule seems to be "Date anyone you want, but if it starts to cause trouble for your supervisor or work group, you'll be in big trouble."[3] There are a number of commonsense steps that people can take to manage the complications created by office romances (this advice assumes that both parties are single). First, all employees should learn their supervisor's and organization's view of workplace relationships. This information may be available through informal channels, but once a relationship becomes serious, a frank conversation with one's supervisors is warranted (it's almost always best for partners to coordinate the timing of these conversations). Second, decide when and how to go public. Advisors differ on this issue. Some say that it's best to come clean about the relationship immediately after the talk with your supervisor. Others say that keeping it private is the best strategy. Your goal should be to minimize hearsay and innuendo, and *especially* to make sure your relationship does not interfere with your work. In some situations, those goals can best be achieved by keeping quiet; in others, the honest approach is less disruptive. If the relationship does become a problem for the organization, the job of the lower-ranked partner (or least difficult-to-replace partner) is most at risk. Third, be discreet. Always maintain a professional relationship at work. Richard Phillips, a career counselor in Palo Alto, California, reminds employees that "what you consider to be lovey dovey [interaction] between the two of you may make your coworkers [want to] retch. You're forcing them into a situation they don't want to be in" (quoted in Eng, March 14, 1999). Don't hold hands in the hallway, play footsie at meetings, or anything else that is perfectly appropriate in romantic relationships but completely inappropriate in professional relationships. And make sure your partner knows that your "aloof" behavior at work is not an indication that you're cold and uncaring toward him or her. Finally, have an exit plan. Discuss what the two of you will do if the relationship ends. Of course, these conversations are about as romantic as negotiating a prenuptial agreement, but they are just as important. Then do it.[4]

Washington Post columnist Marc Fisher once wrote a column that vividly described how awkward office romances can be to coworkers. One of his coworkers accidentally sent him an email that was meant for her romantic partner, probably by clicking the wrong line of her address book directory. The message started out in a friendly tone, but very quickly became erotic. To make things worse, Marc knew the woman and her husband (who was *not* the recipient of the message); in fact he had been invited to their home for dinner that night. What should he do? Respond in a businesslike tone: "Your message of 9:46 on Sunday morning was misdirected to me. Have a good day"? Notify the husband of what was going on? Keep quiet? Find some excuse for canceling the dinner date? He asked his friends for advice (so much for the secrecy of email). Most of the women told him to stay out of it; most of the men wanted him to find out all the sordid details and then tell them all about it (so much for the myth that only women are interested in gossip). He decided to do nothing.

Then, another message arrived, one that was even more intimate than the first. He went to dinner, sat between husband and wife, and felt very nervous throughout the evening. He squirmed during a private after-dinner conversation when the husband told everyone about his dreams for the couple's future years together. Fisher went home rattled and vowed to not have anything more to do with either of them. Then he went to a stationery store and bought note cards and envelopes – a more appropriate medium for private messages (Fisher, June 1, 1999).

Applying What You've Learned

1. In what ways did the characters in Fisher's account violate the advice typically given to romantic partners in organizations? In what ways did they follow it?
2. Would a formal organizational policy about office romances have prevented this problem? What effects did the romance seem to have on the functioning of the organization?

Questions to Think About and Discuss

1. What would you have done had you been in Marc Fisher's place? What should you have done had you been in his place?
2. What does your answer to question 1 reveal about your personal values? And about your view of the extent to which you have different values for working relationships at work than for nonwork relationships?

Notes

1 See Bridge and Baxter (1992); Winstead, Derlega, Montgomery, and Pilkington (1995); and Sias and Cahill (1998). Jablin (2001) makes the distinction between these two functions.
2 The recession data are from Losee and Olen (2010); also see Mainiero (1989).
3 Cautionary tales are provided by Weinstein (2008) and Powers (1999).
4 See note 1.

Just as we create relationships through conversation, we also create "organizations." Thirty years ago, scholars thought of organizations as "things" or "containers" within which people sent chunks of information to one another through stable "channels" or "conduits" in order to meet shared goals. There is a grain of truth in this view. In fact, it is the view of communication that characterizes the traditional strategy of organizing that we will examine in Chapter 3. But, the container or conduit perspective has three weaknesses. First, it oversimplifies communication by reducing it to simple information exchange. Second, it depicts organizations as much stabler than they really are. Third, it depicts employees as relatively inactive automatons who routinely react to the messages they receive. By the late 1970s organizational theorists started to view organizations as dynamic, ever-changing groups of people who were actively trying to make sense out of the events that took place around them, while pursuing their own individual goals as well as goals they shared with their coworkers. At the same time organizational communication theorists started viewing communication as more than the transfer of information, but as a complex, multidimensional process through which organizing took place (Putnam, Phillips, and Chapman, 1996; Weick, 1979).

During the late 1990s, an influential group of organizational communication scholars went even farther, arguing that organizing and conversing are the same thing. Through communicating, we create shared views of organizational life. A group of people does not become a "work group," much less a "team," until members start talking about themselves in those terms. Once they do that, they start thinking of themselves as a "group" or "department" or "organization." Once that happens, the collective takes on something of a life of its own. We talk about "what this organization does" or declare that the "auditing committee says" or "the legal department thinks" as if *organizations* can act, *committees* can speak, or *departments* can think, when it is the people who make up those groups who do all of those things. Communication theorists use the term **reification** to describe this process through which people come to think of something that *they* have created as having its own identity, existence, and power. In organizational settings, reification is one of the most important dimensions of communication. For example, it is much more difficult to question the decisions of "the auditing committee" than it is to disagree with "John, Julie, Fred, and those folks from Arthur Andersen who they hired to go over the books with them." It also is much more likely that an employee will be seen as credible when she or he speaks for "the organization" than when he or she speaks for himself or herself alone. In fact, the miracle of organizational communication processes is that they allow large numbers of people from very different backgrounds, ways of thinking, needs, and goals to coordinate their actions and create "organizations" that at least *seem* to be stable containers within which information flows from person to person (Cooren and Taylor 1997; Taylor and van Every, 2000).

THE FUNDAMENTAL PARADOX

The concept of strategy enters into our perspective on organizational communication at two levels. One level is that of the organization. Most people have learned to think of organizations as places where large numbers of members efficiently cooperate with one another to achieve some shared objectives. According to this view, disagreements, conflicts, inefficiencies, and communication breakdowns are avoidable evils – failures that could have been avoided had the organization and its members only worked the way they are supposed to work. They should happen very rarely, and when they do, members of the organization should dispassionately analyze their causes and take corrective actions.

In this book we will take a very different perspective. We will suggest that the notion that organizations normally run like "well-oiled machines" not only is unrealistic but also can be damaging to organizations and to their members. It is more realistic, and in the long run more productive, to view organizations as sites in which multiple tensions exist. They are not aberrations, but are inevitable aspects of the way organizations function and the way people function within organizations. They must constantly be managed if the organization is to succeed in meeting its members' goals. Some organizations experience more internal tension than others; and some are more often in conflict with members of other organizations and the surrounding society. But all organizations face at least one *fundamental tension*: a tension between individual members' needs and the needs of their organizations. People have needs for **autonomy** (the feeling that they are in control of their actions and destinies), **creativity** (feelings of pride that comes from making something that did not previously exist or in doing something better than or in a different way than anyone else), and **sociability** (the feeling that they have meaningful interpersonal relationships with other people). They also need an adequate degree of structure, **stability**, and **predictability** in their lives. They need to know who they are, where they fit in their organizations and society, and how they and their peers are likely to act in different circumstances.

Organizations also have needs that must be met. The most important of these are control and coordination. Organizations exist because the tasks that people must perform are sufficiently complex that members must cooperate with one another to achieve their goals. In essence, organizations require us to sacrifice some of our independence – our ability to be self-sufficient – and replace it with interdependence. In modern societies, few persons have the skills, experience, or opportunities to do everything personally that are necessary to live a productive life. Most modern people actually can do very little. We are constantly at the mercy of electricians, plumbers, appliance-repair technicians, auto mechanics, and organizations in which we work. What people can do, we do very well. Modern human beings have traded independence for **specialization** and have become far more efficient as a result. But our efficiency depends almost wholly on coordinating our activities with the activities of others. Different cultures vary in the degree of interdependence that exists within them, as do different organizations and the various departments within them. Research-and-development divisions usually have low interdependence, relying only on computer operators, purchasing and receiving departments (which order and deliver raw materials), and the physical plant operators (who keep equipment secure and functioning). For them, coordination within the division is crucial; coordinating their activities with outsiders is less important. For other divisions, coordination is a more complex and critical problem. But to some degree, all organizations need to coordinate their members' activities.

Organizations also need to control their members' interpersonal relationships, in terms of both who they form relationships with and how they communicate within their work relationships. Some version of the military command that officers cannot "fraternize" with enlisted personnel exists within almost all organizations, and enforces the rule by transferring offenders to different departments. But, they may not restrict dating among one's peers, as long as the members are discreet and the relationship does not get in the way of task performance. Others forbid any romantic relationships among any members of the same department; a few forbid them with anyone in the same organization. Often the command is never spoken because it need not be. Sometimes these informal rules are more specific. Associates (recent graduates) in law firms learn by observation that they should not initiate conversations with senior partners, but should respond immediately when partners initiate communication with them. Assembly workers at Dana Corporation learn that they are expected to have lunch with upper management, and individuals in upper management learn that they are expected to have friendly but relatively superficial interpersonal relationships with rank-and-file workers. In both cases, the organization subtly controls the kind of interpersonal relationships that employees form and maintain. Organizations do vary in how tightly they control their members' actions and relationships, but all organizations must exercise at least a minimal level of control if they are to survive.

However, these two sets of needs – those of a society or organization and those of their individual members – create a fundamental paradox. If a society or organization successfully controls its members, the individual needs for autonomy, creativity, and sociability are frustrated. But, if the society or organization fails to control its members, it loses the ability to coordinate its members' activities, and fails. So, societies or organizations must find ways to meet their members' individual needs while persuading them to act in ways that meet the society or organization's needs. They do so through adopting various *strategies of organizing.* Conversely, if members of organizations are to meet their own needs, they must find ways to *communicate strategically* within the situations they face in their organizations. This book is about this fundamental paradox, and the role that communication plays in managing it.

THINKING STRATEGICALLY ABOUT ORGANIZING AND COMMUNICATING

For more than 2000 years, communication scholars have believed that people communicate most effectively if they adapt their communication strategies to the situations they face.[3] To communicate effectively, employees must be able to analyze the situations they encounter in their organizations, determine which communication strategies are available to them in those situations, select the best of those strategies, and enact them effectively. However, selecting appropriate communicative strategies is a challenging process. All organizational situations contain rules that tell employees how they are supposed to act and communicate. Some of these rules guide and *constrain* their actions – they are the secular equivalent of the commandments in theologies. Other rules provide members of an organization with *resources* that they can draw up to achieve their goals – interpersonal relationships and commitments, shared interests, potential lines of argument, acceptable forms of persuasive appeal, and so on.[4] After entering a society or organization, people begin to learn these rules through communicating. Although some members may have a better understanding of them than others, everyone is sufficiently knowledgeable to successfully navigate the situations they face. But, this does not mean that the process of communicating in strategically appropriate ways is either simple or easy.

For example, one of the most common comments that newcomers to an organization hear is "That's just not how we do things here" (we will discuss the experiences of new employees at length in Chapter 5). Most will respond with a comment such as "OK, so that's how to do this task; thanks for the information." But, think carefully about the comment, about what it says and what it does not say (the fancy term is to **deconstruct** it), and about the range of responses that are possible. It implies that there are expectations in place regarding how an employee is to act and/or how a task is to be performed. It also implies that these expectations are not random, but have emerged and developed over time, and have been accepted by other employees. Organizations have histories, and part of those histories are a set of rules and resources that have been **legitimized** as the *natural* (that is, obvious and beyond debate) and *normal* (that is, expected and morally correct) ways to do things. There may or may not be any rational basis for them – as we explain in Chapter

2, there always are many different ways to achieve the same goal – but they are *treated* as being rational and true in a particular organization at a particular point in time. The comment also implies that the newcomer will not be accepted as a legitimate member of the organization unless she or he learns, accepts, and practices those guidelines and constraints. That is, if the newcomer is going to become part of the "we" in the statement, they must start "doing things in this way." It implies that the two people involved in the conversation also have their own individual histories. Differences in their life, work, or other experiences may simplify or complicate their working together. The comment also may imply something about the current employee's expectations about their future together. Oldtimers have little incentive to take the time and effort needed to teach newcomers unless they expect them to be working together for some time, something that interns and temporary employees often discover the hard way (Gossett, 2001, 2008). So, every conversation is embedded in both the past (history, rules, and resources) and the future (expectations).

But, most important, the comment says something about the *power relationship* that exists between the two employees. The oldtimer is acting *as if* she or he has the legitimate *right* to correct and teach the newcomer. It is not clear from the comment why this is so – being older, having more organizational experience, occupying a superior position in the organizational hierarchy, and a host of other attributes may have become legitimate bases for domination in this particular organization. It is not even clear that the oldtimer actually believes that he or she is superior. The comment may be an effort to *establish* a superior power position. It invites the newcomer to accept a subordinate position, but it does not guarantee that he or she will do so. The power relationship will depend on the newcomer's response. The most common response ("OK, so that's how to do this task; thanks for the information") says that the newcomer accepts his or her inferior position in the power relationship, accepts the oldtimer's *right* to tell the newcomer what to do and how to do it, and accepts the assumption that the advice given really does explain the "right" (legitimate, wise, efficient, or other form of "correctness") way to do the task.[5] The response "I know that's how this task has been done for years, but I learned in school and my internship that there's a much better way to do it" challenges the oldtimer's assertion that she or he is legitimately the newcomer's superior, challenges the "rightness" (correctness) or the advice and instruction, and may even challenge the definition of power that has been legitimized in the organization by placing "book learning" or "having a new perspective" above experience, seniority, or tradition. Of course, the interchange will not be complete until after both parties respond to their initial exchange. We will explain all of this in more detail in Chapter 8, but at this point it is important to realize that every conversation in an organization conjures up rules of "right" in both senses of the term – who has the right (power) to dominate and what kinds of statements are treated as "right" (correct) – and derives its meaning and importance from the *interaction* between the parties, rather than from an individual comment.[6] Organizational situations, and the communication produced within them, are embedded in time and permeated with power.

The comment also suggests that situations and communication are embedded in "space." But, the term "space" is a deceptively simple term because it encompasses physical location, economic role, and political positioning. It includes the site(s) of a particular organization, of course (we are "here," at Amalgamated Tool and Die, for example). But, it also is a statement about where the organization is located in the economy. For example, is it a for-profit, or not-for-profit firm? Does it operate in the private sector or is it a governmental agency or NGO (nongovernmental organization)? What sector of the economy does it operate within? Does it act locally, or only within one state or province, or regionally, or throughout its home country, or internationally? Is it a marginal "player," or does it dominate its sector of the economy, or the economy of its city, state, region, nation, and so on? How much political power does it have, and at what levels (local, state, national, and/or international)? The answers to these questions are important because they contribute to the set of rules and resources that organizations and their members have available to them. In the remainder of this chapter, we will examine this multilayered concept of space, and explain how it guides and constrains strategic organizational communication. For an extended illustration of the concepts developed in this section, see Case Study 1.2.

Case Study 1.2

Can You Trust Anyone Under Thirty?

When managers, professors, and reporters think about workforce diversity, they usually think in terms of race, gender, ethnicity, or nationality. Each of these sources of difference is important, and we will examine them in detail in Unit III. But, an often-overlooked source of difference in today's organizations involves age, and the experiences that accompany being part of a particular generation. The most common contrast is among the baby boomers, who were born between 1946 and 1964; Generation X, born between 1969 and 1979; and the Y-generation or Millennials. Boomers were raised in the post-World War II era of social stability and relative prosperity. Divorce was relatively rare; schools were safe, and jobs secure. Single-earner households with a clear division of labor between men and women were normal, for perhaps the only time in US history. Their fathers and role models were the "organization men" described in William Whyte's 1956 book by the same name, and dramatized in the popular TV series *Mad Men*. They were loyal to their organizations, learned to pay their dues patiently and wait for the opportunity for advancement, and largely defined themselves and their success in terms of their organizational rank. It was an era during which white-collar workers in US organizations believed and acted as if they had an unspoken contract with their organizations. If they worked hard, were loyal and productive employees, and followed the rules of their organizations, they expected to stay with their organizations as long as they chose to do so, to be rewarded for their contributions, and eventually to be supported during their golden years by an adequate pension.[1]

In contrast, Xers, who now make up about one third of the US workforce, grew up in two-career families, where divorce rates were increasing rapidly. They are the products of daycare; technology, including television; and, perhaps most important, downsizing. From 1985 until 1995, the Xers' formative years, two thirds of white-collar employees experienced downsizing or major restructuring. The fastest growing sector of the labor market between 1990 and 1995 was the category of temp and employment agencies. (The next fastest growing categories were restaurants and bars, local government, recreation, and hospitals.) Richard Florida, a Carnegie Mellon University professor who studies employee retention, observes that Xers (and Millennials) "expect corporate disloyalty. A 24- or 25-year old says, 'I am responsible for my own life. No one's going to take care of me, [I know] because they threw my dad out of work'" (Franken, 2000). Adding to the fear and insecurities that Xers' parents felt was a growing resentment that stems from the disparity between skyrocketing firm profits and upper-management incomes and the experiences of both white-collar and blue-collar workers. Average worker pay rose 28 percent between 1990 and 1998, only 5.5 percent faster than the inflation rate. But average compensation of the top two managers in large companies rose 481 percent over the same time period. Consequently, the ratio of the base salaries of CEOs of US firms to their average employee's salary in 1992 was 140:1 compared to 15:1 in Germany, 13:1 in Japan. In 1995, the ratio in the United States rose to 187:1 overall and 212:1 at the 30 largest US companies; in 1999, the ratio was approximately 350:1; and in 2008, it was around 500:1 (1000:1 in the largest US firms), even though there is very little evidence that CEO salaries are related to organizational performance. Over the course of a single decade, the 1990s, CEO pay jumped 535 percent, five times the increase in corporate profits and 17 times the increase in average worker pay. Had the average pay for US factory workers increased at the same rate as it did for CEOs between 1989 and 1999, it would have been $114,035 at the end of the period (instead of $23,753); had the federal minimum wage increased at the same rate it would have been $24.13 instead of $5.15. These trends *accelerated* in the United States during the first decade of the new century.[2]

As a result everywhere Xers are advised to "consider themselves to be free agents," keep their résumés polished, and keep their network connections alert to opportunities in other firms. They must plan their own careers, and seek out opportunities to develop new, marketable skills and opportunities to grow. And they seem to be listening. Traditional values like long-term commitment and loyalty to the firm aren't very popular with them. They refuse to make the kinds of sacrifices that their parents made – being subservient to their bosses, accepting multiple cross-country moves, putting in long hours, or accepting overnight travel. They are fiercely independent, aggressive, hardworking entrepreneurs, even if they are working in corporate structures. They concentrate on developing computer, leadership, and communication skills, in part to make them valuable to their current firms, but also as a means of going out on their own as soon as possible. They move on quickly, voluntarily changing jobs nine times by the time they're in their thirties. They are willing to take the risks of self-employment or job changes to get the greater rewards and freedom that accompany being their own bosses. But they also tend to form relatively superficial and inauthentic relationships in the workplace. Knowing that they may not be around very long, they make little investment in getting to know their supervisors and coworkers as people, and their supervisors and coworkers spend little energy getting to know them. This makes it easier to exit the organization – they can do so without leaving close friends or commitments behind – and makes it more likely that they will do so. Ironically they need to be given clear road maps about organizational life, and want lots of performance feedback.

The Boomers and Xers do have one thing in common – they increasingly have to work with an even younger generation. Alternatively labeled the "Y Generation," "Next Generation," or "Millennials," they were born between 1980 and 2002. There are more of them (81 million) than any generation in US history save the Boomers (87 million). While teenagers they had more disposable income than any group in US history, and they also are more technologically sophisticated. Millennials seem to accept both the traditional values of hard work and individualism – in one poll, 94 percent said they shared their parents' values – *and* share the Xers' self-reliance and mistrust of organizations and other institutions. They trust their established interpersonal relationships (families and long-term friendships), and their extensive competence using electronic technologies allows them to maintain those nonwork relationships, even over long distances. One of the best examples of this is the development of "helicopter parenting," although the most interesting question about the phenomenon involves the children, not the parents: why does this group of adolescents and young adults, who presumably are psychologically wired to be *separating* from their parents, so happily accept, even encourage, them to helicopter? The answer seems to be simple – they need to maintain the relationships they trust.

Millennials also seem to rely on themselves – their ability to plan their own lives and strategically adapt to the situations they face. They are team oriented, but realize that the relationships formed in organizational teams are transient, and focused on tasks, not people. So, they see relationships formed at work as means to other ends, not as something to be cultivated for their own sake. They are optimistic, but it is an optimism based on their self-assessment, not their faith in organizations or institutions. Some observers say the Millennials are cynical and disconnected from their communities, while others draw the opposite conclusion that they engage in high levels of social activism. Both observations make sense if observers recognize that Millennials do act, but do so outside of established institutions. They did volunteer work in high school, but *decidedly not* in order to get National Honor Society points. As adults they often contribute a great deal of time and energy to meeting social needs, but they are more likely to do so through informal groups or grassroots organizations than through the United Way or Sierra Club (Green, 2007). If they participate in the political process, they do so because they are excited about an individual candidate or cause, not because of party identification or a broad sense of patriotism or political responsibility. As a result they are highly optimistic and see a world of opportunities in front of them. They are already trying to distance themselves from the Xers – for example with softer music and different clothing. Like the Boomers, they are maturing in a time of sustained economic growth; have become accustomed to material possessions – cars, stereos, phones, computers, and the right clothes; and believe in working hard in the short term for the promise of a big payoff in the long term. But, all of this may already be changing. They are the safest generation in US history – their parents were obsessive about car safety seats, bicycle helmets, and so on. The events of September 11, 2001, may have undermined their sense of invulnerability. The corporate scandals and recession of the early 2000s put the optimism of the older Millennials to the test; the collapse of the financial industry in 2008 and the related Great Recession did the same thing for younger Millennials. The two groups who have been most hurt by these events are the Boomers and the Millennials. For both groups, the 2009–2010 job market was the worst since the Great Depression, even for those with college degrees. It is too early to assess the long-term impact of these new economic realities, but they clearly violate the Millennials' expectations and worldview (Kamanetz, 2005).

It is clear that these differences have generated tensions and conflicts at work. For example, some Boomer supervisors view Xers as slackers – one JC Penney manager complained, "When I started out, I worked long hours. I did whatever they wanted me to do. They come in at 8 and leave at 5." They see the Xers are unrealistic about organizational rewards and the amount of time it will take them to be promoted – "If they don't get what they want, they'll leave – they're just not loyal." Xers question their supervisors' decisions and authority. They ask questions that are unheard of to the Boomers, such as "If I don't like what my boss says, can I go to the next level?" and even do so during job interviews. In contrast, Xers sometimes view their Boomer bosses as burned-out relics of a bygone era. They want rewards to be based on performance, not seniority. They want to know what those rewards will be, and know them in advance of taking on a task. They communicate in ways that Boomers find excessively blunt – a direct, bold, cut-to-the-chase style. Boomers like to think that the Xers are just in a passing phase, that in time they'll settle down into a traditional mold. But, Xers plan to retire long before they settle down. Some organizations are already encountering serious conflicts between the two groups.

The Boomers and Xers are unified to a degree by their frustrations with the Millennials. Xers often view them as demanding, self-absorbed, and presumptuous. Both groups complain about their short attention spans and habits like talking to friends via cell phone or instant messaging or downloading music or playing computer games while at work. They seem to think they are entitled to special projects rather than "pay their dues" doing mundane tasks. And they think everything is negotiable: "Mr. Lankford, a health care recruiter, said that young workers often challenged company policies on matters like tuition reimbursement. 'Their attitude is "Why won't you pay for this?"' he said. 'Instead of accepting that these are our policies, they'll say: "Let's talk about making an exception." Or "Let's change the policies"[3] Education and training are other areas of negotiation because they know that they have to keep their skills current if they are to remain competitive. Many experts think that this model of constant negotiation cannot be sustained over the long run because it focuses attention on individual gain and away from the organization's needs. From the Millennials' perspective, these behaviors are a rational response to a contingent, constantly changing society and economy with few trustworthy rules or commitments. In a society in which nothing is stable, constant negotiation is necessary for survival. But bosses also admire their willingness to "take on tasks they know nothing about . . . and fearlessly march ahead" (Connelly, 2003, 4). And for the Millennials, there are those Baby Boomers and Generation Xers who still seem to be hanging around, reducing their opportunities for advancement.

Applying What You've Learned

1. What expectations do each of these generational groups have about life and about organizations?
2. What messages and experiences have contributed to those expectations?
3. Over what issues are the three groups likely to have conflicts? Why?

Questions to Think About and Discuss

1. To which, if any, of the three generational groups do you belong? (Generationalist research has long been criticized for a tendency to overgeneralize. This is especially true of research on the "Millennials," because that generation is more racially and ethnically diverse than any other generation in US history (one in five has at least one immigrant parent and one in ten has at least one parent who is not a citizen) *and*, ironically, has developed in one of the most politically and economically polarized contexts. For example, public schools in US cities are more segregated now than they were when the US Supreme Court announced its *Brown v. Board of Education* decision in 1954. So, it's especially important to realize that generational membership depends on one's experiences, not one's age.) How do *your* expectations and experiences correspond to those of the three generalized groups? Over what issues are you likely to have conflicts with members of the three groups? Why?
2. Have the economic events since early 2008 – the collapse of the financial industry and the Great Recession – altered your expectations? If so, in what ways? Why or why not?
3. Are the strategies chosen by Generation Xers appropriate to the situations they face? Generation Yers?
4. What effects are their strategies likely to have on their relationships with their supervisors in traditional firms? With their coworkers? With their subordinates? Why?

Notes

1 For an excellent database, see Kohut (2007); for a broader time frame, see Strauss and Howe (1991); and for a standard application to workplace issues, see Zemke, Raines, and Filipczak (2000). Relationships between Boomers and Xers are examined in Walker and Moses (1996), Coolidge (1999), and Jackson (1999). For analyses of these trends see Buzzanell (2000), and Neumark (2000).

2 See "Executive Pay Remains Tops" (1999); also see Blau (1999), Galbraith (1998), and Phillips (2002). Management scholar Jeffrey Pfeffer (1988) effectively critiques arguments that high executive compensation, low worker wages, and large gaps between the two are good for organizations and economies in "Six Dangerous Myths About Pay." Each of these trends will be analyzed in more detail in Chapter 12.

3 See O'Briant (2003), Howe and Strauss (2000, 2003), and Cappelli (1999).

CREATING SOCIO-ECONOMIC SPACES

In today's global economy the broadest relevant "space" is the entire world. Every large organization and many small "mom and pop" organizations have a global reach, either in terms of the people who purchase the goods and services they produce or provide, or in terms of the raw materials, including ideas, that they use. But, starting our discussion with such a broad topic could be overwhelming. So we have chosen to introduce the concept of strategic adaptation to space at a simpler level, a single nation, the United States. This is in part because many of our readers are US residents, but also because the system that has developed in the United States, for good or ill, currently dominates the global economy (Stiglitz, 2002; Greider, 1997; Mann, 2003; Soros, 1998, 2000). Consequently, we will begin with what has been labeled the "American system," and discuss its relationship with the global economy at more length in Chapters 2 and 11.

In the United States today, the most influential organizations are privately owned, only loosely regulated by government, allowed (even encouraged) to become very large, and allowed or encouraged to be politically active. They also are very undemocratic, both in terms of how decisions are made and power is distributed, and in terms of how the wealth created by the organization is distributed among its members and outside stakeholder groups. Of course, this is ironic for a society that presumably values democracy very highly. Other countries have developed social, economic, and political systems with some of the characteristics, but none have developed quite the same combination of attributes – it is a distinctively "American system." None of this was inevitable; it emerged over time as the result of a number of strategic choices by hundreds of political and economic actors. A few of these choices were consciously intended to create a particular kind of society. Most were made for a narrower purpose, to solve a specific problem or manage a particular challenge. But they had major **unintended consequences**. Others were made with very little thought, almost nonconsciously. But, they combined in both anticipated and unanticipated ways over a long period of time to create a unique kind of economy and society, one that involves a complex set guidelines and constraints that permeate even the simplest interaction in the smallest organization.

From their beginnings, the societies that eventually became the United States had all of the ingredients necessary for economic growth. Their land and the land around them were rich in natural resources. They had access to a seemingly inexhaustible supply of inexpensive labor from Europe and, later on, Africa and Asia. They developed cultures that celebrated individual achievement and entrepreneurship. Each of these factors was necessary for the development of the American system but not sufficient – our society and economy still could have developed in any number of different ways. But, during the early 1800s, a number of crucial choices were made.[7] First, owners of businesses persuaded courts and legislatures to create "limited liability" corporations. This doctrine meant that if a company fails and cannot pay its creditors and/or workers, its owners (or the managers they hired to run their organizations) could be held liable for those losses only to the extent that they had invested monies in the firm – its owners would not have to pay the company's debts out of their own pockets, regardless of how wealthy they might be, or how risky or foolish their decision making had been. Policymakers at the time realized that this arrangement was risky, so they required corporations to be operated in the interests of the public as a whole and to have public representatives on their boards of directors. Their assumption was that governments would have to become much larger if they were to make the investments necessary for rapid economic growth – building canals, roads, ports, or railroads. But the immigrants who had founded the nation, as well as the ones who came later, brought with them a deep distrust of large powerful institutions, primarily dictatorial governments and an established church. So, limited liability corporations seemed to be a good way to manage all of the risks they faced. Corporations would absorb the economic risks of large investment, and avoided the risks inherent in large, centralized government; indeed, they could serve as a useful counterweight to the power of church and state. Over time, it became easier and easier to incorporate, as states progressively weakened their requirements that corporations be operated in the public interest.

Eventually, owners persuaded legislatures to go even farther, not only to protect them from the risks of investing in large, expensive projects but also to actively subsidize their efforts (Perelman, 2006). These "deals with the devils" were controversial, to be sure, but as long as corporations were small and tightly regulated, the potential advantages seemed to outweigh the risks.

A number of other important choices were made, often by judges rather than legislators. Owners obtained the legal right to sell stock in their companies, and to do so in a way that severely limited stockholders' influence over their decisions or operations. This legal change gave them almost unlimited access to the funds they needed to enlarge their organizations. The US Supreme Court declared that only the federal government had the power to regulate interstate commerce. This was important because, at that time, the federal government was much less powerful than the governments of the largest states. Indeed, the budgets of the largest corporations were many times the size of the federal government's, something that did not change until the New Deal and World War II. Since the states could not regulate interstate corporations, and the federal government was weak, corporations could play the states off of one another, negotiating for the most favorable laws, including preferential regulations and tax systems.[8] They also successfully used the courts to challenge states' rights to restrict their activities (Ritz, 2001, 2007).

However, the most important court decision was made in 1819. In the *Dartmouth* decision, the US Supreme Court declared that corporations were "persons" and thus had all of the constitutional rights and obligations afforded individual citizens, except the right to vote (Cheney, 1993; Cheney and Carroll, 1997). Thus, corporations obtained the legal rights of "persons" 50 years before black Americans and more than a century before women. For many observers, the case seemed rather unimportant – the issue was whether or not the state of New Hampshire could require Dartmouth College to place representatives of the state government on its board of directors in exchange for receiving public money. But, for the key participants, Daniel Webster, who represented the college, and Chief Justice John Marshall, it provided an opportunity to permanently influence US society. As Thomas Cronin, an award-winning political scientist reminds us, "most of our framers ['founding fathers'] were skeptical . . . and even hostile to notions of popular democracy. They had fought their war of independence in large part to get away from monarchy. . . . Yet democracy was regarded as a dangerous and unworkable doctrine. The very term *democracy* appears neither in the Declaration of Independence nor in the US Constitution."[9] In the *Dartmouth* case, Webster explicitly argued that private corporations must be *protected from* democracy, from "the rise and fall of popular parties and the fluctuations of political opinion." Chief Justice Marshall favored Webster's position, and delayed the case until the Court had a pro-corporation majority and a series of lower court decisions to use as precedents. Yale sociologist Charles Perrow concludes, "The Dartmouth decision . . . was not a mistake, an inadvertence, a happenstance in history, but a well-designed plan devised by particular interests" (Perrow, 2002, 41). It was a conscious, strategic choice, but one whose primary impact was delayed for decades.

After the Civil War, the US economy began to change in ways that eventually revealed how important these changes were. Improved transportation and communication systems allowed corporations to grow rapidly as they pursued a growing mass market. But, the rapid growth of interstate corporations also meant that wealth and political power were being concentrated in the hands of a progressively smaller number of people. Still, as late as the early 1890s there were only a few large corporations. Suddenly, the number and the degree of concentration skyrocketed. Between 1898 and 1904 the 200 biggest corporations of the time were formed, many of which still exist. Simultaneously, the Supreme Court re-entered the picture. In 1886 it broadened and strengthened corporations' constitutional rights (the *Santa Clara* decision); in 1889 (*Minneapolis & St. Louis Railroad*) and 1893 (*Noble v. Union River Logging*) it afforded corporate persons all of the due process and equal protection rights that are listed in the 5th and 14th Amendments; in 1906 (*Hale v. Henkel*) it protected them against search and seizure; in 1908 they received the right to a jury trial in criminal cases (*Armour Packing Company v. US*) and so on. Piece by piece, sometimes almost by accident, a unique political, legal, and economic system emerged, one that gave corporations and their leaders a level of social, political, and economic influence that today is unique among the developed capitalist democracies. Of course, for each piece to be implemented, owner-managers had to persuade someone that the changes would meet the needs of the overall society, by increasing economic efficiency, enhancing economic growth and job creation, or whatever. The fact that corporations often were (and still are) *no more* efficient, productive, or socially responsible than the governmental agencies or noncorporate organizations that they replaced is testimony to the success of their persuasive appeals (Perrow, 2002).

Suddenly, the fears and predictions of those who opposed the development of large, limited liability corporations (LLCs) became much more credible. The accelerating economic and political power of the "robber barons" goaded the federal government into trying to slow down or halt the corporatization of the society. In 1900, Congress forbade corporations from directly contributing money to political campaigns, and soon after President Theodore Roosevelt initiated his brief and rather ineffective "trust-busting" campaign. But the die was cast; the American system was born, legitimized, and accepted as normal, natural, and, for many, superior to any other alternative. No king, queen, or elected government created it as a coherent whole. It was institutionalized through the development and implementation of a distinctive set of political, economic, and social structures; perpetuated through a distinctive set of everyday practices, traditions, and habits; and solidified by the development of a congruent set of beliefs and values (see Chapter 2). It established a set of guidelines and constraints that influenced the kinds of organizations that developed within its reach, and the actions taken by members of those organizations.

MAKING ORGANIZATIONS LOOK ALIKE

The key concepts that we introduced in the previous section – institutions, institutionalization, and legitimation – form the backbone of a valuable interdisciplinary perspective called "institutional theory." Its key assumption is that distinctive systems develop social groupings over time. The process is essentially the same regardless of the size of the group. A group the size of a nation or as small as a nuclear family develops parameters that guide and constrain their actions and perspectives that allow them to make sense out of their actions and the actions of people around them. These parameters and perspectives are attractive because they make life seem to be stable and predictable. As a result, they become very difficult to change. This does not mean that change never takes place. Systems and institutions are filled with tensions and contradictions – for example, a faith in democracy in every institution *except* formal organizations – which eventually may generate resistance and change. The elimination of race-based slavery in Western societies provides an example of all of these pressures; its continuation for hundreds of years shows how difficult it is to change institutionalized social and economic systems. But, the very human need for stability and predictability, combined with the forces of habit, history, and tradition, makes fundamental change difficult and slow.[10]

However, even in relatively homogeneous societies, the parameters and perspectives they provide still leave room for people to create distinctive organizational forms (Oliver, 1991, 1992). Early on, institutional theorists recognized that the members of organizations in different sectors of an economy seem to make similar choices. They cluster together into "fields" in which the organizations have similar structures, operations, and practices. Usually these institutional fields are defined by what their member organizations do – educate people, manufacture heavy equipment, develop "high-tech" products, and so on. Sometimes the similarities result from other factors. For example, they may be run by executives with the same background and training, which taught them what their "kind" of organization is "supposed" to look like and how they are "supposed" to operate. If asked to explain these preferences, managers usually say that the approach they favor is more profitable, more efficient, or more flexible and adaptive. But, institutional theorists realized from the beginning that institutional choices are based more on myths and rituals than on rational analysis. They are sustained by symbolic action more than technical efficiency.[11]

For example, consider elementary schools. There is a general expectation that elementary schools should have teachers who work closely with the children to build their basic skills in reading and writing and in physical activities involved in games and the like. Most citizens also believe that an ideal elementary school would teach children to love learning and respect nation, state, locale, government, and other people. In a highly individualistic society such as the United States, there is also an expectation that elementary schools will treat each child as an individual with his or her own distinctive strengths and needs, although elementary schools rarely implement this assumption in their structures and practices. To carry out these duties, elementary schools have developed similar basic structures. They have teachers who work with relatively small numbers of students, 5 to 30 depending on age. They have principals who make sure teachers follow an established curriculum, handle problems, and otherwise manage the school. Classrooms vary a great deal, but they are expected to have educational materials to interest the students, books, appropriate educational media, materials for projects, the teacher's desk at the front, and so on. Although actual schools may deviate from these expectations, they do so at the risk of being judged "inadequate." Consequently, the deviations tend to be related to noncontroversial matters. And, in spite of at least a half-century of claims that US education is in a crisis and must be reformed in fundamental ways, the institution of elementary schools has been remarkably resistant to change.

Institutional theory explains both the similarities and the lack or slowness of change (Scott, 2008). Three types of institutional influences have been identified. **Coercive**

influence occurs when organizations are forced to adopt certain structures or practices by other institutions. Many of these involve larger social and political systems. A **social institution** is a major organizational force in society. Some institutions are actual organizations, like the Federal Communications Commission, which has legal power to regulate organizations in the communications industry; the Congress; and the courts. Organizations are forbidden to discriminate against women or minorities by federal and state legal codes. Other governmental institutions must act indirectly. For example, both the US and Canadian Constitutions say that public education is a responsibility of the states and provinces, not the federal government. So, the federal governments influence the state or provincial educational institutions through funding – conforming to national dictates will be rewarded with extra funds. States and provinces influence local schools in the same way.

In the private sector, coercion also takes place. Sometimes it is informal – prospective employees do not want to work for organizations that are too different from the norms in their "organizational fields." Stockholders and bankers do not want to invest in firms that lack the up-to-date systems and practices that their competitors have. So, they are willing to pay relatively low prices for a company's stock, or they may limit the size of loans or charge higher interest rates. In other cases the coercion is explicit. For example, Walmart recently forced all its suppliers to use wireless digital identification devices on all goods shipped to the merchandiser. Although this was quite expensive for the suppliers, they really had no choice in the matter because losing Walmart's business would be a major blow. These examples illustrate the role of institutional coercion in the adoption of practices and structures by organizations. To be sure, doing these things may also make the organizations in question more effective. However, they are not adopting them for reasons of effectiveness, but because larger institutions make them do so.

A second source of institutional pressure is **normative influence**. Organizations are sometimes influenced to adopt a structure or practice by normative pressure from organizations like themselves. This pressure comes through associations among similar types of organizations and through other channels that indicate what organizations should do to live up to the value systems they subscribe to. To continue our school example, there are numerous organizations to promote effective education, and school district administrators, principals, teachers, school counselors, school nurses, and other staff belong to them, attend their meetings, and read their publications. These organizations have codes of values regarding how to be effective educators, administrators, counselors, nurses, and so on. They advocate various types of innovations and practices in accordance with these codes, and there is pressure to adopt these by people who value and want to live up to the norms of these associations. In addition to associations, most school personnel go through special educational programs to learn how to be a good teacher, principle, and so on, and one of the goals of these programs is to instill a sense of professionalism into their graduates. Values and expectations are an important part of learning to be a professional. When professionals go to work for an organization, they bring these values with them and influence the organization to adapt in ways consistent with professional norms.

Mimetic influence is the third type of institutional effect on organizations. Organizations often seek to be like exemplary organizations of the same type by imitating them. In the early 1990s Eastman Kodak, a high-tech company with a very good reputation for its information and communication technologies (ICTs), decided to "outsource" its information systems to a major contractor, which took over management of Kodak's ICTs. This unusual move, to turn over management of a very important function to another company, was widely reported in the press and grabbed the attention of other large corporations. In the next three years a number of other firms imitated Kodak and outsourced their information systems functions. This sudden move toward outsourcing was dubbed "the Kodak effect," because rather than being driven by independent rational thinking it was traced to imitation of Kodak. Mimetic influence is strongest in situations with high uncertainty, when organizations may not be able to determine the likely consequences of their actions well enough to make a rational decision. When it is difficult to make sense of a situation, organizations often turn to models for guidance. At the time of Kodak's decision, outsourcing of information systems was not well understood by most organizations, and so they turned to exemplary cases such as Kodak for advice. Since it seemed to work out well for Kodak, other companies began to outsource their information systems functions.[12]

How do members of organizations respond to these pressures? The simplest response is to *acquiesce* to institutional pressures. But, there are different versions of doing so. When pressures are strong, well established, and habitual, members may nonconsciously fall into the same practices as in the other organizations that make up its "field." Or, they may consciously imitate other organizations because the situation is so uncertain that no other options seem to be available. Or, they may grudgingly obey rules and accept norms only because they are not powerful enough to resist. Members also may find a way to *compromise* by bargaining with the sources of the pressure, or placate them by appearing to comply while not changing their everyday practices. Third, they may try to *avoid* the pressures, by separating themselves from the other organizations in their field, or changing their goals, activities, or mission completely – moving into a more compatible economic neighborhood. If their organizations are sufficiently powerful, they may *defy* the pressures, by ignoring demands, challenging rules in courts or other venues, or attacking the credibility of the institutions exerting the pressures. The most difficult cases occur when an organization faces inconsistent pressures from multiple institutions, something that is quite common when it operates in many different societies. In these cases it may be necessary to balance competing pressures, never conforming completely to any of them, but adjusting their responses on a case-by-case basis. The choice about how to respond often is not based on rational judgments of what will improve efficiency or effectiveness, but on the basis of any number of nonrational considerations (Oliver, 1991, 1992; Scott, 2008; Bigelow and Arndt, 2000; Kitchener, 2002). Consequently, organizations often wind up in the middle of destructive "bandwagon effects" in which they foolishly adopt popular but unwise fads and fashions.[13] Whatever strategic choices the members of an organization make, it is important to remember that they (1) were choices, not the inevitable results of conformity pressures, and (2) any choice other than acquiescence will make it more difficult for the organization's members to legitimize its actions.

STRATEGIES OF ORGANIZING

The rules and resources that are legitimized and institutionalized at each of the levels we have discussed to this point – the global, national or societal, and organizational fields – influence each of the other levels (we will explain the processes through which this happens in Chapter 2). The next smallest level is the individual organization. In theory, there are an infinite number of different ways in which organizations could be designed and operated. But the rules and resources developed at each of the levels we have examined combine to reduce the number of viable strategies. In Unit II of this book, we will discuss at length the major strategies of organizing that are employed in modern organizations – the traditional, relational, cultural, and network strategies plus a group of newer alternative approaches. Each strategy has a different design and structure, a different system of employee motivation and control, a different communication systems, and different ways of using communication technology. Of course, no organization corresponds perfectly to any of the strategies of organizing that we will discuss; organizational actors draw different attributes from each of the socially legitimate alternatives to create hybrids that are appropriate to the situations they face. Similarly, no strategy works exactly like it is supposed to work and all organizations have a mixture of strategies in place. But, thinking about real organizations in terms of the available strategies of organizing can help members make sense out of their particular organizations and consider potentially productive alternatives.

STRATEGIC COMMUNICATION FOR INDIVIDUAL MEMBERS OF ORGANIZATIONS

A final sense in which communication is "strategic" involves individual employees. In the best of cases, individual employees can assess the guidelines and constraints they face in particular organizational situations, and draw upon the available resources to construct messages that allow them to pursue their goals and the goals of their organizations. In the worst situations, there may be no viable communication strategy available. Organizational situations sometimes paralyze employees, at least momentarily. One kind of paralysis occurs when the guidelines and constraints in a situation are clear, but the resources available to meet them are unclear, unknown, or insufficient. For example, organizational situations may include commands for psychotherapists to "do good work," hospital administrators to "cut costs," or elementary schoolteachers to "stimulate all the students' interests." These "guidelines" may tell employees what they are supposed to do, but they tell them little about how they are supposed to do those things. As a result, employees may become paralyzed while they make sense out of their situations and discover the resources that are available to them. For example, one of our newly graduated students became a stockbroker. Frustrated by being given a desk and a "training session" that was limited to the comment "I hope you'll like it here. Just don't screw up like George, your predecessor, did," he called and asked, "What do I do next?" This kind of paralyzing situation is depressingly common for new employees, and has been shown to be a major source of organizational stress. But, eventually, primarily through informal communication with his coworkers, the student started to understand what he should and should not do.

A more extreme form of paralysis occurs when action is called for, but constraints leave the employee with no available resources. Presumably, Linus' purpose (in Figure 1.1) is to gain the childlike fun that comes from a friendly snowball fight. But Lucy's comments leave him with both a command to act (since dropping the snowball is an act) and no productive way to achieve his purpose. Throwing the snowball will fail; so will not throwing it. Lucy has taken the fun out of snowball fights and has robbed Linus of any opportunity for meaningful choice.

Organizational situations sometimes parallel the *Peanuts* situation. Supervisors may find that they have only one position to allocate and two departments that desperately need

Figure 1.1 Source: PEANUTS © 1976 Peanuts Worldwide LLC. Dist. By UNIVERSAL UCLICK. Reprinted with permission. All rights reserved.

help, have equally strong claims on the position, and will be justifiably angry if they do not receive it. Subordinates may be told to do one thing by one superior and the opposite by another. They may know that one supervisor has a higher rank than the other and that in their organization they are always expected to follow the orders given by the higher ranking person. But they may also know that the lower ranking supervisor might retaliate against them, in ways that will never be detected by anyone else, for violating his or her order. In this kind of situation, the subordinate has no realistic options because no adequate resources are available. Between the two extremes of simple situations and paralyzing ones are the situations that employees normally face at work, situations that give employees a range of viable options.

Employees' strategic choices create and reproduce the guidelines, constraints, and resources that they face – traditional, bureaucratic strategies of organizing exist only because employees choose to act like bureaucrats. They gain acceptance and support from other bureaucrats by strictly applying established, written policies through documented and inflexible procedures. They may notice that being able to legitimately act like a bureaucrat is a valuable resource, both to establish their credibility and to perform their tasks (for example, managing excessively demanding customers).[14] Similarly, some organizational fields are dominated by bureaucracies because traditional strategies of organizing are treated as natural and normal by the organizations within them; and some societies are dominated by bureaucracies because they have developed rules and resources that encourage that strategy. However, employees' choices also may change the situations they face. They find ways to draw upon the resources they have available to them in order to resist objectionable guidelines and constraints, eventually change their organizations, over the long term influence the other organizations in their organizational fields, and so on.

SUMMARY: THE COMPLEXITIES OF ORGANIZATIONAL COMMUNICATION

All societies, and all organizations, must find ways to deal successfully with a fundamental paradox: if they are to survive they must control and coordinate the actions of their members. But, control and coordination frustrate individuals' needs for autonomy, creativity, and sociability. Historically, a number of strategies of organizing have been developed that strive to achieve the organization's goals while managing this fundamental paradox. Each of these strategies relies on communication because it is through communication that organizations emerge, are maintained, and change. Chapter 2 focuses on the process of making sense out of organizational situations, and examines the processes through which core beliefs and values are created, institutionalized, and enacted in organizations. The chapters that make up Unit II examine the dominant forms of organizing used in contemporary organizations. Although we will try to describe each strategy as a coherent whole, we also will continually caution readers not to lose sight of the complexity of organizational life. No strategy of organizing appears in a pure form in any modern organization. This is partly because every organization has its own unique history, membership, and mode of operation, and because each is embedded in a unique set of societal and "field" pressures. As a result, each organization's members develop distinctive mixtures of strategies in an effort to cope with the challenges they encounter every day. As a result, organizational life is much messier than any overall strategy envisions. That messiness makes organizational life interesting, and makes strategic communication especially challenging.

In addition, members of organizations in the early twenty-first century face an increasingly complex array of challenges. The chapters in Unit III examine what we believe are the most important of them – dealing with organizational power and politics (Chapter 7), making effective decisions and managing conflicts surrounding them (Chapter 8), affecting organizational change (Chapter 9), dealing with the challenges and opportunities created by the increasing diversity of organizations' members (Chapter 10), managing globalization (Chapter 11), and dealing with ethical challenges (Chapter 12).

At this point, all of these ideas may seem a little overwhelming. At least, at this point we hope that most readers feel a little overwhelmed. Communication is an exceptionally complex process; organizational communication is an especially complex type of communication. There are a depressingly large number of books, training programs, and consultants' gimmicks that depict effective organizational communication as the simple application of "five foolproof techniques" or some equivalent. Unfortunately, these depictions are as glib as they are misleading. There are a number of principles that employees can use in most organizational situations. But they are neither simple, nor foolproof, nor applicable in every case. Our goal in this book is to explain those principles and indicate how people can analyze the complexities they face at work and choose appropriate strategic responses, recognizing all the while that it was their choices and the choices made by other members of their organizations that created and reproduce the situations they face.

NOTES

1 Cheney, Lair, Ritz, and Kendall (2010, chap. 3) offer a similar analysis of the parallel phrase, "I'm just doing my job.
2 See, for example, Andrews and Herschel (1996, 16–18); and Sobo and Sadler (2002). For similar results in studies of Australian organizations, see Irwin (1997).
3 Kennedy (1980). A similar concept has been developed by rhetorical theorist Lloyd Bitzer (1968, 1980).
4 The concept that unique sets of "working rules" emerge in organizations, are legitimized over time, and guide and constrain employee behaviors has a long history, going back at least as far as Commons (1950). The version of this concept that has had the greatest impact on organizational communication was developed by Anthony Giddens (in 1979, 1984, 1991). It also is a core assumption of what has been labeled "institutional theory," a perspective that we will refer to throughout this book. Institutional theorists who develop explicit links to Giddens' work include Dacin, Goodstein, and Scott (2002).
5 This dual conception of the term "right" is developed at length in Foucault (1980). An excellent summary of Foucault's complicated ideas is available in Barker and Cheney (1994).
6 The notion that power depends on interactions rather than statements is the basis of an extensively researched model called "Leader-Member Exchange (LMX) Theory" and Karl Weick's conception of the "dual interact." For a summary of the former, see Fairhurst (2001); for the latter, see Weick (1979).
7 For an extended analysis of these processes, see Conrad (2011); Roy (1997); and Perrow (2002).
8 The concept of a financially poor, weak federal government is a little difficult for today's US citizens to believe, but the power imbalance continued until the New Deal (Perrow, 2002).
9 Cronin (1987). The classic treatment of this issue is Beard (1913/1986).
10 Institutional theory originated in two key sources Selznick (1957), and Meyer and Rowan (1977). Its development is summarized in Hinings and Greenwood (1988); Dacin *et al.* (2002); and Oliver (1991, 1992). For an application to organizational communication, see Lammers and Barbour (2006).
11 The concept of institutional fields is developed at length by Fligstein (1990, 2001). Excellent summary articles are available in Powell and DiMaggio (1990).
12 Dacin *et al.* (2002) prefer the term "translation" to "mimesis" because they want to focus attention on the interpretive processes that are involved in one organization's employees "picking and choosing" the parts of another organization that they want to implement.
13 For examples of destructive bandwagon effects, see Staw and Epstein (2000); and Kitchener (2002). For an analysis of managerial fads and fashions and the role that managerial "gurus" play in their development, see Conrad (2011), esp. chap. 3.
14 For a case study of how face-to-face communication reproduces strategies of organizing, see Harrison (1995).

REFERENCES

Andrews, P.H. and Herschel, R.T. (1996). *Organizational Communication*. Geneva, IL: Houghton-Mifflin.

Barker, J. and Cheney, G. (1994). "The Concept and Practices and Discipline in Contemporary Organizational Life." *Communication Monographs* 61: 20–43.

Beard, C. (1913/1986). *An Economic Interpretation of the Constitution of the United States*. New York: Free Press.

Bigelow, B. and Arndt, M. (2000). "The More Things Change, the More They Stay the Same." *Health Care Management Review* 25: 65–72.

Bitzer, L. (1968). "The Rhetorical Situation." *Philosophy and Rhetoric* 1: 1–14.

Bitzer, L. (1980). "Functional Communication," in White, ed., *Rhetoric in Transition*. University Park: Pennsylvania State University Press.

Blau, J. (1999). *Illusions of Prosperity*. New York: Oxford University Press.

Bridge, K. and Baxter, L.A. (1992). "Blended Relationships." *Western Journal of Communication* 56: 200–225.

Buzzanell, P. (2000). "The Promise and Practice of the New Career and Social Contract," in Buzzanell, ed., *Rethinking Organizational and Managerial Communication from Feminist Perspectives*. Thousand Oaks, CA: Sage.

Cappelli, P. (1999). *The New Deal at Work*. Boston: Harvard Business School Press.

Cheney, G. (1993). "The Corporate Person (Re)presents Itself," in Toth and Heath, eds., *Rhetorical and Critical Approaches to Public Relations*. Hillsdale, NJ: Lawrence Erlbaum.

Cheney, G. and Carroll, C. (1997). "The Person as Object in Discourses in and Around Organizations." *Communication Research* 21: 593–630.

Cheney, G., Lair, D., Ritz, D. and Kendall, B. (2010). *Just a Job*. New York: Oxford University Press.

Commons, J.R. (1950). *The Economics of Collective Action*. Madison: University of Wisconsin Press.

Connelly, J. (2003). "Youthful Attitudes, Sobering Realities." *New York Times on the Web*, October 28, p. 3.

Conrad, C. (2011). *Organizational Rhetoric*. London: Polity.

Coolidge, S.D. (1999). "Boomers, Gen-Xers Clash." September 1. www.abcnews.go.com/sections/business.

Cooren, F. and Taylor, J. (1997). "Organization as an Effect of Mediation." *Communication Theory* 7: 219–260.

Cronin, T. (1987). "Leadership and Democracy." *Liberal Education* 73: 35–38.

Dacin, M.T., Goodstein, J. and Scott, W.R. (2002). "Institutional Theory and Institutional Change." *Academy of Management Journal* 45: 45–57.

DeWine, S., Pearson, J. and Yost, C. (1993). "Intimate Office Relationships and Their Impact on Work Group Communication," in Berryman-Fink, Ballard-Reisch, and Newman, eds., *Communication and Sex Role Socialization*. New York: Garland.

Dillard, J. and Miller, K. (1993). "Intimate Relationships in Task Environments," in Duck, ed., *Handbook of Personal Relationships* (pp. 449–465). New York: John Wiley & Sons.

Dillard, J., Hale, J.L. and Segrin, C. (1993). "Close Relationships in Task Environments." *Management Communication Quarterly*, 7: 227–255.

Eng, S. (1999). "Love in the Office Can Be Risky Affair," *Houston Chronicle*, March 14, p. C1.

"Executive Pay Remains Tops" (1999). ABCNews.com, August 30. http://abcnews.go.com/sections/business.

Fairhurst, G. (2001). "Dualisms in Leadership Research," in Jablin and Putnam, eds., *The New Handbook of Organizational Communication*. Thousand Oaks, CA: Sage.

Fisher, M. (1999). "What's the Proper Etiquette for a Scarlet E-mail?" *Houston Chronicle*, June 1, p. C1.

Fligstein, N. (1990). *The Transformation of Corporate Control*. Cambridge, MA: Harvard University Press.

Fligstein, N. (2001). *The Architecture of Markets*. Princeton, NJ: Princeton University Press.

Foucault, M. (1980). *Power/Knowledge*. New York: Pantheon.

Galbraith, J.K. (1998). *Created Unequal*. New York: Free Press.

Giddens, A. (1979). *Central Problems in Social Theory*. Berkeley: University of California Press.

Giddens, A. (1984). *The Constitution of Society*. Berkeley: University of California Press.

Giddens, A. (1991). *Modernity and Self-Identity*. Palo Alto, CA: Stanford University Press.

Gosset, L. (2001). "The Long-Term Impact of Short-Term Workers." *Management Communication Quarterly* 15: 115–120.

Gosset, L. (2008). "Falling Between the Cracks." *Management Communication Quarterly* 19: 376–415.

Green, H. (2007). "The Greening of America's Campuses." *Business Week*, April 9, 62–66.

Greider, W. (1997). *One World, Ready or Not*. New York: Simon & Schuster.

Harrison, T. (1995). "Communication and Interdependence in Democratic Organizations," in Deetz, ed., *Communication Yearbook 17*. Newbury Park, CA: Sage.

Hinings, R. and Greenwood, R. (1988). "The Normative Prescription of Organizations," in Zucker, ed., *Institutional Patterns and Organizations*. Cambridge, MA: Ballinger.

Howe, N. and Strauss, W. (2000). *Millennials Rising*. New York: Vintage Books.

Howe, N. and Strauss, W. (2003). *Millennials Go to College*. Washington, DC: American Association of Collegiate Registrars and Admissions Officers.

Irwin, H. (1997). *Communicating With Asia*. Sydney, Australia: University of New South Wales.

Jablin, F. (2001). "Organizational Entry, Assimilation, and Disengagement/Exit," in Jablin and Putnam, eds., *The New Handbook of Organizational Communication*. Thousand Oaks, CA: Sage.

Jackson, M. (1999). "Business Bends to Include Generation X Workforce." *Bryan/College Station Eagle*, January 31, p. E1.

Kamenetz, A. (2005). "Call This Passive? We're Young and We Do It Our Way." *The Washington Post*, August 28, p. B3.

Kennedy, G. (1980). *Classical Rhetoric in Its Christian and Secular Traditions from Ancient to Modern Times*. Chapel Hill: University of North Carolina Press.

Kitchener, M. (2002). "Mobilizing the Logic of Managerialism in Professional Fields." Organization *Studies* 23: 391–420.

Lammers, J. and Barbour, J. (2006). "An Institutional Theory of Organizational Communication." *Communication Theory* 16: 356–377.

Legg, N.A. (1992). Other People's Kids: Decision-Making About Sexual Education. Master's Thesis, Texas A&M University.

Losee, S. and Olen, H. (2010). *Office Mate*. New York: Adams Media.

Mainiero, L. (1989). *Office Romance*. New York: Rawson.

Mann, M. (2003). *Incoherent Empire*. London: Verso.

Meyer, J.W. and Rowan, B. (1977). "Institutionalized Organizations." *American Journal of Sociology* 83: 340–363.

Neumark, D., ed. (2000). *On the Job: Is Long-term Employment a Thing of the Past?* New York: Russell Sage Foundation.

O'Briant, D. (2003). "Move Over, Gen-Xers." *Houston Chronicle*, August 13, p. D1.

Oliver, C. (1991). "Strategic Responses to Institutional Processes." *Academy of Management Review* 16: 145–179.

Oliver, C. (1992). "The Antecedents of Deinstitutionalization." *Organization Studies* 13: 563–588.

Perelman, M. (2006). *Railroading Economics*. New York: Monthly Labor Review Press.

Perrow, C. (2002). *Organizing America*. Princeton, NJ: Princeton University Press.

Pfeffer, J. (1998, May/June). "Six Dangerous Myths About Pay." *Harvard Business Review* 76: 109–111.

Phillips, K. (2002). *Wealth and democracy*. New York: Broadway Books.

Powell, W. and DiMaggio, P., eds. (1990). *The New Institutionalism in Organizational Theory*. Chicago: University of Chicago Press.

Powers, D. (1999). *The Office Romance*. New York: American Management Association.

Putnam, L., Phillips, N. and Chapman, P. (1996). "Metaphors of Communication and Organization," in Clegg, Hardy, and Nord, eds., *Handbook of Organization Studies*. London: Sage.

Ritz, D. (2001). *Defying Corporations, Defining Democracy*. New York: Apex.

Ritz, D. (2007). "Can Corporate Personhood Be Socially Responsible?" in May, Cheney, and Roper, eds., *The Debate Over Corporate Social Responsibility*. New York: Oxford University Press.

Roy, W. (1997). *Socializing Capital*. Princeton, NJ: Princeton University Press.

Selznick, P. (1957). *Leadership in Administration*. New York: Harper & Row.

Sias, P. and Cahill, D. (1998). "From Coworkers to Friends." *Western Journal of Communication* 62: 273–299.

Sobo, E. and Sadler, B. (2002). "Improving Organizational Communication and Cohesion in a Health Care Setting Through Employee-Leadership Exchange." *Human Organization* 61: 277–287.

Soros, G. (1998). *The Crisis in Global Capitalism*. New York: Public Affairs.

Soros, G. (2000). *The Open Society*. New York: Public Affairs.

Staw, B.M. and Epstein, L.D. (2000). What Bandwagons Bring: Effects of Popular Management Techniques on Corporate Performance, Reputation, and CEO Pay. *Administrative Science Quarterly* 45: 523–556.

Stiglitz, G. (2002). *Globalization and Its Discontents*. New York: W.W. Norton.

Taylor, J. and van Every, E. (2000). *The Emergent Organization*. Mahwah, NJ: Lawrence Erlbaum.

Walker, C. and Moses, E. (1996). "The Age of Self-Navigation." *American Demographics*, September.

Weick, K. (1979). *The Social Psychology of Organizing*, 2nd ed. Reading, MA: Addison-Wesley.

Weinstein. B. (2008). "The Ethics of Office Romances." *Bloomberg Business Week*, February. www.businessweek.com/managing/content/feb2008/c2008212-702316.htm.

Winstead, B.A., Derlega, V.J., Montgomery, M.J. and Pilkington, C. (1995). "The Quality of Friendships at Work and Job Satisfaction." *Journal of Social and Personal Relationships* 12: 199–215.

Zemke, R., Raines, C. and Filipczak, B. (2000). *Generations at Work*. New York: AMACOM.

CHAPTER 2

KEYS TO STRATEGIC ORGANIZATIONAL COMMUNICATION

Don't look back . . . something might be gaining on you.
Satchel Paige, baseball Hall of Famer

CENTRAL THEMES

- Systems models can be used to describe organizations and to explain their processes.
- Principles of systems thinking include the complexity of causation, the importance of indirect effects, the need to look carefully for the levers that can change systems, understanding that the whole is greater than the sum of its parts, understanding the system by analyzing its subsystems and suprasystem, and the importance of organizational learning and renewal.
- Critical analysis is designed to discover and escape from the limitations of assumptions that are embedded in organizations.
- Diversity presents a challenge because organizations tend to value homogeneity, but it is important to take advantage of the resources that diversity provides for the organization.
- Globalization may lead in any of three directions – homogenization, polarization, or hybridization of cultures.
- Over the past 50 years, there has been a transition from a production economy based on the physical production of goods in factories to a knowledge society in which most value is added through information and knowledge-related activities.

Strategic Organizational Communication: In a Global Economy, Seventh Edition.
Charles Conrad and Marshall Scott Poole.

- The impacts of information and communication technologies (ICTs) on organizations and their members are neither simple nor deterministic but are shaped by social processes in the organizations and by the strategy of organizing they utilize.
- A number of ethical and policy problems arise due to organizational use of ICTs, including privacy issues and the degree of surveillance that organizations should be allowed to undertake.

KEY TERMS

organizational system
workflow
process system
principles of systems thinking
wholeness
levers
suprasystem
subsystem
environment
hegemony
laissez-faire capitalism
futility thesis
perversity thesis
jeopardy thesis
diversity
cultural homogenization
polarization
hybridization
knowledge work
information work
convergence
internetworking
intranets
software as a service
cloud computing
bandwidth
wireless technologies
geographic information system
Global Positioning System
ubiquitous computing
cyberespionage
cyberwarfare
electronic data integration
knowledge management
telework
outsourcing

Effective strategies respond to the demands of the situation. In general, the situation facing today's communicators is more complex, more dynamic, and more uncertain than ever. With each new edition of this book, we have had to include more material on dealing with change and responding to complex challenges, and this one is no exception. This chapter presents five keys to effective organizational communication in a complex and changing world. These are not "tips" for how to communicate better, but ways to think about organizations that will foster more intelligent and discriminating responses to the challenges we face day to day. Basically we believe that effective organizational communication rests on cultivating the ability to:

- Discover connections among seemingly unconnected phenomena
- Critically assess the assumptions, often unknown to us, that shape our behavior
- Take advantage of the new ideas and different skills that diversity brings to organizations
- Understand how globalization is changing organizations and society
- Understand the critical role information and communication technology has played in transforming modern organizations and how it can be used to make organizations more effective and enrich organizational life

This chapter introduces these keys, which will be developed throughout this book.

SEEING CONNECTIONS: THE IMPORTANCE OF SYSTEMS THINKING

People Express Airlines was an amazing success story that turned into a spectacular failure.[1] It provided low-cost, high-quality air service on the east coast throughout the early 1980s and quickly grew to be the USA's fifth largest air carrier. It had a reputation as a corporate pioneer, based in part on its emphasis on its people. The airline had a number of innovative human resource policies, such as job rotation, team management, employee stock ownership, and a flat hierarchy, that have since been widely adopted. These innovations kept its employees happy and committed to the organization and enabled the airline to offer excellent low-cost service. The airline grew rapidly and bought Frontier Airlines to help provide the capacity it needed to continue growing.

Despite its enviable position, People Express ran into trouble. Demand for the airline's flights far outstripped the available seats, and the overload resulted in delays and passenger complaints. Service on the flights deteriorated, and its customers left in droves. By 1986 the airline had lost over $130 million and was "rescued" (read "absorbed") in a buyout by Southwest Airlines.

Many theories were advanced to explain People Express's collapse. Some commentators traced the problems to a human resource policy that was "too lenient" and did not control employee costs. Others argued that the takeover of Frontier had been poorly planned and left the company strapped for cash, so that when its debtors called in loans it was unable to pay them.

However, these accounts do not give much insight into how the troubles at People Express developed. It is always easy to identify "causes" of an organization's problems from the outside, but to really understand the situation it is important to consider the processes that created and worsened the problems.

People Express "crashed and burned" because of a complex system of causes and events (Senge, 1990, chap. 8). The first of the "low-fare" airlines, People Express introduced an innovative concept – low prices, no frills, and high-quality air service. It gained a reputation that led to an increasing number of new customers. In its early days, People Express's innovative human resource practics and employee stock ownership kept morale high and motivated its employees to work hard to maintain excellent service levels. However, as the number of customers rose, there were not enough staff to handle them and current employees were overworked. Hiring more employees was slowed by its progressive human resource practices, which required lengthy training and the development of new employees.

At the same time, demand for bookings continued to increase, because reports in the media and word of mouth continued to tout the airline as a great bargain. This drove the price of People Express's stock higher, to over $20 a share. As a result, many of People Express's employees were wealthy. Though they were fatigued, they were happy and positively motivated.

However, the crush of new passengers led to increasing customer complaints due to service problems, ticketing delays, overbooked flights, and overloaded employees. The overworked staff had few resources with which to address these problems. For many employees, passenger complaints soured the one thing they had to hold on to, their love of working with people. As problems persisted, customers began turning to other airlines. This resulted in decreased revenues, which led to a fall in the stock price. Once employees realized that their hard work was not going to be rewarded by stock appreciation, their motivation declined further. This led to a further decline in service quality and more customer flight, which further worsened the bottom line. Paradoxically, the very human resource plans that had originally made People Express distinctive ended up resulting in lower motivation and declining service.

Increasing the size of its fleet by acquiring Frontier Airlines promised to help address the airline's capacity problems and offered an opportunity to improve service. But implementing the progressive human relations policy in Frontier meant a delay in utilizing this new capacity, because Frontier's employees needed to be trained. Service quality continued to erode, and the new capacity really just added to the problem because employees were overworked and saw little reward from working still harder. The end result of this complex set of processes was a worsening spiral that led to the ultimate demise of the airline. These processes are shown in Figure 2.1.

People Express did not necessarily have to fail. Studies of People Express and similar airlines showed that it could have turned these negative processes around by either raising ticket prices by 25 percent (not an excessive increase in view of the economical prices currently offered) or maintaining its high level of service, if it had acted soon enough. However, by the time the downward spiral developed momentum, raising ticket prices would have driven the airline's most loyal customers away and maintaining high levels of service is difficult with a demoralized and overworked staff. These measures should have been enacted well before the spiral worsened.

People Express failed because of a lack of systems thinking. Its managers should have realized that if rising stock prices made workers happy and motivated, falling stock prices might do the opposite. They should have recognized that growing as fast as it did would stress service quality in People Express. Managers should have known that in the face of demand a slight increase in ticket prices would not have been a problem and might have even reduced customer overload somewhat, giving a window of time in which to renew service quality. Employees should have recognized that they were the key to turning the airline around and rising stock prices. However, neither the employees nor the managers were able to see these things. Instead, they stayed focused on their immediate jobs, assuming what worked in the past would work in the future. They were not able to recognize the system of forces that inevitably drove People Express out of business.

Systems thinking does not come naturally. Several tendencies prevent us from seeing the system. Most of us have been taught to break problems down, to focus on a single problem and look for its cause. This is useful in some cases, because it enables us to act relatively quickly and is straightforward. However in the case of People Express – and in most organizations – there was not a simple single problem, but a chain of interconnected factors that interacted in a complex way. Focusing on one part of the system led to overlooking other important factors. Another barrier to systems thinking is the narrowing of perspective that comes from working in a particular position in an organization. Over time members tend to see things mostly in terms of their position or department and reduce problems to their perspective. For example, the human resources people viewed the problems confronting the organization as human relations problems, while the finance people viewed them as cash flow issues, and the operations management people viewed them as scheduling and capacity problems. While each of these diagnoses captured a part of the problem, none recognized the whole system.

The system model offers a general way to understand the world that takes its complexity into account. As this section will show, many different kinds of things – organizational structure, work processes, and causal processes – can be modeled as systems. We will use

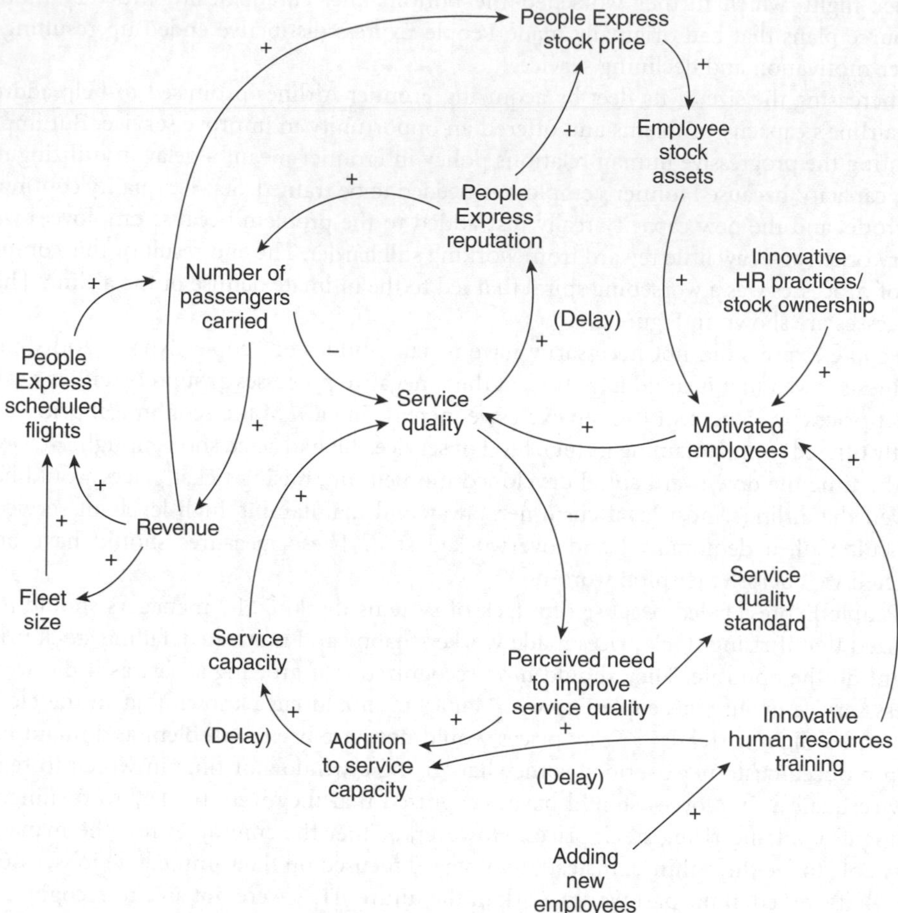

Figure 2.1 The system of factors influencing the effectiveness of People Express.
Note: A plus sign by an arrow means, "The greater the X, the greater the Y." For example, the greater the fleet size, the more flights People Express can schedule. A minus sign by an arrow means "The greater the X, the lower the Y." For example, the more passengers carried, the lower the quality of service (more passengers put more stress on flight attendants; they are rushed and their quality declines). Any cycle with all positive sign (for example, Number of passengers carried +→ Revenue +→ Fleet size +→People Express scheduled flights +→ Number of passengers carried) is a reinforcing cycle. These cycles result in ever-increasing values, a "runaway" system. Any cycle with an odd number of negative signs (for example, Service quality +→ People Express reputation +→ Number of passengers carried −→ Service quality) is a dampening cycle. The negative links counteract the influence of the positive ones, creating a "balanced" cycle.

systems concepts throughout this book, and their ability to yield insights will become evident. In the following paragraphs, we will introduce systems thinking in general terms.

The basic constituents of a system are its components and the relationships among them. In thinking about organizations, two important types of systems must be distinguished. First, the *organization itself* can be viewed as a system. **Organizational systems** can exist at several levels, depending on whether the components are individual members of the organization, departments, or units, or even entire organizations. The types of relationships that hold the system together may vary depending on the nature of the components. If the components are individuals, then the relationships among them include authority (who reports to whom), communication (who talks to whom about what), work roles (who works with whom and what do they do), and interpersonal relationships (who is friends with whom). A common way to map such systems is in the form of a network diagram, which is called a communication network if the relationship in question is communication of various types. We will discuss communication networks in more detail in Chapter 4.

If the components of the system are units or departments, relationships include authority (which department has authority over the other), communication (which department communicates with which), and work (where do departments fit into the **workflow** of the organization, and which departments work with which). The same types of relationships hold when the components of the system are organizations. We will discuss systems of organizations in more depth in Chapter 6, which introduces the networked organization. Figure 2.2 depicts several different organizational systems.

Second, the *processes* that affect the organization and its members can be modeled as a system of interacting factors, as we did in the People Express example. In this case the components of the system are variables that play a part in its operation. The relationships among the variables include causation and influence in this type of system. Figure 2.1 presented an example of a **process system**. Whereas the organizational system gives a description of the organization, the process system gives us an understanding of the processes that influence the organization. Most of the theories presented in this book are process systems theories.

Several **principles of systems thinking** help in understanding organizations and developing strategies for organizational communication:

1. The Whole Is More Than the Sum of Its Parts

Systems are more than just the parts that make them up. A cake is created from separate ingredients, but the cake is totally different from the raw ingredients. In much the same way, an organizational system is more than the sum of its individual members and units or their particular relationships to one another. For example, most charitable fundraising agencies are composed of office staff, telephone and personal fundraisers, advertising and promotion staff, accountants and bookkeepers, managers, and a board of directors. Each individual member has particular skills, values, strengths, and weaknesses. Joined into units, such as the accounting department, individuals' skills and strengths can compensate for others' weaknesses, and together, they can achieve things they could not on their own. The units become wholes in their own right; they evolve their own goals and operating procedures, and they develop a set of values and culture of their own.

Joined into an organization, the units, too, can achieve different outcomes and have different values than they could on their own. Accounting units keep the fundraisers honest. Advertising and promotion keep the whole charity visible in the community, increasing revenues. But advertising and promotion would have no budget for their operations without the fundraisers (nor would the accountants be paid without those they monitor). In a very real sense, the charity functions as it does only because of its entire configuration of people and units. But the people and units would not be what they are without the whole. It is through their place in the charity that they realize their potential.

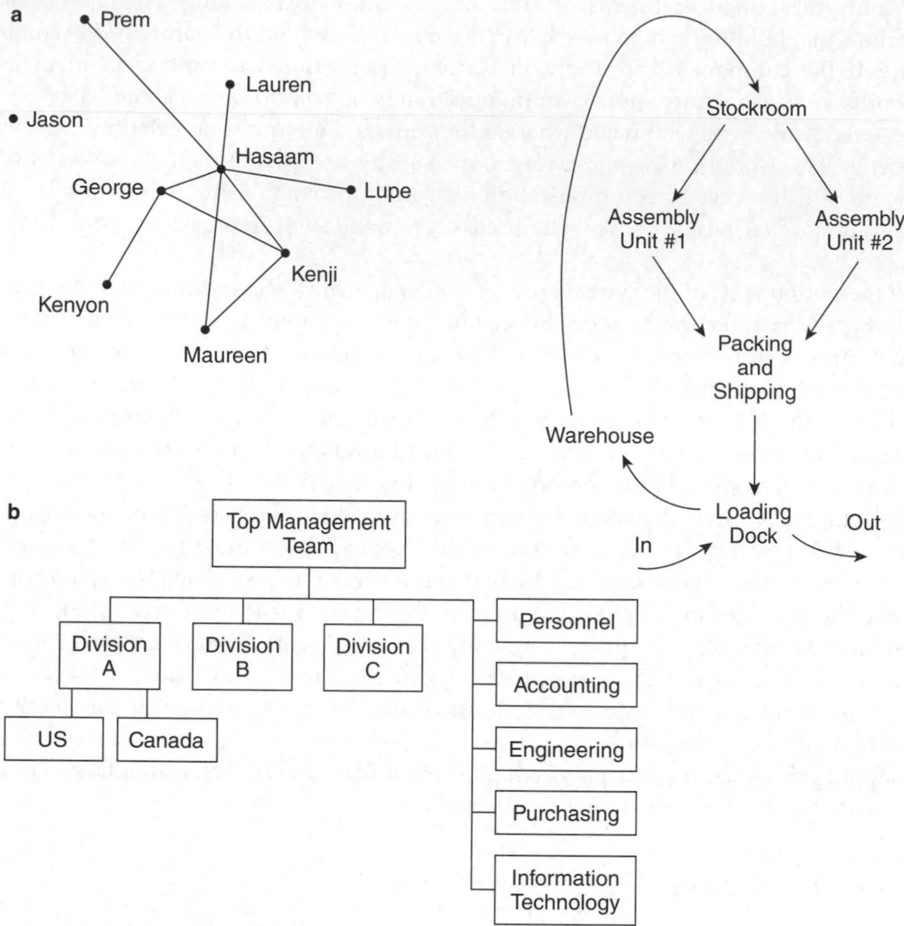

Figure 2.2 Examples of organizational systems.
Note: (a) A communication network, (b) a multidivisional organization, and (c) a workflow system in a small assembly plant. The two units build products, which are shipped from the loading dock.

This process, through which a dynamic interdependence of parts and whole creates a unique overall system, has been called *emergence* by systems researchers.

Wholeness also applies to process systems. The variables can be defined independently of one another, but their influence is due to how they interact with each other in the system. The set of relationships in Figure 2.1 forms a whole system of influences that drove People Express. The variables act as a set, and if the organization is altered to introduce another variable the entire system changes its character.

2. Cause–Effect Relationships in Systems Are Complex

Because all of the parts of a system are interconnected, it is not possible to find a single, simple cause for events or problems in the system. In the People Express process system service quality affects the reputation of the airline. However, is it the ultimate cause of reputation? Quality is influenced by the number of passengers carried and by service capacity, which are themselves influenced by the flight schedule and additions to service capacity. But since the system runs in loops, these variables are influenced by service quality. Where is the cause for the systems behavior? The answer is "In the entire system." Because all variables are linked together, it is impossible to find a single ultimate cause for a problem or, for that matter, for success. Systems thinking warns us against trying to find a single variable or process to blame for a problem or to attribute success to. While individual variables or processes certainly play an important role in the organization, problems or success stem from the system as a whole.

In the same vein, trying to find a person or unit in an organizational system that is responsible for a problem or for success is often fruitless. Though organizations often place blame on a person or unit or reward someone or some unit for successes, because all people and units are interconnected, they all play a role in problems or successes. This is why a commonplace of quality improvement programs is "Don't assign blame – change the system." This does not mean that individuals do not have responsibility and that they cannot create problems in a system. Personal responsibility is critical to effective systems, but it is not the only thing that causes systems to break down.

Many important effects in organizational systems are indirect. In Figure 2.1, additions to service capacity have an effect on reputation, but the effect is indirect. In Figure 2.2, George may well influence Maureen, but this effect will come indirectly through George's effect on Hasaam and Kenji. It is easy to overlook such indirect effects, but they are often quite important. This is particularly likely if the effect is delayed, because the further apart things are in time, the easier it is to miss the connections between them. This is a classic example of systems effects in that Maureen may seem to be reacting to Hasaam, but really it is George's influence on Hasaam that affects Maureen.

3. It Takes Time to Find the Right Levers

Because indirect effects are hard to uncover and often overlooked, we often fail to find the really important variables, people, or units in the system. While systems are wholes and their parts are interdependent, some variables, people, and units are particularly important. These parts stand at central points in the system where they are in a position to influence a number of other variables, people, or units or where they can filter or moderate the effect of other variables. In Figure 2.1, service quality is a centrally located and hence important variable. In Figure 2.2, Hasaam is particularly critical because he ties together a number of other members.

These critically important parts of the system represent **levers** that can be used to change and control the system. Finding a way to maintain service quality or adding other variables into the system that can increase quality would have given People Express a better chance of survival. Of course, critical parts of a system are not always easy to change or control compared to other parts. If we cannot change or control some element of system, it cannot serve as a good lever.

4. To Understand a System, Don't Just Focus on the System Itself

Every system is embedded in a group of larger systems (**suprasystems**) and that every system is made of a number of smaller, interdependent **subsystems**. For example, the loading crew of a freight company is a system made up of a number of subsystems (workers, their interpersonal relationships, and so on), which are made up of smaller subsystems (each worker's perceptual processes, tasks, information-processing activities, memories, expectations, family, church, and social ties, and so on). But the loading crew is only one part of the production suprasystem of the organization, which is only one part of the freight company (supra-suprasystem), which is part of the even larger trucking industry, and so on. At any given time, the actions of any of the many employees or subsystems of employees in the organization (the loading crew, for example) may be influenced by the actions of any of the other interrelated subsystems or suprasystems of people.

Information is input into a system through one or more of its subsystems. As information moves through the system, it is interpreted, acted upon, and communicated to other members of the system. In systems theory language, it becomes output that is interpreted, acted upon, and communicated to other systems and subsystems.

5. Systems Must Adapt or They Perish

It is not only other systems that influence a system. Every system is embedded in an **environment**, that is, in a complex set of pressures. In the case of private organizations this environment includes its customers, its competitors, its stockholders or owners, government regulators, and economic conditions in general. In the case of government or nonprofit organizations, the environment includes consituents or clients, the public, other government agencies, and economic conditions in general.

To thrive, and sometimes to survive, organizations must adapt to their environments. If the environment changes, or if they move into a new environment, the organization must change as well. During the early 1990s, fast-food chains in the United States adapted to the healthy-lifestyles movement by adding salad bars and vegetarian burgers, and moving into high schools and colleges, where their customers were not as concerned with health issues and regularly go through french-fry withdrawal. Some chains shut down their outlets in health-conscious areas and reopened new ones where health was not such a hot issue. When the healthy-lifestyles movement faded, many of the salad bars and almost all of the veggie burgers have disappeared (except in a number of different varieties in India). Today, with increased concern over obesity and public health, lifestyle is once again becoming an issue and healthy foods are again being reintroduced.

In adapting to environmental pressures, an organization must balance the need for change and the stability provided by the older systems. Because organizational systems are made up of people and not parts, they cannot always change on a dime. People who have worked in the organization may resist some types of changes, and they may be slow in adopting even those they accept. The organization's culture may preclude some types of change, or at least make them difficult to implement. Organizations that successfully adapt are able to acknowledge that stability as well as change is needed.

6. History Is Important in Organizational Systems

It is important to remember that organizational subsystems, systems, and suprasystems are made of people, not things. Each organizational member brings a complex set of beliefs, values, history, and expectations into the system. These beliefs, values, histories, and expectations have an important effect on how members interpret, respond to, and communicate the information they obtain. For example, if employees believe that dishonesty is the normal way of conducting interpersonal relationships in their organization, inevitable communication breakdowns (like those discussed in Chapter 3) are likely to be interpreted as dishonest manipulation. It matters little that the breakdowns may be the result of harmless organizational processes. Within the interpretive frameworks of employees of this organization, they will be interpreted as intentional manipulation. Conversely, in an organization whose employees value openness and honesty, the same breakdowns might be interpreted quite differently; employees will act differently on that information, and they will communicate it to others in very different ways.

Consequently, employees define the situation(s) they face at work in their own ways. Those definitions change as the employees perform new and different tasks, participate in interpersonal relationships that develop and grow, receive and interpret new information, and confirm or disconfirm interpretations. Their strategic choices are influenced by the entire matrix of pressures, goals, and concerns that they experience, all of which also are emerging and changing. As a result, individual employees may make decisions that are difficult for other employees to understand. From the position they occupy in their organizational system, their choices probably make perfect sense to them, but they may not make sense to someone in a different position.

7. Systems Must Constantly Learn and Renew Themselves

A vigorous, adaptive organizational system remains so because of the processes of learning and self-renewal. Organizations, made up as they are of people and machines, need to replace these parts as they grow old, unable to perform, or unwilling to adapt. One way in which organizations renew themselves is by making sure to bring in fresh, new people and technology. The danger in this case is that the new people and machines will too radically challenge a structure and culture that has worked well. In many cases, self-renewal is most effective if it replenishes and refreshes rather than changes the organization. How new members can be integrated into organizational relationships and how cultures can be produced and sustained are important topics discussed in later chapters.

However, an organization must learn too, and this is also an important part of self-renewal. It is not only important to maintain, but to expand perspectives, to try out new things, to experiment. For years 3M Corporation has maintained a reputation for being one of the most innovative firms in the United States. A standard policy at 3M is to give its members license to "steal" time to work on new ideas and to reward people even for failures, as long as they keep trying to generate new ideas and products. Google does the same thing, encouraging employees to take one work day per week to develop a new service or idea.

Another form of learning is to take advantage of unexpected opportunities and events. Open systems expose themselves to their environments and thus are open to many unanticipated happenings. They can use these surprises to make themselves stronger and more adaptive. Sometimes these unexpected opportunities come by accident. The story is told that one of 3M's biggest successes, the ubiquitous Post-It Note, came about because of an accident that produced an adhesive that held only temporarily and could be easily peeled off. Rather than throwing out this batch of adhesive, creative 3M staff members tried to figure out what it could be used for. The result has replaced many a thumbtack, paper clip, or piece of tape. Opening up organizational systems to learning is critical to their growth and survival. Remaining open to new ideas and opportunities to learn is not always easy or even pleasant. But the organizations that are able to do so reap great benefits.

Case Study 2.1

There Go the Lights, Here Come the Babies?

In 1984 Yale University organizational sociologist Charles Perrow published a very influential book entitled *Normal Accidents*. Perrow's interest in accidents started in 1979, when he testified before a presidential commission established to examine an accident at the Three Mile Island nuclear power plant near Harrisburg, Pennsylvania. The committee concluded, as most of these investigations do, that the accident resulted from operator error (US-Canada Power System Outage Task Force, 2003).

Perrow disagreed with the findings of the committee because the available evidence indicated that the power plant operators acted in completely sensible ways given their training and the (ambiguous, incomplete, and incorrect) information that was available to them. Blaming *individuals* for organizational failures and crediting *individuals* for organizational successes is completely consistent with the *individualistic* assumptions of US society. Sometimes it *is* both fair and accurate – people do make mistakes that they should have avoided. But, the explanation often is misleading and counterproductive.

Accidents in complex organizations occur, Perrow argued, when unique combinations of events, pressures, and incentives come together. The more complex a system is, the larger the number of possible, unique, accident-producing combinations there are. In retrospect it is easy to see how all of the elements came together to create a particular problem, and to determine what the operators *should* have done. But it is virtually impossible to anticipate all of these unique combinations ahead of time, or to recognize that they are taking place when one is in the middle of one. When the systems also are **tightly coupled** (which means that when something goes wrong in one part of the system, other parts are effected almost instantly), operators have no chance of obtaining the information they need to correctly diagnose the problem, much less intervening to stop the process.

In some cases, systems actually encourage the "errors" that lead to accidents. For example, in the maritime industry getting a ship to its destination on time, or better yet, early, can mean thousands of dollars to the company. Most shipping companies share this windfall with the captains of the ships that arrive on time. As a result, they have significant financial incentives to take risks. On the other hand, they have few disincentives for doing so. Unlike automobile insurance rates, which go up significantly if a driver has an accident, shipping insurance rates are not based on accident records. Although some countries use safety records in decisions about licensing of ships or companies, other countries do not. So shipping companies can simply obtain licenses in the least demanding countries (traditionally, these have been Panama and Liberia).

In addition, the costs of accidents usually are shared with many people outside of the company, and companies can limit their liability through a variety of legal tactics. Consequently, accidents like the 1989 wreck of the Exxon *Valdez* in Prince William Sound, Alaska (and the more than 50 larger maritime oil spills that have occurred worldwide since 1989), are virtually guaranteed. Preventing them would require a complete redesign of the "accident-inducing system," to use Perrow's phrase, something that in many situations simply is not possible.

The 2003 electricity blackout in the northeastern United States and southern Canada is an example of a systems error. It was not the first such blackout – similar events took place in 1965 and 1977 – and a systems-level analysis suggests that it almost certainly will not be the last. And, like Three Mile Island, the initial investigation concluded that no one could have anticipated a massive power outage on a calm, warm day, an event that could only have happened if multiple safeguards had broken down simultaneously. Secretary of Energy Spencer Abraham commented,

> When the procedures are followed and equipment works properly, the grid's delicate balance is maintained – even when things go wrong. But, when something does go wrong – and very important proce-

dures aren't followed and critical transmission monitoring and control equipment fails – the likelihood of major problems intensifies. (Cited in Behr, 2006, E5)

The primary cause, concluded the committee, was "operator error."

At 3:06 P.M. on August 14 a power line owned by FirstEnergy of Ohio came into contact with untrimmed trees and shorted out. Power was automatically redirected to another line, which could not handle the load, overheated, and failed. Power was again redirected, and that line also failed at an energy breaker that connected FirstEnergy to the larger power grid. Had the operators known, they could have intervened, but the alarm system in their control room was not working, and they did not know that it wasn't working.

But, the committee concluded, had they been adequately trained, they would have notified the other utilities in the grid that they were experiencing failures, and would have conducted "contingency analyses" to detect those unknown failures and taken appropriate action. By cutting 1500–2500 megawatts of power to the Cleveland and Akron area, they could have contained the outage. But they had not been trained to assume that their systems were malfunctioning even when no alarm had been sounded, or to assume that automatic safety systems can cause problems rather than prevent them. By 3:46 P.M., 40 minutes after the first powerline failure (at Three Mile Island, the bulk of the damage was done in the first eight minutes), it was too late to stop the blackout from cascading throughout the web.

Two minutes later, power surged wildly into throughout the grid. The power system in upstate New York automatically acted to shut itself off from the surge by disconnecting itself from the Canadian grid. But, this prevented New York power plants from sending power outside of the state, which caused their power plants to overload (including two nuclear plants), and they shut down. At 4:10 P.M., the blackout spread to Michigan where a coal-fired power plant shut down and two transmission lines failed. A minute later, a power plant and several more lines failed in Ohio. Toronto and New York City went black; one-fifth of the US power grid shut down, closing twelve airports, darkening more than 100 power plants, leaving 50 million people in the dark, and causing over $6 billion in economic losses.

Had anyone been able "to see the whole picture and put the pieces of the puzzle together" (Kuttner, 1996, 270) – to "connect the dots," using the phrase that became popular after September 11, 2001 – all of this could have been avoided. But no one did. To understand why, we need to examine the "supra-system" of the power industry. From 1900 until 1975, "electric companies dwelt in a stable and predictable realm where steadily declining costs of production and steadily increasing consumption were natural complements." Although the electrical power market was tightly regulated, a number of private companies were able to enter the market and succeed. In fact, the protections provided by regulation actually encouraged them to innovate and take risks, because they knew that they would be able to recoup the costs of doing so over the long run.

The federal regulatory system was created during the 1930s in response to widespread abuses in the industry during the 1920s. Power companies had grown so large that they crossed state boundaries, and thereby avoid state-level regulation. Rate increases during the 1920s led to multiple government hearings that uncovered widespread fraud and monopoly abuse in the industry. Federal regulation allowed companies to retain the efficiencies of monopolies while protecting customers and suppliers. However, after the energy crises of the 1970s and in a political atmosphere that encouraged deregulation (the Carter administration deregulated the airline industry in 1978 and other industries quickly followed), controls were weakened, both in the United States and in the United Kingdom.

The nature of the industry makes it virtually impossible to create a complete free market in electricity – it makes little sense to have separate power lines from competing utility companies go to the same house, for example. So, the level of deregulation is different for the three activities involved: producing power, distributing it over long distances, and marketing it with individual consumers. This mixed system is an open invitation for fraud and abuse, as California residents learned in the summers of 2001 and 2002. It also creates a maze of interconnected but independent firms, each trying to maximize its profits, with no overall control.

For example, in the US Midwest there are 23 different companies that share responsibility for maintaining the grid. Unfortunately, maintenance is an expensive proposition: Mark Mills, a partner in Digital Power Capital, a venture capital group that invests in utilities, noted that the problems that led to this blackout are easy to cure, but "in this environment we've created in the last decade, utilities don't invest in expensive things (quoted in Wald, 2002, 2). It simply may make more financial sense for a company to set up systems to protect itself from other companies than to spend money on maintaining their part of the grid. Similarly, each company could share information strengths and weaknesses in their part of the grid to other companies, but in a competitive market divulging that information could be used by competitors to the company's disadvantage.

The Midwest Independent System Operator (MISO) watches over the grid, but membership in it is voluntary, as is obeying its recommendations. The Federal Energy Regulatory Commission (FERC) has been trying for years to force utilities to join regional grid organizations and follow their recommendations, but the effort has generated strong opposition among utility companies. In fact, those utilities persuaded their congressional representatives to insert a provision in the 2003 energy bill that would delay implementation of FERC's plans until after 2007. Although the bill did not pass during the 2003 session, its history suggests that the electrical power industry will continue to be fragmented and only loosely regulated.

Six months after the accident, no changes had been made to the system. No federal agency can compel the companies that were involved to take corrective action, or even to reveal what they have (or have not) done to prevent future blackouts. In October 2003, the North American Electric Reliability Council, a voluntary agency founded after the 1965 blackout to "prevent recurrences and fend off government regulation" (Wald, 2002, 1), asked each of its 167 member companies to describe how they manage swings in power, communicate with other companies, train their employees, and keep trees trimmed. By mid-December, fewer than one-third (55) had responded.

Most consumer advocacy groups, and state (and provincial) Public Utility Commissions would like to see stronger regulations, but that would require federal legislation, which the industry is likely to oppose quite strongly. In January 2004, Federal Energy Regulatory Commission Chairman Pat Wood announced that his agency would act to force the utility companies to comply with standards that currently are voluntary. As predicted, industry spokespersons opposed the plan ("FERC Says Grid Fix Can't Wait," 2004, B2).

Applying What You've Learned

1. Using the terms described in this section, assume that FirstEnergy of Ohio is the "system" that you are examining. If that is so, what is the "supra-system"? What are the important "subsystems"? How are they interrelated?
2. What pressures and incentives does FirstEnergy have to focus on prevention of future breakdowns? What pressures and incentives does it have to not do so?

Questions to Think About and Discuss

1. Whose "fault" was the 2003 blackout? If one takes a systems perspective, does this question make sense?
2. On April 5, 2004, the panel investigating the blackout issued its final report. It listed 46 recommendations for changes designed to prevent another blackout. The first was that the voluntary rules that had been in place for years, but strongly opposed (and largely ignored) by the industry be written into federal law and linked to significant penalties if they are violated (Perez-Pena, 2004). Given what you know about the blackout, how likely do you think it is that this recommendation will be implemented? Why? (After you read Chapter 8, on organizational power and politics, and Chapter 12, on organizational ethics, return to your answer to this question and evaluate it given the new information provided in those chapters.)

3. Do some research on the 2010 Deepwater Horizon blowout in the Gulf of Mexico. Analyze the system involved in drilling and maintaining the platform and in government regulation of deepwater oil exploration and production. Can blame be assigned in this case? How did the complex system contribute to the accident? What levers were available to change the system? How did the system's environment change after the blowout?

Conclusion

Oh, about the babies. There's a heated debate among scholars about that, one that pits demographers, who study population trends, and ob/gyns who deliver babies. The ob/gyns often report that areas which experience blackouts for whatever reasons seem to have abnormally high numbers of births around 9 months later. This seemed to happen in Houston, Texas, after Hurricane Ike knocked power out for an extended period of time. Dr. Rakhi Diminio, an ob/gyn at Houston Women's Care Associates whose first child was conceived during the Ike blackout, was asked by *Houston Chronicle* reporter Cindy George, "What was happening at the Dimino home those two and a half days?" Dr. Dimino responded, "What everybody else in Houston was doing. . . . You can only do so much when there's no television, nothing open and there's nowhere to go" (2009, 1A). But, demographers generally say that the blackout–baby link is an urban legend that does not accurately depict what people do during blackouts. For example, many go stay with family or friends when the lights go out, something that mitigates against sexual activity (see, for example, *Science Daily*, 2004). Assume that both groups of scholars are correct – some blackouts lead to baby bumps; some don't. Can you develop a systems-related perspective that would explain why? What factors or processes are part of the system? How do they function?

UNCOVERING ASSUMPTIONS: THE IMPORTANCE OF CRITICAL THINKING

The society from which an organization draws its members provides a context – a complex web of taken-for-granted assumptions, meanings, expectations, and interpretive processes – through which people make sense out of their experiences at work. This context guides and constrains their actions at work and in turn guides and constrains the kinds of organizational strategies they will enact. These assumptions tend to be accepted uncritically; in fact, that is the primary source of their power. But, understanding the organizations that exist within a society and understanding how communication functions in them involves assessing them critically, that is, *not* taking them for granted.

Societal Values and Social Myths

The dominant values of a society are articulated in social myths. These myths may or may not be true in an empirical sense, but they are believed to be true by members of a society. They are important because they tell citizens what their values are, how they should think, and how they should act. They also are important because they function as a powerful form of control, one that social theorists have labeled **hegemony.** Of course, no set of assumptions is accepted by all of a society's members all the time. Some people will constantly question some of the assumptions, and during times of social change large numbers of people may question many of the taken-for-granted assumptions of a society. The burgeoning distrust in financial, corporate, and government institutions in the wake of the 2008–2010 financial crisis and taxpayer bailouts is an example of this. But taken-for-granted assumptions are amazingly stable, because members of a society are constantly exposed to messages that support these assumptions, learn to interpret ambiguous information so that it confirms them, and tend to ignore or rationalize information that disconfirms them. By learning and accepting the assumptions of a society its members become qualified to participate in that society. By learning how people are supposed to think and act, members of a society also accept limitations on how they think and act (Therborn, 1980; Mumby, 1988).

Because organizations exist within societal particular societal contexts, the communication strategies that their members choose are strongly related to the taken-for-granted assumptions of the societies from which they come. Those strategic choices in turn lead us to act in ways that make their taken-for-granted assumptions seem normal and natural, and accurate, and legitimate. Societal myths provide people with stable and predictable lives, both inside and outside of their organizations. This concept often is difficult to understand because doing so forces us to quit taking for granted the taken-for-granted assumptions of our society. It asks us to treat our most basic beliefs about what is natural and normal as socially influenced choices, not as absolute truths. Normally we do not think about such things, and as a result, the assumptions provide powerful guidelines and constraints on our actions and the actions of our organizations.

Two examples from Anglo-US society will help to clarify these ideas. The first taken-for-granted assumption involves the "proper" nature of an economic system. Historically, and increasingly since 1980, US citizens have been taught that the optimal economic system is ***laissez-faire* capitalism**. This theory is based on the assumption that a free-market economic system has sufficient checks and balances in place to ensure that the legitimate interests of all members of a society will be met. Individuals compete with other individuals, and organizations compete with other organizations in pursuit of their own self-interests, and an invisible hand ensures that over the long term good individuals and organizations will triumph and bad ones will disappear. If left alone, markets will move toward an equilibrium, and an equilibrium is the most efficient way for a society to allocate its resources. The competitive dynamics of a free marketplace ensure that no individuals or organizations can unfairly impose their own wills on others. In this theory, government should have only a limited role in the economy. It may sometimes need to ensure that economic markets remain competitive (through antimonopoly laws, for example) or that property rights are protected. But, with these few exceptions, government is best when it does the least.

This view of government's role in the economy is grounded in three assumptions. A **futility thesis** states that governments simply cannot effectively direct a society or economy. The presumed "miracle" of the free market is that its processes work "invisibly," and thus do not have to be understood or managed. The presumed lesson of the demise of the Soviet Union is that centralized economic planning by a government is doomed to fail. When governments act, they do so on the basis of an incomplete understanding of social and economic processes and often base their decisions on considerations other than market values (that is, what one person is willing to pay another in a free economic exchange). In very rare instances, governments may actually do what the market needs to have done at a particular moment, but these instances are purely accidental. It is much more likely that government "intervention" will worsen the condition that the action is designed to solve (a **perversity thesis**). Even more important, government activities inevitably produce serious, perverse, unintended, and unanticipated consequences. As a result, whenever government acts, it is likely to jeopardize the virtues of a society or the economic gains that have been achieved through the free market (a **jeopardy thesis**).[2]

For individual citizens, free market assumptions lead to a focus on individualism, and articulate it in a "Horatio Alger" myth, named after the writer of a series of short books published during the late nineteenth century. In them, the key character, always someone from a highly disadvantaged background, faced a series of challenges. But, thanks to personal grit, talent, and determination, and the unbounded opportunity provided by the US free market economy, he (all of the Horatio Alger heroes were male) eventually overcame these challenges to become an economic and social success. Unlike Europe, the stories go, the United States is a classless society in which the only limit to success is individual competence and effort. A more recent version of the story with a high-tech twist is Apple Computer's Steve Jobs, who started in a garage in California.

However, like all social myths, these should not be taken literally. Very few sectors of the US economy fit a strict definition of *laissez-faire* capitalism. While the model works well in some sectors, in other sectors a mixture of government regulation and free market principles is more effective and efficient than a pure free market, and in still others government is more efficient than the private sector. In addition, the claims about the success of *laissez-faire* systems depends on making a number of unrealistic assumptions (see Kuttner, 1996; Chapters 11 and 12, this volume). There are a wide variety of capitalist economies in the world, each with a distinctive mixture of governmental and private sector operations, all of which fulfill the very different goals of their citizenry quite well. For example, the Chinese system of authoritarian capitalism, which combines government and party control with room for freewheeling enterprise, is challenging the *laissez-faire* model. The 2008–2010 financial meltdowns and the associated unemployment and other social ills stemming from relatively deregulated *laissez-faire* capitalism have made alternative models of economic organization, such as the Chinese economy seem more plausible.

At an individual level, the viability of the Horatio Alger myth has generally been exaggerated (in part because the United States has fewer overt symbols of class differences than other societies), and its accuracy has varied significantly over time. During the 30 years after World War II, it reached its peak – among men whose fathers were in the bottom 25 percent of the country's social and economic status, 23 percent made it into the top 25 percent, which supports the validity of the myth. But, since 1973 income and wealth distribution in the United States have become more and more unequal (especially if inflation and total tax burden are taken into account). During this period, the average real income of the bottom 90 percent of the US population has fallen by 7 percent, while the income of the top 1 percent rose 148 percent. Within this top 1 percent, the income of the top 0.1 percent rose *343 percent*, and the income of the top 0.01 percent rose *599 percent*. As a result, the upwardly mobile percent of the male population has fallen to 10 percent, roughly the same level as during the 1890s when the Horatio Alger books were written.[3]

Between 2000 and 2008 median income actually fell, for the first time since the figures were first compiled during the 1960s. The number of poor people in the United States grew by 5.2 million (to 40 million), a 15.4 percent increase, more than double the overall rate of population increase. More than half of the increase took place among people who lived in the suburbs, traditionally the locale of greatest economic stability and growth. Unemployment rates in Chicago for people aged 16–24 equaled those of the Great Depression, especially for minority males. More than 30 percent of the US population (92 million people) fell below 200 percent of the federal poverty level, $22,000 for a family of four. The declines accelerated after the start of the Great Recession in 2008. As a result, in 2008 the United States ranked tenth in upward mobility among the 12 members of the Organization of Economic Cooperation and Development (the developed countries, abbreviated OECD), with only Italy and the United Kingdom having less upward mobility. In Denmark, Australia, Norway, Finland, and Canada, upward mobility was more than twice the US level.[4]

Communication and Societal/Organizational Tensions

Core beliefs and values make up only one dimension of the context surrounding organizations. Just as societies shape dominant values and beliefs, they also are composed of tensions and contradictions within and among those beliefs. For example, although Anglo-US society is highly individualist, a number of social scientists have long observed that even there, a fundamental tension exists between individuality and community. Alexis de Tocqueville toured the United States soon after it became a nation. He observed that Anglo-US people were so individualistic that they found it difficult to recognize their common needs and interests and to develop a sense of community. Almost 200 years later, sociologist Robert Bellah and his associates interviewed hundreds of people from all walks of life. They found that European Americans' obsession with individualism and their isolation from one another had expanded and deepened since the end of World War II.[5]

Of course, tensions between and within a society's core values can be managed, sometimes through organizations and sometimes through communication. For example, de Tocqueville concluded that the United States remained cohesive because so many people were involved in informal nonwork organizations that provided a sense of community – churches, lodges, and so on – which compensated for the extreme individuality that European Americans face in their work organizations. Sociologists like Robert Putnam (2000) recently have noted that declining participation in these informal organizations has further isolated US residents from one another. This decline in involvement in nonwork organizations has made communication an even more important means of managing societal and organizational tensions. It is not accidental that Horatio Alger stories are most prevalent in the mass media during eras of limited upward mobility. In sum, all societies have characteristic myths, expressions of core beliefs and values of that are rarely even questioned, much less examined carefully and critically. Myths may or may not be true in an empirical sense, but they are treated as if they are true by members of a society. Articulated in stories and rituals, societal myths both express the core values and beliefs of a society and help to manage its core tensions (see Chapter 5).

Critique as a Strategy for Understanding Organizations

Taking a critical stance toward organizations can yield insights that we would not have if we took the organization "at face value." A critical approach assumes that "things are not what they seem," and presumes that current arrangements in organizations often favor some types of people at the expense of others. It invites us to look "below the surface" of the organization for deep-seated power relationships that render the playing field in the organization uneven and advantage those currently in ascendance over groups not in power. Such power relations are often masked in the types of myths and ideologies previously discussed in this section. This book will often take a critical perspective, not simply for the sake of questioning and critique, but because it is useful to ask the question "To whose benefit?" Arrangements in organizations are often arbitrary and serve no useful functions, but are preserved because those in power benefit from them. Very often the advantaged groups have no idea they have advantages – they overlook them because they take for granted that the organization is organized in an efficient and effective manner. But here is the rub – when organizations are irrational and arbitrary, they often function less effectively than they can. By surfacing the arbitrary aspects of organizations, we can often make them more effective and more pleasant places to work and live in.

VALUING DIFFERENCES: THE ADVANTAGES OF DIVERSITY[6]

Organizations often homogenize the types of people they hire, assign to units, or promote. In some cases, this is due to demographics. In countries such as Scandinavia, Ireland, and Japan, for example, a single ethnic group makes up most of the labor force, and hiring from this group is unavoidable, resulting in a homogeneous organization.

In other cases homogenization occurs due to preconceptions (prejudices) about the characteristics of various social groups. Until recently, women in the United States tended to be relegated to low-level positions and men were preferentially promoted into management. This was because management was presumed to require rational, cool-headed thinking, and men were assumed to be better at this than women. In Mexican *maquiladoras* – factories where many products for the United States and Canadian markets are assembled – owners and managers prefer to hire women as shop floor workers, because they are thought to be docile and more easily controlled than male employees.

Another impetus for homogenization is the desire of management to reduce uncertainty. If employees are as similar as possible, the thinking goes, they are more likely to be able to understand one another and work together. As a result there will be less need for management to intervene to manage conflicts or misunderstandings and the organization will operate more efficiently.

Homogeniety can also be encouraged by deep-seated cultural assumptions like those discussed in the previous section. In the United States, for example, the positive value of homogeneity has been supported by an additional societal myth, the melting pot. This myth suggests that all people – regardless of their race, gender, ethnicity, or country of origin – can become Horatio Alger figures if they only embrace the distinctively European-US values of hard work, determination, and loyalty. Any hierarchies and inequities that exist in the society are attributed to individual differences in merit, not to different opportunities based on race, ethnicity, gender, or class. As those living in the United States learn these predominant assumptions, they come to accept its hierarchical relationships as *natural* (that is, inevitable) and *normal* (that is, expected and morally correct).

As people *internalize* the values and assumptions of their societies they also internalize its class-, race-, gender-, and ethnicity-based hierarchies. In many societies, educated middle- and upper-class men of the dominant racial and ethnic backgrounds have been (and often still are) assumed to be superior to everyone else in terms of the skills and attributes needed in organizations. However, during the past decade, this dominant perspective has been challenged by two processes – diversification and globalization.

In many ways the dominant view is based on assumptions of *distance* and *separation.* In many cultures, managers are physically, sociologically, and psychologically separated from workers. Each group tends to view the *other* as fundamentally different people with different tasks, interests, personalities, and motivations. Social groups can separate themselves from other social groups by living in homogenous communities, separated by time and space as well. This way of viewing reality simplifies and stabilizes everyone's world and provides a degree of comfort and predictability. But, today's societies and today's organizations are becoming increasingly heterogeneous. While this phenomenon first occurred in industrialized societies that attracted workers from other nations, it is now spreading worldwide. The *separation* between groups of *others* has declined significantly, creating new challenges, new opportunities, and new demands on communicative processes. White, male, middle- to upper-class managers are no longer separated from nonwhite people or from women. These *others* comprise an increasing percentage of their employees and sit with them in executive dining rooms. Indeed in 2010 in the United States the number of females holding jobs exceeds the number of males (Rosin, 2010).

Moreover, the internal separation between workers and managers – who in the United States traditionally have been white, educated, middle- to upper-class, heterosexual males – has started to dissolve as women and nonwhite employees have moved into professional and managerial positions. Simultaneously, many employees have rejected the arbitrary elevation of work over home that characterizes the dominant view. For many people, relationships and family take precedence over work and career, and balancing the two has become a significant challenge (Kirby, Wieland, and McBride, 2006). No longer are employees willing to treat home and work as separate "containers" that are separate and independent of one another.

These changes in the United States and other countries such as South Africa are in part due to long and difficult struggles of "others" for greater equality. However, other powerful forces are also driving the diversification of organizations. In parts of Europe, traditional social groups are not reproducing at a rapid enough rate to replenish the needed supply of workers. As a result, immigrant groups like the Turks in Germany and Koreans in Japan fill the void. In the United States, women now make up 60 percent of college students, and as a result in the future there will not be enough educated men to fill management positions, even if they could be reserved only for males. Global movement of populations diversifies countries and their workforces. Homogeneity – at least in terms of social or ethnic group – will be difficult if not impossible to maintain in the future.

Unfortunately, organizational policies and practices have often been slow to adapt to these new realities (see Chapter 10 for a more detailed analysis). For example, in the United States women long have been and still are paid substantially less than men for the same or comparable work. A 2008 study by the US Census Bureau showed that on average women earned only 77 percent as much as their male counterparts. Since the beginning of the Great Recession this gap has narrowed, primarily because more men have lost their jobs, been forced to work part-time, or moved to lower paying industries.[7] There are a number of reasons for these differences, although one of the most important is that in the past women tended to be concentrated in sectors of the economy that have relatively low salary rates (for example, teaching or nursing). As the proportion of women in these occupations increased, the level of prestige afforded the occupations, and the wage rates paid to the people in then fell steadily until the occupation was approximately 50 percent women. When the proportion exceeds 50 percent, wages plummet.

There are two possible explanations for this pattern. One explanation is based on societal myths, in this case the myth that women's work is worth less than men's work. The second explanation is an economic one: when the number of applicants for a particular type of job increases, the heightened competition forces wages down. When women enter the workforce and compete for jobs in education and nursing they increase the number of workers, male and female, competing for jobs, and the result is a decline in wages.

The cultural explanation has been shown to be more valid. Women are paid less than men in comparable jobs because their work is perceived to be less valuable, and our society has taught us that women's work is less valuable because they are paid less. The taken-for-granted assumptions of our society and organizations lead us to believe that a wide variety of hierarchical relationships are normal and natural. In turn, we act and think in ways that support those assumptions (Pfeffer and Davis-Blake, 1987; Clair and Thompson, 1996).

An organization that is quite diverse in terms of race, gender, and ethnicity may, however, cultivate a different type of homogeneity. Rather than homogeneity in terms of visible characteristics, organizations may pursue homogeneity in terms of attitudes and values. It may do this by selective hiring, through the ways in which it socializes and trains new employees, and practices that reward certain attitudes and values. This type of homogenization has often been recommended under the rubric of "teamwork" in which organizational members have a shared model of the organization. However, homogenization of attitudes and values can lead to less effective decision making and lower levels of innovation, because everyone thinks alike and no one notices problems or opportunities that differ from the shared model.

We often tend to view **diversity** in terms of the challenges it poses, and this blinds us to the potential advantages of diversity. As we will see in Chapter 10, diversity brings the potential for new ideas and different views of the situation, different ways of interacting, and different orientations to taking action. Diversity, in short, is an opportunity if handled properly. Getting past the myths that keep people from appreciating the contributions of those different from them is one key to strategic organizational communication.

THINKING GLOBALLY: THE CHALLENGES OF GLOBALIZATION

Increasingly, new technologies and the elimination of Cold War barriers to economic activity mean that organizations also are becoming globalized. Increasing levels of education in the non-Western world, especially among women, have combined with the creation of a truly global flow of capital and trade to create a new environment for organizations the world over (Stohl, 2005). The increasing diversity of the employees of contemporary organizations challenge traditional modes of operating from the inside. The increasingly global operations of major organizations is challenging them from the outside. Workers, and organizations, compete directly with people half a world away as well as with people down the street. The insulation, comfort, and predictability provided by traditional barriers are rapidly disappearing and the "others" who once were so far away are now right next door. When multinational organizations based in Western societies enter a new area, they bring with them a distinctively Western set of values – individualism, commercialism, separation of church and state, liberty, and *laissez-faire* economics – that are alien to Islamic, Confucian, Japanese, Hindu, Buddhist, or Orthodox cultures. Many of their products, from rock music to fast food to cosmetics, are also distinctively Western.

Another force shaping globalization is global migration. The United Nations estimates that there are 214 million migrants across the globe, an increase of 37 percent over the past two decades. The ranks of migrants have increased by 41 percent in Europe and by 80 percent in North America over the same period (DeParle, 2010; Fix *et al.*, 2009). In the United States and Europe, migration tends to be framed in terms of illegal immigration from less developed countries. But, while the movements of the nineteenth century were primarily transatlantic and transpacific, today Mongolians work in Prague and Thais in Israel. In Ireland a Nigerian was elected as the nation's first black mayor in 2008. Most of this migration seems also to be related to making a living. Migrants sent home $317 billion last year, propping up many economies. And if current trends continue, women will soon make up the majority of migrants for the first time in history. Technology enables migrants to stay in touch with their families and homes much more effectively than in the past. A cell phone or the internet enables "a nanny in Manhattan . . . to talk to her child in Zacatecas, vote in Mexican elections, and watch Mexican television shows" (DeParle, 2010, 1, 4).

Some observers argue that these trends will lead to **cultural homogenization**, a bland world in which the rich cultural diversity that currently exists will be squeezed into a single, standardized, Western or US pattern. Different writers have created their own clichés for these trends – McWorld, Coca-Colonization, McDonaldization, or McDisneyization – but they all refer to the same processes. Other observers advance a **polarization** thesis, which warns that people in non-Western societies will be progressively more alienated and angered by this cultural invasion, resulting in an increasingly hostile world. A third group argues that culture is far more resilient and flexible than either of the extreme positions suggest. Historically peoples throughout the world have accepted some characteristics of "invading" cultures, modified others to fit their core values, and maintained their distinctive character. This **hybridization** thesis suggests that the challenge imposed by globalization is for countries and individuals to find a healthy balance between preserving a sense of identity, home, and community while living and acting within a global economic system.[8] Each prediction suggests different challenges for multinational organizations.

There is a great deal of anecdotal evidence to support the homogenization thesis – McDonalds, Walmarts, Coca-Cola, and so on now exist in every conceivable corner of the world. Western consumerism is distinctively oriented toward consistency and name-brand identification. Everyone who discusses globalization has his or her own story. Sociologist Peter Berger talks about a visit to Hong Kong. He went into a Buddhist temple and found a middle-aged man in a business suit and stocking feet, standing in front of an altar, facing a large statue of Buddha, burning incense and talking on a cell phone. Cultural homogenization is fueled by mass advertising and the status that accompanies Western (or US) products in much of the world. In fact, the phenomenon seems to be closely linked to the emergence of a global economic elite, people who have become wealthy as a result of the global economy and who are increasingly tied to one another and increasingly isolated from non-elite people in their own societies. George Cheney, for instance, reported that in a visit to Monterey Tec, a technical university in Mexico, some of the students commented that "they identified more with a technologically savvy elite around the work than with the majority of their fellow Mexicans" (Cheney and Barnett, 2005, viii). In the long run, homogenization will minimize the challenges faced by global organizations – once the process is complete, differences will be minimized. The challenge is in the short term.

A second group of observers see much more negative forces at work. When the world becomes a smaller place, cultural differences become *more visible* and *potentially more alienating*. Cultural conflicts are much more difficult to resolve than economic or political ones – compromise on the terms of a trade contract is a fundamentally different thing than compromise on moral or religious truths (Barber, 2000; Huntington, 2000; Kaplan, 2000). When globalization creates or exacerbates disparities of wealth and income, as has been the case in much of the developing world, these cultural differences may lead to an increasing polarization both within societies and between them. The current backlash against globalization is most intense in societies suffering both economic and cultural dislocation, and it tends to be focused on the United States and US-based organizations. The targets of the September 11, 2001, attacks were not chosen at random – they were the headquarters of the US military and US global organizations. Whether or not it is accurate or fair to single out the United States and US organizations, it is quite clear that polarization is significant and, in some areas, growing. And, ironically, the same forces that created globalization can be used to resist it. Protests held outside meetings of the World Trade Organizations and international trade and finance organizations were organized via the internet, and the size and scope of those demonstrations was transmitted instantaneously throughout the world by CNN and Al Jazeera.

A final group of observers argue that the most likely outcome of globalization will be the development of a number of hybrid societies that combine local and Western cultural characteristics. This, they argue, has been the primary lesson of history – from Hellenization to Christianization, local societies have found ways to accept some aspects of outside cultures while retaining the core of their culture. Thomas Friedman calls this process "glocalizing," a term that originally was developed in Japan as a label for marketing products to fit local tastes. John Tomlinson explains,

> Culture simply does not transfer in this [simple linear] way. Movement between cultural/geographical areas always involves interpretation, translation, mutation, adaptation . . . as the receiving culture brings its own cultural resources to bear . . . upon cultural imports. (1999, 84)

The use of English as the global language of commerce provides an excellent example. On the one hand, it is obvious that English dominates the global economy. There is no inherent reason for English to dominate – it is not easier to learn, more precise, more flexible, or more capable of expressing emotions. One third of the world's population (1.6 billion people) use English in some form today. Eighty percent of the content posted on the internet is in English (although the percentage is declining), even though one half of internet users speak a different language at home. Corporations in English-speaking countries account for 40 percent of the world's economic activity. English dominance reflects the political, economic, and military power of English-speaking countries. In many ways, it has created a new system of global haves and have-nots. Being able to speak and read English opens up opportunities for knowledge and career advancement that are not available to people who do not speak the language. Career ads in French newspapers published in Belgium are in English, because multinational corporations (MNCs) increasingly require English-language skills of their professional employees.

But, regional languages have not disappeared. In fact, differences among dialects of non-English languages are becoming more pronounced, and regional languages are increasingly popular ways of bridging linguistic differences. Mulitlingualism is becoming the world-wide norm, everywhere except in the United States. The language that a person uses with family and friends may be different than the one used with coworkers, which may be different than the one used with bosses or government. Many countries have reacted to the growing use of English by forbidding its use in settings where it is not required. As a result, local language use is becoming hybridized, just as local cultures are becoming "glocalized." Instead of becoming impoverished, as the homogenization thesis suggests, world cultures are being enriched by processes of hybridization. Instead of creating an increased potential for hostility, globalization has provided more opportunity for connection. However, glocalization may present the greatest challenge for multinational organizations. Cultural hybridization is a slow, highly selective, and context-dependent process (Drohan and Freeman, 2000; Fishman, 1998/1999). It maximizes proximity and difference, while creating an infinite number of issues that must be negotiated successfully for the organization to thrive.

Understanding the impacts of globalization on organizations and society is a key to strategic organizational communication. The effects of globalization are felt not only around the world, but in the United States as well. Manufacturing job losses in recent years are one effect of the opening up of the global economy. But globalization has also opened up markets to US firms, so that US computer sellers such as Dell and heavy equipment manufacturers like Caterpillar are prospering in Europe and India. Effective organizational communication and organizational effectiveness depend on taking globalization into account, however difficult it might be to project its influence.

UNDERSTANDING TECHNOLOGY: A RADICAL FORCE FOR CHANGE

Peter Drucker, an astute observer of society and of organizations, wrote in 1994,

> No century in recorded history has experienced so many social transformations and such radical ones as the twentieth century. . . . In the developed free-market countries – which contain less than a fifth of the earth's population but are the model for the rest – work and work force, society and polity, are all, in the last decade of this century qualitatively and quantitatively different not only from what they were in the first years of this century, but also from what has existed at any other time in history: in their configurations, in their processes, in their problems, and in their structures. (1994, 53)

Perhaps the most far-reaching change has been the transformation of the United States and most of the developed and developing world to a knowledge society. For most of this century and the last, the economy focused largely on production, on the laborious work in farm and factory that resulted in tangible products. Before World War I, farmers were the largest single group of workers in most countries. From 1920 to 1950, the farm population declined, although the production of food increased. In the 1950s, blue-collar workers accounted for 40 percent of the American workforce, representing the emphasis on factory production through manual labor of that period. However by 1990, blue-collar workers accounted for less than 20 percent of American workers and farmers less than 5 percent.

The largest classes of workers in 1990 were those employed in what Drucker terms "knowledge work" and what has been called "information work."

Knowledge work involves creating and applying knowledge. Examples range from research scientists, engineers, attorneys, and financial analysts on the high end of the scale to teachers and X-ray technicians on the low end. Several things differentiate knowledge work from production work. Working with knowledge involves performing abstract operations and its product – knowledge – is intangible. Indeed, the only tangible outcome of much knowledge work is a document. However, despite its intangible nature, knowledge is the critical factor in the development of new products and the delivery of services such as legal and financial advice. Knowledge work organizes other forms of work, including production work. Knowledge work adds value to materials and to information, making them more useful or desirable or effective. An engineer's designs turn sand, copper, and aluminum into computer chips; an attorney's interpretive and negotiation skills create business partnerships from indecipherable (to any ordinary person) legal tomes and discussions among the parties involved. Knowledge-based work requires formal education (as opposed to apprenticeships or trade school) and an ability to acquire and apply abstract theoretical and analytical knowledge. It also requires a commitment to continuous learning; the knowledge worker's best and only asset is his or her expertise, which must be developed constantly through experience and further schooling.

Information work supports knowledge work. It involves gathering, entering, formatting, and processing information. Examples of information workers include clerical jobs, data entry, and telemarketing. These jobs are generally lower paying than the lowest rungs of knowledge work. They have been called "pink-collar" work, because they are often office positions staffed largely by women.

Together knowledge and information workers comprise about 40 percent of the workers in manufacturing firms and up to 80 percent in service organizations. They have become the largest class of workers in our society. This does not mean that production work is no longer important. It is, after all, what actually creates the products that knowledge workers design and that information workers catalog and sell. However, production work has become subsidiary to knowledge work in the new social arrangements. Advances depend far more on increases in knowledge than on production per se. Production is often separated from knowledge work, as we see when designs for products developed in the United States or Europe are manufactured in the industrial zones of China.

The increasing importance of knowledge and information work has put a premium on information and communication technologies. The last 20 years of the twentieth century and the first decades of this century will surely be remembered as the time when information and communication technology exploded. The most obvious indication of this is the phenomenal and continuing growth of the internet. This is only the tip of an iceberg of changes that include the spread of business integration systems, the takeoff of mobile telecommunications, extraordinary advances in communication technologies such as interpersonal messaging and videoconferencing, the advent of virtual organizations, and reengineering of countless private, public, and nonprofit organizations to incorporate information technology.

Some scholars argue that information and communication technology (ICT) does not really change organizations.[9] They regard it as simply another factor that influences organizational communication by increasing the speed, accuracy, and efficiency of information exchange. However, the past decade suggests that this position vastly underestimates the potential of ICTs to transform organizations and communication. Most organizations could not operate effectively without ICTs. Wal-Mart, for example, could not deliver such low costs without its computerized supply chain management systems and even small corner groceries depend on electronic debit and credit processing. Amazon.com and eBay are examples of organizations that exist only on the internet. Take away ICTs and these organizations would disappear. Farmers rely on ICTs to determine how much fertilizer to apply and when to sell their crops, law firms conduct their research through online services, and local government agencies collect bills and taxes through online payments. ICTs play just as important a role in today's organizational communication as a face-to-face conversation or a telephone call.

Trends in the Development of Information and Communication Technologies

Everyone is aware of how rapidly ICTs are changing. As consumers, we are amazed at the variety and increasingly sophisticated functionality of devices like camcorders, televisions, and mobile phones. The diffusion of ICTs into organizations has been equally rapid, though sometimes we are not as directly aware of it. While it began rather slowly in the 1970s and 1980s, it has consistently picked up speed through the 1990s and early 2000s and shows no sign of slowing. The increasing rate of ICT implementation and its growing impact on organizations and society can be traced to several developments (Applegate, Austin, and McFarlan, 2003).

The **convergence** of formerly separate technologies, such as computers and telephones, was inevitable given the spread of digital technology. Once information like text, audio, and pictures has been converted into digital form – as it is, for instance, when we type into our computers or take a picture with a digital camera or camcorder – it can be easily moved from one kind of ICT to another.[10] For instance, a digital picture can be sent along with an email message or to a printer to make a paper copy. Convergence makes it possible to link together and sometimes even merge separate applications, which makes integration of information in organizations much easier. For example, electronic medical records can combine textual notes made by physicians with digitized radiological pictures and other types of documents in a single database. Still another is the growing number of organizations that are moving their telephone systems to the internet rather than relying on the phone companies' dedicated lines. Movies are now being viewed on portable phones and tablets and literally thousands of apps are turning our phones into all purpose digital devices – how long will it be before the word *phone* is a quaint anachronism?

Henry Jenkins (2006, 1–2) describes a series of events that illustrate the unpredictable consequences of convergence. Right after the 9/11 bombings, a Filipino-American student combined digital images of Osama bin Laden and *Sesame Street*'s Bert culled from the internet into a collage which he posted on his humorous website "Bert Is Evil." A Bangladeshi entrepreneur scanning the web found this image and printed it on posters and T-shirts sold all over the Indian subcontinent. It is not clear that he knew who Bert was, since *Sesame Street* is localized in Bangladesh and he had probably not seen Bert before. Demonstrators in Pakistan, probably not knowing who Bert was either, wore the T-shirts and carried the posters in a gathering praising Bin Laden. CNN broadcast news of these demonstrations that showed the images of Bert and Bin Laden together. The producers of *Sesame Street* were outraged and threatened to sue (though who they could wasn't clear because intellectual property is not protected in Bangladesh under US laws and the entrepreneur was a Bangladeshi local – maybe the poor student?). Coming back around the world, the image inspired other amused college students to link other *Sesame Street* characters with evil ones.

This incident also shows the impacts of **internetworking**, the use of the internet to deliver and access ICT applications. Technologies discussed in the previous edition of this text – office automation, electronic data interchange (EDI), groupware, videoconferencing, workflow management – previously were implemented in stand-alone proprietary systems that were difficult to connect to each other. Over the past ten years, these applications and many others have moved to the internet. Organizations have implemented **intranets**, which are internal, private internets that operate essentially in the same way that the public internet operates. For example, an organization might install an intranet to handle its electronic mail, allow employees to move documents around the organization rather than passing paper copies, and retrieve needed information from the company database. These intranets are often directly connected to the more open internet and can be accessed by employees from wherever they are. There has also been a move to open source software that is not owned by any specific company but are maintained by a voluntary community of developers. Overall, then, internetworking has resulted in an opening up of previously closed systems and much greater levels of interconnection among systems.

Organizations have been embracing internetworking. Building applications on the internet makes it much easier for people to access them and enables organizations to reach customers or clients from a distance. We do our banking online, trade stocks online, order goods and services online, and file our taxes online. Once a web application is created and once information is online, it is essentially free to the organization distributing it, and so can be distributed at low cost and still yield a profit. Governments can reach out to their citizens much more easily through the internet and by putting information on line, they can be much more transparent. For example, the US government has been putting vast amounts of information about budget, government operations, and the state of the nation online, opening up access to people all over the country.

The internet is becoming a ubiquitous ICT, carrying phone and video traffic, as well as traditional "packets" of email or web pages. Rather than using traditional stand-alone computers, organizations increasingly run software across the internet, taking advantage of a new development termed **software as a service** (SaaS). Through SaaS, applications such as word processors and spreadsheets are accessed across the internet and not housed on the user's computer as separate programs. SaaS utilization is spreading due to reduced cost for software and maintenance. Salesforce.com, for example, offers customer relationship management through the internet. Customer relationship management is a holistic approach to dealing with customers that integrates sales, service and support, and marketing in a seamless software application. Customers can come to a company's website and click for advice, technical support, scheduling service calls or complaints (and of course new purchases!). Salesforce.com handles all the technical details and tailors each site to the organization's needs. This enables even small companies that normally could not support such large scale applications to offer extensive customer service and appear quite sophisticated in the bargain.

As one of the pioneering SaaS companies, Salesforce.com also pioneered in offering cloud computing services. **Cloud computing**, which houses data and programs on "clouds" of computers maintained by companies like Yahoo, Amazon, and Google, also seems to be a trend of the future (Nichols, 2010). Users access the cloud through the internet and run

SaaS applications through their browsers (think Google documents and spreadsheets, for instance). In this case there is literally no need for a PC. The cloud can be accessed through small network computers, cell phones, or tablets. While most users and companies still retain their PCs to keep important information locally and for ease of use, there is a trend toward moving to "the cloud," and as it becomes more reliable and established, this trend is likely to increase.

The growth of the internet and developments such as SaaS and cloud computing have been enabled by the ever-increasing **bandwidth** offered by telecommunications services. Connections between ICTs, whether a telephone wire or a fiberoptic cable, can be likened to pipes through which digital signals "flow." The diameter of the pipe determines how much water can flow through it: More water can flow more quickly through a 9-inch pipe than through a 2-inch one. Bandwidth is analogous to the diameter of "pipe" (the connection) between ICTs. The greater the bandwidth the more information and the more quickly this information can flow. When the internet was first developed, it could only support transmission of small amounts of information, such as that included in text messages. Transmissions that included greater amounts of information, such as an audio recording or video picture, moved so slowly that they were not satisfactory. Each new generation of the internet increased bandwidth and was capable of more satisfactory transmission of richer information. Today streaming video on the internet sometimes yields pictures similar to the video signals received by television sets. In the next few years, there will be yet another upgrade of the internet that should provide adequate bandwidth for almost any type of communication or data that can be envisioned. This will fuel still further growth.

Another major development has been the emergence of **wireless technologies**, such as cell phones and other handhelds. Unlike most ICTs, which typically are implemented first in the most advanced countries – the United States, Japan, Europe – and then come much later to less developed areas, cell phones and other wireless communication devices are being implemented rapidly all over the world, in Africa and the Middle East nearly as much as in the United States. This is because there is no need to build up the costly infrastructure of transmission lines and switching boxes that traditional wired telephone systems require. Instead, cell phones can be supported by transmission towers, which can be built relatively quickly and do not take up as much real estate, and satellites, which are costly, but once in operation are easily and constantly available. This infrastructure is much easier to build and maintain in less developed areas than wired phone systems. Cell phones also operate on batteries and are less likely to be rendered inoperable by power outages. Thus, the unreliable electric utilities common in less developed countries are not as much of a problem as they would be for a physically wired telephone system, which must have continuous power to operate. Wireless communication truly is integrating the world.

Wireless applications have burgeoned in recent years. Wireless markers attached to pallets and even individual products help organizations keep track of inventory. The clips attached to clothes that set off alarms when the clerks forget to remove them are "dumb" examples of these devices. Handheld computing devices, such as personal digital assistants and palm computers connected into wireless networks, make computer networks much more flexible and adaptable. Most traffic departments in medium to large cities, for example, use wireless PCs or tablet computers to write tickets and record them in their databases. These integrated systems allow them to check for unpaid tickets and other relevant information (much to our distress sometimes!). Utility companies give employees wireless computers that tell them what their next repair job is, give them directions to the location, and provide maps and diagrams of the installed utilities to guide their work and make sure they don't accidentally cut through the wrong wires or pipes. There is almost no limit to the range of uses to which wireless ICTs can be put.

More and more wireless applications are run by smart phones. The term "app" has entered common parlance in recent years. One interesting aspect of the apps distributed by Apple and Google for their phone operating systems is that they are proprietary and closed to anyone not using the operating system in question on their phone. Hence, they reverse the openness that has been the trend on the internet and are opening up a new era of nonconnected systems. Whether phone apps will follow the same trajectory as the internet and open up is an open question; they could just as easily lead to a new generation of disconnected, proprietary systems. The same is true of currently burgeoning social networking sites, like Facebook. They are closed systems that people have to belong to in order to participate.

Geographic information systems (GIS) – which "integrate hardware, software, and data for capturing, managing, analyzing and displaying all forms of geographically references information – are diffusing throughout society."[11] They are powerful because a picture (in this case, a map-based vizualization) is worth a thousand words. GISs enable us to see relationships that statistics and texts cannot easily convey. Banks use GIS to study real estate deals, governments to plan how to deal with natural disasters such as earthquakes,[12] and researchers to study trends in population movement. A related ICT, the **Global Positioning System**,[13] a space-based global satellite system provides reliable information on locations. This network of satellites beams location information back to earth that can be picked up by anyone with a GPS receiver. It forms the basis for the various navigation systems in cars and ships and, embedded in cell phones and other devices, can be used to locate where workers are and to track their activities. For example, at Texas A&M the parking monitors are tracked using GPS so that their supervisors can see where they are (and, potentially, if they are doing their jobs).

Most organizations are fairly conservative in their adoption of ICTs. They tend to wait until the utility of ICTs have been shown to adopt and utilize them. Until recently this meant following the lead of industry leaders, like Walmart, which pioneered in the use of ICT to keep inventory and restock stores and continues to innovate in "supply chain" applications. However, as ICTs become smaller, more portable, and cheaper, individuals often lead in the adoption of new ICTs. Examples include mobile phones, electronic "books," and tablet computers. Individuals see the value of these and then encourage the organization to adopt them. So-called 3G and 4G mobile devices such as the iPhone and Google's Droid have found their way into the workplace because workers see their potential and sell the organization on them. One commentator put it this way, "What's happened over the past 5–10 years is that enterprise IT has fallen behind consumer IT, especially from a user-experience perspective. A recent client told me 'I feel like I take a 15 year step backward when I come in to work'" (Nichols, 2010, n.p.). Workers are reacting to this and the knowledge they have that things could be done more easily and effectively to become change agents with respect to new technology.

The advent of wireless ICTs, combined with their ever increasing miniaturization, is likely to fuel the spread of **ubiquitous computing**, in which computers are embedded in almost everything. Computers are being developed that can be sewn into clothing, incorporated into sheets of paper, painted onto almost any surface. Envisioned applications of

Case Study 2.2

Working in the Virtual Future: An Optimistic View (Looking Back)

In previous editions of Strategic Organizational Communication, *we included the following case, which was based on what we envisioned work would be like in the twenty-first century, based on predictions then being made by information technology scholars. Well, 2010 has come and gone. How accurate were we in projecting how work would be in the twenty-first century?*

As her train picked up speed on its trip from Philadelphia to Boston, Tara Rodgers linked her personal digital assistant to the onboard computer linked into the armrest of her seat. Tara was on her way to Boston to facilitate a meeting for a scientific team that Worldwide Consulting Group was organizing for InuitAid International. InuitAid International (IAI) was a network organization of social service and health agencies that was being developed to address a health crisis among the Inuit peoples of Northern Canada. For the past three years, starting in 2008, Inuit children and elders had been contracting respiratory infections at three times the rate of 2007. Deaths in both groups had increased sharply, and a number of Native American tribes and organizations had urged the governments of Canada and the United States and the United Nations for help with this crisis.

Tara had a degree in communication, with a specialization in intercultural and group communication, and seven years of experience working with international scientific teams. She had started with a major accounting firm, but soon left to set up her own private agency with two of her colleagues. They had begun working with medical research teams in Boston and later along the East Coast. They developed expertise in helping teams whose members worked in several locations develop virtual organizations. Tara specialized in teamwork and facilitation and her other two partners were experts in contract law and information technology, respectively. The partners learned from each other and each pitched in to help with all sides of the business, but having these three deep specialties enabled the partners to cover most of the important aspects of scientific collaboration. Tara's firm affiliated with Worldwide's group of consulting agencies three years ago and had worked on several contracts for Worldwide. Tara and her colleagues liked having their own independent firm, because it gave them flexibility to work on projects they believed in, like this one. Being one of Worldwide's affiliated partners had brought them a good deal of business, plus some wonderful opportunities like this one.

Tara's immediate job was to facilitate the organizing meetings of the diagnostic group of the IAI. She envisioned that the first set of meetings for this group would take about two months. Following this, Tara (and her associates if they were needed) would continue to work with the IAI to facilitate meetings, assist with problems and help manage conflicts, and help to keep project teams on schedule for the remainder of the project.

The IAI had been quickly assembled by Posi Sistrunk, the broker from the UN Agency for International Relief. She succeeded in getting commitments from the Centers for Disease Control, the UN Health Service, the Canadian Health System, and the Novosibirsk Hospital in Russia. The Centers for Disease Control brought expertise in tracking down the causes of outbreaks of disease or mortality; the UN Health Service had years of experience in delivering care in rugged terrain; the Canadian Health System had first documented the problem and would be in the front line of care provision. The Novosibirsk Hospital had dealt with a similar incident among native peoples in Siberia four years before. In that case the cause had been found to be heavy metals from industrial sites in southern Siberia. Two major drug companies had agreed to provide medicines for the network, if any were needed. As with all network organizations, it was important that all partners commit themselves fully and develop good working relationships and clear ground rules from the beginning.

Using the onboard computer, which had a brighter and larger display screen than her personal digital assistant, Tara downloaded her email and found she had received biographies of the 17 people who would attend the workshop. This was a diverse group, and Tara knew that their different nationalities and scientific backgrounds would make coordinating this group a challenge. From hard-won experience, Tara knew that it was particularly important that everyone agree on definitions of key concepts, such as quality control. Scientists from different disciplines often assumed that others assigned the same meanings that they did to terms. As a result, needless disputes could arise; one scientist might disagree with another's quality assessment, for example, because the two had different definitions of the type of data needed to measure quality. Tara knew that it was important to spend several meetings agreeing on definitions and standards, even though the scientists might grumble that all they were doing was agreeing on words.

Tara knew three of the scientists well, and had heard of several others. She patched through a video call to Stanley Marsh, an epidemiologist with another firm in Worldwide's network who knew most of the scientists. After inquiring about each others' families, Tara and Stanley discussed the members of the group. Tara realized that Stanley was getting more and more interested in the project, so she asked him if he'd like to come on board as co-facilitator; his scientific expertise and evident trust in Tara would give extra weight to Tara's attempts to guide this group. Following this, Tara put in a video call to Scientific Associates International, a nonprofit group dedicated to promoting scientific cooperation among nations, and downloaded case studies of effective scientific health teams and statistics on how long start-up periods for multidisciplinary scientific groups typically were. These would help her make her case for a slow but thorough start-up period for IAI.

In Boston Tara walked from the train station to Worldwide's telecommunications station. Participants would be linked into a virtual meeting tomorrow, and Tara wanted to familiarize herself with the meeting room. On one side of the room was a video screen that could hold full pictures of up to 18 separate meeting sites; the three-dimensional holographic technology made them seem as though they were just different parts of the same room. She knew that not all sites had this technology; the Russians, in particular, had only two-dimensional videoconferencing walls with a capacity for four meeting sites. So she knew she would have to make sure to indicate carefully who wanted to be recognized to speak in the meeting so that the Russians could switch to that site if it was not up on their screen already. Tara also spent some time setting up the conferencing software that would link the group's work over the next year. It allowed textual and data transfer, online data analysis, and video links for impromptu meetings of a few of the scientists in the network. This conference environment would be the team's virtual home for the next year. Finally Tara arranged for a direct video interview of several Inuit leaders. She planned to lead off the meeting with this to highlight the plight of the Inuit, thus providing a common ground for fast, cooperative action in IAI.

Tara walked out of the Worldwide building a happy woman, looking forward to the meeting tomorrow. Sure, there would be some problems and unpleasant arguments, but she looked forward to tackling them. Making IAI work was a challenge, but it would help so many people.

Applying What You've Learned

1. What things about Tara's scenario are consistent with how communication and information technologies have developed during the early twenty-first century? What things are inconsistent?
2. Are communication and information technologies in the twenty-first century more advanced than the case depicts? Less advanced?
3. IAI will bring together people from very different organizations and cultures. What might Tara do to help these people work together?

Questions to Think About and Discuss

1. Will technological advances help us to address the challenges posed by diversity and globalization?
2. What might be the downside of working in this organization for Tara? Can you identify any problems she might face or stresses she might experience?

these devices range from the mundane – keeping track of inventory and preventing theft, monitoring diabetics' blood sugar level continuously – to the exotic – triggering changes in room temperature and lighting as a person walks from room to room. While most applications of ubiquitous computing are still a few years off, it seems safe to assume that ubiquitous computing will have major impacts on the way we live and on organizations over the next decade or two.

One downside of all this interconnection is that it has become increasingly difficult to secure computers and the information they contain because interconnection makes them more accessible. Security experts in many organizations report that there are hundreds of probes by intruders into their servers and systems every day. The impacts of computer viruses, worms, and other "malware" have been common knowledge for at least a decade. The SANS Institute listed among its top cyber security threats for 2008 "increasingly sophisticated website attacks that exploit browser vulnerability," botnets, mobile phone threats, spyware, and cyberespionage. **Cyberespionage** occurs when outsiders hack into organizational ICT for the purpose of stealing valuable information, such as credit card numbers or trade secrets, or planting malware in the system (Messmer, 2008).

An even larger threat comes from terrorists or other governments engaged in **cyberwarfare.**[14] Cyberattacks by another country or group can potentially cripple power grids, which are controlled by computers, and other critical infrastructure. In 2008, for example, hackers infiltrated the US Department of Energy's Oak Ridge National Laboratory. Laboratory Director Thom Mason commented that it was part of "a sophisticated cyber attack that now appears to be part of a coordinated attempt to gain access to computer networks at numerous laboratories and other institutions across the country." Some security experts suggest that the attack originated in China.[15]

Functions of Information and Communication Technologies in Organizations

ICTs play a number of important roles in today's organizations. Table 2.1 list some examplary ICTs and their functions. Most obvious is their capacity to *facilitate communication* within and between organizations. Communication technologies vary considerably in the richness of information they can transmit and the immediacy with which responses come (see Chapter 6), and they can facilitate communication in several respects. They can speed up communication by making it more efficient to contact others (as email and instant messaging do) and to convene meetings of people in different locations (as videoconferencing and computer conferencing do). Email, computer conferences, and weblogs facilitate communication between people who are on different schedules, because messages and entries can be read and answered whenever convenient for the receiver. Several of these ICTs also allow the sending of broadcast messages – requests or memos sent to a large group of recipients, even to the whole organization. This capability enables people who do not know whom to ask to gather information and form relationships.

ICTs also function, of course, to help with the actual work of the organization. Most readers of this book will not recall the time when typewriters were commonplace. The tedious work of hitting keys that required a lot of force to move, "whiting out" typographical errors, retyping pages with lots of errors, and making carbon copies have been made a thing of the past by word processors. It is interesting that many of the features of the word processor were adapted from the typewriter.[16] Often new technologies resemble existing

Table 2.1 Functions of ICT in Organizations

Function	*Representative technology*	*Examples and detail*
Facilitate communication	• Email • Telephone • Audioconferencing • Computer conferencing • Videoconferencing • SMS (IM) • Blogs • Wikis	• Gmail • AT&T; Vonage • AT&T; FreeConferenceCall.com • Adobe Connect; WebEx • Skype; OOVOO • Any instant messaging service • Any weblog • Wikis are like shared bulletin boards
Do the work	• Word processors • Spreadsheets • Computerized machine tools • Media editing and creation • Medical technology • Robotics	• Word; Google document • Excel; Google spreadsheet • Shop machinery • Adobe Premier • CAT scanner • Auto assembly robots
Coordination and integration of work processes	• Electronic data interchange (EDI)	• Automatic exchange of data between organizations; for example, banks exchanging financial information and factories sending suppliers automatic notifications about needed supplies
	• Computer-aided design and computer-aided manufacturing (CAD/CAM)	• Integrates the design of parts with their manufacturing; for example, engineers would use a CAD system to design a tool and then the ICT would transmit specifications to various machine tools and robots in a factory that would assist in its manufacturing
	• Office workflow systems (WS)	• Help organize and manage the flow of information through an organization; for example, a human resources system that serially processes a job listing, information on applicants, justification for a hire, and intake into payroll all online, with each step being conducted by a different person; this system organizes and speeds up the work of hiring and intake
	• Enterprise systems	• Multipurpose systems that link EDI, CAD/CAM and WS with other functions to provide a "total information system" for an organization; examples include SAP, an enterprise resource planning system that can be used to automate all functions in an organization and Banner, a financial control system used by many universities
Knowledge management	• Knowledge databases • Enterprise search • Expertise maps	• Lotus Notes • Coveo • CI-KNOW

ones when they first emerge, because of relatively limited imagination of developers and users. Once launched, however, technologies diverge from the past as new, unimagined functions are added. Today's word processor allows us to do much more than the typewriter ever could.

A third use of ICTs is in the *coordination and integration* of work processes. The improvements in quality and efficiency of work provided by ICTs are well known. Even greater benefits can be realized when ICTs are used to integrate organizational work processes. For example, **Electronic data integration** (EDI) systems enable the management of data exchange among units, divisions, and companies that have to coordinate their work. Organizations use EDIs to set up automated exchanges of information needed to coordinate key tasks.

One of the earliest and most famous examples of EDI is American Hospital Supply (AHS) (Johnston and Vitale, 1988). This system, orginally developed by a regional sales manager, enabled hospital clerks to order supplies over telephone lines using punch cards and primitive computers. It was extremely successful and increased sales markedly. When the executives of AHS realized that the system gave them a direct connection to their customers that competitors did not have, they developed the organization's strategy around this system, reorganizing their sales force and inventory around the computerized purchasing system. They refined and improved the system until it became so simple and reliable that customers "self-served," rather than relying on the sales force as much as they had in the past. This strategy enabled AHS to reduce costs and increase market share, and made it the leader in its industry. It also transformed the organization. Sales representatives no longer devoted most of their time to selling supplies, but instead sold the purchasing system. The sales function became much less important in the company, while the information systems function became much more important. Facilities and personnel were organized around supporting the purchasing system, which required redefinition of jobs and changes in work processes. AHS also used the information flowing from the automated sales transactions to help it predict demand from its customers, which allowed it to adjust inventory levels to keep up with demand and reduce wastage. AHS's customers, too, were changed by the system; AHS helped them redesign their purchasing and supplies systems to fit the new online process.

Building on this concept, in March 2000, five major health care supplies – Abbott, Baxter, GE Medical, Johnson & Johnson, and Medtronic – started the Global Healthcare Exchange (GHX) (Applegate *et al.*, 2003, 35–38).[17] GHX was designed as an electronic marketplace that would enable purchase of health care supplies, but it also offered much more. It promised to enable hospitals to increase the efficiency of their entire health care supply chain, from placing orders to receiving delivery. The five founding partners handled over 70 percent of the supply business at the time of GHX's founding, and were joined by 70 additional firms in the next few years. This "one-stop shopping" approach was attractive to hospitals, but it was also beneficial to suppliers, who no longer had to compete in an open market. They could set prices higher than they might have been in open competition and they could also count on having "captive" customers, once hospitals redesigned their purchasing procedures around the GHX system.

The evolution from AHS to GHX shows how ICTs have fundamentally changed organizations. Today many organizations are literally (re)designed around ICTs. Rather than being just a tool for organizations to use, ICTs are the major component of the organization.

The monetary cost of electronic workflow integration is substantial, since it typically involves design of complex hardware configurations and integrating software across many applications. Even with substantial investment, problem-free integration of the various parts of a system is difficult. Many office automation projects, for example, remain unfinished, because incompatible software and hardware make it impossible to link the various subsystems together. There may also be human resistance to workflow integration. Automating integrating functions may eliminate jobs. It also tightens up surveillance, which may cause resentment, even as it increases quality and control. However, the gains from electronic workflow integration can be substantial, in terms of effectiveness and efficiency. So long as the process being integrated constitutes a substantial part of the organization's critical work and the implementation of the integration is competent, the gains outweigh the costs.

A fourth application of ICTs is to help organizations manage knowledge that has been developed and accumulated over the years. One of an organization's greatest assets is the knowledge that its employees develop. **Knowledge management** refers to the practices and procedures that organizations use to identify, catalog, harness, and utilize valuable knowledge.[18] Two kinds of knowledge can be distinguished. One important type of knowledge, *organizational knowledge*, consists of accumulated experience in an area, such as an extensive database of customers or experience with developing and operating a specialized product, for example computer-assisted inventory systems. A second type of knowledge is the *expertise* of employees. While this knowledge may seem to be solely the property of the employee, the organization has a stake in it as well, because it often pays for employee education and training and gives the employee a context in which to develop this knowledge. For example, an employee who develops expertise in website design has done this using his or her talents and initiative; but the organization has supplied the computers and software and time for programming that enabled the employee to become an expert. Both organizational and employee-based knowledge have come to be regarded as assets that organizations can use to add value to their products and services, and organizations have attempted to develop knowledge management processes to capitalize on these assets.

ICTs play an important part in knowledge management, because once an organization identifies key knowledge, it wishes to preserve it in a form that makes it easily available and manipulable. Knowledge management systems can take a number of different forms. In some cases, organizations compile databases listing customers, problems that have occurred with products, and other organizational knowledge. Linking these together provides an elementary knowledge management system. Still other organizations actively solicit information and knowledge from employees, who enter it into a shared system such as Lotus Notes. This, however, is quite time-consuming for employees and they are not always willing to comply fully with such requests. (Indeed, some are probably afraid that if they put everything they know into the system, they would be let go because there is no longer a need for them!)

Another approach that does not require codification of knowledge in databases employs search engines within the organization that scour email, documents, web pages, and other digitized information for a requested topic. Coveo and Nexis-Lexis, for example, have both developed applications that do this. Coveo's[19] identifies people who have worked on a topic, emails related to it, and relevant documents such as meeting minutes. Noshir Contractor and his associates developed a system to identify knowledge networks that did not rely on content, but rather identified expertise among the members of an organization (Huang, Contractor, and Yao, 2008).[20] He used a two-part mapping strategy in his CI-KNOW software: The first part involves identifying networks of who-knows-what knowledge that is relevant to a project; the second step is to identify people "who know who knows what," that is individuals who are particularly knowledgeable about where expertise lies in the organization. If one could not locate a needed expert from the first map, one could use the second map to find someone likely to know someone else who had the knowledge you needed. One application of CI-KNOW was by the National Institutes of Health, which wanted to map expertise on smokeless tobacco, its effects, and how to encourage cessation.

Knowledge management is still relatively new, and several problems must be solved before it can reach its full potential. As we have already mentioned, knowledge management requires cooperation of organizational members. In this time of overworked, overstretched workers, it may be difficult to obtain the needed inputs. Second, knowledge itself is often difficult to identify. Much knowledge exists in a form that can be expressed verbally and written down or stored in databases; just as much or more knowledge is tacit knowledge, know-how that cannot be put into words, but instead is in the hands of the experienced worker or the judgment of the manager or expert. Most organizational knowledge management systems cannot easily capture this type of knowledge. Finally, some have doubted that effective knowledge management is even possible, given the fact that knowledge is a community property and changes constantly.

Impacts of Information and Communication Technologies

The widespread use of ICTs in modern organizations has several important effects. First, use of ICTs tends to *open up communication and increase accessibility* of people in organizations. Studies show that email, for example, tends to increase lateral communication, contacts across organizational levels, and the flow of ideas compared to more traditional communication media (Rice and Gattiker, 2001, 563). Moreover, rather than substituting for traditional channels such as face-to-face communication, email usually adds to the total communication flow in organizations. As we will see in Chapters 4 and 6, the more open the communication system, the more adaptable and responsive the organization is likely to be.

Second, ICTs promote the *spacial dispersion of organizations*. Prior to the advent of ICTs, organizations either had to situate employees working on highly independent tasks in the same place or allow for delays due to the time taken to manage interdependence via letter, memo, or phone. However, electronic linkages are so fast, reliable, and provide such rich interaction that organizations can now plan to have work dispersed to the locations where it can be done most effectively and integrate via electronic communication. For example, a sales team working with a firm purchasing industrial equipment can work directly with engineers back at the home office to determine if alterations desired by customers are feasible and to price the changes. Where this may have taken a week or more in the "old days," electronic linkages make it fast and relatively easy. **Telework**, a work arrangement in which employees spend at least part of the time working at home or off site, is a growing trend supported by new ICTs.[21] The number of full-time telecommuters accounted for 3.9 percent of US workers in 2006 and more that 23 percent of US workers worked from home at least one day per month in 2005. The number of teleworkers is projected to expand to 14.2 million over the next few years (Cox, 2009, 4). Many organizations, including the US government, are promoting telework as a "green" alternative to commuting and have realized considerable savings by implementing telework programs (Cox, 2009). The capability of ICTs to facilitate coordination and support work is also one major reason for the globalization of organizations.

A third impact of ICTs has been to foster *interorganizational linkages* (Rice and Gattiker, 2001, 569–572). Organizations have always entered into joint ventures, alliances, and other types of collaborative agreements with other organizations. However, ICTs have made it much easier for organizations to develop integrated activities, particularly since the spread of internetworking. Ventures such as GHX, described above, would be much more difficult to manage without the internet, which enables the companies to easily combine their product listings, make them available to customers, take and route orders, and make the accounts for the venture available to each partner. Network and virtual organizations, discussed in Chapter 6, are often comprised of allied organizations linked together through the internet. Another type of interorganizational linkage which is increasingly common is **outsourcing**, in which one organization contracts with another to perform certain functions. For example, it is becoming common for organizations to hire contractors to set up and maintain helpdesks. In many cases calls or emails are routed to helpdesk contractors located in other countries. Until recently Dell Computer, for example, had its helpdesks run by a subcontractor in India.

Recent developments in ICTs have raised issues related to *privacy.* ICTs enable organizations to monitor their employees relatively unobtrusively. Employees working on networked computers may have their keystrokes counted, emails perused, and the websites they visit recorded. Managers often justify these measures on the grounds that they have a right to make sure their subordinates are actually working. However, employees may feel violated in that what were previously private activities are laid open to scrutiny. We will explore issues related to privacy and surveillance in organizations in Chapter 3. ICTs also enable organizations to collect and integrate personal information in unprecedented ways. Records can be made of the websites a person visits and their internet purchases. ICTs can also compile databases of information on individuals, such as major purchases, credit ratings, and travel. In the US this information is not the property of the individual, but of the organization compiling it. The recent dispute over plans by the Department of Homeland Security to employ Carnivore, a powerful search engine, to scan email and other internet communications for suspicious activity is one example of how an organization may compromise private information and intrude on citizens' privacy.

In concluding this brief discussion of impacts of ICTs, we want to register an important qualification. If one thing is certain from the research, it is that effects are strongly dependent on the context in which the ICT is implemented – which include the organizational culture, the goals of the different parties involved in its implementation, the specific problems or opportunities the ICT is brought in to addresses, and social influence processes at workgroup and individual levels (Rice and Gattiker, 2001, 567–569). To be sure, ICTs have certain potentials or tendencies, but they are just that – tendencies. This should also be a lesson to managers or planners. Technology is not a silver bullet that can be used to fix or reengineer the organization. Managers who assume it is will find that the bullet often hits different targets than those at which they aim.

SUMMARY

The term "strategy" derives from the ancient Greek for "artifice" or "trick," and its early use referred to surprising the enemy in battle (Onions, 1996). The person who conceived the strategy, the *strategos*, was a general. The roots of the word imply that the strategist has sufficient insight to devise a trick and enough control to carry it out. But the ancient Greeks were subtle. They knew that situations often changed and that the strategos had to adapt. Hence strategy has an element of improvisation and cannot follow a rigid plan.

The five keys to strategic organizational communication do not offer a simple formula. In our rapidly changing world, formulas are unlikely to work. Rather, the keys are what rhetoricians call "commonplaces" or *topoi*, issues to start from and ways of thinking that will help to generate insights into the challenges facing today's organizations. In complex and dynamic situations, it is important not to freeze one's thinking by trying to adhere to a few simple rules. Maintaining an open mind and responsiveness to the cues in the immediate situation is the key to intelligent and flexible response.

While they deal with different aspects of organizations, the five keys are interrelated. Systems thinking works in synergy with critical thinking to help people become aware of unaknowledged structures that influence organizations. Both of these help us to understand globalization, diversity, and ICTs, which are often driven by subtle forces that are difficult to fathom. ICTs are enablers of globalization, and globalization feeds into the development of ICTs. In turn, globalization is one of the trends that confronts us with the challenges and opportunities of diversity.

As you read on and think about the organizations in your life, we hope you will come to understand these connections and uncover insights of your own.

NOTES

1 The principles of systems thinking are discussed in more detail in Peter Senge's excellent book, *The Fifth Discipline: The Art and Practice of the Learning Organization* (1990).

2 Albert Hirschman (1991). For an extended summary of this argument and an excellent application of it to the recurring debate in the United States about increasing the minimum wage, see James Aune (2001, esp. chap. 1).

3 For a brief summary of these data, see Paul Krugman (2003). More extensive analyses have been published by authors across the political spectrum. At one pole is conservative economist and (until recently) lifelong Republican Kevin Phillips (1990, 2002); at the other is a series of reports issued by the liberal Economic Policy Institute and written by Lawrence Mishel, Jared Bernstein, and Heather Bousley (2003).

4 See Anna Cristina d'Addio (2007). Also see T. Vogel (2006), who found less positive results for the United States after 1990; and M. Corak (2006).

5 See Bellah, Madsen, Sullivan, and Tipton (1995); Reynolds and Norman (1988); and Bennis, Parikh, and Lessem (1994, esp. chap. 10). For a summary of de Tocqueville's observations and their applicability today, see Cawelti (1974); and Deetz (1992).

6 In our discussions of different social groups we have chosen to use the terms that we do to refer to different groups of nonwhite employees because they seem to be preferred by members of each group in the United States. The reasons for our choice of terminology for persons of Spanish descent is a bit more complex. We use the terms *Latino* and *Latina* as *generic* terms to refer to men and women of Spanish descent respectively. We use the term *Mexican American* to refer to residents of the United States who were born in Mexico or whose families immigrated from Mexico. We do not use the term *Hispanic* at all because it is used in so many different ways, even in the scholarly literature, that its use is inevitably confusing. These terminological distinctions are important because the experiences of Latino persons in American organizations are very different depending on their heritage. In particular, people who immigrated from or whose families immigrated from Central and South America

or the Caribbean face different attitudes and have had different experiences than those with roots in Mexico.

7 US Census, American Community Survey (2008), presented on www.aauw.org. In the science and technology professions women do somewhat better, earning on average 88 percent as much as men, according to a report by the US Department of Labor, Bureau of Labor Statistics (2008). However, only 27 percent of the workers in these professions are women.

8 Key advocates of the homogenization thesis include Howes (1996), Ritzer (1993), and Ritzer and Liska (1997). Advocates of the polarization thesis include Barber (1995), Said (1978), and Huntington (1996). Advocates of the hybridization thesis include Friedman (1999) and Hannerz (1992).

9 This opinion is expressed by Winter and Taylor (1996), who argue that new IT-supported organizational forms resemble those found in the pre-industrial era.

10 The phenomenon of convergence and some of its impacts are discussed in Castells (2001) and Jenkins (2006).

11 GIS.com offers an informative overview of geographic information systems and some of their applications: see www.gis.com.

12 An example of using GIS to plan for disasters can be viewed and explored at the Mid-America Earthquake Center at the University of Illinois, which has developed MAEviz, an application that can be used to predict damage from earthquakes of varying degrees of severity. See http://wiki.ncsa.illinois.edu/display/MAE/Home.

13 Information about Global Positioning Systems can be found at www.gps.gov.

14 An excellent resource on cyberwarfare in its many guises, including "cyberterrorism," and "electronic jihad," can be found online at http://staff.washington.edu/dittrich/cyberwarfare.html.

15 Ibid.

16 For a brief history of the word processor, see www.cs.umd.edu/class/spring2002/cmsc434-0101/MUIseum/applications/wordhistory.html and www.computernostalgia.net/articles/HistoryofWordProcessors.htm.

17 For more information about Global Healthcare Exchange, go to www.ghx.com.

18 The website for KM World has a list of the "100 Companies That Matter in Knowledge Management," indicating how much activity there is in this area. There are a number of other papers and other types of information about knowledge management at www.kmworld.com.

19 See www.coveo.com/en.

20 See also http://isda.ncsa.uiuc.edu/ecid/ECID_ciknow.htm.

21 Cox (2009). See also Konradt, Schmook, and Malecke (2000, 63–99). We will examine telework in more detail in Chapter 3.

REFERENCES

Applegate, L.M., Austin, R.D. and McFarlan, F.W. (2003). *Corporate Information Strategy and Management*, 6th ed. Boston: McGraw-Hill.

Aune, J. (2001). *Selling the Free Market*. New York: Guilford Press.

Axley, S. (1984). "Managerial and Organizational Communication in Terms of the Conduit Metaphor." *Academy of Management Review* 9: 428–437.

Barber, B.R. (1995). *Jihad vs. McWorld*. New York: Random House.

Barber, B. (2000). "Jihad vs. McWorld." *The Annals of the American Academy of Political and Social Sciences* 570: 23–33.

Behr. P. (2003). "Blackout Report Cites Ohio Utilities: Michigan Panel Points to Failure to Isolate System." *The Washington Post*, November 6, E5.

Bellah, R., Madsen, R., Sullivan, W. and Tipton, S. (1995). *Habits of the Heart*, 2nd ed. Berkeley: University of California Press.

Bennis, W., Parikh, J. and Lessem, R. (1994). *Beyond Leadership*. Cambridge, MA: Basil Blackwell.

"Blackout Baby Boom a Myth, Duke Professor Says." (2004). *Science Daily*, May 12, B2. www.sciencedaily.com/releases/2004/05/040512044711.htm.

Castells, M. (2001). *The Internet Galaxy*. Oxford: Oxford University Press.

Cawelti, J. (1974). *Apostles of the Self-Made Man*. Cambridge, MA: Harvard University Press.

Cheney, G. and Barnett, G.A. (2005). "Introduction," in Cheney and Barnett, eds., *International and Multicultural Organizational Communication*. Creskill, NJ: Hampton Press.

Clair, R.P. and Thompson, K. (1996). "Pay Discrimination as a Discursive and Material Practice." *Journal of Applied Communication Research* 96: 1–20.

Corak, M. (2006). *Do Poor Children Become Poor Adults?* IZA discussion paper. Bonn: IZA.

"Corporate Women." (1992). *Business Week*, June 8.

Cox, W. (2009). *Improving the Quality of Life Through Telecommuting*. Washington, DC: Information Technology and Innovation Foundation.

d'Addio, A.C. (2007). *Intergenerational Transmission of Disadvantage*. www.oecd.org/els.

Deetz, S. (1992). *Democracy in the Age of Corporate Colonization*. Albany, NY: SUNY Press.

DeParle, J. (2010). "A World on the Move," *New York Times*, June 27, pp. 1, 4.

Drohan, M. and Freeman, A. (2000). "English Rules." *Annals of the American Academy of Political and Social Science* 570: 428–434.

Drucker, P. (1994). "The Age of Transformation." *Atlantic Monthly*, September, 53.

"FERC Says Grid Fix Can't Wait for New [Energy] Bill." (2004). *Houston Chronicle*, January 8, B2.

Fishman, J. (1998/1999). "The New Linguistic Order." *Foreign Policy* 113 (Winter): 116–142.

Fix, M., Papademetriou, D., Batalova, J., Terrazos, A. and Mittelstadt, M. (2009). *Migration and the Global Recession*. Washington, DC: Migration Policy Institute. www.migrationpolicy.org.

George, C. (2009). "Houston Expecting a Baby Bump." *Houston Chronicle*, May 12, 1A.

Hannerz, U. (1992). *Cultural Complexity*. New York: Columbia University Press.

Hirschman, A. (1991). *The Rhetoric of Reaction*. Cambridge, MA: Belknap Press.

Howes, D., ed. (1996). *Cross-Cultural Consumption*. London: Routledge.

Huang, Y., Contractor, N.S. and Yao, Y. (2008). "CI-KNOW: Recommendation Based on Social Networks." *DG.O*: 27–33.

Huntington, S. (1996). *The Clash of Civilizations and the Remaking of World Order*. New York: Simon & Schuster.

Huntington, S. (2000). "The Clash of Civilizations?" *The Annals of the American Academy of Political and Social Sciences* 570: 3–22.

Jenkins, H. (2006). *Convergence Culture*. New York: New York University Press.

Johnston, H.R. and Vitale, M. (1988). "Creating Competitive Advantage with Interorganizational Information Systems." *MIS Quarterly* 12: 7–21.

Kaplan, R.D. (2000). "The Coming Anarchy." *The Annals of the American Academy of Political and Social Sciences* 570: 34–60.

Kirby, E.L., Wieland, S. and McBride, M.C. (2006). "Work-Life Communication," in Oetzel and Ting-Toomey, eds., *Handbook of conflict communication*. Thousand Oaks, CA: Sage.

Konradt, U., Schmook, R. and Malecke, M. (2000). "Impact of Telework on Individuals, Organizations and Families: A Critical Review." *International Review of Industrial and Organizational Psychology* 15: 63–100.

Korn/Ferry International (1993). *The Decade of the Executive Woman*. New York: Korn/Ferry International.

Krugman, P. (2003). "The Death of Horatio Alger." *The Nation* online, December 20. www.thenation.com.

Kuttner, R. (1996). *Everything for Sale*. Chicago: University of Chicago Press.

Martin, L. (1992). *Pipelines of Progress*. Washington, DC: US Department of Labor.

Messmer, E. (2008). "Cyberespionage Seen as Growing Threat to Business, Government." *Network World*, January 17.

Mishel, L., Bernstein, J. and Bousley, H. (2003). *The State of Working America, 2002/2003*. Ithaca, NY: Cornell University Press.

Mumby, D. (1988). *Power in Organizations*. Norwood, NJ: Ablex.

Nichols, R. (2010). "Cloudsourcing the Enterprise." *Computerworld Online*, June 29. http://blogs.computerworld.com/16422/discussing_cloudsourcing_and_corporate_transformation_with_an_execution_specialist. Also at energy.gov.

Onions, C.T., ed. (1996). *The Oxford Dictionary of English Etymology*. Oxford: Oxford University Press.

Perez-Pena, R. (April 6, 2004). "Utility Could Have Halted '03 Blackout, Panel Says." *New York Times* online. www.nytimes.com.

Perrow, C. (1984). *Normal Accidents*. New York: Basic Books.

Pfeffer, J. and Davis-Blake, A. (1987). "The Effect of the Proportion of Women on Salaries." *Administrative Science Quarterly* 32: 1–24.

Phillips, K. (1990). *The Politics of Rich and Poor*. New York: Broadway Books.

Phillips, K. (2002). *Wealth and Democracy*. New York: Broadway Books.

Putnam, R. (2000). *Bowling Alone*. New York: Simon and Schuster.

Reynolds, C.W. and Norman, R.V., eds. (1988). *Community in America*. Berkeley: University of California Press.

Rice, R.E. and Gattiker, U. (2001). "New Media and Organizational Structuring," in Jablin and Putnam, eds., *New Handbook of Organizational Communication* (pp. 554–581). Thousand Oaks, CA: Sage.

Ritzer, G. (1993). *The McDonalization of Society*. Newbury Park, CA: Pine Forge Press.

Ritzer, G. and Liska, A. (1997). "McDisneyization and Post-Tourism," in Rojek and Urry, eds., *Touring Cultures*. London: Routledge.

Rosin, H. (2010). "The End of Men." *Atlantic Magazine*, July–August. www.theatlantic.com/magazine/archive/2010/07/the-end-of-men/8135/.

Said, E. (1978). *Orientalism*. New York: Penguin.

Senge, P. (1990). *The Fifth Discipline*. New York: Doubleday.

Stohl, C. (2005). "Globalization Theory," in May and Mumby, eds., *Engaging Organizational Communication*. Thousand Oaks, CA: Sage.

Therborn, G. (1980). *The Ideology of Power and the Power of Ideology*. London: Verso.

Tomlinson, J. (1999). *Globalization and Culture*. Chicago: University of Chicago Press.

US Census Bureau (2008). "American Community Survey." www.aauw.org.

US Department of Labor, Bureau of Labor Statistics. (2008). *Women in the Laborforce: A Databook*. Report 1018. Washington, DC: US Department of Labor.

U.S.-Canada Power System Outage Task Force. (2003). November 19. Washington, DC: US Department of Energy.

Vogel, T. (2006). *Reassessing Intergenerational Mobility in Germany and the U.S.* Discussion paper 2006-055. Berlin: School of Business and Economics, Humboldt University.

Wald, M. (2002). "Few Indications that Efforts to Cut Blackout Risks Are Underway." *New York Times* online, December 13. www.nytimes.com.

Winter, S.J. and Taylor, S.L. (1996). The Role of IT in Work: A Comparison of Post-Industrial, Industrial, and Proto-Industrial Organization. *Information Systems Research* 7: 5–21.

UNIT II

STRATEGIES OF ORGANIZING

CHAPTER 3

TRADITIONAL STRATEGIES OF ORGANIZING

The foreman should never be authorized to enforce his discipline with the whips if he can accomplish it with words.

Varro of Rome, *ca.* 100 BCE

If the words of command are not clear and distinct, if orders are not thoroughly understood, the general is to blame.

Sun Tzu of China, *ca.* 500 BCE

CENTRAL THEMES

- Traditional strategies of organizing attempt to control employees through rules, norms, and systems of rewards and punishments, all of which rely heavily on communication. But all control systems lead to resistance.
- If information is filtered as it passes through the formal chain of command, decision makers may have too little relevant information to make good decisions; if it is not filtered, they may be too overloaded with information to make good decisions.
- Both structural and personal/interpersonal factors lead to omission and distortion of information as it passes through formal channels.
- When the environment surrounding an organization is stable or not competitive, traditional strategies of organizing may function well; when the environment is turbulent or competitive, weaknesses in formal communication systems make it difficult for traditional strategies to succeed.

Strategic Organizational Communication: In a Global Economy, Seventh Edition.
Charles Conrad and Marshall Scott Poole.

- In traditional strategies of organizing, leadership primarily involves managing, that is designing and implementing formal systems of communication, motivation, and control.
- Information and communication technologies offer ways for traditional organizations to avoid some of the problems that the strategy creates.

KEY TERMS

specialization
hierarchy
centralization
chain of command
bureaucracy
legal authority
time–motion studies
information overload
decentralization
unintended consequence trained incapacity
informal communication networks
redundancy
counterbiasing
face management
distributive justice
procedural justice
surveillance
regressing
working to rule

As the ancient comments at the beginning of this chapter suggest, neither the study of organizations nor that of communication in organizations is terribly new. Whenever people have depended on one another to complete tasks or meet their needs, they have formed organizations. By the time human beings joined together into families and clans, they had become involved in the economic activities of hunting and gathering. They had started to organize, which required them to communicate with other workers. After humans had become farmers, they developed more complex organizations with more complicated communication needs. With farming came villages and the need to govern large groups of people; with villages came the concepts of citizenship and community welfare, which created the dual needs of defense and the management of the village's economy.

As villages became city-states, it became necessary for their managers to plan the operation of the society and to keep permanent records of the rules and procedures that they developed. The oldest written documents in existence deal with religion, management, and government, a combination that makes great sense when one realizes that the earliest managers also were governors and priests. As ancient religious and political civilizations expanded, their needs for effective economic organizations and effective organizational communication multiplied. As early as 2000 BCE, leaders recognized the importance of communication. Pharaoh Ptah-hotep instructed his sons and managers in the importance of listening skills, the need to seek advice and information from their subordinates, the importance of staying informed about what was taking place around them, and the necessity of clearly explaining each worker's tasks and documenting these instructions in writing. The Chinese emperors Yao and Shun (*ca.* 2300 BCE) also searched for ways of opening communication channels between themselves and the peasants and advocated consulting their subordinates about the problems faced by the government. By the first century CE, Greek and Roman scholars had already suggested many of the key concepts of modern organizational communication theory. But it was the growth of the nation-state and the mercantile system that created separate roles for governors, managers, and priests. The large and complex firms of the Industrial Revolution made it clear that control and coordination could be achieved only through effective communication.

Unfortunately, the people who operated these organizations had few reliable guidelines. They had some experience in business and thus could rely on hunch and intuition. But peoples' memories often omit or redefine their failures and overemphasize their successes, so experience often is not a reliable guide (Feldman and Feldman, 2006). Managers also could try to apply the principles used to run military organizations, which were the major large, complex organizations that existed before the Industrial Revolution (Mutch, 2008). But, overall, owners' decision making suffered from a lack of concern for efficiency and a virtual absence of reliable information.

In addition, owner-managers often treated their employees in arbitrary, capricious, and even inhumane ways. Proslavery politicians of the 1800s defended that institution by arguing that the lives of slaves were better than the lives of workers in Northern textile mills. There was enough of a parallel to make the argument credible. As a result, workers began to organize politically and form unions. Labor–management relations became increasingly hostile, and confrontations between labor and management were often violent. The broad, rapid economic growth of the 1800s came to a screeching halt in the Crash of 1873. The economy never recovered fully, and living standards and social stability were devastated by a series of economic depressions during the 1890s, each one more severe than the last. By the early 1900s, both managers and scholars recognized that Western organizations faced serious problems in design and operation. In response to these observations, a group of organizational theorists proposed an alternate strategy of organizing, one that sought to manage the paradox between organizational and individual needs by enhancing efficiency, creating stable and predictable organizational situations, eliminating arbitrary supervisory behavior, and motivating workers through economic rewards and a sense of personal achievement.

TRADITIONAL STRATEGIES OF ORGANIZATIONAL DESIGN

A large number of people were involved in the development of the traditional strategy of organizing. One group, the *bureaucratic theorists*, attempted to improve organizations from the top down, by improving the effectiveness of administrative employees. Their perspective is associated with sociologist Max Weber. A second group developed *scientific management*, an approach that tried to improve organizations from the bottom up, by reforming workers' tasks, efficiency, and rewards. The approach was developed by an engineer, Frederick Taylor. Both groups had the same primary concern – replacing the arbitrary, capricious, and inefficient practices of contemporary organizations with systematically designed, objective, and fair systems of management and supervision.

Traditional Structure and Communication

All organizations are structured. Indeed, it is structure that distinguishes organized enterprises from disorganized ones. Structure is important to members of organizations because it makes life predictable and clarifies each member's area of responsibility. With predictability come feelings of stability and trust. Structure also makes formal authority relationships clear to everyone involved in the organization, and it lets every member know where to go for different kinds of information and expertise (Handy, 1995; Morand, 1995).[1] But, the structure that emerges in a particular organization is not random or determined by outside forces. It depends on a series of choices that employees make.

Bureaucracy and Structure Both the scientific managers and the bureaucratic theorists believed that organizations should be segmented into a matrix of formal positions that can be represented in a triangular "organizational chart." The tasks that must be performed in the organization are *divided* among various groups of employees who have the **specialized** skills necessary to complete those tasks efficiently and effectively. The organizational chart also shows how the various positions are arranged, so that lines of authority are clear to all. The positions are arranged in a **hierarchy**; supervisors are directly responsible to their own immediate supervisors for their own actions and for those of their immediate subordinates. Decisions about major issues, policies, and procedures are **centralized** at the top of the hierarchy. This means that all the major decisions facing the organization are made by the people who occupy the positions located at the top of the organizational hierarchy. Of course, all members of the organization are responsible for making *routine*, day-by-day decisions in their areas of responsibility. But, they must base their decisions on *policies* and *procedures* that are established by the people at the top of the organization. When communication does take place outside of the immediate work group, it is formal, both in tone and in terms of the way in which it is communicated, and follows an established **chain of command**. That is, subordinates send messages to their immediate supervisors, who relay the information to *their* immediate supervisors if they deem it appropriate to do so, and so on. No one goes over his or her supervisor's head. Of course, communicating in this way is slow, cumbersome, and vulnerable to many different kinds of communication breakdowns (examined in more detail later in this chapter). Because this particular organizational structure is so widespread, it is easy to forget a number of basic facts about it. The most important fact is that organizational structure results from choices. It is one of a large, perhaps infinite, number of ways in which an organization can be structured.

The kind of structure that we have just described is called a **bureaucracy**. As sociologist Max Weber noted a century ago, it is especially appropriate to Western capitalist democracies. To people raised in those societies, bureaucratic structures are so common that they *seem* to be *natural,* and *normal* (recall Unit I). As members of these societies mature, they learn that formal rules are necessary for the efficient operation of societies and organizations. Rules also protect people from arbitrary or harmful treatment by more powerful people. They are taught that societies "of law" are better than societies of "men [*sic*]." They come to value individuality, to believe that individuals have rights and that individuals are responsible for their actions. They learn to accept what Weber called **legal authority**, the notion that societies and organizations should be organized around a formal, objective (and thus unbiased), written set of rules, policies, and procedures. They begin to view people in terms of the roles that they play in society and organizations, and to view a person's value, rights, and obligations in terms of the formal positions they hold. These taken-for-granted assumptions mask the fact that the bureaucratic structure is only one of a large number of available strategies of organizing. They also tend to obscure the fact that traditional strategies of organizational design have distinctive strengths and particular weaknesses.

In an organization using a traditional strategy, applicants are hired for a position solely because they are able to demonstrate that they possess the special expertise needed to perform their required tasks, not because of their political connections. Employees base their everyday decisions solely on the written policies, procedures, and rules of the organization, and document all of their actions in writing. To prevent favoritism, all employees must maintain detached, impersonal relationships with clients and coworkers, and keep emotional considerations from influencing their actions. Since communication is restricted to the chain of command, it is easy to determine who is responsible for any communication breakdowns, and corrective action can be taken. The bureaucratic theorists valued this kind of structure because they thought it would bring fairness and accountability to organizations, and also increase organizational efficiency. Everyone in the organization would know who was responsible for each task that needed to be performed. If those tasks were performed well, the correct people would be rewarded; if not, the responsible people would be punished. Every employee would also be held responsible for communicating relevant information up and down the chain of command. After they successfully completed a probationary period, employees would be guaranteed a job for life (assuming their performance continued to be adequate), and an adequate pension. As a result, they could not be pressured to show favoritism to powerful clients or supervisors. Organizations, and all their members, would be accountable for their actions, and the organization would be highly efficient.

Scientific Management The second group of people who helped develop the traditional strategy of organizing advocated *scientific* management. Like the bureaucratic theorists, they were concerned with both accountability and efficiency. Frederick Taylor, the father of scientific management, was very disturbed by the common practice of managers blaming and punishing workers for their own bad decisions. The practice reduced organizational efficiency because it failed to hold managers accountable for *their* errors, giving them no incentive to improve their performance. It also inevitably drove a wedge between labor and management, and management's primary goal should be to foster cooperative and productive relationships with their workers.[2]

Although these attitudes may not seem to be all that radical today, they were to Taylor's contemporaries. They were palatable only because Taylor coupled them with a set of efficiency-enhancing techniques that he could demonstrate had significant short-term economic benefits. Taylor believed that by using these techniques, firms would be able to increase their profits and the incomes of *all* their employees, including managers. Over time increased efficiency would allow these firms to reduce their prices, benefiting the entire society. The best known of these techniques was the **time–motion study**, in which a supervisor or consultant observes workers completing a task, breaks the process down into its elements or motions, and then redesigns it to minimize the number of movements necessary to complete it. By using the improved techniques, workers could increase their productivity, their income, and the organization's profits. For example, Charley Conrad helped fund his college education by working summers and vacations in a metal-processing foundry. Initially he operated a drill press. But, the company conducted a time–motion study and found that workers taller than 6 feet could not efficiently operate the equipment. They had to bend over to reach some of the levers and as a result got tired sooner than the shorter workers did. Like every other operator who was taller than 6 feet, he was transferred to a section that had tasks that could be efficiently performed by people of his height. Even today, a century later, consulting firms, armed with sophisticated video technology, conduct time–motion studies and make recommendations that improve efficiency and reduce worker strain and fatigue, in both manufacturing firms and "high-tech" organizations.

Taylor stressed that time–motion studies, and all of the other techniques he developed, should be used in close consultation with workers and in an atmosphere of cooperation and mutual gain. If they are used without first consulting workers, as they often are, they generate strong resistance, especially if there is a low level of trust between labor and management.

Today firms such as the ones Taylor envisioned are often viewed as sweatshops where workers are treated like inhuman cogs in a giant industrial machine, just as they were in Taylor's time. In addition, the term "bureaucracy" has a number of negative connotations – images of inefficient bureaucrats producing little save exhaustive expense accounts; of customers and employees alike being buried in red tape and treated as nonhuman cogs in a vast administrative morass; and of stubbornness when action is required, blind obsession with unchangeable policies when flexibility is necessary, and interminable delays when speed is crucial. These images of the traditional strategy of organizing are really quite ironic (Sewell and Barker, 2006b). The original purpose of this strategy was to create efficient and productive organizations in which people were treated fairly and equitably. The arbitrariness and capriciousness that Taylor and Weber observed in the organizations of their time were to be replaced by policies and procedures that treated everyone – workers, customers, and clients – in the same way. The biased and inefficient decision making of early firms was to be replaced by objective, data-based considerations. Although the strategy focused on meeting the organizations' needs for coordination and control, it also was intended to meet individual employees' needs for stability and autonomy. Bureaucratic structure is clear, stable, and predictable. But the traditional strategy is also problematic in two ways. Perhaps most important, its key elements – specialization, hierarchicalization, and centralization – place a great deal of pressure on an organization's formal communication system. Consequently, communication breakdowns are highly likely. Second, the strategy sacrifices flexibility and responsiveness for consistency and predictability. This is neither an accident nor the result of "pointy-headed bureaucrats gone mad." Bureaucracies are based on the universal application of predetermined, written rules, policies, and procedures. Everyone is *supposed* to be treated alike, and individual circumstances, needs, and differences are *supposed* to be ignored (Perrow, 1986). Although this trade-off is appropriate for some organizations, it creates serious problems for others.

Communication Breakdowns in Formal Communication Systems

For the traditional strategy of organizing to succeed, information must flow freely up and down through the chain of command. The decision makers at the top of the organization must receive accurate, complete, concise, and timely information about the extent to which orders have been carried out and tasks have been completed. They must also be informed about problems that have developed or are likely to develop in the future. In addition, decision makers must benefit from the specialized expertise of each employee along the chain of command. If that expertise is not available to individuals in upper management, their decision making will suffer. Similarly, information must flow from supervisors to subordinates, including information about policies, procedures, reward and rule systems, and the optimal means of performing each subordinate's assigned tasks. If any of these communication processes breaks down, the organization will function at less than optimal efficiency. If the margin of error available to the organization is small, these communication breakdowns may threaten its survival (Snyder and Morris, 1984).

The Filtering Paradox Unfortunately, processes of information exchange create a fundamental paradox. On the one hand, upper-level decision makers depend on receiving accurate, timely information from employees located lower in the hierarchy. However, if information flowed through the chain of command without any restriction, the upper-level managers would soon be overloaded and overwhelmed. For example, envision a moderate-sized hierarchical organization (one in which each supervisor has only four subordinates and the organization chart has seven levels). Each employee sends only one message a day up the chain of command. If no messages are filtered out, 4096 messages would reach upper management each day, creating serious problems of **information overload**.[3] But, if every employee screens out only half of the information received, 98.4 percent of the information generated in the organization would never reach its decision makers. Consequently, the traditional strategy of organizing requires employees to both rely on formal channels for the information they need while simultaneously restricting the flow of information through these channels.

Structural Barriers to Information Flow A number of factors complicate the filtering paradox. Some of these barriers to information flow involve the formal structure of the organization and the nature of human communication. These structural barriers exist regardless of who works in the organization, regardless of their individual characteristics or relational skills.

When one person communicates a message to another, each of them interprets it. The words that make up the message are meaningless until some human being makes sense out of them.[4] When people communicate, they exchange their *interpretations* of information, not information in a "pure" form. When they interpret messages, they alter the message's meaning. People *condense* messages, making them shorter and simpler; people *simplify* messages into good or bad, all or none, or other extreme terms; they *assimilate* new messages so that their meaning is consistent with information received in the past; they *whitewash* messages, so that they will not upset the people to whom they are sent; and people *reductively code* messages by combining them with other information to form a sensible overall picture. In the process of interpreting a message, people simplify and clarify it. They absorb some of the uncertainty and ambiguity in the message. But, they also change it. Interpreting information is inevitable because all messages carry some degree of ambiguity, and some degree of uncertainty about how they should be interpreted. When messages are interpreted, they are changed.

Interpersonal Barriers to Information Flow A number of personal and interpersonal factors also complicate information flow (see Table 3.1). If people have different levels of organizational power and status, they exchange little information with one another. When they do communicate, it tends to be in writing (physical or electronic) rather than face to face. Their messages focus on tasks, with little informal or social content. Written messages are more ambiguous than those exchanged in open, face-to-face encounters, which makes it more likely that the parties will misunderstand one another (Albrecht and Bach, 1996). Differences in interpretations tend to reduce trust, which leads employees to rely even more heavily on written communication in order to protect themselves, and so on in a downward spiral. Supervisors *could* offset these effects by deemphasizing status differences, training their subordinates in communication skills, rewarding their subordinates for keeping them informed (especially about negative events), and encouraging them to seek clarification of

Table 3.1 Factors That Distort Vertical Communication

Structural	*Personal and relational*
1. Processes of interpreting messages Condensation Accenting Assimilation to past Assimilation to future Assimilation to attitudes and values Reduction	1. Power, status differences between parties
2. Number of links in communication chain	2. Mistrust between parties
3. Trained communication Incapacity Perceptual sets Language barriers	3. Subordinates' mobility aspirations
4. Large size of the organization	4. Inaccurate perceptions of information needs of others
5. Problems in timing of messages	5. Norms or actions that discourage requests for clarification
6. Problems inherent in written communication	6. Sensitivity of topics

ambiguous messages. However, they often do the opposite by verbally or nonverbally communicating, "I don't want to hear about it now."

Supervisors may talk only while on the run, use an annoyed tone of voice, physically move away from the subordinate, and allow other people to interrupt the conversation. Or they may simply fail to acknowledge or act on the information their subordinates provide, which discourages them from providing information in the future. Ironically, the supervisors who most strongly say that they want their subordinates to keep them informed seem to be most likely to discourage them from doing so.[5]

If subordinates do not trust their supervisors, other factors come into play. Subordinates who wish to be promoted or recognized for past achievements and believe that the supervisor will have an influential voice on promotions are especially prone to withhold negative information from supervisors they do not trust. Those effects are increased when subordinates believe that their supervisors do not pass negative information on to them. They are especially unlikely to communicate negative information or information that deals with controversial or sensitive issues – precisely the kind of information that supervisors most need to have. In highly political organizations, withholding information is even more likely, especially when it is negative. As Chapter 8 explains, information is a potent source of power, but only if it is not widely available. Political battles – among individual employees and among units of the organization – often are information battles, and the side that is best at obtaining and exploiting secret information wins (Fulk and Mani, 1986).

Although this section has focused on barriers to the upward flow of information through the chain of command, the same factors and processes also hamper downward communication. One of the most consistent findings in research on organizations is that subordinates want their supervisors to keep them informed and feel that they receive too little relevant and useful information from their supervisors, even information that is necessary for them to do their jobs well. It also seems to be true of feedback about the subordinates' performance, something that is especially frustrating for members of the Generation X and

Millennial groups (recall the "Generations" case study in Chapter 1). Downward communication is selected, filtered, interpreted, and withheld in much the same way as upward communication. In addition, when supervisors believe that they should give their subordinates information only on a "need to know" basis, they filter an even higher proportion of downward communication, frequently withholding even crucial information.

As a result of these processes, cycles of communication are formed and perpetuated. Some cycles are positive; others are negative. Supervisors whose communication is considerate, frequent, and reliable tend to have subordinates whose communication is similar. Because they better understand their supervisors' information needs, they can better summarize the information they receive without leaving out important details, thus reducing problems of information overload. These subordinates keep their supervisors informed, which makes them seem trustworthy, and when people trust one another their communication is more open and direct. The distortions related to differences in status and power are reduced. Conversely, supervisors who withhold information from their subordinates have subordinates who withhold information from them or bury them in detail. These subordinates view their own actions as a necessary way to protect themselves against an untrustworthy supervisor; the supervisor may see the subordinates' actions as compelling evidence that they are hostile or unmotivated, which justifies the supervisor's withholding information, and so on. No one individual is to blame (or should receive credit) for these cycles, although supervisors' higher formal power means that they have a greater effect on the direction the cycle will take. These patterns result from complex, interacting systems of meaning creation and should be understood as complex systems of communication for which all parties are partly responsible.

How Traditional Strategies Complicate Information Flow Each of the sources of communication breakdowns described in this section are present in all organizations. But, they are more of a problem in organizations that employ traditional strategies of organizing than in organizations that rely on other strategies. One of the key characteristics of traditional strategies is centralization of power and decision making. If an organization is highly centralized (that is, if its organizational chart is "tall") messages will be exchanged, interpreted, and altered many times before they reach the decision makers at the top of the organization. In addition, it takes a long time for information to flow through long chains of command, so it may reach decision makers too late for it to be useful. Conversely, the decisions that are made at the top of the hierarchy – the policies and procedures that are created – will be exchanged, interpreted, and altered many times before they reach the people at the bottom of the organization who will implement them. They also may arrive too late to be useful. Communicating through formal chains of command is exhausting and time-consuming, as any student who has needed to change a registration for a course or find a "lost" student aid check is painfully aware. In Chapter 4 we will explain that organizations can choose strategies of organizing that reduce these problems. In them, decision making is distributed throughout the organization (that is, if it is **decentralized**) and messages are exchanged fewer times before action is taken on the information they contain. Fewer exchanges mean less interpretation and less alteration.

A second element of the traditional strategy of organizing is *specialization*. It increases organizational efficiency by making sure that tasks are performed by people with the relevant expertise. But, an **unintended consequence** of specialization is that it complicates information flow. As people are trained in an increasingly specialized set of skills, they become less and less capable of performing other tasks. They develop a kind of **trained incapacity**. The most obvious incapacity involves differences between upper management and lower-level workers. Managers often become incapable of understanding the processes through which their workers perform their tasks, even if they once did those jobs themselves. Conversely, lower-level workers become less able to understand complex, abstract thought. But, trained incapacity permeates the entire organization. Employees who play specialized roles interpret the messages they receive in a manner appropriate to those roles. Personnel officers interpret messages in terms of what they imply about future needs for hiring, firing, or training employees; and financial officers attribute meaning to messages based on the economic impact that they imply. As their training and experience progress, employees become less capable of taking the perspectives of other members of the organization when they construct or interpret messages.

Sometimes they may even create their own languages. Corporate attorneys learn to talk like corporate attorneys, IT personnel learn to talk like IT personnel, and so on. As employees become literate in the artificial language of their position or unit, they become less capable of translating their ideas into a language that other people can understand (Spence, 1978; Jablin, 2001). As a result, misunderstanding across specialties is quite common. The size of an organization in itself does not seem to increase problems of trained incapacity, but when an organization is highly specialized, trained incapacity can create severe problems.

Finally, traditional strategies of organizing attempt to formalize communication, which highlights power and status differences, and stipulates that relationships between supervisors and subordinates should be impersonal and governed by established policies and procedures. As a result, trust is reduced, written communication dominates, and misunderstanding becomes more likely. It is precisely in this kind of situation that the personal and interpersonal sources of distortion are most potent. In summary, traditional strategies rely heavily on formal, chain-of-command communication and paradoxically create a number of barriers to successful information flow. If organizational communication really did function as it is supposed to in the traditional strategy, most people would not know what was going on most of the time. (For an extended illustration of the concepts presented in this section, see Case Study 3.1, which begins on p. 83.)

Compensating for Communication Problems of Traditional Strategies of Organizing

So far in this chapter, we have argued that traditional strategies of organizing rely heavily on formal systems of communication and that it is normal for these systems to break down. That analysis may lead readers to wonder just how these organizations manage to survive. The answer is that many organizations have minimal needs for rapid and accurate task-related communication. Some organizations exist in extremely stable environments that place limited demands on communication. Problems can be anticipated and situations can be understood rather easily because they almost always are like those faced in the past, and tried-and-true solutions are generally available. Expertise, decision making, and authority can be centralized, communication can be restricted to the chain of command, and so on. Information can usually be obtained through formal channels, and the kinds of communication breakdowns that are discussed in this chapter can be anticipated and offset.

In stable environments, traditional strategies of organizing cope quite well with the limited amount of uncertainty that they face. In contrast, organizations in highly

Case Study 3.1
Feel Safer Now?

Within days of September 11, 2001, pundits and politicians alike were trying to explain the intelligence breakdowns that allowed 20 or more terrorists to carry out attacks on the World Trade Center and Pentagon. Some commentators explained the event as the result of vast conspiracies.[1] Others explained the breakdowns in less exciting terms. Like in the case of organizational accidents (recall the blackout case in Chapter 2), the dominant impulse was to blame "operator error":

> [T]here were people at the borders who let these people in even though they didn't have proper papers. . . . There were F.B.I. people who, when they got reports from Phoenix and Minnesota and elsewhere, didn't think they were important enough to buck up to the higher-ups. There were security officers at the airports who let these people onto airplanes even though they were carrying materials that weren't allowed on airplanes. (Thomas Kean, chairman of the September 11 Investigating Panel, cited in Shennon, 2003)

It is clear that people, both inside and outside of formal organizations, often make errors in judgment that result from well-understood cognitive processes, biases that may "blind people to emerging threats." We will examine these individual sources of "nonrational" decision making at length in Chapter 8. At this point, we only mention one dimension – information itself is meaningless until it is interpreted. But, interpretation is impossible without a frame of reference that allows decision makers to understand how the individual pieces of information they possess fit together. In this sense, decision making is a little like putting a 100-piece jigsaw puzzle (the items of information) together without having the picture on the boxtop (the frame of reference) available to guide the process. To make matters worse, much of the information available to decision makers is not relevant to a particular decision. Without a frame of reference, it is very difficult to know which of the pieces will be useful and which ones are "noise." So, it is a little like taking four or five puzzles, dumping all of the pieces into a large box, shaking them around, and then giving them to the decision makers to assemble (again, without them having access to any of the pictures on the boxtops). Of course, after the event takes place, *everyone* has a frame of reference available that will make all of this clear (it's like finding all of the boxtops), which is why hindsight is always better and "Monday morning quarterbacks" always seem to be smarter than the ones on the field. Keep this image in mind as we work through the events leading up to 9/11.

There was a second kind of explanation offered for 9/11: almost as soon as the investigations began, informed (and uninformed) experts started attributing those breakdowns to "communication problems" in the US intelligence community that prevented "the necessary integration of information until it is too late" (Bazerman and Watkins, 2008). We will focus on this organizational explanation in this case study. Our story begins at the end of World War II, not in 2001. Myriad federal agencies have been in some way involved in national safety, from the Department of Agriculture to the Federal Aviation Administration to the US Coast Guard. Almost all of these organizations also have other responsibilities, ones that are either irrelevant or only tangentially related. The most visible and most important federal agencies are the Federal Bureau of Investigations (FBI), Central Intelligence Agency (CIA), and National Security Agency (NSA). When World War II ended, a proposal was made to continue the wartime Office of Secret Service as the CIA. The head of the FBI at that time, J. Edgar Hoover, fought the creation of the CIA, primarily on the grounds that the two bureaucracies were unnecessarily duplicative (see Riebling, 1994). Hoover lost the battle, but was able to ensure that the two agencies would have separate intelligence functions: one to anticipate and prevent actions by targets outside of the United States (CIA) and one to investigate and convict criminals who had acted within the United States (FBI). At the time, critics questioned this division of labor, since spies and saboteurs regularly cross national borders. But, it made sense as a political compromise. Over time the two bureaucracies developed different ways of doing business, different rules for operating and making decisions, and even attracted a different kind of employee. During the same era the operations of the CIA became progressively more secretive, even after the creation of the even-more-secret NSA maintaining secrecy came to be valued so highly that employees in one agency refused to share information with employees in another agency except on a "need-to-know" basis. But, if one agency doesn't know the information that has been collected in the others, its members cannot know what they "need to know," and cannot determine whether other agencies actually do need to know the information they have requested. The agencies became separate "stovepipes" or "silos" which house different collections of information, analyze that information in different ways for different purposes, and share with other agencies only in very rare circumstances. The silo problem means that the total amount of information *available* to decision makers in any organization at any given point in time is always less than the total amount of information possessed by all of the organization's employees. Bazerman and Watkins describe this combination of silo structures and a demand for secrecy as the "fundamental paradox of intelligence gathering." All organizations experience structural distortion in information flow – that was one of the main points of this chapter. But, intelligence organizations also must be committed to secrecy, which makes structural distortion even more likely.

However, and ironically, the intelligence community also experienced serious problems of information overload. Sometimes leaders of one or more of the agencies complained that counterterrorism offices gathered very little information, especially given the size of their budgets – at least $30 billion per year (since the budgets of the NSA and CIA are secret, this figure is only an estimate). But, after 9/11 it seemed clear that their greatest problem was collecting *too much* information relative to the intelligence community's capacity to process and interpret that information (the overload problem discussed earlier in this chapter). Processing the information was complicated further by the fact that much of the information collected was irrelevant to the upcoming 9/11 attacks. Indeed, former FBI Director Louis Freeh concluded that there was so much information available that "analyzing intelligence information can be like trying to take a sip of water coming out of a fire hydrant" (cited in Helm, 2002).

The "communication breakdown" explanation for the US intelligence community's "failures" before 9/11 is based on information that had been collected on three of the hijackers, Khalid al-Midhar, Nawaf al-Hazmi, and his brother Salim al-Hazmi; all three were aboard the plane that crashed into the Pentagon (Hill, 2002). Evidently, no government agency had any relevant information on the other 16 prior to 9/11. During 1999 the intelligence community began a worldwide effort to monitor people connected with al-Qaeda and Osama bin Laden. The community closely monitored a meeting in Malaysia, where the CIA discovered new information about al-Midhar (his full name, passport number, etc.) and learned that he was leaving Malaysia on a plane with Nawaf al-Hazmi. Eventually they decided that none of this information was important enough to pass on to the other agencies. The NSF's (ultra-secret) database also included the name Nawaf al-Hazmi, along with information indicating that he was linked to al-Qaeda. A lower-level CIA employee, whose job it was to improve communication between the CIA and FBI, did brief the FBI and summarized the briefing for other CIA agents, but no one raised any "red flags" about this information. Later, an overseas CIA agent notified his headquarters that al-Hazmi had entered the United States, but the information was not communicated to the FBI because he had done nothing illegal or threatening (in fact, it evidently was not read by many people within the CIA). While investigating the October 12, 2000, attack on the USS *Cole*, the CIA uncovered links between al-Qaeda and a second hijacker, al-Midhar, and in at least one case passed the information on to the FBI. When the FBI agent asked why the CIA was following al-Midhar, he was told that the information could be given only with permission from his supervisor (a silo/secrecy effect). No formal request was made. The CIA had so many resources tied up investigating the attack on the USS *Cole* that it could not follow up on these leads, and the FBI did not do so because no crime had been committed. Consequently, it risked litigation and/or criticism for racial profiling had it investigated a group of Middle Eastern men when there was no evidence of criminal activity.

The most egregious example of "not connecting the dots," at least according to the US media, involved a presumed almost-hijacker, Zacharias Moussaoui. He had been in the United States for some time attending various pilot schools. When he made it clear to a trainer in Egan, Minnesota, that he did not want to learn how to take off or land, the instructor became suspicious and called the local FBI office. When he refused to allow agents to search his laptop computer, he was arrested on a charge of visa violations that the FBI had constructed in order to keep him in custody while conducting an investigation. They learned from French intelligence officials that he had connections to al-Qaeda. Local agents asked the Washington office to obtain a search warrant for Moussaoui's computer. The Washington office made the request to the special US national security court, but did not include the French reports in the request. The request was denied, leading to a heated and now famous memo from Minneapolis Special Agent Coleen Rowley to the Washington office. Other agencies experienced similar errors – the NSA intercepted a message – believed to be a recorded telephone conversation – that referred to a "big event" planned for September 11, but it was in Arabic and was not translated until after the attacks (a resource/overload problem).

A year later, in June 2002, President Bush reported that "the CIA and the FBI are now in close communications, there's better sharing of intelligence." The next day White House spokesman Ari Fleischer amended the president's comments to contend that the needed changes were gradually being implemented. Eighteen months later, the independent Markle Task Force on National Security in the Information Age was less optimistic, concluding that information sharing "remains haphazard and still overly dependent on . . . personal relations among known colleagues" (an example of using informal communication networks to compensate for breakdowns in formal ones). In addition, there seems to be some confusion about the roles of two agencies created since September 11, the Terrorist Threat Integration Center, created to coordinate information gathered by the CIA, FBI and other agencies, and the Department of Homeland Security. As the chart at the end of this case study illustrates, each of the steps taken to improve communication in the intelligence community has added layers of bureaucracy to the intelligence community and/or communication links to its formal network (Arnold, 2003).[2]

Using What You Have Learned

1. Which of the sources of breakdowns in information flow described in this chapter seem to have been present prior to September 11? To what extent were the identified problems a function of insufficient amounts of information, inadequate flow of information, or errors in interpreting the information that was available?
2. As we indicated in Chapter 2, one of the difficulties in assessing the causes of accidents in separating actual system problems from what only seem to be problems because of the advantages gained by hindsight. For example, airport screeners were trained to search for bombs and the materials that could use to build bombs, not to think of an airplane filled with fuel *as* a bomb. Of the "errors" made before September 11, which were errors, and which merely seem to be errors in hindsight?

Figure 3.1 is an organizational chart from the Department of Homeland Security (which does not include the FBI, CIA, or NSA).

Questions to Think About and Discuss

1. Using what you know about the sources of communication breakdowns in bureaucratic organizations, assess the likelihood of

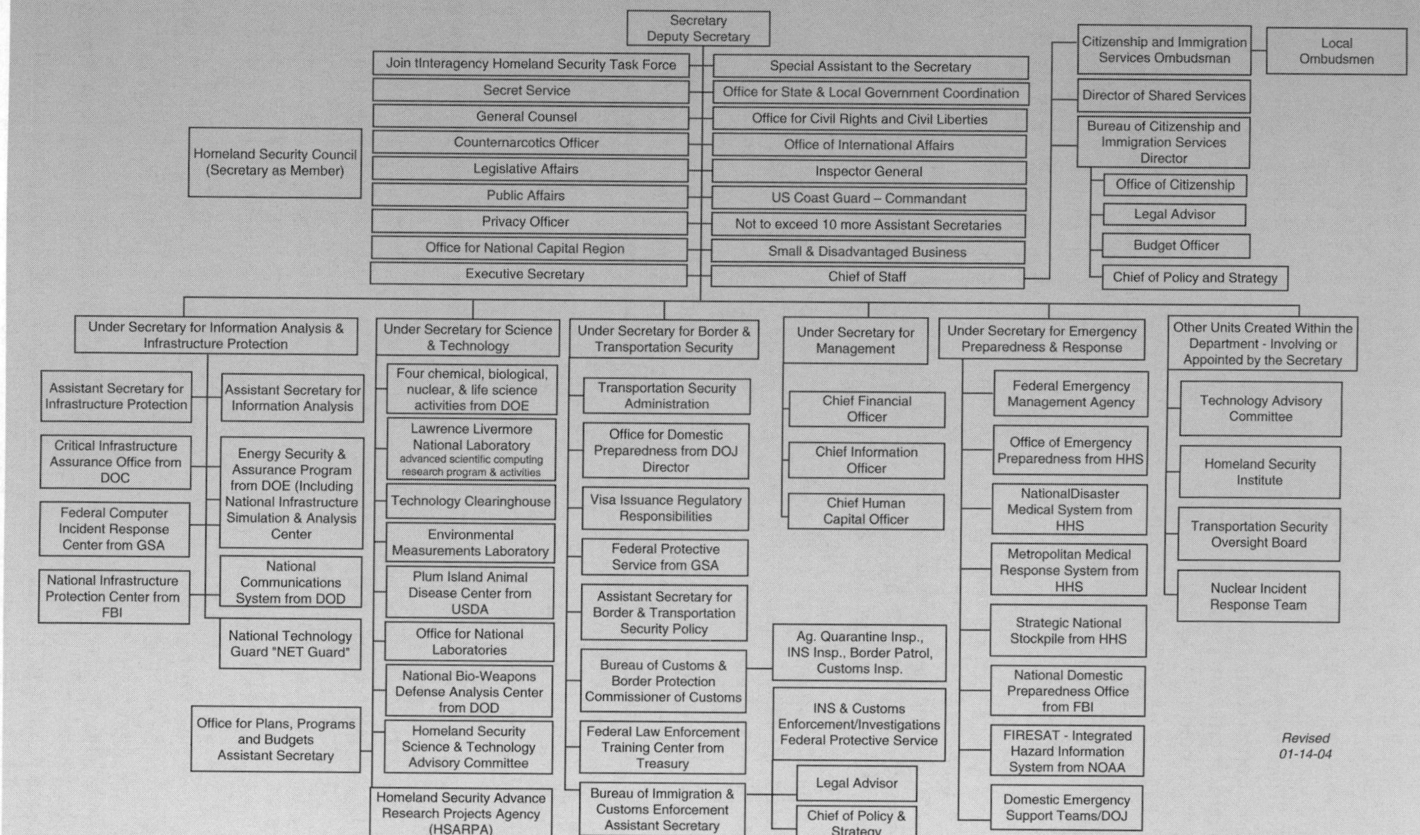

Figure 3.1 Department of Homeland Security – organizational chart.

Note: This chart is a shortened version of the complete chart, which is 25 pages long. The complete chart is available at www.ndu.edu/library/docs/crs/crs_rl131500_20feb04.pdf.

communication breakdowns in the new department, and among the new department and the FBI, CIA, NSA, and Terrorist Threat Integration Center.

2. What strategies would you recommend in an effort to compensate for any potential sources of communication breakdowns? Why would they work?
3. (The next two will take a little extra research). To what extent do the factors and processes described in this case study explain the communication breakdowns prior to the 2002 decision to invade Iraq (WMDs that didn't exist, etc.)? What additional factors, if any, were involved in that decision? Good starting points for your research include the chapters in part 2 of Edwards (2007), and Whitney (2005). A somewhat less academic analysis is available in Drogin (2007).
4. On April 1, 2011, the US government located Osama Bin Laden living in a suburban compound in Pakistan. A team of Navy Seals attacked his compound, killed him and a number of his followers, and captured others. What does the success of this mission tell us about the effectiveness of the US intelligence community? Of the Department of Homeland Security? Be careful to not deal in generalities. Instead focus on the nature of the tasks involved in the two cases (predicting and preventing 9/11, and finding and eliminating Bin Laden), the intelligence agencies that were involved, the communication processes with and between them, and the usual problems involved in "connecting the dots."

Notes

1 For example, see the debate between David Griffin (2004) and the editors of *Popular Mechanics* magazine (Dunbar, 2006).

2 Also see US Senate Select Committee on Intelligence and US House Select Committee on Intelligence (2003). Also see *The Spy Factory*, especially the first half of the episode, at www.pbs.org/wgbh/nova/insidenova/2010/06/spy-factory.html.

competitive, rapidly changing, turbulent environments are effective when their work and communication structures allow a free, open, and rapid flow of information, not the restricted, formal, and slow chain of command. This was first explained during the late 1950s by two British sociologists, Tom Burns and G.M. Stalker, and developed further during the late 1960s by US management scholars Paul Lawrence and Jay Lorsch. Their findings have been replicated by many people in multiple cultures, to such an extent that there now is a consensus: "Both practitioners and theorists agree that organizations today face enormous competitive pressures and must be highly responsive to rapid changes in the external environment if they are to survive."[6] Open communication structures (such as those of the "relational," "cultural," and "networking" strategies described in Chapters 4, 5, and 6) allow information about sudden environmental changes to be diffused more rapidly throughout the organization.

Fortunately, there are a number of steps that employees who find themselves in organizations that employ traditional strategies or organizing can do to compensate for the communication problems that are inherent in them. One strategy is to grow. Since competition and turbulent environments magnify the problem of "traditional" organization, managers can take steps to reduce those pressures. Large firms can pay other organizations not to produce competing products. They can purchase, and then dissolve, competitors, or they can become even larger. Monopolies and oligopolies are able to influence (perhaps even control) the prices and availability of inputs and sales in ways that reduce the environmental turbulence they face. Pharmaceutical firms have used all these strategies to prevent or forestall having to compete with low-cost generic drugs.[7] In addition, managers also can often persuade government to insulate them against environmental pressures, by placing patent or copyright restrictions on their competitors, or by using tariffs or other restrictions to make foreign competitors' products excessively expensive. Most US residents believe that government regulations and regulatory agencies were created to protect consumers or workers from organizations. This sometimes is true, but historically it has been much more common for regulatory systems to be created in order to protect existing organizations from competitors (see Conrad, 2011; and Wilson, 1974). Or they can shift their activities to sectors of the economy that have relatively stable environments and/or little competition.

The history of the largest US tobacco firms shows how these anticompetitive strategies can be used together. During the 1980s, they diversified, often merging with industries such as food production, which were located in more stable sectors of the economy and received less criticism from advocacy groups. For example, in 1985 tobacco giant Philip Morris purchased General Foods, and four years later it acquired Kraft Foods. Diversification also allowed them to use political and financial pressure to insulate them from external pressures. For example, television news organizations, which might have been tempted to air highly popular *exposés* of the tobacco industry, risked losing the massive advertising revenues that they receive from the tobacco companies' food subsidiaries. Once tobacco firms had shifted much of their production and marketing to Asia, the link was no longer as useful, so they spun off many of their food operations (for example, Kraft Foods is no longer part of Philip Morris). In 2009, after decades of fighting proposals to allow the Food and Drug Administration (FDA) to regulate nicotine, Philip Morris suddenly supported regulation. Industry experts and Morris' competitors complained that the change was designed to reduce competition. Morris' internal research showed that its Marlboro brand had captured such a large market share that regulating the industry would be to the company's advantage. Limits on advertising that would come with regulation, and difficulty obtaining FDA approval for new tobacco products would make it almost impossible for their competitors to ever catch up (Wilson, 2009). Of course, especially in a society that presumably values "free and open competition," these activities raise important ethical and legal questions (see Chapter 12), so they must be implemented quietly and/or justified through appeals to socially acceptable values. But, they all reduce the competitive pressures that organizations face. Finally, organizations can rely on information and communication technologies to help them get around some of the liabilities of the traditional mode of organizing.

Employees also can compensate for the communication problems inherent in the traditional strategy. If they often find that their supervisors leave them "out of the loop" on important topics, they can strategically develop relationships with other people in the organization who are "in the know." The **informal communication networks** they develop gives them the information that they should have received through formal channels (see Chapter 4). In addition, they can build **redundancy** into their own communication networks. If they suspect that they are receiving distorted information, they can engage in **counterbiasing**, in which they determine the probable biases of each person who communicates with them, adjust their interpretation of the message to compensate for these biases, and then actively seek out opinions from people who have differing biases. Fortunately, these compensating networks seem to emerge quite naturally unless managers actively suppress them, so they are there to be used.[8] By acting strategically in their own interests, employees compensate for the weaknesses of traditional strategies of organizing.

TRADITIONAL STRATEGIES OF MOTIVATION, CONTROL, AND SURVEILLANCE

One of the goals of the traditional strategy of organizing was to replace the arbitrary and capricious treatment of workers that often took place in turn-of-the-nineteenth-century organizations with a scientifically designed and rationally implemented system of incentives and disincentives. The strategy assumed that all employees work to achieve goals, primarily economic ones, and a system that rewards them for following established rules and procedures and maximizing their own productivity would be in everyone's self-interest. Labor–management hostility would be replaced with cooperative, mutually rewarding relationships. As traditional rule-and-reward systems were implemented, practitioners and scholars alike came to understand that those systems can succeed if and only if they are supported by effective communication.

Rules, Rewards, and Persuasive Communication

Like traditional organizational structures, rule and reward systems make our worlds stable, predictable, and in some ways simpler. Organizational theorist Karl Weick has noted that rules place parameters around our interactions with other people. Without those rules, we would constantly have to negotiate and renegotiate how we will act toward one another, leaving little time and energy for accomplishing tasks or pursuing other goals. For example, when hospitals provide parents of pediatric patients with a written list of rules about who (parents or nurses) will be responsible for different aspects of their child's care, both the parents and the nurses are more satisfied. The rules make an ambiguous and stressful situation less difficult and allow the parties to spend their time and energy making detailed decisions about their child's special needs (Weick, 1979; Adams and Parrot, 1994). Rules constrain our actions, but they also simplify our organizational lives. However, it is surprisingly difficult to design effective rule-and-reward systems or to implement them successfully. Doing so depends on communication and on being able to persuade members of an organization that the rules and rewards in the system are *legitimate* and *fairly administered.* Success also depends on the systems themselves, and how they deal with *unintended consequences.* To succeed, rules must be clear enough to be easily understood, specific enough to give employees precise guidelines for acting, and general enough to be applicable to a wide range of day-by-day situations. Rules will be seen as legitimate only if members believe that they are applied equitably to everyone in the organization and are produced by the organization, rather than by an individual supervisor acting on his or her own whim.[9] Rules will be perceived as illegitimate if they are applied outside an accepted range of activities. For example, rules about employees' private lives will not be accepted if employees perceive that their employer does not have a legitimate right to enforce them. At one time employees, especially managerial and supervisory personnel, gave their organizations the right to control much of their private lives. Today employees often refuse to accept company rules about where they should live, how they should spend their income, or what they should do with their leisure time.

For example, the management of Dell Computer Company created an uproar when it distributed a memo informing employees that their "Code of Conduct" for behavior at work also applies to the games of the local AA baseball team, the Round Rock Express (who play their home games at the Dell Diamond). Heckling visiting players and booing members of the home team are forbidden because they are "disruptive, unprofessional, offensive, or potentially slanderous"; acting "responsibly with respect to consumption of alcohol" is required. Dell employees are accustomed to rules that impinge on their private lives – 60 hour work weeks for its sales staff or mandatory overtime for technical support people – and generally view those intrusions as legitimate business requirements. But many of them believe that regulating their conduct at a minor league baseball game goes too far.

Rules systems also must be connected to a credible reward system. Employees must perceive that the rewards they receive are both substantial and important. Pay seems to have these characteristics, especially for employees whose incomes are low, whose tenure in the organization has been brief, whose commitment to the firm is low, and who feel that their pay is inappropriate when compared to the pay of other workers. The promotions and status that usually accompany pay increases also seem to be important to most people, especially those with a high need for achievement. Praise also is salient to most people and is positively related to both improved performance and job satisfaction.

Employees must also be persuaded that the reward system is fair. They must believe that rewards are based on performance, rather than on friendships or biases, and that individual employees are primarily responsible for their level of performance, and the rewards they receive. This is a difficult undertaking because people tend to attribute their successes to themselves or to factors within their control and their failures to others or to factors they cannot control.[10] These problems are reduced when objective, quantifiable measures of an employee's performance are available; they are magnified if an employee is involved in creative or managerial work which is more difficult to quantify. But, in the end, the key is a supervisor's ability to provide persuasive performance feedback (Tracy and Eisenberg, 1990/1991). Feedback should both clearly confront a problem (or clearly encourage continuation of excellent performance) and allow all parties to save face. **Face management** is complicated by an employee's status, race, gender, and ethnicity. For example, face saving is especially important to people who culturally have communitarian orientations – women and people from Latin, Asian, and Middle Eastern backgrounds (Nathan, Mohrman, and Milliman, 1991).

At least for people from Western societies, a reward system is seen as fair only if it also is seen as *equitable*. Employees do not evaluate the rewards (or punishments) they receive in a vacuum; they compare them to what others receive and what they believe others *should* have received. If they perceive that the rewards allocated by the organization are just, their job satisfaction is higher than if they believe the distribution of rewards are unjust (labeled **distributive justice**). Similarly, if they perceive that the *process* through which the rewards are allocated is fair (**procedural justice**), their trust in and evaluation of their supervisors, and their commitment to the organization will be higher (McFarlin and Sweeney, 1992). If they perceive that the reward system is not just they will be frustrated and may respond by reducing their effort, negotiating for increased rewards, leaving the organization, or rationalizing the inequity.

Supervisors have a number of persuasive strategies available to convince their subordinates that a reward system is just. Some strategies are overt – giving workers information that proves that they are being treated equitably; and others are covert – withholding information about the other employees' rewards, for example. It is difficult to employ the first strategy successfully, as professors remember each time they try to respond to a student's complaint that "I worked much harder than so-and-so and received a lower exam grade." It is equally difficult to implement the second strategy, although organizations often try to do so through rules that forbid employees from discussing their raises (or salaries) with others. The primary effect of these rules seems to be to encourage employees to obtain the forbidden information, since the very existence of the rules creates the impression that the reward system must be inequitable. The fact that these rules often fail may be the best evidence in support of the equity theory's assumption that people are very much concerned with the equity of reward systems.[11]

Fortunately, supervisors seem to recognize just how important perceptions of equity are in the success of reward systems, and how difficult it is to allocate rewards in a fair manner. When they believe they have reliable performance information on their employees, and they can realistically determine which employee was responsible for which outcomes (positive and negative), they try to allocate rewards based on performance, even though they know that doing so can create competition and hostility within a work group. But when the situation is less clear-cut, or when the supervisors are concerned about "team building," they tend to give approximately equal rewards to each of their subordinates. As a result, in departments in which people work closely together and are similar to one another in backgrounds, experience, and interests, rewards are more alike and there is less difference among the salaries of the various employees (Meindl, 1989; Pfeffer and Langton, 1988).

To complicate matters even further, employees' responses to issues of equity seem to be culture specific. In a study of employees in two individualistic and masculine cultures (the United States and Japan) and a culture that is less individualistic and less masculine (South Korea), Kim and his associates found that all three groups of employees preferred equity-based reward systems over across-the-board systems, although the preference was stronger with the US and Japanese employees. This should not have come as a big surprise. A century ago, Max Weber noticed that in traditional Catholic, European peasant communities, raising the sum that workers received for each item they produced often actually *reduced* their output. Workers found that with the increased pay rates, they could maintain the same income with less effort. At some point, leisure time became more important to them than increased income, so working harder made little sense given their complex set of goals. With the coming of Protestantism, and its emphasis on wealth and consumption as evidence of moral goodness, increases in pay have a more positive effect on performance.[12] In sum, there is no doubt that traditional organizational control systems influence employees' actions and attitudes. However, there also is a great deal of evidence that these systems may have many unanticipated consequences. Implementing control systems requires that a number of requirements – communicative and otherwise – be met, and even if they are met, employees will still make their own decisions about how to interpret and respond to them. (For an extended illustration of the concepts presented in this section, see Case Study 3.2, which begins on page 92.)

Avoiding Unintended Consequences of Rule–Reward Systems

Unfortunately, rule–reward systems may inadvertently encourage behaviors other than those that were intended. In what has become a classic essay on reward systems, Steven Kerr provided a number of examples of "the folly of rewarding A while hoping for B." For

Case Study 3.2

The Power of Rewards at Industry International[1]

Industry International is a manufacturing firm with about 2500 employees in a number of plants. It is often touted as a monument to the power of financial reward systems. In an industry that has been battered by foreign competition for three decades, it has remained highly profitable, in large part because its workers are 2½ to 3 times as productive as those of its competitors. Their compensation is also three times the average salary for US manufacturing employees. They are not unionized, have no paid vacations, and work 45–50 hours per week. Much of their income comes from a year-end cash bonus. Each year, after company taxes and dividends have been paid, the board of directors determines the size of the bonus pool, which is divided among the employees based on their base salary and individual merit ratings. From 1943 to 1994 the bonus percentage ranged from 55 percent to 104 percent; in 1994 it was 61 percent, meaning that an employee earning a $30,000 base salary and receiving a 100 percent merit rating would receive a bonus of $18,300.[2] Base salaries and bonuses have increased faster than inflation since. The bonus is kept secret from October until a meeting-celebration in December. When the meeting ends the employees rush to their cars, bonus checks in hand, and tie up traffic for hours going to their favorite places of celebration.

Most employees use the money to pay accumulated bills, in fact many spend far in excess of their base salaries and then put off paying bills and loans until the bonus checks come in. Other employees use the money for less mundane activities. One got his bonus in $100 bills, spread them on the living room floor, and, along with his wife, rolled around on them (among other activities) in celebration. Some made major purchases like houses, cars, and luxury items in cash. A few (mostly younger employees) used the money to gamble, hire prostitutes, or buy illegal drugs. When asked why they spend the money as they do, three answers were commonly given – to live the good life so valued in the United States, to assert their autonomy (one said, "Spending bonus money is the one thing they [management] ain't telling me what and how to do"), and for the social status that money provides:

> "As soon as they [friends and neighbors] find out you work there, they think you have money coming out of your ears"; [another said] "They think I'm the richest s…o…b [ellipses mine] in the world"; [another recalled that] "years ago we made more money than professional football players."

What they don't tell their envious neighbors is what they went through to get the bonus. Merit points are based on output, quality, dependability, and personal characteristics. The first two can be quantified, leading employees to "work like dogs" until dangerously exhausted by long hours and difficult working conditions; the last two cannot, creating a highly political atmosphere in the plant; most echoed one worker's conclusion that

> "if you don't go along with the system [managers], you could be the hardest worker in the world . . . and you would still be way short because you have not gone with the flow and you would be blackballed, and they give you what they want to give you."

But, circumstances do change for Industry International. Recessions led to lowered bonuses (55 percent in the recessions of the 1980s). Many workers lost their homes and cars because they were relying on large bonuses to pay mortgages and loans. Workers attributed the decline to many things, but primarily to management greed and incompetence – a "fat managerial level and more men at the top," embezzlement, and mismanagement of overseas accounts. Whatever the reason, the recession made it clear to workers just how dependent they were on Industry International, and how much things had changed: "The whole philosophy [established by the founder and maintained until 1983] was that you worked hard and got compensated for it. You busted your ass, but you got compensated. Now you bust your ass and you don't get compensated for it." But, they have very few options. Most are too old to start over somewhere else and are limited by their education and training to manufacturing jobs, and high-paying manufacturing jobs are becoming very rare in the United States, a trend that has increased during the Great Recession of 2008 and beyond (Rich, 2010; also see Chapter 12 of this book). And, when the economy recovers, bonuses increase and the company expands.

So, they sometimes talk about resisting management. They fear that management will eliminate the bonus system, replacing it with a form of profit sharing that is not as lucrative for the workers. Many predict a massive walkout or work stoppage if that happens. Others talk about unionizing the firm. Management has persuaded them that the bonus system relies on a non-union shop, but if the bonus system is eliminated they have no reason not to unionize. Others predict that employees would quit the company; still others predict plummeting productivity and quality, others threaten physical violence against management and sabotage of the plant. "If they got rid of bonus, they wouldn't have the control over anyone. Bonus is what they have to keep the hold on you" (also see Campbell and Pritchard, 1976; Greene and Podsakoff, 1981).

Applying What You've Learned

1. A number of factors need to be present for rule–reward systems to succeed. Which of those factors were present at Industry International? Which, if any, were absent?
2. What resistance strategies are available to these employees? What could they do to keep from being so dependent on the system? What effects would those actions have on the system? Why?

Questions to Think About and Discuss

1. There is a substantial amount of research evidence indicating that pay is the most powerful motivator for US workers, more so than for workers in some other countries. Why?
2. Would this kind of motivation and control system work differently in different societal contexts, for example, in a society that was not as consumption oriented as the United States or in a country with extensive social support systems for unemployed workers and their families (see Freeman, 1994)?
3. If you were the CEO of Industry International, what kinds of public economic policies would you want the government to follow? (Would you want the Federal Reserve Board to focus on keeping inflation low or keeping unemployment low? Would you want corporate income taxes to be a primary source of government funding or personal income taxes?) Why?

Notes

1 This case is based on Hancock and Papa (1996), and Gibson and Papa (2000).

2 Since Papa and his associates have never identified the real company that they called Industry International, it is impossible to update these figures. However, the Lincoln Electric company operates very much like Industry International. It gave comparable bonuses during the years covered in this case, and gave out average bonuses of $11,800 in 2002 and $10,800 in 2003 and comparable amounts in subsequent years.

example, in politics, US citizens say they want candidates for office to make their goals, values, plans, and sources of campaign funding perfectly clear so that they can make informed choices. But, repeatedly, voters reject candidates who do so and reward those who deal with images and personalities rather than issues and solutions. Citizens want state adoption agencies to place children in good homes, but they also want state agencies to run as efficiently (which usually means as cheaply) as possible. So, legislators enact regulations that base adoption agencies' budgets, prestige, and staff size on the number of children enrolled (that is, the number *not* placed in homes). Consequently, employees and administrators are inadvertently encouraged to make it difficult to adopt these children – by requiring prospective parents to not smoke, be of the same religion, have never been divorced, have a separate bedroom for the child, and so on. Similarly, universities are supposed to teach students, but tend to reward research activities that have only an indirect positive effect on teaching quality, especially in undergraduate courses. Students are supposed to go to college to learn something, but are rewarded by employers and graduate schools largely based on the grades they receive regardless of what they have learned, thereby encouraging them to take easy classes (which reduces their opportunities to learn), focus on getting high grades instead of on mastering of the material, and so on (Kerr, 1975).

Reward systems may also ignore the intangible rewards that employees receive from their jobs. Some professors in research universities actually do spend time and effort on undergraduate teaching, in spite of the organization's formal reward system, because they receive intangible rewards from their interactions with their students. Kerr studied a medical insurance company that rewarded claims adjusters for quickly and accurately paying good claims and rejecting bad ones. But the size of the reward was too small to offset the hassles they received from turning down a claim. So, newcomers quickly learned, "When in doubt, pay it out!" It is the "net" reward, as perceived by individual employees, that determines the extent to which a reward system motivates them to act in ways desired by the organization's leaders.

Finally, some tasks are complicated in ways that make it virtually impossible to design an effective reward system. For example, William Ouchi examined the reward systems in a number of retail stores (Ouchi, 1977).[13] He found that those salespersons paid on a commission basis sold a lot of merchandise, but ignored other necessary tasks – ordering and arranging inventory, or training new salespeople. In contrast, people paid an hourly wage completed all the necessary tasks, but didn't sell much merchandise. People paid on commission also had strong incentives to engage in unethical behavior. Presumably, it is possible to design reward systems that discourage unethical activities and encourage employees to complete support tasks. But, if salespersons receive no rewards for maintaining high ethical standards or completing support activities, especially in the short term, they will do what they *are* rewarded for doing (Kerr and Slocum, 1987).

In sum, rule–reward systems are complicated because human beings are complicated. People actively perceive, interpret, and strategically respond to the guidelines and constraints they face. The people who design the systems clearly do not *intend* the systems to have these effects; indeed they cannot even *predict* that they will do so. Reward systems are powerful motivating agents, but their impact is determined more by the employees who interpret them than by the systems themselves.

Surveillance and Rule–Reward Systems

All organizational control systems require some form of **surveillance**, some process through which supervisors can determine the extent to which employees conform to policies, procedures, rules, and motivational systems. This is particularly true of traditional strategies of organizing because the primary function of supervision is worker control and because supervisors exercise control over everything from major policies and procedures to microscopic elements of task design and completion. The simplest form of control involves supervisors constantly looking over the shoulders of their subordinates. This kind of surveillance is still common in newly industrialized economies. In a Malaysia-based microchip plant, male supervisors constantly pressured female workers to increase their productivity; even trips to the locker room were penalized. Workers complained about being constantly spied upon and felt that they had no place to hide. The company set up an in-house "union" to serve as an additional watchdog (Ong, 1991). However, simple surveillance systems have two important disadvantages. First, they are highly inefficient, requiring organizations to hire and pay large numbers of supervisors to watch over their employees. This managerial overhead is especially large in US firms (almost three times as large as in Japanese organizations, and almost four times as large as in European firms), and it has steadily increased since the end of World War II. Second, they are very *obtrusive* (visible and "in your face"), which generates a great deal of antagonism between supervisors and subordinates.[14]

Today supervisory surveillance is made much easier by the advent of sophisticated computer technologies. A 2000 study by the American Management Association found that almost 80 percent of US firms used some form of electronic surveillance during the previous year, a number that had increased by an astonishing 67 percent over the previous year. Annual surveys since 2000 have had similar results. The most common activities were monitoring internet use, listening in on or recording telephone conversations, storing and reviewing computer files, using video equipment to guard against employee theft and sabotage, and recording computer use (number of keystrokes per minute, time taken between entries, etc.) Indeed, computer monitoring is more common in the workplace than in any other part of society, in part because modern organizations are technology intensive, making it easy to monitor employees. For example, Metron Enterprise Behavior Analysis's appliance helps managers identify which media employees use to communicate, identify groups of employees who communicate frequently, measure the productivity of each employee and each of the informal groups that the system identifies, and detect messages from employees who disagree with the policies or actions of a company or a particular supervisor (Dubie, 2007; Findlay and McKinlay, 2008). Historically, women are more likely to be monitored than men, and minority women are the most heavily monitored group. This is because it is easiest to monitor people whose jobs can be quantitatively measured – clerical work, data entry, or routine computer programming – and those tasks are largely performed by minority women. But, with the development of more sophisticated software, the range of jobs that can be closely monitored has been expanding.

Some computer monitoring is widely accepted, particularly in North America because of widespread acceptance of the doctrine of "employment at will," which means that employers have the right to set almost any condition of employment and to fire workers for almost any reason. Like anything else, electronic surveillance must be justified, legitimized through day-by-day conversations among workers, and limited to acceptable behaviors. The most common justification is that management has a legitimate right to make sure that all employees are working hard, and to discover, expose, and control employees who disagree with company policies and/or may act in ways that disrupt smooth operations.[15] A variant of this "coercive" rationale asserts that using electronic surveillance to detect and control workers shows that the organization "cares" about protecting compliant, productive workers from a lazy, disruptive, or incompetent few. Although two-thirds of North American workers accept these justifications, especially if they are managers and/or if the surveillance is being used to monitor other people rather than themselves, they also believe that the practice should not be used to monitor personal matters (anything done outside of work, or personal phone calls or emails unless they were in some way interfering with an employee's work), or observe people while in "private" spaces such as restrooms or breakrooms. In addition, employees perceive that much of the information collected should not be made public. For example, the number of bathroom breaks that employees take in a day, or the duration of those breaks, should not be posted in public. Some technologies also tend to be viewed negatively, such as genetic screening of prospective employees, and the information collected should not be used to discriminate on the basis of race or gender. In 1996 a number of women workers at Mitsubishi Motors' Chicago area plant filed a sexual harassment suit (we discuss this issue in Chapter 10). Management retaliated by threatening to make their health records public, information that it had collected when they filed claims with the company's health insurance provider. Evidently, Mitsubishi's management thought that a public revelation of the workers' sexual history – forms of birth control used, abortions, treatment for sexually transmitted diseases, and so on – would coerce them into dropping the suit (Keyton *et al.*, 2006). Not only did the strategy fail, but also it generated heated opposition from every woman in Congress, among others. Finally, and ironically, workers should be told about the surveillance system, preferably when they are hired or during new-employee orientation, but its operation should be unobtrusive, so that workers do not *feel* that they are constantly being watched.

Assessing the effects of computer surveillance systems is difficult. They have often been linked to a number of negative outcomes, especially among employees in Europe who tolerate less corporate invasion of their privacy, or those who see the systems as unethical. Adverse effects include lower job satisfaction, higher absenteeism and turnover, adverse health effects (including increased stress and anxiety), feelings of lost privacy, lower commitment to the organization, and high levels of resentment about being monitored. Ironically, they also can harm supervisor–subordinate communication. Supervisors who receive daily printouts of their subordinates' activities feel less of a need to talk with them face to face, which harms their relationships and reduces their access to complicated information.

Heavily monitored employees often perceive that management does not trust them and treats them like children and fear that they are being set up for punishment or dismissal. Some resist the systems, often in creative ways. If the systems are obtrusive – for example, they flash messages such as "work harder" or "concentrate" on the workers' computer screens when they slow down – the negative effects are more likely and more severe. Surveillance systems also can harm performance, especially for employees who perform complex tasks. Employees begin to believe that management is concerned with quantity of output, *but not quality*, and respond accordingly. They provide lower-quality service to customers and find ways to bypass complicated or otherwise time-consuming clients or activities. However, properly designed and implemented electronic surveillance may have net positive effects, especially if employees are actively involved in their design and implementation. Monitoring is perceived favorably if it is restricted to legitimate, performance-related activities, if it increases the fairness of the organization's rule–reward system, and if it is linked to effective performance feedback. In these senses, employee responses to computer monitoring are very much like employee responses to rule–reward systems in general.[16]

Resistance to Rule–Reward Systems

Resistance is an inevitable aspect of social or organizational control because control systems inevitably reduce members' autonomy and creativity (recall the dilemma discussed in

Chapter 1).[17] The simplest forms of resistance are withdrawal and open rebellion. The former leads people to be progressively less involved in and committed to their jobs; the latter can culminate in sabotage. The disastrous chemical leak at Bhopal, India, in 1985 resulted in part from an employee's rebelling against being punished (fired) for breaking what he perceived as illegitimate rules. A cleaning woman once admitted that she retaliated against an especially controlling employer by using her employers' toothbrush to clean her commodes – for years. Employees also may resist rules by **regressing**, that is, by reducing their performance to the minimum acceptable standard that the rule–reward system allows. Employees resist electronic surveillance systems by finding ways to fool the computers, sabotaging the systems, or filing lawsuits.

Other forms of resistance are more complex. Employees sometimes rebel against their organizations by following rules exactly, robbing their organizations of the common sense and flexibility to make rule systems work. In Mexican *maquiladoras* workers covertly resist pressures to speed up production by engaging in *tortuosidad*, literally "working at a turtle's pace." Since their supervisors (US and Mexican) viewed their workers as "lazy," they often failed to recognize that the slowdowns were strategic (Pena, 1987; Young, 1987). During 1991, a small number of American Airlines pilots resisted management by following FAA regulations to the letter – filing very complete flight plans, requesting detailed weather reports, and engaging in other activities that are completely legal but rarely absolutely necessary for flight safety. The number of flight delays and cancellations skyrocketed. Management retaliated by giving the pilots assignments that reduced their income (while denying in public that they were doing so). Pilots countered by following the rules even more exactly, eventually paralyzing the airline through their strategy of malicious obedience. Similar actions in 1997 and 2000 cost American $70 million and $225 million respectively. In 1997, United Airlines pilots virtually shut that airline down by obeying rules regarding overtime exactly; in 2000 the same strategy cost the airline $225 million. Even flight attendants, who have substantially less bargaining power, were able to force concessions from US Airways in 2000 after costing the company $40 million by **working to rule** (Goldberg, 2000).

Whether the consequences are massive or minor, all forms of resistance serve the same purpose: They allow employees to rebel against rule–reward systems, enhancing their feelings of autonomy and, sometimes, their need for creativity. Unfortunately for organizations, supervisors often respond to resistance by tightening the rule–reward system, which increases the probability of further resistance. The organization then finds itself immersed in destructive cycles of disobedience and dictatorial management. Unfortunately for employees, resistance rarely leads to major changes in organizations or organizational rule–reward systems. The nature of the traditional strategy makes it difficult to locate and resist real sources of organizational control. When resistance actually does threaten to force changes on an organization, high-powered members are usually able to change the systems to undermine resistance strategies. Finally, resisting rule–reward systems focuses attention on them and can unintentionally legitimize them. For example, resisters can be depicted as troublemakers, which adds credibility to the "caring" rationale for electronic surveillance. In addition, while resisters usually raise questions about the legitimacy of a particular rule–reward system or the way in which it is being implemented, they usually accept the legitimacy of *some* system of organizational control (they are resisters, not revolutionaries). Thus the relationship between control and resistance is paradoxical: Control inevitably creates resistance, which often supports systems of control.[18]

TRADITIONAL STRATEGIES OF LEADERSHIP

Most contemporary organizational theorists view "leadership" as a process through which charismatic people develop and persuasively articulate a vision that challenges an organization to excellence and constant improvement. These perspectives contradict the traditional strategy of organizing, which focuses on stability (see Chapters 4 and 5 for more detail on contemporary views of leadership). In contrast, the traditional strategy dictates that supervisors will be "managers," people who implement an existing set of plans, or "administrators," people who develop routines for efficiently accomplishing particular tasks (Fine and Buzzanell, 2000). Traditional organizations are comprised of a kind of class or caste system that fosters clear distinctions among a managerial power elite, a "new working class" composed of lower-level managers and people with technical skills, and lower-level workers that must appear to be "like" upper management, both in terms of overall attitudes and behaviors and in terms of the images they project. People who advance through traditional hierarchies tend to come from the same schools, wear the same clothes, and develop the same communication styles and mannerisms of their higher ups. They must learn to please their superiors by accommodating their every whim and meeting their every need. "Good" subordinates will anticipate their superiors' demands, prevent or solve the problems they encounter, and "help a superior perform well and look good," even if doing so involves taking blame for the superior's errors and giving him or her credit for the subordinate's successes (Goffee and Jones, 2001; Smith, 1970; Kelley, 1992, 2004).[19] They must demonstrate loyalty, both to the organization and to their sponsors in the power elite. They must keep their distance from people below them in the hierarchy. The most promotable ones develop a near obsession with following established rules because doing so is their only source of protection. Above all, they do not make waves; creative approaches and new ideas threaten the stability and predictability that are hallmarks of the traditional strategy of organizing. As a result, the people who are hired for upwardly oriented jobs tend to already have the appropriate credentials and behavioral styles. And, "fitting in" gets progressively more important as one moves up the organizational hierarchy.

Omar Aktour has provided an excellent example of these processes in a study of two breweries, one in Montreal and one in Algiers. Although there were some differences in the two settings, there were striking similarities in how one became promotable in these two very traditional organizations. From the day they arrived in the organization, employees who eventually became worthy of promotion engaged in a particular pattern of behavior. They were obsessed with doing more – a machinist who used his breaks to clean his machine or a quality control officer who repeatedly phoned the plant on his days off to make sure things were going well. They showed a strong capacity to keep lower-level workers in line and showed unconditional obedience and submission to their superiors. They kept their distance from the regular workers and took care to master the language of the elite – managerial jargon, including the most recent managerial fads, and upper-class accents. They zealously enforced rules and quotas, boycotted all unionizing activities (or informed on pro-union workers), appeared to suffer from their workload and worries, and constantly stayed on their bosses' coattails. In both plants the formal job descriptions of managers and the official reward/evaluation system focused on objective performance criteria such as production per machine or number of equipment breakdowns. But, upper management described a "good" (promotable) subordinate in terms that had little to do with technical expertise or objective performance. To them, good subordinates are submissive, punctual, serious (absorbed in their tasks), malleable, and ambitious. As a result it is not surprising that the workers in these plants complained about the technical incompetence of their supervisors as well as about their untrustworthiness and political game playing (Aktouf, 1996).

Consequently, by the time people are promoted to managerial positions in traditional organizations, they have developed ways of thinking and acting that preclude their being "leaders" in the contemporary definition of that term. The only legitimate vision is that of maintaining the existing systems and structures; the only possible challenge is to do what the organization has always done more rapidly and efficiently. Such people are likely to be excellent "managers" and "administrators," but not leaders.

INFORMATION AND COMMUNICATION TECHNOLOGIES (ICT) IN TRADITIONAL STRATEGIES OF ORGANIZING

Overcoming the Limitations of the Traditional Organizational Strategy

As we have emphasized throughout this chapter, the principles of the traditional strategy of organizing often create problems in their own right. To reap the efficiencies of bureaucracy, organizations must manage employees through hierarchical arrangements that can lead to resentment and resistance on the part of workers. The friction generated by intrusive managers reduces efficiency and saps employee energy. In order to avoid constant oversight by managers, the traditional strategy relies on rule governed coordination of work, often supported by technologies such as assembly lines. However, the rules must be kept relatively simple or employees will lose track of them, and simple rules promote a degree of inflexibility. When organizations try to build flexibility into rules by making them more complex, the rule books become dense and time consuming to consult. Almost any college catalog is a good example of this; aside from the standard curriculum, the rules are somewhat different for each major and degree and the result is a tome that must be carefully consulted when contemplating graduation or changing majors.

Another problem is that applying complex rules often requires access to information that front line employees do not have access to. When the authors bought their first houses over 30 years ago, they filled out applications that listed assets and debts and documented credit worthiness, but the bank employee who took the application had no idea whether this information was correct or not. It took several days, sometimes as much as a couple of weeks of telephone calls and formal requests for information, to verify that the authors were not deadbeats out to cheat the bank or ne'er-do-wells who would default on their loans.

These problems have in the past imposed limits on organizations employing the traditional strategy. However, in the past 30 years, the new developments in ICTs have enabled organizations to minimize the effects of these problems. ICTs make it much easier to support consistent use of complex rule systems and to provide needed information to front line employees than has previously been the case.

Workflow systems can route documents through channels just as efficiently as the assembly line routes physical objects. In some insurance companies, for instance, a claim application submitted by a field adjustor at her portable PC is automatically evaluated by a machine-based expert system to determine whether it needs further scrutiny by higher level employees. If it does not, the claim is routed through the system for direct payment;

if it requires another look, it is routed to a manager, who evaluates it and may communicate via email with the adjustor regarding any questions, finally routing it on for payment or further scrutiny. The documents and related messages are all handled by the workflow system and the routing is almost instantaneous. The system uses a complex set of rules more rapidly and consistently than any person with a manual could.

ICTs can also be used to provide front line employees with information to guide them as they apply rule systems. For example, in today's loan process the information that the authors provide is entered into a workflow system that enables the loan officer to verify information and check credit status much more rapidly than in the past. Often a same-day response is possible for even complicated loan applications. In a different field, sales of large computers, servers, and networks are facilitated by systems that the frontline sales associate can use to customize complex systems and networks via his or her laptop. These systems enable sales associates to give quotes for complex networks of computers and memory devices in real time, greatly enhancing the sales process. Many of the most compelling examples of how ICTs revolutionize traditional organizations are in the sales sector, but they also abound in manufacturing as well. In the 1950s and 1960s, machine tools were limited in the number of parts they could manufacture. It often took hours to "retool" to a machine so that it could make a different part and this often had to be done with the assistance of a foreperson or engineer. Modern computer controlled machine tools can make literally hundreds of different parts. "Retooling" is done by programming and the operator is generally trained in how to do this. Computerized machine tools enable the front line worker to control the process, increasing responsiveness and efficiency, yet still delivering adequate control over the work.

At the turn of the twenty-first century, Aviall Inc., an aviation parts distributor headquartered in Dallas, implemented an integrated IT inventory management system to enable it to have more control over its work processes. In 1999 the company lost 20 percent of its accounts and $70 million in business, in part because of a botched effort to implement an inventory system. The company conducted a major overhaul of its systems in 2000, installing an extranet for customers to use in purchasing parts. This system enabled the company to offer 380,000 parts to the company's 17,000 customers, using 20,000 different pricing schemes. Web sales rose 60 percent and cost per order declined from $7 by phone to 39 cents via the web. The company also upgraded its inventory control and warehouse system enabling managers to track products in inventory and move it around more effectively. This system enabled sales managers at Aviall to know what was in stock and initiate sales incentives on overstocked products. The system also enabled Aviall to know what sorts of parts its customers ordered, which gave salespeople the information needed to target their sales pitches. Customers were able to cut expenses in the order process and track shipment using the system. They are even able to download invoices and see them ahead of receiving the order. This system enabled Aviall to "have their cake and eat it too" (Melymuka, 2003). Aviall continued to upgrade its systems throughout the first decade of the twenty-first century. In 2010 it linked its system with Pentagon 2000 using a web-based system that makes Aviall's inventory easily accessible for Pentagon 2000s aerospace customers (PRNewswire, 2010). Pentagon customers will have a direct web link to Aviall's parts network utilizing the latest technologies which will shorten time to fulfill orders and increase efficiency.

ICTs enable organizations to exert control over work processes in a very efficient, complete, and relatively unobtrusive manner. They enable organizations to implement systems of rules to regulate work that are complex enough to be flexible. They enable organizations to give front line employees detailed information and support so that they can operate independently using the rules. As the next section illustrates, ICTs also enable organizations to extend the workplace into the home.

Telework

As noted in Chapter 2, telework refers to a wide range of arrangements in which employees work outside the traditional office and conduct a large portion of their work via computer or telecommunications linkages. A survey of information technology executives from 120 private firms in 2007 found that 20 percent of the employees of these firms telecommute and most of them were planning to increase telework (Dubie, 2007).

While not all telework is performed in traditional organizations, a good deal is, and this raises some issues that are worth considering at this point. The nature of telework varies widely. Some teleworkers conduct all their business from home; the telephone salespersons for some catalog companies mentioned in the previous section are one example; but many other professional employees work out of their homes as well. Some employees telecommute only part time, working at home a few days a week or month, and going into a regular office the rest of the time (Konradt, Schmook, and Malecke, 2000). Another type of teleworker is the road warrior. The advent of reliable ICTs, as we have seen, makes it possible to coordinate complex work, such as sales of high ticket items with complex specifications at distant locations or in the field.

Many insurance firms have done away with central offices, assigning agents and underwriters to the field, where they work out of cars and hotel rooms via telecommunications and email. At AT&T, about 5 percent of the company's 373,000 employees do their work from cars or hotels. These road warriors save their companies millions in overheads each year. But they also complain of the lack of a feeling of belonging to their organizations and of the stress of living on the road many weeks a year.

Telework is feasible for any job that centers on paperwork and information processing. There are a number of incentives for telework. For organizations, the attraction stems from lower overhead since they don't have to maintain office buildings and, for the many teleworkers who work on a part-time basis, don't have to pay benefits. For the worker, advantages include closer contact with home and family (except for the road warrior), a more relaxed lifestyle away from the formality of the office, avoidance of office politics, and fewer long commutes. There are also advantages for the public, since less commuting means less expense for highways and other infrastructure and less automobile pollution. Evaluations of telework support its advantages. The majority of studies suggest that teleworkers are more productive and less costly than those based in the office.

There are several prerequisites for teleworking arrangements to succeed. First and foremost, the technological infrastructure must be developed. Often this means that high-speed transmission lines must be installed by the phone companies or other communication carriers. The organization must also purchase the proper technology (computers and high-speed modems) for processing and moving the information. Second, all involved must have developed "communication discipline," that is, they must be in the habit of using their email, workflow, and other ICTs to stay in contact and coordinate their work. These new media require users to develop new patterns of behavior based on different communication modes (usually written) than the verbal channels with which most people are accustomed.

Managers must be able to trust that commands issued via communication technology will be followed; employees must learn to understand what managers mean over media such as email that do not offer the direct personal contact that often provides extra information and detail. A final prerequisite for effective telecommuting is that home workers must create a work environment in their homes. Provisions must be made so that family matters do not constantly intervene in work. Some employees take on considerable expenses in setting up and equipping home offices. Since some office equipment is too expensive to be installed in the homes of all workers, many companies have set up satellite offices where employees can come when they need office facilities. Satellite offices are also places where employees can work with information too sensitive to transmit over public media.

A major barrier to effective telework arrangements is the discomfort of managers who can no longer see what their employees are doing. Before they become accustomed to electronic media, many middle and upper managers are wary of supervising employees they cannot see. "Management by walking around" is premised on visual contact and face-to-face communication. Managers do not know what they will find, but walk around to see what is happening; in the process they see things that work and should be done more and problems that have to be addressed. Management is very different with teleworkers. The information technology provides ways to monitor work, but understanding and working with the information requires managers to learn new procedures and skills. Managers who do not have these, or who are uncomfortable with new technologies in general, are likely to perceive a loss of control due to telework. A manager at a major truck manufacturer learned that sending blunt emails similar to the orders he gave in person could cause problems. "People would say, 'Why did you ask me that? Are you angry at me?' said the manager. "If you see them every day, they figure, 'That's just Dave – he has to get stuff done.' But if you're not seeing them on a frequent basis, you have to explain yourself." Managers in new telecommuting programs are often counseled to take communication courses to avoid this type of problem (Brandel, 2002, 50).

Telework may also present some problems for the employee. The line between work and private or family time often blurs for teleworkers. Telework may be convenient in the sense that it gives the employee a more informal and flexible work environment; but it also makes it more convenient for others to reach the employee. Most teleworkers – and almost all road warriors – report that they work more hours. When work intrudes into the family space, there is nowhere for employees to escape work-related stress and get a break from the pressure. Teleworkers must exert considerable effort to keep their nonwork lives intact.

Despite these disadvantages, telework is here to stay. It is simply too attractive to both organizations and employees. Some futurists predict that telework will reverse the growth of cities and suburbs. If a travel agent can work as effectively from a farm 100 miles from Minneapolis as in the city, there is nothing to keep him or her in the city. A corporation that can locate satellite offices around the country in cheaper rural locales could be sorely tempted to vacate its high-priced suburban campus. It is possible that telework will encourage dispersion of the population and a general move away from the cities. The result may be further deterioration of cities and, eventually, suburbs, as those holding the highest paying jobs disperse more evenly around the country.

Ethical Issues in the Use of ICTs

The use of ICTs helps classical organizations overcome several of their inherent limitations. However, the use of ICTs for purposes such as monitoring employee use of ICTs and keeping track of their activities raises ethical issues. How far should organizations be able to go in monitoring employees? Some argue that if an organization provides the ICTs to employees they should be able to monitor and control everything that goes on in the system. The organization is not paying for personal facilities for its employees; they should use the system for work and nothing else. Further, if an employee engages in illegal or questionable behavior – sexual harassment of a coworker, fraudulent use of the internet, or lobbying a politician – the organization will be held liable, because it provided the means to the perpetrator.

The other side of the argument holds that even in the workplace employees expect some degree of privacy. While it is true that the organization provides the ICT, personal use with reasonable bounds should be allowed, particularly since the company often expects employees to check their email or voicemail from home on their personal time and may request that employees work extra hours. Being able to take a few minutes to order Christmas gifts from the office is reasonable compensation for the organization's infringement on personal time and private life. The vast majority of employees do not engage in questionable activities using ICTs and they should not be penalized for the misdeeds of a few. Moreover, employees will always make some personal use of organizational resources; they make phone calls related to private matters and use the photocopier for their tax returns. Is there really any difference between this and some private use of the internet? There is no clear resolution to this issue at present.

An overwhelming proportion of employees use the internet for personal reasons at work. A study by Verton (2000b) indicated that costs to the organization of this behavior can be substantial. A company with 1000 internet users who do personal web surfing for one hour per day can lose more than $35 million in productivity costs each year. However, the study also indicated that the great majority of firms were not concerned about this type of cost, because they believed that increased morale among employees more than compensated for it. Most organizations in the survey indicated that they tolerate private use of the internet as a perk for their employees. Over 80 percent of the firms surveyed indicated that they have a written internet use policy to guide employees.

The ever-increasing capacities of network ICTs to keep track of what employees are doing has encouraged firms to ask their information technology departments to monitor employees to detect illegal or illicit activities (recall the discussion of cyberspying in Chapter 2). The ethical issues involved have put some staff in IT departments in a difficult position. Their relationship with their users is sometimes compromised by users' resentment of monitoring, and this distrust can compound problems in keeping complex systems running. As one manager commented, "Our [IT] department philosophy is that if users fear us the job gets ten times harder. Fear leads to cover up and spin. When we are trying to find [the cause of] a problem, what we need is the truth." This can extend beyond possible misuses to almost all problems with ICTs, resulting in breakdowns in the communication system and other key systems the organization needs to operate effectively. To counteract this, IT departments try to develop clear statements of monitoring policy and informally reassure other employees they are not trying to catch them out, but instead their primary goal is to maintain security.

A second privacy-related problem concerns organizations' use of private information about customers and employees. The increasing integration of computer networks enables information from different databases to be linked and shared within and across organizations. Information about employees' health histories, for example, might be compiled and shared among companies. Since employees with health problems often result in higher insurance costs and more time missed from work, some organizations might use this information in their hiring decisions. There has long been a debate about the appropriateness and legality of compiling and using this type of information, and laws and standards have been proposed. This issue is clearly on the public's mind. Fear of having health problems included in a company database and ultimately disclosed has led some people to avoid seeking treatment for serious maladies or to seek private treatment that they pay for themselves.

Information about consumer preferences can also be captured by ICTs. A group of 70 electronic commerce companies, including IBM and First Union Corporation have been developing a data-sharing specification called Customer Profile Exchange (Verton, 2000a). This promises to enable companies to compile massive databases on customers and to comb through them to discover purchasing patterns, lifestyle information, and other information about customers. This possibility has raised concerns that the companies are overstepping the bounds of their customers' privacy. More recently, Facebook and Google have been in the news because of similar concerns about the information they capture about users and clients.

Case Study 3.3
Scenes From the Electronic Sweatshop

Barbara Garson, playwright and investigative journalist, investigated how computers were transforming office work. Her book *The Electronic Sweatshop* documented some negative consequences that occurred when information and communication technologies (ICTs) were used to coordinate and control work in traditional organizations. Here are two vignettes based on her book that illustrate the dark side of ICTs:

Until the late 1970s, *airline reservation agents* were valued, long-term employees of the major airline companies. They had to learn and remember the companies' fares, routes, and policies and apply this knowledge to solve problems for customers on an individualized basis. This made them highly skilled employees who were difficult to replace. Some made as much as $15 per hour in the early 1980s, good money at that time.

However, once computerized reservation systems were developed, companies attempted to redefine the work of the reservation agent. Much of the problem solving was built into the system: the agent simply had to type in the place of departure and destination, and the computer listed the available times and seats. There was, however, still need for a human in the loop, because each customer's circumstances were so different that adjustments had to be made.

However, while the airlines still had to have people on line, they wanted to regulate their behavior as much as possible to maintain strict cost and quality control. Based on studies of the work process involved in making a booking, conversations between agent and customer were broken into typical segments, with recommended scripts and prompts assigned to each. For example, if a customer called up knowing what he or she wanted, agents were instructed in ways to get the reservation down as quickly as possible, so they could go on to the next customer. In cases in which customers were fare shopping, agents were taught ways to probe for a sale; for instance, one strategy was to tell the customer that there were limited seats at the low fare and that the seat could be held for 24 hours at no cost, which insured that many customers would call back and offer another opportunity to close the deal. Agents were also told never to ask yes or no questions such as "Would you like to book?"; instead they were to ask, "Would you like the 10 A.M. or the 2 P.M.?" All transactions between agents and customers were tightly scripted. Supervisors listened in without the agent's knowledge and graded them on how well they kept to the script and efficiently booked passengers. Too much small talk or empathy could get the agent a lower grade. The companies also set performance targets: in the company Garson studied, agents were supposed to make a sale during 26 percent of their calls.

Time on and off line was carefully monitored by the computer system as well: AHU ("after hang up") time, the time between calls, was supposed to be 14 seconds on average if the agent wanted a raise. To keep one's job and get raises, the agent had to be available, plugged in, 98 percent of the time for bookings.

For this, the new agents were paid $5.77 an hour.

The Automated Social Worker

When New York State installed a computer system to keep track of its welfare system, it took a job that it would seem is impossible to automate and turned it into a series of steps. Most social workers take up the profession because they want to help people. They are taught in school that every person is an individual and that it is important to take each individual's needs into account to help them. People attracted to this field typically enjoy working with others and hope to make a difference in people's lives. However, the computerization of work in New York did not take this approach.

Job analysis divided the social worker's tasks into units and assigned a time value to each. For example, making a food stamp change counted 0.5, authorizing funeral and burial expenses counted 0.7, and replacing a lost or stolen welfare check counted 0.4, where the numbers stood for tenths of an hour. As a worker does each of these tasks, they are toted up to give a figure for hours of work done. Once a worker reaches his or her allotted 160 hours (actually the target is about 120 hours per month, because 40 hours are required for staff meetings, maintaining work records, and other activities), he or she is done for the month. An experienced worker can do most of these tasks in much less time than the official time figure, so they can get credit for 160 hours with much less work.

So do the workers stop working when their credits reach their limit? Although we have not provided a full list of tasks here, suffice it to say that activities such as making exceptions for clients, trying to help them with their special problems when the help goes outside procedures, and providing sympathy are not among the officially sanctioned list of tasks. The tasks list refers only to bureaucratic operations involved in registering parties for welfare and delivering their services, not to the human side of welfare. Garson found that the social workers spent the time they had left after satisfying their hourly credits on these other activities – coaching clients in how to get the best benefits, giving them sympathy and support, and working around the system – and also in helping and counseling each other. The social workers made the system human by "gaming" the system.

Sadly, social workers who really try to help clients within the system often receive poor performance evaluations. If they diligently carry out their work, it takes more time than is allotted in the work analysis. One social worker commented,

> Now if you is a person with a problem, you don't want to just tell it to everyone. You want to feel it out first. "This [social] worker, does she have some sensitivity to my problem? Can she hear me?" But I can't hear her. I can't listen to her. I'm just trying to get my points. The whole system is survival. And she goes away feeling as bad or worse than when she came down here. . . . [S]ome people come here, they are at the end of their rope. They think, "You is a social worker. That's something. Maybe you can help me." And they start telling me about a child that is getting out of hand, starting to drink, not coming home.

This woman was a dedicated social service employee who wanted to do the best she could for her clients. But engaging a client in this way was not efficient and did not earn her the points she needed to make her hours. She had been "written up for Corrective Action" three times in the previous four months. Garson concluded, "The fact is that Jo Martin is not an efficient [social worker]. But a human service department that's organized so it can't use her true skills is profoundly inefficient."

The system used to organize social workers was very similar to the scientific management systems set up to control work under the traditional strategy of organizing. However, unlike the studies of physical labor conducted by management scientists, New York's studies made a profound error. Sympathy for the client and advocacy for his or her needs are an important part of the social worker's job that were simply omitted from the analysis; the system captured all the physical motions of being a social worker, but ignored the spirit of the profession. This may have been inevitable in a system that was intended to enable computerization of social work. Behaviors that could be counted were emphasized because number crunching is what the computers at that time did best.

A good deal of the social worker's time was spent filling out papers that documented all the papers they filled out for clients, so that their work records could be entered into the computerized system. The next step was to set up the system so social workers could enter their activity records into networked computers themselves. As the system developed further, the workers would enter in data about their clients directly, and the system would guide the social worker through the steps of authorizing burial expenses and other activities. In theory this might eliminate the labor of filling in forms, freeing the social worker up to engage their clients. However, judging by how the system had been developed at the time of Garson's interview, it is doubtful that this was the direction it would take. Instead the social workers would simply have their case loads increased.

Ironically, the dedication of the workers to their clients kept this system going. Garson had the following conversation with one of the supervisors:

G: What do you think of the time standards and point system?

S: I blame the union for the way it's operating.

G: You mean because they're sabotaging it?

S: No, because they're not sabotaging it.

G: What do you mean?

S: If they followed the rules the department issued them, this system would have collapsed in three months. . . . If I were a worker and a union activist, the first time I did 100 percent in the first 3 weeks of the month I'd stop work. And if they tried to make me do anything over 100 percent, I'd fill out an overtime form. The problem is that all the workers have developed systems of their own to get the points they need and still deliver timely service. That's what keeps this place going.

Since Garson's book was published, ICTs have transformed work and work relationships in almost every occupation and organization.

Applying What You've Learned

1. Are the airlines and the social work agency engaging automating or informating their work? (See the section below on the impacts of ICTs on work.)
2. How do these organization apply the principles of the traditional bureaucracy in their systems? What are likely reactions of employees to the system controls?

Questions to Think About and Discuss

1. What are some of the benefits of the computerization of work discussed in these cases for the employees involved? For customers or clients? For the organizations?
2. Would you like to work in these jobs (assuming that pay was up to your standards)? Why or why not?
3. Do you agree with the supervisor's suggestion concerning how the social workers could shut down the system? What might management do if the social workers tightly conformed to rules?

Note

This case is based on Garson (1988).

Postscript: Automating versus Informating The impact of ICTs on organizations and their employees depends in part on how they are used. Once applications are in the office or on the work floor, employees can begin to master computers themselves. They can use the computers to analyze their work and improve it. Shoshanna Zuboff argued that the preferred strategy for organizations is not simply to use computers to *automate* work and replace employees with machines. Instead she advocated using information technology to *informate* work, to enable workers to learn which processes are effective and which are not. Informating is possible because computers – properly programmed and utilized – can generate information on how the work is done and the output associated with different configurations of steps or methods. This makes workers smarter about their work and also better able to suggest and make improvements. As the case on the Electronic Sweatshop illustrates, computers are sometimes used in a very different way, to deskill employees and turn them into servants of the machine.

For informating to succeed, those at the top of the organization must be willing to share power with those lower down. Those at lower levels must feel some control over their work and some power to make changes before they are willing to take the initiative to change how they work based on the new information. While management often initiates the empowerment of workers, distributed technologies themselves may also shift the balance of power downward. Enhanced communication via email and other telecommunications facilities make it possible for lower-level employees to form coalitions and share information that increases their power in the organization.

CONCLUSION: COMMUNICATION AND TRADITIONAL STRATEGIES OF ORGANIZING

We have spent a substantial amount of space discussing traditional strategies of organizing because they are so relevant to modern employees. The traditional strategy, with its tight hierarchy, focus on the structure, formal communication, rule–reward systems, and written policies and procedures, is still the dominant strategy used in the United States for governmental agencies, educational institutions, and many private firms. Bureaucratic modes of management are the norm rather than the exception throughout the world. Although very few organizations conform completely to the strategy, many employees entering organizations today find themselves in situations much like the traditional bureaucracy. Procedures and policies are documented in writing; job-related communication flows through the chain of command; positions require specialized skills and are filled at least in part because applicants fulfill established, written criteria; and decision making is centralized near the top of the organization. The development of ICTs promises to enhance the effectiveness of the traditional strategy and has in a real sense revitalized it.

Of course, real organizations – even those in which the traditional strategy is in evidence – deviate in a number of important but predictable ways from what the traditional theorists envisioned. But, understanding the traditional strategy is important because many people will spend most of their lives working in organizations that are "traditional" in many ways.

NOTES

1 This section is based on two sources, McPhee (1988) and McPhee and Poole (2001).
2 For excellent summaries of Taylor's ideas, see Taylor (1978) and Locke (1982).
3 This is why computerized management information systems, recently installed in virtually every major organization, have had perplexing effects. Computer information systems do not filter information. In theory, they allow every employee, no matter where in the organization, to instantly access any part of its information base. However, no one can process all the information. Unfiltered formal communication will literally bury upper-level managers in information, at least until they learn to use the equipment to screen out messages. High-speed computer systems may only allow them to be buried more quickly. The "solution" to the problem of communication overload is for upper management not to use the systems, which defeats the purpose of installing them in the first place. See Rice and Gattiker (2001).
4 The "classic" study of sources of communication breakdowns is Roberts and O'Reilly (1974). Also see Jablin (1987), McPhee and Poole (2001), and Eisenberg (1984).
5 See Downs and Conrad (1982) and Fairhurst (2001). For an extended analysis of how one's nonverbal cues influence interpersonal communication, including communication by the other members of the relationship, see Burgoon, Buller, and Woodall (1995); and Manusov and Billingsley (1997).
6 See St. Clair, Quinn, and O'Neill (2000, 244). The original studies were published as Burns and Stalker (1961) and Lawrence and Lorsch (1967). An excellent summary of subsequent research is available in Sutcliffe (2001).
7 See Conrad and Jodlowski (2008) and Angell (2004). One strategy alone, paying generic drug companies to delay the introduction of competing drugs, is predicted to have cost US consumers $35 billion, and the US treasury an additional $2.6 billion, between 2010 and 2020 (see "Drug Company Payoffs," 2010).
8 See Monge and Contractor (2001). Employees also compensate for weaknesses in traditional motivation and control systems (see Katz, 1964; Williams and Anderson, 1991).
9 For an excellent analysis of how difficult it is to design policies that provide equity (which is not the same thing as "equality"), see Stone (2002).
10 Explanations of these processes are part of "attribution theory," a model summarized effectively and applied to organizational reward systems in Bettman and Weitz (1983) and in Staw, McKechnie, and Puffer (1983).
11 An excellent summary of the importance of equity in Western societies is available in Sampson (1986); a fine cross-cultural comparison is available in Kim, Park, and Suzuki (1990). Summaries of the effects of perceived distributive and procedural justice are available in Brockner, Tyler, and Cooper-Schneider (1992); and in McFarlin and Sweeney (1992).
12 See Weber (1958). Initially, this relationship was constrained by Protestant concepts of self-restraint and saving for the future. Over time the concept of financial gain eclipsed self-denial in Protestant theology, especially in the United States. See Valeri (2010).
13 This concept is developed in greater detail in the final sections of Chapter 9.
14 The best source for data on managerial overheads is Gordon (1996). Superb summaries of these ideas are available in Aronowitz (1973), Braverman (1974), Burawoy (1979), and Edwards (1978).
15 The two justifications were first developed by Sewell and Barker (2006a). A useful model for understanding negotiations about the boundaries of acceptable surveillance was developed by Petronio (2002), and applied to organizational surveillance by Allen, Coopman, Hart, and Walker (2007).
16 See Allen *et al.* (2007), Adler and Tompkins (1997), Aiello (1993), Aiello and Svec (1993), Balitis (1998), Botan (1996), and Kidwell and Bennett (1994).
17 Hannah Arendt (1958) provides an explanation of the inevitability of resistance. Michel Foucault (1977, 1980, 1984), a theorist whose work we will cite frequently in this book, draws similar conclusions. Foucault's work is difficult to understand, but an excellent summary is available in Barker and Cheney (1994).
18 Charles Conrad (1995) summarizes the research underlying these conclusions and examines the relationship between leadership and resistance in Conrad (in press). The most important background sources are de Certeau (1984), Burawoy, (1979), Clegg (1976), and Ferguson (1984).
19 For an alternative perspective, see Chaleff (2003) and Banks (2008). The primary source for this section is Ferguson (1984).

REFERENCES

Adams, R. and Parrot, R. (1994). "Pediatric Nurses' Communication of Role Expectations of Parents to Hospitalized Children." *Journal of Applied Communication Research* 22: 36–47.

Adler, G.S. and Tompkins, P. (1997). "Electronic Performance Monitoring." *Management Communication Quarterly* 10: 259–288.

Aiello, J.R. (1993). "Computer-based Work Monitoring." *Journal of Applied Social Psychology* 23: 499–507.

Aiello, J.R. and Svec, M.J. (1993). "Computer Monitoring of Work Performance." *Journal of Applied Psychology* 23: 537–548.

Aktouf, O. (1996). "Defamiliarizing Management Practice," in Linstead, Small, and Jeffcutt, eds., *Understanding Management*. London: Sage.

Albrecht, T. and Bach, B. (1996). *Organizational Communication*. Ft. Worth, TX: Harcourt.

Allen, M.W., Coopman, S., Hart, J. and Walker, K. (2007). "Workplace Surveillance and Managing Privacy Boundaries." *Management Communication Quarterly* 21: 172–200.

Angell, M. (2004). *The Truth About the Drug Companies*. New York: Random House.

Arendt, H. (1958). *The Human Condition*. Chicago: University of Chicago Press.

Aronowitz, S. (1973). *False Promises*. New York: McGraw-Hill.

Balitis, J.J., Jr. (1998). "Care Needed with Electronic Monitoring." *Business Journal (Phoenix)* 18: 71.

Banks, S., ed. (2008). *Dissent and the Failure of Leadership*. Cheltenham, UK: Edward Elgar.

Bazerman, M. and Watkins, M. (2008). *Predictable Surprises*. Cambridge, MA: Harvard Business School Press.

Bettman, J. and Weitz, B. (1983). "Attributions in the Board Room." *Administrative Science Quarterly* 28: 165–183.

Botan, C. (1996). "Communication, Work and Elec-tronic Surveillance." *Communication Monographs* 63: 294–313.

Brandel, M. (2002). "Distant Messages." *Computerworld*, December 9.

Braverman, H. (1974). *Labor and Monopoly Capital*. New York: Monthly Review Press.

Brockner, J., Tyler, T.R. and Cooper-Schneider, R. (1992). "The Influence of Prior Commitment to an Institution of Reactions to Perceived Unfairness." *Administrative Science Quarterly* 37: 254–271.

Burawoy, M. (1979). *Manufacturing Consent*. Chicago: University of Chicago Press.

Burgoon, J., Buller, D. and Woodall, W.G. (1995). *Nonverbal Communication*. New York: Harper & Row.

Burns, T. and Stalker, G.M. (1961). *The Management of Innovation*. London: Tavistock.

Campbell, J. and Pritchard, R. (1976). "Motivation Theory," in Dunnette, ed., *Handbook of Industrial and Organizational Psychology*. Chicago: Rand-McNally.

Chaleff, I. (2003). *The Courageous Follower*, 2nd ed. San Francisco, CA: Berrett-Koehler.

Clegg, S. (1976). "Power, Theorizing and Nihilism." *Theory and Society* 3: 65–87.

Conrad, C. (1995). "Was Pogo Right?" in Wood and Gregg, eds., *Communication Research in the 21st Century*. Creskill, NJ: Hampton Press.

Conrad, C. (2011). *Organizational Rhetoric: Resistance and Domination*. London: Polity Press.

Conrad, C. and Jodlowski, D. (2008). "Dealing Drugs on the Border," in Zoller and Dutta, eds., *Emerging Perspectives in Health*. Mahwah, NJ: Lawrence Erlbaum.

De Certeau, M. (1984). *The Practice of Everyday Life*. Berkeley: University of California Press.

Downs, C. and Conrad, C. (1982). "A Critical Incident Study of Effective Subordinancy." *Journal of Business Communication* 19: 27–38.

Drogin, B. (2007). *Curveball*. New York: Random House.

"Drug Company Payoffs." (2010). *New York Times* online, July 7. www.nytimes.com/2010/07/07/opinion/07wed.html?ref=opinion.

Dubie, D. (2007). "New Tool for Monitoring Employee Behavior." *PC World*. www.pcworld.com.

Dunbar, D., Reagan, B. and McCain, J. (2006). *Debunking the 9/11 Myths*. New York: Hearst.

Edwards, R. (1978). *Contested Terrain*. New York: Basic Books.

Edwards, G. (2007). *The Polarized Presidency of George W. Bush*. New York: Oxford University Press.

Eisenberg, E. (1984). "Ambiguity as Strategy in Organizational Communication." *Communication Monographs* 51: 227–242.

Fairhurst, G. (2001). "Dialectical Tensions in Leadership Research," in Jablin and Putnam, eds., *The New Handbook of Organizational Communication*. Thousand Oaks, CA: Sage.

Feldman, R. and Feldman, S. (2006). "What Links the Chain?" *Organization* 13: 861–887.

Ferguson, K. (1984). *The Feminist Case Against Bureaucracy*. Philadelphia: Temple University Press.

Findlay, P. and McKinlay, A. (2008). "Surveillance, Electronic Communication Technologies and Regulation." *Industrial Relations Journal* 34: 305–318.

Fine, M. and Buzzanell, P. (2000). "Walking the High Wire," in Buzzanell, ed., *Rethinking Organizational and Managerial Communication from Feminist Perspectives*. Newbury Park, CA: Sage.

Foucault, M. (1977). *Discipline and Punish*. Harmondsworth, UK: Penguin.

Freeman, R. and Katz, L. (1994). "Rising Wage Inequality," in R. Freeman, ed., *Working under Different Rules*. New York: Russell Sage Foundation.

Fulk, J. and Mani, S. (1986). "Distortion of Communication in Hierarchical Relationships," in M. McLaughlin, ed., *Communication Yearbook 9*. Newbury Park, CA: Sage.

Gibson, M. and Papa, M. (2000). "The Mud, the Blood, and the Beer Guys." *Journal of Applied Communication Research* 28: 68–88.

Goffee, R. and Jones, G. (2001). "Followership." *Harvard Business Review* 79 (11): 146–152.

Goldberg, L. (2000). "Slowdowns Hit Airlines," *Houston Chronicle*, December 6, 1C.

Gordon, D. (1996). *Fat and Mean*. Ithaca, NY: Cornell University Press.

Greene, C., and Podsakoff, P. (1981). "Effects of Withdrawal of a Performance-Contingent Reward on Supervisory Influence and Power." *Academy of Management Journal* 24: 527–42.

Griffin, D. (2004). *The 9/11 Commission Report*. New York: Olive Branch Press.

Hancock, M. and Papa, M. (1996). "Employee Struggles with Autonomy and Dependence: Examining the Dialectic of Control through a Structurational Account of Power." Paper presented at the International Communication Association Convention, Chicago.

Handy, C. (1995). "Trust in Virtual Organizations," *Harvard Business Review* 73: 40–48.

Helm, M. (2002). "Former Director Defends FBI," *Houston Chronicle*, October 9, 7A.

Hill, E. (2002). *The Intelligence Community's Knowledge of the September 11 Hijackers prior to September 11, 2001*. September. Washington, DC: Government Printing Office.

Jablin, F. (1987). "Formal Organizational Structure," in Jablin, Putnam, Roberts and Porter, eds., *Handbook of Organizational Communication*. Newbury Park, CA: Sage.

Jablin, F. (2001). "Communication Competence and Effectiveness," in Jablin and Putnam, eds., *The New Handbook of Organizational Communication*. Thousand Oaks, CA: Sage.

Johnson, K. (1994). "Many Companies Turn Workers into High-Tech Nomads." Minneapolis *Star-Tribune*, April 3, 1J.

Katz, D. (1964). "The Motivational Basis of Organizational Behavior." *Behavioral Science* 4: 131–133.

Kelley, R.E. (1992). *The Power of Followership*. New York: Doubleday.

Kelley, R.E. (2004). "Followership," in Burns, J.M., Goethals, G.R. and Sorenson, G.I., eds., *Encyclopedia of Leadership*. Thousand Oaks, CA: Sage.

Kerr, J. and Slocum, J. (1987). "Managing Corporate Culture through Reward Systems." *Academy of Management Executive* 1: 99–108.

Kerr, S. (1975). "On the Folly of Rewarding A While Hoping for B." *Academy of Management Journal* 19: 769–783.

Keyton, J., Clounak, T., Fischer, C., Howard, C., Topp, S. and Zlatek, M. (2006). "Ethical Storm or Model Workplace?" in May, ed., *Case Studies in Organizational Communication*. Thousand Oaks, CA: Sage.

Kidwell, R.E., Jr. and Bennett, N. (1994). "Employee Reactions to Electronic Control Systems." *Group and Organization Management* 19: 203–219.

Kim, K., Park, H-J. and Suzuki, N. (1990). "Reward Allocations in the United States, Japan, and Korea." *Academy of Management Journal* 33: 188–198.

Konradt, U., Schmook, R. and Malecke, M. (2000). "Impact of Telework on Individuals, Organizations and Families: A Critical Review." *International Review of Industrial and Organizational Psychology* 15: 63–100.

Lawrence, P. and Lorsch, J. (1967). *Organizations and Environments*. Cambridge, MA: Harvard Business School.

Locke, E. (1982). "The Ideas of Frederick Taylor." *The Academy of Management Review* 7: 14–24.

Manusov, V. and Billingsley, J.M. (1997). "Nonverbal Communication in Organizations," in Byers, ed., *Organizational Communication*. Boston: Allyn and Bacon.

McFarlin, D. and Sweeney, P. (1992). "Distributive and Procedural Justice as Predictors of Satisfaction with Personal and Organizational Outcomes." *Academy of Management Journal* 35: 626–637.

McPhee, R. (1988). "Vertical Communication Chains." *Management Communication Quarterly* 1: 455–493.

McPhee, R. and Poole, M.S. (2001). "Organizational Structure, Configurations, and Communication," in Jablin and Putnam, eds., *The New Handbook of Organizational Communication*. Newbury Park, CA: Sage.

Meindl, J. (1989). "Managing to Be Fair." *Administrative Science Quarterly* 34: 252–276.

Melymuka, K. (2003). "Going for Broke." *Computerworld*, March 26.

Monge, P. and Contractor, N. (2001). "Emergent Communication Networks," in Jablin and Putnam, eds., *The New Handbook of Organizational Communication*. Thousand Oaks, CA: Sage.

Morand, D.A. (1995). "The Role of Behavioral Formality and Informality in the Enactment of Bureaucratic Versus Organic Organizations." *Academy of Management Review* 20: 831–872.

Mutch, A. (2008). "Organization Theory and Military Metaphor." *Organization* 13: 751–769.

Nathan, B., Mohrman, A. and Milliman, J. (1991). "Interpersonal Relations as a Context of the Effects of Appraisal Interviews." *Academy of Management Journal* 34: 352–369.

Ong, A. (1991) "The Gender and Labor Politics of Postmodernity," *Annual Review of Anthropology*, 20 (1991).

Ouchi, W. (1977). "The Relationship between Organizational Structure and Control." *Administrative Science Quarterly*, 22: 95–113.

Pena, D. (1987). "Tortuodidad," in Ruiz and Tiano, eds., *Women on the U.S.-Mexican Border*. Boston: Allen & Unwin.

Perrow, C. (1986). *Complex Organizations: A Critical Essay*. New York: McGraw-Hill.

Petronio, S. (2002). *Boundaries of Privacy*. Albany, NY: SUNY Press.

Pfeffer, J. and Langton, N. (1988). "Wage Inequality and the Organization of Work." *Administrative Science Quarterly* 33: 588–606.

PRNewswire. (2010). "Aviall, Pentagon 2000 Software Provide Customers with Direct, Instantaneous Access to Parts and Materials." www.bloomberg.com/apps/news?pid=conewsstory&tkr=BA:US&sid=asPqfD3kqaZ0.

Rice, R. and Gattiker, U. (2001). "Communication Technologies and Structures," in Jablin and Putnam, eds., *The New Handbook of Organizational Communication*. Thousand Oaks, CA: Sage.

Rich, F. (2010). "Still the Best Congress Money Can Buy." *New York Times* online, November 27. www.nytimes.com/2010/11/28/opinion/28rich.html.

Riebling, M. (1994). *Wedge*. New York: Knopf.

Roberts, K. and O'Reilly, C. (1974). "Failures in Upward Communication." *Academy of Management Journal* 17: 205–215.

Sampson, E.E. (1986). "Justice, Ideology, and Social Legitimation," in Bierhoff, Cohen, and Greenberg, eds., *Justice in Social Relations*. New York: Plenum.

Sewell, G. and Barker, J. (2006a). "Coercion versus Care." *Academy of Management Review* 31: 934–961.

Sewell, G. and Barker, J. (2006b). "Max Weber and the Irony of Bureaucracy," in Korczynski, Hodson, and Edwards, eds., *Social Theory at Work*. Oxford: Oxford University Press.

Shennon, P. (2003). "Chief of Sept. 11 Panel Assesses Blame but Holds Off on Higher-Ups." *New York Times* online, December 19. www.nytimes.com.

Smith, R. (1970). "How to Be a Good Subordinate." *New York Times*, November 25, 16F.

Snyder, R. and Morris, J. (1984). "Organizational Communication and Performance," *Journal of Applied Psychology* 69: 461–465.

Spence, L. (1978). *The Politics of Social Knowledge*. University Park: Pennsylvania State University Press.

"The Spy Factory." (2010). *Nova*. www.pbs.org/wgbh/nova/insidenova/2010/06/spy-factory.html.

St. Clair, L., Quinn, R. and O'Neill, R. (2000). "The Perils of Responsiveness in Modern Organizations," in Quinn, O'Neill, and St. Clair, eds., *Pressing Problems in Modern Organizations (That Keep Us Up at Night)*. New York: AMACOM.

Staw, B., McKechnie, P. and Puffer, S. (1983). "The Justification of Organizational Performance." *Administrative Science Quarterly* 28: 582–600.

Stone, D. (2002). *Policy Paradox*. New York: W.W. Norton.

Sutcliffe, K. (2001). "Information Processing and Organizational Environments," in Jablin and Putnam, eds., *The New Handbook of Organizational Communication*. Thousand Oaks, CA: Sage.

Taylor, F. (1978). "The Principles of Scientific Management," in Shafritz and Whitbeck, eds., *Classics of Organizational Theory*. Oak Park, IL: Moore.

Tracy, K. and Eisenberg, E. (1990/1991). "Giving Criticism." *Research on Language and Social Interaction* 24: 37–70.

US Senate Select Committee on Intelligence and US House Select Committee on Intelligence. (2003). *Joint Inquiry into Intelligence Community Activities Before and After the Terrorist Attacks on September 11, 2001*. S. Rpt. 107-351, JH. Rpt. 107-792. Washington, DC: Government Printing Office.

Valeri, M. (2010). *Heavenly Merchandize: How Religion Shaped Commerce in Puritan America*. Princeton, NJ: Princeton University Press.

Verton, D. (2000a). "Senator Attacks Data Sharing." *Computerworld*, December 11.

Verton, D. (2000b). "Employers OK with E-Surfing." *Computerworld*, December 18.

Weber, M. (1958). *The Protestant Ethic and the Spirit of Capitalism*. New York: Scribners.

Weick, K.E. (1979). *The Social Psychology of Organizing*, 2nd ed. Reading, MA: Addison-Wesley.

Whitney, C.R. (2005). *WMD Mirage*. New York: Public Affairs Press.

Williams, L.J. and Anderson, S.E. (1991). "Job Satisfaction and Organizational Commitment as Predictors of Organizational Citizenship and In-Role Behavior." *Journal of Management* 17: 601–617.

Wilson, D. (2009). "Philip Morris' Support Casts Shadow Over a Bill to Limit Tobacco." *New York Times* online, April 1. www.nytimes.com/2009/04/01/business/01tobacco.html.

Wilson, J.Q. (1974). "The Politics of Regulation," in McKie, ed., *Social Responsibility and the Business Predicament*. Washington. DC: Brookings Institution.

Young, G. (1987). "Gender Identification and Working-Class Solidarity among *Maquila* Workers in Cuidad Juarez," in Ruiz and Tiano, eds., *Women on the U.S.-Mexican Border*. Boston: Allen & Unwin.

CHAPTER 4

RELATIONAL STRATEGIES OF ORGANIZING

If thou art one to whom petition is made, be calm as thou listeneth. . . . Do not rebuff him before he has . . . said that for which he came. . . . It is not [necessary] that everything about which he has petitioned should come to pass, [but] a good hearing is soothing to the heart.

Pharaoh Ptah-hotep to his managers, *ca.* 2700 BCE

If a leader maintains a close relationship with his soldiers they will be more eager to be seen performing some honorable action, and more anxious to abstain from doing anything that was disgraceful.

A lesson learned by Alexander the Great from the Persian King Cyrus, *ca.* 325 BCE

CENTRAL THEMES

- Relational strategies of organizing substitute decentralization and participatory decision making for the centralized, hierarchical, specialized organizational design of the traditional strategy. Employees sometimes resist these strategies, and their effects depend on a number of factors.
- Informal communication networks are an inevitable aspect of organizations, and they can benefit organizations and their members in many ways.
- Teams are a basic building block of the relational strategy. Teams enable relational organizations to respond flexibly to their challenges, but they may also function to control their members rather than empowering them.

Strategic Organizational Communication: In a Global Economy, Seventh Edition.
Charles Conrad and Marshall Scott Poole.

- Relational strategies rely on creating open and supportive supervisor–subordinate relationships, achieved through "transactional" leadership tactics.
- ICTs to support groups and relationships include email, instant messaging, and group support systems.
- Critical theories of organizational communication argue that relational strategies obscure differences among the interests of owner, managers, and workers.

KEY TERMS

participatory decision making
familia
power distance
production/service team
action team
project/development team
quality improvement team
integrating team
uniplex relationship
multiplex relationship
clique
closeness
centrality
prestige
liaison
bridge
isolate
centralization
density
weak ties
hierarchy of needs
job enrichment/enlargement
routinization
deskilling
ratebuster
principles of team effectiveness
boundary spanning
self-managing teams
concertive control
transactional leadership
unified messaging
wiki
groupware
systematically distorted communication

In the modern world, people can accomplish relatively little acting alone. In fact, the reason formal organizations developed after the agricultural revolution was because the everyday tasks that societies needed to perform could not be accomplished efficiently by individuals or family groups acting on their own. Organizations are made up of people involved in complex webs of relationships with one another. Relational strategies of organizing focus on interpersonal relationships as the key to managing the "fundamental paradox" described in Chapter 1.

Like Chapter 3, this chapter discusses organizational design, motivation/control/resistance, leadership, and technology. However, the amount of space that we devote to each of these topics is quite different. Traditional strategies of organizing focus on organizational design and motivation/control/surveillance at length, and deemphasize leadership. "Communication" is defined very narrowly, as the movement of information from one point in the organization to another. Relational strategies of organizing reverse that priority, largely taking organizational design for granted and focusing on motivation/control/surveillance and interpersonal relationships among workers, including leadership. "Communication" is defined more broadly, to encompass both information exchange and the development and maintenance of interpersonal relationships.

RELATIONAL STRATEGIES OF ORGANIZATIONAL DESIGN

There is one important design-related difference between relational and traditional strategies – decentralization. In traditional strategies of organizing centralization and hierarchicalization – the notions that organizations should be shaped like a multilevel triangle and decision making should be located at the top of the triangle – were central concepts. Lower-level employees are allowed to make decisions, but only about implementing the rules, policies, and procedures that are established on high. The relational strategy relaxes both assumptions, asserting instead that organizational hierarchies should be "flattened" and decision making should be decentralized. This means that lower-level employees would be empowered to make decisions about a wide range of issues that directly affect them and their jobs, and that there would be fewer links in the formal chain of command.

Decentralization and Participation

Decentralization and **participatory decision making** (PDM) are two sides of the same coin. If an organization adopts a decentralized organizational structure, the number of managers drops significantly, as does the number of levels of management. As a result, lower-level employees must be allowed to make everyday decisions because there is no one else available to do so. In addition, those managers that are left in the organization are required to supervise much more "loosely" than are managers in the traditional strategy. "Tight" supervision is alienating and increases the likelihood that workers will resist management. Loose supervision involves granting workers more autonomy, allowing them to determine how to accomplish their assigned tasks, and expecting them to make the decisions that influence them most. Supervising loosely allows each supervisor to manage a much larger number of employees. Furthermore, decisions would be made by the employees who are most directly concerned with them and most knowledgeable about the day-to-day activities of the organization. Formal communication would cross fewer levels, thus reducing the potential for structural breakdowns (recall Chapter 3).

Necessary Features for Successful PDM Participatory decision making is time-consuming and costly for organizations, but if it is properly handled, these costs are often more than offset by the increased morale, improved decision quality, and enhanced information flow that result. PDM comes in a variety of different forms that are called by many different names. Examples of PDM approaches include the following:

- Delegation: In this case employees are authorized to make decisions and solve problems that arise in connection with day-to-day work.
- Management by objectives: A program in which managers and employees jointly set goals for the employee, goals by which the employee is later evaluated.
- Quality improvement programs (one version of which is called "quality circles"): A program in which employees, usually working in groups, develop and implement ideas to improve the organization, their work, and working conditions. The employees are allowed to determine what problems to address and how to solve them, subject to management approval (more about this later in this chapter and in subsequent chapters).
- Self-managed teams (also called "self-directed work teams"): Groups of employees who have "collective responsibility for managing themselves and their work with minimal direct supervision. Usually they plan and schedule work, order materials and handle budget expenditures, make production-service related decisions, monitor productivity, and act on matters once reserved for management" (Seibold and Shea, 2001, 680).

PDM in its various forms is implemented in order to empower employees, under the assumption that the desirable results just mentioned are most likely to result when employees are empowered.

Merely implementing a PDM program does not, however, guarantee good results. PDM will increase organizational performance only if several requirements are met:

1. Subordinates must want to be involved in decision making, must be involved in complex tasks, and must be given substantial control over how they complete their tasks.
2. Supervisors must be willing to allow their subordinates to participate legitimately and must listen and respond to their ideas, and to encourage them to contribute.
3. The issues being discussed must be important to the participants. Workers usually believe that any decisions that directly affect them or their jobs are important and that decisions about more general company policies are less important. They especially would like to have influence over decisions about how to do their own work, scheduling of work, awarding raises and promotions, and hiring and firing of coworkers.
4. All the participants must have expertise and information relevant to the problems being discussed.
5. Managers must foster and support the beliefs, values, and attitudes necessary to legitimize participatory systems. Publicly recognizing employees' contributions and creating positive feelings of success make employees feel that they really do have the authority to act on their own, and thus are important determinants of feeling empowered.[1]

Resistance to PDM Sometimes resistance is grounded in the societal context surrounding an organization. It seems logical to expect PDM systems to be more successful in societies that have a strong democratic tradition, like the United States. However, US society has long separated the political and business realms – political rights that are taken for granted (freedom of speech and dissent, majority rule, due process, and so on) have never been required in private sector organizations (Cheney, Christensen, Zorn, and Ganesh, 2004; Stohl and Cheney, 2001). Since the United States also has had a history of adversarial relationships between workers and management, it is difficult to achieve the level of trust and cooperation necessary to make PDM systems work well. In some societies, people learn that supervisors should make and enforce decisions simply because they are supervisors, a concept that Max Weber labeled "traditional authority" (see Cheney *et al.*, 2004; Stohl, 1993). For example, Asian workers often find it difficult to challenge higher-status members of their organizations. For them, PDM can be alienating and frustrating.

Sometimes resistance is based on a lack of trust or skill. Many workers, especially blue-collar workers, do not wish to participate in decision making because they would rather not share the responsibilities that accompany the systems. This is especially true when workers are new to PDM or when a previously hierarchical organization decides to implement PDM, because workers are not sure may fear that management will use the systems to penalize them when they make inevitable mistakes. It also is true in more mature PDM systems, when people with high levels of expertise but weak communication skills are often frustrated by PDM. They expect to have a great deal of impact on decisions because of their expertise. But, their limited communication skills reduce their impact and they become frustrated. To overcome this problem, some organizations employ "coaches," who help employees identify issues related to their communication and decision making skills and work on improving them (McLean, 2006).

People with high levels of communication anxiety may also find participation threatening and may respond by withdrawing. The organization loses the expertise of such employees and their satisfaction with their jobs drops. In less participatory arrangements, these people would have opportunities to communicate privately with a single supervisor. Since privacy provides back stages where they can plan and rehearse their messages for this single, known listener, their anxiety may be reduced. For them, consultative decision making may be more satisfying and may allow the organization to benefit more from their expertise.

Participation may also increase employee stress by creating communication overload. Participatory strategies require everyone involved to communicate more actively. Some PDM systems ask employees to meet after work or on weekends. Especially when their jobs are demanding, this may be difficult for employees. The problem is even more serious when employees, for whatever reasons, wish to participate less than they are asked to do. When the amount of participation is either more or less than employees desire, they report higher stress, lower job satisfaction, and poorer performance than when participation matches their preferences (Seibold and Shea, 2001; Richmond and Roach, 1992; Stohl and Cheney, 2001).

Supervisors may also resist PDM. People become supervisors, at least in part, because they have a desire for power and an ability to obtain and use it to their advantage. They often gain substantial rewards from their superior positions – salary, status, and most important, the legitimate right to exercise authority over others. PDM works best, both in terms of enhancing productivity and in terms of increasing job satisfaction, if it reduces the power "gap" between supervisors and their subordinates. If the strategies succeed in equalizing power, they threaten the superiority, and thus the self-esteem and self-images, of precisely those people who hold power most dear and who have the greatest personal and practical reasons to want to hold on to the power they have gained over the years.

Power holders may resist sharing their power overtly by refusing to use participatory strategies, by using them only for trivial issues, by acting in ways that split the group or otherwise impede its ability to make effective decisions, by refusing to carry out the group's decisions, or by sabotaging the decision when it is implemented. They may also resist in more subtle fashion, for example, by withholding valuable information from subordinates, so that they will make bad decisions. The manager then steps in and "fixes" things, leading their subordinates to perceive them as exceptionally expert and competent. Thus their ability to control the group's decisions in the future is increased.

In a series of studies of power-sharing strategies in European firms, Mauk Mulder found that in addition to having greater access to information, supervisors typically also have superior communication skills their subordinates. They are more persuasive, argue positions more effectively, and are more adept at interpreting other employees' communication and responding appropriately. In participatory systems, these advantages allow them to influence the views of other employees. In time a "power elite" develops whose membership seems to be determined by their greater communication skills, but also is related to their formal positions. Eventually less powerful members communicate less and less and more

Case Study 4.1

Going South?[1]

USA Home Products (a pseudonym, as are all of the company names in this case study) is a US multinational company that has been operating in Mexico for more than 40 years. It has more than 100,000 employees in 80 countries and markets more than 200 brands to nearly 5 billion consumers worldwide. Unlike many US firms that have moved to Mexico solely to reduce labor costs, USAHP did so because they long ago saw Latin America as an important market for their products. In order to expand its operations in Mexico, it purchased a state-of-the art plant in Lourdes State (also a pseudonym) from a Mexican corporation, MEXCO. The two companies had very different ways of doing business. MEXCO valued having a local workforce, so it hired largely through family connections (like Industry International, one of the case studies in Chapter 3).

Lourdes State is a unique place. Its largely native population is very proud of the fact that it was never conquered by the Aztecs. It allied itself with the conquistadors, and gained special treatment by the Spanish. As a result, it is culturally and economically very different than neighboring states, especially Azteca State (another pseudonym) which surrounds Lourdes on three sides. Azteca is much more sophisticated (the home of a number of universities), much more accepting of foreigners, and wealthier than its smaller neighbor. The two peoples eat different types of food, have different forms of entertainment – the Aztecans' most important sport is soccer, which is not that important in Lourdes. Citizens of Azteca are "foreign," almost as foreign as Anglos from the United States.

MEXCO's management believed that employees could learn by trial and error and did not need more than an elementary school education. Salaries, especially of managers, were based more on interpersonal relationships with the owner and Board of Directors than on performance. Both practices are completely consistent with the Latin concept of **familia –** strong values attached to family and community, as well as a commitment to hard work, achievement, and aiding people who are in need – as ways of honoring one's family. These practices had a major effect on the plant's reward system. The favored managers had salaries much higher than employees of USAHP who held a similar rank in the company, while the salaries of lower-level employees (especially the technicians who operated the high-tech machinery) were much lower than USAHP standards.

Mexico is a high **power-distance** culture, which means that its people learn to accept and value hierarchical power relationships. For the technicians this meant that they accepted having management make decisions and them then following their orders, and they gained a sense of pride from their technical skills, especially in comparison to workers who cleaned the plant and its equipment, and staff personnel who worked in the company's offices. They also gained a degree of pride from their ability to "make do," an attitude that is quite common in societies that experience scarcity. The plant never had allocated much money for maintenance and repair of equipment. When things broke down, the technicians found ways to get them running again. Most of the solutions they discovered were nonstandard – "spit and baling wire" – but they worked. In effect their motto became "If it ain't broke, don't fix it," and when it did, the "fix" was almost never anything that would be included in an operations manual or a university course.

When USAHP took over the plant, they immediately moved to change its operations to be like those in its other plants, both in the United States and in Latin America. Part of the change was a complete revision of the selection and reward system. USAHP wanted its machine operators to have technical training, preferably a degree from a respected university, and fluency in both written and spoken English. Very few people with this level of education lived in Lourdes, which has one of the weakest educational systems in Mexico. Instead of helping improve Lourdes' educational system, something that local leaders expected,

USAHP decided to hire new employees from the universities in Azteca. To make matters worse, the **expatriates** (US employees that USAHP transferred to the new plant) decided to live in Azteca, where the schools are better, the climate cooler, and the lifestyle more sophisticated.

Suddenly, the plant was being run by people who were doubly foreign – Anglos allied with Aztecans. In addition, many of the overpaid managers were fired, and the ones who had the technical skills USAHP desired had their salaries frozen until the rest of the employees caught up to USAHP's salary scale. USAHP's headquarters saw these changes as making the plant's salary structure fairer; many of MEXCO's workers had a very different definition of "fairness," one based on tenure and loyalty, not technical qualifications. The supervisors who stayed were unhappy, but glad they still had jobs; the workers who remained were afraid because the interpersonal connections that had given them a sense of security suddenly were irrelevant.

However, the biggest change involved USAHP's "AM" system, based on two principles borrowed from Japanese managerial practices (ones based on the work of American J. Edwards Deming). These were "continuous improvement" and constant monitoring of performance using advanced statistical techniques. For the technicians this meant that they would now be responsible for cleaning and maintaining their own machines. They could no longer blame equipment breakdowns on the maintenance department, and they suddenly were responsible for performing tasks that they perceived as beneath them. They were evaluated in part on a very ambiguous criterion of "support for the AM" system, even though Mexican culture is known for its low tolerance of ambiguity. (Interestingly, the company's efforts to shift to AM in its US plants during the 1990s had failed because it violated US workers' "If it ain't broke don't fix it" attitudes, and because AM was a Japanese system. The company had greater success in Latin America, because, they believe, the culture is more supportive of following orders sent from "the top down.") Upper management realized that they had to persuade local management to support AM or they would not be able to overcome resistance by the workers. The parent company transferred managers from other Latin American plants that had successfully shifted to the AM system, and paired them with local plant managers.

Unfortunately, they failed to persuade Mr. Suarez, a supervisor from Lourdes State who had worked in the plant for decades. They also failed to explain the changes and the reasons for them to the workers, evidently assuming that in a "top-down" culture, they would quickly accept changes that were mandated by their supervisors. The technicians resisted the changes in every way they could. After 2½ years, only one of 40 teams had successfully completed the first phase of the program.

It is somewhat surprising that USAHP's upper management realized that the new system was failing – US managers have long been known for a tendency to persist in failing courses of action long after failure is abundantly clear (Tegar, 1980). But, they learned from their mistakes and started implementing AM in a way that was appropriate to Mexican and Lourdian culture: they completely revamped the reward system so that it could encourage acceptance of the change, broke down the solidarity around the previous opposing leader, and improved the skill level of the workforce.

In order to recover from the initial failure, USAHP replaced the ambiguous practice of rewarding people for showing their commitment to the new system with rewards based on achieving a set of clearly stated objectives. New procedures and metrics to evaluate the involvement of the personnel in AM were implemented, such as attendance to AM-related meetings and activities. All AM teams meet each week to share their results and assign each member with specific responsibilities, ensuring that all of the employees were actively involved in the implementation process. The operators still have a lot of pressure to produce but now they have pre-established hours to receive training in AM. Teams were given small rewards for achieving the set goals and recognition will be given to those completing important milestones in the AM process. The team decides when it will be audited to see if it is ready to move on to the later phases of implementation and they are told ahead of time precisely what criteria will be used in the evaluation.

Mr. Suarez was relocated outside of the production division where he could be consulted for technical advice, but where he no longer supervised the technicians. He was replaced by two production managers who are familiar with and committed to the new system. Three technicians with long histories in the plant were selected to receive initial training, and then to train the other technicians in the division. In order to break the tight solidarity among the workers from the previous company, a new leadership team was formed, which included members from all of the production areas. New subcommittees were created in each area composed of a functional leader (a worker with AM experience), the leader of the area, and an AM planner.

Applying What You Have Learned

1. In general, why do people resist participatory programs? Which of those sources of resistance were evident in this case?
2. What aspects of Mexican and Lourdian culture made the shift to a more participatory system more complicated? What aspects made it (or should have made it) easier?

Questions to Think About and Discuss

1. Will this program be successful over the long term? Why or why not?
2. Is this case study primarily about cross-cultural differences or about resistance to change or about attitudes toward participation? How are these factors interrelated?
3. If you were to develop a manual on cross-cultural communication based on this case, what would it say? Why?

Note

1 The research on which this case is based was partially funded by both the Consejo Nacional de Ciencia y Tecnología (CONACYT – Mexico), contract No. 35981-U; and the National Science Foundation (NSF–USA), contract No. DMI-0116635.

powerful members begin to dominate the decision-making process. Thus, the opportunity for more open communication, which is the strength of participation, may lead to increased power gaps rather than to power sharing (Bass and Bass, 2008; Mulder, 1971; Mulder and Wilke, 1970).

The Organization as a Tier of Teams

The work team is the basic unit of the relational strategy of organization. The relational strategy does not do away with managerial structure altogether. There are still top managers and some middle managers, as well as line-level work teams. However, the concept of the hierarchy so critical to the traditional strategy is replaced with the concept of the organization as a tier of teams. One of the primary advocates of the relational strategy, Rensis Likert (1961), developed a model of relational organizational design that may help clarify these concepts. He proposed that organizations should be structured around overlapping teams of employees instead of with the independent divisions of the bureaucratic model. Each team would make any decisions that affect it or its members. Each team would be linked to every other group with which it was interdependent by a "linking pin," an employee who was a member of both teams (see Figure 4.1).

In this structure, the linking pin enables each team to better understand the needs and problems of the teams it is linked to (and also to other teams linked to those teams, if communication worked properly). This arrangement would minimize the problems of trained communication incapacity and specialized languages (discussed in Chapter 3) because they would always have translators available – the linking pins. Intergroup conflict can be reduced because communication breakdowns between the two teams would be less frequent. Group decision making should be enhanced because each linking pin would have access to different kinds of information as a result of his or her contact with other teams. In effect, this system (which Likert called System IV) created an organizational structure designed around the concept of PDM. Unfortunately, linking pins are placed in difficult and stressful positions. When things go wrong, they are handy scapegoats, and they are often not rewarded for their efforts.[2]

Several different kinds of teams can be distinguished (Sundstrom, De Meuse, and Futrell, 1990). The most common form of group in organizations is the **production/service team**, such as a factory assembly team, a sales team, or a crew of flight attendants. Production/service teams are formal units that range in size from three to over 50 members. They have definite goals and tasks, they tend to repeat their work cycles, and their relationships with other work groups and the larger organization are often specified in formal terms. For instance, in an office equipment maker studied by Scott Poole, production was organized around six to eight member teams that crafted pieces of office furniture. Each team developed its own methods of working together to assemble the furniture (that is,

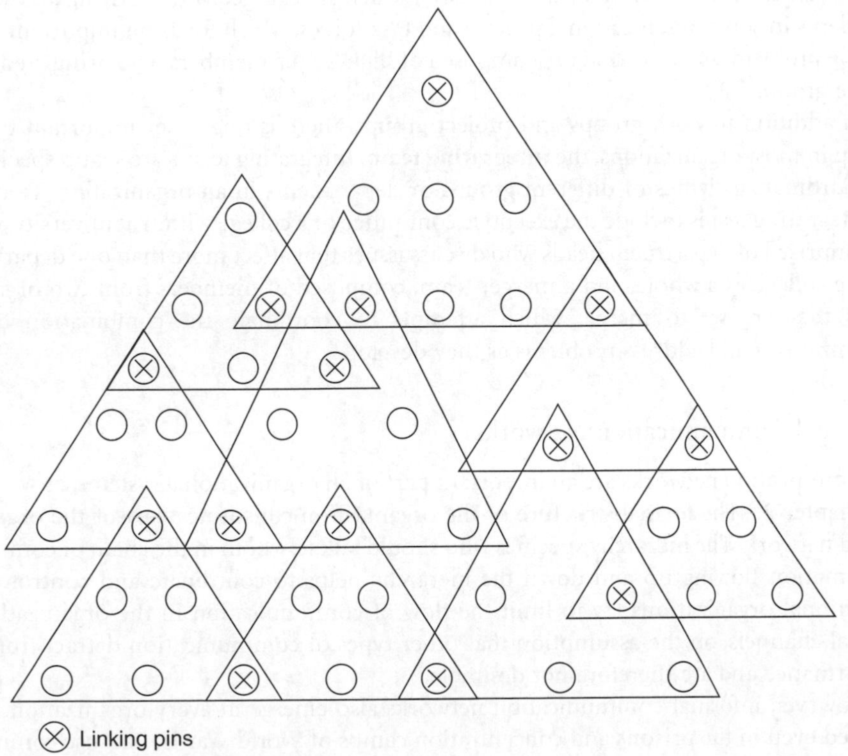

Figure 4.1 Likert's multiple overlapping groups.

the teams were self-organizing) and to coordinate two teams in the shipping department that packed and shipped the orders. These lower level teams were coordinated by a management team. Under the relational strategy this coordination is carried out through direct communication between the groups, sometimes through linking pins and sometimes via informal representatives. The informal communication system, discussed in the next section, may also play a role in coordinating work groups.

Another type of team is the **action team**. These teams engage in brief performance episodes that have clearly defined goals and end points. Examples include emergency medical teams, fire fighting crews, and surgical teams. They typically have members with different specialized roles and tight coordination of activities is essential to their effectiveness.

Project/development teams are set up on a temporary basis to carry out a specific task within a specified time frame, which may vary from a few months to several years. Members are typically assigned to project teams on a limited basis and are often on loan from their home department or group. Organizations often create project teams to develop new products and activities or to solve persistent problems, as when McDonald's Corporation formed the Chicken McNugget team to bring this interesting fast food to market (Larson and LaFasto, 1989). The Chicken McNugget team had members from the product development and marketing departments, which made it a cross-functional project team. Cross-functional teams are constituted to ensure that the perspectives of different departments or functions are brought to a project and that all aspects of the organization that must participate in the project are involved. Other examples of project teams include **quality improvement teams** (introduced previously), which are charged with studying and solving problems in some organizational process and task forces, which focus on important, high-profile problems or issues and are composed of high-status members who bring credibility to the group.

In addition to work groups and project groups, there is one other important type of group in most organizations, the **integrating team**. Integrating teams are set up specifically to coordinate activities of different groups or departments in an organization. Examples of integrating teams include the executive committee of a college within a university, which is comprised of department heads who discuss issues that affect more than one department or the college as a whole, and a merger team, composed of members from two organizations that are set to merge, which attempts to coordinate the combination of the organizations and address problems as they develop.

Informal Communication Networks

Communication networks are an important part of all organizational systems, as we noted in Chapter 2.[3] The formal structure of the organization constitutes part of the organizational network. The hierarchy specifies who should talk to whom in the chain of command. Information flowing up and down the hierarchy helps to coordinate and control work. Traditional organizations try to limit the flow of communication in the organization to formal channels, on the assumption that other types of communication detract from job performance and are therefore not desirable.

However, informal communication networks also emerge in every organization. They formed even in the prisons and concentration camps of World War II. Because communication through informal ties is outside management's control, supervisors in traditional organizations often try to suppress their development. Informal networks often initially develop parallel to the organization's formal structures, which constrain and shape initial opportunities for interaction, but over time they depart considerably from formal networks and take on a configuration and a life of their own (Monge and Contractor, 2003).

Relational strategies suggest that informal communication networks are an important part of the organization's structure. Through informal networks employees form meaningful interpersonal relationships, gain a sense of self-respect, meet their sociability needs, and exercise some degree of control over their working lives. People who are actively involved in informal networks have higher morale, job satisfaction, and commitment to their organizations; know more about how their organizations operate; and are better able to meet others' communication needs than employees who are not actively involved (Albrecht, 1984; Jablin, 1985; Eisenberg, Monge and Miller, 1983).

At this point we will introduce some basic communication network terminology that we will use in the remainder of this book. There are two types of ties in organizational communication networks. Some relationships are **uniplex**, which means that the parties always talk about the same topic (for example, work or sports). Others are **multiplex** relationships in which the parties communicate about a wide variety of topics and play a number of different roles with one another (for example, boss, collaborator on a key project, tennis partner, and so on). Multiplex relationships tend to be long term, emotionally intense, influential, trusting, and more predictable than uniplex relationships. Communication in multiplex relationships tends to be deep, involving a good deal of self-disclosure and rich, providing much emotional and cognitive detail. Multiplex relationships provide parties with social support and opportunities to vent frustrations, thus helping manage stress and make positive changes. They also may increase stress because it takes time and emotional energy to maintain intense relationships. Informal communication networks tend to have more multiplex ties than formal communication networks.

Sets of people who are tightly interconnected are called **cliques**. Cliques can arise from formal work groups or units whose members interact a lot, but they may also result from informal interactions. Figure 4.2 shows a communication network in which there are three interconnected cliques. There are also other important properties related to the position that an individual has in a communication network. **Closeness** refers to the ease with which a person can reach others in the communication network. The more people one can reach without having to go through others, and the fewer others one has to go through, the higher one's closeness. An example of a person high in closeness is the administrative assistant of a unit; typically that person has close contacts with everyone else in the unit and can contact them immediately to route a phone call or request.

Centrality is the degree to which an actor is central to a network. The more one can "control" the flow of information in a network, the more central one is. The administrative assistant in a department is typically highly central. Centrality and closeness are often correlated in organizations. **Prestige** is the degree to which a person is contacted by others as opposed to having to contact them. Studies have shown that people with high status and power are sought out by lower ranking, less powerful people, and therefore typically receive more contacts and communications than they must send. It is interesting to note that prestige is not necessarily correlated with closeness or centrality. Some prestigious people are high in centrality and closeness, but others are not.

Several key roles in communication networks have been identified by previous research. A **liaison** links cliques that would not otherwise be linked but is not a member of either

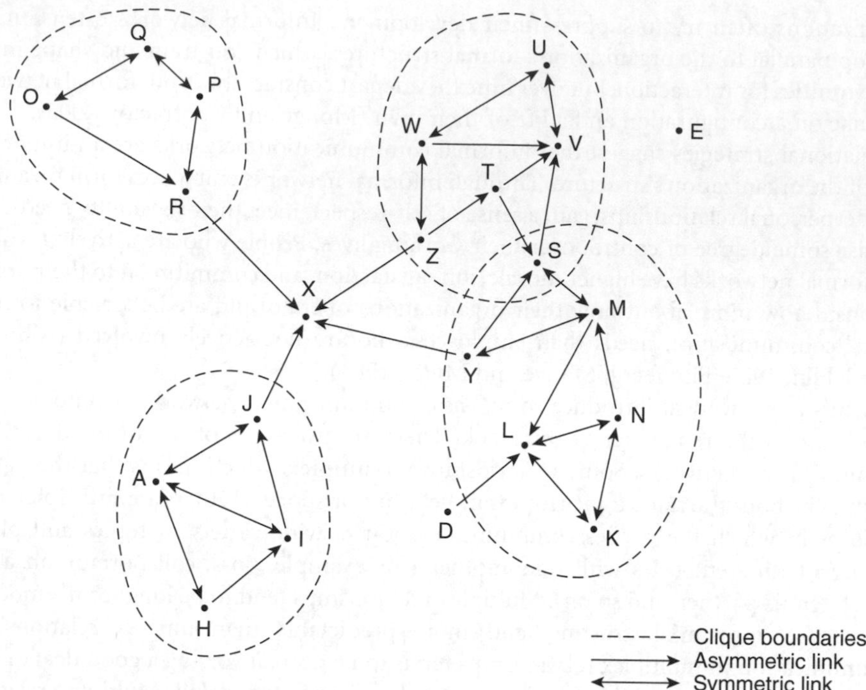

Figure 4.2 A communication network.

clique. Person in Figure 4.2 is a liaison. Liaisons are important roles in networks because they provide linkages between groups that would not otherwise be linked. Liaisons are often managers or highly respected people and they tend to score high in prestige (they are contacted a lot but they may not directly reciprocate those contacts). They may also be members who perform a specialized role, such as one of the linking roles described in Chapter 6. A **bridge** (person S) also links two cliques but is a member of both of them. An **isolate** (person E) is someone who has few or no links to others in the network. It is tempting to think of isolates as people who are not valuable to the organization, but some are isolated because they are so committed to their work that they do not communicate with many others. Other people are isolates because of their work schedules. The janitor who cleans after hours may be an isolate, but he or she performs a valuable function.

One important characteristic of communication networks as a whole is their **centralization**, the degree to which one or two members can control most of the flow in the network. Networks with a few members very high in centrality and most others with relatively low centrality tend to be centralized. The organizational hierarchy characteristic of traditional organizations is centralized, whereas participatory networks characteristic of the relational strategy are lower in centralization.

Density refers to how dense the communication network is and is measured by the ratio of how many links are actually in the network and how many links there could potentially be between members. The organizational hierarchy of the traditional organization is low in density on purpose, because the traditional organization wants to restrict information flow to a relatively few formal channels. It regards additional links beyond what is required to maintain the hierarchy as wasteful. On the other hand, the relational strategy seeks to create denser networks. Table 4.1 summarizes key terms used to characterize communication networks.

It takes effort to develop and sustain dense, connected informal networks. It takes time for people to find one another and much successful communication for them to come to understand and trust one another. Sometimes they must learn to compensate for the problems of trained incapacity that were discussed in Chapter 3. Informal networks must regularly be used or they tend to atrophy. Unless two people communicate on a fairly regular basis they will forget the language and frame of reference used by the other person. Just as competence in a foreign language wears off with disuse, learning the frame of reference of other employees also wears off. Then, when a crisis occurs in which employees need to communicate, they find it difficult to do so. Typically, informal networks are maintained through gossip – the sharing of personal information that is irrelevant to specific tasks or organizational decisions. But without interactions such as gossip that activate them and keep them active, informal networks tend to decay (Knoke, 2001; March and Sevon, 1982).

Generally speaking, informal networks help organizations in three ways: by compensating for the weaknesses in formal communication, by improving organizational decision making, and by fostering innovation (Knoke, 2001; Monge and Contractor, 2003; Johnson, 2009). Formal communication networks allow people to handle predictable, routine situations, but they are inefficient means of meeting unanticipated communication needs, for managing crises, for dealing with complex or detailed problems, sharing personal information, or exchanging information rapidly. In a now classic study, Keith Davis (1953b) found that during a quality control crisis in a large firm, the information that was needed to solve the problem was rapidly disseminated using informal networks, not formal channels. Informal communication may also be more reliable than formal communication. Because informal communication is less restricted by differences in power and status, it is richer in content than formal communication. Mutual give and take is less inhibited in informal communication, so communicators provide more detail in their messages and are more willing to give and receive feedback.

Even gossip and rumors – messages whose accuracy cannot immediately be determined by management – often provide accurate information. Job-related rumors originate because employees are not adequately informed through formal channels. Although some gossip and rumors may be false, when compared to formal communication, with its inherent problems of withholding and distortion (recall Chapter 3), informal communication may often be more accurate. Informal networks also tend to be self-correcting. Once an employee is caught spreading false rumors, his or her credibility is reduced. Formal communication networks are not based on interpersonal relationships, so they tend not to self-correct (Planalp, Hafen, and Adkins, 1999).

Informal networks can also foster innovation. Sometimes people have access to a wealth of valuable information that they are not "officially" supposed to possess. Informal relationships with those people provide an invaluable source of information, especially information that is not supposed to be public knowledge. Employers can release "trial balloons" and monitor employees' reactions while never having to admit officially that the proposal was even being considered. Being able to talk off the record seems to improve organizational decision making, especially when organizations are in the early stages of defining problems and searching for solutions. Through his 20-year study of bureaucratic organizations, Peter Blau found that informal communication allowed employees to obtain advice

Table 4.1 Properties of Communication Networks (refer to figure 4.2)

Measure	*Definition*	*Examples*
Measures of Network Ties		
Frequency	How many times or how often the link occurs.	X talks to Y 5 times per week.
Multiplexity	Extent to which two members are linked together by more than one relationship.	X and Y work together, belong to the same club, and share gossip.
Strength	Amount of time, emotional intensity, intimacy, or reciprocation.	X and Y interact a lot and spend a lot of time together.
Direction	Who initiates the link.	In an asymmetric link, Y asks X for advice, but X does not ask Y for advice. In a symmetric link, M and Y both ask each other for advice.
Measures Related to Individuals in the Network		
Centrality	Extent to which member is centrally located in a network (there are lots of ways to measure this).	X is central.
In-degree	Number of directional links coming to a member from other members.	X has 4 in-degrees.
Out-degree	Number of directional links going from the member to other members.	Y has 3 out-degrees.
Closeness	Extent to which member is close to or can easily reach all the other actors in a network.	X has high closeness. K has low closeness.
Measures Related to Individuals in the Network		
Prestige	How many asymmetric links an actor has in which he or she does not initiate contact measured by in-degree.	X is high in prestige.
Network Roles		
Star	An actor highly central to a network.	X is a star.
Liaison	An actor who has links to two or more cliques that would otherwise not be linked, but is not a member of either clique.	X is a Liaison.
Bridge	An actor who belongs to two or more cliques.	S is a bridge.
Isolate	A person who has no links or relatively few links to others.	D and E are isolates.
Gatekeeper	A member who mediates or controls the flow between one part of the network and another.	X, Y, and Z could be gatekeepers.
Measures of Entire Network Properties		
Density	Number of links in the network compared to the number that could potentially form. Dense networks have lots of links.	The network is moderately dense.
Centralization	Degree to which a few members could control most links in the network.	The network is highly centralized.
Connectivity (also called Reachability)	Extent to which actors in the network are linked to one another by direct or indirect paths.	The network is moderately high in connectivity.

and assistance without "really" admitting that they needed it and provided them with politically safe opportunities to think out loud about new ideas or experiences. In general, the more dense and less centralized an organization's communication system is, the more innovative its employees will be. Through informal networks, people share innovative ideas, obtain feedback that allows them to improve those ideas, and eventually obtain support for those innovations. Informal networks allow (but do not guarantee) people to come to a shared understanding of new ideas and their importance to the organization and thus stimulate them to take collective innovative action.[4]

Whereas dense, connected communication networks enable organizations to implement new ideas more effectively, the *source* of new ideas is more often the **weak ties**. Weak ties are connections to others with whom one has only occasional contact. Because they represent ties that are seldom used, weak ties typically do not show up in network diagrams like the one in Figure 4.2. However, they are critical for moving new information into existing networks. People tend to talk about the same types of things and have much in common with those to whom they are strongly tied. Continuous communication in formal and information networks tends to homogenize thinking. New ideas more often come from the outside, from someone we meet on an airplane, or at a conference, or party, someone who has a different perspective, different ideas and knowledge. Sociologist Scott Granovetter (1973) conducted one of the first studies of weak ties and found that, contrary to common expectations, most people found a new job not through contacts they regularly communicated with, but through weak ties.[5]

RELATIONAL STRATEGIES OF MOTIVATION, CONTROL, AND SURVEILLANCE

Traditional strategies of motivation and control are based on the assumptions that workers find work to be alienating and must be tightly controlled and motivated by the promise of economic gain (the view that James McGregor once labeled "Theory X"). Relational strategies are based on what McGregor called a "Theory Y" (see Table 4.2) view of human beings and work – people have important needs for autonomy, creativity, and sociability, needs that are frustrated by organizations' (and societies') needs for control and coordination. Supervisors can align those individual needs with the needs of their organizations by making work meaningful and fostering positive supervisor–subordinate relationships. They can do this by enlarging and enriching jobs, and by adopting transactional leadership strategies.[6]

Job Enrichment and Enlargement

Two of the most influential advocates of this approach to motivation and control were Abraham Maslow and Chris Argyris. Maslow (1987) posited that people have five kinds of needs that are arranged in a hierarchy: physiological (expressed in feelings of thirst, lust, and so on), safety (feeling free from danger, harm, and the fear that physiological needs will not be met), belongingness (a desire for meaningful relationships with other people), esteem or ego (feelings of accomplishment and recognition), and self-actualization (a concept that Maslow never explained clearly but that seems to be related to the feeling that one has done or is doing what one is meant to do). Once lower-level needs are fulfilled,

Table 4.2 McGregor's Theory X and Theory Y

Theory X

1. Workers must be supervised as closely as possible, either through direct oversight or by tight reward and/or punishment systems.
2. Work is objectionable to most unless it is made less offensive by the actions of organizations.
3. Most people have little initiative, have little capacity for being creative or solving organizational problems, do not want to have responsibilities, and prefer being directed by someone else.
4. People are motivated by economic factors and a need for security.

Theory Y

1. People usually do not require close supervision and will, if given a chance to control their own activities, be productive, satisfied, and fulfilled.
2. Work is natural and enjoyable to people.
3. People are ambitious, desire autonomy and self-control, and can use their abilities to solve problems and meet their goals. Creativity is distributed "normally" across the population, just as is any other characteristic.
4. People are motivated by a variety of needs only some of which involve economics or security.

upper-level needs become salient. Although Maslow's **hierarchy of needs** and its implications have not been supported consistently in subsequent research, his perspective became the basis of a number of strategies for increasing workers' job satisfaction by enlarging and enriching their jobs.[7]

One of the earliest and most influential advocates of **job enrichment/enlargement** was Chris Argyris (1957). He argued that many of the key characteristics of traditional models of organizing frustrated the needs of normal, psychologically healthy people. Jobs that are specialized or **routinized** (performed in the same way day after day), supervisors who control their employees "tightly", and highly competitive, individualistic atmospheres are especially alienating. People respond to these situations by acting in ways that are counterproductive for their organizations – becoming defensive (attacking or withdrawing from coworkers) or apathetic (for example, daydreaming), socializing with other frustrated workers instead of focusing attention on their work, leaving the organization, or attempting to advance to positions that are less frustrating. The traditional strategy focuses on creating precisely these kinds of situations. Managers are charged with **deskilling** jobs – segmenting, simplifying, and routinizing them – making them as "impoverished" and "small" as possible so that people will fit into their roles as parts in the organizational machine.

Presumably, this deskilling of jobs is designed to increase organizational efficiency, but it is so alienating for employees that it often leads to a net loss in individual and organizational productivity. In fact, the real reason for deskilling often is to enhance supervisory control rather than to improve efficiency. Organizations with many deskilled jobs can hire employees who have few alternatives and thus cannot resist management regardless of how alienated they are – high school students, disabled people, or, most recently, residents of developing countries (including children). Deskilled tasks can easily be outsourced (contracted to outside organizations who use their own workers to do the job, often at much lower rates of pay) or assigned to part-time or other "contingent" workers (people who are hired for a specific project only). And, because workers perform tasks requiring few skills, they are easy to replace when they are fired. Arraying deskilled tasks along an assembly line provides workers with little or no opportunity to communicate with one another and forces them to adjust the pace of their activities to the pace of the machines. This makes it more difficult to share grievances, compare the way management treats them, or make plans for collective action.

New technologies can be developed solely for the purpose of simplifying and routinizing jobs even further. For example, at one time the service jobs of grocery-store checker and fast-food sales clerk required at least minimal arithmetical, keyboarding, and memory skills. Today computerized cash registers make it possible to hire people without these skills. The next time you visit your local McDonald's, look closely at the keyboard on the cash registers and ask yourself what skills are necessary to operate it. To see just how deskilled these jobs are, order something that is not represented by a button on the keyboard and see what happens. By the mid-1960s most production workers in the United States were involved in this kind of routine, repetitive, deskilled activity, which failed to fulfill individual needs for creativity, autonomy, or sociability. By the mid-1980s many white-collar workers were involved in similar jobs.[8]

Although deskilling does increase productivity for a time, it also decreases job satisfaction and encourages resistance. Sometimes resistance is informal. For example, salesclerks have long resisted deskilling by creating and using their own informal relational strategies. They are friendly and supportive of one another, huddle together on the floor to foster in-group communication, ignore management's efforts to make them compete against one another, share duties that management assigns to individuals, and meet together outside of work to engage in "rituals of women's culture," such as wedding and birth showers (Benson, 1992). Other forms of resistance involve more overt hostility between labor and management.

An alternative to deskilling is for management to do just the opposite – to "enlarge" or "enrich" jobs. Doing so increases efficiency because it allows organizations to decentralize. It also increases profitability by substituting the upper-level rewards of enhanced creativity and autonomy for expensive lower-level rewards, such as salaries and wages. But, successful enlargement/enrichment relies heavily on relational communication. If a job is too complex, it is frustrating and unsatisfying. If it is too simple, it is boring. Successfully matching workers and jobs, as Fredrick Taylor realized a century ago, requires a high level of open communication and feedback between supervisors and their subordinates. In addition, workers seem to figure out how rich their jobs are both by monitoring what they do and by talking with other workers. Unless people believe that their tasks are stimulating, they will not be stimulated. Workers develop these beliefs when other workers tell them that they envy their jobs. In fact, job satisfaction in general is influenced both by the objective features of employees' jobs and by what their coworkers say about their jobs. Thus, successful job enlargement/enrichment requires both careful job design, and active and supportive relational communication (Pollock, Whitbread, and Contractor, 2000).

Teams and Team-Based Surveillance

The work teams and other informal groups an employee belongs to have an important influence on his or her attitudes and actions in the organization.[9] Attention to group influences on motivation goes back at least as far as the Hawthorne studies of the 1930s.[10]

Groups influence employees in several ways. First, work groups play an important role in socializing members to the organization. Organizations often spend considerable time on formal orientation and training for new members in attempts to socialize them. However, once orientation and training are over, employees spend most of their time in their work groups, which also teach them a great deal about the organization. In work groups employees informally learn things like shortcuts and special techniques for getting their work done properly, which rules the organization will enforce and which are simply window dressing, which supervisors are fair and which are unreasonable. In some cases this learning actually counteracts the formal orientation and training sessions.

Employees also join other groups in the organization, such as the company baseball team, the Windows user's group, and informal groups (cliques) such as the group of other employees they typically have lunch with. These groups shape the way in which the employees make sense out of work experiences. For example, if a company institutes a quality improvement program and an important group interprets an organization's attempts to motivate employees as exploitative, its members are likely to resist the program, no matter how attractive it may seem to those who devise them. On the other hand, if groups buy into job enrichment or other programs, it may significantly increase their motivational impact (Hackman and Oldham, 1980).

Groups also play an important role in connecting individual and organizational identities. Silva and Sias (2010) showed how groups in a community church helped individuals bond to the larger organization through giving them connections to the organization, helping them to restructure their identities so they were consistent with organizational demands, and buffering them from organizational pressures they were uncomfortable with.

Groups also influence their members' productivity. In some cases, these pressures lead individual members to be less productive. **Ratebusters**, people who produce too much or who go along with management too readily, may be punished by coworkers. Sanctions can range from "tutoring," to warnings, to the "silent treatment," and even to physical violence. But, in other cases the pressures may be to increase production. Leonard Sayles notes, "We have other instances on record where the group has sanctioned increasingly high productivity, rejected fellow workers who could not maintain high output, and resisted threats to existing high quality standards."[11] This line of thought is behind recent advocacy of team-based organizations. In theory, properly composed and motivated teams may create a more effective organization than more traditional forms of organizing (Mohrman, Cohen, and Mohrman, 1995).

Principles for Team Effectiveness In recent years there has been an upsurge of research on team effectiveness (Larson and LaFasto, 1989; Salas, Sims, and Burke, 2005).[12] This has long been an elusive subject, but in the past decade several convincing models of team performance have emerged, as summarized in two studies. In the first, Larson and LaFasto conducted an in-depth study of 50 effective teams, ranging from a field team from the Centers for Disease Control to the 1988 Notre Dame football team. In the second, Salas, Sims, and Burke synthesized over 25 models of teamwork and team effectiveness that were advanced between 1975 and 2005. These two studies indicate that effective teams have eight common characteristics:

1. A *clear, elevating goal* that is meaningful and significant to members, clearly stated in familiar terms, measurable, and challenging. Larson and LaFasto concluded that the

main reason for failure in the 50 teams they studied was that personal goals superseded group goals.

2. A *results-driven structure* with clear role definitions, accountability, methods for monitoring performance, and an effective communication system that fosters fast and complete information exchange and documentation of issues and decisions. Using this structure, members engage in mutual performance monitoring and feedback to ensure that the team's goals are being met.
3. *Competent team members* who have technical knowledge and skills necessary for the team's work. Members must also have social competencies as well. They must be able to work with others, desire to contribute to the group, and appreciate others' differences and contributions.
4. *Unified commitment* to the team and its success. This is fostered, first, by promoting participation of all members in making important and day-to-day decisions. Second members must develop "high expectations for each other, expect that everyone else on the team will contribute to the extent that each is capable, and will become disturbed if a member pursues individual objectives at the expense of the team goal."[13] When members see that a teammate is in trouble or who cannot complete his or her tasks, they backup the struggling member.
5. *A collaborative climate*, characterized by open communication operating on the following principles: honesty – bringing all issues before the group and not hiding problems or exaggerating what one has done; willingness to share and receptivity to ideas, opinions, and positions; consistency in behavior; and respectful and dignified treatment of all people.
6. *Standards of excellence* that create pressure to perform at very high levels. Pressure to perform stems from having members who have a high motivation to excel, encouragement by other members to perform, a clear sense of the positive consequences of success and the negative consequences of failure, and external pressure from the organization. High standards are encouraged by models of excellence, especially other high-performing teams. Effective teams also continuously upgrade their standards as they meet or exceed them.
7. *External support* and recognition from the larger organization. The team must be given the resources and authority to succeed and the organization must recognize and reward high performance.
8. *Principled leadership* that establishes a vision for the team and empowers members. The leader must also create change by realizing the need for change, reminding members that change is normal, and helping members through the change process. The goal of the effective team leader is to unify the team and enable members to "unleash their talent" in the team's work.

A group that organizes itself around these principles is designed to motivate its members to contribute to the organization and also to improve their knowledge and skills so they can contribute even more. Teams such as these do not just spring into being with little or no work, but instead are cultivated over a period of time.

Research by Deborah Ancona and David Caldwell (1988, 1992) established the importance of external, **boundary-spanning** activities in communication networks. Teams must interact with individuals and groups in the organization who are important to the team's effectiveness, such as superiors who must evaluate the group, resource providers, customers and clients, and parties affected for good or ill by group activities. Four types of external activities that span the team's boundary with the organization are particularly important:

- *Scouting or scanning activities* through which team members gather intelligence and information that can help them make better decisions.
- *Liaison activities* with those who evaluate and consume the team's work or products to ensure that requirements are understood and needs met.
- *Campaigns* to form good impressions of the team, its activities, and its products in the organization and external community.
- *Buffering* activities that protect the team from external threats and events that might prevent it from attaining its goals. This includes a wide range of protective behavior, for example, keeping team activities secret until the team is ready to go or defending the team and team members from negative comments made by a supervisor in another unit.

Depending on the team's context, some of these four types of activities may be more important than others.

In line with the emphasis on participative decision making in the relational strategy, many organizations, including corporations such as Xerox and Proctor and Gamble, are attempting to promote the development of teams by setting them up so that they are "self-managing." **Self-managing teams** are intended to empower team members by enabling them to organize and govern themselves as they see best. In many cases, the team is also allowed to set its own goals. In a real sense, the team members serve as their own manager and leader. The philosophy behind self-managing teams takes a page from the book on empowerment discussed previously: If members are told what to do and kept in dependent positions, they are unlikely to develop the skills and motivation needed to create an effective team. If, on the other hand, members are given power and responsibility, they will see them as a privilege and rise to the occasion, learning the skills and attitudes of leaders by making their own mistakes and correcting their course. The self-managing team is currently the pinnacle of the relational strategy of organizing.

While teams can be quite rewarding to participants and for the organization as a whole, as the Xel case study (Case Study 4.2) shows, they may also exert their own form of control over their members, control that may cause stress and even lead members to act against their best interests. Several characteristics of teams – their stress on unity and commitment, their emphasis on high levels of performance, ever-increasing standards, and high levels of mutual responsibility among members – can set the stage for the development of extreme pressure to conform on members who are out of line with the group. When groups strongly identify with the organization, as at Xel, this pressure can serve as a stronger controlling force than a traditional hierarchical manager exerts. Tompkins and Cheney (1985) call this **concertive control** because although it has many of the same results as control by top managers, it arises from the concerted action of peers. In such cases, the team becomes just another body that represents managerial interests at the expense of worker development, empowerment, and other desirable results of the relational strategy. Members of controlling teams tend to fall back into a cycle of doing things the organization wants them to do, powerlessness, and in some cases the same type of resistance that is common in hierarchical

Case Study 4.2
Empowerment, or Iron Cage?

Xel Communications, a telecommunications manufacturing company located in the Denver suburbs, changed its manufacturing plant from a traditional hierarchy to a flattened design that depended on self-managed teams.[1] Xel made this change because Vice President Joe Painter became convinced that the company could survive in the highly competitive telecommunications market only if it was adaptive and innovative. He concluded that self-managed teams that harnessed all employees' energy and creativity were the most effective way to increase Xel's flexibility.

Self-managed teams in Xcel are peer groups of 10–15 people totally responsible for the manufacture of major components. Members of the team make all the decisions and undertake all the work involved in manufacturing the components; they are also responsible for hiring and firing, obtaining materials, and for general management of the team. If a self-managed team has a problem coordinating with another team, members of the two teams meet to come to a workable decision. Barker, Melville, and Pacanowsky (1993) observe, "These teams fit best in organizations characterized by interdependent tasks, complex processes, time sensitivity, and the need for rapid change and adaptation."

Xel implemented the new program gradually, starting with a trial team that performed well beyond anyone's expectations. Within eight months the plant had been reconfigured to accommodate three self-managing teams, labeled the red, white, and blue. Painter's role became that of a "coach," a consultant the teams could call on for advice and problem-solving suggestions. Otherwise the teams called their own shots, and were proud of their independence. In fact, at one point the white team encountered a crisis and sent their coordinator to ask Joe for advice. When she returned with an "order" from Joe about how to handle the situation, the team rebelled – they were angry and resentful that Joe would "order" a self-managing team to do anything. They confronted Joe and aired their grievance, at which time Joe told the white team that they were absolutely correct that they should make their own decisions and that Alma had misinterpreted his suggestion as an order. The members of the white team were pleased when their independence was confirmed. They felt they had learned to stand on their own two feet and take responsibility. They also had started to feel that the fate of the company rested in their hands. They were responsible for decisions that could make or break Xel.

Over time, the team's empowerment confronted it with a thorny issue: what was it to do with members who had their own ideas about work and did not go along with the group's sense of what should be done? No longer were there supervisors around to write up employees who did not act like the team wanted them to. One particular problem was employees who arrived late and left work early. In theory, members could set their own hours now that the team managed itself, and a degree of flexibility was seen as desirable by some members. However, when these members worked fewer hours than (but received the same pay as) other members, it impaired the white team's ability to deliver orders in a timely fashion.

At one of the team's daily 7 A.M. meetings, when the day's activities were planned and other decisions made, the members decided that everyone should arrive before the 7 A.M. meeting and work until 5 P.M. to meet the backlog of orders. A worker who arrived five or more minutes late would be docked a day's pay. When one late-arriving member protested the penalty, team members scolded her and refused to relax their rules. This and similar incidents had an interesting effect on the members of white team. They noted their fellow members' strictness and became afraid of it themselves. Moreover, having seen the team be hard on its own members, they were also not inclined to let other members "get by" by relaxing the norms. Over time, some members began to resent the rigidity of the white team, but it steadily increased its focus on the control system. Eventually the team wrote more and more rules that were more and more concrete and restrictive. They began to talk more about following their very bureaucratic rules than about teamwork and commitment to Xel.

Stitchco,[2] a textile plant in the United Kingdom, underwent a similar change. Prior to the institution of a team system, all decisions were made by managers and employees were rewarded individually based on their output. Workers who produced more than the "standard minute," determined through the "time–motion" studies described in Chapter 3, were rewarded; workers who did not were sanctioned. In the early 1990s the British textile industry was hit hard by foreign competition. Stitchco responded by closing half of its plants without warning to the employees or community, and by converting the other half to a teamwork system. Management's goal was to increase flexibility and speed of manufacturing. The division was told that it would constantly be in competition with external suppliers, with a clear threat that manufacturing would be completely shifted outside the firm if it failed to compete successfully. It was clear that an influential contingent of the company's top managers wanted to close manufacturing altogether, and that the division had been excluded from the decisions to close some operations and restructure the others. A complex accounting system was implemented to monitor the performance of the division in comparison to external producers.

Teams were made up of members who were classified as high, medium, and low performers based on their previous records. Workers were paid a flat rate, and bonuses based on the performance of their teams as a whole. Initially the high performers resisted the change because they feared that their incomes would decline, but once the system was in operation those fears dissipated. Team performance was monitored twice a day, and the results were posted where everyone in the plant could see them. Management hoped that the combination of team-based rewards and public displays would motivate the strongest performers in each team to teach and motivate the weaker performers to improve. Unfortunately, the strategy failed: "team members were not necessarily committed to improving or maximizing their collective output, especially if it meant compensating for . . . other team members [or resolving] conflicts over the allocation of work within the teams" (Ezzamel and Willmott, 1998, 379). In short, the self-managing teams refused to self-manage.

The failure stemmed from a number of factors. Perhaps most importantly, the workers understood the system too well: one machinist explained that "I prefer line work and piecework . . . [under teamwork] you've got to be the supervisor as well as the machinist. When you're working in a line you earn the money that you get. If you're having a bad day . . . the other girls don't suffer." The machinists received no training in supervisory skills, and no separate rewards for playing that role. Others simply were not interested in the bonus system – they knew that they would get the "flat rate" if the group performed at 80 percent of the expected rate, and since they didn't have families to support, that was fine with them. Interpersonal problems also were quite frequent. Management placed workers on teams based solely on their past performance, which meant that some teams had members who had longstanding grievances with one another over issues like boyfriends. As a result, plant managers spent much of their time sorting out disagreements over issues that had nothing to do with the tasks being performed. In something of a paradox, the groups never coalesced into "teams" because they felt too connected to one another to "order one another around," but not connected enough to feel responsible for their peers' incomes.

Applying What You've Learned

1. What forms of control are characteristic of relational strategies of organizing?
2. How do those forms of control differ from control in traditional strategies?
3. A basic assumption of the now-extensive literature advocating the use of team systems is that teamwork provides a better quality of work life for employees, while improving organizational efficiency. Was this assump-

tion correct in these two case studies? Why or why not?
4. What personal and interpersonal factors are involved in the success (or failure) of "relational" strategies like teamwork?

Questions to Think About and Discuss

1. Were the members of white team empowered, or trapped in a control system of their own creation?
2. Barker *et al*. (1993) conclude that employees who strongly identify with a firm are generally tougher managers for each other than hierarchical supervisors are. Do you agree or disagree with this?
3. Why might employees entrusted with managing their own team develop the strong surveillance and control system over other members that they did at Xel? Why might they refuse to do say, as they did at Stitchco?
4. Barker *et al*. argue that excessive (and even exploitative) control of self-managing teams over their members is harder to recognize and resist than the same type of control by managers. This is because members believe that rules they are enforcing are legitimately made by a democratic process. As a result, they see the rules as more objective and legitimate than they might if a manager imposed them from outside. This seemed to be true of the white team at Xel but not the machinists at Stitchco. Why were the machinists able to avoid the cycle that appeared at Xel? Is it possible for the white team break out of the spiral of control it has fallen into? What recommendations do you have for how it could do this?

Notes

1 The first part of this case is based on Barker (1993) and Barker, Melville, and Pacanowsky (1993). Similar findings, in an overseas operation of a Japanese-owned electronics manufacturing plant, are available in Sewell (1998).
2 The second part of the case is based Ezzamel and Willmott (1998). For a similar study of an organization in which team-based control was rather ineffective, see McKinlay and Taylor (1996).

structures. However, concertive control is particularly effective because it is often much harder to recognize than control by managers or top-down rules. This is because members of the team have inadvertently developed the control system themselves, and they see it as a normal outgrowth of their work and tend not to recognize how it undermines participation. Concertive control is a special case of unobtrusive control, a strategy of control that figures importantly in the cultural strategy of organizing, which will be discussed in Chapter 5.

Other kinds of teams, such as quality improvement teams, have been criticized for similar reasons. Cynthia Stohl (1985) argues that though quality circles are often intended to enable employees to improve their work through participation, they frequently become tools of managerial control. Only those suggestions that management is comfortable with are implemented, which in effect takes participation out of employee hands and turns quality-improvement efforts into instruments of organizational control. This is why ex-members of quality circles are among the least satisfied employees (Stohl, 1995). Scott Poole observed examples of this in a large medical organization he worked with; several members of quality improvement teams commented that had they known that their efforts would be used to promote the agendas of management, they would not have participated in the first place. However, this reaction was not uniform: Other members found the quality teams a great source of satisfaction and felt their voices had been heard; some also believed participation helped them develop their leadership skills and would help their careers. As with all systems of surveillance and control that develop in participative programs, control is less than perfect, resistance is possible, and some participation is real and meaningful.

RELATIONAL STRATEGIES OF LEADERSHIP

Although there are a large number of different relational strategies of leadership, they all focus on improving supervisor–subordinate relationships through making them more trusting and more predictable. These goals are achieved by fostering open and supportive communication and by engaging in **transactional leadership**.

Fostering Open and Supportive Supervisor–Subordinate Communication

Early research on relational strategies of leadership found that high-producing organizations had supervisors who were both highly competent in the technical aspects of their jobs and were employee centered and considerate. Effective supervisors express respect for, trust in, and a genuine concern about their subordinates. They set high but achievable performance goals for their units and communicate a kind of contagious enthusiasm about achieving them. They supervise loosely and actively encourage their subordinates to participate in decision making. They do not engage in superficial "pat-on-the-back" or "first-name" gimmicks, but emphasize a deeper concern for the group members' needs. They also do not make their subordinates feel uncomfortable or defensive.

When people feel that they are being judged (even praise creates discomfort if it is excessively strong or too public), manipulated (tricked into believing that they have an important role in the organization when they do not), controlled, or "preached at," or otherwise treated as an inferior, they become defensive and withdraw from the relationship. Supervisors can create supportive, nondefensive climates by communicating in ways that are descriptive and objective rather than evaluative; that focus on working together to solve important problems; that are spontaneous, open, and honest; that affirm the subordinates' competence; and that encourage them to initiate communication, even if doing so involves negative topics or information. Even orders can be given in a supportive way. The orders themselves need to be clear and specific, be perceived as logical and appropriate, and be legitimate in the sense that Weber used that term (that is, accepted as normal and proper by workers). Orders also need to be communicated in a way that allows subordinates to retain a sense of personal pride, self-respect, and autonomy (to "save face," a concept that will be developed in Chapters 7 and 11) – to feel that they are making a free and open choice to obey the order.[14]

Supportive communication also depends on the supervisor's listening skills and his or her ability to avoid disconfirming communication. Messages carry meaning at both content and relational levels – they provide information and they make a statement about the interpersonal relationship that exists between the communicators (see Chapter 7 for a more detailed discussion). Disconfirming communication occurs when a supervisor communicates in a way that does not acknowledge a subordinate's worth. For example, a young accountant waited two weeks to see her supervisor. After having meetings canceled, rescheduled, and canceled again; telephone calls cut off; and chance meetings in the hallway in which the supervisor did not even stop walking to say hello, the accountant finally got into a meeting. After explaining that she did not understand new tax laws on capital gains rates, her supervisor said, "This isn't my problem. Talk to the training department." Her long-awaited meeting lasted three minutes. Clearly, she concluded, her supervisor does not recognize that she exists, much less that she is an important part of the team. This does not mean that supervisors cannot disagree with their subordinates, because one can reject or question the content of persons' communications without rejecting their identities (Richmond and McCroskey, 2000; Remland, 1987; Jablin, 1979, 2001). Open and supportive communication enhances trust, reduces withholding and distortion of information, and serves as a basis for transactional leadership.

Transactional Leadership

Supervisor–subordinate communication is a two-way, interactive process. Although supervisors tend to have a greater impact on communicative relationships than their subordinates because of their formal authority, interpersonal relationships develop because of the mutual exchanges that take place between the parties. This is the primary assumption underlying transactional views of leadership (Northouse, 2010). Leaders, according to this model, must legitimize their position – formal rank alone does not make one a leader – but legitimation is a two-way street. Leaders and each of their followers negotiate working relationships. (Chapter 8 examines the negotiation process in more detail.) Both parties align themselves with one another; they converge toward the same set of values, are able to solve complex and unprecedented problems together, and have a relaxed, mutually supportive relationship. Eventually, they become co-oriented – they reach agreement on the rules that guide their relationship (for example, what topics they will discuss and what topics they will avoid, whether they must schedule meetings or can just pop in to one another's office, whether to use first names or titles, or whether they interrupt one another or quietly wait until the other is finished talking to respond). They negotiate a trusting relationship, one in which their motives, intentions, openness, and integrity are consistent; in which they are dependably competent, willing, and able to help one another with job-related problems; and in which the judgment is reliable.

Even supportive communication is mutual and transactional. Trust, respect, and task factors, such as risk taking and innovation, have all been shown to be greatest when supervisors are supportive of their supervisors and their subordinates perceive that they receive high levels of support. In other words, both the level of support and the level agreement about the level of support are important factors. Supervisors and subordinates support one another in a number of ways: by talking about how organizations work (for example, discussing potential career moves and their likely effects), by helping develop new skills or giving one another tangible assistance when it is needed (for example, a director of programming jumping in to help solve a knotty language problem and doing so cheerfully without a "this-will-cost-you-later" attitude), by providing an outlet for venting anger or frustration (serving as a sounding board), or by offering praise, acceptance, or reassurance. Regardless of the specific technique that is used, it is the mutual support that supervisors and subordinates give one another that is important (Albrecht and Halsey, 1992; Albrecht and Adelman, 1988).

In sum, transactional views of leadership focus on the development of particular kinds of supervisor–subordinate relationships. They recognizes that neither person is wholly in charge of the process and that supervisors will often have different kinds of relationships with different subordinates.

Leadership and Group Decision Making

In Western societies people are taught to assume that groups must have a designated leader or leaders. In most organizations, the leader is identified before the group begins its work, either explicitly when person X is ordained as chairperson, or implicitly when members realize that person X is the group member who has the highest status in the organization. If no leader is appointed or selected for the group, the group has three options: Designate one person as leader from the outset; take a chance that a leader will emerge, or hope that the different members of the group can share leadership tasks efficiently and smoothly. The second and third options have their advantages, but they are also risky. When the group allows a leader to emerge naturally, the person best suited to the task and group often rises to the occasion. Emergent leaders are generally more effective than leaders appointed by management. However, the danger in the emergence option is that no leader will emerge or that competing candidates will split the group. Sharing among all members develops every member's skills and commitment to the group; but members must be very conscientious or important issues may slip through the cracks.[15]

Groups with clearly identified leaders are often more efficient, have fewer interpersonal problems, and produce better decisions, provided the leader is competent and effective at organizing the group. This does not mean that leaderless groups are doomed to failure. It just means that they will have problems unless members have the right mix of leadership skills and exercise them effectively. Another strategy for a leaderless group or self-managed teams is to rotate leadership; this builds all members' skills and also gives the team one clear point of responsibility without giving power to one person on a permanent basis.[16]

What role should a leader play in group decision making? Leaders have three options: They can make the decision themselves; they can consult with the group and make the decision themselves; or they can have the group make the decision. An important model developed by Victor Vroom and Peter Yetton advanced some rules to help leaders decide which method to use. According to their model, either consultation or group decision making should be used when quality of the decision is critical and when the leader does not have sufficient information to make the decision him or herself. The group model should also be used when members' acceptance of the decision is important. On the other hand, the leader should make the decision or consult if members do not share the organization's goals. If quality is not important, any of the methods can be used, depending on what seems best for the group at the time.[17] Two additional factors that must be considered are the amount of time the group has to make a decision and the cost of convening the group. If time is short and cost high, the recommendation is to have the leader make the decision or consult in an efficient manner.

When the group is making the decision, the leader's role should fulfill three functions. Leadership means influencing members' *perceptions of themselves* – motivating them to contribute to the group and to feel committed to it and its task. Leadership also involves influencing members' *perceptions of the group.* It means focusing the group's attention on the group's goals and the role that each step has in the group's meeting those goals. Making members feel that the group is an autonomous entity by minimizing references to outside pressures, involving members in decisions about tasks and procedures, taking each member's comments seriously, and building the group's confidence that it can make a good decision.

Finally, leadership means influencing the *pace* and *direction* of the discussion and the *decisions* made by the group. In general, leaders should avoid acting like advocates, especially early in the group's history; they should adopt a participative style that invites members' contributions and follows their ideas (Bass and Bass, 2008). If the leader jumps in too early or too forcefully, members are discouraged from sharing their ideas and expertise, reducing the advantages of group decision making. However, leaders are generally selected because of their perspective or expertise, and there are times when the group needs to have that information made available.

Members who are not identified as leaders also play important roles. Group tasks are too large or complex to be performed by individuals. Consequently, the group needs the expertise and efforts of all members. But commitment is rarely high or equal among all members. One problem in groups, especially those larger than six or seven members, is the "free-rider" problem, where several members do not contribute their effort fairly and take advantage of other members' work (Thompson, 1967). You may have experienced this yourself with classroom group projects. The opposite extreme, when members are excessively committed to the group, is equally damaging. Groups benefit from disagreement, from constructive conflict. When members agree for the sake of agreeing, the group does not benefit from their expertise or from the careful testing of ideas and evidence that comes from positive confrontation. The primary obligation of group members is to act as valuable members of a cooperative activity and to undertake communication functions, such as summarizing, contributing ideas, encouraging other members, and energizing the group (Thompson, 1967, chaps. 5–6).

INFORMATION AND COMMUNICATION TECHNOLOGY AND THE RELATIONAL STRATEGY

Several information and communication technologies (ICTs) support participation, groups, and informal networks, the keystones of the relational strategy. The most familiar is electronic mail. Email is a fast and effective linking mechanism, for several reasons. Email enables communication between people who are on different schedules, because it can be read and answered whenever convenient for the receiver. It is also less intrusive than a phone call or face-to-face contact; the recipient can reply on her or his own schedule. Hence, email encourages communication between people who do not know each other well, who differ in status, or who are in different units that do not have formal relationships. Email also allows the sending of broadcast messages – requests or memos sent to a large group of recipients, even to the whole organization. This capability enables people who do not know whom to ask to gather information and create links. The end result is that email tends to increase lateral communication between people at the same level of the organization and contacts across organizational levels, enhancing relational linkage in organizations (Rice and Gattiker, 2001).

When email systems are implemented, the total amount of communication within an organization or work group increases and the use of the telephone and written memos does seem to decrease, although the use of face-to-face communication increases. Thus the electronic media seem to supplement, rather than replace, traditional media (Rice, 1984).

The information exchanged via electronic media does not seem to be any more or less accurate than information exchanged through other media, although people tend to be less confident of its accuracy. In face-to-face communication, we rely on vocal cues (pitch, rate of speech, loudness) and nonverbal cues to confirm our interpretations of the meanings of the words that people use. Because these cues are less readily available or are absent in mediated communication, we feel less secure in our interpretations.

Use of email seems also to be affected by the user's relationships. Studies have shown that the adoption and degree of use of email are significantly influenced by the user's closest coworkers and others in their communication network. These effects were even stronger in cohesive groups (Fulk, 1993; Rice and Aydin, 1991). Once formed, groups joined by email seem to reinforce members' continued use.

There are also costs to email, notably message overload. In email-intensive organizations, it is not unusual to receive more than 50 messages a day. (One manager in an information technology firm came back from a two-week vacation to find over a thousand messages waiting!) Sorting through this to separate the junk mail from the important messages can take much time and energy. Some have worried about the impersonal nature of computer-mediated communication. However, studies have generally shown that this medium can be as personal as any once users master it (Sproull and Kiesler, 1986; Finholt and Sproull, 1990; Rice and Love, 1987; Walther, 1992). The style of electronic messages often is less formal than in written messages, and people seem to think less about social norms and hierarchical relationships when constructing electronic messages than when constructing messages for other media. Their communication may be less inhibited – they may express extreme emotions overtly (a process called "flaming") and swear more often. Of course, groups of people develop and enforce cultural expectations that require users to refrain from flaming or to engage in other patterns of communicating, such as reading and responding to email messages within a specified period of time (Yates and Orlikowski, 1992; Sproull and Kiesler, 1986; Rafaeli, 1990; Steinfeld, 1991).

Other ICTs that enable messaging, including instant messaging, short messenger services, wireless mobile devices, paging, and voice mail have a similar effect to email. All enlarge the social networks of users and hence enable relational connections to be made more easily (Monge and Contractor, 2003). One advance that is just beginning to diffuse through organizations worldwide is **unified messaging**, systems that integrate email, voice mail, and faxes in a single message system.[18] These systems, offered by a number of vendors, attempt to decrease the complexity of communication. In developing African countries, for example, unified messaging has been used to improve citizen access to services such as healthcare and education from their low-end mobile phones.[19]

The availability of electronic message networks also allows people to address messages by topic rather than by the name of the recipient. Employees who are unhappy about a recent management decision or consumers unhappy with a produce or service can instantaneously locate other people who also are unhappy and share their complaints, and sometimes organize actions against the organization (Brandel, 2010).

Social networking technologies such as **wikis** are also being used to foster relationships in organizations.[20] A wiki is an online space that allows users to freely create and edit web page content and links from their web browsers. It allows open, collaborative editing by multiple users. The US Department of State, for example, has set up a wiki called "Diplopedia" for internal use by its staff.[21] It is open to the contributions of all who work in the State Department. So, if the Italian ambassador is visiting Washington, DC, anyone on staff who knows about Italy, the ambassador, or pending issues with Italy can enter a memo into Diplopedia. It can be accessed by anyone via computer or cell phone and hence is open to consultation at all times. The capability for multiple users to enter information into wikis like Diplopedia makes them ideal for pooling information and knowledge. This speeds up turnaround in information sharing. Since wikis are "permanent" documents (entries can be edited and changed), they also serve the useful function of serving as a source of history for the organization. By increasing participation and access to information, these also have the potential to empower members. The playful and informal style common in wikis builds connections among members and between them and the organization.

Wikis, blogs, and photo- and video-sharing sites also offer the opportunity for an organization to build relationships with its customers or clients. Consumers and citizens use blogs to discuss all sorts of things, and among them are compliments or complaints about their experiences with companies or products. Sites like "I Hate Microsoft" attract people who want to complain and many user forums for products feature discussions about problems or complaints.[22] Discussions in online forums and chat rooms often center on good or bad aspects of organizations or products. Organizations can use various tools or services to find and analyze what is being said about them in blogs, forums, chat rooms, and video-sharing and social-networking sites. Often what is being said is good, which is good news for the organization, but if there are problems, the organization can respond to them rapidly. For example, if a customer complains about a long wait time for customer service, the organization might send a note of apology and offer a small gift certificate in compensation. Southwest Airlines takes this approach to monitoring social media. This helped it quickly respond to a storm of Twitter messages (tweets) that occurred when film director Kevin Smith complained in a message that he had been forced off a Southwest flight for being overweight (Brandel, 2010, 55). This sort of rapid monitoring and response enables the organization to build relationships with external parties because it seems very personal and responsive. It also gives organizations insights into how they can improve and adapt to the needs of customers and clients.

Another type of technology useful for the relational strategy of organizing is **groupware.** Groupware refers to networked ICT that enables members of a group to make decisions and coordinate their work in both short- and long-term projects. Some types of groupware, such as Lotus Notes and Microsoft Exchange, are proprietary systems that must be purchased and installed on an organization's network. Other types of groupware, such as Google Groups and Yahoo Groups, are free and are hosted in computer clouds and can be accessed using browsers.

The proprietary groupware systems are generally fairly complex and combine features from office automation, electronic workflow linkage, and computer conferencing systems into a bundle of tools for a group; these tools can be used by groups working in the same office or building or by geographically dispersed groups. A typical workgroup support system, such as Lotus Notes, includes document management, scheduling features, email notification, and computer discussion groups. The discussion groups are similar to computer conferences in that they contain discussion threads, which are lines of discussion on a single topic arranged in statement–response format. Discussion topics can vary widely, from a general discussion of policies to specific updates on a particular task. Other features that may be incorporated into a workgroup support system include audio- or videoconferencing over the internet, project management tools that keep a diagram of the project and monitor progress, and libraries to store commonly used documents. In addition, organizations may program their own specific applications into the system; an accounting firm, for example, may want to have its software connect with the workgroup system.

The free, cloud-enabled groupware systems typically do not have as much functionality as the proprietary ones. However, this is changing as online applications such as Google Groups, Documents, and Sites include ever more features.

Teams that use workgroup support systems typically have to change their mode of operation, because the systems require members to diligently check in and enter their own work and documents. These systems generally encourage groups to be more structured in how they work and make decisions, because the group has to "think out loud" about how it is going to proceed as it decides how to break up its work into tasks and decides on discussion topics. While groups initially try to use their own typical procedures in the system, over time their style of working adapts to the system itself. For example, a team that typically did not get feedback from all members on an idea would be likely to develop a norm favoring more input and feedback if it faithfully used the discussion features of a workgroup system.

While the most direct application of workgroup support systems is for the groups themselves, the systems can also be used to link teams and people across entire organizations. Teams can be given access to each other's discussions and timelines, and discussion groups that anyone interested may join can also be set up. For example, a major oil company used Lotus Notes to set up project support for over 30 teams and gave members of other teams limited access to most of these "team spaces." This enabled members of related teams to find out what other teams were doing, helped coordinate work between teams, and enabled teams to learn from each other. In addition, general discussion groups were initiated on various topics, including general interest topics, such as Movies and the company's Charitable Projects, and specific topics, such as Microsoft Office and Techniques for 3-Dimensional Analysis of Oil Deposits. These general discussion groups enabled people from all over the organization to get to know one another and share ideas; they also built organizational cohesiveness. A few executives complained that these general discussion groups wasted company time, because they were not related to specific project support. However, the chief information officer argued for and succeeded in preserving the discussion groups on the grounds that they encouraged employees who otherwise might be unwilling to learn the new technology to try it out and generally led to a more connected organization.[23]

ASSESSING RELATIONAL STRATEGIES

There are many criteria that might be used to evaluate a strategy of organizing and its associated motivation and control strategy and approach to leadership. Two commonly used criteria are employees' job satisfaction and organizational performance and profitability.

Relational Strategies and Employee Job Satisfaction

Relational strategies, both PDM and transactional leadership, do lead to increased job satisfaction. This impact has been shown to be rather small from a practical standpoint, but it does seem to occur consistently, regardless of the kind of organization being studied or the specific research method employed. The relationship is strongest for employees near the bottom of the organizational hierarchy and with people who need large amounts of information to do their jobs well. But, regardless of the specifics of a work situation, employees in open, supportive communication climates are satisfied employees (Guzley, 1992; Infante and Gordon, 1991).

Creating and maintaining high levels of job satisfaction are important for a number of reasons. Perhaps most important, teams composed of satisfied people simply are more pleasant places to work. Since most people spend much of their lives at work, this may be sufficient justification for the use of relational strategies. There also are some more tangible benefits. Job dissatisfaction has consistently been linked to high levels of absenteeism and voluntary turnover. When employees who perform important tasks are missing, other employees feel increased stress and organizational performance declines. When the costs of searching for and training replacement personnel are high, voluntary turnover is costly. When the economy is strong, as it was from 2003 to 2008 in the United States, voluntary turnover can be extremely expensive. For example, to enhance employee satisfaction, Ford Motor Company agreed to establish 30 round-the clock "Family Service and Learning Centers" at their largest locations. These centers will provide child and elder care, formal and informal education programs, health screenings, and limited health care. They are primarily designed to address the lack of affordable child care for working parents, especially for those who work the night shift. Ford President Jacques Nasser said, "It's not low cost, but we're not wasting a cent. This is an effort to attract and retain talent because turnover costs money."[24]

PDM and Individual/Organizational Performance

Participatory systems have a number of positive effects. In US firms, formal, company-wide programs of participation still are rare, although their popularity has increased during the last few years (see Chapter 8). Informal programs of participation, where supervisors ask their most productive employees for advice or information, are more widespread. Subordinates respond with useful advice, which increases their supervisors' trust in their judgment and encourages them to seek further advice, and their job satisfaction increases, which reduces absenteeism and voluntary turnover. Somewhat surprisingly, these positive effects do not result from subordinates feeling that participation gives them greater power, primarily because PDM in US firms are structured and operated in ways that largely maintain gaps in power. Instead, it results from their being better informed about what is going on in the organization (Miller and Monge, 1986). During participatory interactions, supervisors provide information and a more open and satisfying communicative relationship is created.

Systems of participation have more limited effects on performance and productivity. In general, the quality of decisions made by participatory groups is better than that of decisions made by the "average" member of the group but is worse than the decision that would be made by the group's most expert individual (Brown, 2000). This does not suggest that better decisions would be made by a supervisor acting alone, for the simple reason that the supervisor may or may not be the most expert member of a work group. It just suggests that the positive effects of PDM depend on a number of factors, including the distribution of expertise in the group. Research on the effects of participation on productivity is less favorable. Some studies have found that participation does motivate workers to perform more effectively and more efficiently. In other cases, participation gives supervisors an opportunity to persuade their subordinates to accept high performance goals. But, overall, research on participation indicates that participation does not automatically increase organizational productivity (Bass and Bass, 2008; Harrison, 1985).

Cynthia Stohl and George Cheney have explained these results by focusing on the paradoxical nature of participatory systems. They identify four basic paradoxes of participation. One group of paradoxes relate to the design and operation of PDM systems (what they call "paradoxes of structure"). Typically, PDM systems are imposed by management, so that the overall message given to employees is "Be spontaneous, creative, vocal, and assertive *in the way that we have planned!*" (emphasis added). Along with this often comes another message, "Be democratic, but don't take much time doing it." Over time, the process becomes so tightly constrained, and so routine, undermining its advantages. "Paradoxes of agency" occur because employees are told to "Do things in your own way, but make sure that's our way." This undermines attempts at empowering members. "Paradoxes of identity" harken back to the "fundamental paradox" that we described in Chapter 1 because the message sent is "Be *self*-managing, but do so in order to meet the goals of the organization." "Paradoxes of control" occur when participatory groups are more controlling than traditional strategies, a process that we will examine in the following section. We would add, as a final paradox, that managers tend to adopt PDM systems because they are a popular fad and thus help legitimize managers as "up-to-date" experts in their fields (see Chapter 12), or as a last resort when their firms are failing.

Ironically, some very successful PDM systems were created after firms closed. For example, when Argentina's economy collapsed in early 2002, many managers simply shut the doors of their factories and walked away, often owing their employees months of back pay. Instead of giving up, many workers, backed by neighborhood associations, persuaded the bankruptcy courts to let them reopen the plants. Eighteen months later, at least 150 factories employing more than 10,000 people were being run as cooperatives. They are run by plant councils, which, like plant managers, are elected by the workers. By equalizing wages – everyone from the plant manager to custodians get the same salary – they have been able to double the average wages paid to the workers. Workers are willing to make sacrifices for the organization because of "the commitment we feel to something that is our own." Of course, the cooperatives face continuing challenges (we will discuss the difficulties facing alternative forms of organizing in Chapter 6). Their ability to expand is limited because the banks are unwilling to make loans to them, but they have managed to find other sources of funding. Now that the economy has improved, many of the former owners have gone to court in an effort to regain control of the properties. But, at this point, the Argentinean cooperatives provide testimony to the effectiveness of truly participatory systems (Rohter, 2003). A similar takeover occurred at the Republic Windows and Doors factory in Chicago, Illinois, in 2008.[25]

Transactional Leadership and Individual/Organizational Performance

Transactional leadership is based on the assumption that improving communication will increase morale and motivation, which in turn will increase individual and organizational performance (Northouse, 2010). Ironically, at least in production-oriented firms, relational strategies do have positive effects on performance – but not for the reasons typically ascribed to it. First of all, the primary assumption of the relational strategy does not seem to be accurate: High levels of job satisfaction do not inevitably lead to high levels of individual or organizational performance. Of course, it does makes sense intuitively that satisfied workers will work harder and perform better than dissatisfied workers; if people are happy at work, they should be more committed to their organization and thus should want to work harder to make sure their organizations succeed. However, 50 years of research on the relationship between job satisfaction and performance have not found strong relationships between the two. The average correlation is 0.14, which means that about 2 percent of differences in employees' performance can be attributed to differences in their job satisfaction. Instead, this research indicates either that high performance leads to high job satisfaction (because workers feel pride in a job well done) or that other factors simultaneously increase both satisfaction and performance. For instance, if workers value hard work and high levels of performance for its own sake, or if they believe they will receive tangible rewards from high performance, they tend to be both satisfied and productive. If they do not hold these beliefs, they tend to be both dissatisfied and relatively unproductive regardless of the strategy of organizing used in their organizations. People who are trapped in an autocratic, alienating organization because they have few employment opportunities, because of their race, gender, ethnic background, lack of education, disabilities, or because of the general economic situation, are often dissatisfied but highly productive, because they are afraid of losing their jobs. Conversely, people whose nonwork lives are fulfilling may expend only the minimum amount of effort necessary to keep their jobs regardless of how satisfied they are at work. In short, the work world seems to be relatively full of people who smile a lot and do very little and people who smile very little and do a lot (Fisher, 1980; Bass and Bass, 2008; Allen, 1996).

Relational strategies do not necessarily improve productivity by increasing morale, but they do seem to pay off for other reasons. Open and supportive supervisory communication helps compensate for the problems in formal communication that were described in Chapter 3. Openness creates trust, and trust reduces the withholding or distorting of information. Open and supportive communication is especially valuable for subordinates who have complex and ambiguous jobs. These employees need a great deal of task-related information and advice that only their supervisors can provide. It is difficult to ask for help from a closed and unsupportive supervisor. If employees do not ask for information or help, it is more difficult for them to master their complex tasks, which makes it more likely that they will make errors. Subordinates who make frequent mistakes lose their supervisors' trust, which perpetuates the negative cycle (Gioia and Sims, 1986; Fairhurst, 2001).

These advantages are especially important to organizations in highly competitive, turbulent environments. Relational leadership (as well as decentralized structures and PDM) creates open, relatively free-flowing communication systems. Boundary spanners can obtain information from the environment and rapidly disseminate that information to other employees who will be able to draw on multiple kinds of expertise to solve complicated, unprecedented problems. For example, Taiwan and Hong Kong, and more recently mainland China, have built their economic success around family businesses. These organizations have thrived in highly competitive, global environments because they are more flexible, less bureaucratic, and have greater employee commitment than large private or state-owned companies. They also innovate more rapidly and are quicker to adopt new product lines (Dana, 1999).

Relational strategies also seem to have a positive influence on the performance of service-related organizations, which now comprise more than half of US firms. When employees communicate with clients or customers, they tend to mirror their communication relationship with their supervisors. If their supervisors are not warm, supportive, and open with them, they will not be with their clients and customers. Alienated subordinates create alienated customers, who may take their business elsewhere. For example, the late 1990s were a disastrous time for Northwest Airlines, the fourth-largest carrier in the United States. Beginning with serious labor problems in 1995, the public's opinion of the airline plummeted, culminating in a 1999 snowstorm in Detroit when angry passengers were left sitting in planes for eight hours. Faced with economic disaster, Northwest's management asked some of its best customers (then a small and rapidly declining number of people) to tell them what they could do to turn the airline around. The customers blamed the airline's image problem on poor supervisor–subordinate relationships. One told them that "Your employees do care and a lot of them are frustrated by lack of response from Northwest's management;" another advised them to "Focus on respect for your employees and they will undoubtedly deliver." Management responded by trying to improve supervisor–subordinate communication. Within a year, Northwest's regular customers saw a difference. Tom Bagget, a customer from Memphis, Tennessee, noted that "Northwest is going from an almost adversarial relationship with employees to cooperation." It is too early to tell whether the improved relationships will continue, but Northwest's experience, and the experiences of similar firms like Southwest Airlines and Kaiser Permanente of Oakland, California, make it clear that improving superior–subordinate communication pays immediate dividends in improving employee–customer relationships. For service organizations, high customer satisfaction yields bottom-line benefits: It increases profit margins, reduces marketing costs while increasing them for the competition, enhances the organization's reputation, and lowers many of the costs of doing business (Mills, 2000; Cameron and Thompson, 2000; Weidlich, 2002).

THINKING CRITICALLY ABOUT RELATIONAL STRATEGIES

Throughout this chapter we have examined relational strategies largely in terms of organizational performance and effectiveness. This is the dominant taken-for-granted criterion used among managers and management theorists. However, an important part of understanding organizations and organizational communication is being able to think critically about taken-for-granted assumptions. On the surface, relational strategies do seem to create better work situations than traditional strategies, but that impression masks some important realities about all strategies of organizing. Two key concepts are especially important for understanding critical theories of organizing – interests and legitimate participation.[26]

Thinking Critically About Interests

At one level, owners, managers, and workers all seem to have many interests in common, including the long-term survival of their organization. On a closer look, it becomes clear that all three groups have some self-interests that is different from, and contradictory to, the interests of the other groups. For example, workers almost always have a strong vested interest in the continued operation of their firms in a particular locale and with stable or increasing real (adjusted for inflation) wages. When plants are closed or relocated, workers usually lose their jobs and find it difficult to find comparable employment elsewhere. Even if they are offered employment in other plants, relocating is psychologically and financially costly, especially when the workers have not previously moved. Similarly, reductions in wages or benefits can be devastating for workers, and programs to increase organizational productivity through technological innovations often lead to layoffs or a lowered standard of living.

Managers, on the other hand, usually benefit less from maintaining the long-term viability of their organizations or increasing their workers' job security. This is because managers are rarely owners, especially in large firms. They are not the entrepreneurs whose vision, ideas, and hard work built an organization to which they are psychologically and financially committed. Indeed, their careers often involve moving rather quickly from one organization to another. Their rewards are based on the short-term profitability of the firm, especially in cases in which a large portion of the managers' total income is based on year-end performance bonuses. Consequently, managers may have little self-interest involved in the firm's long-term success and a great deal of interest in downsizing, reducing workers' wages and benefits, and replacing workers with new technologies. Since each of these steps is likely to increase the firm's short-term profitability, they will increase the managers' economic gains. They also may increase managers' salaries, bonuses, and job security because they also serve the financial interests of investors. For example, Alan Downs found that in US firms during the 1990s, the number of jobs that a CEO eliminated was a better predictor of her or his compensation than the overall performance of his or her firm.[27] Similarly, successful strategies of motivation and control tend to serve management's interests much more than workers' interests. Even if they do lead to increased organizational effectiveness and profitability, most of the resulting rewards will go to management and investors, not to workers.

This has been the case over the past 40 years in the United States. During the 1980s, Frank Lorenzo was the CEO of Texas Air, the parent company of Continental Airlines and Eastern Airlines. Although Continental and Eastern regularly lost $200 million or more each year and entered bankruptcy proceedings three times, Lorenzo regularly received annual performance bonuses of more than $1 million. When Eastern finally went out of business, its owners (creditors) received approximately 3 cents for each dollar they had invested in the airline. Similarly, during the late 1980s and early 1990s, Lee Iacocca decided to move much of Chrysler's production operation overseas (primarily to Mexico and the Far East). These steps cost thousands of autoworkers their jobs, but they also increased Chrysler's profits (or, initially, reduced its losses) and the value of its stock. Iacocca was rewarded with multimillion-dollar annual performance bonuses and one of the largest retirement bonuses in American history. Iacocca could have taken a different approach to revitalizing Chrysler – reducing stock dividends and reinvesting the funds in improved production technologies, as many German automakers did, or reducing the massive gap between worker income and managerial salaries as Japanese automakers did, or reducing overhead by restraining managerial salaries. There is little evidence that Chrysler's management (or the management of virtually any large US organization) ever seriously considered these approaches.

Most of the corporate scandals that rocked the United States during 2001–2003 (see Chapter 12 for a more detailed analysis) involved egregious behaviors that enriched upper management at the expense of all other stakeholders. And the excesses in payments to upper management in banks, investment firms and hedge funds in the United States, Britain, Netherlands, and Iceland, among others, are well known. These very same firms sewed the seeds of the financial crisis of 2008 and the subsequent great recession in the United States and Europe. In sum, actions that may be in management's self-interest may violate the short- and long-term interests of workers and owners and vice versa.

However, the conflicting nature of these interests is often disguised by the discourse of modern organizations, a process that Jürgen Habermas (1972, 1979) has labeled **systematically distorted communication**. One way of disguising the contradictions is to treat one set of interests (for example, management's) as everyone's interests. Installing a computerized system for monitoring employees' work is usually justified in terms of its increased efficiency and the firm's enhanced ability to compete (recall Chapter 2). Efficiency and increased competitiveness are presented as being in everyone's interests. In the long run, they may or may not be, depending on a large number of considerations. But in the short term, the new system increases management's control and workers' stress and has no guaranteed effects on either workers' or stockholders' incomes, because management may not choose to pass the savings on to either group.

Another way of disguising the contradictions is to simply deny that they exist.[28] Simple forms of denial include refusing to discuss a topic or to deny that one's actions meant what they seemed to mean ("Of course I wasn't trying to get rid of you; I just wanted you to have the excitement of working in Mongolia"). A more complicated mode of denial is pacification, a process through which legitimate conflicts are treated as unimportant, or mere communication breakdowns. An example of this is when managerial discourse suppresses grievances through defining the organization as a team or family in which all the members are in it together. Another way of disguising contradictory interests is disqualifying some interest groups, as in "This is a managerial problem, and you just don't have the information necessary to understand it fully." If events are also defined as inevitable or unavoidable (layoffs during recessions, for example) or as value neutral ("We have to base our personnel decisions on the data, not on how we feel"), they cannot be discussed, much less challenged. (Recall the discussion of hegemony in Chapter 2.)[29] Whatever the specific technique, the effect of organizational discourse often is to disguise or redefine the conflicting interests of workers, managers, and owners. Relational strategies often disguise this conflict.

Thinking Critically About Empowerment

Legitimate programs of participation and transactional leadership have the effect of empowering workers throughout the organization. To be legitimate, PDM must be valued for its own sake, as a means of ensuring that the legitimate interests of all organizational groups are represented in decisions. This means that they cannot be justified solely because they increase organizational efficiency, unless they involve guarantees that increased efficiency will fulfill the interests of all organizational stakeholders. Legitimate participation entails equal opportunities to communicate. This sounds simple, as when women's consciousness-raising groups use "talking sticks" (a system adopted from Native Americans in which someone must be holding a particular object in order to be allowed to speak) to ensure that all members get an equal number of speaking turns. Contrast this system with

Michael Huspek's study of communication in a lumberyard. Although the company presumably had an "open door" policy for workers to express their grievances, managers demanded that those discussions take place in the technical, legalistic language of management. Since workers literally did not know how to speak that language, they were often literally unable to say a word during grievance sessions. As important, their inability to express themselves led them to believe that they did not know enough to have the right to challenge their supervisors (Huspek, 1987). The research on supervisory resistance to PDM that was summarized earlier in this chapter provides additional examples of relational strategies that depower instead of empower.

Legitimate empowerment programs also ensure equal opportunities to influence a work group's decisions. Doing so involves giving all employees all of the information that is relevant to the decisions being made and valuing all of the conceptions of truth expressed by members of the group. For example, single parents' reports of their own frustrating experiences finding adequate child care should be respected as much as the results of management's surveys on child-care issues. Empowerment also means that conflicts within the group will not be resolved through appeals to some external higher authority (as in "It's a great idea, but the CEO will never buy it").

The relational strategies that are used in contemporary organizations often include only an illusion of empowerment. As long as participatory systems are used without making major changes in organizational power relationships, managerial interests will be privileged. The existence of the hierarchy and the right of management to make final decisions – including how, when, where, over what issues, and with what outcomes participation will occur – will continue to be treated as natural and normal. When workers are trained to participate in decision making (or quality control programs or quality of working life groups), they are taught to make decisions on criteria (like efficiency) and through processes that favor the interests of management.[30] But the discourse surrounding relational strategies of organizing often presents them as systems for fulfilling the interests of all stakeholders.

NOTES

1 See Chiles and Zorn (1995, 1–25). The concept of empowerment is popular in contemporary organizational theory, and will appear repeatedly throughout this book. One of the most important lines of research underlying the relational strategy was conducted by Arnold Tannenbaum and his associates. They found that in many kinds of organizations in both capitalist and socialist countries, employees believe that they exercise far less influence over decisions that affect them directly than does upper management. In contrast, Tannenbaum found that the most productive organizations and departments were ones in which all employees, even those at the bottom of the organizational hierarchy, perceived that they had substantial influence over decisions (see Tannenbaum, 1962, 17–42).

2 See Organ (1971, 73–80). For an extended critique of Likert's model, see Marrow, Bowers, and Seashore (1967).

3 This section draws heavily on Peter R. Monge and Noshir S. Contractor's (2003) excellent book. They provide a definitive discussion of this topic.

4 See Albrecht and Hall (1991a, 1991b), Bach (1991), Bastien (1992), Ellis (1992), and Rice and Aydin (1991).

5 See also Monge and Contractor (2003, 147–148).

6 McGregor found that supervisors really do tend to communicate to their subordinates in ways that are consistent with one of these two sets of assumptions. Also see Courtright, Fairhurst, and Rogers (1989, 773–802).

7 See Locke and Latham (2004); a classic reference is Locke (1976).

8 See Edwards (1978) and Dandeker (1984). An excellent example of the alienating effects of deskilling is provided in "The Lordstown Auto Workers" (1979).
9 One of the classic studies that established the influence of groups on employees is Sayles (1957).
10 See Roethlisberger and Dickson (1939). In *The Human Group* (1950), George Homans gives a readable account of the findings from the Hawthorne Studies on work group influences on members.
11 See Sayles (1957). With few exceptions, group research since 1980 has focused on work teams and how they can be made more effective. This has greatly decreased the number of recent studies of the impacts of work teams on workers. Most of the really good work on this was done between 1935 and 1960.
12 For a similar model of teamwork, see Hackman (2002). For an excellent recent treatment of teams, see Thompson (2010). For a more general book on groups, see Gastil (2010).
13 See Larson and LaFasto (1989, 82–83).
14 Much of this foundational research is summarized in Likert (1961) and in the first and second editions of Fleishman and Associates (1961, 1967). An excellent summary of research on leadership communication is provided by Fairhurst (2001).
15 Kramer (2006, 141–162) discusses a case when the designated leader did not fulfill her role and members of the group divided leadership tasks among themselves. There were a number of things that "slipped through the cracks" in this group, but by improvising they handled them.
16 Bormann (1990). Also see Bass and Bass (2008).
17 The classic source on this model, which is simplified in this discussion, is Vroom and Yetton (1973).
18 See Wikipedia (n.d.).
19 See "Safaricom" (2010).
20 See Roy (2010).
21 See Cohen (2008).
22 There is even a site called Complaints Board (n.d.), where all sorts of general complaints about hundreds of products and services are aired: see www.complaintsboard.com.
23 Personal interview with an IT professional in a major oil corporation, conducted by Scott Poole.
24 "Ford, Union," (2000, C1) and Zipkin (2000). A study by Anthony Nyberg on turnover among high performers showed that pay growth and satisfaction both related to retention of high-performing personnel. The unemployment rate had a negative effect on turnover; the higher the unemployment rate, the lower the rate of turnover. See Nyberg (2010, 440–453). Denise Segura (1997) argues that what satisfies workers varies with their level in the organization, but not with their gender or ethnicity. Craig R. Scott and his associates (1999) and Mike Allen (1996) both found that there also is a direct relationship between communication and turnover – communication in itself influences turnover intentions and also influences satisfaction, which has an additional effect on turnover.
25 "Laid-Off Chicago Workers Take Factory, Demand Pay" (2008).
26 The best analysis of the development of critical theory and its many versions is Held (1980). An excellent application to organizational theory is Alvesson and Wilmott (1992), and to organizational communication is Deetz (1995, 2000).
27 Downs (1995); also see Deetz (1992, esp. chap. 9) and Conrad (2011, esp. chap. 3).
28 See Forester (1989). This section is based in part on Therborn (1980). A fine summary of the issues regarding the concept of ideology is available in Kersten (1993).
29 See Jehensen (1984). For analyses of how seemingly objective organizational "data" are manipulated symbolically to privilege management's interests, see Ansari and Euske (1987), and Sless (1988).
30 See, for example, Alvesson (1987a, 1987b). Classic studies of nonlegitimate participatory systems are available in Abrahamsson (1977), Perrow (1986), and Clegg (1975).

REFERENCES

Abrahamsson, B. (1977). *Bureaucracy or Participation?* Beverly Hills, CA: Sage.

Albrecht, T. (1984). "An Overtime Analysis of Communication Patterns and Work Perceptions," in Bostrom, ed., *Communication Yearbook 8*. Beverly Hills, CA: Sage.

Albrecht, T. and Adelman, M. (1988). *Communicating Social Support*. Newbury Park, CA: Sage.

Albrecht, T. and Hall, B. (1991a). "Facilitating Talk about New Ideas." *Communication Monographs* 58: 273–288.

Albrecht, T. and Hall, B. (1991b). "Relational and Content Differences between Elites and Outsiders in Innovation

Networks." *Human Communication Research* 17: 535–561.

Albrecht, T. and Halsey, J. (1992). "Mutual Support in Mixed Status Relationships." *Journal of Social and Personal Relationships* 9: 237–252.

Allen, M. (1996). "The Relationship between Communication, Affect, Job Alternatives, and Voluntary Turnover Intentions." *Southern Communication Journal* 61: 198–208.

Alvesson, M. (1987a). "Organizations, Culture and Ideology." *International Studies of Management and Organization* 17: 4–18.

Alvesson, M. (1987b). *Organization Theory and Technocratic Consciousness*. New York: Walter de Gruyter.

Alvesson, M. and Wilmott, H., eds. (1992). *Critical Management Studies*. Newbury Park, CA: Sage.

Ancona, D.G. and Caldwell, D.F. (1988). "Beyond Task and Maintenance: Defining External Functions in Groups." *Group and Organization Studies* 13: 468–494.

Ancona, D.G. and Caldwell, D.F. (1992). "Demography and Design: Predictors of New Product Team Performance." *Organizational Science* 3: 321–341.

Ansari, S. and Euske, K. (1987). "Rational, Rationalizing, and Reifying Uses of Accounting Data in Organizations." *Accounting, Organizations, and Society* 12: 549–570.

Argyris, C. (1957). *Personality and Motivation*. New York: Harper & Row.

Bach, B. (1991). "The Effect of Multiplex Relationships upon Innovation Adoption." *Communication Monographs* 56: 133–150.

Barker, J.R. (1993). "Tightening the Iron Cage: Concertive Control in Self-Managing Teams." *Administrative Science Quarterly* 38: 408–437.

Barker, J.R., Melville, C.W., and Pacanowsky, M.R. (1993). "Self-Directed Teams at Xel: Changes in Communication Practices During a Program of Cultural Transformation." *Journal of Applied Communication Research* 21: 297–313.

Bass, B. and Bass, R. (2008). *The Bass Handbook of Leadership*, 4th ed. New York: Free Press.

Bastien, D. (1992). "Change in Organizational Culture." *Management Communication Quarterly* 5: 403–442.

Benson, S. (1992). "The Clerking Sisterhood," in Mills and Tancred, eds., *Gendering Organizational Analysis*. Newbury Park, CA: Sage.

Bormann, E. (1990). *Small Group Communication: Theory and Practice*, 3rd ed. New York: Harper-Collins.

Brandel, M. (2010). "Are You Listening?" *Computerworld* 44: 13–15.

Brown, R. (2000). *Group Processes*. Malden, MA: Blackwell.

Cameron, K. and Thompson, M. (2000). "The Problems and Promises of Total Quality Management," in Quinn, ed., *Pressing Problems in Modern Organizations (That Keep Us Awake at Night)*. New York: AMACOM.

Cheney, G., Christensen, L., Zorn, T., Jr. and Ganesh, S. (2004). *Organizational Communication in an Age of Globalization*. Prospect Heights, IL: Waveland Press.

Chiles, A.M. and Zorn, T., Jr. (1995). "Empowerment in Organizations." *Journal of Applied Communication Research* 23: 1–25.

Clegg, S. (1975). *Power, Rule and Domination*. London: Routledge and Kegan Paul.

Cohen, N. (2008). "An Internal Wiki That's Not Classified." *New York Times*, online, August 4. www.nytimes.com/2008/08/04/business/media/04link.html.

Complaints Board. (n.d). [Home page]. www.complaintsboard.com.

Conrad, C. (2011). *Organizational Rhetoric: Resistance and Domination*. London: Polity Press.

Courtright, J., Fairhurst, G. and Rogers, L.E. (1989). "Interaction Patterns in Organic and Mechanistic Systems." *Academy of Management Journal* 32: 773–802.

Dana, L.P. (1999). "Small Business as a Supplement in the People's Republic of China (PRC)." *Journal of Small Business Management* 37: 76–81.

Dandeker, C. (1984). *Surveillance, Power and Modernity*. New York: St. Martin's Press.

Davis, K. (1953a). "A Method of Studying Communication Patterns in Organizations." *Personnel Psychology* 6: 301–312.

Davis, K. (1953b). "Management Communication and the Grapevine." *Harvard Business Review* (September–October): 43–49.

Deetz, S. (1992). *Democracy in the Age of Corporate Colonization*. Albany, NY: SUNY Press.

Deetz, S. (1995). *Transforming Communication, Transforming Business*. Creskill, NJ: Hampton Press.

Deetz, S. (2000). "Critical Theories of Organizational Communication," in Jablin and Putnam, eds., *The New Handbook of Organizational Communication*. Thousand Oaks, CA: Sage.

Downs, A. (1995). *Corporate Executions*. New York: AMACOM.

Edwards, R. (1978). *Contested Terrain*. New York: Basic Books.

Eisenberg, E., Monge, P. and Miller, K. (1983). "Involvement in Communication Networks as a Predictor of Organizational Commitment." *Human Communication Research* 10: 179–201.

Ellis, B. (1992). "The Effects of Uncertainty and Source Credibility on Attitude about Organizational Change." *Management Communication Quarterly* 6: 34–57.

Ezzamel, M. and Willmott, H. (1998). "Accounting for Teamwork." *Administrative Science Quarterly* 43: 358–396.

Fairhurst, G. (2001). "Dialectical Tensions in Leadership Research," in Jablin and Putnam, eds., *The New Handbook of Organizational Communication*. Thousand Oaks, CA: Sage.

Finholt, T. and Sproull, L. (1990). "Electronic Groups at Work." *Organization Science* 1: 41–64.

Fisher, C. (1980). "On the Dubious Wisdom of Expecting Job Satisfaction to Correlate with Performance." *Academy of Management Review* 5: 607–612.

Fleishman, E. and Associates (1961). *Studies in Personnel and Industrial Psychology*. Homewood, IL: Dorsey.

Fleishman, E. and Associates (1967). *Studies in Personnel and Industrial Psychology*, 2nd ed. Homewood, IL: Dorsey.

"Ford, Union to Open 30 Child-Care and Family-Service Centers for Workers." (2000). *Houston Chronicle*, November 22, C1.

Forester, J. (1989). *Planning in the Face of Power*. Berkeley: University of California Press.

Fulk, J. (1993). "Social Construction of Communication Technology." *Academy of Management Journal* 36: 921–950.

Gastil, J. (2010). *The Group in Society*. Thousand Oaks, CA: Sage.

Gioia, D. and Sims, H. (1986). "Cognition-Behavior Connections: Attribution and Verbal Behavior in Leader-Subordinate Interactions." *Organizational Behavior and Human Performance* 37: 197–229.

Granovetter, M. (1973). "The Strength of Weak Ties." *American Journal of Sociology* 81: 1287–1303.

Guzley, R. (1992). "Organizational Climate and Communication Climate." *Management Communication Quarterly* 5: 379–402.

Habermas, J. (1972). *Knowledge and Human Interests*. London: Heinemann Educational.

Habermas, J. (1979). *Communication and the Evolution of Society*. London: Heinemann Educational.

Hackman, J.R. (2002). *Leading Teams*. Cambridge, MA: Harvard Business School Press.

Hackman, J.R. and Oldham, G. (1980). *Work Redesign*. Reading, MA: Addison-Wesley.

Harrison, T. (1985). "Communication and Participative Decision-Making." *Personnel Psychology* 38: 93–116.

Held, D. (1980). *Introduction to Critical Theory*. London: Hutchinson.

Homans, G. (1950). *The Human Group*. New York: Harcourt Brace.

Huspek, M. (1987). "The Language of Powerlessness." PhD dissertation, University of Washington.

Infante, D. and Gordon, W. (1991). "How Employees See the Boss." *Western Journal of Speech Communication* 55: 294–304.

Jablin, F. (1979). "Superior–Subordinate Communication," in Ruben, ed., *Communication Yearbook 2*. New Brunswick, NJ: Transaction Books.

Jablin, F. (1985). "Task/Work Relationships," in Miller and Knapp, eds., *Handbook of Interpersonal Communication*. Beverly Hills, CA: Sage.

Jablin, F. (2001). "Communication Competence and Effectiveness," in Jablin and Putnam, eds., *The New Handbook of Organizational Communication*. Thousand Oaks, CA: Sage.

Jehensen, R. (1984). "Effectiveness, Expertise, and Excellence as Ideological Fictions." *Human Studies* 7: 3–21.

Johnson, D. (2009). *Managing Knowledge Networks*. Cambridge: Cambridge University Press.

Kersten, A. (1993). "Culture, Control, and the Labor Process," in Deetz, ed., *Communication Yearbook 16*. Newbury Park, CA: Sage.

Knoke, D. (2001). *Changing Organizations: Business Networks in the New Political Economy*. Boulder, CO: Westview.

Kramer, M.W. (2006). "Shared Leadership in a Community Theater Group: Filling the Leadership Role." *Journal of Applied Communication Research* 34: 141–162.

"Laid-Off Chicago Workers Take Factory, Demand Pay." (2008). *Houston Chronicle*, December 6. www.chron.com/disp/story.mpl/front/6150673.html.

Larson, C.E. and LaFasto, F.M.J. (1989). *TeamWork*. Newbury Park, CA: Sage.

Likert, R. (1961). *New Patterns of Management*. New York: McGraw-Hill.

Locke, E. (1976). "The Nature and Causes of Job Satisfaction," in Dunnette, ed. *Handbook of Industrial and Organizational Psychology*. Chicago: Rand-McNally.

Locke, E.A. and Latham, G.P. (2004). "What Should We Do about Motivation Theory?" *Academy of Management Review* 29: 388–403.

"The Lordstown Auto Workers." (1979). In Kanter and Stein, eds., *Life in Organizations*. New York: Basic Books.

McKinlay, A. and Taylor, P. (1996). "Power, Surveillance, and Resistance: Inside the Factory of the Future," in Ackers, Smith and Smith, eds., *The New Workplace and Trade Unionism*. London: Routledge.

March, J. and Sevon, G. (1982). "Gossip, Information, and Decision Making," in Sproull and Larkey, eds., *Advances in Information Processing in Organizations*, vol. 1. Greenwich, CT: JAI Press.

Marrow, A., Bowers, D. and Seashore, S. (1967). *Management by Participation*. New York: Harper & Row.

Maslow, A. (1987). *Motivation and Personality*, 3rd ed. New York: Harper and Row.

McLean, G. (2006). *Organization Development*. San Francisco: Berrett-Koehler.

Miller, K.I. and Monge, P. (1986). "Participation, Satisfaction, and Productivity: A Meta-analytic Review." *Academy of Management Journal* 29: 727–753.

Mills, K. (2000). "Northwest on a Flier-Satisfaction Mission." *Houston Chronicle*, May 14, 6D.

Mohrman, S.A., Cohen, S.G. and Mohrman, A.M. (1995). *Designing Team-Based Organizations*. San Francisco: Jossey-Bass.

Monge, P. and Contractor, N.S. (2003). *Theories of Communication Networks*. New York: Oxford.

Mulder, M. (1971). "Power Equalization through Participation?" *Academy of Management Journal* 16: 31–38.

Mulder, M. and Wilke, H. (1970). "Participation and Power Equalization." *Organizational Behavior and Human Performance* 5: 430–448.

Northouse, P. (2010). *Leadership: Theory and Practice*, 5th ed. Thousand Oaks, CA: Sage.

Nyberg, A. (2010). "Retaining Your High Performers: Moderators of the Performance–Job Satisfaction–Voluntary Turnover Relationship." *Journal of Applied Psychology* 95: 440–453.

Organ, D. (1971). "Linking Pins between Organizations and Environments." *Business Horizons* 14: 73–80.

Perrow, C. (1986). *Complex Organizations*, 3rd ed. New York: Random House.

Planalp, S., Hafen, S. and Adkins, A.D. (1999). "Messages of Shame and Guilt," in Roloff, ed., *Communication Yearbook 23*. Thousand Oaks, CA: Sage.

Pollock, T., Whitbred, R. and Contractor, N. (2000). "Social Information Processing and Job Characteristics." *Human Communication Research* 26: 292–330.

Rafaeli, S. (1990). [Electronic message to computer-mediated hotline]. April 26. New York: Comserve Electronic Information Service.

Remland, M. (1987). "Leadership Impressions and Nonverbal Communication." *Communication Quarterly* 19: 108–128.

Rice, R. (1984). *The New Media*. Beverly Hills, CA: Sage.

Rice, R. and Aydin, C. (1991). "Attitudes toward New Organizational Technology." *Administrative Science Quarterly* 36: 219–244.

Rice, R. and Gattiker, U.E. (2001). "New Media and Organizational Structuring," in Jablin and Putnam, eds. *The New Handbook of Organizational Communication*. Newbury Park, CA: Sage.

Rice, R. and Love, G. (1987). "Electronic Emotion." *Communication Research* 14: 85–108.

Richmond, V.P. and McCroskey, J.C. (2000). "The Impact of Supervisor and Subordinate Immediacy on Relational and Organizational Outcomes." *Communication Monographs* 67: 85–95.

Richmond, V.P. and Roach, K.D. (1992). "Willingness to Communicate and Employee Success in U.S. Organizations." *Journal of Applied Communication Research* 20: 95–115.

Roethlisberger, F. and Dickson, W. (1939). *Management and the Worker*. Cambridge, MA: Harvard University Press.

Rohter, R. (2003). "Workers in Argentina Take Charge of Abandoned Factories." *New York Times* online, July 6. www.nytimes.com.

Roy, A. (2010). "Internal Wikis." July 21. www.gaebler.com/Internal-Wikis.htm.

"Safaricom Brings Mobile Email and Online Chat to Subscribers in Kenya." (2010). *IT News Africa*, May 28. www.itnewsafrica.com/?p=7804.

Salas, E., Sims, D.E. and Burke, C.S. (2005). "Is There a 'Big Five' in Teamwork?" *Small Group Research* 36: 555–599.

Sayles, L. (1957). "Work Group Behavior and the Larger Organization," in Whyte, ed., *Research in Industrial Human Relations*. New York: Harper.

Scott, C.R., Connaughton, S., Diaz-Saenz, H., McGuire, K., Ramirez, R., Richardson, B., Shaw, S. and Morgan, D. (1999). "The Impacts of Communication and Multiple Identifications on Intent to Leave." *Management Communication Quarterly* 12: 400–435.

Segura, D. (1997). "Chicanas in White-Collar Jobs," in Lamphere, Razone' and Zavella, eds., *Situated Lives*. New York: Routledge.

Seibold, D. and Shea, C. (2001). "Participation and Decision-Making," in Jablin and Putnam, eds., *The New Handbook of Organizational Communication*. Newbury Park, CA: Sage.

Sewell, G. (1998). "The Discipline of Teams." *Administrative Science Quarterly* 43: 397–428.

Shaw, S. and Morgan, D. (1999). "The Impacts of Communication and Multiple Identifications on Intent to Leave." *Management Communication Quarterly* 12: 400–435.

Silva, D. and Sias, P.M. (2010). "Connection, balancing, and buffering: The Role of Groups in the Individual-

Organizational Relationship." *Journal of Applied Communication Research* 38: 145–166.

Sless, D. (1988). "Forms of Control." *Australian Journal of Communication* 14: 57–69.

Sproull, L. and Kiesler, S. (1986). "Reducing Social Context Cues." *Management Science* 32: 1492–1512.

Steinfeld, C. (1991). "Computer-Mediated Communication in the Organization," in Sypher, ed., *Cases in Organizational Communication*. New York: Guilford.

Stohl, C. (1985). "Bridging the Parallel Organization: A Study of Quality Circle Effectiveness," in Burgoon, ed., *Communication Yearbook 10*. Beverly Hills, CA: Sage.

Stohl, C. (1993). "European Managers' Interpretations of Participation." *Human Communication Research* 20: 108–131.

Stohl, C. and Cheney, G. (2001). "Participatory Processes/Paradoxical Practices." *Management Communication Quarterly* 14: 349–407.

Stohl, S. (1995). *Organizational Communication: Connectedness in Action*. Thousand Oaks, CA: Sage.

Sundstrom, E., De Meuse, K.P. and Futrell, D. (1990). "Work Teams." *American Psychologist* 45: 120–133.

Tannenbaum, A. (1962). "Control in Organizations." *Administrative Science Quarterly* 7: 17–42.

Tegar, A. (1980). *Too Much Invested to Quit*. New York: Pergamon.

Therborn, G. (1980). *The Ideology of Power and the Power of Ideology*. London: Verso.

Thompson, J. (1967). *Organizations in Action*. New York: McGraw-Hill.

Thompson, L. (2010). *Making the Team*, 3rd ed. Englewood Cliffs, NJ: Prentice Hall.

Tompkins, P.K. and Cheney, G. (1985). "Communication and Unobtrusive Control in Organizations," in McPhee and Tompkins, eds., *Organizational Communication: Traditional Themes and New Directions*. Beverly Hills, CA: Sage.

"Unified Messaging." (n.d.) Wikipedia. en.wikipedia.org/wiki/Unified_messaging.

Vroom, V.H. and Yetton, P.W. (1973). *Leadership and Decision Making*. Pittsburgh, PA: University of Pittsburgh Press.

Walther, J.B. (1992). "Interpersonal Effects in Computer-Mediated Interaction." *Communication Research* 19: 52–90.

Weidlich, T. (2002). "Who Says Unions Must Dislike the Chief?" *New York Times* online, December 15. www.nytimes.com.

Yates, J. and Orlikowski, W.J. (1992). "Genres of Organizational Communication." *Academy of Management Review* 17: 299–326.

Zipkin, A. (2000). "Bosses Become Nice to Try to Keep Employees from Leaving." *Houston Chronicle*, June 4, 5D.

CHAPTER 5

CULTURAL STRATEGIES OF ORGANIZING

The reality of the [social] world hangs on the thin thread of conversation.
Peter Berger and Thomas Luckmann

CENTRAL THEMES

- Cultural strategies of organizing assume that managers can influence employees' beliefs, values, and perceptions of reality and that employees actively create their own beliefs, values, and perceptions. Organizational cultures are communicative creations, embedded in a history and a set of expectations about the future. They are usually heterogeneous, composed of multiple subcultures.
- Cultural strategies of motivation and control rely on self-surveillance, which is accomplished through systems of unobtrusive control, emotional regulation, and discursive practices.
- Cultural strategies of leadership focus on "transformational" processes through which leaders communicate a vision of the organization and help employees "frame" everyday events.
- Organizational symbolism – metaphors, stories, myths, and rituals – facilitates unobtrusive control.
- Communication technologies have cultural assumptions embedded in them, and the way they are used in a given organization is influenced as much by the organizational culture as by the characteristics of the technologies themselves.

Strategic Organizational Communication: In a Global Economy, Seventh Edition.
Charles Conrad and Marshall Scott Poole.

KEY TERMS

corporate culture perspective
organizational culture perspective
cultural traffic
subcultures
externalization
objectification
internalization
identities
reality shock
anticipatory socialization
identify/identification
disidentification
stories
myths/mythologies
storytelling
codes
rituals
ceremonies
display rules
surface acting
deep acting
obtrusive/unobtrusive control
self-surveillance
charisma
transformative vision
framing
leadership moments

In Chapter 1 we suggested that a central tension in all societies is between *individuality* and *community*. The traditional strategy of organizing focuses on the individual pole of this tension and relies on the structural dimension of communication to manage it. The traditional strategy assumes that rewarding employees for their *individual* competence and performance will motivate them to act in ways that meet their organizations' needs for control and coordination. Feeling emotional connections to one's coworkers and/or one's organization is either ignored or treated as a potential threat to organizational control. Although some versions of the traditional strategy did consider the pride that people feel when they successfully perform their tasks, traditional strategies view human beings as predominantly rational, not emotional, beings. In contrast, relational strategies retain the rational, individualistic focus of traditional strategies, but also recognize that human beings are emotional, community-oriented creatures. For this reason they offer a more complete view of human experience. Relational strategies recognize that people have sociability needs and that interpersonal relationships are important aspects of work groups and teams. But, these additions still offer an impoverished view of the rich texture of beliefs, values, feelings, and personal connections that characterize life in modern organizations.[1]

Cultural strategies of organizing attempt to develop a more complete view of organizations and organizational communication. They accept the underlying assumptions of both the traditional and relational strategies, but strive to integrate concepts that often are treated as different or conflicting. They recognize that emotional ties, both to one's organization and to one's coworkers, are powerful influences on how people choose to act and communicate at work. They suggest that employees do make reasoned, strategic choices based on their individual beliefs, values, and sense-making processes. They put the individual at the center of organizational analysis, and focus on the ways in which people's identities – their conception of who they are and how they should act – are created, modified and enacted in the choices that they make every day. As important, cultural strategies recognize that each of these dimensions are interrelated and are constantly undergoing change. Each dimension, and their interrelationships, influence employees' choices of communication strategies, and are influenced by communication. As a result, motivating and controlling employees' behavior are tenuous and complicated processes that depend on persuading them to accept the organization's core beliefs, values, and frames of reference as their own. The tension between organizational and individual needs that was described in Chapter 1 is managed by creating and sustaining a sense of community within work groups and organizations. As in the other strategies of organizing, cultural approaches also incorporate a distinctive form of leadership, and posit unique relationships with communication technologies.[2]

However, from its beginnings the cultural strategy was defined by a core tension. One version, which gained the label **corporate culture**, suggested that *managers* could make their organizations succeed by learning to use some seemingly simple and relatively inexpensive tools for controlling their subordinates' behaviors, while increasing employee morale, commitment, and productivity. The key assumption of this version of the cultural strategy is that people are both rational beings (as described in traditional strategies) and nonrational creatures. Rule and reward systems can be developed that persuade employees to act in the ways that are desired by management. But, managers also can persuade employees to accept a desired set of beliefs, values, loyalties, feelings, and ways of viewing reality. Through mastering traditional forms of communication – persuasive messages, rituals, rites, and so on – managers can generate significant short-term increases in the competitiveness and profitability of their firms. It probably comes as no surprise that this "corporate culture" perspective quickly became very popular among managers and US schools of business.[3]

Almost as soon as the corporate culture perspective was articulated, its underlying assumptions were criticized. Cultures, both natural and organizational, are composed of active, thinking human beings who interpret and respond to management's messages in their own ways. Sometimes they even interpret management's attempts to mold beliefs, instill values, and manipulate perceptions and emotions as offensive and manipulative (regardless of how management interprets them). Employees may even resist positive changes, and in general make "culture management" exceptionally difficult. The resulting **organizational culture** perspective proposed that both managers and workers jointly create, sustain, and transform organizations. Organizations do not *have* cultures that can be easily manipulated by leaders, as suggested in the corporate culture perspective, but they *are cultures* – complex, ever-changing collectives which are defined, stabilized, and sometimes transformed by the *mutual* actions of knowledgeable.[4] Subordinates were depicted as competent actors whose decisions to ignore and/or resist "leaders" comprised a rational response to complicated situations. Organizational success or failure was the outcome of actions by all employees. Cultures simply cannot be managed in the ways envisioned in the corporate culture version. This organizational culture perspective continued to occupy an important place in the thinking of scholars in departments of sociology and communication in the United States and in management programs in Europe and the countries of the former British Commonwealth.

DEFINING KEY TERMS: CULTURES AND ORGANIZATIONAL CULTURES

Although "cultures" have been studied informally for thousands of years – every time a person has contact with people who seem to be "different" – and formally for a century or so, the concept still is ambiguous. Anthropology and sociology, the fields that long have viewed culture and/or subcultures as their primary focus of research, seem to agree that a culture is located *both* in the minds of its members and in their communication with one another (Alvesson, 2002b). But, neither minds nor communicative interactions are simple. Part of "culture" is a way of viewing the world and events that take place within it that is distinctive among a group of people who interact with one another – the "taken-for-granted" assumptions that we have discussed in earlier chapters, assumptions about what is natural, normal, right, wrong, and so on. But, these assumptions usually are held at a non conscious level, so we are not aware of them until we encounter someone with a different set of assumptions (who view the world differently and therefore act in ways that we do not expect) or encounter an event communication that does not immediately make sense (and thus ask ourselves, "Why did they say or do *that*?" or, more importantly, "Why did *I* say or do *that*?"). Moreover, even in homogeneous cultures there are variations. The "flip side" of taken-for-granted assumptions is characteristic modes of expression – from everyday communication to ritualized behavior to cultural artifacts – that also are often nonconscious. For example, record a conversation that you have with your friends and then record the "fillers" that you use without thinking about them ("whatever," "you know," etc.) Then do the same thing with an acquaintance whose communication style bothers you. Or, define the term "flip side" that we just used, and write down what it means to you and what you think about people who actually use terms like that (if you've never heard it, you can Google it). Members of a culture have different backgrounds, experiences, emotions, thought processes, and interpersonal connections, so their taken-for-granted assumptions vary at least a little from those of the people with whom they interact. People whose daily lives lead them to interact with people from multiple, different cultures or subcultures tend to develop more individualized interpretive frames than those who do not, and they tend to be more aware of the "taken for granted" assumptions of each culture or subculture because they constantly are having to translate from one to another. So, cultures are complicated because they are *both* conscious *and* nonconscious, individual *and* collective, stable (thus comforting) *and* changing (thus exciting and frightening), constraining and enabling, and located in *both* our minds/perceptions *and* in our actions and communication. Moreover, they are simultaneously accepted and contested, and linked in fundamental ways to members' identities, which also are complex, developing, and both individual and cultural.[5]

Organizational cultures, at least according to cultural strategies of organizing, are essentially like naturally occurring cultures. Their members learn a pattern of assumptions that tell them how to interpret events, actions and communication, and how to respond to them. Organizational cultural assumptions eventually are taken for granted, and are represented in characteristic patterns of acting and communicating, rituals, and artifacts, and so on. Those choices can be (and are) legitimized by pointing to beliefs and values that are shared by members of the organizational culture. Culture and organizations are inextricably tied to one another – through creating shared understandings, interpretations, actions, and so on ("cultures"), groups of people become "organized" into collectives who cooperatively pursue shared goals, as well as their own interests and desires (See Cooren and Taylor, 1997; Taylor and van Every, 2000). Conversely, the "organization" becomes the key concept that people use to make strategic choices and to evaluate their own actions and the actions of other members. It *seems* to be a stable, entity that operates independent of its members, and we often talk of it in those terms – "the organization" says, or does, or succeeds, or fails, or requires, or allows, or any number of other actions that inanimate objects simply cannot do. But, organizations are embedded in broader cultural contexts. Their members bring a complex and varying set of understanding with them when they enter the organization, and these "imported" perspectives change as the surrounding cultures change. Mats Alvesson refers to this ongoing process as **cultural traffic**: "changes involving environmental protection, gender and ethnic relations, age, attitudes toward work, new ideas on business and management, and so on, affect people not only outside but also inside of their workplaces" (Alvesson, 2002b, 160).[6] Differences in background and experiences mean that many different belief systems are present within each organizational culture and potentially compete with one another. Some are persuasively shared with some members but not with others. Some become primary aspects of the organization's overall culture – a cultural center or core. Others are more peripheral, accepted but treated with "lip service." Consequently, "managing" organizational cultures is an exceptionally difficult process, just as "managing" British, or US, or French culture would be. But, the assumption that cultures can be strategically managed is the key assumption of many (but not all) cultural strategies of organizing.

CULTURAL STRATEGIES OF ORGANIZATIONAL DESIGN

Although most advocates of cultural strategies of organizing were comfortable with relational conceptions of organizational design – decentralization, participation, and so on – issues of organizational design were relatively unimportant to them.[7] The values, beliefs, language, symbols, and meaning systems that hold an organization together are much more important to them. Initially they argued that organizational cultures could be managed strategically, and rather easily. Upper management merely had to communicate persuasively the core values of the organization to all employees and provide tangible and intangible rewards to employees who act in accordance with those values. Eventually, a homogeneous and harmonious "strong" culture would emerge, one in which employees throughout the organization – regardless of their rank, tasks, networks of interpersonal relationships, or formal roles – would share the same goals, have the same kinds of feelings about the organization, and interpret the culture in the same way. This strong culture would be the key to managerial control, worker commitment, and organizational effectiveness.[8]

In some cases, this deceptively simple perspective did seem to work. For example, Gideon Kunda's study of a high-tech engineering firm found that management did seem to succeed in establishing a planned organizational culture. They started by developing a coherent set of beliefs, and values, an ideology, that was articulated over and over through a variety of different media, from mission statements to slogans to meeting agendas to theme parties. Moreover, they designed the firm in ways that were consistent with that ideology, assigning roles, devising reward systems, and developing evaluation systems that were consistent with, and thus reinforced, that ideology. Similar processes seemed to succeed in organizations that are themselves ideological – churches and nonprofit organizations such as Alcoholics Anonymous, for example (Kunda, 1992; Witmer, 1997).

However, even if a strong culture exists, not all employees will participate in it equally or in the same ways. It may be accepted by one cluster of employees who regularly communicate with one another, but not by other clusters, creating a collection of distinct but connected **subcultures**. In this sense, "culture" is located both inside of each member's head *and* in their communication with one another. Employees tend to form communicative ties with people who share their view of their organization. Different subcultures emerge – groups of people whose shared interpretation of their organization helps bind them together and separate them from other groups of employees. Subcultures usually form along formal lines – the tasks that people perform require them to interact with some people and not with others. But, subcultures can be based on almost any similarity – geography (different plants or offices in the same company may develop distinctive subcultures), generation (recall Chapter 1), and organizational hierarchy all have been shown to generate distinct subcultures. Consequently, it is more likely that an organization will be composed of many distinct and different subcultures rather than a homogeneous culture consciously defined and guided by upper management. And, usually unfortunately, different subcultures tend to be talked about in terms of opposition – us versus them.[9]

For example, Charley Conrad once visited the technical writing division of a major computer firm as part of a consulting project. He entered through the front door and was examined by the security team at the front desk. Then he was led down corridor after corridor past each of the major divisions of the firm into a separate building that housed the writing staff. One of the first things he noticed was the staff's coffee room. On the wall was a poster of the firm's newest product, an exceptionally powerful portable computer that was not yet on the market. But unlike the hardware division, which had an entire wall covered with the posters, or the software group, which had arranged to have one of the posters professionally framed and displayed in the center of their workroom, the technical writing group had only one poster and displayed it in a dark corner. In front of the poster was a Norfolk pine that all but obscured it from view.[10]

Prominently displayed in the center of the room was a poster of a penguin jumping off an ice cliff into the ocean with a long row of penguins following it. Someone had written the division head's name next to the lead penguin and the other writers' names next to the others. Significant symbols reveal a great deal about the culture (or subculture) of an organization. In this organization, the poster symbols suggested that technical writing was a subculture – a strong and stable one – that was separate from the other units of the organization. They perceived themselves as writers, not as employees of Computer Firm X. They proudly told Charley that they were in their isolated building because they had asked to be there. He recently re-visited the plant. It has grown as the company has grown, but 20 years after his first visit the Tech Writing division still is located in its own area. Sometimes the different subcultures make up an organization, but coexist peacefully; in other cases their values, patterns of acting, sense-making processes, and so on are conflicting and irreconcilable.

To complicate matters further, subcultures, like the communication networks that underlie them, are fluid and changing, and different patterns of cultural traffic lead subcultures to change in different ways. In addition, individual employees usually are members of more than one subculture or network. As a result they develop their own, unique set of cultural understandings, which are sufficiently like those of other employees to allow them to work together successfully, but sufficiently different to allow them to maintain separate identities. Somewhat ironically, it is the complexity and ambiguity of organizational cultures, symbolism, and identities that allow people to simultaneously be connected to and separate from one another.[11] The existence of multiple, ever-changing organizational subcultures does not mean that implementing cultural strategies of organizing is impossible. In some cases, the organization's core beliefs and values are so powerful and communicated so persuasively that individual interpretations and subcultural differences are overwhelmed. But, cultures are communicative creations. They emerge and are sustained by the communicative acts of all employees, not just the conscious persuasive strategies of upper management (Wilkins, 1989).

CULTURAL STRATEGIES OF MOTIVATION, CONTROL, AND SURVEILLANCE

Cultural strategies of control rely on three communicative processes – socializing newcomers into the taken-for-granted assumptions of the organization, reinforcing those assumptions through organizational symbolism, and regulating emotions. The goal of all three processes is to encourage employees to monitor and control their own behavior in ways that meet the organization's needs.

Socializing Newcomers

Sociologist Peter Berger has described the process through which people learn and accept the core values and beliefs of their society; to learn "who I am and how I should act." In the first phase, **externalization**, people notice the ways in which others interpret and respond to their surroundings. To fit in, they begin to act as the "locals" do. Eventually, they may enter the second phase, **objectification**. They begin to believe that the way the people in their societies or organizations act is the only correct (that is, normal and natural) way of acting. They begin to "objectify" the thought processes and action patterns of their society or organization and not to be consciously aware of how those societal or organizational assumptions influence their everyday lives. Eventually they forget that the people in their societies *choose* to act as they do, and that they could have chosen any number of different courses of action. The concept of objectification implies that cultures (and organizations) are maintained nonconsciously, as much through habit as through conscious deliberation. Routine decisions can be made automatically, and with little expenditure of time or energy. In the final **internalization** phase people begin to evaluate themselves and their actions in terms of the society's or organization's assumptions. They begin to see themselves as good, productive, or righteous only if they think and act in accordance with the core beliefs and values of their society. Their self-concept begins to depend on their continually thinking and acting in ways that are normal in their organizations. Their self-esteem depends on doing what is valued by their society or organization. If they ever do act in ways that violate those core beliefs and values they will view themselves negatively and be motivated to change their behavior. As we will explain later in this chapter, their sense of who they are as people – their **identities** – are tied to their society and its accepted assumptions.

When people enter a new organization or a new division of their existing organization they go through a similar process. They bring with them a lengthy and complex history.[12] They have learned to perceive their organizational worlds in their own ways and have developed patterns of acting and communicating that have succeeded in the past. But, every organization is unique in some ways. Consequently all newcomers experience some degree of **reality shock** – the sudden realization that what they took for granted in their previous organization is not what people take for granted in their new one. So, the first challenge that newcomers face is *making sense out of* their new organization, of coping with the surprises that their new experiences bring. The organization's management has an incentive to assist newcomers in this process – after all, if they quickly accept the key components of the organization's culture they will be more productive and more easily managed or controlled – and do so both informally and through formal orientation or mentoring programs. But, newcomers usually need additional information and perspective, so they *proactively* seek it on their own.[13] Much of this learning involves task performance, and organizational culture. But, it also involves emotions, including the emotions of being a newcomer – feeling lost, confused, inept, or alien. For example, new firefighters learn what to feel when someone they are trying to save dies, when they get into a life-threatening situations because of their own stupidity or irresponsibility and in the process put them or their coworkers in severe danger, or when someone asks these highly trained experts to leave their station to get a cat out of a tree (an example of what the firefighters call a "bullshit call"). They also need to learn how to control their emotions so that they will be motivated to act quickly and decisively, but in a controlled and productive way. Through communicating with others, newcomers begin to manage the ambiguities and uncertainties that they feel (Scott and Myers, 2005). Of course, some newcomers are better able to cope with new situations than others. People who are inner directed, that is, who rely on their own beliefs, values, and analytical skills, cope more easily than people who are outer directed, who usually rely on the opinions and interpretations of others.[14] Consequently, outer-directed people are more likely to be influenced by cultural strategies of control than inner-directed people. However, the need to make sense out of a new situation makes all newcomers susceptible to persuasion from their new organizations. Sense making is a complicated combination of thoughts and feelings, and is both the process of entering a new organization and the process through which people cope with their new organizational worlds (Ashforth, 2000; Ashforth and Sacks, 2002).

Anticipatory Socialization Newcomers who have had many and varied work experiences deal with the reality shock of the entry experience more successfully than people with few work experiences. They are better able to anticipate their own feelings and information needs, and are better able to the culture of their new organization as a chosen strategy. In many cases, the newcomers will have had some indirect experience with the organization before they enter it. For example, everyone knows that the best source for leads on new jobs is friends and family members. Conversations with those sources give a potential newcomer insight into the organization before they even apply. In Chapter 3 we introduced Industry International, an organization with an especially powerful system of financial rewards. But, Industry also relies on organizational socialization as a mechanism of control. Its employees learn to accept its core beliefs and values long before they ever enter its doors. The organization hires its workers, which are frequently relatives of its current employees, from local blue-collar communities. From childhood, they have been told that Industry is a stable and highly successful organization. By the time they are adolescents, they have learned a strong work ethic – to be dependable, conscientious, and concerned about the quality of their work, and to work very, very hard. They learn that real men put food on their family's table, and that only "real men can make it at Industry International."[15] In fact, being able to withstand the body-punishing rigors of blue-collar life and being willing to celebrate the strength, stamina, and manual dexterity required by Industry work are the sources of the worker's identity and self-esteem. For Industry's employees, these attributes make them superior to people who make a living by shuffling papers. Industry's employees internalize the organization's values at their dinner tables and look forward to someday becoming one of "the mud, the blood, and the beer guys."

By the time people apply to work at Industry, they know what will be expected of them, what it means to be part of a cohesive work group, and what kinds of financial rewards they can obtain. This pre-employment indoctrination makes it easy to adopt the core beliefs of the organization. As Roy, a 17-year-old employee notes,

> You walk in there and you know you're not going to get days off. You know you're not going to get sick days. You know that you don't just say "Im not feeling well and I'm going home." If the person after you doesn't show up [for the next shift], you know that you're not leaving. Your group depends on you to keep the line going.

Employees also know that if they ever slack off, they will be reminded by the men with whom they are working. Deon (an old-timer at 25) explains, "When I see these kids in here who do not know how to work, I kinda' take them under my wing. I show them how to work hard." Jim personalizes the issue: "If my kid or relative went there and wasn't working hard, I'd go down and kick his ass. No way he's shamin' me by not working as hard as I said he could." Some of the most powerful identification messages come from employees' supervisors and coworkers (Kramer and Miller, 1999). But, if workers really have identified with their organizations, few messages are necessary. They act as the organization wants them to because they believe that it is natural and normal to do so.

Colleges and universities provide the same kind of **anticipatory socialization** for potential "white collar" employees. Students in US universities are taught to expect that they will someday get a "real job," one that pays well (the realest ones have six-figure salaries), is full-time, involves managerial tasks, includes perks (independence and a large private office) and the possibility of advancement, and is with a reputable company (Clair, 1996; Clair, Bell, Hackbarth, and Mathes, 2008). In real jobs, supervisors are competent and do not mistreat their subordinates. These expectations are elitist, and they are stereotypically masculine because the "realness" of a job depends on traditionally male considerations, such as financial gain and upward mobility. Stereotypically feminine values like improving society or nurturing and caring for others, are characteristic of jobs that are not quite "real" jobs. Students' perceptions of real jobs include a particular kind of organizational life and a specific set of criteria for evaluating an organization, a job, and the people who fill them. But, some of the first jobs that new college graduates obtain, if they obtain them – as many have discovered during the recessions of the twenty-first century – are not "real" jobs, and their expectations are not being fulfilled.

Other expectations are more specific. As soon as a person has accepted a new position she or he begins to anticipate what the new job will be like. For some people these expectations will be relatively accurate; for others they will not be. Sometimes selection processes and negotiations over terms of employment create inaccurate expectations. During these processes, the firm and the applicant engage in communication that is similar to romantic courtship, where each party strives to present the best possible image. But, as in many marriages, the reality may be quite different from the expectations.[16] Sometimes unfulfilled expectations involve organizational tasks and perks. But, just as often they involve the employee's personal life or family – their subdivision was not as welcoming, or their children's schools were not as good, or the weather was not as balmy, or the local theater not as good, as they had anticipated. Organizations do a great deal to help newcomers prepare for their jobs, but they often fail to realize that people also have identities and lives that go beyond the workplace. Failing to adequately prepare newcomers for their nonwork lives is just as alienating, perhaps more so, than failing to prepare them for their tasks. The most memorable experiences that people have in their organizations involve their first few weeks.

Unfortunately, if these memories involve unmet expectations, the disappointment and hurt feelings may never disappear (Stohl, 1983; Jablin and Kramer, 1998). When expectations are violated, people feel betrayed, and their trust in the other parties is reduced. As Chapter 3 explained, low levels of trust reduce the amount of and accuracy of communication. As the quality of communication between newcomers and old-timers is reduced, it becomes progressively more difficult for either side to understand the other. New expectations are formed, based on patterns of withholding or distorting information. Since these expectations are unrealistic, they are easily violated. As employees become less predictable to one another they tend to withdraw, making it even more difficult for them to communicate effectively. Their expectations become less realistic, their orientations toward one another less trusting, open, or cooperative. In contrast, if the expectations are fulfilled, the newcomers are likely to feel psychologically connected to their organizations and begin to identify with it.[17]

Identification and Organizational Socialization Members of organizations, especially managers, encourage employees to **identify** with their firms – that is, to begin to see their continued connection to the organization as an important part of who they are as people. Identification messages use a variety of communicative strategies and are distributed through a number of different media, from face-to-face interactions to more formal organizational discourse – newsletters, annual reports, and so on. Sometimes these messages laud the *team atmosphere* that presumably exists between workers and the organization. Other identification strategies involve *expressing concern for individual employees* and *recognizing contributions* that individual employees or work groups have made to the organization or to the larger society. Other messages *invite* employees to become increasingly involved (or remain involved) in some worthwhile organizational activity; others *brag* about the dedication and sacrifice shown by an individual or work group on behalf of the organization. The Bank of America newsletter includes a regular feature in which employees talk about their contributions to the company. Sometimes messages encourage employees to identify with their organizations by identifying a common enemy. When Steve Jobs served his first term as head of Apple Computer, Inc. he expressed respect for IBM as a "national treasure" and galvanized Apple's employees by telling them that Apple was the only thing that kept IBM from "total industry domination." Each of these communicative strategies attempt to create a corporate "we" between workers and the organization – a feeling that "we" are inextricably tied together, teammates in a shared struggle against common enemies (Pondy, 1993; Martin and Powers, 1983; Smith and Simmons, 1983).

Employees respond to these messages in a number of ways. Many do identify with their organizations. They begin to feel close ties to the employees who are mentioned in the messages and feel connected to the organization through their positive feelings about those people. They may feel that they really are part of the organization or feel pride in being involved in an organization that cares for its members. Or they may feel a strong connection to their peers or to their organizational community. Other employees may interpret the messages as mere transparent motivational appeals that serve to entertain the workers, or as "mere rhetoric" which fails to fulfill its persuasive goals. They may feel that their own experience contradicts the messages, may see them as a waste of organizational resources, or feel that their work group or its members are not given enough recognition.

Employees also respond differently to the identification process, as well as to the content of identification messages. Like almost every other aspect of organizational communication, identification processes are filled with tensions and contradictions. One tension is familiar because it exists in all interpersonal relationships, a tension between retaining one's individuality while being part of a "we." Like dating relationships, in which one or both partners sometimes feel "smothered," employees may psychologically withdraw when organizational identification pressures become too intense. Another tension exists between stability and change. People grow, and in the process their sense of who they are and how they are related to their organization also changes. In the process of adjusting their new identity, their relationship to their organization becomes a little less stable and a little less predictable. Conversely, our organizations and our images of them also change. Organizational identification is influenced by "the way they [members of an organization] believe others see the organization, to gauge how others are judging them." If the organization's image among outsiders is positive, members "bask in its reflected glory"; if it is negative they may feel stress, become depressed, disengage from their work, or even leave the organization. For example, after the wreck of the Exxon *Valdez*, Exxon employees often had to defend themselves and their organization in social settings; as a result of the Deep Water Horizon drilling rig explosion and oil leak, BP employees were being forced to defend themselves and their employer on a daily basis for months. Similarly, NASA's muddled efforts to manage its image after the multimillion dollar Hubble telescope was launched in unusable condition created identity problems for its employees as well.[18] Employees who identify strongly with their employer experience these criticisms as threats to their personal identities. Some respond by identifying more strongly with their firms, others **disidentify,** and all are forced to consciously think about issues that normally are nonconscious.

A third tension that influences the extent to which employees identify with their organizations involves concrete, everyday experiences. If they become dissatisfied with their pay, their working conditions, or the degree of autonomy they have at work, they are less likely to identify with their organizations and are more likely to interpret identification messages as manipulation (Alvesson, Ashcraft, and Thomas, 2008; Russo, 1998). A final tension stems from the complex and multifaceted identities that human beings develop. For example, both authors of this book simultaneously are husbands, fathers, researchers, teachers, organizational communication scholars, employees of different communication departments, colleges and universities, and a number of other people. We are simultaneously involved in multiple, sometimes overlapping, communication networks whose members produce and share different identity messages with one another. As we receive and interpret messages from people who know only one or two parts of our composite identities, we are constantly creating and re-creating our sense of who we are and how we should act.[19] Like everyone else, we tend to identify most closely with the people who are most central in our communication networks – our immediate families and our immediate work groups – and we identify most closely with organizations and relationships that we have been part of for a long time. We interpret each identification message we receive through lenses that are made of complex webs of attachment and identification. As a result, it is unlikely that we would ever identify *completely* with any one of the many organizations or groups of which we are members.

To summarize, some people strongly identify with their organizations and their identities are relatively stable over time. Others identify only in part, for example when their own beliefs, values, and interests happen to coincide with those of the organization. They understand where they fit in the organization, take pride in their contributions to its success, and feel commitment to its continuation. They may accept some of the accepted assumptions of the organization; but they do so because they actually believe in those values, not because someone in their organization tells them that they should. Other employees are aware of the assumptions that members of their organizations take for granted, but do not accept them uncritically. An employee's level of identification also varies across time and with different organizational experiences. But when identification is strong, it is a powerful mode of organizational control.

ORGANIZATIONAL SYMBOLISM AND CULTURAL STRATEGIES OF MOTIVATION AND CONTROL

Organizational symbolism – metaphors, stories, myths, rituals, and ceremonies – have a dual relationship to cultural strategies of organizing; they express the taken-for-granted assumptions of the culture and, when articulated, reproduce those assumptions. Cultures are ambiguous and difficult to describe in sentence form. Symbols carry a great deal of information, but they also express more abstract and amorphous dimensions of culture. In the process they integrate disparate thoughts, feelings, assumptions, and meanings into a coherent and powerful image. As a result, symbolic action triggers the core beliefs, values, sense-making processes, and accepted patterns of action that people know, but usually retain at a nonconscious level (Alvesson, 2002a; Rafaeli and Worline, 2000). Advocates of *corporate culture* perspectives assume that upper management can motivate and control employees by strategically managing organizational symbols. Advocates of *organizational culture* perspectives argue that this view seriously oversimplifies the nature of symbolism and organizational cultures. Employees are human beings, and humans actively perceive, process, and often choose to respond to symbolic acts in their own idiosyncratic ways. They interpret stories and other symbolic forms in the same way that they interpret more traditional messages – in terms of their individual needs, experiences, and perspectives. Different employees or different subcultures of employees may interpret the same symbolic act in different ways. They also may tell different stories, create their own rituals, or describe their organization or unit through the use of different metaphors. Upper management may tell one story in an effort to explain an organizational disaster (or success); production workers may tell a very different one. People in marketing may tell stories that blame the research and development division for failed product lines, while research and development employees may tell the same story in a way that satirizes members of the marketing. In some cases, storytelling may increase managerial credibility and control; in others, organizational symbolism may actually reduce managerial control and motivate employees to act in ways that are not desired by management.

Metaphors These are symbols in which one image is used to describe another one. They are symbolically powerful means of suggesting similarities *and* difference. Metaphors often are used to describe an entire organization. More importantly, they also imply acting, and acting in certain ways but not in others (Ortony, 1993; Grant and Oswick, 1996; Inns, 2002; Tsoukas, 1991).

Frequently used organizational metaphors are military machines ("Working here is like being in the army"), families ("These people are my closest friends [or my family]" or "This desk is my home away from home"), and games ("To survive here you have to play the game" or "Pretend to be what the big shots want you to be"). For 50 years, a large West Coast toy manufacturer has been described by its employees as an "army under siege." Although the enemy has changed many times, from profit-hungry East Coast companies during the 1950s to wily foreign importers who keep their workers in poverty during the 1960s and 1970s to computer firms that care about wires and chips, not children, in the 1980s, the guiding metaphor has remained the same. Employees talk about "fighting the battle," which means constantly working hard to maintain efficiency; "taking no casualties," which means having everyone constantly monitor quality (including a company program in which samples are donated to employees provided they take them home and see how long it takes their children to destroy them); "everyone being a spy," which leads most employees to regularly take their children to toy shops just to see which of their competitors' products are popular and ought to be duplicated; and "foot soldiers in the battle," which both involves every employee in the mission of the organization and justifies a hierarchical, rule-governed style of management. But the most powerful expressions of the metaphor are borrowed from the larger culture: "Be all that you can be" is used to justify voluntary overtime, and "lean, mean fighting machine" is used to explain reductions in the number of middle managers. Almost every normal work experience is explained in language reflecting the army-under-siege metaphor; almost every behavior desired of workers can be justified by referring to the metaphor. In cases like this one, management and employees share the same metaphorical description of their organization and define that metaphor in the same way. Motivation and control are enhanced.

However, metaphors are highly ambiguous. First of all, they usually are caricatures of "real" symbols. For example, British scholar Alistair Mutch has pointed out that very few of the employees who use the "military" metaphor have had any direct experience with military life. As a result, their image of military life probably is archaic and overly simplistic. But, even metaphors that are close to employees' "real" experiences also are ambiguous and can be interpreted in a number of different ways (Mutch, 2008; also see Pondy, 1993; Martin and Powers, 1993; Smith and Simmons, 1983).

If employees think their organizational "family" is like the *Simpsons*, the Barones (*Everyone Loves Raymond*), or the Griffins/Pewterschmidts (*Family Guy*), they are likely to interpret and respond to the metaphor very differently than they would if their image of "family" is the Lopezes (*The George Lopez Show*), Hudsons (*Glee*), or Hummels (*Glee*). Whatever the definition, if they accept the family metaphor, they will perceive employees who behave in un-family-like ways as being problematic members of the organization. The metaphor "says" that employees should put the organization ("family") above themselves and, at least in the short term, not question the basic power relationships that exist within it. The meanings attributed to metaphors also change over time and with events. Ironically, people rarely interpret instances in which coworkers violate the metaphors as evidence that the metaphor may be inaccurate. Metaphors are important because they guide and constrain peoples' interpretations of everyday events. They also provide stability because people tend to perceive reality in ways that confirm their metaphors. They articulate and reproduce the power relationships of an organization because they accept *a* way of thinking and *a* way of seeing which precludes alternative perspectives. But, metaphors also can serve as a source of independence and resistance. For example, Peter Fleming and Andre Spicer studied workers who created their own metaphors in order to escape the "official" metaphors used in their organizations. Workers who talked about their organizations as *playgrounds* (as in the US sitcom *The Office*) were able to escape, at least for a time, the mind-numbing elements of everyday life in bureaucratic organizations. Similarly, workers who described their organizations as "like Parliament," conjuring up the image of a rowdy House of Commons confronting the prime minister during weekly questioning times, were more likely to dissent against organizational rules and practices (Sennett, 1998, 2006; Fleming and Spicer, 2007).

Stories and Storytelling Human beings are *storytelling* animals. From childhood fairy tales to the tales told during executives' weekend retreats, stories provide concrete, vivid images of what life is or will be like and what behaviors our culture values or prohibits. They are emotionally involving, and thus potentially powerful, because they require audiences to be "active" listeners. They can help people negotiate differences because telling a story from one person's point of view invites others to share a similar story from their perspectives.[20] **Stories** present events in sequence rather than in a list or chart, which makes some events seem to be the causes and effects of other events. At least in Western cultures, stories are based on a dramatic conflict between a protagonist and an antagonist. Stories are relevant to the needs and experiences of members of the organization. An event is worthy of a story only if it involves a deviation from what is normal, and the deviation can be either positive (action beyond the call of duty) or negative (against the culture and its members). Stories are told most often and are most powerful when people are confused and concerned about what is going on in their organizations (for instance, when a person is entering a new organization or when the organization is undergoing major changes). They provide explanations of events, policies, procedures, and so on that are beyond doubt or argument. They function as social **myths**, not in the sense that they are untrue (although they may be), but in the sense that their "truths" are taken for granted by the people who tell and listen to them. Like stories, the power of myths stems from their coherent, vivid details, their ability to help people make sense of their surroundings, and their consistency with other organizational stories and myths.[21]

Stories and myths usually coalesce to form **mythologies**, groups of interconnected symbols that support one another. In short, stories and myths tell people how things are to be done in a particular group and provide a social map that points out potentially dangerous topics, events, or persons present in at least one of an organization's subcultures. To be credible, stories must express a value, purpose, or philosophy that is consistent with the taken-for-granted assumptions of the culture or subculture and must provide employees with guidelines for acting. They often tell employees what management wants them to believe is valued and rewarded in the organization; they sometimes tell employees what management really rewards and who really has power. And, sometimes they may do both. Stories and myths also gain power from the processes through which they are told. **Storytelling** (and mythmaking) is an interactive process in which the teller presents his or her version of a story, usually leaving out many details, while others jump in and challenge, reinterpret, and revise the storyteller's version. The process allows each of the storytellers to link his or her own experiences to the experiences and interpretations of other storytellers. Through this process of mutual interpretation and reinterpretation employees may learn to better understand the beliefs, values, biases, and experiences of other employees; at an emotional level it can help them bond with one another. But, stories and storytelling are almost never neutral. They normalize and naturalize the preferences, values, and so on of the most powerful members of the organization and denigrate alternative views and actions. In this sense, they are inherently linked to issues of power and politics. Thus, through a complicated process, the values and accepted assumptions of the group are produced, reproduced, and revised.[22]

Of course, the observation that organizational symbolism can be powerful does not imply that its effects are always positive. Tom Hollihan and Patricia Riley's study of a "Toughlove" group provides an excellent example. Toughlove is a self-help voluntary organization composed of parents who have troubled teenagers. Toughlove meetings are like "testimonial services" in Protestant churches. Members come to tell stories about their experiences and their successes in overcoming their problems. Their individual stories combine to form a complicated mythology that unifies the members through their common experiences. The core experience is suffering brought on by the actions of their delinquent children; the common salvation is recognizing that adolescent children choose to behave as they do, realizing that parents have rights to peaceful homes and productive lives, and taking action to regain control of their lives instead of remaining victims of the tyranny of their children. Their stories are filled with villains and nostalgic images of a peaceful past. The villains are child service professionals – teachers, social workers, therapists, and counselors – who are too quick to blame the parents for their children's delinquency and who are responsible for the modern "permissive" view of child raising that the parents believe has created the problem of delinquent children. The nostalgia is of their childhoods when visits to the woodshed led them to both fear and respect their parents and learn to behave in socially acceptable ways.[23] By listening to stories members of organizations learn the values that bind the culture together and discover what they must say and do if they are to become accepted members of the culture.

Performances: Rituals and Ceremonies A final form of organizational symbolism involves performances: codes, rituals, and ceremonies. Like *storytelling*, these forms gain their power from *both* the act of participating in them and the meanings that people extract from them. **Codes** are repetitive behaviors that regulate work relationships. *Courtesies* are behaviors such as letting someone with only a page or two to copy cut in line; *pleasantries* involve adjusting one's actions or communication to the specific people who are present in a particular situation; and *privacies* differentiate, guide, and constrain where a particular message should be exchanged, and can include something as specific as honoring different employees' sense of personal space. One of the most interesting codes is organizational humor. Sometimes the function of humor is to help employees make sense out of events that are incongruous in some way – irrational, incoherent, inappropriate, or just unexpected. Sometimes it is a way of providing emotional release – an act of disguised aggression, a way of attacking a coworker with whom other workers are "fed up," or an act of bonding in the face of maddening work situations. Humor is the cause and effect of bonding – it creates "in-groups" (and out-groups), and cohesive groups generate humor in order to clarify membership and boundaries. But, most research of humor views it as a mechanism of organizational control and resistance. High-power employees use humor to keep dissidents in line; resisters use it to challenge organizational power relationships without admitting that they are resisting.[24]

Rituals are informal celebrations that may or may not be officially sanctioned by the organization. **Ceremonies** are planned, formal, and ordained by management. When a work crew gets together at a local bar on Friday evenings, it is a ritual – an informal gathering. When all the employees of a department store are asked by their supervisors to appear at a media event designed to kick off a new line of clothes, it is a ceremony. Participating in rituals and ceremonies helps individual employees understand the political and interpersonal nuances of their organization. If they perceive that the ritual or ceremony is meaningful, participating also may increase their commitment to the organization because it makes them feel like they are a part of the organizational community.

Harrison Trice and Janice Beyer have observed that there are five primary types of organizational ceremonies. *Ceremonies of passage* tell everyone that a person has changed organizational roles and now has a new set of responsibilities, behavioral guidelines and constraints, and interpersonal relationships. *Degradation ceremonies* assign responsibility for errors or problems, refocus attention on the kinds of performance that is expected by management, and remove the guilty party from the power structure of the organization (usually through demotion, reassignment, or resignation). *Enhancement ceremonies* (for example, Mary Kay Cosmetic seminars) reemphasize the goals of the organization and create instant heroes who symbolize those goals. Regular awards ceremonies for the top salespersons can serve this function. *Renewal ceremonies* (such as annual executive retreats complete with motivational speakers) create an image of action and deflect attention from underlying organizational problems. *Integration ceremonies* redefine the organization as a community and tell each employee that she or he is a part of it. However, ceremonies almost always do many of these things. For example, "employee of the week/month/year" awards are enhancing for one employee and degrading for many others. Giving every employee an identical Christmas ham is an integration ceremony for some, but may be an alienating ritual for others.[25] The foundry that Charley Conrad worked in during his undergraduate years (recall the time–motion study described in Chapter 3) had a Christmas ceremony during which the owner stood in the back of a truck and gave a ham to each worker. But, Charley did not receive one, something that everyone quietly noticed. After distributing the hams, the owner took him aside and explained in private that he was worried that giving a ham to a part-time (summers and holidays) employee would make the ceremony less meaningful for the full-time workers, and might even cause resentment. Ironically, some of the workers interpreted it differently. The next day the workers in his section of the plant took him aside and told him that they felt bad that he had been left out. They explained that they thought the oversight was because he was not the head of a family as they were and thus didn't need the gift as much. Then they presented him with a ham that they had purchased during lunch with money they had collected from the other workers. Interestingly, although the two meanings were very different, they both recognized that the ceremony was meaningful to the owner and workers alike. Like all symbolic forms, ceremonies can be interpreted in many different ways and their power to motivate and control employees depends on the extent to which they are perceived to be meaningful and on the meanings that individual employees attribute to them. (For an extended illustration of the concepts discussed in this section, see Case Study 5.1 on p. 171.)

Emotion Regulation and Unobtrusive Control

So far we have discussed cultural control in terms of employees' thoughts – the ways in which they come to identify with the dominant beliefs and values of their organizations. But, human beings are not only thinking creatures. We also are emotional beings, and our thoughts and feelings are interconnected in fundamental ways. Emotions are relevant to cultural forms of motivation and control in three ways. First, organizations can overtly manipulate employees' emotions by telling them which emotions are legitimate

Case Study 5.1

It's My Party and I'll Do What I Want To[1]

In a study of annual ceremonies at a Philadelphia-area advertising agency – a Christmas party and an annual breakfast – Michael Rosen illustrates the subtle and powerful ways in which ceremonies function as forms of cultural control. Shoeneman and Associates' annual Christmas party has characteristics of work and a party. Although it was held after hours on the Friday before Christmas, attendance was required. No spouses or family members were allowed to attend (except the boss's family), and a formal program – a four-page list of the evening's activities printed on heavy yellow paper – was provided. But it also is a party. It was held at a rustic bar away from work, where people seem to eat, drink, and "make merry" with one another as equals regardless of their formal rank, and where the boss acts more like a host than like a supervisor – wearing casual clothes and circulating from table to table making small talk at each stop. But the tension between the two identities is also quite clear. As one married member put it, the structure of the event tells employees that "your work is your life, and these are your friends. It's so f— weird. There's dancing later. I don't want to dance with people that I work with." The party *did* require employees to be away from their families for an extended period during the most family-oriented time of the year. But, perhaps because of the timing – the holiday season – or the location, most of the employees seemed to think of the event as more party than work.

After dinner was over, the program began – a series of jokes and skits that are carefully prepared and professionally executed. All of them were funny; all were ambiguous; most made fun of the higher-ups in the firm. Together they created a joking relationship that seemed to help flatten the hierarchy of the firm. They celebrated the bosses' problems. All three top managers were going through divorces. The employees joked about them and presented a skit entitled *The Mating Game* (a take-off of the TV series *The Dating Game*) that included a voluptuous blonde asking pointed questions about the sexual appetites and exploits of the three divorcing upper managers. Other jokes and skits made fun of the managers' status symbols and of one manager's inability to keep secretaries because he was so obnoxious. The humor also commented on the pace and work hours of the agency – one skit raffled off a coupon for electroshock psychotherapy treatments, and many of the jokes were about the craziness of the work environment. They also made fun of other workers. One skit spoofed the large number of female employees who dyed their hair blonde; another made fun of the different attire of the business side of operation (dark blue suits and ties) and the creative side (almost anything else).

At one level, the humor made it seem that the organization's hierarchy had disappeared and suggested that the organization was a community of equals. After the program ended, the participants adjourned to the bar and dance floor. During this very informal part of the ceremony bosses and subordinates buddied around with one another, arms on shoulders, joking and laughing. Workers commented on how the skits and jokes had skewered the bosses. Some were even honest with management. The obnoxious manager asked the (lower-ranked) office manager what people thought of him. Thinking, "What the h—?" she told him that people think he is a bastard and is the most disliked person in the agency, something she admitted that she never would have said at work. She could get by with saying it on this night because they were at a party. In Western societies eating signals community, and drinking alcohol symbolizes freedom, especially from the drudgery of work. Parties are times of unusual license, and frictions encountered in the presence of alcohol tend to be forgiven. It *seemed* that the rules of the party were very different than the rules at work.

But, behind the scenes hierarchy and formal power/authority relationships were subtle, but still in place. People seemed to dance with one another as equals; but even during the most informal part of the party, the women (most of whom are secretaries) danced with males who were their own age or older and who occupied higher positions in the organization. The skits that skewered upper management were written by a skits *committee* only after a lengthy negotiation process, and were revised many times before being approved by the committee chair. As one member put it, "We really had to watch our asses, but we had a f— ball putting this thing together." A skit at the previous year's party had superimposed a picture of the boss over a picture of a farmer in overalls, boots, and pitchfork, with the title "Big Wally [their boss] Sells B—s— (advertising) Cheaper." Walter had made it very clear that the picture was out of bounds, primarily because it was a permanent record that could leave the party, not a joke or skit that could be remembered but not reproduced. Through censorship, the rules of the work game invaded the party game, and actions that were permitted under the party rules were not to be repeated "at work." In addition, much of the party celebrated and legitimized the rules of the work game. One of the most important work rules was that work comes before anything else – that all employees were expected to sacrifice their personal and family lives to meet deadlines and satisfy clients' every whim. Much of the humor at the party focused on the frenetic pace of the organization – even divorces could be celebrated, because everyone knew that they resulted, at least in part, from the demands of the workplace. Even the party itself required employees to sacrifice time that could be spent with outside relationships.

Interactional rules were constantly being negotiated, but negotiated in a way that maintained the underlying power relationships. Subordinates *could* make fun of their supervisors, but only in approved ways. Supervisors *could* fraternize with their subordinates, but only in ways that maintained the hierarchy of the firm. Supervisors *could* ask for frank reports on how they were perceived by others; but they alone could decide what to do with that information. Subordinates *could* give frank responses, but only in private and only when asked. Some kinds of communication were out of bounds and other kinds were permitted. Although the bounds were different at the party than they were at work, boundaries did exist, and in negotiating them everyone was reminded that underneath it all was a power relationship that could not be challenged.

While the Christmas ceremony was a party that retained vestiges of the power and authority relationships at work, the breakfast ceremony was work with some of the trappings of a party. Held at one of Philadelphia's most posh hotels, everyone – even the servers – were dressed in formal attire. In one way everyone was alike – even the lowliest employee could experience opulence at least once a year just by being part of the team. For a moment, even they were being served. But in other ways the opulence focused attention on hierarchy – everyone knew that most of the employees could never have afforded this place on their salaries, and that for a short time everyone was looking and consuming *as if they were managers*, not as if they were regular employees. It also obscured differences between the business and artistic sides of the organization.

After breakfast, the speeches started. Unlike the Christmas party, the boss (Walter) was clearly and overtly in control of the entertainment part of this ritual. Walter congratulated everyone for the firm's success and noted that it occurred in spite of a recession, in spite of "problems" in the public relations division, and because of their hard work and sacrifice (late hours and frenetic work pace). Walter gave gifts to retirees and recognized their loyalty to the firm. Walter talked about the "things the agency does for *us*," like funding the pension program (not mentioning that the "agency" [that is, Walter] has a legal obligation to do so, that "it" did so instead of giving year-end bonuses that were customary in other advertising agencies and once had been customary at Shoeneman's, or that it could do so because of the dedication and skills of the workers). After a slide show that made fun of the creative side of the firm, Walter announced that the money that would have gone to bonuses reluctantly had to be retained "for the good of the firm." Although managers would benefit from the decision, because it would increase the value of their stock in the firm, it meant that the workers' incomes actually fell because of the effects of inflation. And, raises and bonuses would occur only when management decided that they should be given, and no one knew when that might happen. One accountant referred to this tendency to leave potentially troubling details out of his announcements about the munificence of management as a "Walterism."

Finally, the vice president of public relations spoke. He talked about how important the division was, admitted that it had problems and failures, and confessed that all of those problems were his fault. For him, the breakfast was a degradation ceremony; for others, it was a time of enhancement. After the confessional, Walter returned to the podium and led the celebrants in a pep rally, focusing on telling versus listening ("If everyone in this agency told and listened, we'd have 15 percent more revenue"), me versus we ("If we can get all of the ambitions of the Me under the We, Shoeneman and Associates could add another 15 to 20 percent to our revenues"), and drive/win ("Laid-back people have no place in this agency . . . drive is what it takes to win . . . let's get back to work").

Although still subtle, the discourse at breakfast enacted the organization's power relationships in a much more overt form than the Christmas party. *Walter* decided who would be rewarded, who would be chastised, and who would be allowed to talk. *Walter* defined and celebrated the values of the organization and legitimized them in terms of increased revenues. And *Walter* decided how those revenues would be distributed. Although at least some of the employees understood all of these things, they said nothing, for saying nothing is how *they* play the Walter game.

Applying What You've Learned

1. What were the taken-for-granted assumptions about supervisor–subordinate relationships at Schoeneman's?
2. How did the behaviors at the parties enact those rules? How did they undermine them?

Questions to Think About and Discuss

1. Rosen argues these political rituals are important because they obscure the organizational power relationships while enforcing them. How would the employees' interpretations and responses have been different if Walter had been overt and direct about his expectations about employee performance and his evaluations of their work? Why?
2. What would have happened if an employee who understood what was going on had spoken up? How would the other employees have responded? Why?

Note

1 This case is based on Rosen (1985, 1988).

(and which are not), what events they should (and should not) get emotional about, and how and when they should (or should not) display their emotions. The emotions may be positive, as in ceremonies of enhancement. Often employees receive recognition based as much on complying with the organization's demands as on making tangible contributions. In any case, public recognition of subordinates serves to solidify the supervisor's power position, because she or he makes the decision about whom to recognize and how to do so. Negative emotions serve the similar control functions. For example, many observers of the downsizing, outsourcing of jobs, and reengineering of tasks that have dominated US firms since the 1980s believe that the practices are designed more to frighten and control workers than to enhance organizational efficiency.[26] Creating and manipulating negative emotions reduces employees' self-esteem and makes them more compliant. They follow orders more readily and are less likely to see emotional manipulation as a control strategy. For example, stewardesses (the old-fashioned term for flight attendants) who had been made to feel shame about their age, weight, or sexual orientation were less likely to oppose management and/or support their union than those who had not been degraded. First-line supervisors who were made to feel embarrassed for mixing with their subordinates tend to withdraw from them and become more autocratic.[27]

Control also is exercised when employees learn to interpret emotions in ways that are preferred by the organization. Emotional responses are highly ambiguous. Fear and excitement *feel* very much the same, so they have to be interpreted. The core beliefs and values of an organization often include taken-for-granted assumptions that tell employees how to interpret their emotional responses. For example, they may be trained to feel pride when the organization's goals are met, but not when their own objectives are fulfilled.

Finally, employees may learn to actually feel the emotions that are desired by their organizations. The process begins when employees are taught to obey particular **display rules** as part of their jobs. For example, people who work in the leisure and tourism industry are required to constantly display positive emotions and to elicit them in their clients or customers. Stewardesses, cruise ship employees, and resort workers are expected to be happy, perky, and concerned about meeting their customers' needs and making them feel happy. In contrast, bill collectors are expected to display negative emotions, such as disgust, to elicit other negative emotions (guilt) from the people they contact. Still other employees must display neutral (or no) emotions, even in crisis situations, to calm other people. No matter how trivial a call to 911 might seem to be (the Chicago-area 911 gets many calls regarding parking just before Bears' home games) or how much of a crisis is involved (people who actually have a burglar in their homes), operators are expected to remain calm, collected, and emotionally distant. Employees manage these demands in three different ways. They pretend to feel the emotions that they display, a process that usually is labeled **surface acting**. But, surface acting is exhausting and psychologically uncomfortable. It can lead to burnout, reduced self-esteem, depression, and cynicism. In many ways, it is easier to manage the dissonance and discomfort created by displaying inauthentic emotions by learning to actually feel them, to engage in a kind of **deep acting**. By learning to actually feel the emotions demanded by management, employees can increase their job satisfaction, enhance feelings of connectedness and community at work, and believe that they are performing their tasks well and having a major impact at work. This is why employees who have been in careers that require emotion management for a long time experience less dissonance and less effort than newcomers to a profession.[28]

Summary: Unobtrusive Control and Self-Surveillance

Both the traditional and the relational strategies of organizing relied on systems of motivation and control that are **obtrusive**, that is, known by and visible to workers. Indeed, if employees are not aware of and understand systems of reward and punishment, or of policies and procedures, or of job enrichment, those systems will not succeed.[29] Similarly, **concertive control** – when peers monitor and control one another in some kind of team arrangement – relies on workers being aware of and accepting organizational rules, regulations, and practices. Obtrusive control systems are difficult to administer because employees may interpret them in unanticipated ways, and because they often have unintended consequences. In addition, the more obtrusive a control system is, the more it robs employees of a sense of autonomy and the opportunity to be creative. As a result, they often choose to overtly resist obtrusive motivation/control/surveillance systems. In contrast, cultural strategies of organizing focus on **unobtrusive** forms of control. In effect, organizational surveillance becomes **self-surveillance**, a process in which employees act in ways that are desired by the organization because they have internalized its core beliefs and values, identify with it, and feel positive emotions when they comply with its commands. Since employees perceive that they are voluntarily acting in organizationally prescribed ways, unobtrusive control is simultaneously the most potent and most fragile form of control. Persuading people to change deeply held values, beliefs, and identities is an exceptionally difficult process. In addition, any number of events can undermine its effects. Organizationally sanctioned core beliefs and values will not be seen as legitimate if they contradict the experiences and messages that workers encounter outside of the work setting. In addition, negative events at work can lead people to critically analyze the organizations core beliefs. Resistance, even by a handful of employees can have the same effect. If any of these events lead employees to perceive that unobtrusive control is manipulative, it is likely to fail, and to alienate. As management scholar Gareth Morgan points out, "there is an important distinction to be drawn between attempts to create networks of shared meaning that link key members of an organization around visions, values, and codes of practice . . . and the use of culture as a manipulative tool" (Morgan, 1997, 151). In extreme cases, employees may "unidentify" with their organizations, and leave, taking their expertise, experience, and organizational intelligence with them. Consequently, organizations tend to rely on a mixture of obtrusive and unobtrusive control systems.

Case Study 5.2

Resistance and Control in Three Service Organizations[1]

As we have indicated throughout this book, resistance is an inevitable aspect of systems of motivation and control. This is true even of cultural forms of control, although in theory unobtrusive control is largely invisible, so it is less likely to generate resistance than other control systems. Sometimes resistance is overt and public. But, it is more likely that resistance to unobtrusive control will be covert. It may take place in private places and times, be sufficiently ambiguous that it appears to be compliant, or be disguised in complex symbolic forms such as humor. This case is about control and resistance in three service-sector organizations, a cruise ship (the *Radiant Spirit*), the kitchen of a five-star hotel (*Hotel*), and *Pairs*, an upscale, all-inclusive Caribbean resort. The names have been changed to protect the innocent – and guilty. *Pairs* and *Radiant* cater to people from all over the world, but primarily from Europe and North America; *Hotel*'s clients primarily come from the southeastern United States, but national and international conferences often are held by nearby organizations, so customers can be a diverse group. According to all three organizations' marketing rhetoric, from brochures to television ads, they are places where clients are catered to in every way. At *Pairs*, frontline employees, all of whom are black, are taught that they are to perform the "happy-go-lucky" attitude that tourists expect of Caribbean people. Employees on the *Radiant,* all of whom are white, learn to mimic the behaviors of the performers on the old television series *The Love Boat*, which means that they constantly are to be smiling and "perky." In both organizations, employees learn that the customer is always right, and that employees will act like smiling, happy servants regardless of the situation. One *Pairs* staff member said, "A guest coming here could be a thief or a murderer, but we have to be nice to them no matter what." Cassie, a *Radiant* employee, told about a man at the ship disco who

> asked me to dance. He was grabbing and holding me close . . . and saying these weird things

> . . . [like] 'have you ever thought of coming over to the dark side?" I just played dumb. . . . In this type of situation you don't want to piss someone off. . . . I didn't know what I could get away with and what I could not. I was so frustrated that I had no control. (Tracy, 2000, 110)

When Cassie reported the incident to her supervisor she was told to walk away when things like that happen. But, after a training program that included the motto "We never say no," she really didn't know what to do, and blamed herself for not knowing.

Both organizations supplement unobtrusive control with other forms. At *Pairs* each guest is given an evaluation sheet that includes a section where she or he is asked to comment on the performance of the staff by name. Twice a month the public relations office posts the comments for all employees to see. Cash rewards (recall the analysis of traditional forms of control in Chapter 3) are given to employees who receive many positive comments, and punishments are given those with negative comments. The *Radiant* uses a similar system, and it works so well that employees believe that the passengers are their "second bosses," who control the employees' actions and emotions. But their cash awards seem to focus on control as well as service – one employee won an award to suggest that mirrors be installed throughout the ship so that employees could constantly monitor their appearance. The employees themselves help discipline one another. *Pairs* posts summaries of customer comments. When the sheets are posted, the staff excitedly huddles together behind the reception desk to read the results. Workers read positive comments aloud for all to hear; workers with the highest points receive congratulations from their peers; workers with negative comments and low points are talked about behind their backs for the rest of the week. When Ken, a bellman, walked by the desk, Simone teased him by saying, "I don't see your name here." He immediately turned the pages of the report until he found a remark that included his name: "It only takes one," he said. If any of the *Radiant*'s workers complain, their coworkers will tell them, "It's a tough job. If you can't handle it, go home."

The control system does *seem* to work. Most of the workers are like Trendy, about whom *Pairs* workers commented, "I have never seen Trendy get mad. I'm not telling a lie. In all the years I've been here I've just seen her smile [when guests or supervisors are present]." A *Radiant* employee said, "Our job is to be happy, and there will be times when you don't feel that way. You have to put it aside and look as though you're enjoying your job" (Tracy, 2000, 106). The employees' performances are so fluid and so convincing that they seem to be scripted. But most of the workers see their performances as just that, a strategic way of behaving that fulfills management's commands while making their lives easier. *Radiant* employees complained bitterly that management shoved the customer service program down their throats. And, behind the scenes – in the galleys of airliners, the back rooms of resorts, and the tiny employee staterooms on cruise ships – "servanthood" is a different thing entirely. When safely out of the hearing of guests or management *Pairs* staffers often complained about customers who clearly were not "right." A *Radiant* employee told all his peers about a customer who asked if the ship generates its own electricity, and wondered "what if I would have told him, 'No, we run an extra long electric cord back to port?'" A US tourist asked Sandy if he could mail his postcards with US stamps. Sandy, in his best British English, explained that the guest would have to use local stamps "because each country uses its own stamps and postal system." As the guest departed, he immediately shifted into his local dialect and we talked at length about how little US residents, including his friends at school, knew about Caribbean or West Indian culture. In fact, one of the dominant topics of conversation involved the various failings of the guests – their stupid questions ("Why is it raining?" or "What language are the staff members speaking?" [the answer is English]), their arrogance (for example, one US resident who repeatedly demanded that the desk clerk check his bill for unauthorized long-distance calls after seeing his maid using his phone, even after being told that the maids *always* use the room phones to notify the desk when they have finished cleaning a room), their paranoia (the German couple who would not leave their luggage for a moment lest a staff member steal the tacky palm leaf hat, and the couple who demanded to know the location of the American embassy in case of civil unrest, something that had not happened on this island in almost a century), and their racism. Telling these stories to one another seemed to have three purposes – they place the worker in a superior role vis-à-vis the guest, thus reversing subservient role demanded by their organization; they help cushion the worker from negative comments by the guests, making it less likely that they will blame themselves when they encounter rude behavior; and, paradoxically, they allow the worker to continue to play his or her assigned role while simultaneously rejecting it.

The situation at *Hotel* is more complicated (Lynch, 1998). There are almost no "private" spaces in the kitchen, so covert resistance has to take other forms. The primary tensions are between managers, professional chefs, short-order cooks, and chefs in training. Chefs are highly trained professionals, and see their expertise and creativity as an important part of their identities. Managers may or may not have any culinary expertise, and are viewed at best as friendly strangers, and at worst as hostile intruders in the chefs' world. As the food service industry has been "McDonaldized," managerial values of efficiency and consistency have increasingly conflicted with professional values of autonomy and creativity (Fine, 1996). Managers often use humor to gain compliance while avoiding overt conflicts with the chefs. As long as they use teasing or practical jokes that are accepted by the "in group" in the kitchen, they can exert control without making workers lose face, become embarrassed, and feel an overwhelming need to defend themselves. Chefs asserted their own power when they played pranks on other chefs or cooks who were being lazy or inattentive. Some pranks served to solidify the hierarchy, as when a chef sent a trainee to the storeroom to retrieve a can of steam or when a senior chef heated up the handle of a pan being used by a lower-level chef who had developed a reputation for being lazy and inattentive. When the target, who had not been paying very close attention to his work, grabbed the pan, he burned his hand rather seriously. A morning ritual consisted of making the soup of the day. When it was finished, the responsible chef invited other chefs to taste it, which led to a boasting contest that enacted the chefs' legitimate right to comment on one another's creative efforts. But, if a manager tasted and admired it, the chef would respond by devaluing the effort and the compliment – chefs have the right to judge, but managers do not. Insiders were given humorous nicknames – receiving one and accepting it was a rite of passage that recognized a chef's special skill and symbolized his legitimate membership in the kitchen in-group. Managers were not given nicknames, and were roundly condemned if they used a chef's nickname. Naming became tied up with resistance in another way. A new manager decided that there was just too much talking in the kitchen. So, he decided to separate the talkative chefs by giving everyone an assigned work station identified by a name tag, much as an elementary school teacher would separate talkative children. Not only did this move challenge the chef's autonomy, but also it upset a production process in which they helped one another on matters of taste and creativity. The chefs responded by having the personnel department make them all nametags that said "John." When the manager walked in the next day, expecting to see his new plan in action, he wisely laughed and dropped his crusade.

The goal of this case study has been to contrast the overt, official meanings of employees' performances with their private, often resistant meanings. The greater the power gap between controllers and controlled, the more different these two types of meanings will be. If one looks at public performances and meanings alone, it will seem that unobtrusive control is total – employees' beliefs, values, and feelings *seem to* correspond with the desires of their organizations. But, if one also examines their hidden performances/meanings a much more complex picture emerges. Workers in all three organizations do seem to have internalized the core beliefs and values, of their organizations and do seem to be willing to enforce behavioral constraints on themselves and their peers. This is especially true in public but also seems to be true to some degree in private. But, they also engage in complex processes of resisting sometimes in public, and often in private. Organizational life seems to involve a "dance of resistance and domination" (Tracy, 2000, 99).

Applying What You've Learned

1. What evidence is there that the employees of these tourist organizations have identified with their organizations and roles in them? What evidence is there that they have not done so?
2. How does surveillance work in these organizations? Who does it? How do they do it, and with what effects?

Questions to Think About and Discuss

1. How do the various forms of control used at *Pairs*, *Radiant*, and *Hotel* support one another? How would the points or bonus system work differently if there was no system of managers watching the employees? No system of guests being encouraged to watch and report on the employees? No training program or messages that support the organizations' core beliefs and values?
2. What functions does resistance play for the workers? What effects does it have on the functioning of the organization? On the organizational control system? Why?
3. Some theorists argue that unobtrusive control soon will go the way of the dinosaurs. Recent trends toward short-term employment (recall Chapter 1) mean that employees will not be in a company long enough to even learn its core beliefs and values, much less identify with it. Others argue that people are getting more and more isolated from one another, so that their workplace is the only source of community that is available to them. As a result, unobtrusive control will be even more powerful. What do you think? Why?

Note

1 This case is based on Carnegie (1996), Lynch (2009), and Tracy (2000). Key sources for all three studies are Scott (1990) and Fine (1996). For analyses of resistance in a very different kind of organization, see Collinson (2002) and Roy (1958).

CULTURAL STRATEGIES OF LEADERSHIP

We noted earlier in this chapter that there is a key tension within cultural strategies of organizing. On the one hand they assume that organizational cultures can be managed strategically. But, on the other hand they assert that employees actively perceive, interpret, and strategically respond to their organizational situations. Thus, employees may come to believe, feel, and act in different ways than management assumed they would. Cultural strategies of leadership recognize that this tension exists and strive to deal with it through what have been labeled "transformational" processes. The most important of these processes are called visioning and framing.

Visioning and Transformational Leadership

Both transformational and transactional leaders are characterized by their consideration for employees and their needs, by their willingness to actively involve their subordinates in decision making (even encouraging them to question the basic assumptions of the organization or unit), and by their willingness to supervise loosely. Both forms of leadership involve similar communicative strategies: Leaders clarify the challenges that the organization or unit faces while encouraging, supporting, and inspiring their subordinates to use their own abilities to meet those challenges. Transformational and transactional leaders both maintain close communicative ties with their subordinates.

But, transformational leaders also differ from transactional leaders. Their authority is based on what Max Weber called **charisma**, the image that they possess some divine, supernatural, or otherwise special talents or attributes. At the heart of charismatic leadership is the ability to create a vision of where the organization or unit is going and how it is to achieve those goals and persuade others to accept that vision.[30] Visionary leadership involves communicating a mission for the organization or unit that is noble or otherwise meaningful for employees. The vision encompasses each employee's hopes, desires, and so on (even if it requires the leader to sacrifice some of her or his own gains). Visionary leadership involves a great deal of impression management – displays of personal integrity and a willingness to take reasonable risks and give of oneself for the good of the organization and demonstrations of personal warmth and charm, including showing concern for employees and their nonwork lives (Gardner and Cleavenger, 1998). Transformational leaders are able to adopt their subordinates' creative ideas and actions in ways that further the mission of the organization or unit and do so without embarrassing them or claiming ownership of their ideas.

Of course, not just any vision will do. A **transformative vision** is realistic and credible. It is consistent with the history of the organization or unit and fits the realities of the current situation, and it is attractive. It provides goals that beckon commitment and stimulate productive action. The genius of transformational leadership is the ability to "assemble – out of all the variety of images, signals, forecasts, and alternatives – a clearly articulated vision of the future that is at once simple, easily understood, clearly desirable, and energizing."[31] Visions provide a picture of the future, a sense of purpose, a framework for making sense out of events and actions, and guidelines for acting on an everyday basis. They allow each employee to find his or her own role in the organization, his or her own way to contribute to the mission, and in doing so, they release new energies and enthusiasm. They emerge over time, with experience, and through mutual consultation with subordinates. They are flexible and adaptive. They include long-term goals that help define a series of short-term goals, which in turn both guide and are influenced by goals that emerge out of everyday experience. For example, when Dr. Barbara Barlow was appointed chief of pediatric surgery at Harlem Hospital Center, her goals focused on successful treatment of patients. But she and her staff noted that many patients were hospitalized because of injuries suffered from falling out of buildings, playing on unsafe playground equipment, and improperly operating their bicycles. So, her goals changed to focus on preventative care as well as acute care – increasing the number of window gates in apartment buildings, teaching children safety rules and street smarts, and so on. Her unit now pursues long-term, short-term, and emergent goals simultaneously, and each kind of goal influences the pursuit of the others.[32]

Finally, visions are *appropriately* ambiguous. It is somewhat ironic that transformational leadership *relies* on ambiguity, because ambiguity complicates cultural strategies of motivation and control. When situations and symbolic acts are ambiguous, employees have much more freedom to reinterpret them and act in ways that differ from what the leader intended. But, ambiguity may be intentional and strategic. Employees from many non-Western societies, especially those in Asia and the Middle East are likely to have learned to be comfortable with ambiguity. If meanings lie in relationships and situations, formal, contractual obligations and explicit bargains are unnecessary, maybe even offensive. But, employees from Western societies probably have been taught to value clear communication. Their security stems from the "letter of the law," not interpersonal relationships and tacit commitments. Of course, regardless of one's cultural background, some situations do call for a high level of clarity and specificity – communicating technical standards for precision equipment, for example. But, in other cases, ambiguity may actually be helpful. It allows different people to interpret the same message in different ways, helping to maintain a diversity of viewpoints within the same organization. When the organization faces problems that are new or particularly difficult, or when it goes through major organizational changes, this diversity of ideas can lead to innovative solutions. Ambiguity may also allow parties involved in conflicts to avoid having to blame anyone for an impasse or escalation, thus saving everyone's face. It also may allow employees from multiple cultural backgrounds to successfully communicate even if they do not have the same definitions for key terms. For example, "teamwork" is an important dimension of both transactional and transformational leadership, but it means different things in different societies. In Japan it implies *loyalty* to one's company; in Sweden it refers to one's *membership* in a work group; in Anglo societies it evokes images of team sports – rugby, cricket, fútbol (soccer), baseball, or basketball – which require cooperation with one's own group and competition with (or even hostility to) others. Since these definitions differ from one another, ambiguity allows people to perceive that they are part of the same "team" even if they define the term differently. Similarly, good visions are both sufficiently focused to energize employees and give them a sense of direction, but ambiguous enough to allow flexibility. According to cultural/transformational strategies of leadership, this dilemma is managed through processes of framing.

Framing and Transformational Leadership

In addition to persuading employees to accept a particular set of beliefs and values, transformational leadership involves persuading them to see their organizational world in a particular way.[33] It may be as simple as persuading them to view a new situation as a challenge rather than a problem. The ambiguities of organizational life create spaces within which transformational leaders can act. **Framing** begins when a leader develops her or his own view of reality and makes sense of the organization's past, present, and future in terms of that view. It continues when she or he communicates that view to subordinates. In this sense, the key to framing lies in employees' memories. If a leader's interpretation makes sense and seems to be spontaneous, honest, and motivated by a legitimate concern for the organization and employees, it may be credible; if it is perceived as being manipulative, controlling, or uncaring, it will not be (Sgro, Worchel, Pence, and Orban, 1980). When employees later encounter a new situation, they will automatically approach it through the supervisor's frame of reference. Eventually the entire work group or organization begins to share the same way of making sense out of the world.

In some cases, members of the organization may develop a language that is consistent with their frame of reference. They will think in terms of a particular set of metaphors and categories, interpret events in accord with stories and myths that they share, and infuse their new language with beliefs and values that are especially meaningful. So, the key to persuading subordinates to accept a transformational leader's frame of reference is not overt persuasion. Instead, persuasion occurs when a leader uses a particular frame in his or her everyday activities to make sense out of events. By paying attention to some things and ignoring others, expressing honest emotions of anger in response to some things and joy in response to others, and reacting to critical incidents and crises in particular ways, we let other people know how we make sense out of life, and in the process we let them know what we really value. The supervisor–subordinate relationships that emerge can be empowering for workers, because they capitalize on enthusiasm and create feelings of significance, competence, and connectedness to others who share a common purpose (Fine and Buzzanell, 2000).

For example, a new resort was about to open. The employees were anxious because they knew about a neighboring resort that had recently experienced a disastrous opening day; everything that could have gone wrong did. Recognizing how nervous everyone was, the CEO convened a meeting of all employees and said,

> We have all noticed the bad press about [another resort's] opening day. You can't help but feel the pressure. Despite our confidence and all that we've done to get ready for tomorrow, you can be sure that something will go wrong. But that's not what makes a bad opening day. It's how you deal with what goes wrong that makes the difference. Tomorrow, you will see people walking around looking lost. You'll be lost too. Instead of sitting there feeling insecure, walk up to our guests and introduce yourself, Say, "I'm new here too, but I'm going to do my best to try to help you."

He went on to tell other stories about people bringing order out of chaos and thereby replaced the failure scenario that the employees had been circulating with a more positive one. The exchange helped put people at ease and contributed to a successful opening day (O'Conner, 1997).

Of course, leaders do communicate their frames of reference in more formal ways. During planning sessions, a leader sets an agenda for a group by guiding the discussion toward a certain set of priorities or suggesting that the group view a particular event or problem in a certain way. Leaders also send powerful messages about what they actually value when they appraise employees' performance and distribute rewards. But, the most powerful way to communicate a frame is by everyday behavior, by seizing what Fairhurst and Sarr call **leadership moments**, opportunities to suggest a particular way to view events, messages, and communication.

TECHNOLOGY AND CULTURAL STRATEGIES OF ORGANIZING

It is common to think of information and communication technologies (ICTs) as neutral products of science and engineering. Certainly science, engineering, and design are important factors in the production of technologies. However, ICTs also embody cultural assumptions and political influences.[34] Take the personal computer, for example. Until very recently the PC was designed for people with good vision; a person with a visual impairment was unable to use most of the features on a PC. Voice activated computers were an accommodation that developed in response to problems people with visual impairments had with PCs, which are still largely visual in orientation. PCs are also difficult to use for people who have trouble understanding or processing visual information of the type that appears on the computer screen. While most people younger than 50 find PCs fairly natural, to the authors' parents and to many of your grandparents the PC seemed unnatural and alien. Some of them never managed to grasp what an icon was or how word processors worked. PCs also are heavily oriented to those with good typing skills. Despite the graphical interfaces of most PCs today, the most efficient mode of inputting large amounts of information is still via keyboard. People who favor handwriting and have never learned to type and those who prefer or are forced to speak their input have been, until recently, out of luck. Further, PCs are organized around an office metaphor. Microsoft explicitly uses the desktop metaphor in its software and other operating systems implicitly model the computer screen as a table. For those who do not work in offices, this is an unnatural metaphor and it takes such users considerable time to master the desktop idea. Systems designed for use in warehouses and other active workplaces typically a type different interface, often organized around buttons, that seems more natural to these users.

It was not inevitable that PC designs favor vision over other senses or the office or table over other situations. Their makers were not forced to adopt these designs. The designers' thinking was channeled by choices that seemed natural and obvious to them, but also reflected certain values. The dominance of visual thinking in Western scientific inquiry tended to favor visual over other approaches to PC design. The IBM PC, which set the standard for design, was designed for office workers because this was the biggest market for PCs at the time, so a desktop metaphor seemed natural. However, as we have observed throughout this chapter, what seems natural to one person or culture may seem strange and artificial to another.

ICTs, like all cultural artifacts and symbols, play an important role in creating and sustaining organizational culture. They embody assumptions of the broader culture, as the PC illustrates, but they also are tailored to embody the organizational culture. In an organization that seeks to create a highly work focused professional culture, PCs in organizations are likely to have standard logos and applications, and the software on them and their use is likely to be tightly controlled by the information systems department. An organization with a looser culture that looks to its employees for creativity may allow users to put whatever graphic – however strange or irreverent – on their PC screen and allow employees to play computer games and surf the internet while they incubate ideas.

Organizations also use ICTs to symbolize and shape their cultures. Over the past five years, customer relationship management (CRM) systems, a type of work integration ICT that enables companies to keep track of and provide enhanced customer service, have been growing in popularity. Implementing a CRM requires the organization to redesign how its employees work with customers and this often requires redesigning the entire work process. For example, a CRM enables companies to identify their most loyal customers and calls up a special script for dealing with them, which may contain special offers or extra services. Installing a CRM is a strong signal that the organization has a customer service orientation and is cultivating a customer-centered culture. Some organizations use this to reinforce already existing aspects of their cultures, while others may implement a CRM in an effort to change their culture. The CRM not only changes member behavior, but also is an expensive and potent symbol of the value of customer service.

Culture also has a reciprocal effect on ICTs. ICTs not in line with organizational culture will often meet with resistance. For example, a university system whose culture stressed the autonomy of local campuses attempted to implement a financial management system that was uniform across all units in the system. The new system met considerable resistance from the campuses, especially those that were large and brought in large amounts of research funding. The end result was that three of the 20 units in the system did not use the system and some of the other units used it, but kept their own unique accounting systems that ran in parallel with the financial management system (Chae and Poole, 2003).

ICTs are also used differently in different organizational cultures. An interesting study of a computerized calendar system found that use varied according to organizational culture. An organization with a very work oriented, rigid culture used the calendar system as a control device. They set it so that everyone could see everyone else's calendars. In this culture a blank spot on an employee's calendar was interpreted to indicate that the employee was free for a meeting or (worse) that he or she was not working hard enough. And heaven help the employee who typed "gone golfing" into a time period when others were working. In a different organization whose culture emphasized autonomy and flexibility, calendars were used quite differently. Large blank spaces were interpreted to mean the employee was taking some time to think through a new idea or design a new product. Managers did not check calendars to make sure they were filled and the employee was working hard. Instead the calendar was mainly used as a coordination device for the many meetings required in this participatory culture.

THINKING CRITICALLY ABOUT CULTURAL STRATEGIES

There is no question that cultural strategies of organizing have dominated management thinking during the past 20 years. For example, Tom Peters and Robert Waterman's *In Search of Excellence*, one of the founding documents of the cultural strategy, sold more copies in English than any other book save the *Living Bible*, a total of 5 million copies within a decade. When combined with income from sequels, media events, and consulting contracts, it generated an annual income for its first author larger than that of many small nations (Kleiner, 1996). It also is clear that the popularity of the strategy resulted primarily from the promise that its use would increase organizational performance, and do so at minimal financial cost. Unfortunately, after scores of related studies, the evidence of a link between cultural strategies and organizational performance is far from convincing. Even the initial research supporting the perspective has lost its credibility. Twenty years after *In Search of Excellence* was published, Peters admitted that he and Waterman had invented the "data" used to link their leadership advice to organizational performance:

> This is pretty small beer [unimportant], but for what it's worth, okay, I confess: We faked the data. A lot of people suggested it at the time. The big question was, how did you end up viewing these companies as "excellent" companies? A little while later, when a bunch of the "excellent" companies started to have some down years, that also became a huge accusation.

Peters's confession came as no surprise to academics who had questioned the book's database from its first appearance on the scene.[35]

The weak relationship between culture–management strategies and organization performance seems to result from three factors. As advocates of the *organizational* culture framework argued, employees are active, thinking agents. Consequently, "the CEO, president, founder, or the top management team cannot dictate all aspects of an organization's culture. . . . No one person or team can control the communicative activity of all organizational members. . . . Culture is self-organizing, and always evolving – being shaped and reshaped, but never in an absolute way" (Keyton, 2005, 73). Second, even if managers could successfully use cultural strategies to impose their preferred beliefs, values and so on, and even if doing so led to high levels of motivation and performance, there are many other factors that contribute to organizational performance. Economic conditions, technological changes, and organizational decision making all influence outcomes – in short, if a strong culture organization is making a product that no one any longer wants to buy, it does not matter how motivated or loyal its workforce is. Third, if everyone in an organization actually does strongly adhere to upper management's preferred set beliefs, values, and frame of references, the organization may find it very difficult to adapt and change when conditions warrant its doing so (we discuss the complexities of planned organizational change in Chapter 7). So, an organizational culture that generates positive returns at one point in time actually may reduce the firm's performance at a later date. Finally, if it is as easy to use cultural strategies as the corporate culture perspective says it is, there is no reason why *every* organization in a particular sector of the economy cannot do so. Indeed, as our discussion of institutionalization and institutional theory in Chapter 1 pointed out, organizations in the same sector tend to adopt similar strategies. But, if all of the competing organizations implement the same strategy, no organization gains a long-term competitive advantage.

However, these limiting factors do not warrant rejecting the concept of *organizational* culture. Just as the taken-for-granted assumptions of overall cultures guide and constrain their citizens' actions, the key characteristics of an organization's culture also influence employees' choices and actions. But, those choices are influenced by a number of factors and processes. One, but only one, of those factors is communication by upper management. What managers say is important, but its effects may be very different than what they intended. Organizations do develop distinctive cultures, and in some cases those cultures can give them a competitive advantage. But, the advantage stems from the people who make up the organization, and the unique combination of expertise, insight, and cooperative action that emerge over time within them, not because of a perspective imposed by upper management.[36]

NOTES

1 See Fineman (1999), and Miller, Considine, and Garner (2007).

2 For an interesting analysis of the link between organizational culture and sense making, with an application to an important issue, see Dougherty and Smyythe (2004).

3 See Barley, Meyer, and Gash (1988). The popularity of the perspective is explained in Conrad (1985).

4 Although the work of a large number of social theorists served as the basis of this perspective, the most important one was Anthony Giddens and his theory of structuration (see Giddens, 1984; Conrad and Haynes, 2000).

5 See Geertz (1973), Keyton (2005), Eisenberg and Riley (2001), Sackman (1997), and Carbaugh (1988a, 1988b).

6 Also see Alvesson and Berg (1991); Parker (2000); Mills, Bgoylstein, and Lorean (2002); Schein (1992); Martin (1992); Schoenberger (1997); and Stackman, Pinder, and Conner (2000).

7 Karl Weick has argued that decentralization and participation are necessary for cultural strategies to succeed (1987). Also see Weick (2000).

8 For an extended analysis of the development of the cultural strategy, see Eisenberg and Riley (2001). The primary proponents of this view were Tom Peters and Robert Waterman (1982), Deal and Kennedy (1982), Ouchi (1981), and Ouchi and Jaeger (1978). Peters and Waterman's (1982) *In Search of Excellence* still is the most popular book on organizations ever published. It generated a series of follow-up books, videotapes, and consulting programs, and by 1987, three years after its publication, Peters's consulting firm was grossing about $3.5 million. The dominance of the perspective is examined by Barley, Meyer, and Gash (1988).

9 See Parker (2000); Ouchi and Wilkins (1983); Gregory (1983); Hatch (1997); and Willinghanz, Hart, and Leichty (2003). For an interesting example of how subcultures "play out," see Rosenfeld, Richman, and May (2004).

10 For examples of subcultural differences, see Rosen (1985), Young (1989), and Baxter (1994).

11 This concept was introduced into communication studies by Kenneth Burke (1945, 1949). It is central to the concept of organizational identification that we will examine later in this chapter. For an analysis of the impact that simultaneous membership in multiple communication networks has on subcultures and individuals, see Gregory (1983), Isaac and Pitt (2001), and Kuhn and Nelson (2002).

12 The entry experience usually is thought of as occurring in stages, but doing so can easily be misleading. It is made up of the processes that occur throughout a person's experience in an organization – they are continuous and overlapping, and do not occur in a fixed sequence. There do seem to be key "turning points" that, in retrospect, signaled the declining importance of some thoughts, emotions, and communication processes and the increased importance of others (Barge and Musambria, 1992; Bullis and Bach, 1989). Excellent summaries of research on the entry experience include Miller and Jablin (1991), and Jablin (2000). Two classic articles are Louis (1980) and van Maanen and Schein (1979).

13 For analyses of proactive communication by newcomers, see Kramer (1993); Miller and Jablin (1991); Comer (1991); and Kramer, Callister, and Turban (1995).

14 A summary of these personality variables is available in Albrecht and Bach (1996, esp. chap. 7). Also see Edwards (1990) and Louis (1990). Personality variables seem to not be important for people involved in job transfers (see Jablin and Kramer, 1998).

15 Cited in Gibson and Papa (2000). The classic study of anticipatory socialization of blue-collar workers is Sennett and Cobb (1972). For a similar case study in organizational control at the US Forest Service, see Bullis and Tompkins (1989). For analyses of the processes through which identification occurs, see Pratt (2000).

16 Ralston and Kirkwood (1995). It also is disorienting when the organization changes around its employees, which often happens during mergers and acquisitions (see Pepper and Larson, 2006).

17 For an excellent, communication-centered model of the different phases involved in entering an organization, see Wilson (1984).

18 The Exxon example is developed by Dutton and Dukerich (1991). Also see Dutton, Dukerich, and Harquail (1994); and Dukerich, Golden, and Shortell (2002). The BP observations are based on Charles Conrad's conversations with friends who work for oil companies in Texas; and the NASA example is explained by Kauffman (1997). For an additional example of the link between identification and organizational image, see Gioia and Thomas (1996), and Aust (2004).

19 See Ashcraft and Alvesson (2007), and Clair (1999). Also see Cheney (1991); Scott, Corman, and Cheney (1998); Larkey and Morrill (1995); and Scott (1997).

20 See Gargiulo (2005). A number of sources have investigated the relationship between stories and cultures, organizational and otherwise. An extended treatment of the relationship between stories and societal control is available in Mumby (1993). For extended analyses of organizational stories, see Trice and Beyer (1993). For an extended distinction between lists and stories, see Browning (1992) and Weick and Browning (1986).

21 Keyton (2005) examines the story-worthiness of organizational events. The standard analysis of story credibility was presented in Fisher (1984).

22 The distinction between stories and storytelling is developed at length in Pacanowsky and O'Donnell-Trujillo (1983), and in Pacanowsky (1989). Also see Knuf (1994) and Boje (1991). For analysis of the interrelationships among power, politics, stories, and storytelling, see Coopman and Meidlinger (2000), Mumby (1988), and Putnam and Fairhurst (2001).

23 Hollihan and Riley (1987). For a similar analysis of a group that has more positive outcomes, see D.F.

Witmer's (1997) study of an Alcoholics Anonymous group.

24 For valuable models of organizational humor, see Collinson (2002), Holmes (2000), and Holmes and Marra (2006). Excellent case studies in organizational humor include Boje (1991); Lynch (2009); and Tracy, Myers, and Scott (2006).

25 See Trice and Beyer (1984). For an excellent analysis of the ritualized nature of the concept of communicating via the chain of command, see Golding (1996).

26 See Tourish, Paulsen, and Bordie (2004). Also see Casey, Miller, and Johnson (1997); Kets deVries, and Balzazs (1997); Burke and Cooper (2000); Boje (1997); Grint (1994); and Grint and Case (1998).

27 See Flam (1993). For the examples presented in this section, and others, see Planalp, Hafen, and Adkins (2000).

28 Emotion management has become a major focus for organizational communication scholars (for a summary of work before 2000, see Kruml and Geddes, 2000; for a post-2000 update, see Miller, Considine, and Garner, 2007). The classic studies were by sociologist Arlie Hochschild's *The Managed Heart* (1983), which focused on stewardesses (flight attendants), and management scholar Gideon Kunda's *Engineering Culture* (1992). Alexandra Murphy (1998) revisited flight attendants. Additional exemplars include Sarah Tracy (2000, 2005), Tracy and Tracy (1998), Miller and Koesten (2008), Shuler and Sypher (2000: 50–89), and Ashford and Humphrey (1993).

29 The ideas that we will present in this section are similar to those of Mats Alvesson (1994).

30 See Barge (1994); Bass (1985); Hackman and Johnson (1991); Pavitt, Whitchurch, Glurg, and Peterson (1995: 243–264); and Bennis, Parikh, and Lessem (1994).

31 Bennis *et al.* (1994, 58); also see Senge (1990).

32 The example and the analysis of different kinds of goals are from Gail Fairhurst and Robert Sarr (1996), who based their analysis on Wilson and Putnam (1990). Also see Hellman (1995). An excellent discussion of the need for visions and goals to be adaptive and flexible is available in Hitt, Keats, Harback, and Nixon (1994).

33 The best treatment of the concepts discussed in this section is Fairhurst and Sarr (1996), and Fairhurst (2005).

34 See Deetz (1990) and Chesboro (2000).

35 See Peters (2007). The "excellence" series even spawned a parody; see Chapman (2006). For an early critique, and summary of other early critiques, see Conrad (1985). For an extended analysis of the evidence linking cultural strategies and organizational performance, see Alvesson (2002); Cheney, Christensen, Zorn, and Ganesh (2004); and Siehl and Martin (1990).

36 See Barney (1986); also see Alvesson (2002), Sorenson (2002), McKenna (2003, 12–15), and Mitchell and Yates (2002).

REFERENCES

Albrecht, T. and Bach, B. (1996). *Organizational Communication.* Fort Worth, TX: Harcourt Brace.

Alvesson, M. (1994). "Cultural-Ideological Modes of Management Control," in Deetz ed., *Communication Yearbook 16.* Newbury Park, CA: Sage.

Alvesson, M. (2002a). "Organizational Culture and Discourse," in Grant, Hardy, Oswick and Putnam, eds., *Handbook of Organizational Discourse.* London: Sage.

Alvesson, M. (2002b). *Understanding Organizational Culture.* Thousand Oaks, CA: Sage.

Alvesson, M. (2004). "Organizational Culture and Discourse," in Grant, Hardy, Oswick and Putnam, eds., *The Sage Handbook of Organizational Discourse.* London: Sage.

Alvesson, M., Ashcraft, K. and Thomas, R. (2008). "Identity Matters." *Organization* 15: 5–28.

Alvesson, M. and Berg, P.O. (1991). *Corporate Culture and Organizational Symbolism.* Berlin: De Gruyter.

Ashcraft, K. and Alvesson, M. (2007). "The Moving Targets of Dis/Identification." Paper presented at the annual meeting of the European Groups for Organizational Studies, Vienna, Austria.

Ashford, B.E. and Humphrey, R.H. (1993). "Emotional Labor in Service Roles." *Academy of Management Review* 18: 88–115.

Ashforth, B. (2000). *Role Transition in Organizational Life.* New York: Psychology Press.

Ashforth, B. and Sacks, A. (2002). "Feeling Your Way," in Lord, Klimoski and Kanfer, eds., *Emotions in the Workplace.* New York: Jossey Bass.

Aust, P.J. (2004). "Communicated Values as Indicators of Organizational Identity." *Communication Studies* 55: 515–534.

Barge, J.K. and Musambria, G.W. (1992). "Turning Points in Chair-Faculty Relationships." *Journal of Applied Communication Research* 20: 54–77.

Barge, K. (1994). *Leadership*. New York: St. Martins Press.

Barley, S., Meyer, G.W. and Gash, D. (1988). "Cultures of Culture." *Administrative Science Quarterly* 33: 24–60.

Barney, J. (1986). "Organizational Culture." *Academy of Management Review* 11: 656–665.

Bass, B. (1985). *Leadership and Performance Beyond Expectations*. New York: Free Press.

Baxter, L. (1994). "'Talking Things Through' and 'Putting It in Writing.'" *Journal of Applied Communication Research* 21: 313–328.

Bennis, W., Parikh, J. and Lessem, R. (1994). *Beyond Leadership*. Cambridge, MA: Basil Blackwell.

Boje, D. (1991). "The Storytelling Organization." *Administrative Science Quarterly* 36: 106–126.

Boje, D. (1997). "Restorying Re-engineering." *Journal of Applied Communication Research* 6: 631–668.

Browning, L. (1992). Lists and Stories in Organizational Communication." *Communication Theory* 2: 281–302.

Bullis, C. and Bach, B.W. (1989). "Socialization Turning Points." *Western Journal of Speech Communication* 53: 273–293.

Bullis, C. and Tompkins, P. (1989). "The Forest Ranger Revisited." *Communication Monographs* 56 (1989): 287–306.

Burke, K. (1945). "Container and the Thing Contained." *Sewanee Review* 53: 56–78.

Burke, K. (1949). *A Rhetoric of Motives*. Berkeley: University of California Press.

Burke, R. and Cooper, C., eds. (2000). *The Organization in Crisis*. Oxford: Blackwell.

Carbaugh, D. (1988a). "Comments on 'Culture' in Communication Inquiry." *Communication Reports* 1: 38–41.

Carbaugh, D. (1988b). "Cultural Terms and Tensions in the Speech at a Television Station." *Western Journal of Speech Communication* 52: 216–237.

Casey, M., Miller, V. and Johnson, J. (1997). "Survivors' Information-Seeking Following a Reduction in Force." *Communication Research* 24: 755–781.

Chae, B. and Poole, M.S. (2003). *"A Tale of Two Systems: Technology Acceptance of Mandated Technologies."* Unpublished manuscript. Manhattan: Department of Management, Kansas State University.

Chapman, R. (2006). *In Search of Stupidity*, 2nd ed. Berkeley, CA: Apress.

Cheney, G. (1991). *Rhetoric in an Organizational Society*. Columbia: University of South Carolina Press.

Cheney, G., Christensen, L., Zorn, T., Jr. and Ganesh, S. (2004). *Organizational Communication in an Age of Globalization*. Prospect Heights, IL: Waveland Press.

Chesboro, J.W. (2000). "Communication Technologies as Cognitive Systems," in Wood and Gregg, eds., *Toward the 21st Century*. Creskill, NJ: Hampton.

Clair, R.P. (1996). "The Political Nature of the Colloquialism, 'A Real Job.'" *Communication Monograph* 63: 249–267.

Clair, R.P. (1999). "Ways of Seeing." *Communication Monographs* 66: 374–381.

Clair, R.P., Bell, S., Hackbarth, K. and Mathes, S. (2008). *Why Work?* West Lafayette, IN: Purdue University Press.

Collinson, D. (2002). "Managing Humor." *Journal of Management Studies* 39: 269–288.

Comer, D. (1991). "Organizational Newcomers' Acquisition of Information from Peers." *Management Communication Quarterly* 5: 64–89.

Conrad, C. (1985). "Review of *A Passion for Excellence*." *Administrative Science Quarterly* 30: 426–429.

Conrad, C. and Haynes, J. (2000). "Key Constructs," in Jablin and Putnam, eds., *The New Handbook of Organizational Communication*. Newbury Park, CA: Sage.

Coopman, S.J. and Meidlinger, K.B. (2000). "Power, Hierarchy, and Change." *Management Communication Quarterly* 13: 567–625.

Cooren, F. and Taylor, J. (1997). "Organization as an Effect of Mediation." *Communication Theory* 6: 219–259.

Deal, T. and Kennedy, A. (1982). *Corporate Cultures*. Reading, MA: Addison-Wesley.

Deetz, S. (1990). "Representation of Interests and the New Communication Technologies," in Medhurst, Gonzales and Peterson, eds., *Communication and the Culture of Technology*. Pullman: Washington State University Press.

Dougherty, D. and Smythe, M.J. (2004). "Sensemaking, Organizational Culture, and Sexual Harassment." *Journal of Applied Communication Research* 32: 293–317.

Dukerich, J., Golden, B. and Shortell, S. (2002). "Beauty is in the Eye of the Beholder." *Administrative Science Quarterly* 47: 507–533.

Dutton, J. and Dukerich, J. (1991). "Keeping an Eye on the Mirror." *Academy of Management Journal* 34: 17–554.

Dutton, J., Dukerich, J. and Harquail, C. (1994). "Organizational Images and Member Identification." *Administrative Science Quarterly* 39: 239–263.

Edwards, R. (1990). "Sensitivity to Feedback and the Development of Self." *Communication Quarterly* 38: 101–111.

Eisenberg, E. and Riley, P. (2001). "Organizational Culture," in Jablin and Putnam, eds., *The New Handbook of*

Organizational Communication. Thousand Oaks, CA: Sage.

Fairhurst, G. (2005). "Reframing *The Art of Framing*." *Leadership* 1: 165–185.

Fairhurst, G. and Sarr, R. (1996). *The Art of Framing*. San Francisco: Jossey-Bass.

Fine, M. and Buzzanell, P.M. (2000). "Walking the High Wire," in Buzzanell, ed., *Rethinking Organizational and Managerial Communication from Feminist Perspectives*. Thousand Oaks, CA: Sage.

Fineman, S. (1999). "Emotion and Organizing," in Clegg, Hardy and Nord, eds., *Handbook of Organization Studies*. Thousand Oaks, CA: Sage.

Fisher, W. (1984). "Narration as a Human Communication Paradigm." *Communication Monographs* 51: 1–22.

Flam, F. (1993). "Fear, Loyalty, and Greedy Organizations," in Fineman, ed., *Emotion in Organizations*. Newbury Park, CA: Sage.

Fleming, P. and Spicer, A. (2007). *Contesting the Corporation*. Cambridge: Cambridge University Press.

Gardner, W. and Cleavenger, D. (1998). "The Impression Management Strategies Associated with Transformational Leadership at the World-Class Level." *Management Communication Quarterly* 12: 3–41.

Gargiulo, T. (2005). *The Strategic Use of Stories in Organizational Communication and Learning*. Armonk, NY: M.E. Sharpe.

Geertz, C. (1973). *The Interpretation of Culture*. New York: Basic Books.

Gibson, M. and Papa, M. (2000). "The Mud, the Blood, and the Beer Guys." *Journal of Applied Communication Research* 28: 78.

Giddens, A. (1984). *The Constitution of Society*. Berkeley: University of California Press.

Gioia, D. and Thomas, J.B. (1996). "Identity, Image Management, and Issue Interpretation." *Administrative Science Quarterly.* 41: 370–403.

Golding, D. (1996). "Management Rituals," in Linstead, Small and Jeffcutt, eds., *Understanding Management*. London: Sage.

Grant, D. and Oswick, C. (1996). *Metaphor and Organizations*. London: Sage.

Gregory, K. (1983). "Native-view Paradigms." *Administrative Science Quarterly* 28: 360–372.

Grint, K. (1994). "Reengineering History." *Organization* 1: 179–200.

Grint, K. and Case, P. (1998). "The Violent Rhetoric of Reengineering." *Journal of Management Studies* 35: 222–238.

Hackman, M.Z. and Johnson, C.E. (1991). *Leadership: A Communication Perspective*. Prospect Heights, IL: Waveland Press.

Hatch, M.J. (1997). *Organization Theory*. Oxford: Oxford University Press.

Hellman, P. (1995). "Her Push for Prevention Keeps Kids Out of ER." *Sunday Examiner and Chronicle Parade Magazine*, April 19, 8–10.

Hitt, M., Keats, B.W., Harback, H.F. and Nixon, R.D. (1994). "Rightsizing." *Organizational Dynamics* 23: 18–32.

Hochschild, A. (1983). *The Managed Heart*. Berkeley: University of California Press.

Hollihan, T. and Riley, P. (1987). "The Rhetorical Power of a Compelling Story." *Communication Quarterly* 35: 11–20.

Holmes, J. (2000). "Politeness, Power, and Provocation." *Discourse Studies* 2: 159–185.

Holmes, J. and Marra, M. (2006). "Humor and Leadership Style." *Humor: International Journal of Humor Research* 19: 119–138.

Inns, D. (2002). "Metaphor in the Literature of Organizational Analysis." *Organization* 9: 305–330.

Isaac, R.G. and Pitt, D.C. (2001). "Organizational Culture," in Golembiewski, ed., *Handbook of Organizational Behavior*, 2nd ed. New York: Marcel Dekker.

Jablin, F. (2000). "Organizational Entry, Assimilation and Exit," in Jablin and Putnam, eds., *The New Handbook of Organizational Communication*. Newbury Park, CA: Sage.

Jablin, F. and Kramer, M. (1998). "Communication-related Sense-making and Adjustment during Job Transfers." *Management Communication Quarterly* 12: 155–182.

Kauffman, J. (1997). "NASA in Crisis," *Public Relations Review* 23: 1–10.

Kets deVries, M. and Balzazs, K. (1997). "The Downside of Downsizing." *Human Relations*, 50(1997): 11–50.

Keyton, J. (2005). *Communication and Organizational Culture*. Thousand Oaks, CA: Sage.

Kleiner, A. (1996). *The Age of Heretics*. New York: Doubleday.

Knuf, J. (1994). "'Ritual' in Organizational Culture Theory," in Deetz ed., *Communication Yearbook 16*. Newbury Park, CA: Sage.

Kramer, M. (1993). "Communication and Uncertainty Reduction during Job Transfers." *Communication Monographs* 60: 178–198.

Kramer, M. (1994). "Uncertainty Reduction during Job Transitions." *Management Communication Quarterly* 7: 384–412.

Kramer, M., Callister, R.R. and Turban, D.B. (1995). "Information-receiving and Information-giving during Job Transitions." *Western Journal of Communication* 39: 151–170.

Kramer, M. and Miller, V. (1999). "A Response to Criticisms of Organizational Socialization Research." *Communication Monographs* 66: 362–368.

Kruml, S. and Geddes, D. (2000). "Exploring the Dimensions of Emotional Labor." *Management Communication Quarterly* 14: 8–49.

Kuhn, T. and Nelson, N. (2002). "Reengineering Identity." *Management Communication Quarterly* 16: 5–38.

Kunda, G. (1992). *Engineering Culture*. Philadelphia: Temple University Press.

Larkey, L. and Morrill, C. (1995). "Organizational Commitment as Symbolic Process." *Western Journal of Communication* 59: 193–213.

Louis, M.L. (1990). "Acculturation in the Workplace," in Schneider, ed., *Organizational Climate and Culture*. San Francisco: Jossey-Bass.

Louis, M.R. (1980). "Surprise and Sense-making in Organizations." *Administrative Science Quarterly* 25: 226–251.

Lynch, O.H. (2009). "Kitchen Antics." *Journal of Applied Communication Research* 4: 444–464.

Martin, J. (1992). *Cultures in Organizations*. New York: Oxford University Press.

Martin, J. and Powers, M. (1993). "Truth or Corporate Propaganda," in Pondy, Frost, Morgan and Dandridge, eds., *Organizational Symbolism*. Greenwich, CT: JAI Press.

McKenna, T. (2003). "Culture as a Competitive Weapon." *National Petroleum News* 96: 12–15.

Miller, K., Considine, J. and Garner, J. (2007). "'Let Me Tell You about My Job.'" *Management Communication Quarterly* 20: 231–260.

Miller, K. and Koesten, J. (2008). "Financial Feeling." *Journal of Applied Communication Research* 36: 8–32.

Miller, V. and Jablin, F. (1991). "Information Seeking during Organizational Entry." *Academy of Management Review* 16: 92–120.

Mills, T.L., Bgoylstein, C.L. and Lorean, S. (2002). "'Doing' Organizational Culture in the Saturn Corporation." *Organization Studies* 22: 117–143.

Mitchell, M.A. and Yates, D. (2002). "How to Use Your Organizational Culture as a Competitive Tool." *Nonprofit World* 20: 33–34.

Morgan, G. (1997). *Images of Organization*. Thousand Oaks, CA: Sage.

Mumby, D. (1988). *Communication and Power in Organizations*. Norwood, NJ: Ablex.

Pavitt, C., Whitchurch, G.G., McGlurg, H. and Peterson, N. (1995). "Melding the Objective and Subjective Sides of Leadership." *Communication Monographs* 62: 243–264.

Pratt, M. (2000). "The Good, the Bad, and the Ambivalent." *Administrative Science Quarterly* 45: 456–493.

Putnam, L. and Fairhurst, G. (2001). "Discourse Analysis in Organizations," in Jablin and Putnam, eds., *The New Handbook of Organizational Communication*. Thousand Oaks, CA: Sage.

Rafaeli, A. and Worline, M. (2000). "Symbols in Organizational Culture," in Ashkanasy, Wilderom and Peterson, eds., *Handbook of Organizational Culture and Climate*. Thousand Oaks, CA: Sage.

Ralston, S. and Kirkwood, W. (1995). "Overcoming Managerial Bias in Employment Interviewing." *Journal of Applied Communication Research* 23: 75–92.

Rosen, M. (1985). "Breakfast at Spiro's." *Journal of Management* 11: 31–48.

Rosen, M. (1988). "You Asked for It: Christmas at the Bosses' Expense." *Journal of Management Studies* 25: 463–48.

Rosenfeld, L., Richman, J. and May, S. (2004), "Information Adequacy, Job Satisfaction, and Organizational Culture in a Dispersed-Network Organization." *Journal of Applied Communication Research* 32: 28–54.

Rothschild, J. and Miethe, T.D. (1994). "Whistleblowing as Resistance in Modern Work Organizations," in Jermier, Knights and Nord, eds., *Resistance and Power in Organizations*. London: Routledge.

Russo, T.C. (1998). "Organizational and Professional Identification." *Management Communication Quarterly* 12: 72–111.

Sackman, S., ed. (1997). *Cultural Complexity in Organizations*. Thousand Oaks, CA: Sage.

Schein, E. (1992). *Organizational Culture and Leadership*. San Francisco: Jossey-Bass.

Schoenberger, E. (1997). *The Cultural Crisis of the Firm*. New York: Wiley.

Scott, C. (1997). "Identification with Multiple Targets in a Geographically Dispersed Organization." *Management Communication Quarterly* 10: 491–522.

Scott, C., Corman, S. and Cheney, G. (1998). "Development of a Structurational Model of Identification in the Organization." *Communication Theory* 8: 298–336.

Scott, C. and Myers, K.K. (2005). "The Socialization of Emotion." *Journal of Applied Communication Research* 33: 67–92.

Senge, P. (1990). *The Fifth Discipline*. New York: Doubleday.

Sennett, R. (1998). *The Corrosion of Character*. New York: W.W. Norton.

Sennett, R. (2006). *The Culture of the New Capitalism*. New Haven, CT: Yale University Press.

Sennett, R. and Cobb, J. (1972). *The Hidden Injuries of Class*. New York: Vintage Books.

Sgro, J., Worchel, P., Pence, E. and Orban, J. (1980). "Perceived Leader Behavior as a Function of Trust." *Academy of Management Journal* 23: 161–165.

Shuler, S. and Sypher, B.D. (2000). "Seeking Emotional Labor." *Management Communication Quarterly* 14: 50–89.

Siehl, C. and Martin, J. (1990). "Organizational Culture," in Schneider, ed., *Organizational Climate and Culture*. San Francisco: Jossey-Bass.

Smith, K. and Simmons, V. (1983). "The Rumpelstiltskin Organization." *Administrative Science Quarterly* 28: 377–392.

Sorenson, J.B. (2002). "The Strength of Corporate Culture and the Reliability of Firm Performance." *Administrative Science Quarterly* 47: 70–91.

Stackman, R.W., Pinder, C.C. and Connor, P.E. (2000). "Values Lost," in Ashkanasy, Wilderom and Peterson, eds., *Handbook of Organizational Culture and Climate*. Thousand Oaks, CA: Sage.

Stohl, C. (1983). "The Role of Memorable Messages in the Process of Organization Socialization." *Communication Quarterly* 34: 231–249.

Taylor, J. and van Every, E. (2000). *The Emergent Organization*. Mahwah, NJ: Lawrence Erlbaum.

Tourish, D., Paulsen, N. and Bordia, P. (2004). "The Downsides of Downsizing." *Management Communication Quarterly* 17: 485–516.

Tracy, S. (2000). "Becoming a Character for Commerce." *Management Communication Quarterly* 14: 90–128.

Tracy, S. (2005). "Locking Up Emotion." *Communication Monographs* 72: 261–283.

Tracy, S., Myers, K. and Scott, C. (2006). "Cracking Jokes and Crafting Selves." *Communication Monographs* 73: 283–308.

Tracy, S. and Tracy, K. (1998). "Emotion Labor at 911." *Journal of Applied Communication Research* 26: 390–411.

Trice, H. and Beyer, J. (1984). "Studying Organizational Cultures through Rites and Ceremonials." *Academy of Management Review* 9: 653–669.

Trice, H. and Beyer, J. (1993). *The Cultures of Work Organizations*. Englewood Cliffs, NJ: Prentice Hall.

Tsoukas, H. (1991). "The Missing Link." *Academy of Management Review* 16: 566–585.

van Maanen, J. and Schein, E. (1979). "Toward a Theory of Socialization," in Staw, ed., *Research in Organizational Behavior*, vol. 1. Greenwich, CT: JAI Press.

Watson, T. (2008). "Managing Identity." *Organization* 15: 121–143.

Weick, K. (1987). "Organizational Culture and High Reliability." *California Management Review* 29: 112–127.

Weick, K. (2000). *Making Sense of the Organization*. London: Blackwell.

Weick, K. and Browning, L. (1986). "Argument and Narration in Organizational Communication." *Journal of Management* 12: 243–259.

Wilkins, A. (1989). *Managing Corporate Character*. San Francisco: Jossey-Bass.

Willinghanz, S., Hart, J.L. and Leichty, G. (2003). "Telling the Story of Organizational Change," in Millar and Heath, eds., *Responding to Crisis*. New York: Lawrence Erlbaum.

Wilson, C. (1984). "A Communication Perspective on Socialization in Organizations." Paper presented at the annual meeting of the International Communication Association, San Francisco, May.

Wilson, S. and Putnam, L. (1990). "Interaction Goals in Negotiation," in Anderson, ed., *Communication Yearbook 13*. Newbury Park, CA: Sage.

Witmer, D.F. (1997). "Communication and Recovery." *Communication Monographs* 64: 324–349.

Young, E. (1989). "On the Naming of the Rose." *Organization Studies* 10: 187–206.

CHAPTER 6

NETWORK STRATEGIES OF ORGANIZING

The connective mechanism that enables parts of the [network] organization to coordinate with one another and with other organizations is communication.

Janet Fulk and Gerardine Desanctis[1]

CENTRAL THEMES

- Over the past 50 years, there has been a transition from a production economy based on physical production of goods in factories to a knowledge society, in which most value is added through information and knowledge-related activities.
- The knowledge society gives rise to different types of organizations than did the production economy and to two new types of workers, knowledge workers and information workers.
- Along with the knowledge society came an increased rate of change in the growth of knowledge and in markets, products, and competition, much of it spurred by the globalization of the economy.
- The increased complexity and required speed of response has led organizations to emphasize flatter structures with more lateral links; a number of different types of integrating methods have been developed to coordinate these organizations.
- The network organizing strategy has evolved to handle very high levels of uncertainty due to complexity and rapid change in the environment.
- The network organization has four characteristics: flexible modular structures, team-based units, flat organizational design, and use of information technology to integrate the organization.

Strategic Organizational Communication: In a Global Economy, Seventh Edition.
Charles Conrad and Marshall Scott Poole.

- Motivation and control in network organizations are handled through developing trust and engaging in significant tasks and formal control systems.
- Network strategies of organization rely on leaders to be symphony conductors rather than top-down managers. The manager must be coach, negotiator, problem solver, and improviser, rather than simply a director.
- Several problems confront network organizations, including their complexity, a tendency for power to "recentralize" despite efforts at empowerment, and the disadvantages of permanent "temporariness."
- There are additional organizing strategies beyond the network, including the cooperative and the heterarchy.

KEY TERMS

liaison role
task force
integrating teams
matrix organization
telepresence
work integration technology
knowledge management systems
managerial linking role
media richness
symbol-carrying capacity
network organization
broker
virtual organization
cooperative
heterarchy

One of the striking developments of the past 30 years has been the increased instability, complexity, and turbulence of organizational environments. We discussed the roots of these changes in Chapter 2. There we noted that the growth of knowledge and know-how has increased technological change, and this in turn has sped up the pace of economic and social change.

Along with increasing rates of change has come increased complexity of organizational environments. Globalization of the economy has introduced many new competitors into the United States and, in turn, made opportunities available in many more places than was previously envisioned by most US organizations. The rapid change and growth in knowledge and technology have increased competition as well, as companies strive for advantage. The public, too, has become more aware of the impacts of organizations on the quality of life in general. As a result, organizations have to deal with increasing regulation, lawsuits from disgruntled parties, and consumer protests. As time goes by, the environment of many organizations becomes more crowded with stakeholders who are more tightly interconnected.

While organizations in the private sector, such as manufacturers, food companies, and retailers have been most immediately affected by these changes, they are reverberating through the government and nonprofit sectors as well. President Barack Obama has promoted an initiative to move the US government online, increasing transparency and speed of service delivery, as are state governments in the United States and governments all over Europe and Asia. In the United States and many other developed countries, government agencies are also having to compete with private organizations bidding to provide the same services. The same tendencies can be seen in nonprofit hospitals, charitable organizations, consumer advocacy groups, and many other organizations in the nonprofit realm. Indeed, the first decades of the twenty-first century seem likely to bring about changes in public and nonprofit sectors comparable to those in the private economic sector in the 1990s.

The upshot of these cumulating and accelerating changes is that many organizations must deal with extremely uncertain conditions. They employ changing technologies and face environments that are unstable and highly complex. None of the strategies for organizing that we have introduced is well suited for this situation. The most flexible of the three strategies, the relational strategy, is appropriate for organizations facing moderately high rates of change, but not the rates of flux that a significant number of today's organizations confront.

In the "good old days" organizations would have had to throw up their hands and cope as best they could. However, now there is a wild card – information and communication technologies (ICTs). As we have seen, ICTs open many options to organizations that were previously simply too time-consuming or costly. In particular, information technology has facilitated the emergence of the network strategy of organizing as a major trend in the twenty-first century.

NETWORK STRATEGIES OF ORGANIZATIONAL DESIGN

Network strategies of organizing are premised on the need to balance integration and change. As previous chapters have observed, a major purpose of organizations is to integrate the activities of many people and units to achieve goals too ambitious for smaller, informal groups or individuals. Organizations achieve this coordination by integrating members and their work through structures, relationships, and cultures, using strategies discussed in Chapters 3, 4 and 5. But as the world changes around them, organizations must change how they operate if they are to achieve their goals, and this often means that they must change their structures, relationships, and cultures.

A major problem faced by organizations is balancing flexibility needed for change with the structure needed for integration. An organization faced with a low to moderate amount of change in its environment can often effectively change simply by tinkering with structures, relationships, and cultures as described in the earlier chapters of this unit. A bureaucratic organization can amend its procedures and rules to take new circumstances into account. An organization using a relational strategy can involve its employees in a change program whereby they would diagnose needed alterations in relationships and implement them. Organizations also undertake steps – sometimes more and sometime less successfully – to alter their cultures. However, tinkering has its limits, and when the need to change passes a certain point, it becomes difficult to use the three strategies to integrate organizations.

There have been other times when organizations faced the need to integrate in the face of great change and uncertainty. The Manhattan Project, which created the atomic bomb in World War II, and NASA's project to put a human on the moon in the 1960s both confronted these conditions and had to develop new strategies and tactics for integration. These strategies have continued to develop, culminating in the development of the network strategy from a specialized approach to a common form of organizing in the 1980s and 1990s. To understand the network strategy it will be useful first to make a short detour to consider ways of integrating organizations.

Methods for Integrating Organizations

Over 30 years ago, Jay Galbraith (1987) identified a number of methods organizations use to integrate themselves in order to cope with uncertainty, and the list has grown in recent years. Galbraith was concerned with how the organization can reduce uncertainty about how to respond to changing environments to manageable levels while maintaining as low a cost in money and time spent communicating as possible. Of particular interest to us are methods for creating lateral relationships, those that facilitate communication and coordination across different units or organizations. One limitation of Galbraith's analysis is that it focused primarily on linkages within organizations. However, today linkages between different organizations are just as important. In this section we will discuss examples of three major methods for integrating organizations: structural integration methods, information and communication technology (ICT) integration methods, and legal integration methods.

Structural Integration Methods These methods rely on organizational structure and people to do most of the work of integrating the units or organizations. Structural methods differ in cost – money, time, effort – involved in implementing them, and we have arranged them in order of increasing cost.

Liaison Roles In this structure personnel are assigned specifically to link two units or organizations. This may be a part-time or full-time assignment. For example, the assistant to the director of a local social service agency was asked to be liaison to the County Health Department. This assignment took one day a week and involved keeping contact with the Health Department to ensure that the social service agency's soup kitchen and homeless shelter complied with codes and to represent the agency to the Health Department. By having a "person on the spot," the social service agency ensured that it had some input on the writing and enforcement of regulations. Filling the liaison role usually has beneficial career development consequences, because it broadens the liaison's outlook and sharpens his or her communication skills. The major disadvantage is that the liaison may come to identify more with the unit he or she visits than with the home unit or organization. This alienation can cause problems with coworkers and lead the liaison to put the interests of the organization they are linked to before those of the home organization or unit.

Task Forces As mentioned in Chapter 4, these are short-term teams set up to deal with a specific problem or project. Members are drawn from several different units based on special knowledge about the issue and the interests their units have in it. Task forces typically dissolve after a set time or when the project is finished. A key challenge for the team is to overcome communication barriers posed by the fact that its members come from different units (and sometimes different organizations) and have to deal with differences in experiences, terminology, and interests. If this problem can be surmounted, task forces often outperform other teams. When Texaco faced charges that it systematically discriminated against black managers, it formed a blue-ribbon task force to find the roots of this problem and work out a solution (see more on this in Chapters 10 and 11). The task force went to work, quickly made some recommendations, and was dissolved. Interorganizational task forces are also common. For example, standards for new technologies such as cloud computing services are typically worked out by task forces representing the manufacturers, government regulators, and professional information technology standards bodies, such as the International Standards Organization.

Integrating Teams Sometimes a problem or project continues indefinitely or recurs regularly. In this case, a dedicated team is formed on a permanent basis. Assignments to this team become a permanent part of the members' jobs. Many universities have ongoing committees dedicated to increasing the number of women and minorities they hire. These integrating teams have representatives from all parts of the university. In the technology standards area, some task forces have been in existence so long due to the complexity of the technologies that they have evolved into integrating teams.One company that designed integrated computer hardware and software systems had several teams working on different parts of its new System Alpha. To deliver System Alpha on time and in shape, it was vital that each team's work be compatible with that of the others. The company created an Alpha Management Team whose assignment was to coordinate the work of the System Alpha teams. An engineer who had informally worked on coordinating the teams involved in System Alpha was appointed manager of the Management Team. She was given a budget for personnel to test the compatibility of products that the different teams were creating and to provide extra help for teams having problems. This extra heft that the manager had enabled her to stimulate the teams to action, and System Alpha was delivered on schedule.

Joint ventures between organizations are often managed by integrating teams. For example, NASA and the 3M Company negotiated a joint venture to conduct materials engineering experiments in the vacuum of outer space. It was handled by a team of people drawn from both organizations and headed by a 3M manager.

Matrix Organizations Sometimes organizations face tasks of high complexity that require them to constantly adjust and coordinate the activities of a great many specialties and departments. In these cases it is useful to shift to a dual-authority system in which members of specialized departments are assigned to one or more projects and report to both the integrating manager of their project team and to their department manager. The most common type of dual-authority structure is called the matrix.[2] As Figure 6.1 illustrates, the matrix is literally a matrix structure in which members of project teams report to two managers: the project manager and their department manager.

To accomplish the incredibly complex and daring feat of landing a person on the moon, NASA developed one of the first matrix organizations. Members of various departments were assigned to one or more special projects. For example, a materials engineer specializing in forming parts from metal alloys might be assigned to the Nosecone Team for 50 percent of his or her time, to the Booster Team for 30 percent and spend the remaining 20 percent back in the Materials Engineering Laboratory. On both teams, the engineer would lend her or his special expertise in materials to creating the best possible nosecone or booster, working closely with other engineers and scientists with different specialties. Back at the home lab, the engineer could consult with other materials engineers about problems that needed solving on his or her teams and catch up on the latest knowledge in materials engineering.

The advantage of dual structures, such as the matrix, is that teams keep the work focused on tangible products and outcomes (nosecones and boosters). Reporting back to their home department helps members keep their skills sharp and keep up to date on the latest developments in their fields. So our engineer is kept focused on nosecones by the project emphasis of the Nosecone Team. Other members of this team keep the engineer from applying only a materials perspective to the problem and she or he will keep other

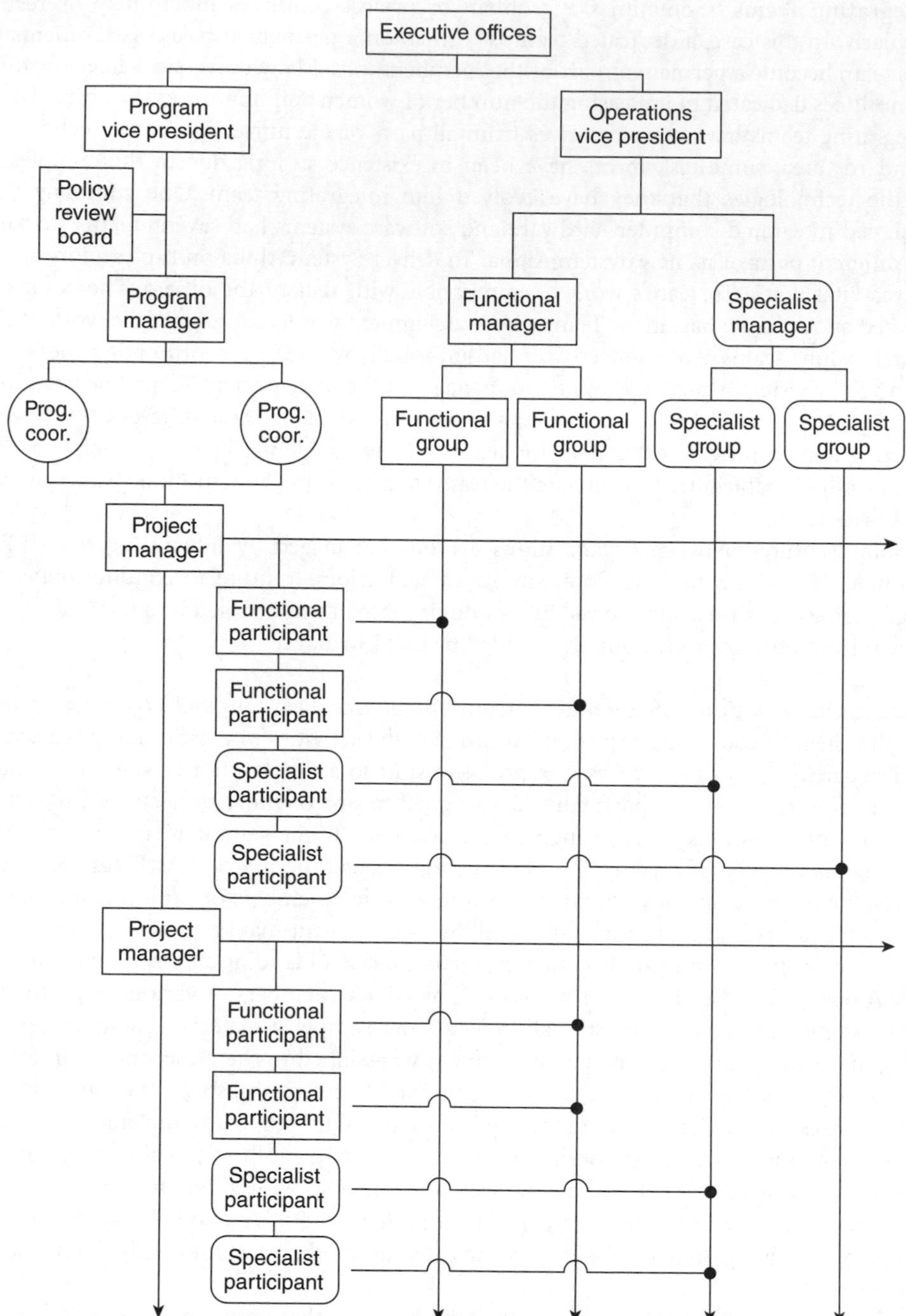

Figure 6.1 Diagram of a dual-authority matrix structure.

team members "honest" by making sure that materials issues are considered each time the team makes a decision. Upon return to the materials department, the engineer is able to consult with other materials engineers about the materials-related problems that the team has encountered. This sharpens the engineer's own expertise and makes her or him more valuable to the project team.

The matrix structure as a whole also helps ensure that the various project teams and departments are coordinated. The project managers meet as a team and with their integrating managers to ensure that the various projects come together into an effective whole. Using a structure such as this, NASA succeeded in putting a man on the moon by 1969, after starting almost from scratch in 1961. No one, not even NASA managers, thought it could be done. But the matrix organization was up to the task.

The matrix structure attempts to ensure effective performance on complex tasks by dividing them among highly focused project teams. However, to ensure that the personnel on these teams are highly qualified and current in their fields, they are drawn from specialized departments with which they keep in touch (Daft, 1989). The overall structure of the matrix coordinates the work of the various project teams. The glue that holds the matrix together is intensive communication. Through many team meetings, liaisons between teams, integrating teams across projects, and communication with functional departments, members of the matrix create a deep and complicated flow of information and ideas throughout the organization. For the matrix to work, communication within project teams and in specialized departments must create team and organizational cultures that promote open communication, innovation, constructive criticism, and high standards of excellence.

This communication-intensive organization has costs as well. Serving more than one supervisor can create ambiguities in the chain of command and tensions for workers who are torn between the mandates of two or more bosses. The requirement of continuous open communication can cause overloads and stress in its own right. Meetings, meetings, meetings can drive workers to distraction. And the solution to these problems is often even more communication. The matrix keeps all workers on their toes, but can be exhausting as well. In addition, this form works only if the integrating managers can coordinate the various projects, bringing them to completion on schedule so that one project does not hold up other interdependent ones.

Matrix structures proliferated during the 1970s and are still common today in large complex organizations. These corporate matrix structures have formal reporting systems (often utilizing ICTs) and use the matrix to organize the divisions of the organization. For example, in the 1980s Dow Corning set up a matrix in which the organization was divided into groups representing different regions of the world (Africa, East Asia, North America, etc.) and divisions representing the different product types the company offered (industrial chemicals, agricultural chemicals, glass, etc.). The units within Dow Corning reported to both group and division managers. For example, the manager of Dow's pesticide plant in India was responsible both to the division management for agricultural chemicals and to group management for South Asia, and this person had to draw personnel from functions such as marketing, which had a corporate-wide department. The rationale was similar to that for the NASA matrix: local plants need to be both excellent in their function (e.g. manufacturing pesticides) and responsive to their region (e.g., South Asia). However, at the plant or facility level within the matrix, each plant or facility was organized along either structural or relational lines, depending on what it did. For instance, the pesticide plant used continuous production processes similar to those in an oil refinery and was staffed mostly by professional engineers and mechanics and so used a relational strategy for organizing. Continuous adaptation, quality control, and problem solving were best served by the flatter, team-oriented relational strategy. A warehouse where pesticides were moved to facilitate marketing would more likely be organized in a traditional fashion, with managers exerting hierarchical control over lower-level employees.

The corporate matrix is thus a hybrid with a matrix for higher-level management and other strategies for particular plants or facilities. While it uses matrix principles to some extent, it has to a great degree sacrificed the flexible, open communication orientation of the original matrix structure. These days organizations needing flexible adaptative structures are more likely to adopt the network strategy, which will be described below.

ICT Integration Methods As we discussed in previous chapters, ICTs offer a wide variety of ways to integrate organizational units and organizations. Here we will mention some again and distinguish three different ways to integration organizations – through communication links, through work process integration, and through developing a shared knowledge base.

Communication Technologies As discussed in Chapters 2 and 4, technologies such as email, computer, audio, and videoconferencing, blogging, wikis, and instant messaging can be used to knit disparate parts of the organization together. As we noted, these technologies typically increase linkages both within and across units and organizations at all levels. They are advantageous for the formation of informal relationships and networks. But they are perhaps more valuable as linking methods when combined with one of the structural integration methods, as when a liaison uses email or a computer conference to maintain contacts with the units or organizations he or she is responsible for.

One technology that has matured in recent years is **telepresence**, videoconferencing that delivers very high-quality video and audio. It is expensive and requires specially outfitted rooms, but can be used to simulate in-person meetings at a distance because it delivers lifesized images of distant members that enable participants to pick up nonverbal cues that are lost in most videoconferencing systems. One participant in a recent telepresence conference commented, "I was in San Francisco looking into the eyes of people in New York, and it felt like they were just across the table. They were the right size to be seated across the table, their voices seemed to come directly from their mouths, and they sounded natural – not at all artificial, as they would with so many remote sound systems" (Dickenson, 2007, 47).

Today many integrating teams are "virtual teams" which maintain contact and meet mostly via email or conferencing because their members are spread over geographically dispersed units or belong to different organizations. They coordinate their work by using online document repositories such as Google Docs and Dropbox to share documents and wikis as online bulletin boards.

Work Integration We have discussed many examples of ICTs used to manage organizational work processes. Each of these, of course, offers a method for integrating the organization. So enterprise resource and planning (ERP) systems, electronic data interchange (EDI) systems, and office automation systems can be used to integrate organizational units and organizations.

For example, CNA Insurance Corporation uses a virtual office to integrate employees in its many units and divisions.[3] Any employee can access an intranet portal, which runs a steady feed of insurance industry news and company announcements, plus links to a corporate knowledge base and an e-learning area where employees can take training modules in different aspects of the virtual office. On the left of the portal are buttons that employees can use to go to the virtual teams they are members of or to go into the virtual office that has their applications, such as tools for calculating rates a word processor, and forms that can be entered into the office document workflow system. The virtual office also gives workers access to a general discussion space, project management and budgeting tools, and status reports on how the company and various projects are progressing. The CNA information systems department is constantly working to improve and further integrate this office portal.

Work integration can also link together different organizations. Jones and Stokes, an environmental consulting firm, uses an extranet to link staff, clients, and subcontractors from the Western United States to prepare environmental impact reports to submit to the EPA for major construction and reclamation projects (Robb, 2002, 30). The virtual office application used by Jones and Stokes has a library with thousands of references and manuals useful in preparing environmental reports. Once a document is authored, the virtual office application automatically notifies the next person in the workflow that it's ready to be reviewed and edited. GHX, the medical supply purchasing exchange discussed in Chapter 2, is another type of work integration technology that provides linkages among firms.

Knowledge Management Systems Developing a knowledge management system, as discussed in Chapter 2, offers another way to integrate organizations through technology. Whereas work integration systems link people and units through the common work they perform and communication systems integrate people by enabling contact and communication, knowledge management systems link people by building a common knowledge base that they can draw on in their work.

Intec, an engineering and project management firm that serves the petroleum industry, is one example of how integration through knowledge management can be done (Melymuka, 2003). In 2002 the company found that it was becoming more and more difficult to keep track of and access information and knowledge that had been accumulated over years and many projects. The company formed a learning team to put together a knowledge management system that would compile and make useful knowledge available so that Intec engineers could learn from one anothers' experiences and weren't always reinventing the wheel when they undertook a new project. The learning team put together a database system that integrated existing knowledge resources such as manuals and previous bids, automatically located experts on various topics, facilitated the identification of best practices, and captured information from engineers' work automatically, all with an easy-to-use interface. While this sentence makes it sound easy, it took the learning team over a year to do this and they had the assistance of an excellent knowledge management vendor. The resulting system enabled engineers to capitalize on the firm's knowledge and saved the company over $200,000, not to mention improving the quality of its work.

Knowledge management systems integrate an organization not by directly linking work processes or people, but by providing a shared resource that employees come to. When they draw on the system in their work, employees are bringing a common stock of knowledge and experience to bear and adding to it as well. The system is a growing shared resource for the organization, a contact point to draw its members together.

Legal Integration Methods **Contracts** are the third class of methods for integrating organizations. Legal agreements are, of course, a common means of specifying how two different organizations will work together. For example a building developer might contract with a food service company to bring its employees lunch on site. Traditionally contracts have been thought of as means of keeping organizations independent of one another: the contract specifies each organization's rights, responsibilities, and rewards and each treats the other as a separate entity. However, this is an idealized view of contracts and ignores the function of a contract as a basis for a relationship. The term "marriage contract" expresses the relational nature of contracts well. An effective contract not only spells out what both parties should do and their rights and responsibilities, it also provides a basis for trust, because parties know they have legal recourse if other parties do not meet their obligations. As the relationship between the parties develops, the importance of the contract may decrease, as trust and a lasting bond forms between them.

Contracts have often been viewed as methods of integrating separate organizations, as when one organization contracts with another for some service. However, many large organizations are moving to models that emphasize each of its major units as essentially its own organization with internal and external customers. The information systems department of an organization, for example, might have to bid competitively against outside companies for a job to develop a database for another unit in the organization. If the department wins the bid, it would sign a contract with the unit just as would an outside organization.

Contracts vary in how specific they are. Some are basically just "handshakes" that rely on the goodwill of both parties. Others are much more detailed, specifying not only what products or services should be delivered but also levels of quality and service. For example, when organizations contract with another company to maintain their computer network, it is common to put in the contract the bandwidth of the network, what percentage of down time will be accepted, and what penalties the provider will incur if these are not met. Generally the rule of thumb is, the more detailed the better when it comes to contracts. However, it is impossible to be completely specific and there is always interpretation and negotiation involved when people or organizations work under contract.

Which Integration Method to Use? Organizations often combine more than one integrating method. For example, an organization might employ an integrating team and communication technology to link personnel involved in a particularly important project. An organization entering a joint venture might use work integration technology for routing key documents, a managerial linking role to manage it, and liaisons between units of the two organizations that need to coordinate.

How does one choose among and combine these integration methods? One thing to consider is the cost of the method compared to the benefits it offers. Benefits of the structural methods depend on each method's effectiveness in handling the level of uncertainty the organization experiences. Liaisons and task forces are effective for moderate to moderately high levels of uncertainty. Organizations facing high levels of uncertainty will be more effective if they utilize approaches further up the list, including integrating teams, **managerial linking roles,** and matrix designs. But costs must also be considered: These include personnel expenses, the time spent learning to use the method and getting it to work smoothly, the information load imposed by the method, and the amount of stress members experience.

The ICT integrating methods also differ in benefits and costs, depending on the situation. Workflow integration will work better under conditions of moderate uncertainty, though it can be useful when uncertainty is high. Both communication and knowledge management ICTs work fine with higher levels of uncertainty. There are also cost considerations for ICTs. Integrating technologies that are already installed, such as electronic mail or internet applications that are standard, such as internet messaging, are less costly than purchasing a special system, like the knowledge management system used by Intec. Maintaining security for ICTs to avoid attacks or intrusions also adds to their cost, as does training users, providing support, and maintaining the systems. Contracts too have costs in addition to the benefits they offer in terms of uncertainty reduction. Monitoring whether the other party is living up to their side of a contract is one cost, as is enforcing the contract in the courts, if it comes to that.

From the cost–benefit standpoint, an organization should select the least costly method that meets its needs. For example, an organization in a very complex, unstable environment with a highly difficult task may have to choose a highly flexible, yet costly form, such as the matrix. On the other hand, an organization in a more stable situation that has one difficult problem may be able to handle things with a task force. A second variable is the degree of geographical dispersion of the organization, that is, how many different locations the employees and units that need to be linked are spread across. Organizations that are widely dispersed must often choose an ICT based linkage system.

Another variable to consider in choosing a linking method is the culture of the organization. The values, traditions, and history of an organization may predispose it to be more comfortable with some integration methods than others. Selecting a method the organization is not accustomed to requires a period of learning and change. For example, implementing a task force is not simply a matter of assigning people. More important is getting people from different departments that have very different views on an issue to work together. In organization that emphasize teamwork and inclusion, this will be easier than in those built around competition and individualism.

No single integration method will work under all circumstances or for all organizations. The balance among cost–benefit considerations, geographical dispersion, and culture depends on which is more important to the organization or the task at hand. In many cases, organizations settle on integration modes after a period of experimentation in which different methods are tried and rejected.

Limitations of the Integrating Methods The integrating methods have proven extremely useful. However, they do not offer a complete solution to problems of uncertainty. Many of these methods are suitable for addressing limited individual problems, but not capable of integrating organizations as a whole by themselves. The matrix and the ICTs offer solutions for the whole organization, but they tend to work best for moderately high uncertainty and not for extremely uncertain conditions that require flexibility. The matrix tends to become inflexible after it is used for some time. Members learn to think of it as a framework much like the bureaucracy, and the matrix is flexible as long as managers keep it so; but once they start to think about it as a standard operating procedure, it can become as much of a cage as a bureaucracy. ICTs offer some degree of help in dealing with high levels of uncertainty, but they must be supplemented by structural measures and contracts as well.

Box 6.1
Choosing Communication Media

All activities in organizations, including integration, depend on communication and communication occurs through various media. We have discussed the ever-growing set of media options available to members of today's organizations, including face-to-face conversations, face-to-face meetings, speeches to large assemblies, memos (handwritten and typed), formal reports and documents (similar to essays in form), recorded video and audio for wide distribution, telephone, fax, email, audioconference, videoconference, computer conference, web pages, intranets, interpersonal messaging, blog, and wiki. How do we decide which to use?

Trevino, Lengel, and Daft (1987) developed a framework for media choice based on the relative richness of the media. **Media richness** depends on the number of cues the medium can carry (verbal and nonverbal), the timeliness of feedback via the medium, the use of natural language as opposed to numbers or other information, and the degree to which the medium allows the message to be personalized. A highly rich medium would carry many cues, and allow immediate feedback, a wide variety of languages, and a high degree of personalization of messages. Less rich media are deficient in one or more of these respects. Based on this definition, media can be ranked according to richness as shown in Table 6.1. The media are arranged in rough

Table 6.1 Some Media Rated on Media Richness Dimensions

Medium	*Number of cues*	*Timeliness of feedback*	*Natural language*	*Personalization*
Face-to-face (ftf) communication	High	High	Yes	High
Ftf small group meeting	High	High	Yes	Medium
Ftf address to large assembly	Medium high	Medium	Yes	Low
Group videoconference	High	High	Yes	Medium
Telephone call	Medium[a]	High	Yes	High
Conference telephone call	Medium[a]	High	Yes	Medium
IM/SMS	Low	High[b]	Yes	High
Blog/wiki/website	High[c]	Low[d]	Yes	Low
Twitter	Low	Medium[b]	Yes	Low
Email	Medium low	High[b]	Yes	High
Paper memo to single receiver	Low	Low	Yes	High
Paper memo to broad audience	Low	Low	Yes	Low
Statistical report	Low	Low	No	Low

a. It allows verbal cues and nonverbal audio cues.

b. Provided the recipient checks his or her email, phone, or the like often.

c. It allows printed words, pictures, videos, audios, and links to other pages.

d. Since Wikis can be collaboratively edited, they can sometimes have highly timely feedback. If others are reading the wiki, they can give feedback in the form of edits or comments on entries right after they appear. Reports indicate that this is a common occurrence in Wikipedia, for example.

order of overall richness with the richest media at the top and the least rich at the bottom.

The richest medium is face-to-face conversation, because it allows people to exchange a wide range of vocal, nonverbal, and verbal cues, and receive immediate feedback; uses natural language; and can be adapted specifically to the partner. Telephone calls screen out nonverbal cues and thus are less rich than face-to-face conversation, but they still permit immediate feedback, use natural language, and allow some personalization. Email also screens out vocal cues and most nonverbal cues (except emoticons), but it allows immediate feedback, uses natural language, and allows a degree of personalization. Written paper memos sent to a number of people are low in richness (i.e., lean), because they use only a single cue, tend to elicit feedback slowly, and cannot be personalized.

Daft *et al.* posited that media should be selected based on the nature of the message, the need for response, and the cost in time and effort (note the similarity between their criteria and those for selecting integrating mechanisms). A simple, routine message that has low probability of being misunderstood and does not require an immediate answer or reaction (e.g., "Remember, our staff meeting is at 4 P.M. this week.") is most effectively sent via a paper memo or a broadcast email, because these are the low-cost alternatives. On the other hand, more complex messages, and messages that require immediate feedback or sensitive communication processes, such as negotiating or managing disagreements and conflicts, should be conducted in rich media, such as a videoconference or face-to-face small-group meetings.[1] In these cases, communicators need to monitor emotional responses and determine how a message influences their interpersonal relationships so nuances that can only be detected by paying attention to multiple cues and fast, immediate feedback are essential.

Subsequent research has suggested that other factors should be taken into account in choosing media. One important factor is norms regarding media use. Norms regarding what media are appropriate for different kinds of messages and different communication processes are socially constructed. Employees learn the accepted assumptions of their cultures or subcultures about media use the same way that they learn other assumptions – indirectly, by observing what other people do, and directly, through conversations with others, particularly those in their immediate groups (Fulk, Steinfield, Schmitz and Power, 1987; Rice and Gattiker, 2001). After an advertising account representative lost an important account because the recipient was offended by the brevity and impersonality of an email message, all the executives started using the telephone or face-to-face meetings with their clients. An engineer asked his associates how to deliver bad news to the manager of another division of the organization. One colleague advised using lean media for this message, another recommended using a written memo sent through the normal chain of command to signal respect for the other division, and still another told a story about what happened the last time an engineer communicated with the other division via a memo. Together, the engineers established a set of their own "rules" for choosing appropriate media. Although considerations such as the inherent richness of a medium are important, those considerations must be interpreted within the cultural context of the organization.

A third consideration is raised by Sitkin, Sutcliffe, and Barrios-Choplin (1992): One should also consider the symbolic impact of media choice. They note that immediate goals and norms are not the only influences on communicators' media choices. Instead, communicators also consider the **symbol-carrying capacity** of the medium. Symbol-carrying capacity manifests itself in at least two ways. First, media vary in their ability to transmit the core values of the organization. For example, an organization that values efficiency will find email, which can deliver a message almost instantaneously, a better device for signaling this value than snail mail: regular postal delivery that could take several days for the same message. Symbol-carrying capacity is also evident in the symbolic value that the medium itself comes to hold. During World War II, parents of a soldier serving at the front shuddered when they saw the Western Union delivery person, because the news of deaths was announced in telegrams; telegrams came to symbolize death and mourning. For many of today's communicators, using email symbolizes being technologically savvy and innovative; whereas sending the same message in a handwritten note indicates backwardness. Because the form of a message is often as important as its content, symbol-carrying capacity is an important criterion to consider in choosing a medium. Of course, organizational cultures and coworker attitudes also shape what a medium symbolizes. Symbol-carrying capacity may vary a great deal from organization to organization.

Together, richness, cultural norms, and symbol-carrying capacity provide a useful set of criteria to guide media choice. The only problem arises when the recommendations made by different criteria conflict with each other. Probably the most basic criteria is the organization's culture. There are indications that it shapes both perceptions of richness and symbol-carrying capacity.

One limitation of the media choice research just discussed is that it does not take the user's skill with a given medium into account. Even if all the criteria point to a face-to-face encounter as the most effective medium, a shy and retiring person may not be nearly as effective with this medium as he or she might be using email. Carlson and Zmud (1999) found that experience with a medium and with the organizational context in which it was used increased perceptions of the richness of the medium. So a middle-aged manager who is "all thumbs" with social media when instant messaging is first introduced in his organization might find it quite useful and fairly rich as he gains experience with it and sees how it improves speed of response to customer questions. And many of us know how involving and rich interpersonal messaging can be, once one gets the hang of it.

One final development related to media choice is an interesting theoretical analysis that suggests paradoxical effects of media on our abilities to think about messages critically. Lionel Robert and Alan Dennis (2005) argue that, in view of our brain's limited information processing capabilities (more on this is in Chapter 9 when we discuss decision making), there are limits on how much information we can absorb. They speculate that rich media are very good at motivating people to attend to a message, but that the very richness causes us to be less effective in analyzing the message, because the greater amount of input in rich media absorbs so much of our information processing capacity. On the other hand, lean media leave us sufficient capacity to think critically and analytically about the incoming message, but they are not as effective at motivating us to think about the message. So with rich media, if we want our receiver to think about what he or she is hearing, we must find ways to give him or her time to analyze what we are saying. And with lean media, we must find ways to impress the hearer with the importance of thinking about our message. Their theory has not yet been put to an effective test, so far as we know, but it is food for thought.

Note

1 When messages are not complex, personal preferences seem to determine which media people use (Trevino, Lengel, and Daft, 1987). For example, people with high levels of oral communication anxiety seem to avoid face-to-face media unless the complexity of the message absolutely requires them to use it (Alexander, Penley, and Hernigan, 1991).

The Network Organization

Network organizations are aggregates of organizations whose component units are assembled to meet a particular set of demands. They are referred to by a number of names including dynamic networks, federated organizations, "cloverleaf" forms, virtual organizations, and post-bureaucracies. Network organizations take a wide variety of forms: In some cases the units are from the same organization, whereas in others, different organizations comprise the network; some network organizations are assembled on a long term basis; but others are set up for temporary projects. The Japanese *keiretsu*, a dense network of interrelated organizations that develops lasting and stable business relationships, is a good example of a long-term networked organization. In the Japanese automobile industry, firms such as Nissan and Toyota develop networks of suppliers, shippers, and financial institutions that depend on the central firm's business for their livelihood and in turn give the central firm exceptional quality, effort, and dependable support.

Some textbook publishers offer examples of temporary, project-centered networks, illustrated in Figure 6.2. Older publishing companies have traditionally consolidated the acquisition of new books, their design and layout, printing, and sales in a single organization. More recently publishers have been farming out some, and in some cases all, of these functions. The publisher may acquire the book and then hire a graphics firm to handle layout, an independent printer to produce the books, and several firms, including the publisher's own staff, to market the book. Special types of books are produced for the publisher by smaller independent firms, themselves dynamic networks, often founded by former employees of the publisher who have gone out on their own. Publishing is a very different game today than it was 30 years ago.

While the example of textbook publishers shows how a number of different organizations can be combined into a network, large firms often create networks within themselves for special projects. One common case is when firms assemble temporary networks to develop a new product and bring it to market. The network might be put together by an integrating project manager who would assemble units for the project: Design might be carried out by a team assigned from engineering, production would be from a particular

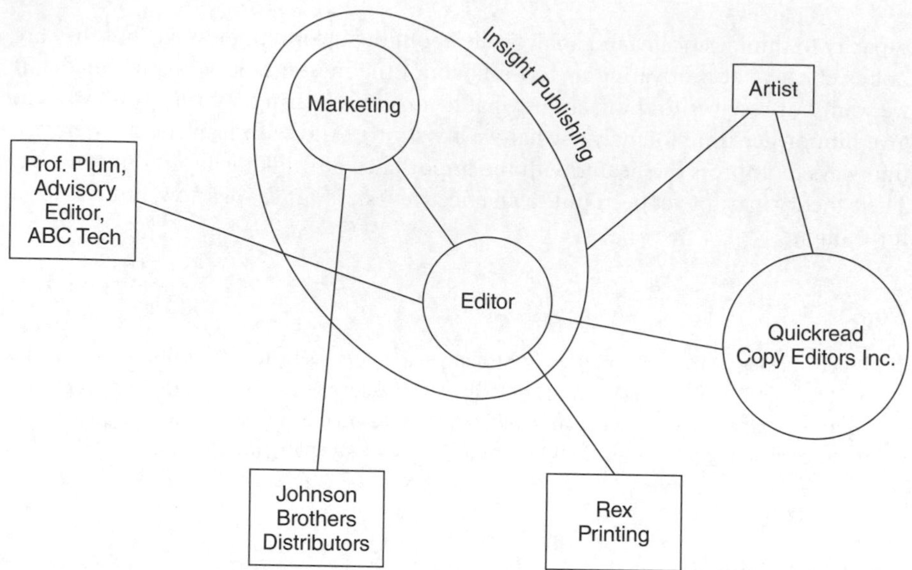

Figure 6.2 A network organization: textbook publishing.

plant with excess capacity, inventory would be handled by suppliers on a just-in-time basis, marketing would be the responsibility of a sales team reassigned from a downsizing division, and the accounting department would handle bookkeeping. The project manager would start with no organization and through negotiation and competitive bidding get units together to bring the product out. After the product was out and sales had begun, it might be transferred to an existing functional unit of the organization and the dynamic network disbanded.

Characteristics of Network Designs The network is not a new organizational design (Winter and Taylor, 1999; Malone and Laubacher, 2003). Building contractors have long employed this structure. They assemble reliable subcontractors into a temporary structure that they coordinate to the needs of each unique project. Before the 1980s, network structures were utilized mostly by specialized industries such as construction and movie production; but in the past twenty years, they have become ubiquitous. The modern network organization generally has four characteristics (Poole, 1999; Knoke, 2001):

1. Flexible, modular organizational structures that can be readily reconfigured as new projects, demands, or problems arise. As noted previously, these structures may be composed of units of a single larger organization, or they may be different organizations joined through various types of interorganizational alliances. Rearrangement of organizational units is important to the ability of networked organizations to adapt. For example, a network of community mental health agencies might find that its clients need help with job placements. It could then approach a job-training and placement agency and arrange for it to join the network. Typically a **broker** (either a central person or an organization) assembles and coordinates the network organization.

2. Team-based work organization that emphasizes autonomy, self-management, and initiative. This is generally combined with emphasis on quality and continuous improvement. To be effective, network organizations must be designed so that they promote effective teamwork, as discussed in Chapter 3. So they must work to define clear goals that specify the overall mission of the organization and the contribution of each unit, so that units can manage their own processes to contribute to the overall mission. Team-based work organization also involves empowerment of employees, just as in the relational strategy, because only if they have the necessary resources and authority can teams adapt to the needs of the situation. Cross-functional teams that bring together people from different units and organizations are particularly important in network organizations. There is also an expectation that members of network organizations will be proactive and work hard to deliver quality and excellence to the product or service being delivered.
3. Flat organizational structures that rely on coordination and negotiation rather than hierarchy to manage relationships among teams and units. As organizations move to network structures, they lose layers of middle managers and generally have fewer employees than traditional organizations.
4. Use of ICTs to integrate across organizational functions and geographically dispersed units to reengineer production and service processes, and to create tighter interdependence among activities. Technologies, such as email and telecommunications, discussed in Chapter 2, can be used to ensure that people from different units coordinate their activities. These units may be different departments in a single location, units spread across a wide distance, or a combination.

One pharmaceutical company that Scott Poole worked with used a computer conferencing system and teleconferences to develop a team of 11 salespeople, each stationed in a different Asian or African country. The team members met face-to-face a few times a year, but conducted all other business through the internet and teleconferences. Members of the team not only had to manage their own sales strategy, but also had to coordinate with other sales teams that had responsibility for other geographical areas and with production units in Europe and the United States on a frequent basis. Without ICTs this team could not possibly have managed its work.

ICTs also enable organizations to redesign and rethink how they do their work. As networked organizations rely more and more on ICTs, the nature of their work changes. For example, an organization may decide to use an automated inventory control system that relies on input of stock levels through handheld computers. It also is likely to find that it does not have to keep as many parts on hand, since the computer system enables it to keep track of them easily and automatically reorders them through the internet. As a result, it might enlarge the jobs of stockroom clerks so that they are also responsible for reordering needed parts, which eliminates some jobs in the procurement department, but greatly reduces the costs incurred in storing parts.

Finally, ICTs can also enable units to automate their coordination. For example, a group of companies planning a complex offshore oil project can automatically share updates to designs through computer networks. When a unit in charge of designing the pipes for bringing the oil from the seafloor to the platform changes its design and specification, the plans of each other unit would be instantly altered to reflect this. Unit members could then determine whether the alterations would cause any problems or require any action on their

Box 6.2
What Might Have Been

There have also been times in the past when network organizations were just as common as they are becoming today (Perrow, 2002, chap. 4; Knoke, 2001, chap. 6). The textile industry was the first major industry to emerge in the United States. During the period of 1820–1880, there was much uncertainty and change in this industry. Technology was changing fast, concentrated work in factories was a novelty, since most people were used to working on farms, in small workshops, and at home, and new entrepreneurs were uncertain about where to get capital to start new ventures. As a result several different types of industry organization emerged. In Massachusetts, the heavily capitalized, large corporations we are familiar with today were beginning to develop. They favored large plants that concentrated workers. But around Philadelphia, a network of textile companies developed. They were smaller and required less capital, and they formed and went out of business relatively rapidly. They regularly worked together for periods of time without merging or consolidating. For example, if one weaver won a larger order than he could deliver, he would often have several other weaving companies help to fulfill the order. Companies specialized in certain aspects of textile preparation and cooperated with others who fulfilled other functions to produce the finished product. For instance, one company might dye and make the yarn, another weave it into cloth, and a third finish the cloth and sell it to local stores.

The large factories of Massachusetts were fairly inflexible because they had to invest a great deal of money and time in machinery suitable for a single type of textile. During the Civil War, for instance, when the supply of cotton from the South dried up, the factories in Massachusetts had to shut down, because they were only set up to handle cotton. The textile firms around Philadelphia were more flexible and could adapt better to the current demand for cloth. If wool was not available at an acceptable price, they could shift to cotton or linen fairly easily. They were not as dependent on inflexible technologies and could adjust their looms accordingly. And some companies would simply go out of business when demand changed and their owners or employees would either start up new companies suited to current demand or find jobs with other firms in the network.

The network of textile firms around Philadelphia in the mid-1800s was much like the network organizations we see today. So in a real sense, today's firms are "reinventing the wheel."

Charles Perrow argues that the Philadelphia network model might have become the pattern for our economy if the large, heavily capitalized firms like those in Massachusetts had not influenced legislation and the structure of the economy and if our federal government had not been so weak. Instead, we developed an economy that favored the types of firms that are described in the chapter on traditional organizations. Many argue that today our economy is undergoing a fundamental change that will increasingly favor network organizations.

part. In all three functions, information technology speeds up production and response time and enables the organization to adapt to customer needs and environmental demands in highly specific ways.

Network Organizations and Boundaries Peter Monge and Noshir Contractor (2003) have commented that "network organizations create what have come to be called 'boundaryless' organizations." In network structures, it is not always clear where one organization begins and the other leaves off. Organizations and units in networks share practices, knowledge, and often members. No longer is it necessary to think of organizations as self-contained entities with definitive structures. Instead they can be composed, rearranged, and stuck together by various integrating methods, as the occasion demands. Organizations become "mix-and-match" systems. The network offers a good description of the various joint ventures, cross-firm alliances, and consortia that are becoming increasingly prevalent today.

An example of this type of venture network is SEMATECH, the Austin, Texas-based research-and-development consortium developed by more than ten leading information technology companies (Browning, Beyer, and Shetler, 1995). Typically firms assign researchers to SEMATECH, where they work with employees of other companies to develop cutting-edge products and share insights into solving production problems. The rationale behind such a consortium is that the United States needs a prosperous, technically advanced group of information technology companies if it is to remain among the world leaders in this area. Such firms are usually seen as temporary ventures; but some are so successful that they exist for a long time. SEMATECH now is more than fifteen years old.

Case Study 6.1

al-Qaeda: A Network Organization?

It is well known that many underground movements set themselves up as networks. News reports in the wake of the September 11 attacks have repeatedly described al-Qaeda and related Islamic terrorist groups as "networks." But what is it about the network strategy that makes it so useful for underground groups?

The members of al-Qaeda are organized into small cells, groups of 5–20 members, who communicate only with each other and often do not know the members of any other. Cells are linked through their connections to a few prominent members. The resulting network has densely connected groups that are linked to other groups only through their contacts, who do not move information between cells unless absolutely necessary. The result is a network of moderate density in which groups are relatively close to other groups in the network, but do not directly relate to them.

For example, the cell in Madrid, Spain, that trained a number of the September 11 hijackers was led by a used car salesman, Imad Yarkas, who had a Spanish wife and five children. Muhammed Zouaydi, the cell's financier, ran construction and real estate companies that funneled money from Islamic supporters to the cell. Other members of the cell ran normal businesses such as carpentry shops and a ceramics factory. Members were recruited by Yarkas, and Yarkas and Zouaydi were the primary contacts to the larger al-Qaeda organization. Occasionally higher-level cell members would meet with members of other cells to plan large scale operations, like the September 11 attacks. However, for the most part the cell kept to itself. The members of the cell have cultivated very strong ties to one another – often they have met one another years before in school or on the job – and interact with others outside the cell only on a more superficial level unconnected with the cell's mission, selling them cars, for example.

Networks made up of cells like the one in Madrid are very efficient communication mechanisms. The cells are linked by a number of central liaisons and the number of links between any two cells is very small. So information about operations, attempts to capture the members of the network, and related issues moves very quickly from cell to cell.

Such a network is a remarkably resilient organization. If the members of one cell are captured or destroyed, the other cells can go on basically undisturbed. They are insulated because the members of other cells do not know them or what they are doing well enough to supply useful information. So, although the Madrid cell is now broken up, it is likely that there are other cells unknown to us going about their business.

The most logical approach to breaking up a terrorist network would seem to be to capture or kill the most prominent members, on the assumption that if the leaders are taken out of action, the group will founder. Paradoxically, taking out the leaders of a terrorist network will not necessarily disable it. The leaders are important links, but the cells can survive without them because they are so strong by themselves. Studies of networks similar to al-Qaeda suggest that eliminating the central leader would not disable the network, because there are multiple connections between cells. In time one or more of the liaisons would emerge as a new leadership. Capturing the person who is the most central link in this type of network may even strengthen the power of individual cells for a while. They may take more initiative than they might when linked to a leader they feel a need to seek permission from. Hence, rather than disabling the terrorist network, capturing the central leader may stimulate more attacks. These attacks might be interpreted by leaders of the opposing forces and the media as "revenge attacks," when in fact they are simply a product of the cells feeling more potent and in control of their own affairs. Network research suggests that the killing of Osama bin Laden, however satisfying to the West, will hardly end al-Qaeda's activity. Arquilla, Ronfeldt and Zanini (1999) caution,

> It is important to avoid equating the bin Laden network solely with bin Laden. He represents a key node in the Arab Afghan terror network, but there should be no illusion about the likely effect on the network of actions taken to neutralize him. The network conducts many operations without his involvement, leadership, or financing – and will continue to be able to do so should he be killed or captured. (63)

Indeed, there is reason to believe that terrorist organizations form a "network of networks." al-Qaeda is linked to other terrorist organizations in the Philippines, Kurdistan, and Morocco that have their own base and causes to fight for. The organizations exchange information and sometimes resources. In the late 1970s there was a formal agreement among the Palestine Liberation Organization, the Red Brigades in Italy, the Irish Republican Army, and other terrorist groups to assist one another with training, procuring arms, and planning attacks. There is less evidence that this holds true today, but there are ties among the various terrorist networks.

Information and communication technologies are very important to the maintenance of terrorist networks. Email and telephones are important tools for maintaining a far-flung network. ICTs also offer a way to locate members of terrorist networks and trace their activities, but the terrorists have become very good at using pseudonyms and other means of disguising their accounts and use of these technologies. ICTs enable networks to operate over vast distances, whereas without the technology members would need to be located close together. These ICTs enable "cyberplanning" of terrorist operations. This makes terrorist networks even more difficult to disrupt. Some authorities have argued, for example, that the invasion of Afghanistan has made terrorism even more difficult to deal with, because it dispersed all the terrorist groups that were moving to Afghanistan all around the world, as they fled to escape UN forces.

ICTs also enable sympathizers with al-Qaeda and similar groups to proselytize and recruit over vast distances, thus refreshing terrorist causes. Anwar al-Awlaki, a cleric and US citizen recently killed in Yemen, became a major recruiter of terrorists. Dubbed "the bin Laden of the internet," he posted videos of lectures exhorting young men and women to attack the United States on YouTube and other sites, and there is evidence that these attracted potential terrorists. Nidal Hassan, the Muslim US Army officer who killed 13 people at Ft. Hood, Texas, listened to al-Awlaki's lectures and contacted him by email several times prior to his attack. al-Awlaki also inspired Farouk Abdulmutallab, the Nigerian who tried to blow up a Northwest Airlines jet on Christmas Day 2009, and Faisal Shahzad, a naturalized US citizen who tried to set off a bomb in Time Square in May 2010. ICTs enable terrorist networks to survive and grow.

Applying What You've Learned

1. In what way is al-Qaeda like the network organizations described in this chapter? How does it differ?
2. What are some of the weaknesses of an organization like al-Qaeda? Is it subject to any of the problems that network organizations face, discussed at the end of this chapter?

Questions to Think About and Discuss

1. Drawing on the principles and practices of a network organization, what suggestions would you have for stopping al-Qaeda and disrupting its network?
2. Networks are complex systems. Which of the principles of systems thinking discussed in Chapter 2 might give us insights into al-Qaeda and how it might be stopped?
3. Although very little of the trove of information that was captured during the raid that killed Osama bin Laden at the time had been released this book went to press, some of it was relevant to the strengths and weaknesses of network organizations. For example, it was quickly discovered that bin Laden very much wanted to launch an attack on the United States on the tenth anniversary of September 11, 2001. But, nothing happened. It also seemed that, while he had frequently communicated with al-Qaeda cells during the intervening decade, few of his directives were carried out. What does this information tell you about al-Qaeda? About network organizations? What additional information has been revealed since this book went to press? What does it tell you about al-Qaeda in particular, terrorist organizations, or network organizations? Why?

Note

This case draws on a number of sources, including Stohl and Stohl (2007); Woolls (2004); Bergen (2002, 2004); Arguilla, Ronfeldt, and Zanini (1999); Thomas (2003); and Madhani (2010).

Virtual Organizations A **virtual organization** is one that has no physical location (Lucas,1996; Burton, DeSanctis, and Obel, 2006). It has no building, no campus, and no office. Instead it exists across a computer network. Many catalog companies' sales divisions are virtual organizations, with independent individual sales agents operating out of their homes. The catalog companies link them via high-speed computer lines to a central database that handles order delivery and other functions. Compaq Computer Corporation moved its sales force into home offices and reported a 50 percent reduction in sales expenses as a result.

The California flower company Calyx & Corolla is a good example of a virtual organization (Lucas, 1996). The organization is really a virtual network composed of a negotiated agreement between three organizations. Calyx & Corolla mails catalogs showing flower arrangements to potential customers and takes orders using an 800 number and an order center located in a suburb of San Francisco. The orders are then forwarded via computer network or fax to flower growers who have also agreed to package the flowers in arrangements prior to shipping them. Calyx & Corolla has negotiated an agreement with Federal Express to pick up and deliver the arrangements the next morning to any place in the continental United States. Orders are tracked and monitored via a computer system that also handles accounting and distribution of payments to the various components of the organization. Calyx & Corolla itself is relatively small, but the virtual organization it has put together is much larger and is composed of the growers and Federal Express. Consumers cannot differentiate the different organizations that make up Calyx & Corolla; from the point of view of the customer, Calyx & Corolla looks like a traditional florist who delivers.

One characteristic of virtual organizations is that to outsiders they appear to be like older self-contained organizations. They deliver the same or better product or service with the same or better efficiency. Information technology and telecommunications enable these dispersed organizations to coordinate their activities and maintain coherent work processes. Each part of the virtual organization is able to focus on its particular function, resulting in competent and even excellent performance. By staying small, the component organizations keep their costs for management and overheads down, enhancing efficiency. Smallness also makes communication easier within the components, opening them up for fast development and testing of new ideas.

Informal Network Organizations Just as there are informal networks between people in organizations, there are also informal networks of organizations. In some cases, these form around a particular purpose and interaction is regular enough that though they are not held together by formal contracts or structures, these networks can be called "network organizations." In industries where technology is rapidly changing, knowledge is complex, and expertise is distributed among a number of organizations, knowledge networks often form whereby organizations can uncover new knowledge and insights. The biotechnology industry – to which we owe the new advances in DNA analysis and development of new bioengineered therapeutic drugs – is an example of this type of field. Studies of small biotech firms have documented that they develop densely connected networks for the exchange of new knowledge, information about competitors, and new directions in the biotechnology industry (Powell, Koput, and Smith-Doerr, 1996; Liebeskind, Oliver, Zucker, and Brewer, 1996).

Some of these informal connections eventually evolve into more formal connections. For example, the eWater Cooperative Research Centre in Australia emerged from an informal network of scientists, policy makers, and practitioners (e.g., water companies) who were interested in how water use affected the environment (Johnson, 2009). However, the absence of formal contracts or connections among these organizations increased their flexibility to seek new connections and also decreased the potential problems associated with sharing information that might be proprietary if developed in a formal network organization.

Other areas around which informal network organizations often develop include organizations that are heavily dependent on certain ICTs, such as the GHX medical supply exchange discussed in Chapter 2 (in response to the power that this exchange gives the suppliers, several informal buyer groups have formed, and they are beginning to develop more formal ties), organizations developing standards for new technologies, products, or services, and school districts attempting to deal with the unusually demanding budget and legislative restrictions that have occurred in the past few years (e.g., the "No Child Left Behind" Act).

Case Study 6.2
Evolving Into a Network Organization[1]

Industrial controls maker ICG has long been in the forefront of its industry. It had been among the first firms of its kind to implement a computer integrated design and manufacturing (CAD/CAM) system (explained in more detail in Chapter 6). The CAD/CAM system enabled engineering and manufacturing units to work on a common set of plans stored in a database; as the units made alterations and adjustments in either design or manufacturing, they were automatically entered into the plans. This system was met with some resistance from engineers who were used to paper drawings, but their enhanced ability to consult with manufacturing noticeably improved the quality and time-to-market for the various product lines offered by ICG. These teams worked in a paperless environment with the CAD/CAM system as the linking pin for their efforts.

As ICG worked with the CAD/CAM system, top managers realized that the company was not capitalizing on its potential. To take advantage of the system, they felt, it would be necessary to develop cross-functional teams that would own product development from womb to tomb, so to speak. ICG constituted product teams with representatives from marketing, engineering, manufacturing, scheduling, and quality assurance that would be responsible for product performance in terms of quality, cost, time-to-market, and profit. These product teams were formed by top management and charged with managing a set of products and allocating resources among them. While many ICG employees were skeptical about the new teams because they had been ordered by top management, they were eventually won over as it became clear that management were going to give the teams full control over their own decisions. Working on product teams enabled employees to develop their skills in management, teamwork, communication, and leadership, as well as increasing their commitment to ICG.

Its experience as a leader in CAD/CAM led to ICG's next advance. It worked with a major computer maker to create the Pyramid Integrator, a computer system that incorporated CAD/CAM and had the ability to integrate all of a company's design and manufacturing across multiple products. The Pyramid Integrator facilitated standardization of designs across products, reducing costs and enabling companies to build on previous designs as they created new products in a rapid and flexible process. It also made it much easier to tailor products to customer needs, since customers could work with ICG personnel, in effect to design their own systems. The first product lines ICG designed with the Pyramid Integrator were a great success and won the company national recognition and an award from a manufacturing publication. The Pyramid Integrator also became a profitable product for ICG.

ICG had moved to a team-intensive organization, but it was still hierarchically organized around divisions that corresponded to product lines. The excessive amount of work entailed by the various teams and the fine-tailoring of products for customers put pressure on the product-oriented divisions, which were better suited for relatively large production runs of similar products. Moreover, the divisions tended to be concerned mainly with their own success and did not think in terms of the success of the entire enterprise of ICG. Each division focused on its narrow line of products, which utilized a certain technology, and sought to be a world leader in its products. This narrow focus sometimes put divisions at odds with each other, as they introduced products that conflicted or went in very different directions. It also confused the sales force and ran the risk of overstretching resources across too many product lines.

The executive vice president decided that ICG needed to reorganize. He argued that the success no longer depended on technologies or new products, because technology was beginning to diffuse rapidly through the industry; rather success would depend on how well the company could respond to the particular needs of its customers. Therefore, ICG should be organized around its customers and projects for them rather than around product-focused divisions. After considerable analysis of customer needs, the management group determined that the core business for ICG lay in two product lines and that everything else the company did basically added value to these lines.

ICG was reorganized as a concentric organization with the two core control businesses at the center. A second ring, Communication and Information Systems, would focus on tying these core technologies together using information systems. The third and outer ring, application services, would package integrated control systems according to customer needs. General service functions, such as human resources, marketing, planning, and operations, were consolidated from the old divisions into single units in orbit around these three rings to provide support for them as needed.

The company reorganized its efforts to cut down the number of products it offered and focused on customer groups, reducing its number of projects to about one-third of those in the old divisionalized structure. It developed a number of self-managed teams to handle various projects and customer groups. Teams sometimes operated at one layer of the concentric circles; for example, a team might specialize in controls for canning companies and work with teams in the control and communication and information systems layers to tailor these. In other cases, teams bridged layers; for example a team attempting to develop new control devices to combine with other company products in an integrated system might be composed of personnel drawn from the core and second layers of the ICG. Teams could be formed only with the approval of an upper-level management team, which was called an executive sponsor team. The executive sponsor team scanned for business opportunities and identified personnel and resources for the teams that undertook them. Once formed, the teams were largely self-managing. Supervisory business teams were formed to coordinate sets of related teams and to argue for and make decisions about resources and other organizational-level issues for their teams. The result was a network of teams and a shallow three-level hierarchy with little direct authoritarian control over the bottom-level teams. Just as teams were created at need, they were phased out when their projects had run their course, and the personnel were reassigned to other teams.

ICG also included personnel from its suppliers on some teams, creating networks with its suppliers. As it developed deeper relationships with some particularly effective suppliers, ICG reduced the total number of suppliers it dealt with by about 50 percent. Cross-organizational teams of ICG and supplier personnel embarked on quality improvement projects to ensure that parts and materials met the highest quality specifications; they also embarked on some joint ventures in which both the supplier and ICG developed parts of a new product. ICG also reached out to competing firms to engage them in developing standards and sometimes in joint ventures.

Over a 15-year period, ICG moved from a traditional divisionalized form to a networked organization best characterized as a team of teams.

Applying What You've Learned

1. What characteristics of a network organization does ICG exhibit? Which ones are missing, if any? Is ICG a "poster child" for network organizations?
2. Why did ICG evolve from a divisionalized form to a networked organization? Were any of the forces discussed at the beginning of this chapter in operation?

Questions to Think About and Discuss

1. Based on the discussion in Chapter 3, we would expect that teams in ICG are not always completely satisfactory experiences for their members. What are some of the problems that might arise in ICG's teams? How might these problems carry over into networks of teams?
2. The change at ICG was instituted on the initiative of top management. What measures did management take to ensure that employees accepted and cooperated with these changes? What might management have done to increase the probability that employees would go along with the changes at ICG? What would have happened to ICG if it had not changed? Would it have been as successful? Why or why not?

Note

1 This case is based on Nohria and Berkley (1994).

NETWORK STRATEGIES OF MOTIVATION, CONTROL, AND SURVEILLANCE

The lack of hierarchy and the accompanying empowerment of members in network organizations poses new challenges for coordination and control. While members of the units that comprise the network are likely to feel loyal to their units, there is no intrinsic reason for them to feel the same loyalty toward the network. Consider the case of a computer programmer whose software firm contracted to develop a new inventory system for a major company. This software firm is part of a temporary network formed to bring a major new product to market. The programmer's future is with the software firm, not the company; any raises come from the firm, and personal ties exist with coworkers in the firm, not with "those other guys" in the big company. The software firm and the project itself form the programmer's frame of reference. The programmer uses the standards of her firm and profession when planning and evaluating her work and that of others. The big company's standards are relevant only if her managers emphasize them. The programmer is influenced by the software firm's culture, and much less by the culture of the distant company. To the extent she orients to the big company at all, her main concern is to ensure that the software company delivers on its contract and is judged favorably by the larger firm.

Motivation in Network Organizations

How do network organizations motivate the members of individual units to collaborate? This problem cannot be solved by a leader's dictates, because the flatter network organization does not have hierarchical authority over its constituent units or their members. Indeed, hierarchical authority would undermine the flexibility and adaptability that are the greatest advantages of the network form. Another challenge arises from the fact that the network gives units a degree of freedom in how they organize their work and the effort they put into the larger enterprise. This situation makes it possible for some units to take advantage of the others by "free riding" and taking shortcuts so they maximize their profit by putting in the bare minimum that others will accept.

Network organizations motivate and control their units and their members through three complementary routes. First, they attempt to cultivate *trust* in the network. Trust is the ideal cement for the network organizations. They have little or no hierarchy, so hierarchy cannot be the source of authority to coordinate and control. Moreover, networks are often composed of numerous different organizations, each with its own culture, so culture cannot be the basis for control. Trust is a special property of the relationships among members of the network that enables them to act on the assumption that others will fulfill their own responsibilities in good faith. It is achieved through engaging in cooperative action with others and through observing their competence and their willingness to live up to their commitments. To cultivate trust, the managers of the new product network might ask our programmer to work in the field for a couple of weeks with programmers from other components of the network. If their work goes well, programmers from the various firms come to trust each other and carry back good reports to the rest of the network. Trust will also be built in this network as various units carry out their responsibilities on time and effectively (Mayer, Davis, and Schoorman, 1995; Hart and McLeod, 2002; Wang and Emurian, 2005). One interesting finding about trust online is that it is often built most effectively by focusing first on the work at hand; this "swift trust," centered around tasks and activity, forms the basis for developing interpersonal trust (Hart and McLeod, 2002).

For example, a major retailer, with approximately 1200 stores throughout the United States, forms a virtual organization with some of its suppliers. This retailer supplies data about sales and sales forecasts to about 20 percent of its most trusted suppliers, who can use it to set up their production schedules to meet the retailer's needs (Ghosh and Fedorowicz, 2008). Sharing this information enables the retailer to cut costs by speeding delivery and to ensure it has the stocks that it needs. However, these sales forecasts are critical information and if they were shared with the retailer's competitors, they would place the retailer at a significant disadvantage. The retailer is willing to share this information because trust has developed between the retailer and some of its suppliers. Initially the retailer "tests" whether the supplier can be trusted by first providing only 16 weeks of forecasts. If the supplier acts in a trustworthy manner, longer term forecasts are shared. Once the relationship has developed, the suppliers are asked to make their own forecasts for sales for the retailer and the retailer and suppliers compare and discuss discrepancies in the forecasts, creating a knowledge management system, which further increases trust.

Trust can also be based on reputation; we tend to trust people who are recommended by those we trust or who have a reputation for integrity. If the programmers report back to their managers that other firms' programmers are competent and good to work with, this in turn enhances the managers' trust in the network. Generally trust is assessed informally through direct experience of others. Hence organizations are most likely to enter into networks with those they already know and respect. Research shows, for example, that managers and decision makers tend to turn first to well-established networks of associates and advisors, rather than broadly searching for "strangers" who might be competent (Monge and Contractor, 2003). However, there are also formal indicators of trustworthiness. Professional credentials and certifications, such as those a computer programmer is likely to have, can also form the basis for trust.

In recent years online systems have emerged that enable network brokers to find trustworthy employees and organizations. For example, Elance.com (n.d.) is a site that connects potential employers with freelance employees and organizations who are available on a project-by-project basis. Professionals and organizations looking for work register on the site and brokers and employers who want a freelancer or network member can read their profiles, which include resumes, photos, testimonials from previous clients, and other information. Potential employers can also post jobs online and ask for bids on them. Elance includes a "water cooler," a discussion space where jobseekers can trade advice and tips, and "Elance University," which provides the information you need to get started on the site and also education on freelance work in general (Star Reviews, n.d.). Elance also includes a reputation system, which rates its jobseekers and is modeled after the reputation system on eBay, the online auction site (Dellarocas, 2006). Elance's system asks employers to rate and comment on employees they have found through Elance. Average ratings for the past six months give potential employers information on potential employees' reputations.

A second source of motivation in network organizations is *an inspiring, meaningful task*. Network organizations are typically task- or product-focused, and this gives all members a common frame of reference. A meaningful task or goal can inspire the units and individuals in the network to work hard and ensure that they coordinate with other units. For example, the goal of the networked floral company, Calyx and Corolla, is to deliver the best possible flower arrangements faster than any other company and at a good price. This goal unifies the efforts of each part of the network: the flower growers try to deliver high-quality flowers; the arrangers work out innovative designs; the express delivery companies configure their operations to make sure the flowers get there fresh; and the coordinating unit, Calyx and Corolla itself, works hard to make sure that the parts of the network connect smoothly with each other as the process moves from flowers in the field to flowers on the table. A survey of contributors to Wikipedia, the online encyclopedia, indicated that the top two motivations for their participation were that it was "fun" to work on Wikipedia and their belief that they were contributing to a novel project that upheld the open source model of offering free information to the world (Nov, 2007).

One important thing to bear in mind, however, is that an inspiring task can hold a network together only for so long; in the longer term, members must also develop trust in each other. If some part of the network does not deliver – for example, if a grower delivers poor-quality flowers – the best efforts of other units will not succeed. In this case, the network either begins to malfunction and fall apart or finds another, better grower.

A third source of motivation and control in network organizations are network-based *formal systems* for monitoring and controlling members and their activities. In addition to trust, networked organizations may also attempt to develop structures to formally coordinate unit activities. These systems are based on contracts among the units in the network that provide a formal, written understanding among the units concerning their responsibilities and compensation. The retailer discussed a few paragraphs ago also requires all its suppliers to sign contracts and nondisclosure statements in order to provide a backup for trusted relationships. Because contracts are legal documents, any unit that does not fulfill its contract can, of course, be sued. However, since legal actions often take years, they are not effective in coordinating ongoing activities. A more effective means of coordination is first, to develop a project or workflow plan that specifies what should be done and in what sequence and second, provide methods to enable units to monitor each others' activities. When these are formally integrated with ICT, the result is a full-disclosure **accounting information system**, a work integration system likes those discussed above, that enables units to know what other units are contributing to the network and what earnings they are getting from it.

The accounting information system is simply a set of databases accessible to all participating units that shows them whether other units are meeting their responsibilities and the level of return obtained by the organization as a whole and by each unit. For example, units in the new product venture could determine from this data whether suppliers are on time with their deliveries, whether other units are putting in a fair effort (based on their expenditures and the payments they have received), and where they stand vis-à-vis other units in the network in terms of expenses and profits. This accounting information system reassures units that others are holding up their end of the bargain and puts pressure on them to hold up their own end. As units see that others are faithfully fulfilling their obligations, they come to trust them and trust builds over time.

Also important in this trust-building process are timely and effective use of electronic communication systems such as email, teleconferencing, and groupware, discussed in Chapter 6. Direct, rapid communication and response help the network coordinate work and iron out problems. Both the accounting and communication systems help to build trust, and trust is a self-reinforcing cycle: Open communication builds trust, which leads to more open communication and to more trust, in an ever-increasing spiral (Knoke, 2001).

The *keiretsu*, the networks of Japanese manufacturers and suppliers discussed previously, provide an interesting example of the mix of strategies used to hold networks together. Contracts among members of a *keiretsu* network are "short and remarkably imprecise, essentially committing the parties only to work together to resolve difficulties as they emerge" (Holmstrom and Roberts, 2003). Trust, embodied in the shared understanding that the supplier will have the business into the foreseeable future so long as the supplier delivers quality parts in a timely fashion, is the major glue that holds these networks together. Satisfying interactions over the long term reinforce this trust and cement the network so that when models change, suppliers know they have a good chance of remaining in the network. In a study of an 11-year period, only three of 150 suppliers was dropped from Toyota's supplier network.

What is the future of the individual employee in the world of the networked organization? The temporary and fluid nature of many networks and their projects does not provide the type of job security that the traditional employment contract has been based on. The freelance artist who works in networked projects with publishers, advertising agencies, and other organizations does not have access to the type of package that provides health care, retirement savings, and other benefits which is provided by long-term employers. Rather than looking to their employers for these things, Robert Laubacher and Thomas Malone (2003) argue, employees in networked organizations will rely on what they term "guilds," organizations of professional employees that provide these same services in return for a percentage of the members' income or surcharges paid by the broker of the networks they serve in. A well-known example is the Screen Actors' Guild (SAG), which, beyond giving its famous yearly awards, provides health care and pension systems for its members. Construction workers' unions and the World Wide Web Artists' Consortium provide similar services.

CHALLENGES FOR CONTROL SYSTEMS IN NETWORK ORGANIZATIONS

Systems for motivation and control in network organizations are an amalgam of methods used in the relational strategy (trust, an involving task) and the traditional strategy (formal control systems). The network strategy, however, extends relationships over a much greater distance than does the relational strategy, and it calls for more flexibility in the control system than is typically allowed for by the traditional strategy.

Just as team control sometimes becomes overwhelming in the relational strategy, control can be excessive and uncomfortable in the network. The project management system and full-disclosure information systems give information to all parties. This information can be used to make judgments about the effort of any given unit and bring pressure on that unit to get into line. The fact that these systems and their plans were approved by all units and are open to everyone gives negative information an objective force that can be used to embarrass and harass individuals or units. The resulting control structure can be just as oppressive as the team-based systems discussed in Chapter 4, creating defensiveness that makes the network less flexible than it could be if each unit were not holding all the others to strict standards of accountability.

There is also a mismatch between the types of rewards and incentives acceptable in US culture and those needed to make a network organization function properly. Team-based organizations should give rewards to teams rather than basing salaries and promotions on individual performance. But most people in the USA are accustomed to expect rewards on an individual basis, as specified in the traditional strategy and passed on to the relational strategy. Anne Donnellon and Maureen Scully (1994) argue that organizations like the network form must move beyond traditional assessment and reward practices in which the manager assesses the employee, who receives an individual reward based on the assessment. Instead they argue for assessment by fellow team members and team-based rewards supplemented by individual rewards. In addition, they argue that organizations ought to avoid using terms like "merit," a symbol that implies that individual characteristics are responsible for good performance. Such a term is misleading in network organizations, where good performance is dependent on collaboration and teamwork among individuals and units.

LEADERSHIP IN NETWORK ORGANIZATIONS

Leadership in network organizations is not as clear cut as it is in the traditional, relational, or cultural strategies, simply because networks are, by definition, somewhat diffuse. It is useful to distinguish top leadership, in which there is a central figure who provides leadership for the network, and leadership at the unit and interunit levels.

As we have noted many network structures are assembled by brokers, a manager or firm that identifies appropriate units and builds them into a network, and brokers are the "natural" leaders of the network. The broker may be an integrating project manager, as in the new product development example introduced at the beginning of this chapter. Alternatively, the broker may be an independent agent or organization. Building contractors, who coordinate the work of carpenters, plumbers, electricians, and others, are a familiar examples of brokers. In other cases, leaders emerge as symbols or spokespeople for the central organization in a network. The president of SONY, for example, could serve a leadership role for the *keiretsu* that developed in association with SONY.

These top leaders may take either transformational or transactional roles in the networked organization. A founder or renewer of the network may play the role of a transformational leader, described in Chapter 5. The founder or renewer sets the values and basic directions for the network, and its members look to him or her as an inspirational model. Frances Hesselbein, the CEO of the Girl Scouts of America, is a good example of transformational leadership in a network organization.[4] When Hesselbein took over the reins of the Girl Scouts in the 1970s, the organization was on the decline, buffeted by the conflicts and changes occuring in society that made many question the relevance of organizations such as the Girl Scouts. Hesselbein commented, "The Girl Scouts had suffered the same traumas of the 1960s and 1970s that so many great firms had. Organizations did not know who they were any more; it was a new world and you could not repeat the mistakes of the past." She greatly diversified the reach of the Girl Scouts, including every type of girl, from a chapter on a Navajo Reservation to one in picket-fence New England, and succeeded in revitalizing the organization. In doing this, she moved the Girl Scouts from a traditional hierarchical organization to a network form "with the CEO in the middle looking across, not at the top looking down." She also engaged the Girl Scouts in interorganizational networks with interested companies, government agencies and foundations. According to Hesselbein. "Alliances, partnerships, and collaborations are the language of the future." Transformational leadership such as Hesselbein's has been shown to increase members' trust in other members and commitment to the network (Joshi, Lazarova, and Lao, 2009).

A broker or manager of a network is more likely to take a transactional approach, as detailed in Chapter 4. The role of transactional manager in newer designs, such as the networked organization, has been described as more like that of a symphony conductor than anything else. The individual units and their members have high levels of specialized knowledge and skill, and, like individual musicians, they know best how to perform their part in the organization. Rather than telling them what to do – micromanaging – an effective leader instead sets up conditions that enable units and members to perform up to their capabilities and helps them to coordinate their work with other units.

With respect to leadership within units, the network form poses several challenges for managers (Ancona, Kochan, Scully, Van Maanen, and Westney, 1999). The team-based structure of network organizations implies that leaders must be able to promote teamwork as described in Chapter 4. Since teams are self-managing, leaders should take on the role of coach rather than directive leader, advising the team and helping it to solve problems. The flatness of networked organizations necessitates a negotiator role for the manager as well. The negotiator must be able to represent the unit and its interests in negotiations over schedules, division of labor, and problems between units. The flexibility of network organizations means that managers must be able to deal with workforce management in a responsive, creative manner. For example, if serving a client means that someone has to travel to a distant plant and fix something, who in the unit is to do it? How does that person get compensated for his or her time within a fixed budget without causing perceptions of unfairness on the part of other employees? These and other sorts of issues arise during the process of constant adjustment necessary for flexible response. So the manager in the networked organization must be coach, negotiator, problem solver, and improviser, rather than simply a director.

Managers and members of units in networked organizations must also manage relationships with other units and organizations, because integrating functions are so important. Some of the communication functions involved in spanning the boundaries between units will be discussed in Chapter 9. In addition, units in network organizations face a new problem. Whereas previously the problem was how to relate to another set of units one is more or less stuck with, in the network it becomes how to maintain credibility in a network of units, some of which may be potential competitors seeking to replace your unit. The problem in this case is how to project an image of competence, efficiency, and quality. In a real sense each unit – even within intact organizations – becomes an independent small business vying with many potential competitors. This situation requires a very different strategy for communicating with other units than do the three strategies discussed in Chapters 3, 4, and 5.

CHALLENGES AND PROBLEMS FOR NETWORK ORGANIZATIONS

Organizations employing network strategies face a number of problems. For one thing, network organizations – with their flexible structures and complicated relationships among units – are extremely complex. This complexity introduces problems. It is often not easy to determine who is responsible for what in network organizations. Unless units specifically work out how they coordinate activities and constantly communicate with each other, important things can fall between the cracks.

In complex systems, as we noted in Chapter 2, it is often impossible to determine the cause of problems. Consider a relatively simple organization composed of three units: one that designs widgets, a second that produces them, and a third that markets and distributes them. The marketing unit may find that there is not enough of product X to meet the demands of an important customer. Its initial tendency is to blame production, which has immediate responsibility for making the X. But production may be having trouble due to a design problem that causes a part of the product to break when it is removed from the stamping presses. The blame then seems to shift to design. However, the design unit used the flawed plan for product X, because it had not gotten any feedback from production on the problem. Moreover, design understood from marketing that customers really appreciated the part of X that tended to break off in production's machines, so they wanted to keep it. Does the problem then trace back to production's lack of feedback or to marketing's insistence that the part of the design that caused problems be retained? The answer is that none of these can be said to be the sole cause of the problem. Causality in networks is often ambiguous. The problems persist because of the organizational system as a whole, a system in which design does not communicate with the other units, in which production is not particularly proactive about problems it encounters, and marketing is out there selling stuff without considering whether other departments can meet the delivery schedules it sets. In cases where it is difficult to determine the causes of problems, it is also difficult to solve them. When eliminating the source of a problem means changing the entire system, the problem may recur, because systems change slowly at best.

Network organizations also have a tendency to become more limited, rigid and inflexible over time. One reason for this is that "once organizations have chosen partners, they tend to spend less time seeking other partners" (Monge and Contractor, 2003, 192). A lot of effort is typically put into finding suitable network partners, ascertaining whether they can be trusted, and negotiating working relationships with them. Once organizations find suitable partners they are not as likely to put new effort into finding additional ones. As a result, networks tend to contain the "same old" organizations who are not likely to bring new ideas or new skills to the table. Another reason networks tend to become rigid is that, the units highest in prestige, centrality, and closeness tend to grow more powerful over time. They have information that other units do not have; they enjoy status due to their centrality, and they can control the flow of information. The extent of their power is in direct proportion to how much they control the key communication paths in the network. This slight (and sometimes not so slight) advantage can set up a self-reinforcing cycle whereby the more centralized units use their power to exert some control over the network, thereby increasing their reputation and power still more and so on. However, centralized control over the network weakens the ability of units to adapt flexibly to the demands of the situation, defeating the purpose of using a network system. Centralization also takes power away from some units, sapping the initiative that self-management gives them. The heterarchy, described in the next section, is an adaptation of the network form that promises to be more flexible and responsive. A fourth problem with network organizations is that, although they may enable their members to develop their own professionalism and careers, they do so at the expense of making "temporariness" permanent. No longer can employees assume they'll be working for the same company for 30 or 40 years. By their very nature, network organizations force their employees to think of a future in which they'll have to find new contracts and new positions in a new organization. This can undermine loyalty to the organization, making it hard to develop and sustain an organizational culture. It is also an uncomfortable situation for individuals who desire stability in their lives. Although it may seem something of a paradox, stability of employees is critical for maintaining the flexibility and adaptability that the network emphasizes. When employees know the organization and their jobs well, they are generally better able to see what needs changing and how to change it.

BEYOND NETWORKS: ALTERNATIVE STRATEGIES OF ORGANIZING

The network and other new organizational forms continue to evolve. However, as we have noted, they did not spring up new and fully formed in the 1990s. Versions of the network organization have been around for decades, if not centuries. At least two alternative strategies of organizing should be recognized. They are not as common as the four discussed to this point, but one or both of them may emerge as a major organizing strategy in the future.

Cooperatives

Organizations have been designed and operated in accordance with distinctive philosophical beliefs for millennia. Historically in the United States alone, Christian monastaries long have produced wine; the Shaker communities once produced household products, including furniture that continue to be valued – almost revered; and the Amana colonies long produced appliances. In each of these cases, the operant organizational strategy was based on a particular set of beliefs, usually that in some way separated the believers from the surrounding society.

Throughout US history, groups have formed **cooperatives** and other types of collective organizations around specific economic philosophies. Many of them, especially in agriculture, were designed to empower small producers in the struggle against monopolies, primarily banks and railroads. There was an upsurge in the development of cooperatives in the United States in the late 1960s and 1970s, and the recent economic crisis has stimulated a similar surge. In the Bushwick neighborhood of Brooklyn, New York, for example, a number of cooperatives and communes have sprung up, including traditional food cooperatives, clothing stores, neighborhood farms, and apartments (Lipinski, 2010).

In Mexico and among Mexicans living in the United States, the *tanda* (which means "to take turns") and *cundina* ("to increase in volume" or "go a long way") allow people to avoid the fees and interest charged by banks for personal loans (Gama, Medrano, and Medrano, 2010). Friends, relatives, or coworkers deposit a set amount of money per week into a communal pot. The participants determine when they will pay money out to members, and what the money can be used for. Sometimes loans are used to start businesses. More often they are used for more personal projects – home remodeling, automobiles, and so on. They work because the members have trusting relationships with one another. Although banks have tried to compete by creating their own *tanda* systems, they have had limited success for the simple reason that the people trust one another more than they trust the banks.

The best known alternative organizations among organizational communication scholars are on opposite sides of the world – Spain and Bangladesh. The first is the Mondragón Cooperative Corporation in the Basque region of northern Spain. For almost a decade, George Cheney studied the Mondragón Cooperative Corporation in the Basque region of Spain, making extended visits in 1992, 1994, and 1997. Founded in 1956 by a priest and five young engineers, the cooperative has been based on a radical strategy of organizing – democracy. Organizational decisions, including selection of managers, are made on a one-person, one-vote system. Each of the 170 co-ops, which range in size from eight to 9000 employees, are worker owned. A system is in place that is designed to ensure that employee welfare and relationships with the surrounding community is as important as productivity and profit in organizational decision making. Originally, only participants in the collectives could own stock in them. In Bangladesh, one of the poorest countries in the world, the Grameen Bank was created in order to help women gain a measure of economic independence. Bangladeschi women typically are confined to their homes, either by cultural limits or by the demands of child care. So, the Grameen Bank established a system of giving them small loans in order to help them set up home businesses, usually producing textiles (Moreno, 2002; Papa, Auwal, and Singhai, 1995).

These organizations face unique challenges because they are alternative organizations. Sometimes the challenges are internal. The educational programs at Grameen Bank were designed to challenge male domination over women, but were presented in a paternalistic manner by the males who started and managed the bank – customers, mostly women, were given information to be used as a guide for better lives, but were not empowered to use that information in their own ways. The bank's loans helped the women escape from the oppression of traditional moneylenders, but did not overcome cultural and economic barriers to selling their goods. As a result, the impact on their incomes was limited. People who worked for the organization were so committed to its social change-oriented values that they often made excessive sacrifices of their own needs. Other challenges came from the outside. After Spain entered the European Union in 1992, the Mondragón cooperatives suddenly had to compete with German, Swedish, Japanese, and US firms. Pressures for greater productivity and faster responses to customers led to a more centralized, bureaucratic, strategy of organizing. Differences in wages grew, leading one group of co-ops to leave the association. Originally, "participation" (recall Chapter 4) meant the right or power to influence organizational decisions and policies. Today it has become more centered on daily tasks and on managing competition. Like many of the PDM programs described in Chapter 4, it has the potential to become participation without democracy.

Heterarchies

Heterarchies are organizations (or networks of organizations) in which different units (organizations) are allowed to choose and develop their own particular organizational strategy and practices. These practices may vary and no uniformity is imposed on the units (organizations) that make up the heterarchy. In heterarchies, different units may adopt different ways of doing the same work, different ways of relating to other units, different methods of decision making, and so on. Units will have different value systems as well. Some units may emphasize efficiency and low cost, others quality despite cost, still others development of their members' skills. The organization accepts and tacitly encourages these different approaches. However, it does not require them or try to organize them. Each unit is allowed to develop as it sees fit (Stark, 1999).

One example of a heterarchical organization is a new media advertising firm that serves its clients through multiple media, including traditional channels, such as television and print media and new channels, such as the internet and blogs. In this organization, each department – the creative department, designers, marketers, technologists, and top management – must organize itself as best it sees fit to deal with the particular demands of its own task, which are continuously in flux. The ways in which departments organize themselves also may vary when they specialize on different media or sectors of media, since each medium has its own demands. The departments must still coordinate their activities with one another for the firm to be effective, and each will be held accountable by the value sets of all the departments it coordinates with, because there is no "chain of command" in a heterarchy. So, for example, the marketing department must initiate and sell ads in a way that enables the creative department to produce good, effective art and the technologists to deliver a reliable product via state of the art technologies. It must meet two different sets of criteria and adjust its activity to satisfy them. In turn, the creative department and the technology unit must satisfy the marketing department and adjust their activities so that they smoothly fit. The various parts of the advertising firm are very much like the different animals in an ecological system; they go their own way, but must also fit themselves into the system to continue to survive in it.

The rationale for a heterarchy is that it offers the best way to enable the organization to cope with extreme levels of uncertainty. In some cases, not only is the environment of organizations changing, but also the nature of the environment is changing. For example, the advance and spread of new ICTs are changing the work of the advertising firm so rapidly that practices that used to work no longer is guaranteed to work with new media such as wireless communications. These media are developing so fast that there is literally no standard practice like there once was for print ads, and they change so quickly that by the time a "standard" is recognized it may be outmoded. At the same time the technology is changing, new trends in public taste are developing, spurred and magnified by increasing concentration in media ownership that enables media firms to shape tastes much more strongly than previously. This type of radical change makes it difficult for organizations to understand their environments well enough to plan coherently. So numerous variations by different units offer the best way to hit on new ideas and practices. Each individual unit knows its own particular problems and its own situation best, and therefore is able to adapt more effectively than if directed by a superior unit, common culture, or coordination mechanisms in a network. Heterarchies are truly self-organizing systems.

As our example of the advertising agency illustrates, though units may adapt independently there are still interdependencies among units that must be carefully managed for the organization to be effective. Interdependencies tend to be managed by improvisation at first and as units understand each other better, they fall into more regular patterns. For instance, in the ad agency, the creative unit may want to try a new wireless campaign and would need to coordinate with the technology department to make sure the ads were designed for the narrower bandwidth of cell phones. Members of the creative unit would need to work with the "wireless guys" in the technology department, which would involve working out ways to collaborate effectively; once done, future contacts on wireless projects would be much easier. If this collaboration proved to be unusually fruitful, it might later be imitated by other units of the agency.

What is life like in a heterarchy? On the one hand, it is interesting and can be exhilirating because it involves continuously confronting the situations before one and working out answers. There is no "rulebook" for a heterarchy. Members are free to organize things in ways comfortable for them and to put their stamp on the organization. On the other hand, it is likely to be exhausting as well from time to time with the need to balance off satisfying many different units. Recall the ancient Chinese curse "May you live in interesting times." People with low tolerance for ambiguity will likely not be happy in a heterarchy. Those who like rules and clear structure will not function well either.

Box 6.3
Postmodern Organizations?

One of the most influential and most controversial views of society and organizations that has developed during the past 30 years is postmodernism. Although it is impossible to describe this perspective at length in this chapter, it is based on the assumption that sometime during the twentieth century, human society underwent a fundamental change. For millennia human beings had looked for a source of stability, an explanation of natural and human events that made sense in all situations, and could thus be used to predict future events and prepare for them. In some societies that explanation was primarily religious; in others it was primarily philosophical; in the West it was primarily scientific, at least after the Enlightenment. Of course, in all societies the three forms of explanation mixed together in complex and often contradictory ways, but there was a common assumption that *some* stable explanation was possible – that a "grand narrative" was being constructed that made sense out of human experience. Eventually, this changed. People realized that the world had become fragmented, rapidly changing, and global. The narratives that we construct are unstable, so much so that they are illusions (postmodernist theorist Jean Baudrillard [1981] calls them **simulacra** because they are mere simulations of a "reality" that does not really exist). They also are highly political, in that they legitimize some form of domination of one group of people by other groups. Authority should not only be critically questioned, as the student movements of the 1960s through 1990s claimed, but it should also be resisted. In fact, there is no such thing as "fact" – all "truth" is constructed through communication, and its claims should be taken apart (through techniques usually labeled "deconstruction") and examined (Derrida, 1976).

How, one might ask, could an "organization" be postmodern, since the whole idea of postmodernism is a rejection of the concept of organizing? First, in postmodern forms of organizing, image is central – in fact, it may be all there is. Postmodern organizational theorists Eric Eisenberg and H. Lloyd Goodall (2001) point to a BMW plant in South Carolina as a stereotypical example of postmodern forms of organizing. BMW makes automobiles, but doing so is only a sidelight, or a mechanism, for selling a corporate image. Its logo means wealthy, sophisticated, European, and technological (even though its actual operations are much less technologically sophisticated than those of its competitors). It is so completely focused on adapting its products to different global markets, that it can be "different things for different people." An automobile is an automobile, but that is a decidedly modern way of thinking – BMW is not an automobile, it is an image.

Of course, if everything is image, then communication is crucial. It also is unlimited. BMW rejects the notion of boundaries. It is actively involved in every community it touches. It uses communication technology to keep each of its employees directly connected with its customers and suppliers. It emphasizes shared accountability among all of its employees. Everyone, regardless of rank in the organization, wears the same uniform and is accessible to everyone else. It celebrates ambiguity and difference – cultural, linguistic, racial, and ethnic – and stresses that what might be viewed as "communication breakdowns" (recall Chapter 3) are opportunities for dialogue and discussion (Eisenberg and Goodall, 2001). In short, postmodern strategies of organizing take all of the trends that we discuss in this book – from globalization to technological change to organizational image – and extend them as far as possible.

Do heterarchies eventually evolve into one of the other organizational forms? For example, if the rapid advance in the ICT industries slowed, the advertising firm might well eventually stabilize as the particular practices that were effective were preserved and others died out. In this case it might shift toward a relational or network strategy, which are the ones that best fit the type of work advertising firms do. However, in cases in which the environment continued to be uncertain and rapidly changing, the heterarchy would continue to renew itself. Heterarchies may also be preserved if the organization and its members value them. Some critics of the control organizations exercise over their members argue that heterarchies are an organiazational form that preserves members freedom and allows them voice.

Heterarchies must address several types of challenges to be effective. For one thing, they require a lot of energy from their members. If the matrix structure and network strategy are communication intensive, then the heterarchy is *really* communication intensive for its members. Problems of overload and burnout are likely to be common. Second, the heterarchy works only if its constituent units or organizations remain fairly equal in terms of power or influence over the system. Once one or a few units or organizations gain control, they may begin to favor some ways of organizing over others and impede the random variation of approaches taken by different units that is at the heart of the heterarchy's effectiveness. Third, coordination of units or organizations ina heterarchy is by no means a trivial matter. Since coordination depends on relationships among units, there are cases where it will break down. Breakdowns can be the source of new ideas and practices that further enrich the heterarchy, but it may also lead to problems or even failure for the organization.

CONCLUSION

Network organizations have become more prominent in the past 20 years, but they have always been with us. As we have noted, building contractors and movie producers typically operate network organizations. Acting as brokers, they contract with carpenters, plumbing companies, electrical contractors, and others to perform the work necessary to build a house or store.

The gradual evolution of the knowledge society in the last half of the twentieth century set the stage for the explosive rate at which the emphasis on knowledge and information work has developed over the past 20 years. Along with this came the globalization of the economy, rapid growth in knowledge and technology, and increased environmental turbulence. The rapid development of ICTs has facilitated and fed on these changes. Computer and telecommunications technologies have permeated organizations and made many types of structures and communication systems possible that were only visions before 1980.

To deal with the increased pace of change and adapt to turbulent environments, organizations must incorporate integrating communication methods for coordination. We discussed a number of different methods for integrating organizations and suggested that they be evaluated on the basis of benefits and costs to the organization, the degree of geographical dispersion of the organization, and the organization's culture. Ideally the least costly method that can adequately meet the organization's needs should be chosen. In practice this is not always possible due to limitations in member knowledge and willingness to use a given method and due to lack of fit with the organization's culture. These coordination methods will help organizations employing the traditional, relational, and cultural strategies to deal with changing technologies and environments; but they can only go so far. When uncertainty is high due to environmental change, internal complexity, or other factors, a different strategy of organizing is needed.

The network strategy of organizing is appropriate for organizations that must cope with high levels of uncertainty. It approaches organization as a network, with a flexible, modular set of interrelated units, a relatively flat hierarchy, emphasis on teams and self-management, and use of information technology to coordinate units. Networks can be changed relatively easily to incorporate new units or to rearrange themselves to respond to new demands from their work or environment. The network organization relies on employees to be independent, knowledgeable and team oriented. Rather than rigid structures, the network uses mutual trust among members, member's commitment to their work, contracts, and open communication systems to hold the network together. Units in the network coordinate through communication and negotiation rather than through authority.

The network is the newest widespread approach to organizing, but it is also important to remember that there are other approaches, including cooperatives and heterarchies. Either of these – and perhaps some other heretofore unknown strategy – might turn out to be the next popular approach to organizing.

NOTES

1 Fulk and DeSanctis (1999).

2 A readable account of the matrix organization can be found in Youker (1977, 18–24). Also see Galbraith (1987).

3 Robb (2002, 30). Despite the continued development of enterprise-level applications since this article appeared, this still remains a good example of how they can be used to integrate organizations. For a more recent discussion of enterprise systems, see McKeen and Smith (2004).

4 See "Why Peter Drucker" (2010). All quotations in this paragraph taken from this source.

REFERENCES

Alexander, E., Penley, L. and Hernigan, I. E. (1991) "The Effect of Individual Differences on Managerial Media Choice." *Management Communication Quarterly* 5: 155–173.

Ancona, D., Kochan, T., Scully, M., van Maanen, J. and Westney, D.E. (1999). "The New Organization: Taking Action in An Era of Organizational Transformation," in *Organizational Behavior and Process*. Cincinnati, OH: South-Western.

Arguilla, J., Ronfeldt, D. and Zanini, M. (1999). "Networks, Netwar and Information Age Terrorism," in Lesser, Hoffman, Arquilla, Ronfeldt and Zanini, eds., *Countering the New Terrorism*. Santa Monica, CA: Rand.

Ashcraft, K.L. (2001). "Organized Dissonance: Feminist Bureaucracy as Hybrid Form." *Academy of Management Journal* 44: 1301–1322.

Ashcraft, K.L. and Kedrowicz, A. (2002). "Self-Direction or Social Support?" *Communication Monographs* 69: 88–110.

Baudrillard, J. (1981). *Simulacra and Simulations*. Minneapolis: University of Minnesota Press.

Bergen, P. (2002). "Al Qaeda's New Tactics." *New York Times*, November 15. www.nytimes.com/2002/11/15/opinion/al-qaeda-s-new-tactics.html.

Bergen, P. (2004). "Defining al-Qaeda: Is It a Group? Is It a Movement?" *Houston Chronicle*, January 4.

Browning, L., Beyer, J. and Shetler, J. (1995). "Building Cooperation in a Competitive Industry: SEMATECH and the Semiconductor Industry." *Academy of Management Journal* 38: 113–151.

Burton, R.M., DeSanctis, G. and Obel, B. (2006). *Organizational Design: A Step-by-Step Approach*. Cambridge: Cambridge University Press.

Carlson, J.R. and Zmud, R.W. (1999) "Channel Expansion Theory and the Experiential Nature of Media Richness Perceptions." *Academy of Management Review* 42: 153–170.

Charles Perrow. (2002). *Organizing America*. New Haven, CT: Yale University Press.

Cheney, G. (1999). *Values at Work*. Ithaca, NY: ILR of Cornell University Press.

Daft, R. (1989). *Organization Theory and Design*, 3rd ed. St. Paul, MN: West.

Dellarocas, C. (2006). "Reputation Mechanisms," in Hendershott, ed., *Handbook on Economics and Information Systems*. Amsterdam: Elsevier.

Derrida, J. (1976). *Speech and Phenomenon*. Evanston, IL: Northwestern University Press.

Dickinson, J. (2007) "Videoconferencing That Works. Finally!" *Computerworld*, September 10, 46–48.

Donnellon, A. and Scully, M. (1994). "Teams, Performance, and Rewards: Will the Post-Bureaucratic Organization Be a Post-Meritocratic Organization?" in Heckscher and Donnellon, eds., *The Post-Bureaucratic Organization: New Perspectives on Organizational Change*. Thousand Oaks, CA: Sage.

Edley, P. (2000). "Discursive Essentializing in a Woman-Owned Business." *Management Communication Quarterly* 14: 271–306.

Eisenberg, E. and Goodall, H.L., Jr. (2001). *Organizational Communication: Balancing Creativity and Constraint*. Boston: Bedford/St. Martin's Press.

Elance.com. (n.d.). [Home page]. www.elance.com.

Freeman, J. (1976). "The Tyranny of Structurelessness." *MS*, July.

Fulk, J. and DeSanctis, G. (1999). "Articulation of Communication Technology and Organizational Form," in DeSanctis and Fulk, eds., *Shaping Organization Form: Communication, Connection and Community*. Newbury Park, CA: Sage.

Fulk, J., Steinfield, C.W., Schmitz, J. and Power, J.G. (1987) "A Social Information Processing Model of Media Use in Organizations." *Communication Research* 14: 529–552.

Galbraith, J. (1987). "Organizational Design," in Lorsch, ed., *Handbook of Organizational Behavior*. Englewood Cliffs, NJ: Prentice Hall.

Gama, R., Medrano, D. and Medrano, L. (2010). "The Anthropology of Money in Southern California." www.anthro.uci.edu/html/Programs/Anthro_Money/Tandas.htm.

Ghosh, A. and Fedorowicz, J. (2008). "The Role of Trust in Supply Chain Governance." *Business Process Management Journal* 14: 453–470.

Hart, R.K. and McLeod, P.L. (2002). "Rethinking Team Building in Geographically Dispersed Teams: One Message at a Time." *Organizational Dynamics* 31: 352–361.

Holmstrom, B. and Roberts, J. (2003). "The Boundaries of the Firm Revisited," in Malone, Laubacher, and Scott-Morton, eds., *Inventing the Organizations of the 21st Century*. Cambridge, MA: MIT Press.

Johnson, J.D. (2009). *Managing Knowledge Networks*. Cambridge: Cambridge University Press.

Joshi, A., Lazarova, M.B. and Lao, H. (2009). "Getting Everyone on Board: The Role of Inspirational Leadership on Geographically Dispersed Teams." *Organization Science* 20: 240–252.

Knoke, D. (2001). *Changing Organizations: Business Networks in the New Political Economy*. Boulder, CO: Westview.

Laubacher, R. and Malone, T.W. (2003). "Retreat of the Firm and the Rise of Guilds: The Employment Relationship in an Age of Virtual Business," in Malone, Laubacher, and Scott-Morton, eds., *Inventing the Organizations of the 21st Century*. Cambridge, MA: MIT Press.

Liebeskind, J.P., Oliver, A.L., Zucker, L. and Brewer, M. (1996). "Social Networks, Learning, and Flexibility: Sourcing Scientific Knowledge in New Biotechnology Firms." *Organization Science* 7: 428–443.

Lipinski, J. (2010). "A Commune Grows in Brooklyn." *New York Times*, style sec., September 9, 1, 8.

Lott, C. (1988). "Redwood Records: Principles and Profit in Women's Music," in Bate and Taylor, eds., *Women Communicating*. Norwood, NJ: Ablex.

Lucas, H.C. (1996). *The T-Form Organization: Using Technology to Design Organizations for the 21st Century* San Francisco: Jossey-Bass.

Madhani, A. (2010). "What Makes Cleric al-Awlaki So Dangerous?" *USA Today*, August 25, 1–2.

Malone, T.W. and Laubacher, R. (2003). "The Dawn of the E-Lance Economy," in Malone, Laubacher, and Scott-Morton, eds., *Inventing the Organizations of the 21st Century*. Cambridge, MA: MIT Press.

Martin, J., Knopoff, K. and Beckman, C. (1998). "An Alternative to Bureaucratic Impersonality and Emotional Labor: Bounded Emotionality at the Body Shop." *Administrative Science Quarterly* 43: 429–469.

Mayer, R.C., Davis, J.H. and Schoorman, F.D. (1995). "An Integrative Model of Organizational Trust" *Academy of Management Review* 20: 7–9.

McKeen, J.D. and Smith, H.A. (2004). *Making IT Happen: Critical Issues in IT Management*. New York: Wiley.

Melymuka, K. (2003). "Smarter by the Hour." *Computerworld*, June 23: 43–44.

Monge, P.R. and Contractor, N. (2003). *Theories of Communication Networks*. Oxford: Oxford University Press.

Moreno, J. (2002). "Old-Fashioned Savings, Loans." *Houston Chronicle*, September 17, B1.

Nohria, N. and Berkley, J.D. (1994)., "Allen-Bradley's ICCG Case Study," in Heckscher and Donnellon, eds., *The Post-Bureaucratic Organization: New Perspectives on Organizational Change*. Newbury Park, CA: Sage.

Nov, O. (2007). "What Motivates Wikipedians?" *Communications of the ACM* 50: 60–64.

Papa, M., Auwal, M. and Singhai, A. (1995). "Dialectic of Control and Emancipation in Organizing for Social Change." *Communication Theory* 5: 189–223.

Perrow, C. (2002). *Organizing America: Wealth, Power, and the Origins of American Capitalism*. Princeton, NJ: Princeton University Press.

Poole, M.S. (1999). "Organizational Challenges for the New Forms," in DeSanctis and Fulk, eds., *Shaping Organization Form: Communication, Connection, and Community*. Newbury Park, CA: Sage.

Powell, W.W., Koput, K. and Smith-Doerr, L. (1996). "Interorganizational Collaboration and the Locus of Innovation: Networks of Learning in Biotechnology." *Administrative Science Quarterly* 41: 116–145.

Rice, R.E. and Gattiker, U.E. (2001). "New Media and Organizational Structuring," in Jablin and Putnam, eds., *The New Handbook of Organizational Communication*. Thousand Oaks, CA: Sage.

Robb, D. (2002). "Collaboration Gets It Together." *Computerworld*, December 9, 30.

Robert, L.P. and Dennis, A. R. (2005). "Paradox of Richness: A Cognitive Model of Media Choice." *IE IEEE Transactions on Professional Communication* 48: 10–22.

Sitkin, S.B., Sutcliffe, K.M., and Barrios-Choplin, J.R. (1992). "A Dual-Capacity Model of Communication Medium Choice in Organizations." *Human Communication Research* 18: 563–598.

Stark, D. (1999). "Heterarchy: Distributing Authority and Organizing Diversity," in Clippinger III, ed., *The Biology of Business: Decoding the Natural Laws of Enterprise*. San Francisco: Jossey-Bass.

Star Reviews. (n.d.). "Elance: Star Review." www.starreviews.com/elance.aspx.

Stohl, C. and Stohl, M. (2007). Terrorism Networks: Theoretical Assumptions and Pragmatic Consequences" *Communication Theory* 17: 93–124.

Thomas, T.L. (2003). "Cyberplanning." *Parameters*, Spring, 112–123.

Trevino, L., Lengel, R. and Daft, R. (1987) "Media Symbolism, Media Richness, and Media Choices in Organizations." *Communication Research* 14: 553–574.

Wang, Y.D. and Emurian, H.H. (2005). "An Overview of Online Trust: Concepts, Elements, and Implications." *Computers in Human Behavior* 21: 105–125.

"Why Peter Drucker Hailed Francis Hesselbein as the World's Best Leader." (2010). *India Times* online, January 10. http://economictimes.indiatimes.com/features/corporate-dossier/Why-Peter-Drucker-hailed-Francis-Hesselbein-as-the-worlds-best-leader/articleshow/5446959.cms.

Winter, S.J. and Taylor, S.L. (1999). "The Role of Information Technology in the Transformation of Work: A Comparison of Postindustrial, Industrial, and Protoindustrial Organization," in DeSanctis and Fulk, eds., *Shaping Organization Form: Communication, Connection, and Connectivity*. Newbury Park, CA: Sage.

Woolls, D. (2004). "Al-Qaida Suspects Had Normal Lives." *Houston Chronicle*, January 20, 9A.

Youker, R. (1977) "Organization Alternatives for Project Managers." *Project Management Journal* 8: 18–24.

POSTSCRIPT TO UNIT II

CONTINGENCY PERSPECTIVE ON ORGANIZING STRATEGIES

There is no one best way to organize.
Any way of organizing is not equally effective.
Jay Galbraith

CENTRAL THEME

- Which organizing strategy is most effective depends on the type of technology the organization employs and the nature of the organization's environment

KEY TERMS

contingency theory   technology   environment

You may have detected a theme that runs through Chapters 3 through 6: There is no one best way to organize. The answer to the question "Which strategy for organizing is best?" is "It depends." Advocates of traditional and relational strategies thought they had found the single best way to organize. So did the early proponents of cultural strategies, who viewed strong cultures as a universally applicable strategy. However, much research and practical experience has shown that they were mistaken. Under some conditions, the bureaucratic strategy works best, while under other conditions, the relational, cultural, or networking strategies are superior.

Strategic Organizational Communication: In a Global Economy, Seventh Edition.
Charles Conrad and Marshall Scott Poole.

This was first noted in the late 1950s by two English sociologists, Burns and Stalker (1961). They found that when the environment in which the organization operates is stable, a well-planned, efficient organization, which is epitomized by the bureaucracy, outperforms all other types because it is the most efficient organization. Other types of organizations may do well for a while; but ultimately the bureaucracy outraces them, because it produces the best results with the least input. It will have superior profitability and efficiency and more funds to reinvest in improving its product or service.

However, Burns and Stalker found that when the environment is unstable and turbulent, the bureaucracy is too slow to adapt. Its formal structures, standard operating procedures, and centralized decision making limit its members' ability to recognize the need for change and make it inflexible when change is necessary. A more "organic" structure with a flatter hierarchy, more open communication, and more flexibility in procedures and rules, performs best in this environment. The conclusion Burns and Stalker drew is that the most effective structure for an organization is *contingent* on the nature of the organization's environment.

Burns and Stalker's study initiated a major area of research in organizational studies that attempted to develop a **contingency theory** of organizational design. This contingency theory attempts to specify the key variables that determine the effectiveness of various organizational structures. If we know the values of these variables, the reasoning goes, then we can determine how to design our organization so that it will be most effective.

Forty years of research on contingency theory has identified two key contingency variables: (1) nature of the organization's tasks and (2) the organization's environment. Together these two variables determine the level of uncertainty the organization faces, which many scholars believe is the major factor that motivates organizational design (Burton, DeSanctis, and Obel, 2006). Depending on the values of these variables – and the level of uncertainty that they create – different organizing strategies are recommended.

TASK

The term **task** refers to the activities necessary to transform organizational inputs into outputs (Perrow, 1967; Burton, DeSanctis, and Obel, 2006). This definition means that task refers to the operations by which the work of the organization is done. A social service agency's task, for example, includes patient intake and record keeping, provision of services such as client counseling and therapy, and billing. Executing this series of operations enables the social service agency to serve its clients, which in turn ensures a flow of funds to the agency.

In general terms, tasks vary along a continuum from routine to nonroutine.[1] For a *routine* task, the process by which the work must be done is well understood, and there are few unexpected problems or exceptions. Routine tasks can be broken down into steps and programmed. In many cases, routine tasks can be automated, reducing the organization's reliance on human labor. For example, fast-food restaurants offer limited menus, so the procedures for preparing the food are highly standardized. This is true even in those that claim to be able to let you "have it your way." Machines often do the cooking, and workers follow tightly regimented recipes and portion control formulae. Routinization ensures a consistent product and good returns for the franchise. In fact, the primary appeal of McDonald's is that Big Macs taste the same almost everywhere in the world (except India, where lamb is used instead of beef). Even exceptions can be easily planned for. "Having it your way" involves a relatively limited set of ingredient variations and preparation steps, each of which is planned well in advance. Workers have little or no discretion or control over the work. Engineers, operations management specialists, and other experts analyze the work and determine how it should be done.

At the other end of the scale are *nonroutine* tasks. Because there are many exceptional cases, and because the procedures for doing nonroutine tasks are not well understood, human judgment and discretion must be applied to each case. As the old phrase goes, the work is more of an art than a science. Skilled workers are needed to exercise finely trained judgments in solving problems and doing the work. Strategic planning requires extensive know-how and background. However, planners do not always understand exactly what the right way to respond to the situation they face is. Nor do they know what the situation will be like in the future. Hence they must improvise and project based on their own knowledge and experience.

Generally speaking, uncertainty increases as we move from routine to nonroutine tasks. As a result, traditional strategies of organizing are most effective for highly routine tasks, relational strategies for moderately routine tasks, and network strategies for nonroutine tasks. Cultural strategies that emphasize continuity and stability are more effective for routine tasks; but those that emphasize change and innovation are more effective with nonroutine tasks.

Intermediate cases are more difficult. In such cases, there is less than perfect knowledge of how to do the work and more than a few exceptions occur; however, these intermediate cases do not have the extremely high degrees of uncertainty that nonroutine tasks are designed for. Examples of intermediate cases are clothing design and pattern making, specialty steel manufacturing, legal work, and the performing arts. A typical intermediate strategy is to develop a repertoire of methods or techniques that can be mastered and applied to different cases. The challenge is selecting and combining the right routines to get the job done properly. So the surgical team knows many different procedures (anesthesia, opening the patient, tying off blood vessels), and combines different sets of them in different ways, depending on the type of operation being done and the particular characteristics of the patient.

Organizational communication is quite different in organizations with routine tasks from those with nonroutine **technologies**. The greater the uncertainty, the greater the need for direct, intensive communication and many adjustments. Although most people prefer face-to-face communication, direct and intense communication is costly. It takes a great deal of time to communicate and come to an understanding, to adjust work and plans, and to manage the conflicts that may arise along the way. For best results, a balance must be struck between communication needs and cost: The organization should enact the least costly communication system that can adequately meet its needs for communication and coordination.

If people need to exchange only standard information, such as an order for a meal, placing the order through a more impersonal medium, such as a checklist or email, is adequate because it conveys the same information with less communication cost. For routine technologies, vertical, formal, written communication is most adequate. Since these tasks are predictable and repeatable, there is usually a wealth of documented information and analysis concerning how best to do the work and handle problems. This can be put in formal manuals or work procedures that substitute for direct communication between workers or between workers and managers. For routine tasks, most communication follows the chain of command as managers give orders to and solve problems for subordinates. Low levels of task variety suggest that exceptions requiring extended discussion will be rare and that instructions for handling those that do can be built into procedural manuals.

For nonroutine tasks uncertainty is high, so each task must be approached with a great deal of direct, often unscheduled communication. Face-to-face consultations and long, intense meetings are often the only adequate form of communication to meet the needs of nonroutine work.

For intermediate cases, there is a need for higher levels of communication than routine organization allows for but less than the nonroutine case. The lowest cost method for increasing communication beyond formal channels in such cases is the scheduled meeting, because this can be planned into the work.

To sum up, depending on the nature of the tasks a unit does, the unit will have different levels of uncertainty and different communication needs. To remain effective and viable, the organization must adopt an organizing strategy and communication system that is adequate for the demands placed on it. Assessing a unit's tasks can help us understand why its communication is effective or not and what needs to be done to improve communication.

Environment

The notion of organizational environment has already been introduced in earlier chapters. In this section, we will define environment more systematically and connect it to the design of organizations and their communication systems.

Literally, environment refers to everything outside the organization's boundaries. However, for the purpose of analysis, **environment** can be defined as those institutions, organizations, groups, and people outside the organization that affect it. Environments are made up of many elements, including domestic and foreign competitors, customers and clients, government agencies and regulators, general economic conditions, technological developments relevant to the organization, financial resources, the labor market, raw materials suppliers, and the general culture surrounding the organization. Not all these elements are similar or equally important for every organization; depending on its purpose and location, each organization has a particular mix of these elements as its environment.

Organizational environments can be described in terms of two basic dimensions, complexity and stability (Burton, DeSanctis, and Obel, 2006). The *complexity* of an organization's environment refers to the number of elements in the environment with which the organization has to deal. An organization with a simple environment may have only a few elements to deal with, whereas one in a complex environment may deal with dozens or hundreds of elements. For example, a university library has a relatively simple environment; it has to deal with the university's administration, student and faculty clientele, publishers and other publication sources, and other libraries. Many of the library's dealings with other agencies, such as the Occupational Safety and Health Administration and the Social Security Administration, are handled for it by the university administration, greatly reducing the environmental complexity. On the other hand, a publishing house has to deal with a much more complex environment – stockholders or owners (who may change frequently as a result of mergers), competing publishers, authors (who often miss deadlines), customers, an assortment of government agencies, the financial institutions that provide its capital and operating monies, labor unions, and new technologies that compete with published books, magazines, and journals. Clearly, university libraries and publishing houses experience different environmental demands.

The other dimension of organizational environment, *stability*, can be defined as the rate of change in the elements of the environment and their relationships, a concept mentioned in several previous chapters. Some environments are stable and/or change in a predictable fashion. Before deregulation, the telephone company AT&T had a stable environment. Suppliers and customers were predictable, the telephone company's monopoly status gave it a guaranteed market, and its relations with the regulators ensured it would make a reasonable profit. Change came mainly in the form of new technologies and services that the phone company developed itself. On the other end of the continuum are organizations whose environments are changing rapidly and continuously. These organizations must adapt constantly, and unpredictability is expected and factored into their operation. To deal with instability, these organizations develop special positions and units to monitor and plan reactions to the environment. Firms in the information technology field offer a good example of life in an unstable environment. Driven by the fast pace of technological change and cutthroat international competition, they often change their products, their markets, and their own structures to survive and remain competitive.

Together environmental complexity and stability define four basic situations that can be arranged in order of increasing uncertainty. Simple, stable environments – what Burton, DeSanctis, and Obel call "calm" environments – create relatively low levels of uncertainty. Organizations in these environments can focus on setting up the most effective and efficient organizational design. Examples of such organizations in this cell include soft drink distribution companies and law offices. Complex, stable environments – what Burton *et al.* call "varied environments" – offer medium levels of uncertainty. As a result, the organization must evolve special units or procedures for dealing with uncertainty and anticipate a certain amount of change. Examples of organizations with complex, stable environments include universities and chemical companies.

Moderate to high uncertainty is experienced by organizations in simple, unstable environments, called "locally stormy" by Burton *et al.* Whereas these environments are relatively simple, they undergo continuous change, and organizations must change to survive in them. Examples of organizations with unstable, simple environments include firms in the clothing industry and manufacturers of personal computers who supply the big retail outlets. Finally, unstable, complex environments – what Burton *et al.* call "turbulent" environments – create the highest level of uncertainty. In these environments, the organization must constantly plan for change and react to circumstances beyond its control. To do so, special positions and units are created to monitor and guide reactions to environmental change, and a flexible organizational structure is needed to promote adaptation. Examples of organizations in this quadrant are software, telecommunications, and airline firms.

To be effective, organizations in calm environments should adopt the traditional strategy; those in varied and locally stormy environments should adopt the relational strategy, and those in turbulent environments should adopt the network strategy (Daft, 1992; Burton *et al.*, 2006). Cultural strategies that value stability are more effective in stable environments; those that emphasize innovation and change are more effective in unstable environments. The traditional form is the most effective when the organization can plan its structure and procedures carefully because of its advantage in efficiency. However, when the environment is changing, the flatter, more interconnected relational form is preferred because of its adaptability.

As instability and complexity increase, organizations become more complex and have less stable structures. This situation increases the need for communication and integrating roles in the organization. Integrating roles are those that help different units coordinate their efforts and resolve actual and potential conflicts. Organizations with high levels of instability and complexity in particular have many integrating roles.

Case Study P.1

Steeling Away Into a Different Structure[1]

From the days of Andrew Carnegie and the other steel barons to the late 1960s, the steel industry was dominated by large, vertically integrated companies. The industry existed in a stable environment and the rate of technological advance was steady and gradual. If steel manufacturers could produce steel of good quality at a reasonable price, it could be sold.

Excelsior Steel is 125 years old, employs 2200, and makes 250,000 tons of steel a year. Located in Northern Indiana, it is housed in a huge plant that consolidated all operations under one roof. Excelsior had a centralized, hierarchical structure. From its offices in downtown Gary, top management, with the aid of engineering, made decisions regarding the products Excelsior would manufacture and the level produced. Separate departments handled manufacturing, marketing, metallurgy, field sales, and support for these units. Over the years, top managers forged close contacts with unions, and the unions often worked with Excelsior to determine work rates and how the work should be done.

But all that changed starting in the late 1970s. The inflation of that period, coupled with the recession that followed it and fierce competition from Germany, Japan, and Brazil, brought Excelsior to the edge of bankruptcy. Excelsior was in danger of following many of the other steel giants that lined the southern edge of Lake Michigan out of the steel business. But Excelsior did not become another of those huge abandoned buildings north of Hammond, Indiana. Instead it took aggressive steps to solve problems.

After extensive diagnosis, Excelsior's managers found that their products were no longer keeping pace with the market, 60 percent of the firm's orders ran behind schedule, and profits were eaten up by materials, energy, and labor costs. In this more turbulent environment, the stable, hierarchical structure was not nimble enough. Moreover, technological advances had rendered much of Excelsior's plant outdated. Smaller furnaces equipped with the latest computer-assisted manufacturing devices could turn out many of Excelsior's products at a much lower cost.

In conjunction with outside experts and the union, management at Excelsior concocted a strategy to save the plant. The strategy hinged on shifting production to high-value products tailored for separate markets, while upgrading technology and research.

To get started, Excelsior set up three product task forces: sheet metal, special alloys, and open-die forgings. These task forces had representatives from all departments involved in the products and their charge was to determine how each product could be produced in an independent product group. The task forces formed the basis for permanently integrating teams headed by product managers, each of which was responsible for all aspects of one of the three product areas, including sales. Each product area was also responsible for introducing new products and trimming products that were not successful.

Over time, there were so many orders for different types of specialty steel that the special alloys group subdivided into multiple project teams, instituting a mini-matrix structure within the group. Since it was important to keep the personnel in the special alloys groups trained in the latest technology and metallurgical research, the functional departments assumed increased importance. Functional managers, such as the manager of metallurgy, were responsible for keeping abreast of the latest technical developments and for keeping personnel trained. These personnel were then assigned to one or more projects, under the supervision of the project manager. This structure greatly enhanced communication both within and between specialties.

Excelsior installed electronic mail and voice mail when it implemented an order and inventory tracking system. These greatly increased the ability of Excelsior's employees to keep in touch with each other and increased the flow of ideas. Along with this, Excelsior created a program to cultivate new ideas in which employees who had brainstorms could set up project teams to develop them, provided they could make a good case with the management team. From this program came several new product lines.

Implementation of this new structure was not painless. The company had to lay off workers, because the three product lines did not require as many employees as Excelsior had in its heyday. By the end of the reorganization, Excelsior had only 1300 employees; however, as production increased it hired back about 300 more. Many of the laid-off employees were replaced by technology. The union still hung on, but union and management were much less adversarial than in the past. Union and management worked together to reorganize the plant. Middle managers and foremen were especially confused by the transition to product units and the matrix-based structure. Not accustomed to dealing with ambiguity, they initially resisted the increased number of meetings and negotiation required. Over time the most disgruntled managers and foremen retired, and the new structure, which emphasized horizontal and integrative links as well as vertical communication, took over. Many of the managers who initially resisted this shift have found it to be a growth experience; they try to involve younger employees in new product development and problem solving to develop them for the future.

Excelsior Steel is now back on track. Deliveries are on time better than 95 percent of the time. An average of 20 new products are introduced each year, and profits are up. Market share has recovered as well. Excelsior employees gladly embrace their new motto, "Change or Die."

Applying What You've Learned

1. How did Excelsior respond to changes in its environment and technology? Which of the integrating methods did Excelsior use?

Questions to Think About and Discuss

1. It is not clear that a company in Excelsior's position can ever stop changing. What are some of the disadvantages of continuous change? How could Excelsior minimize them?
2. What communication problems would you expect to occur as Excelsior moved from its old structure and culture to the new one?

Note

1 This case was inspired by Richard Daft (1989).

INTERRELATIONSHIPS AMONG THE CONTINGENCY VARIABLES

The relationship between the task and organizational design takes much the same form as that of the environment to organizational design, if we consider the level of uncertainty each creates for the organization. If the levels of uncertainty created by task and environment are consistent – for example, if the technology is nonroutine and the environment locally stormy or turbulent, both of which create high levels of uncertainty – then design choices are straightforward.

However, what about cases when the two variables are inconsistent with each other? An organization might, for example, have a nonroutine task but confront a calm environment.

The nature of the task suggests that the relational or even network strategy should be used; but the nature of the environment suggests the traditional strategy. Two possible outcomes have been suggested for organizations in this situation. First, some scholars suggest that the organization should adopt the most complex organization indicated by the three variables. At the cost of some inefficiency, the organization would be able to deal with its toughest challenge. Second, other scholars suggest that cases when the variables are inconsistent represent instances when the organization must "suboptimize" or underperform, because it is faced with contradictions. One of the emerging organizational forms, the heterarchy has been advanced as a response to just this sort of case, in which the situation confronting the organization is both contradictory and highly changeable.

CONCLUSION AND TRANSITION

While it is tempting to pick out one organizational strategy as "the best" or "our favorite," the ultimate effectiveness of a strategy depends on the organization's technology and environment. As these two factors vary, so too does the organizing strategy that is most effective.

We now make a transition from general approaches to organizing to specific processes and challenges that face today's organizations. In Unit I of this book, we introduced a perspective that typically is called "institutional theory." It asserts that organizations and organizational communication can only be understood if one considers the broader context(s) within which they exist. At a societal level, people create distinctive sets of structures, practices, and taken-for-granted assumptions. These social institutions emerge over time, piecemeal and sometimes in a rather incoherent way. Sometimes they are developed through the intentional, calculated actions of powerful individuals; sometimes they result from unanticipated and unintended long-term consequences of efforts to address immediate social conditions. But, once they are established they are legitimized – treated as normal and natural – they establish a complex web of guidelines, constraints, rules, and resources that influence both the strategic choices of the organizations that exist within a given society and the communication strategies available to their members. Those strategic choices in turn reproduce institutionalized structures and taken-for-granted assumptions, and in some case lead to their transformation.

In the chapters of Unit III, we return to those key concepts. In Chapter 7 we examine organizational power relationships as a key dimension of institutionalized structures and assumptions, and view organizational politics as the strategic management of power. In Chapter 8 we offer a parallel analysis of organizational decision making and conflict management. Chapter 9 explores organizational change, a key challenge raised in this postscript. In the final three chapters, we return to societal context and examine three core constructs – gender, diversity, and ethics.

NOTE

1 Perrow divides technology into two dimensions: analyzability and variety. Analyzability refers to the degree to which process the technology is designed to carry out, and is known and understood. The second dimension of technology is its variety and the number of exceptions encountered in the course of doing the work. In some work, exceptional cases are very rare; there are only small differences from case to case and

the "inputs" to the organizational systems are relatively uniform. This defines four types of technology. Two are covered in detail in the main text: low analyzability coupled with high variety (nonroutine technologies apply) and high analyzability coupled with low variety (routine technologies apply). The other two cases are engineering and craft technologies. Engineering technologies, with high analyzability but also high variety, are complicated, because many exceptions are encountered. However, because cause–effect relationships are well understood for these tasks, it is possible to develop a set of formulas that can then be applied to the different cases. For engineering technologies, uncertainty is somewhat higher. Manuals and standard procedures describe the various programs the unit can carry out, but members of the unit may need to consult regarding the specific programs that will be used, how they will be coordinated with each other, and what to do if problems arise. Hence, engineering technologies are most adequately served by a combination of written, standardized communication and verbal communication directed to coordinating work and problem resolution.

Craft technologies, with low analyzability and low variety, have a stable set of activities, but the transformation process is not well understood. Extensive training and experience are required to master work techniques and the judgment necessary for applying them. For example, a group of performing artists putting on a play knows the script, but turning that script into a performance requires them to draw on years of slowly accumulated know-how that they cannot put into words. For craft technologies, uncertainty is still higher than for engineering technologies. Because these technologies deal with low-analyzable work, the use of manuals and standard procedures is less feasible. The most adequate way of coordinating craft work is through horizontal verbal communication among those who have to work together. This can often be scheduled. For example, a specialty steel-fabricating plant might have a scheduled weekly meeting to discuss formulations for new orders.

REFERENCES

Burns, T. and Stalker, G.M. (1961). *The Management of Innovation*. London: Tavistock.

Burton, R.M., DeSanctis, G. and Obel, B. (2006). *Organizational Design: A Step-by-Step Approach*. New York: Cambridge University Press.

Daft, R. (1992). *Organization Theory and Design*, 4th ed. St. Paul, MN: West.

Perrow, C. (1967). "A Framework for the Comparative Analysis of Organizations." *American Sociological Review* 32: 194–208.

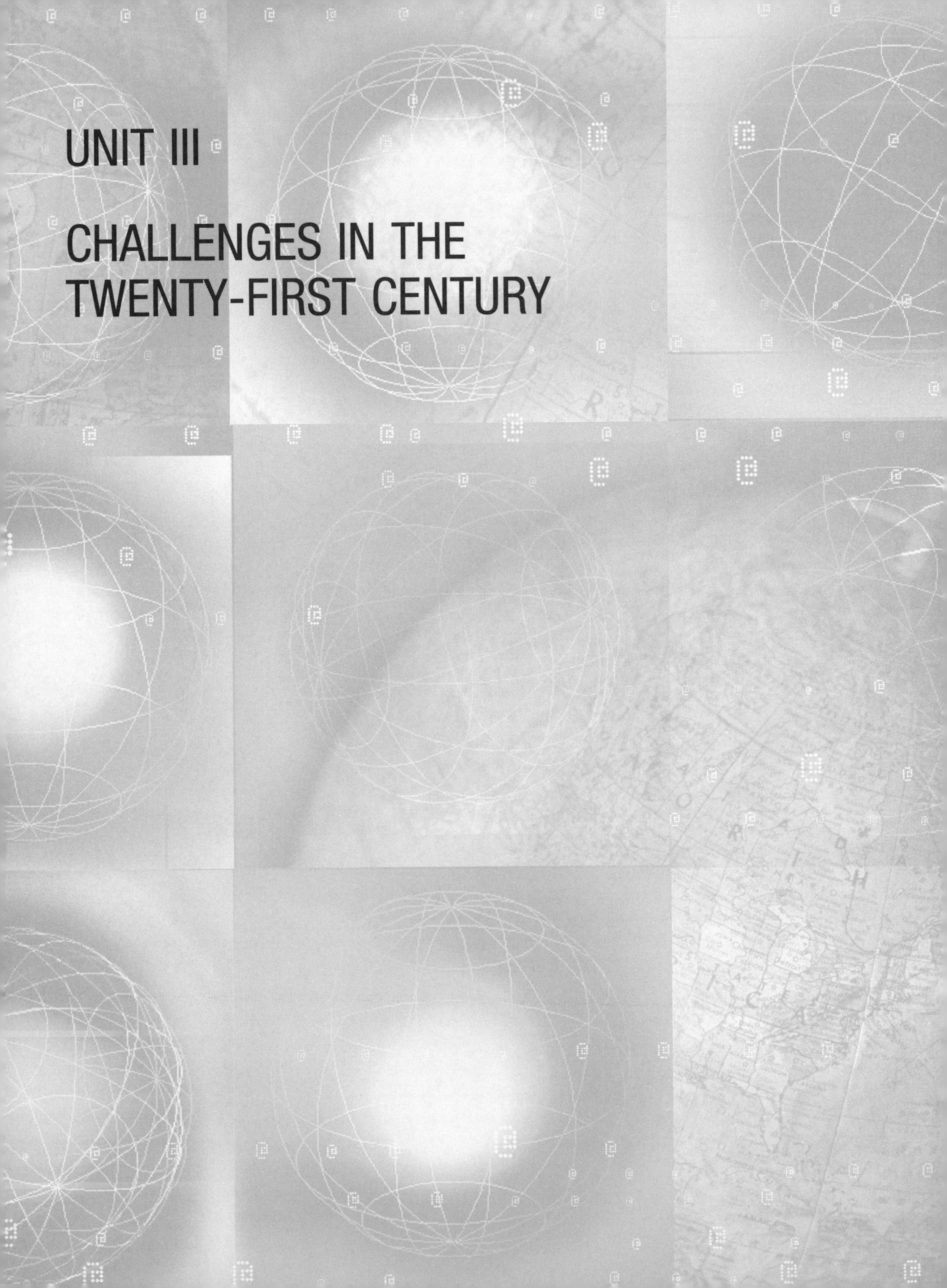

UNIT III

CHALLENGES IN THE TWENTY-FIRST CENTURY

CHAPTER 7

COMMUNICATION, POWER, AND POLITICS IN ORGANIZATIONS

Whatever else organizations may be . . . they are political structures. This means that organizations operate by distributing authority and setting a stage for the exercise of power.

Abraham Zalzenik

Insofar as knowledge is power, communication systems are power systems.

David Barber[1]

"Would you tell me please, which way I ought to go from here?" "That depends a good deal on where you want to get to," said the [Cheshire] Cat. "I don't much care where –" said Alice. "Then it doesn't matter which way you go," said the Cat. "– so long as I get somewhere," Alice added as an explanation.

CENTRAL THEMES

- Power usually is thought of as the "ability to dominate" other people. Not only does this perspective ignore the "accomplishment" aspect of power, but also it seriously oversimplifies its multifaceted nature.
- Power has two components: a "surface structure," which consists of overt displays of power and conscious but unspoken decisions about who, when, and how to challenge power relationships; and a "deep structure," which consists of unconscious elements of power relationships.

Strategic Organizational Communication: In a Global Economy, Seventh Edition.
Charles Conrad and Marshall Scott Poole.

- Power is in the eye of the beholder. Whenever people are able to control resources that others perceive they need, they have a potential base of power.
- Employees can develop power through developing personal characteristics (expertise, interpersonal skills, and access to symbols of power) and through controlling key resources (information, rewards and punishments, and roles in coalitions).
- Power is obtained and exercised through a predictable group of communication strategies.
- One of the effects of social and organizational power relationships is to silence the voices of dissenting individuals. These processes help explain unethical and/or illegal organizational behavior.
- Power also serves to silence the voices of "different" employees. One of the most important sources of resistance to power relationships is raising those voices.

KEY TERMS

sovereign power
disciplinary power
empowerment
surface structure of power
open face of power
hidden face of power
deep structure of power
organizational politics
exemplification
open persuasion
manipulative persuasion
manipulation
justifications
rationalizations
rhetorical messages
strategic ambiguity
indirect questions
self-disclosure
denotative hesitancy
mobbing
collective resistance
testing limits
discursive closure
nullification
whistleblowing
circumvention
development
"practical" questions
"technical" questions

In the first two units of this book we introduced a number of key concepts: organizations and their members are embedded in complex social, political, and economic systems. These systems were created through strategic actions, and in turn guide and constrain the actions of the organizations that exist within them. Similarly, employees must strategically draw upon the rules and resources that are available to them to achieve their goals and the goals of their organizations. But, people are not just workers – they have complex lives and interpersonal relationships, and must find ways to deal with the competing pressures that exist in each of the systems that surround them. Furthermore, they must develop strategies for dealing with all of these pressures, with all of their "identifications" as explained in Chapter 5. Because we are "knowledgeable" actors, we can meet this challenge, and in the process reproduce and sometimes change those systems. In the chapters that make up this unit, we return to those key concepts and apply them to a number of challenges that are faced by employees and organizations in the twenty-first century. In this chapter we examine organizational power relationships as a key dimension of institutionalized structures and assumptions, and view organizational politics as the strategic management of power. In Chapter 8 we offer a parallel analysis of organizational decision making and conflict management. Chapter 9 focuses on communication and organizational change. In the final three chapters, we return to societal context and examine three challenges that stem from organization-society relationships – diversity, globalization, and ethics.

The words *power* and *politics* are used by almost everyone to explain much of what happens in life and at work. Consumers decry their powerlessness in the face of big business. Students complain that they are victimized by arbitrary professors and administrators, and are powerless to do anything in response. Subordinates vow to change their organizations for the better as soon as they advance to positions of authority (but they rarely do). Power influences employees' choices about which audiences to address (and which to avoid) and how to communicate to them. Political considerations tell people what actions must be taken in particular situations and what actions and emotions should be suppressed.

If subordinates see their supervisors as powerful members of their organizations, their job satisfaction tends to increase and their tendency to withhold or distort information decreases. Similarly, if subordinates perceive that their supervisors are actively involved in organizational politics, they may trust them less and be more likely to withhold information (Jablin, 1981). Employees base their choices about how to communicate partly on their assessment of organizational power and politics, and their choices about how to communicate create and reproduce power relationships.

A PERSPECTIVE ON ORGANIZATIONAL POWER

Many discussions of power and politics are based on a misconception about what power is and how it functions in societies and organizations. Traditional views of power focus on what Michel Foucault has called **sovereign power,** the processes through which the people who occupy positions at the top of hierarchies dominate people who are located lower in them. Historically, this kind of "power" is connected to the phrase "abuse of" because having total power often leads to its misuse. However, there are a number of problems with this "power over" view. One is that it fails to recognize that power is dispersed throughout societies and organizations. It exists in every relationship and every interaction, not just those that cross levels of social and organizational hierarchies. As Chapter 3 explained, organizational control sometimes does involve direct surveillance by supervisors, sometimes using computer technologies, and systems of control through rules and rewards. It also may involve team surveillance/concertive control (Chapter 4) and self-surveillance/unobtrusive control (Chapter 5), processes that Foucault calls **disciplinary power**. In modern organizations, disciplinary power is at least as important as sovereign power. Since disciplinary power is largely ignored in "power over" models, they seriously oversimplify power relationships.[2]

Second, traditional views of power forget that abuse stems from *imbalances* of power, not power itself. The accent in Lord Acton's famous dictum that "absolute power corrupts absolutely" should be on absolutism, not on power. When people have a great deal of power over others they begin to believe that low-power people are inferior and untrustworthy. Conversely, if people feel powerless, they tend to become depressed and helpless, feel higher levels of stress, develop physical symptoms such as headaches and hypertension, and impede valuable organizational change and innovation. Powerlessness creates feelings of vulnerability, and vulnerability leads to abuse. People need to feel that they have influence over their lives. One way to offset these effects is to help people understand the relationships between power and communication. All power relationships involve opportunities and strategies for resistance. Although knowledge is often used to dominate people, it also can lead to **empowerment**. Increasing the degree of balance in organizational power relationships reduces the potential for abuse.

Third, a "power over" view of power leads people to overlook the positive role that power plays in mobilizing people and resources to get things done. If members of an organization define power as "accomplishment" rather than "domination," nonproductive and personally destructive power games are less likely. But because the "domination" view of power is a taken-for-granted assumption in Western societies, it is difficult for people to change their frame of reference. The shift can happen, but only through understanding how communication, power, and politics are interrelated.

The final problem with "sovereign" views is that they focus on only the overt, conscious level of power. We will call this level the **surface structure** of power.[3] It has two dimensions. One involves an **open face** that is composed of overt displays of power – threats, promises, negotiations, orders, coalitions, gag rules, and so on. The second dimension of the *surface structure* of power is its **hidden face**. This face works by regulating public and private issues. In organizational life, employees must often make difficult decisions about when and how to challenge power holders. Newcomers soon learn that some issues are not to be discussed in public; some potential solutions are not to be considered openly; and some arguments are not to be made. Open discussions are limited to safe topics (those that power holders are willing to have discussed in public), acceptable alternatives, and unofficially sanctioned premises for making decisions. As a result of these regulatory processes, consensus in open discussions is the rule, not the exception. When disagreements are voiced they tend to be over minor issues and serve the purpose of perpetuating the myth that open, rational, and objective decision making exists in the organization. If individuals violate these constraints, they may either be ignored or attacked by the rest of the group. If they persist they will be "educated" by an unofficial tutor. If they cannot be educated, they may be removed.

But, power also has a second level, a **deep structure** that operates below employees' conscious awareness. Throughout this book, we have discussed the processes through which the taken-for-granted assumptions of a society guide and constrain employees' actions. People act in ways that they have learned are *normal* and *natural* and usually do so without being aware of it. A society's taken-for-granted assumptions tell people who they are, what their role is in society, and where they fit in the formal and informal hierarchies that constitute their society. It is through these nonconscious parameters of action that power normally is exercised. Usually employees never realize that these societal assumptions are part of organizational power relationships.

For example, in Western societies people take it for granted that those who have formal expertise about an issue should have the greatest influence over related decisions. This assumption holds even if the issue being discussed is one for which information and argument are largely irrelevant, for example, an issue that involves values more than "facts." For example, deciding when to terminate life support for a terminally ill patient is a matter of values and emotion at least as much as it is one of information and expertise. But societal assumptions – codified into law in most US states – treat it as an information-based decision to be made by medical experts (Smith, 1992; Vanderford, Smith, and Harris, 1992). Taking one's own life often is a criminal offense, and life insurance companies are protected by law from customers who make these decisions on their own. Although these laws *seem* to be about expertise and rational decision making, they enact a complex set of values about which members of a society have power to make choices for other people, even over the most private of decisions. In turn, when people, or their families, defer to expert opinions in life and death decisions, they legitimize and reproduce the societal assumption that medical experts should dominate these decisions. In doing so, they reproduce the deep structure of power.

In sum, the taken-for-granted assumptions and political/legal structures of societies and their organizations dictate that some people legitimately have power over others. But power is not hierarchical; it is diffuse and dispersed. Some source of power is available to every member of a society or organization. Our objective in this chapter is to examine potential *sources* of power and to describe the communicative strategies that can be used to manage organizational power relationships. In the process, we will discuss the ways in which power is exercised in organizations, a process that we label **organizational politics**.

Case Study 7.1

On Death and Dying

In Unit I, we explained that organizations exist within a multilevel hierarchy of structures and assumptions that have been legitimized – that is, come to be treated as normal and natural – among members of the societies within which they operate. Power holders in the organizations that make up different sectors of an economy make similar decisions about how to manage the guidelines, constraints, rules, and resources that are accepted within those societies. The decision makers in individual organizations do the same, creating the situations that their employees manage every day. In all societies, one of the most fundamental issues involves life and death.

Worker safety is a major concern to employees, organizations, and society as a whole. The US Bureau of Labor Statistics estimates that 55,000 US workers employed by private firms die every year (more than the number who die of breast cancer, double the number who die of prostate cancer, and five times the number who die of skin cancer), and an additional 3.8 million experience disabling injuries. People injured on the job suffer physical, psychological, and behavioral consequences while their organizations lose productivity and incur a variety of additional costs (see Dana and Griffin, 1999; Schulte, 2005). Some occupations are inherently dangerous – farming, ranching, transportation, and extractive industries. But, in virtually every industry some corporations experience far more deaths and serious injuries than others, raising issues of negligence. For example, between 2005 and 2010 BP's (formerly British Petroleum) offshore drilling operations in the Gulf of Mexico reported 47 safety "incidents," more than any other company. BP claims that the number is so large because they have more wells operating in the gulf than any other company. But, Shell Oil, which has the second largest number of wells, had fewer than half as many incidents. BP's onshore record is starker. From June 2007 until February 2010, the US agency regulating workplace safety (OSHA) issued 761 citations for "willful and flagrant" violations of safety rules to petroleum companies; 760, or 99.87 percent, were to BP. The second most serious category of violations are those "with intentional disregard for employee safety and health." Of 91 citations given, BP received 69 (75.8 percent). After a 2005 explosion at its Texas City refinery, BP paid a $21 million fine and agreed to make a number of safety improvements. In 2009, after additional fatal accidents at its refineries in Texas and Ohio and 700 new violations, it was fined an additional $87.4 million for "failing to live up to the terms of its previous settlement." The combined fines represent only a few days of the company's profits. Then came the 2010 explosion and sinking of the Deep Water Horizon rig, which killed 11 workers. By using drilling shortcuts that other oil company CEOs say they would not use, BP saved $5 million of an estimated $100 million cost for Horizon. It will be years before the total cost of the explosion will be known. Ironically, BP's recent record is a 75 percent reduction in BP's accident rate prior to 1999.[1] So, the key question for our purposes is why do some companies continue to have a "systemic safety problem" over long periods of time when others do not?

The simplest answer is that they do not have to improve. It begins at the societal level. In Western societies two dominant taken-for-granted assumptions historically have governed workers safety: (1) employment involves a master–servant relationship, and (2) government should take a hands off (*laissez-faire*) approach to private corporations. Workers are employed at the will of owners (or, more likely in today's firms, managers), and if they disagree with company practices, they should seek employment elsewhere. Government should interfere with management only when it is absolutely necessary. Of course, "necessity" is a hotly contested term, and its definition depends on the outcome of constant negotiations in the courts, between management and union representatives, and in legislative bodies – that is, on social and organizational power relationships. In the United States, workers have two sources of protection. One is the federal government (OSHA). But, Congress has severely restricted OSHA's power. For example, the maximum fine that can be imposed is $7000 *per death*. If you need a bit of context for this number, in August 2009, ExxonMobil agreed to pay the Environmental Protection Agency (EPA) $600,000 in fines and penalties for negligently allowing 85 migratory birds to become trapped in uncovered storage pits ($7058 *per bird*); and in June 2009 a federal judge fined Jammie Thomas-Rasset $80,000 *per song* for illegally downloading music for her own use, in violation of regulations designed to protect corporate copyrights. Most firms quickly pay these fines in order to get the issue (and negative publicity) behind them, but in early 2010 Walmart decided to challenge a $7000 fine imposed on it for negligently allowing a crowd of "Black Friday" (the day after Thanksgiving) sale shoppers to crush one of its workers.[2] An additional problem involves OSHA's budget, which is so small that it in 93 percent of the cases referred to it cannot be pursued, even when they involve repeat offenders.

The second level of worker protection is the legal system. But, litigation is expensive, and large corporations can extend court cases for years and/or win on appeal. For example, in Texas – which executes more criminals each year than all other states combined–condemned death row prisoners are much more likely to win an appeal than an injured employee. In addition, recent sessions of the state legislature have passed "tort reform" legislation that makes it much more difficult to win lawsuits against corporations, and caps damages at such a low level that filing a suit is unlikely to be worth the effort. The laws in Texas are quite similar to those in many other states, and are slowly being incorporated into federal law.[3] Moreover, many states now allow corporations to require their employees to waive their right to sue over safety issues. Two examples illustrate the power imbalance that is created:

> Martha McJimsey was pulling brains out of cow carcasses coming down the line at IBP in Amarillo [TX] when she split one of her fingers wide open. But, before a nurse would stop the bleeding and stitch her up, McJimsey had to sign a waiver not to sue the company, now called Tyson Fresh Meats. It didn't matter that her right hand – her writing hand – was dripping blood. A company representative simply put a pen in her left hand and told her to sign. (1C)

Gabriel Beltran, who experienced a herniated disk in his spine as a result of an injury sustained while working for Houston's Memorial Hermann Hospital, faced a less immediate crisis, but still had little choice about signing a waiver. His medical insurance, which he obtained through his employer, refused to pay his medical bills because the injury happened on the job. The hospital would not let him show the waiver to an attorney before he signed it. Beltran did sign, and explained, "I was kind of stuck. I wouldn't have a paycheck, and who would pay for my medical costs?" Later he complained, but District Judge Patrick Mizell ruled that the waiver was binding because Beltran did not sign it under duress. Hermann estimates that it saves about $8 million per year as a result of the waiver system. Tyson has not reported its savings in public. Even states which restrict injury waivers allow firms to require employees with injuries – or any other grievances – to use company-appointed arbitrators who typically conduct secret hearings – in many cases the employee is not invited to attend – and issue a ruling that is never published, instead of using the legal system (Sixel, 2002, 2003).

Massey Energy corporation is to coal-mining deaths and injuries what BP is to oil company deaths and injuries – leading the pack by a wide margin. Like the oil industry, overall safety has steadily improved in the coal mining industry for the past 40 years, with deaths reaching a 100-year low of 35 in 2009. But, then there is Massey. Its Upper Big Branch mine, which exploded in April 2010 killing 25 miners, was charged with 204 serious violations during 2006 and 2007, nineteen times the national average. Interviews with miners after the blast revealed that management had ordered a company electrician to disable a piece of safety equipment that would have stopped operations when methane gas reached dangerous levels (a methane explosion is the most likely cause of the disaster). Massey avoided penalties for almost all of these violations by reducing their frequency to just above the national average. It received a congratulatory note from Mine Safety and Health Administration (MSHA) regulators, but within a year, the number of violations had doubled, restarting the cycle of violations, warnings, action, and violations (federal law requires the MSHA to remove a mine from its list of those with a "pattern of violations" but reducing the number by 30 percent, but it does not require them to retain their violation list at the lower level). In the two weeks after the Big Branch explosion, Massey received 60 new serious safety violations.[4]

However, none of this came as much of a surprise. The only recent safety violation egregious enough to be deemed criminal took place in a Massey mine, and the most recent mining disaster before Big Branch involved the Massey mine at Sago, West Virginia, in 2006. Twelve miners died in a mine that had received 270 safety citations during the previous two years resulting in fines of $24,000, a relatively minor cost of doing business. The accident did prompt an outcry by state and federal politicians who promised much tighter regulation (the average fine for serious violations is $1000). Legislators at both levels did enact rules that increased the number of mine inspections and improved the ability to *respond* to disasters, extending the lives of miners who *survive* explosions, but did little to require actions designed to *prevent* disasters or create meaningful punishments for safety violations. For example, Congressman Bill Owens's Wrongful Death Accountability Act, which would have made manslaughter due to organizational negligence a federal felony and doubled the penalty for lying to federal inspectors, was killed in committee by a straight party-line vote. This, too, did not come as much of a surprise. In 2009 the coal-mining industry spent $26 million on congressional campaign contributions and lobbying expenses, much of which went to fight increased safety regulations because of the costs they would have imposed. Former Massey CEO Don Blankenship is a bit of a superstar when it comes to influencing the political process. He contributed more than $300,000 to federal candidates over the past two decades, and contributed the federal maximum of $30,400 to the Republican National Senatorial Committee, a small part of his $11.2 million income in 2008 (up from $5.3 million at the time of the Sago disaster). He has been equally active at the state level. In 2004 he spent $3 million to defeat an incumbent justice of the West Virginia Supreme Court. His favored candidate later was the deciding vote in two decisions to throw out *Caperton v. Massey*, a $50 million verdict against the company. Another of the pro-Massey votes cast in the initial appeal came from Elliot Maynard, who recused himself from the second vote after pictures surfaced showing him vacationing in Monaco with Blankenship while the appeal was being heard. Blankenship's influence over the West Virginia Supreme Court was so blatant that in 2009 the pro-business US Supreme Court ruled that state judges must disqualify themselves from ruling on cases involving companies from which they had received "unusually large" campaign donations. The following year Maynard resigned his position on the court and ran for Congress, aided by the maximum allowed campaign contributions from Blankenship, his family, and selected Massey Energy employees (see Mosk, 2010). He lost. After receiving a salary of $17.8 million and a bonus of $27.2 million in 2009, Blankenship resigned from Massey so that it could be purchased by Alpha Natural Resources. The terms and size of his "golden parachute" have not yet been announced. In late 2010, Blankenship's bodyguard and chief of security at Massey, Hughie Stover, was indicted for obstruction of justice – destroying documents and lying to federal agents – in the Big Branch case.

The US Supreme Court decision is important because Massey has so often used the appeals process to defeat or delay penalties for safety violations. In the coal mining industry as a whole, one-fourth of fines (for a total of $210 million) are appealed, often repeatedly, delaying payment by decades. Massey has been even more aggressive, appealing 69 percent of the $1.9 million in penalties imposed on it by lower courts and regulators. Although the state Supreme Court, which will eventually rule on all of these appeals, still is dominated by recipients of Massey funds, in theory the Supreme Court decisions will force them to recuse themselves. For the immediate future, the MSHA will continue its efforts to clear its backlog of cases against 48 mines, some of which include orders to shut down, in spite of limited staff and an inability to subpoena testimony or company records because it lacks the powers of a law enforcement agency.

Applying What You Have Learned

1. What sources of power are available to management in the cases described above? What sources are available to workers?

Questions to Think About and Discuss

1. Contemporary models of power suggest that resistance to power always is possible. Albert Hirschman (1970) notes that there are four possible responses to objectionable practices: exit (leaving the organization), voice (speaking out against organizational practices), loyalty (quietly accepting the practices while working to change them), and neglect (ignoring the objectionable practices). Which of these options is realistically available to employees in these cases? What responses is management likely to make to each of those options?
2. What does your answer to question 1 suggest about the theory that resistance always is possible? Why?

Notes

1 See Thomas, Jones, Cloherty and Ryan (2010). This report is based on Morris and Pell (2010), available at www.publicintegrity.com; Olsen and Nadler (2010); and Steffy (2010).

2 See Greenhouse (2010). For overall data, see the series of investigative articles on OSHA enforcement in the December, 2003 *New York Times*, available on the newspaper's website. For a summary of Texas court decisions, see Elliott (2003).

3 See Mosk (2010). The odds of successful litigation are even smaller in states where judges are elected after expensive, corporate-financed election campaigns. This problem exacerbated by the US Supreme Court's 2010 *Citizens United v. Federal Elections Commission*, which invalidated key provisions of existing limits to campaign contributions *Citizens United*. Most observers predict that its greatest impact will be on state courts. See Kirkpatrick (2010) and the *New York Times* editorials at www.nytimes.com/2010/01/22/opinion/22fri1.html and http://roomfordebate.blogs.nytimes.com/2010/21/how-corporate-money-will-reshape-politics.

4 We would like to thank Elizabeth Odom, currently a graduate student at the University of Texas at Dallas, for her excellent research regarding Massey Energy. Key sources include Cooper, Harris, and Lipton (2010); Eggen (2010); Harris and Eckholm (2010); three items by the *NY Times* editorial board (2006a, 2006b, 2010); and Schone (2010).

SOCIETAL ASSUMPTIONS AND THE BASES OF ORGANIZATIONAL POWER

Power is in the eye of the beholder.[4] It is the belief by some members of a society or organization that they should obey the requests or commands and seek the favor and support of other members. Power is not possessed by a person. It is granted to that person by others. One person may order another to act in a certain way. But the person giving the command has no power over the other until she or he accepts the first person's right to dominate. In this sense, power is a feature of interactions and interpersonal relationships, not of individuals or organizational roles.

Creating perceptions of power is important to every employee. But doing so is especially important for people who depend on others. Even employees located near the bottom of an organization can have power if other employees depend on them. If an employee is relatively autonomous and independent, creating and maintaining power are less important. Consequently, one can develop power either indirectly, by minimizing the number of people and institutions on which she or he depends, or directly, by obtaining socially legitimate bases of power. Only completely self-sufficient people and/or workers need not be concerned with developing power.

Traditional strategies of organizing assume that power and power relationships could be built into the formal structures of organizations; relational strategies assume they could be imbedded in particular forms of leadership and tasks; cultural strategies inculcate beliefs and values that create distinctive kinds of power relationships; and networking strategies conceptualize power as stemming from one's position in a network and alliances among parties. But there are fissures, gaps, and contradictions in all systems of power. Employees can maneuver within these gaps and manipulate these contradictions by acquiring power on their own, independent of their formal position in their organizations (Conrad, in press, 2011; Conrad and Abbot, 2007; de Certeau, 1984). They can do so by demonstrating that they possess one or more valued *personal characteristics* or that they have the ability to control the distribution of resources valued by other people. But characteristics and resources cannot be transformed into power unless they are *scarce* (available in supplies that are smaller than the existing demand), *significant* (employees depend on them to do their jobs), and *irreplaceable* (they can be depleted but cannot be easily replaced).

Gaining Power Through Personal Characteristics

In Western societies, two kinds of personal characteristics are assumed to be a legitimate basis on which some people can obtain and exercise power – *expertise* and *interpersonal relationships*.

Expertise as a Source of Power In Western societies, expertise has at least two dimensions. The first is a person's organization-related *knowledge* (Foucault, 1980). However, knowledge provides power only if other people depend on it and it is scarce, significant, and irreplaceable. This explains why people sometimes do not want to hire the most competent applicant for a job. If the newcomer has the kind of expertise that an old-timer has used to gain power, the newcomer is threatening. When you are the only person who can operate your company's computer system, you have almost complete power. When you are one of two people who knows how to do so, you have little power unless you can form and sustain an alliance with the other expert. It also explains why employees sometimes develop equipment or procedures that only they can use. Secretaries and administrative assistants have known for millennia that if they devise filing systems that only they understand, they may make themselves irreplaceable. Michael Crozier observed a group of mechanics who installed and repaired machinery in tobacco processing plants. Although they had little formal power in the organizational hierarchy, they realized that without their cooperation the plant would come to a grinding halt. Over time they trained new mechanics orally, making sure that there were no written diagrams of equipment or repair instructions around. When they installed new equipment, they modified it in ways that would make it difficult, if not impossible, for outsiders to repair it. As a result, as long as they cooperated with one another, they could virtually force management to act as they wanted. Although their power was fragile, it could be maintained as long as the dependency relationship was maintained (Crozier, 1964).

Communication is necessary to transform expertise into perceived power. Sometimes other employees do not understand why a particular employee's expertise is important to them and to their organization. This is one of the reasons why obtaining and maintaining power is more difficult for staff personnel, who do important work "behind the scenes," than for line personnel, those whose activities and contributions are visible to everyone. In addition, the people who occupy the top positions of organizational hierarchies determine what "counts" as expertise, how much value is attached to different kinds of knowledge, and how it is supposed to be used. The upper managers of chemical firms are usually chemists, not human resource specialists. Engineering firms are usually controlled by engineers, not former directors of personnel. They can understand the value of being able to develop new chemicals or design new equipment. They often find it more difficult to understand why the ability to design and administer a new appraisal system is significant.

Image Management as a Source of Power For millennia communication scholars have recognized the impact that a communicator's image has on her or his messages. As early as 330 BCE, Aristotle observed that the images speakers create of themselves are their strongest persuasive tools. Employees cannot choose between creating an image and not creating one. They *can* choose between creating an image by chance or doing so by design. In highly political organizations, image management is especially important. Some image management strategies, and the impressions they create, usually are viewed negatively by members of Western cultures – intimidation, through which employees seek to appear dangerous or threatening, and self-promotion, through which people tout their competencies or achievements, for example. Others are perceived more favorably – attempting to be likeable (ingratiation), or trying to be viewed as dedicated, loyal, and/or committed to the organization or their work groups (exemplification). Some are viewed positively if balanced by others. For example, trying to be seen as needy (supplication) usually is viewed negatively unless it is balanced by enough self-promotion for the combination to be perceived as evidence of modesty.[5] The use of some impression-management strategies also can benefit an employee's organizational or work group. Ingratiation seems to make other workers feel better about themselves, enhances concertive control (recall Chapter 4), reduces conflicts, and makes groups function more smoothly. **Exemplification**, that is, going "beyond the call of duty" through actions such as arriving at work early, volunteering to take on difficult projects, and helping other employees complete their assigned tasks, almost always enhances one's image and potential influence. Since all of these positive effects are achieved without any additional cost to the organization or the group, they benefit. Of course, performing organizational tasks for selfish reasons can have negative effects, especially if it unproductively consumes organizational resources or distracts an employee (or coworkers) from her or his assigned tasks (Bolino, Tumley, and Niehoff, 2004).

In the end, the impact of impression management depends to a large extent on the employee's motives. Unfortunately, it is difficult for coworkers to know the "real" person of another employee, or fully understand his or her motives. This is partly because of the human need to keep some of one's identity private, a need that is magnified in the close confines of organizations. It also is because everyone has a number of different, and often conflicting, traits, abilities, personality attributes, and motivations. Impression management means accenting some of these characteristics and deemphasizing others. It also results in part from the very human need to keep some of one's identity private. As a result, organizational decisions are based on carefully constructed images. Hiring decisions are based largely on selection agents' conclusions about the extent to which candidates match their images of the kind of person needed for a particular job. Promotions are granted or withheld primarily on the basis of how well an employee's image conforms to decision makers' preferred images. This is especially true in organizations that have no formal performance criteria, or when the nature of one's job makes it especially difficult to unambiguously measure one's performance (Goffman, 1955, 1959; Ferris, Russ, and Fandt, 1989; Giddens, 1991).

In theory, people will become more adept at detecting especially inauthentic image management efforts as they work with one another. Employees live in fishbowls (or given the size of most organizations, in aquariums) in which they are constantly observed and their actions analyzed and interpreted. If the gap between a person's public and private images is too great, impression management is exhausting. Maintaining an inauthentic image is made more difficult by the dynamics of nonverbal communication. Some nonverbal cues are easy to manage; others are not. As any "dress for success" book points out, personal appearance can be consciously managed and has been related to career success, although the size of the effect is small. Cues such as maintaining direct eye contact, actively gesturing, using a relaxed and open body position, and consistently using responsive nonverbal cues (e.g., nodding in agreement and/or leaning forward while talking) are perceived positively and can be consciously controlled with some effort and skill. For example, in job interviews, interviewers' perceptions of an applicant's social skills seem to be more positive if the applicant is animated (gestures actively for a period of time during the interview) and responsive (provides extended and relevant responses to questions), and conforms to expectations regarding attire and appearance (is moderately formally dressed).

Fortunately, "presenting an appropriate self" (as Erving Goffman labels the image maintenance process) is made easier by two elements of interpersonal communication. First, people usually establish working agreements to support one another's public images. If any participants violate the implied agreement, they risk having others retaliate by undermining their images. Image maintenance is also aided by the availability of front and back stages in interactions. Even in organizational fishbowls, there are times and places in which people can rehearse and perfect the communication patterns they are trying to establish.

As a result, image management is difficult, but possible, and can be an important source of power.

Persuasive Skill as a Source of Power A third dimension of expertise is an employee's ability to persuasively *articulate* positions, to argue successfully in favor of preferred courses of action. Analyzing organizational situations provides guidelines about what communicative strategies to use and how to turn those strategies into messages. Of course, one aspect of the situations an employee faces is his or her image because it influences the credibility of any message that she or he might construct, just as the credibility of the messages influence image.

Fortunately, employees have a wide variety of message strategies available to them; unfortunately they do not seem to be very good at selecting persuasive strategies unless they are specifically trained to do so (Wilson, Greene, and Dillard, 2000). The available strategies can be grouped into three categories, *open persuasion*, *manipulative persuasion*, and *manipulation*. **Open persuasion** occurs when employees make their goals and methods clear to their target(s). Some open persuasion strategies are *cooperative,* as when an influencer bases appeals on rational arguments grounded in the available information. Bargaining may also be an open, cooperative strategy if both parties are interested in achieving a mutually beneficial outcome.

Other open persuasion strategies are *competitive,* as when an influencer simply orders someone to do something or threatens or promises sanctions. Threats, promises, and self-centered bargaining are available to all employees; even workers at the bottom of the organization can threaten to quit working or promise to work harder. As one might expect, subordinates rarely use competitive strategies to influence their supervisors; rational strategies are used instead. However, when resources are tight, and competition for them is intense, competitive strategies are more common.[6]

A second type of influence strategy is **manipulative persuasion**, when influencers disguise their strategies but not their goals. "Going over someone's head" (discussed at more length later in this chapter), seeking support from coworkers, and manipulating interpersonal relationships are competitive versions of this strategy. "Wearing a target down" with repetitive influence attempts is another. Ingratiation, making others feel important or humbling oneself, is a common cooperative form. Although ingratiation rarely influences decisions or outcomes, it does seem to make targets like influencers more, which may benefit them in the long run.

The final category involves **manipulation**, disguising one's goals and one's strategies. There is a substantial amount of evidence that manipulation is the most common organizational influence strategy. The reason is simple: the potential costs of failing to influence are smallest when one's intention to influence is hidden. If the influencer fails, he or she can merely claim not to have been trying to influence. Retribution then would be seen by others as arbitrary and capricious behavior. A complex version of manipulation involves overloading a target person with information until the target is confused. The influencer then offers a solution that she or he prefers. Overwhelmed by information, the target goes along with the persuader's recommendation.

Concern for retribution also seems to influence organizational persuaders' choices of *targets* for their efforts. The optimal target is someone who is powerful enough to give the persuader what she or he wants, but is not powerful enough to retaliate against an employee whose persuasive efforts fail. Trying to influence one's immediate supervisor carries risks, because the superior can retaliate if the attempt is offensive. It is safer to choose a target who can impose smaller costs – a peer, group of peers, or employee in another unit of the organization. Thus, two supply sergeants at different bases will bargain with one another for desired materials more than they will bargain with their base commandants. If the negotiations go awry, neither one can punish the other. But, regardless of the target choice, the softer influence strategies (open persuasion or ingratiation) seem to be more effective in persuading other employees to change their beliefs or actions than the harder strategies (Falbe and Yukl, 1992).

Other factors that influence employees' choices of strategies include their *cultural backgrounds* and *goals*, and the *point in the influence effort*. For example, European American managers in US firms seem to use different strategies depending on the issue. When it clearly is within the manager's formal authority (for example, a subordinate not coming to work on time), managers tend to use highly individualistic and dominating strategies – issuing ultimatums or threatening the subordinate with punishment. When the issue is less clearly within the manager's range of formal authority, managers tend to use softer individualistic strategies – requests (such as "I want you to feel free to ask me for help"), promises ("I reward people who have good ideas"), and ingratiation ("I really trust your judgment"). In contrast, Japanese managers seem to use community-related strategies regardless of the issue – altruism and appeals to duty (such as "For the good of the company, please do it") or counseling ("Can I help you get here on time?"). Of course, European American managers also occasionally use community-related strategies and Japanese managers also sometimes use individualistic strategies. But the tendencies of the two groups seem to be quite clear regardless of the kind of organization they work in and clearly related to their cultures of origin.[7]

Communicators' goals also seem to influence strategy selection, at least among European American employees. When the goal is to improve performance or meet organizational objectives, cooperative strategies are more common; when the objective is to get personal assistance or rewards, ingratiation is most common. When the target has high formal status, rational argument is most common; when the target is of low status, competitive and manipulative strategies seem to dominate. Supervisors' personal preferences seem to be a more important influence on their choices of influence strategies than strategic considerations: They use friendly and attractive compliance strategies with subordinates whose communication is friendly and attractive, and they use unattractive strategies with subordinates who communicate in unattractive ways.

Finally, communicators seem to use different influence strategies at different "points in the influence effort." Organizational communicators are similar to modern politicians, who do not try to sway voters with a single brilliant speech or television ad but instead hope to influence them through a lengthy persuasive campaign. Organizational politicians usually begin influence efforts with open and cooperative strategies and shift to competitive or manipulative communication when they encounter resistance or discover that more cooperative strategies have failed (Morris, Gaveras, Baker, and Coursey, 1990).

Three conclusions can be drawn about research on choices of influence tactics. The first is that employees really do communicate strategically, choosing different approaches in different situations. The second is that the choice of influence strategies is reciprocal. Subordinates mirror the influence styles of their supervisors, who in turn mirror their subordinates' communication styles. Third, the influence strategies used in organizations are gendered. Since most organizational cultures are masculine, communicators within them tend to use individualistic and competitive strategies that are goal oriented and rely on gaining or asserting control over other people. They focus on protecting one's identity and feelings. Like any other organizational strategy, a preference for masculine influence styles is a choice, but it is a choice that employees may not be aware they are making because it is grounded in societal assumptions. Organizations could adopt feminine influence tactics, ones that value the ideas of all members of the organization, focus on equality and openness, and value tentativeness and flexibility. These approaches are more likely to be valued when the organization and its practices make sense to all of its members, where people feel *safe* to take risks and self-disclose, and where organizational control systems are not excessively constraining. These conditions do seem to exist some alternative forms of organizing, but even there they are difficult to sustain because masculine strategies are viewed as normal and natural in Western organizations (Wood, 1994; Foss and Griffin, 1995).

Once employees choose appropriate persuasive strategies, they must translate them into messages. Anyone can find facts and arguments to support a position on complex issues. But influence depends on articulating organizationally appropriate reasons. Some explanations are **justifications** (reasons presented in public before an action is taken, a policy is implemented, or an issue is resolved); others are **rationalizations** (reasons presented after a decision or action). Both forms of explanation are essentially the same – they are presented by an image to an audience through some medium of communication and consist of reasons arranged in some order. In the best of times employees carefully choose the reasons, structure, medium, and image. In the worst of times they do not.

The best way to find out which appeals work in a particular organization is to listen. For example, if employees notice that in their organization successful justifications or rationalizations often are based on statistical data of a certain type, they can tentatively conclude that appeals should incorporate this kind of evidence. Conversely, if they find that statistical data are *never* offered successfully as reasons, they can eliminate this kind of information from their list of potential justifications; if they notice that statistical data always are included in persuasive acts, but never seem to matter in the final decisions, they should conclude that including these kind of data are necessary but not sufficient. Eventually, employees can comprise a list of potentially effective, and potentially devastating arguments, appeals, and evidence. Of course, some of the items in the acceptable list are potentially more powerful, and some will be viewed as relevant to some kinds of decisions but not others. For example, moral arguments like fairness, equity, and honesty may be used successfully in personnel decisions but not in budget decisions. In other situations, none of the *usually* acceptable reasons may fit, which requires employees to creatively employ a usually unacceptable reason and create some plausible explanation of why is it appropriate in this particular case. Our point is that the actions of employees determine which reasons are acceptable; audiences sometimes change their minds; and naive employees can get caught in the middle of the shift if they are not careful.

Once employees choose a set of situationally appropriate reasons to support their ideas, they still have to articulate those reasons in a message. In Western societies and organizations, messages are more influential if they are organized, include extensive supportive evidence, are no more ambiguous than necessary, and generally create an impression of rationality. Creating effective messages involves a great deal of editing. In general, messages in which employees blurt out simple, straightforward *expressions* of their feelings or thoughts tend to be minimally effective. Most organizational situations are complex and multidimensional, requiring people to pursue multiple goals simultaneously. For example, subordinates almost always want to construct messages that *both* preserve or strengthen their relationships with their supervisors and achieve one or more tangible goals. Even when a supervisor–subordinate relationship is hostile or otherwise negative, subordinates want to maintain at least the minimum level of civility needed to perform his or her assigned tasks (Waldron, 1991; Waldron and Krone, 1991). Expressive messages tend to be too simple and blunt to achieve multiple goals simultaneously. And, they tend to lock relationships into us-against-them patterns, polarize positions on the issue(s) being discussed, and create ill feelings. If reciprocated, they tend to create rapidly escalating conflicts (see Chapter 8).

Messages that draw on the *conventions* of a society or organization tend to be more effective than expressive messages. But by using the rules and resources that exist in a particular situation of a group, conventional messages reproduce situational rules and tend to create rigid, emotionally distant, formal work relationships. **Rhetorical messages** are those which allow employees to pursue multiple objectives simultaneously – express feelings, create harmony, foster relational development, demonstrate sensitivity to others, obtain and/or use power, and generate productive outcomes. They recognize the unique circumstances faced by the other person or the unique complications that exist in a particular situation. And, they also tend to be strategically ambiguous.[8]

In Chapter 5 we explained that maintaining some degree of ambiguity regarding values, rewards, and so on often has advantages for organizations. **Strategic ambiguity** also can have advantages for individual employees. For instance, it can allow someone to speak without being held accountable for what he or she says. It also allows people to violate expectations – to say things that are not supposed to be said – without overtly doing so. Finally, ambiguity also may allow people to take actions that are necessary but forbidden by existing policies and procedures. A supervisor usually cannot openly tell his or her subordinates, "OK, do it that way, but if you get caught I'll never admit that we had this conversation." He or she can, however, leave instructions so ambiguous that a sensitive subordinate will get the message. Ambiguity provides flexibility, and in highly structured organizations, flexibility may be more important than clarity. However, ambiguity can also be used to unfairly manipulate employees. People are led to believe that commitments have been made that later are not carried out. They take risks and exert time and effort for promised rewards that do not materialize. They become angry and defensive, sometimes resorting to the destructive bureaucratic behaviors that were described in Chapter 3. Cycles of distorting and withholding information are established, and people become more concerned with creating a protective paper trail documenting their activities than in maintaining effective work groups.

In sum, being able to construct rhetorically *appropriate* messages is necessary for employees to successfully perform their tasks and achieve their goals. But it has an additional advantage; it is crucial to successful impression management. Being able to present masterful, logical arguments in support of a proposal is a wonderful skill. But if the proposal is rejected, the advocate's credibility is reduced, regardless of how brilliant his or her arguments might have been. Good proposals often fail solely for political reasons. They may involve scuttling a powerful member's pet (but failing) project or shifting the staff and budget of a powerful department to a less powerful one. Especially good proposals may even provide evidence that a subordinate is more expert than a supervisor, thereby undermining their relationship. In all of these cases, the proposal threatens power holders and is likely to be resisted and, ultimately, rejected. In what may seem to be a kind of perverse logic, expert people are those whose ideas are accepted, and people whose ideas are accepted are perceived as experts.

Interpersonal Relationships as a Source of Power The final source of personal power is the management of *interpersonal relationships.* People have learned that it is natural and normal to comply with the wishes of people with whom they have good relationships. If we believe that refusing to comply with a friend's request may threaten the relationship, we are more likely to comply. Maintaining effective interpersonal relationships also increases a person's power in less direct ways. People view those with whom they have good relationships as being more expert, powerful, and trustworthy than others. They communicate more freely with friends and give them information they can use productively. An employee who has many friends in the organization eventually knows a lot about what is going on and can use that information to create an impression of expertise and power. Because people are attracted to expert, powerful people, they form friendships and share information with them. Sharing provides them with additional information and expertise. In a complex cycle, creating and sustaining interpersonal relationships also enhances an individual's access to other bases of power.

Interpersonal relationships with groups of people also can provide power (Putnam, 1986). Coalitions are particularly important for employees or departments that lack other bases of power. Having allies includes the additional benefits of increasing employees' self-confidence and reducing their stress. Alliances are based on common interests, which are ever changing. When salient issues and interests change, every member has the option of defecting and joining a different alliance. They are also unstable because of the dynamics of size. Alliances are based on the expectation that some form of spoils will be divided up if the coalition is victorious. Each member's reward will be increased and obligations to the other members decreased if the alliance is of the smallest winning size. But employees also must think about the future and the need to implement the decision once it is made. Implementation often requires the cooperation of a large number of people. Their support will be stronger if they are part of the alliance that got it enacted. To gain their support, coalition members must give up some of their potential rewards to these persons. Each member of the coalition thus may be ambivalent about the presence of each other member. Coalitions are unstable, although for many people they may be the only available base of power.

Gaining Power Through the Control of Key Resources

People control resources when they are *key communicators* or *gatekeepers* in communication networks, occupy formal positions that allow them to distribute *legitimate rewards* and *punishments*, or can obtain access to the *symbols* of power.

Controlling Information Especially in societies that value rational decision making, information is a potent source of power. In fact, people who appear to be experts often have no more knowledge than anyone else, but have superior access to information. Information allows people to anticipate organizational problems and either prevent them or be ready with solutions when they do occur. It helps them locate and exploit weaknesses in potential adversaries and locate employees with whom they have common interests. But knowledge is usually acquired only from other employees, primarily through informal communication networks. Employees who occupy a central role in these networks (the key communicators described in Chapter 6) have access to more information than people who occupy peripheral roles.

Being a key communicator and possessing information reinforce one another. When people are confused, they seek out people who are reputed to be in the know. Key communicators can also control the flow of information through their organization. Information gives people power only if it is scarce. If it is disseminated selectively, it can enhance an individual's image as an expert. For example, in a classic study of how an organization chose between two computer systems, Andrew Pettigrew revealed the strategies a middle manager used to see that his preference was purchased. The manager gathered information about both systems from his subordinates, passed little information about the system he opposed on to his supervisors (unless that information was negative), and sent on favorable information about the system he favored. In effect, he created uncertainty about one system and then provided the information needed to resolve that uncertainty. Since he was in a central position in the formal communication network and was able to prevent his subordinates from "going over his head," he was able to control communication. This control gave him influence over both the computer decision and subsequent decisions. Of course, in an organization with an active informal communication network, controlling information flow is very difficult. But since key communicators in formal networks also tend to play central roles in informal networks, it may not be impossible.[9]

There are a number of potential sources of information available to every employee, and there are a number of strategies that can be used to obtain it. Unfortunately, most employees have rather primitive information-seeking skills, are unaware of the possible sources of information that are available to them, and tend to choose sources out of habit rather than doing so strategically. Asking overt questions is the most *efficient* way to obtain information; but it is awkward because doing so reveals one's ignorance (and one's interest in the topic). It is especially difficult for newcomers who have been transferred from other parts of the organization, because they are *supposed* to know what is going on. Consequently, direct questions tend to be used only between people who have high levels of mutual trust. In other relationships, employees tend to avoid using overt strategies of obtaining information until they feel certain that the risks, including the possibility of being embarrassed, are small (see Table 7.1). Instead, they may devour all the written information that is

Table 7.1 Types of Information-Seeking Behavior

	Overt questions	*Indirect questions (hinting)*	*Observing*	*Testing limits*
Employee comfort level	High	Low	Low	High
Fear of being embarrassed	High	Low	High	Low
Source availability and competence	High	High	High	High
Risks	High	Medium	Moderate to high (depending on degree of culture shock)	High

available to them. Still, since face-to-face interpersonal communication is the preferred mode for information-seeking, they learn to ask **indirect questions** about a harmless topic that is related to what they really want to know (Dervin, 1997; Jablin, 2001; Johnson, 1996, 2003; Rice, McCreadie, and Chang, 2001). They may hint or ask other employees about their histories with the firm as a way of finding out about how people advance through the organizational hierarchy. *Joking* about key characteristics of the new organization or **self-disclosing** (revealing a relatively private aspect of one's experiences or identity) may generate informative responses from other employees. For example, a newcomer might tell a supervisor that she or he prefers all-nighters to missing deadlines in the hope that the supervisor will respond by revealing his or her preferences about deadlines and work styles. Newcomers also may simply *observe* other employees completing specific tasks and mimic their actions. As Chapter 5 pointed out, employees can obtain a great deal of insight into the beliefs and values of the organization by closely monitoring key symbolic forms – stories, myths, metaphors, rites, and rituals. Of course, they must be careful to remember that the official meaning of a symbol may be very different from the real meaning that employees attribute to it. Asking third parties is risky, because it may produce incorrect or misleading information, or may lead a newcomer to view the organization in ways that conflict with the supervisor's views. And even more risky are covert strategies involving **testing limits**, when newcomers intentionally violate the informal rules of the organization and observe and interpret other employees' responses to their actions.

However, eliciting information is not sufficient to create power; it depends on effective listening. It may seem simple, but listening is a complex and difficult process. Effective listening depends on understanding the nature of messages and developing a specific set of skills. Every message includes multiple levels of meaning. Messages "mean" on a *cognitive* level – they convey bits of information. They also "mean" at *emotional* and *relational* levels. It is possible to detect a speaker's emotional tone and intensity during face-to-face communication, even though communicators often attempt to hide their emotions, especially in organizations where rationality is valued and emotional displays are frowned on. It is more difficult to assess emotional tone when messages are communicated in modes that do not include nonverbal cues, for example, in written memos. Finally, messages "say" something about the sender's interpersonal relationship with the receivers, with other members of the organization, and with the organization itself.[10]

Simultaneously listening for cognitive, emotional, and relational dimensions of meaning is important for two reasons. First, it gives employees more complete and accurate information about the purposes that underlie communication from others. For example, when an old-timer tells a newcomer, "That's a pretty good idea, for a rookie," the comment may reflect a variety of purposes. It could be intended to focus attention on a good idea (primarily a content purpose), to express a mentor's pride in the accomplishments of a mentoree (an emotional purpose), to remind the newcomer that he or she is a subordinate (rookie, a relational purpose), or any combination of the three. The rookie can accurately understand the comment and its purposes only by thinking about what it means at content, emotional, and relational levels.

Second, listening for multiple levels of meaning also gives employees a sense of what responses are appropriate to different messages. For example, the effects of the rookie's responding, "Yep. . . . Gee, I'm smart, aren't I?" will depend on the old-timer's purpose(s). If it was content, the response would have little impact. If it was emotional, the response could deny the old-timer's right to feel pride in the mentoree. If it was relational, it could challenge the hierarchical relationship that existed between them. In each case, the response would alienate the mentor.

However, listening for multiple levels of meaning is a skill that must often be learned. For example, in Western societies men often do not learn to listen at the emotional and relational levels. Listening for content alone can easily lead to misunderstandings, frustrations, and communication breakdowns. In contrast, Western women often learn to focus on the relational level of meaning and to respond by expressing understanding, sympathy, and emotional support. They learn to treat the content of the message as less important. But, focusing solely on the relational level of meaning also can create misunderstanding and frustration (Mumby, 1993; Wood, 1994).

Just as employees must listen for multiple levels of meaning, they also must listen for the *organizational functions* and *personal implications* that messages contain. Some messages serve a decision-making function. They call for a rational analysis of problems and give permissions to disagree with one another to some extent. Other messages only *seem* to serve a decision-making function but are really organizational ceremonies (recall Chapter 5). For example, when upper-level personnel resign or retire, messages like "What can we ever do to replace Andy?" abound. They may sound like a call for analysis; but responses like "Well, Fred, Jennie, or Stanley could easily move up and do quite well" or "Ah, come on . . . anyone could handle Andy's job" would miss the point entirely.

Messages also include *personal implications.* Every message can influence employees' public images and their private conceptions of themselves. A challenge that all employees face is to understand that the organizational functions and personal implications of messages often do not coincide. It is difficult to construct messages that meet both goals simultaneously, as illustrated by research on organizational friendships. Work fosters the development of friendships, because it places people in sustained contact with one another; because it makes it easier to find common interests, backgrounds, and so on; and because it creates opportunities for people to demonstrate their loyalty to and concern for one another. Contact, similarity, and emotional commitment are the basis of strong interpersonal relationships, in part because they foster high levels of trust.

But work also creates tensions within friendships. One tension is between individuality and community. Friends enjoy contact and interaction; but too much contact can smother the relationships and create tension. Other tensions involve organizational roles. Friendships are most stable if both parties are open, honest, and nonjudgmental. But organizational roles often require people to evaluate one another's work, especially in supervisor–subordinate relationships and in work teams, and organizational situations usually limit the kinds of information that coworkers can share with one another.[11]

Formal Control of Resources Some positions in formal hierarchies involve officially sanctioned control of scarce resources. Resource control gives people power by enabling them to reward or punish (promise gains or threaten losses to) other employees. As long as they threaten subtly or promise tactfully, they will be able to exercise power. Resource control also allows employees to persuade others to share some of the assets that they control. Most societies have deeply ingrained norms of reciprocity. When people voluntarily give something to someone else, the recipient feels pressure to reciprocate.

Although any scarce resource can be used to threaten or promise, the most important is money. Employees and groups who control funds invariably are the most powerful parts of an organization. In all organizations a substantial proportion of the budget is fixed. The allocation of the remainder (usually less than 10 percent) is flexible and can be distributed at someone's discretion. Once it is distributed, recipients begin to depend on it. They start payments on new equipment, hire new staff, or expand sales territories. If the discretionary funds are suddenly withdrawn, the person or unit faces serious problems. Payments will not be met, new staff will have to be fired, and new clients will have to be abandoned. Controlling discretionary funds is a potent source of power, and it provides an exceptionally strong basis for making threats, promises, or bribes. It's a golden rule: "The one who has the discretionary gold makes the rules" (see Pfeffer, 1981, 1993, 2010).

Obtaining Access to the Symbols of Power At first glance it may seem strange to think of symbols as a resource. But power depends on perceptions, and symbols are powerful influences on perceptions. In all societies tangible materials symbolize power: large offices, large desks, royal blue carpets, the keys to the executive washroom, invitations to social events that include high-status people, and even office windows. Symbols create the impression that the person who possesses them should be honored and obeyed. They take on meaning disproportionate to their "real" value.

As a result, some of the most intense and humorous battles ever observed involved an office with a large window or office space that neither combatant really needed. While Charley Conrad was an undergraduate working in the foundry described in Chapters 2 and 4, the key symbol of power was a hard hat – lower-level workers had none, foremen had blue ones, and supervisors white ones. One day Charley and a friend started wearing yellow, plastic, nonprotective hard hats that they had borrowed from a child of his neighbor. For two weeks the foremen and supervisors puzzled over what to do about the toy hats, although they agreed from the outset that *something* must be done. Since there was no official rule about wearing toy hard hats, he and his friend were violating no policy, but they were upsetting the power relationship by violating (and making fun of) its most important symbol. Finally, after a one-hour high-level meeting, a new policy was enacted that forbade the wearing of unapproved hats, "because they provided no added safety for workers," of course. Possessing symbols of power creates the perception of power, but only if some people are denied access to them.

Summary Power is in the eye of the beholder. In this chapter, we have discussed a number of potential sources of power as if they were independent of one another. In real organizations, they are interrelated. For example, people who occupy central positions in communication networks also tend to be perceived as experts and generally are part of many interpersonal relationships. Individuals who are supposed to have powerful allies are often seen as being more expert and having access to more information than other people. Perceptions of others are not separate and discrete. They merge together and overlap into complicated overall images. The communication strategies that employees can use to establish one base of power also influence other bases. Individuals or units of organizations are seen as being powerful or powerless depending on the *composite image* that their communicative acts establish in the minds of other members of their organization.

Case Study 7.2

The Playground Never Ends

There are people, we're told, who successfully navigated the challenges of childhood, adolescence, and college without ever having been the target of bullies. With the advent of internet bullying, the number of people who have done so is getting much smaller. More important for our purposes, it now appears that bullying may be as common at work as on the schoolyard. Depending on the study, between 25 percent and 90 percent of employees report being bullied at some point during their careers; one in ten report that they are currently experiencing it (Tracy, Lutgen-Sandvik, and Alberts, 2006).[1] One reason for this wide range of results is that bullying seems to be more common in some fields than others – from 23 percent of university faculty and staff to 60 percent of retail industry workers, to a whopping 97 percent of nurse managers. Another reason is that employees find it very difficult to determine what is and what is not "bullying." A common academic definition of bullying is "persistent, verbal and nonverbal aggression at work that includes personal attacks, social ostracism, and a multitude of other painful messages and hostile interactions, including insulting remarks, verbal threats, humiliation, and interference with one's work." It is extended over time – the average duration for US workers is 18–20 months, but some cases have lasted almost a decade (Einarsen, 1999; Einarsen, Hoel, Zapf, and Cooper, 2003; Lutgen-Sandvik, 2006). Even this definition is ambiguous. Does a person have to intend to bully someone else for the label to be appropriate? What goals, patterns, or outcomes differentiate bullying from simple boorish behavior? Is a pattern of behavior "bullying" if everyone in a workgroup or department is targeted (said differently, can someone be a jerk [you are welcome to substitute your favorite insulting term] and not be a bully)? Is "bullying" merely a direct and disciplined leadership style? A primary reason for this ambiguity is the lack of an explicit legal definition (Yamada, 2000, 2003). For example, before the advent of laws and court decisions regarding sexual harassment, targets often were unable to understand their experiences, much less talk about them. Once legal terms were created and a widely agreed-upon language for discussing harassment emerged, targets' **denotative hesitancy** (to use the academic term) disappeared and it became much easier to determine what was, and was not, sexual harassment. Bullying may be even more complicated because the word already exists and we may think we know what it means, but the common association with childhood makes it seem less important than it is. This ambiguity is important for substantive reasons – it makes it more difficult for targets of bullying to resist it, and it creates a number of complicated problems for professionals, primarily human resource managers, who must deal with it.

There is, however, no ambiguity about the adverse effects of bullying. Targets experience a host of physical, psychological, and cognitive symptoms, including posttraumatic stress syndrome (PTSD), suicidal ideation, and suicide. Their job performance suffers, as do their relationships with other people both at work and outside of it. Organizations experience increased medical costs, reduced job performance by targets and other members of their work groups, heightened levels of turnover, and significant consulting and/or legal costs (see Lutgen-Sandvik, 2003, 2006; Yamada, 2006; and Yamada, Hoel, Einarsen, and Cooper, 2002). They also lose credibility with outside stakeholders and their reputations suffer. Given these costs, it is surprising that relatively few organizations have formal antibullying policies, although actions that violate established law (assault, sexual or racial harassment, or discrimination) are covered indirectly. This is partly because the ambiguities surrounding bullying make it difficult to craft specific policies, and partly because historically US firms do not implement worker protection policies unless required to do so by the courts or legislation.

The beginning of a bullying cycle, like other forms of employee emotional abuse, seems to coincide with major organizational changes – mergers, financial crises, changes in upper management, or changing the management of a work group or unit. Researchers have not yet sorted out the factors that motivate some people to become bullies, and may never be able to do so since bullies almost always deny being a bully. It is clear that they tend to have more organizational power than their targets, either because of their formal position or their value to the organization (most bullies are supervisors, but some are superstars). It also is not clear why some people are chosen as targets and others are not. Early sexual harassment research found that targets were either threatening to the harasser because of their assertiveness or competence (superstars become targets as well as bullies) or because of their vulnerability (single mothers with few external job prospects, for example). A similar dynamic may explain bullies' selection of targets.[2]

During the initial stage of bullying, targets begin to notice a pattern of communication with a bully that makes them feel intimidated, insulted, or inappropriately excluded. As the behavior persists, they begin to doubt their perceptions, fear going to work or interacting with the bully, and spend a great deal of energy trying to make sense out of their experience. They tend to blame themselves, since their peers are not going through the same experience, and they feel shame about being bullied and being unable to stop it. Coworkers complicate the process by assuming that the target *must* have done something to warrant the treatment. As the bullying escalates in frequency and intensity, as it almost always does, all of these responses become more acute. As bullying moves into its overt stage, the target and coworkers begin to believe the bully's attacks on the target's beliefs, values, personalities, physical characteristics, work, or personal lives. In extreme cases, coworkers join in the abuse, a process that researchers call **mobbing**, a "malicious attempt to force a person out of work through unjustified accusations, humiliation, general harassment. . . . It is a 'ganging up' by the leader(s) who rallies others into a systematic and frequent 'mob-like' behavior" (Davenport, Schwartz, and Elliott, 2002; also see Einarsen, 1999; Lutgen-Sandvik, 2008). Targets observe themselves acting like frightened children in response to increasingly "aggressive, unmistakably abusive acts" and begin to actively work on reconciling their identities as capable adults and their experiences. Kay explained,

> I heard [the bully's] footsteps to the upstairs door, and I *ran* to my computer with my heart thumping. I remember thinking, "I am a highly educated, respected professional woman, and I am *running* to my desk like a child. *What is wrong here?"* I was physically sick at the thought that I'd be *caught*. (Lutgen-Sandvik, 2008, 107)

Many workers resist bullies, although everyone who does seems to realize that it is risky to do so. Resistance is complex, creative, and resourceful, and must be sustained over time as bullies intensify their abuse in retaliation for resistance (something that also is true of whistleblowers, discussed later in this chapter; see Rothschild and Miethe, 1994). Resisting workers typically report lengthy processes of gaining and losing ground over and over. The likelihood of positive outcomes – stopping the abuse, obtaining punishment of the bully, or getting rid of him or her – is greater if the resistance is **collective**, where coworkers pooled their efforts to stop the abuse (which is why mobbing is such a devastating form of bullying). Sometimes resistance starts as individual action, but became collective as other workers spoke out once someone took the first step. The most common collective resistance strategy seems to be leaving (or, to use targets' term, *escaping*) the organization. Coworkers circulate celebratory stories about people who left, encourage one another to do so, help one another find other jobs, and serve as sources of social and emotional support. They also shared their own experiences in order to help targets realize that they are not crazy and the abuse is not their fault. Workers with expertise in workplace bullying shared it with one another, providing advice such as documenting each instance of abuse. Individual strategies include "working to rule" (doing exactly what is required by one's job description, but no more). Some targets eventually reduce their work effort and doing "only enough to get by," although this almost always is used as a second resort after initially doing everything possible to please the bully. Sometimes targets embraced the labels imposed on them by bullies – targets who were labeled "troublemakers." In other cases they used the strategies discussed in this chapter – withholding information from the bully, avoiding the bully, creating safe "spaces," using humor to respond to attacks, or telling everyone about the bully's behavior (Lugen-Sandvik, 2008).

Some targets, often with the aid and support of coworkers, file grievances through formal channels, primarily with human resource professionals. In general, targets involved in research on bullying are very angry about the actions of HR professionals, claiming that they did nothing to stop the abuse and often acted in ways that made it worse (Lewis and Rayner, 2003; also see Cowan, 2009; and Lutgen-Sandvik, 2008). This response is understandable, but it reflects simplistic understanding of the power of HR professionals. Although part of their role *is* to champion the needs and rights of employees, their own job security and influence with upper management requires them to "learn to measure results in terms of business competitiveness rather than employee comfort." Jose explained,

> Well they are management biased [referring to HR]. A lot of employees don't realize that so when they come see me they see me as their advocate. Which is true and it is a balancing act we have to play but at the same time really, ultimately, I am really there for management. It is a misunderstanding that I am not sure we should correct. (Cowan, 2009, 143)

And, the "bottom line" is quite clear:

> [Y]ou kind of tag team with whoever the ultimate authority is over the individuals who are in the situation. As an HR person you have the responsibility to make sure that employee relations are healthy and good, however, you really don't have any authority in the situation. You don't have hiring and firing authority over those individuals (Pat). (Cowan, 2009, 144)

The HR professional first must determine whether or not a pattern of behavior constitutes bullying. Some complainants *are* excessively sensitive; others do "cry wolf." Some managers employ an "aggressive" or "demanding" leadership style or have communication skill deficits or low "emotional IQs." For example, a recent *Parade Magazine* article quotes attorney Victoria Pynchon expressing a common attitude against the creation of laws against bullying (something that has been considered in 17 states), "making a federal or state case over the day-to-day management of a workforce is nuts. At best it's a jackhammer solution to an Emily Post problem. At worst it's a scheme for extortion" (July 18, 2010, 12). Calvin (an HR director) comments,

> I see it [my role] as the unbiased third party as much as possible because the first person who brings you the situation is not necessarily the one who is in the right. I have to be very careful about that. I have to be the passionate, empathetic, but not start picking a side. So, that is a challenge. It is very hard. Because you want to reach out to them but sometimes they are crying, angry, or mad. I see it as my job to try and calm them down as well. I feel that I have to be very emotionally intelligent so I can do that. (Cowan, 2009, 154)

If the HR pro decides that the behavior does constitute bullying, she or he must decide what to do. Counseling the bully usually achieves little because bullies always deny any intent to bully and attribute their behavior to a desire to maximize organizational performance or demanding style. (Since the HR professional's research of the complaint almost certainly has found that only a small number of employees have been targeted, it is easy for him or her to determine that these rationalizations are excuses, they make it difficult to pursue the case any farther.) Bullies also often respond to a visit from the HR pro by intensifying their actions against the target and may retaliate against the HR pro (remember, bullies always have greater organizational power than their targets, and usually have more power than anyone in HR). If the bully's actions violate a law or an explicit organizational policy, the HR pro or the target may be able to go over the bully's head to upper management. But, that rarely is the case. Moreover, tolerance of bullying may be part of an organization's culture, one that is accepted or encouraged by upper management (Lutgen-Sandvik and McDermott, 2008; also see Cowan, 2009). Marty, a senior project director for a large global organization, talked about how her organization was also well known for letting bullies get away with their behaviors:

> It's not handled because again it's considered a culturally acceptable way of grasping your way to the top. For example, the individual to whom I report is a notorious bully in every way, shape, and form. The people that work with him, either

> do as I do which is look him in the eye and say, "Knock it off" or "That's not how you work with me and cut it out." Or they react, and they complain to HR who then go to his boss. I've been in the room with his boss who is actually the CEO of the corporation of 380,000 employees, and he'll say, "What do you expect? That's how he got to where he is. Toughen up and take it." So there's no interest on their part in handling it. That's not considered anything unusual in the normal course of doing business. (Cowan, 2009, 131)

When all of these factors are combined, the reality in many organizations is that the HR pro simply cannot do what targets want – make the bullying stop. They can help, by listening, investigating, providing guidance, and, in rare cases, confronting bullies or advocating for the target. But, they also have to deal with the frustrations that come from this very intense kind of emotional labor (recall Chapter 4):

> It is a very huge part of the job. You still go through all of the emotions. So I feel anger when I find out these things and I feel sadness, and the strong desire to stop it and help. So you still have all of the same emotions when dealing with this stuff. So what I learned to do was well people would say well don't be a part of it, well that is you, I am very emotional, I get involved. So I get very involved. So when you are the type of person that I am it is hard to remove yourself and realize that you are in a setting where these people need you to resolve this issue. You need to be the professional. So I find myself wanting to be fair. I want to give them an opportunity to correct this because everybody makes mistakes. I want you to stop and I want you to get help but at the same token I want to be fair to the person that you are bullying and I want them to feel like they are vindicated. I want to balance that somehow but I still want to send a clear message that this is wrong. The hardest place is to play that balance. It is very tiring. (Alejandra, in Cowan, 2009, 131)

Individual resistance, whether informal or through formal channels, can be successful – Pamela Lutgen-Sandvik's research found that it led to sanctions against the bully in about 25 percent of cases, about one-third the success rate of collective resistance, but led to the target being fired 20 percent of the time.

Applying What You Have Learned

1. What sources of power (or other resources) are available to bullies? To targets? To bystanders? To HR professionals? How are those source and resources interrelated?

Questions to Think About and Discuss

1. How can the various parties involved in suspected bullying differentiate instances of boorish behavior from actual bullying?
2. What kinds of organizational structures and taken-for-granted assumptions enable or encourage bullying? What structures and assumptions limit and constrain it?
3. What communicative strategies, appeals, arguments, and so on are available to bullies who want to continue their actions? What strategies, appeals, arguments, and so on are available to targets and their colleagues?
4. Should organizations have formal, written antibullying policies? If so, what should they say? Who should implement those policies? Should governments have antibullying laws akin to sexual or racial harassment laws? Why or why not?

Notes

1 The higher figure is from Lutgen-Sandvik (2003).
2 Cowan (2009); subsequent citations to this work will be included in the text of this case study. Also see Keashley and Harvey (2006), and Keashley and Jagatic (2003).

ORGANIZATIONAL POLITICS: OVERT POWER IN THE COMMUNICATIVE PROCESS

Politics is power in communicative action (Mumby, 2001). In its simplest form, organizational politics involves using the influence strategies described in this chapter to pursue one's interests. Open politicking is relatively rare in organizations. Employees must appear to be cooperative members of their organizations or units, lest they be perceived untrustworthy. If they undermine their trustworthiness, they risk destroying their credibility and undermining their ability to gain cooperation from others.

When open politicking does occur, it usually is in situations that are confusing or ambiguous. Uncertainty and ambiguity create power vacuums that invite political activity. This explains why organizations are most politically active when changes are taking place – reorganization, personnel assignment (hirings, firings, and promotions), and budget allocation. These issues are directly related to organizational power, partly because they are important and partly because they involve high levels of uncertainty. But open politicking creates uncertainty and ambiguity, which feeds political activity. Politics depends on power, but power often depends on not seeming to be political.

Managing Organizational Politics

Politics is a central element of virtually all organizational situations. The greatest complication in managing organizational politics is their game-like nature (Frost, 1987; Weick, 1995). In some ways "game" is an unfortunate metaphor because it trivializes political action and suggests that there are stable rules that govern organizational politics. Neither notion is accurate. Even what seem to be incredibly trivial political games – fights over corner offices, the largest cubicle, and so on – often are serious processes of negotiating organizational power relationships. Similarly, while organizational political games may *seem* to have rules, the rules are always negotiable and can change at any moment. The old adage that "When English gentlemen can't win playing by the rules, they just change the rules" also is true of people who are not from the United Kingdom and are not men. In all organizations, manipulating the rules is an important part of political action.

Some political games involve the surface structure of power. The strategies used may be relatively transparent, or they may be more covert. When employees interpret events or actions, they label them as either legitimate or illegitimate. Actors who act in ways that are perceived to be legitimate tend to garner support from others, and because they act "legitimately" they tend to maintain or increase their power. People who act in ways that are defined as "illegitimate" generate opposition and reduce their power. As a result, much of organizational politics is covert and subtle, as the following case study illustrates.

The Biggest Game of All: Taking and Silencing Voices

During the 1990s organizational communication theorists started to focus on the concept of *voice*, recognizing that a crucial element of social and organizational power relationships is regulating who gets to speak (and who does not), what they may speak about, and how they must speak in order to be heard. The process of regulating voice occurs at an individual level when organizations suppress dissent, but it also occurs at a broader level. Organizational discourse tends to be discourse by and for a particular group of people – primarily educated white male managers – and tends to exclude the voices of other groups – women, non-management workers, and members of racial and ethnic minority groups. Since these processes of **discursive closure** – the ways in which discussions privilege one viewpoint and exclude or devalue others – are developed in more detail in Chapters 10 through 12, we introduce them only briefly in this chapter.[12] Because discursive closure is essentially a political process, it is important to think about it in terms of organizational power relationships.

Muting Individuals' Voices W. Charles Redding, generally viewed as the father of organizational communication, once summarized a speech given to his class by a high-ranking officer of a *Fortune* 500 firm:

> A single dominant theme emerged from the speaker's lecture. . . . Although the company needs people who, of course, are intelligent and competent, our over-riding objective is to find people who will *fit in*. . . . "Will this applicant become a Company Man or a Company Woman?" (a "loyal" employee who internalizes corporate goals and values). . . . To be sure we heard the conventional wisdom that the company needed college graduates with "ideas," with "creativity and imagination." However class questions elicited the caveat that generating innovative ideas did *not* extend to challenging "basic corporate policies" or "managerial prerogatives." I wrote down at one point the speaker's exact words, which he emphasized with appropriately vigorous gestures: *We don't particularly need boat-rockers.*[13]

A quarter-century later, Redding's point still is appropriate – in most organizations dissent is forbidden, regardless of how principled or correct it might be. Employees are expected to speak in the organization's (that is, upper management's) voice, both inside and outside of the organization.

In most organizations, most of the time, dissent is not even an issue. Every strategy of organizing (recall Unit I) has its own system of controlling employees; every model of leadership includes strategies for preventing or silencing dissent. Every system of control covers what employees do *and* what they say. But no control system is perfect; there is always some space for resistance, and dissent is a potent form of resistance. However, resistance leads to counterresistance (Ashforth and Mael, 1998). When resisting voices are raised, surface-level power strategies come into play. These overt strategies of suppressing dissent typically take place in graduated phases. Initially, organizational power holders attempt to persuade the dissenters that they are wrong or mistaken (a process sometimes called **nullification**). If that fails, the dissenters are isolated from coworkers – disconnecting telephones or revoking computer access codes, removing the dissenters' names from invitation lists for social events, or transferring them to the corporate version of Stalin's Siberia (or nearby – an Enron employee who dared challenge his bosses' wildly inaccurate profit and loss data was transferred to the company's Alberta, Canada office). If nullification and isolation fail (and they rarely do because most people decide that dissent is not worth the cost), direct sanctions are applied – defaming the dissenters or expelling them from the organization.

Research by Jeffrey Kassing and his associates has found a complicated relationship among the issue, the dissenter's standing in the organization, and the audience of the dissent. Employees offer dissent about a wide range of topics, from everyday work activities, to treatment of coworkers, to ethical and safety issues. All employees are very much concerned with the effects that dissenting will have on their image in the organization, and consciously balance those concerns against the risks of retaliation and their individual ethical codes. Sometimes dissenters complain to peers (lateral dissent); sometimes to supervisors (upward dissent); and sometimes to outsiders such as the media or governmental agencies (**whistleblowing**). Those who engage in upward dissent tend to be supervisors themselves, are comfortable arguing, have high levels of job satisfaction and identification with their organizations, have good interpersonal relationships with their supervisors, and believe that their organization values freedom of speech. Employees who engage in lateral dissent have the opposite characteristics. Employees perceive upward dissenters more favorably than lateral dissenters. Sometimes dissenters are motivated by self-interest or self-protection needs, but more often they are concerned about organizational issues. However, if a dissenter's supervisor ignores or dismisses their concerns, responds in a vague and/or ambivalent way, or retaliates, self-oriented motivations may become primary.[14]

In general, the preferred communicative strategy for upward dissent is a direct factual appeal combined with a concrete solution for the problem being raised. Factual evidence includes physical evidence, explicit reference to formal, written policies and procedures, and personal work experience. The combination of fact and solution minimize the chances that a supervisor will feel threatened and respond defensively. In contrast, repetition (calling attention to a condition or to one's complaint over and over again) and threatening to resign generally are ineffective (we examine the dynamics of threats and promises in Chapter 9). The most complicated and most risky strategy is **circumvention**, going around or above one's immediate supervisor to complain to people higher up in the organization. Circumvention inevitably threatens a supervisor's face and invites a defensive response. In organizations where following the chain of command is valued highly, it also violates important organizational rules. It can be a self-centered political maneuver (a very risky one), but often stems from a subordinates' conclusion that someone's (including one's immediate supervisor's) actions need to be questioned on ethical, moral, or professional grounds. Potential *relational* outcomes for the dissenter range from harming one's relationship with one's supervisor and decreasing the likelihood of successful dissent in the future, to prompting compromises which address some of the problem while allowing all parties to save face, to having nothing happen, to having one's supervisor view the issue in a new way and accept the dissenter's recommendations, to having the supervisor express his or her thanks to the subordinate (a outcome that Kassing and his associates call **development**). Supervisors also may respond to circumvention with *understanding*. For example, a supervisor may agree with the dissenter, but be so constrained by organizational policies or by *his* or *her* supervisor that it is impossible to comply. In these cases, circumvention is seen as legitimate and nonthreatening. For example, an employee felt that his annual raise was too small. His supervisor responded that it was the largest raise that the plant manager would allow. The employee then appealed to the plant manager and got the raise. The dissenter's immediate supervisor was not offended because he knew that negotiating for larger raises in this way was "just business," and because the dissenter used rational appeals. Of course, circumvention more often leads to negative outcomes than to positive ones, and it is even less likely that using of the strategy will improve organizational policies, procedures, and practices (Kassing, 2007).

The most complex form of dissent involves whistleblowers. Many studies find that employees often are required to compromise their own values at work. In a typical study, Posner and Schmidt found that 72 percent of employees face pressure to engage in actions that they perceive to be unethical, and that 41 percent admit that they have succumbed to those pressures. A 1995 study of 30 Harvard MBAs revealed that 29 of them had been ordered to violate their own personal ethical standards at least once during the previous five years. Because pressure to act in unethical or illegal ways is so common, examples of whistleblowers are easy to find – every major newspaper publishes at least one story every month.[15] Whistleblowers' stories are amazingly consistent with one another. An employee, usually one with high levels of commitment to their organization, detects something going wrong in their organization. It often involves illegal activity (in the United States, 51 percent of complaints involved criminal activity, 19 percent involved health and safety violations, and 12 percent involved discrimination) and always involves something that the potential whistleblower fervently believes is unethical (Hananel, 2002). She or he then attempts to change the practice through the normal chain of command, using some of the strategies described in this chapter. When internal appeals fail, as they usually do, whistleblowers face an exceptionally difficult decision. They realize that blowing the whistle will add significant risks to their personal life, advancement potential, relationships with coworkers, and personal safety, while the potential for any personal gain is quite small (Kassing and Avtgis, 1999; Kassing, 2001; Kassing and Armstrong, 2002). Because of the stresses involved in fighting a prolonged battle with a powerful organization, whistleblowers sometimes become alcoholics, lose their homes, are divorced, go bankrupt, and/or attempt suicide. But the personal costs of not doing so – reduced self-esteem, guilt, and fear that someone else will report the improper practices, leaving the employee in the role of an accomplice – may also be quite large. Faced with an intense avoid–avoid conflict, only about 10 percent of people who could blow the whistle actually do so, and whistleblowers' complaints are often withdrawn before any corrective action is taken because the pressure becomes too intense.[16]

Organizational responses to whistleblowers are easy to predict. Whistleblowers are subjected to a wide variety of different forms of harassment, from being denied the resources necessary to do their jobs (for example, having their security clearance canceled, losing access to necessary computer files, losing support staff, and so on), to being subjected to repeated psychological evaluations in spite of being declared fit for duty, to being subjected to arbitrary and negative performance reviews. Studies in the United States have found that 90 percent of whistleblowers who refuse to resign lose their jobs or are demoted, and 27 percent are sued by their companies and/or supervisors. One of the longest and most complicated cases involved Vera English, formerly employed at General Electric's nuclear fuel plant in Wilmington, North Carolina. After two years of complaining to GE management about practices which violated both company policy and federal law, English went public. Within a month GE told her that she would lose her job unless she agreed to be transferred to the non-nuclear section of the plant, thereby abandoning her career and sacrificing years of education and experience. She refused, and two months later she was fired. She then filed a complaint with the US Department of Labor, which found evidence of discrimination. GE appealed the verdict. A year later an administrative law judge ordered GE to reinstate her to her original position and pay her $73,007 in damages plus back pay. GE again appealed. The Secretary of Labor reversed the law judge's decision on a technicality – English had not filed her complaint within 30 days of being threatened. She appealed, and after a number of other re-hearings and appeals within the Labor Department, the secretary again dismissed her complaint. English also had sued GE in federal court. A federal district judge found that she had a valid claim, but dismissed her lawsuit on a technicality. Six years after filing her lawsuit, and after two successful appeals, the US Supreme Court ruled in her favor and returned the case to the lower court. Once again her case was dismissed, this time because she had not proven GE's actions to be "outrageous," a decision that was upheld on appeal. In total, English spent eight years fighting her battle, and in the process received favorable rulings by both the US Supreme Court and the Nuclear Regulatory Commission. But, the fight cost her $250,000 in lost wages and legal fees; she received no financial award, and GE paid only a $20,000 fine. Ironically, because potential threats to the public from radioactive events are so great, the Nuclear Power

Industry has among the *strongest* whistleblower protection laws in the United States.[17] The protections are much weaker elsewhere, and many industries have none (for example, a congressional proposal to create whistleblower protections provision for the new US Department of Homeland Security was not passed by the Bush administration).[18]

Unfortunately, dissenters and whistleblowers often find that they also are punished by their coworkers, who ostracize, threaten, or intimidate them (Lipman-Blumen, 2008). People in the United States have ambivalent attitudes about whistleblowers. At one level, they know that because organizations are so adept at covering up their illegal and unethical activities, whistleblowers are absolutely necessary for our justice system to work. Virtually every successful action against corporate corruption and illegality – from Texaco's racism to environmental violations to corruption in the savings and loan, mutual fund, and banking industries – could not have happened without whistleblowers. It is for this reason that *Time* magazine celebrated three dissenters as its "people of the year" for 2003. On the other hand, elementary school children learn to view children negatively who report wrongdoing, and studies of peer harassment of whistleblowers show that these attitudes carry over to adulthood. This seems to be especially true in organizations that rely on cultural strategies of organizing. Employees who identify closely with their organizations interpret any threats to it as a personal threat, and respond accordingly. For example, Dr. Troy Madsen was working the 32nd hour of a 34-hour shift at Johns Hopkins Hospital, the top-ranked hospital in the United States. As a result of exhaustion, he made a mistake that could have killed a patient. His shift violated rules established in 2003 that limited medical residents to 30-hour shifts and no more than 80 hours of work in a single week. Madsen recalled, "People I worked with, people I knew very well, would not look at me, would not talk to me." Unlike most whistleblowers Madsen won his case and forced Johns Hopkins to abide by the new regulations (Straziuso, 2004; Vaughn, 1992). But soon after he moved to Ohio State, not because he was fired, but because of the way he was treated by his coworkers. Like Madsen, a large percentage of whistleblowers regret taking action. Richard Lundwall, the manager who blew the whistle on Texaco's racist promotion policies in 1998, now says, "[I]f there are other Richard Lundwalls out there who have information contrary to their employers' best interest, they would be rather foolish to put themselves at risk."[19] A Tennessee Valley Authority nuclear plant worker echoed the sentiment: "the process doesn't do anything but put a big bull's eye on your back." (See Figure 7.1.)

Figure 7.1 Source: NON SEQUITUR © 2000 Wiley Ink, Inc. Dist. By UNIVERSAL UCLICK. Reprinted with permission. All rights reserved.

Muting Groups' Voices One of the recurring themes of this book is that power and control in organizations are closely linked to sense making and processes of meaning creation. Sense making is guided by social and organizational power relationships; power relationships are managed strategically by creating shared sense making. In turn, sense-making and strategic communication creates, reproduces, and sometimes transforms power relationships. At first glance, the interrelationships among meaning creation, communication strategies, and power relationships appear to be the same for all groups of people. But a number of contemporary views of social and organizational power suggest that taking a closer look will reveal that there are important power inequalities embedded in meaning creation and communication. In short, in most US organizations, what an act means is determined by the beliefs, values, and frames of reference of educated, white, male upper-level managers. Although employees who are nonwhite, lower level, less educated, or female may make sense of an event or action in very different ways, the discourse of organizations tends to privilege to the sense-making processes of dominant groups. For example, the managerial rhetoric that has accompanied the organizational downsizing from 1985 to the present claims that cutting thousands of jobs is an unavoidable adaptation to the pressures of a global economy. They will increase efficiency and productivity, thus making US firms more competitive in the long term and protecting Americans' jobs. In general, members of US audiences have accepted this rhetoric.

Many other interpretations are possible. For example, one could argue that downsizing is a strategic choice that primarily benefits upper management, not workers, stockholders, or society as a whole, one that has little positive effect on efficiency or productivity. Between 1980 and 1995 the 500 largest US firms (Fortune 500) eliminated more than 8 million jobs, while their CEOs' compensation increased 1000 percent (the trends accelerated after 1985). Anthony Downs found that the number of jobs eliminated by a company is a significantly stronger predictor of executive compensation than the 5-year performance of the company. After job reductions are announced, stock prices quickly jump – when IBM, Sears, Xerox, McDonnell Douglas, and Dupont cut between 4500 and 60,000 workers, there was an increase of stock value the next day of between 3.4 percent and 7.7 percent. For executives whose compensation is primarily based on stock price, which includes almost all Fortune 500 firms, the gains were monumental. But, for the organizations and other stakeholders, the impact of downsizing is very different. Only 26 percent of downsized firms report efficiency increases; 19 percent report decreases, and 39 percent report no change. Eleven percent of downsized firms report increased absenteeism; 62 percent report lower morale, and 39 percent report increased voluntary turnover. Within two years of downsizing, firm performance falls, in part because when employees are forced to leave they take a great deal of the corporation's intelligence with them. They may be rehired, usually as consultants or contract workers, whose salaries may be greater than before, but whose benefits packages are much smaller and their job security is nonexistent. For example, during 2009 the Chrysler Corporation declared bankruptcy, downsized, accepted a $12.5 billion taxpayer bailout, and emerged from bankruptcy as a partner of Fiat. By the end of the year they realized that they had eliminated the jobs of the designers and engineers who might have developed new products in order to recapture some market share. As a result, Chrysler showed up at the January 2010 North American International Auto Show with no new products, and consequently was the only manufacturer to not hold a flashy press conference to introduce its new vehicles. All its new management could do was announce plans to hire more engineers and product development specialists (Krishner, 2010; Whoeriskey, 2010).

Over an even longer time frame, 15 years or so, companies whose managers choose strategies other than downsizing are stronger than those who did not (Boje, 1997; Downs, 1996). For workers and middle managers – more of whom tend to be female, nonwhite, less well educated, and less wealthy than upper management – downsizing means lost income, reduced self-esteem, and increased stress and insecurity, not increased profits or a rosy future. The societal *narrative* about downsizing, both within organizations and in the popular media, is *closed*, as people uncritically accept and in turn legitimize the managerial interpretation while ignoring or muting other interpretations.[20]

Processes of elevating one voice and obscuring others also takes place at a microscopic level, in the key terms used to describe organizational policies and practices. For example, think about the term "efficiency." Almost everyone knows what the term means and nonconsciously accept the importance of the concept it represents. However, Roger Jehensen has suggested that, like the rhetoric of downsizing, taken-for-granted definitions of efficiency are "ideological fictions" that privilege the interests of some groups over the interests of others. "Efficiency" is not itself a goal in itself. It is a means of reaching some other goal or outcome. Driving fast, or driving in a fuel-efficient manner (two possible definitions of "efficient" travel), are meaningless unless doing so gets people somewhere they want to go. Presumably, organizational efficiency is important, because it produces something else of value – profits or the continued existence of the organization, for example. If "efficiency" is defined as a *means* to an end, it immediately raises questions about the value of the ends themselves. They will ask what communication theorist Jürgen Habermas has called **practical questions**, questions such as "What level of environmental damage are we willing to accept in order to increase profits?" or "What proportion of a firm's profits should be reinvested in the publicly funded infrastructure (roads, education systems, and so on) that the organization uses to produce its profits?" But when efficiency is defined as an *end* in itself, as it usually is, these value-laden questions are ignored. Instead, people only ask what Habermas calls **technical questions**, about how best to maximize efficiency. Defining efficiency as an *end* obscures value-laden questions about goals and social costs by focusing attention on seemingly value-neutral questions about techniques, and makes the conversation between Alice and the Cheshire Cat quoted at the beginning of this chapter into perfect sense. In the process, narrow, technical kinds of expertise – the expertise that managers are presumed to have – are elevated in importance. And the voices of people who ask *practical* questions that are based on the experiences and values of other groups – workers and members of the communities in which our organizations exist – are silenced.[21] Focusing on *technical* questions instead of *practical* ones privileges the interests of some groups over others. So do the definitions of the key terms that make up the questions themselves. For example, the usual "technical" definition of "efficiency" is output per person hour. But what if "efficiency" is defined in terms of output per dollar of supervisory overhead? Both definitions are justifiable on economic grounds; but the former definition focuses attention on workers, places the burden for organizational success on controlling and motivating *them*, and legitimizes management's efforts to do so. It also suggests that the returns created through increased efficiency should be given largely to management because it was *their* skill at motivating and controlling workers that created the "efficiency." Similarly, the dominant definition justifies blaming workers for negative outcomes because it could only have been *their* lack of effort, ability, and productivity (in-spite of management's best efforts) that caused the losses. This sense-making system further legitimizes management's efforts to motivate and control workers in the future. In contrast, the second definition of "efficiency" focuses attention on managerial overheads, places the burden for organizational success on management's shoulders, suggests that the number of managers and their compensation should be kept as small as possible, and assumes that nonmanagerial managerial personnel do the *real* work of the organization. The former definition elevates the interests and "voice" of managers over workers; the latter elevates the interests and voice of workers.

Box 7.1

An Exploration of Life in Systems of Power

The following poem by Barry Oshrey (1995) explores the inner feelings of those caught up in systems of power. It considers the ways in which dominant parties think, feel, and act, and the ways in which dominated parties think, feel, react and act.

Dominant/Dominated

The other side of dominant is not submissive;
it is dominated.

The Dominant and the Dominated
In many systems,
there are two cultures:
the Dominant
and the Dominated.
The Dominated exist within the Dominant culture:
females in a male dominated society,
acquired companies within an acquiring company,
people of color in a white dominated society,
Native Americans in America,
Soviet states in a Russian dominated empire,
Palestinians in Israel,
Blacks in South Africa,
French Canadians in English-Canadian dominated society,
Serbs in the Ottoman Empire,
Jews in anti-Semitic societies,
Catholic, Japanese, Chinese, and other early immigrants in
the U.S.A.
The Dominated
within the Dominant.

HE: So we're not talking about "minorities"?
SHE: Absolutely right. Minority, majority – that's not the issue. The question is: Who are the Dominant? And who are the Dominated?

The Dominant Culture
The Dominants' culture
is invisible to them;

it is the water in which they swim,
the air they breathe.

To the Dominants,
how they speak
is the way one speaks,
how they dress
is how one dresses,
their values
are *the* values,
their history
is *the* history.

To the Dominants
the culture of the Dominated
is not merely different,
it is wrong –
wrong speech,
wrong dress,
wrong emotionality,
wrong spirituality,
wrong values.

The culture of the Dominated is seen as strange,
sometimes comical,
usually lesser,
inferior.

The Survival of the Dominated
To the Dominated,
the culture of the Dominants
is oppressive –
there is not space for *their* voice,
their dress,
their values,
their history.

How to survive as a Dominated
within the Dominant culture?

Adopt.
We can suppress our culture
and adopt their culture,
become more like them:
white-ish Blacks,
man-ish women,
Gentile-ish Jews,
straight-ish gays.
We can walk like them,
talk like them,
dress like them,
think like them.

We can make our way
as best we can
as one of them
in their world.

Embrace.
We can accept our fate –
the Dominated within the Dominant.
This is our life;
we can chose it,
love it,
embrace it,
and make our way
as best we can.

Separate.
We can separate from them –
from their businesses,
their schools,
their churches
their government.
We can reject their ways
and elaborate our ways,
our culture;
create our own businesses,
churches,
schools,
government.
We can make our way
as best we can
without them.

Rebel.
We can attack the Dominant culture –
try to destroy it,
discredit it,
tear down its heroes,
revise its history
and ours,
paints ours as good
and theirs as evil.
We can try to dominate "Them,"
pass laws to constrain "Them."
We can try to make our way
the dominant way.

Drop out.
We can withdraw from both cultures –
into drugs, alcohol,
insanity.

Crime.
Since the Dominant culture is unfair –
its rules are *their* rules,
its laws, *their* laws,
its opportunities, *their* opportunities –
we can take what we can,
we can steal,
cheat,
lie.
We can break *their* laws,
which isn't crime,
only doing what is fair,
making our way
as best we can
in their culture.

Adopt.
Embrace.
Separate.
Rebel.
Drop Out.
Crime.
All struggling to survive
as the Dominated
among the Dominant.

The Possibility of Transformation
Or we can choose to end the old dance –
first to see it.
then to end it –
to transform the culture
so that it embraces the cultures
of both the Dominant
and the Dominated:
the customs of each,
the speech,
the emotionality,
the history,
the spirituality
of both the Dominant
and the Dominated.

The Dominants will resist –
powerfully.
They will wonder what the fuss is all about.
For them there is no problem,
nothing to solve,
nothing to fix.
Their culture is invisible to them;
it is the water in which they swim,

the air they breathe.
The Dominants are offended
when their culture is made visible,
when it becomes an option
rather than the way things are.
The Dominants will resist,
and if the Dominated persist,
there will be chaos:
A mess,
the disruption of the familiar energy pattern.
And in the chaos,
there is nothing but possibility:
The Dominant crushing the Dominated –
that's possible!
A settling back into the old comfortably uncomfortable
dance –
that's also possible.
A complete rupture of the relationship –
that, too, is possible.
And there is always the possibility of transforming the
culture into some new and unpredictable form.
(Remember when it was unthinkable that women and
Blacks would vote.)
There will be resistance,
but is resistance just resistance?
Or is it also the sound of the old dance shaking?

HE: Dominant cultures have accomplished great things. You're not denying that are you?

SHE: The issue is: Did those great things have to be accomplished over the bodies of the Dominated? That is the blind reflex: What were the possibilities of partnership around the life of these systems? What are the possibilities now?

HE: Are you optimistic about *this* transformation?

SHE: Neither optimistic nor pessimistic, simply painfully aware of the tragic alternatives. Throughout history, the consequences of this dance have been devastating.

CONCLUSION

Traditional models of organizational power define it in terms of domination and through overt displays such as orders, threats, promises, and political strategizing. But power has additional, equally important dimensions. The "surface" structure of power also has a "hidden face," the conscious processes through which employees decide which battles to fight and how to fight them. And power has a deeper structure. Power is perception; it exists in the minds of social and organizational actors, not in a realm independent of our activities. It is inextricably linked to the taken-for-granted assumptions of our culture, both in general and in particular organizational cultures. It is exerted through disciplinary processes that permeate every corner of the organization.

Each of these dimensions of power must be considered if any one dimension is to be understood. Overt displays are influenced by the hidden face of power and its deep structure, *and* both of these dimensions are influenced by overt displays. Similarly, the hidden face is influenced by employees' perceptions of what actions are *normal* and *natural* in their cultures. Their decisions about which battles to fight and how to fight them determine how and when power is displayed in their organizations. Finally, the assumptions of a society are created, reproduced, and transformed by its members' overt actions and hidden decisions about power relationships. One dimension of power simply cannot be understood without simultaneously considering the others.

NOTES

1 See Zalzenik (1970, 47) and Barber (1966). The literature on social and organizational power is almost overwhelmingly large, so much so that it would be impossible to list even a small proportion of the important works here. Particularly valuable items are Mintzberg (1983), Pfeffer, (1981, 1993, 2010), and Mumby (2001).

2 Foucault focused on organizations in which the sovereign's control over others was total – kings, dictators, prison wardens, or directors of mental institutions – but his analysis has been applied to all kinds of organizations. For readable summarizes of Foucault's complicated perspective, see Tretheway (2000) and Barker and Cheney (1994). These sources summarize Foucault (1977/1990, 1978/1990).

3 Multilevel models of power are developed in a large number of contemporary writings. They are summarized in Clegg (1989) and Conrad (1995). For applications of multilevel models to interpersonal relationships in organizations, see Morrill (1992) and Clair (1993).

4 See Berger (1994). For a classic application of this concept to organizations, see Barnard (1968).

5 Ferris, Russ, and Fandt (1989) examine the link between impression management and organizational politics. For analyses of impression management strategies, see Mark Bolino (1999). For an analysis of modesty, see Robinson, Johnson, and Shields (1995).

6 For a summary of subordinates' influence strategies, see Lamude, Daniels, and White (1987). Also see Roberts (1986).

7 Hirokawa and Miyahara (1986). Also see Kim and Miller (1990). For an analysis of relational effects on supervisor strategies, see Garko (1992).

8 See Eisenberg (1984) and Eisenberg and Phillips (1991). For an application to organizational image management, see Kline, Simunich, and Weber (2009).

9 Classic studies of how interdependencies and power are interrelated include Pettigrew (1972) and Emerson (1962).

10 See Watzlawick, Beavin, and Jackson (1967). Perhaps the most important aspect of the "relational" level of meaning involves the relative power that exists among the people who are communicating (Lukes, 1974).

11 This section is based largely on Bridge and Baxter (1992). Also see McAllister (1995), Kramer (1995), Sias and Jablin (1995), and Sias (1996).

12 The term was coined by communication scholar Stan Deetz (1992).

13 See Redding (1985) and Sprague and Rudd (1988). Also see Miceli and Near (1992), Near and Jensen (1983), and Stewart (1980). For an interesting analysis of the intersection between gender and dissent, see Perriton (2009).

14 See Collinson (1994) and Larson and Tompkins (2005). Also see Kassing (2001) and Kassing and Armstrong (2002).

15 See Hegstrom (1995), Kassing (1997), and Posner and Schmidt (1984). Also see Sims (1992). The MBA study and the cost estimates are summarized in Barlow (1996).

16 Data about the United States (and Australia) are available in McMillan (1990) and Grace and Cohen (1995).

17 The primary source for this example was a series of articles published by the *Houston Chronicle* during March and September 1993. For a broad analysis of issues regarding the release of low-level radioactivity, see Gould (1990) and Gould and Sternglass (1996).

18 The Dodd-Frank Act, passed in 2010 in the wake of the 2008 financial industry collapse and bailout, strengthened whistleblower protections (see Hilder, 2010). But, if history is any guide, those protections

will be incrementally reduced over time and only weakly enforced by subsequent administrations.

19 The Lundwall interview is available in "Texaco Whistle-Blower: Much Trouble, Little Reward" (1999).

20 The data presented are based on a September 1996 survey of 5000 companies by the Society for Human Resource Management. A summary was published in the October 1, 1996 *Houston Chronicle* (see Society for Human Resource Management, 1996). Additional data are provided by Gibson and Schullery (2000). For an analysis of the effects of downsizing on both employees who are dismissed and those who stay behind, see Tourish, Paulsen, and Bordia (2004); Boje (1997); and Grint and Case (1998). An excellent summary of muted group theory is provided by Orbe (1998).

21 For an excellent summary of these ideas, see McMillan (2007). Also see Jehensen (1984) and Barker and Cheney (1994). Habermas's work is explained clearly in Mumby (1988) and Deetz (1992). For an analysis of the ways in which technical reason strengthens management's power, see Gowler and Legge (1996).

REFERENCES

Ashforth, B.E. and Mael, F.A. (1998). "The Power of Resistance," in Kramer and Neale, eds., *Power and Influence in Organizations*. Thousand Oaks, CA: Sage.

Barber, D. (1966). *Power in Committees*. Chicago: Rand McNally.

Barker, J. and Cheney, G. (1994). "The Concept of Discipline in Contemporary Organizational Life." *Communication Monographs* 61: 19–43.

Barlow, J. (1996). "Ethics Can Boost the Bottom Line." *Houston Chronicle*, October 31, C1.

Barnard, C. (1968). *The Functions of the Executive*, 30th anniversary ed. Cambridge, MA: Harvard University Press.

Berger, C. (1994). "Power, Dominance, and Social Interaction," in Knapp and Miller, eds., *Handbook of Interpersonal Communication*. Beverly Hills, CA: Sage.

Boje, D. (1997). "Restorying Re-engineering." *Journal of Applied Communication Research* 17: 631–668.

Bolino, M. (1999). "Citizenship and Impression Management." *Academy of Management Review* 14: 82–98.

Bolino, M., Tumley, W.H. and Niehoff, B.P. (2004). "The Other Side of the Story." *Human Resource Management Review* 14: 229–246.

Bridge, K. and Baxter, L. (1992). "Blended Relationships: Friends as Work Associates." *Western Journal of Communication* 56: 200–225.

Clair, R. (1993). "The Use of Framing Devices to Sequester Organizational Narratives." *Communication Monographs* 60: 113–136.

Clegg, S. (1989). *Frameworks of Power*. Newbury Park, CA: Sage.

Collinson, D. (1994). "Strategies of Resistance," in Jermier, Knights and Nord, eds., *Resistance and Power in Organizations*. London: Routledge.

Conrad, C. (1995). "Was Pogo Right?" In Wood and Gregg, eds., *Communication Research in the Twenty-first Century*. Cresskill, NJ: Hampton Press.

Conrad, C. (2011). *Organizational Rhetoric*. London: Polity Press.

Conrad, C. and Abbot, J. (2007). "Corporate Social Responsibility and Public Policymaking," in May, Cheney and Roper, eds., *The Debate Over Corporate Social Responsibility*. New York: Oxford University Press.

Cowan, R. (2009). "Walking the Tightrope." December. Unpublished dissertation, Texas: A&M University.

Crozier, M. (1964). *The Bureaucratic Phenomenon*. Chicago: University of Chicago Press.

Davenport, N., Schwartz, R.D. and Elliott, G.P. (2002). *Mobbing*, 2nd ed. Ames, IA: Civil Society Publishing.

de Certeau, M. (1984). *The Practices of Everyday Life*. Berkeley: University of California Press.

Deetz, S. (1992). *Democracy in an Age of Corporate Colonization*. Albany, NY: SUNY Press.

Dervin, B. (1997). "Given and Context by Any Other Name," in Vakkari, Savolainen and Dervin, eds., *Information-Seeking in Context*. London: Taylor Graham.

Downs, A. (1996), *Corporate Executions*. New York: AMACOM.

Einarsen, S. (1999). "The Nature and Causes of Bullying at Work." *Journal of Manpower* 20: 16–27.

Einarsen, S., Hoel, H., Zapf, D. and Cooper, C. (2003). *Bullying and Emotional Abuse in the Workplace*. London: Taylor & Francis

Eisenberg, E. (1984). "Ambiguity as Strategy in Organizational Communication." *Communication Monographs* 51: 227–242.

Eisenberg, E. and Phillips, S. (1991). "Miscommunication in Organizations," in Coupland, Giles and Wieman, eds.,

"Miscommunication" and Problematic Talk. Newbury Park, CA: Sage.

Emerson, R.M. (1962). "Power-Dependence Relations." *American Sociological Review* 27: 31–41.

Falbe, C. and Yukl, G. (1992). "Consequences of Managers' Using Single Influence Tactics and Combinations of Tactics." *Academy of Management Journal* 32: 638–652.

Ferris, G.R., Russ, G.S. and Fandt, D.M. (1989). "Politics in Organizations," in Giacolone and Rosenfeld, eds., *Impression Management in the Organization*. Hillsdale, NJ: Lawrence Erlbaum.

Foss, S. and Griffin, C. (1995). "Beyond Persuasion." *Quarterly Journal of Speech* 62: 2–18.

Foucault, M. (1977/1990). *Discipline and Punish*, trans. A. Sheridan. New York: Vintage.

Foucault, M. (1978/1990). *The History of Sexuality*, vol. 1, trans. A. Hurley. New York: Vintage.

Foucault, M. (1980). *Power/Knowledge*, trans. C. Gordon. New York: Pantheon.

Frost, P. (1987). "Power, Politics, and Influence," in Jablin, Putnam, Roberts and Porter, eds., *Handbook of Organizational Communication*. Newbury Park, CA: Sage.

Garko, M. (1992). "Persuading Subordinates Who Communicate in Attractive and Unattractive Styles." *Management Communication Quarterly* 5: 289–315.

Gibson, M. and Schullery, N. (2000). "Shifting Meanings in a Blue-Collar Worker Philanthropy Program." *Management Communication Quarterly* 14: 189–236.

Giddens, A. (1991). *Modernity and Self-Identity*. Palo Alto, CA: Stanford University.

Goffman, E. (1955). "On Face Work." *Psychiatry* 18: 213–231.

Goffman, E. (1959). *The Presentation of Self in Everyday Life*. New York: Doubleday.

Gould, J. (1990). *Deadly Deceit*. New York: Four Walls Eight Windows.

Gould, J. and Sternglass, D. (1996). *The Enemy Within*. New York: Four Walls Eight Windows.

Gowler, D. and Legge, K. (1996). "The Meaning of Management and the Management of Meaning," in Linstead, Small and Jeffcutt, eds., *Understanding Management*. London: Sage.

Grace, D. and Cohen, S. (1995). *Business Ethics*. Melbourne: Oxford.

Grint, K. and Case, P. (1998). "The Violent Rhetoric of Re-engineering." *Journal of Management Studies* 35: 222–238.

Hananel, S. (2002). "Whistleblowers Lack Protection." *Houston Chronicle*, September 2, 19A.

Hegstrom, T.G. (1995). "Focus on Organizational Dissent," in Lehtonen, ed., *Critical Perspectives on Communication Research and Pedagogy*. St. Ingbert, Germany: Rohrig University Press.

Hilder, P. (2010). "Law Makes It Easier to Blow the Whistle on Corporate Crime." *Houston Chronicle*, October 17, B8.

Hirokawa, R. and Miyahara, A. (1986). "A Comparison of Influence Strategies Used by Managers in American and Japanese Organization." *Communication Quarterly* 34: 250–265.

Hoel, H., Einarsen, S. and Cooper, C. (2002). "Organizational Effects of Bullying," in Einarsen, Hoel, Zapf and Cooper, eds., *Bullying and Emotional Abuse in the Workplace*. London: Taylor & Francis.

Jablin, F. (1981). "An Exploratory Study of Subordinates' Perceptions of Supervisory Politics." *Communication Quarterly* 29: 269–275.

Jablin, F. (2001). "Organizational Entry, Assimilation, and Disengagement/Exit," in Jablin and Putnam, eds., *The New Handbook of Organizational Communication*. Thousand Oaks, CA: Sage.

Jehensen, R. (1984). "Effectiveness, Expertise, and Excellence as Ideological Fictions." *Human Studie*, 7: 3–21.

Johnson, J.D. (1996). *Information Seeking*. Westport, CT: Quorum Books.

Johnson, J.D. (2003). "On Contexts of Information Seeking." *Information Processing and Management* 39: 735–760.

Kassing, J. (1997). "Articulating, Agonizing, and Displacing." *Communication Studies* 48: 311–332.

Kassing, J. (2001). "From the Looks of Things." *Management Communication Quarterly*: 14: 442–470.

Kassing, J. (2007). "Going Around the Boss." *Management Communication Quarterly* 21: 55–74.

Kassing, J. and Armstrong, T. (2002). "Someone's Going to Hear About This." *Management Communication Quarterly* 16: 39–65.

Kassing, J. and Avtgis, T. (1999). "Examining the Relationship Between Organizational Dissent and Aggressive Communication." *Management Communication Quarterly* 13: 76–91.

Keashley, L and Harvey, J. (2006). "Workplace Emotional Abuse," in Kelloway, Barling and Hurrell, Jr., eds., *Handbook of Workplace Violence*. Thousand Oaks, CA: Sage.

Keashley, L. and Jagatic, K. (2003). "By Any Other Name," in Einarsen, Hoel, Zapf, and Cooper , eds., *Bullying and Emotional Abuse in the Workplace*. London: Taylor & Francis.

Kim, Y.Y. and Miller, K.I. (1990). "The Effects of Attributions and Feedback Goals on the Generation of Supervisor Feedback Message Strategies." *Management Communication Quarterly* 4: 6–29.

Kline, S., Simunich, B. and Weber, H. (2009). "The Use of Equivocal Messages in Responding to Corporate Challenges." *Journal of Applied Communication Research* 37: 40–58.

Kramer, M. (1995). "A Longitudinal Study of Superior–Subordinate Communication During Job Transfers." *Human Communication Research* 22: 39–64.

Krishner, T. (2010). "U.S. Automakers Start to See Improvement." *Houston Chronicle* online, January 11. www.chron.com/fdcp?1263604173320.

Krone, K. (1992). "A Comparison of Organizational, Structural, and Relationship Effects on Subordinates' Upward Influence Choices." *Communication Quarterly* 40: 1–15.

Lamude, K., Daniels, T. and White, K. (1987). "Managing the Boss." *Management Communication Quarterly* 1: 232–259.

Larson, G.S. and Tompkins, P. (2005). "Ambivalence and Resistance." *Communication Monographs* 72: 1–25.

Lewis, D. and Rayner, C. (2003). "Bullying and Human Resource Management," in Einarsen, Hoel, Zapf and Cooper , eds., *Bullying and Emotional Abuse in the Workplace*. London: Taylor & Francis.

Lipman-Blumen, J. (2008). "Dissent in Times of Crisis," in Banks, ed., *Dissent and the Failure of Leadership*. Cheltenham. UK: Edward Elgar.

Lukes, S. (1974). *Power: A Radical View*. London:Macmillan.

Lutgen-Sandvik, P. (2003). "The Communicative Cycle of Employee Emotional Abuse." *Management Communication Quarterly* 16: 471–501.

Lutgen-Sandvik, P. (2006). "Take This Job and . . . : Quitting and Other Forms of Resistance to Workplace Bullying." *Communication Monographs* 73: 406–433.

Lutgen-Sandvik, P. (2008). "Intensive Remedial Identity Work." *Organization* 15: 97–119.

Lutgen-Sandvik, P. and McDermott, V. (2008). "The Constitution of Employee-Abusive Organizations." *Communication Theory*, 18, 304-333.

McAllister, D.J. (1995). "Affect- and Cognition-Based Trust as Foundations for Interpersonal Cooperation in Organizations." *Academy of Management Journal* 38: 24–59.

McMillan, J. (1990). "Legal Protection of Whistleblowers," in Prosser, Wear and Nethercote, eds., *Corruption and Reform*. St. Lucia, Australia: University of Queensland Press.

McMillan, J. (2007). "Why Corporate Social Responsibility: Why Now? How?" in May, Cheney and Roper, eds., *The Debate Over Corporate Social Responsibility*. New York: Oxford University Press.

Miceli, M. and Near, J. (1992). *Blowing the Whistle*. New York: Lexington Books.

Mintzberg, H. (1983). *Structure in Fives: Designing Effective Organizations*. Englewood Cliffs, NJ: Prentice Hall.

Morrill, C. (1992). "The Private Ordering of Professional Relationships," in Kolb and Bartunek, eds., *Hidden Conflict in Organizations*. Newbury Park, CA: Sage.

Morris, G.H., Gaveras, S.C., Baker, W.L. and Coursey, M.L. (1990). "Aligning Actions at Work." *Management Communication Quarterly* 3: 303–333.

Mumby, D. (1988). *Communication and Power in Organizations*. Norwood, NJ: Ablex.

Mumby, D., ed. (1993). *Narrative and Social Control: Critical Perspectives*. Newbury Park, CA: Sage.

Mumby, D. (1998). "Organizing Men." *Communication Theory* 8: 164–183.

Mumby, D. (2000). "Communication, Organization, and the Public Sphere," in Buzzanell, ed., *Rethinking Organizational and Managerial Communication From Feminist Perspectives*. Thousand Oaks, CA: Sage.

Mumby, D. (2001). "Power and Politics," in Jablin and Putnam, eds., *The New Handbook of Organizational Communication*. Thousand Oaks. CA: Sage.

Near, J. and Jensen, T.C. (1983). "The Whistleblowing Process." *Work and Occupations* 10: 3–28.

Orbe, M. (1998). "An Outsider Within Perspective to Organizational Communication." *Management Communication Quarterly* 2: 230–279.

Oshrey, B. (1995). *Seeing Systems*. San Francisco: Berrett-Koehler.

Perriton, L. (2009). "'We Don't Want Any Complaining Women.'" *Management Communication Quarterly* 23: 218–243.

Pettigrew, A. (1972). "Information Control as a Power Resource." *Sociology* 6: 187–204.

Pfeffer, J. (1981). *Power in Organizations*. Marshfield, MA: Pitman.

Pfeffer, J. (1993). *Managing with Power*. Boston: Harvard University Business School.

Pfeffer, J. (2010). *Power*. New York: HarperBusiness.

Posner, B.Z. and Schmidt, W.H. (1984). "Values and the American Manager." *California Management Review* 26: 202–216.

Putnam, L.L. (1986). "Conflict in Group Decision Making," in Hirokawa and Poole, eds., *Communication and Group Decision Making*. Newbury Park, CA: Sage.

Redding, C. (1985). "Rocking Boats, Blowing Whistles, and Teaching Speech Communication." *Communication Education* 34: 245–258.

Rice, R., McCreadie, M. and Chang, S.L. (2001). *Accessing and Browsing Information and Communication.* Cambridge, MA: MIT Press.

Roberts, N. (1986). "Organizational Power Styles." *Journal of Applied Behavioral Science* 22: 443–455.

Robinson, M.D., Johnson, J.T. and Shields, S.A. (1995). "On the Advantages of Modesty." *Communication Research* 22: 575–591.

Sias, P. (1996). "Constructing Perceptions of Differential Treatment." *Communication Monographs* 63: 171–187.

Sias, P. and Jablin, F. (1995). "Differential Superior-Subordinate Relations, Perceptions of Fairness, and Coworker Communication." *Human Communication Research* 22: 5–38.

Sims, R. (1992). "The Challenge of Ethical Behavior in Organizations." *Journal of Business Ethics* 11: 501–513.

Smith, D. (1992). "Stories, Values, and Patient Care Decisions," in Conrad, ed., *The Ethical Nexus.* Norwood, NJ: Ablex.

Society for Human Resource Management. (1996). [Summary]. *Houston Chronicle*, October 1, B1.

Sprague, J.A. and Rudd, G.L. (1988). "Boat-rocking in the High Technology Culture." *American Behavioral Scientist* 32: 169–193.

Stewart, L. (1980). "'Whistle Blowing.'" *Journal of Communication* 30: 90–101.

Straziuso, J. (2004). "New Doctors Find Hours Still Long, but Abuses Fewer." *Houston Chronicle*, January 13, B10.

"Texaco Whistle-Blower: Much Trouble, Little Reward." (1999). *USA Today*, December 29, 24A.

Tourish, D., Paulsen, N. and Bordia, P. (2004). "The Downsides of Downsizing." *Management Communication Quarterly* 17: 485–516.

Tracy, S., Lutgen-Sandvik, P. and Alberts, J. (2006). "Nightmares, Demons, and Slaves." *Management Communication Quarterly* 20: 148–185.

Tretheway, T. (2000). "A Feminist Critique of Disciplined Bodies," in Buzzanell, ed., *Rethinking Organizational and Managerial Communication from Feminist Perspectives.* Thousand Oaks, CA: Sage.

Vanderford, M., Smith, D. and Harris, W. (1992). "Value Identification in Narrative Discourse." *Journal of Applied Communication Research* 20: 123–161.

Vaughn, D. (1992). *Controlling Unlawful Organizational Behavior.* Chicago: University of Chicago Press.

Waldron, V. (1991). "Achieving Communication Goals in Supervisor–Subordinate Relationships." *Communication Monographs* 58: 289–306.

Waldron, V. and Krone, K. (1991). "The Experience and Expression of Emotion in the Workplace." *Management Communication Quarterly* 4: 287–309.

Watzlawick, P., Beavin, J. and Jackson, D. (1967). *Pragmatics of Human Communication.* New York: W.W. Norton.

Weick, K. (1995). *Sense–Making in Organizations.* Thousand Oaks, CA: Sage.

Whoeriskey, P. (2010), "Chrysler Comes to Detroit Auto Show Without a Splashy New Lineup." *Washington Post*, January 13, A14.

Wilson, S., Greene, J.O. and Dillard, J.P. (2000). "Introduction to the Special Issue on Message Production." *Communication Theory* 10: 135–138.

Wood, J. (1993). "Engendered Relationships," in Duck, ed., *Processes in Close Relationships*, vol. 3. Beverly Hills, CA: Sage.

Wood, J. (1994). *Gendered Lives.* Belmont, CA: Wadsworth.

Yamada, D. (2000). "The Phenomenon of 'Workplace Bullying' and the Need for Status-blind Hostile Work Environment Protection." *Georgetown Law Review* 88: 475–536.

Yamada, D. (2003). "Workplace Bullying and the Law," in Einarsen, Hoel, Zapf and Cooper, eds., *Bullying and Emotional Abuse in the Workplace.* London: Taylor & Francis.

Yamada, D. (2006). "The Business Case Against Workplace Bullying." *Business Forum* online. www.businessforum.com/Yamada_01.html.

Zalzenik, A. (1970). "Power and Politics in Organizational Life." *Harvard Business Review* 48 (May–June): 47–60.

CHAPTER 8

COMMUNICATION, DECISION MAKING, AND CONFLICT IN ORGANIZATIONS

Nothing is more difficult, and therefore more precious than being able to decide.

Napoleon[1]

Decide, v. i. To succumb to the preponderance of one set of influences over another set.

Ambrose Bierce

Far from being necessarily dysfunctional, a certain level of conflict is an essential element in group formation and the persistence of group life.

Louis Coser

CENTRAL THEMES

- Both Western culture and traditional models of organizing view individual employees and organizations as rational actors. In contrast, many contemporary perspectives suggest that these assumptions are cultural myths and that actual decision-making processes are often not rational.
- Because our rationality is "bounded" and our choices are "intransitive," we cannot be rational actors. Consequently, we use communication to make choices that are acceptable and not necessarily rational.

Strategic Organizational Communication: In a Global Economy, Seventh Edition.
Charles Conrad and Marshall Scott Poole.

- Traditional views of group decision making are straightforward applications of the rational actor model; contemporary models focus on the processes through which groups deviate from strict rationality.
- To make effective decisions, groups must exchange and analyze information in a critical fashion, maintain a balance between group cohesion and conflict, and counteract hidden agendas.
- A number of situational and interactional factors influence the extent to which a particular organizational decision can or should be made through strictly rational processes.
- Because rationality is a core value of Western cultures, people need to rationalize their nonrationality. However, doing so tends to privilege the interests of managers over those of workers.
- Conflicts are an inevitable part of relationships characterized by interdependence and interaction. People may perceive that a conflict exists when there is no realistic basis for one and vice versa.
- The ways in which people "frame" conflicts and the choices they make during the early phases of conflicts create parameters that guide and constrain the communication during overt conflicts.
- Destructive escalation occurs when major power imbalances exist. They can be prevented or controlled if all parties understand the communication strategies available to them.
- In productive conflicts, many kinds of communication strategies are used; in destructive ones, only a few strategies are employed.
- In dealing with conflicts, employees can employ avoidant or confrontive strategies. Confrontive strategies generally lead to better results.
- Organizational dispute systems are of three types: interest-based, rights-based, and power-based.
- An alternative view of conflict based on feminist principles views conflict and negotiation as an opportunity for communication and transformation rather than as issue-based problem solving.

KEY TERMS

classical rational model
optimizing
availability bias
bounded rationality
satisficing
intuition
standard agenda
group cohesion
groupthink
egocentric influence
sense making
enactment–selection–etention
conflict
latent conflict
mixed-motive situations
perceived conflict
conflict frames
conflict interaction
avoidance
accommodation
personalization
coercion
threats and promises
toughness
reformed sinner
compromise
problem-solving
aftermath
dispute resolution systems
feminist approach of conflict

Many people, especially in Western societies, view organizations as rational, cooperative enterprises. According to this perspective, organizations exist so that people can pursue their goals through the most efficient means, and organizations are efficient only if the people who comprise them are trained to make and be rewarded for making rational decisions. Rational employees actively address problems or challenges; they systematically seek out the information and expertise needed to choose among courses of action and then make careful, objective decisions based on thorough analysis of extensive information.

Rationality is often treated as an obvious, nonproblematic term. Like many concepts discussed in this book, however, the meaning of rationality in organizations has been influenced by a social myth advocated by classical economists that rationality consists primarily in assessing costs and benefits. While there is merit to this position, there are other, more realistic models of rationality, which are advantageous in their own right. If we consider how individuals, groups, and organizations make decisions, we find that people are not and cannot be strictly rational actors in terms of cost–benefit assessment and may sacrifice a great deal by trying to be. Our goal is not to disparage the model of economic rationality. Instead our objective is to suggest that strictly rational theories of decision making simply do not reflect the complex maze of personal, interpersonal, political, and ethical considerations that employees incorporate into their choices. While the economic model of rationality is one ideal that we can use to guide decision making, it is important to recognize the value of other approaches to decision making.

Decision makers – and all members of organizations for that matter – are not always in agreement, and when they are not conflict ensues. In some cases conflicts are fought out in the open and are evident to observers. In others, conflicts are suppressed and simmer underneath the surface. In still other cases, parties actively try to avoid acknowledging that there is a conflict at all, dancing around potential disagreements in the hope of avoiding open disagreement. Managing conflicts effectively is a challenge in all organizations.

COMMUNICATION AND ORGANIZATIONAL DECISION MAKING

When we think about decision making, the first thing that comes to mind is the lone actor, charged with making a choice and bearing the consequences. Individuals do make many decisions in organizations, starting from the CEO down to employees working directly with customers. As decisions become more complex and more knowledge is needed, however, decisions are delegated to groups, committees, and teams (recall our discussion of coordinating mechanisms in Chapter 6). These groups often must gather information and input from many other parts of the organization and from outside of it, and many of the people who provide this input become players in the decision process. The larger organizational context affects decision making as well because the organization is a source of information, norms (culture), authority to make decisions, as well as constraints and limitations on decision makers. Organizations must also account to outsiders – stockholders, voters, clients or customers, government regulators, investors, and the general public – and this shapes decision behavior and also how they represent their decisions and decision process to outsiders. As we will see, what is often presented as a careful, rational decision is often quite different "under the surface."

This section will move from individual to group to organizational decision making. While they will be dealt with in different sections, it is important to bear in mind that all three levels intersect in most organizational decision processes.

Individual Decision Making

The Classical Rational Model of Individual Decision Making According to the **classical rational model** of decision making, people choose among a set of possible actions by comparing the probable outcomes of each alternative on the same criteria and selecting one that promises the greatest return. For example, if a person is trying to choose among three job offers, she or he will begin by selecting a set of evaluative criteria. (For the purposes of this example, we have chosen initial salary, flexibility in working conditions, and two items included in offers given to recent college graduates during periods of economic growth – stock options and signing bonuses.) Next, our decision maker assigns a weight to each criterion and determines how important it is to him or her. Finally, she or he estimates the likelihood that accepting each offer will produce the outcomes that are implicit in each evaluative criterion. He or she then multiplies each weight by its associated probability, adds the products, and, *voilà*, has her or his choice (see Table 8.1).

In our example, a hiring bonus is highly salient to our decision maker because she or he has large unpaid college loans and plans to change firms or start a business as soon as possible. So she or he gives it a weight of 11. Starting salary is almost as salient (a weight of 9) because he or she wants to invest the bulk of it to make enough money to start his or her own business quickly. Stock options are a bit less (a weight of 7) important because she or he anticipates that the firms' stocks will skyrocket in value in the short term, level off by the time she or he changes jobs, and plummet soon after (like dot.com companies did during the late 1990s and in 2000). Flexibility of working conditions is relatively unimportant (a weight of 2) because he or she is single and plans to work incessantly before age 30 and then get a life.

He or she estimates that the probability of receiving handsome stock options from company X is quite high (and attaches a probability of 0.9); getting them from company Z is moderate (probability of 0.4), and the probability of getting them from company Y is quite low (probability 0.1). Negotiating for a large signing bonus is relatively easy with company Z, because a recent and successful initial public offering of stock (IPO) has given it a lot of cash (probability of 0.9); but the likelihood is low for companies X and Y because they are cash strapped at the moment. Company X has won a number of awards for its family-friendly policies and flexible scheduling (so it receives a likelihood score of 0.8). Company Y has just started its flextime and telework programs and still puts lots of limits

Table 8.1 A Classical Rational Model of Career Decision Making

	Stock options		*Flexibility*		*Salary*		*Bonus*		*Total*
Company X	0.9(7)	+	0.8(2)	+	0.1(9)	+	0.2(11)	=	11.0
Company Y	0.1(7)	+	0.5(2)	+	0.1(9)	+	0.1(11)	=	3.7
Company Z	0.4(7)	+	0.1(2)	+	0.3(9)	+	0.9(11)	=	15.6

on them (resulting in a score of 0.4), and company Z still is living in the 1950s on these issues (a score of 0.1). Starting salaries are comparable across the industry; but they are a little bit higher in company Z. So it receives a probability score of 0.3, while the other two companies receive scores of 0.1. When our decision maker performs all the necessary computations, company Z wins. This process, in which the decision maker weighs the pros and cons or all alternatives on the basis of complete information about each, is called **optimizing**.

As this example illustrates, the classical rational process involves a complex set of calculations. For these calculations to lead to the best decision, our decision maker must have quite a bit of information, including (1) sufficient self-awareness to know the criteria that are important to him or her, (2) accurate information about the probability that the various jobs will fulfill the criteria, and (3) the relative importance of these criteria to him or her so that weights can be assigned to the criteria. Economic and philosophical analyses have demonstrated that under this condition – called "complete information" – this approach to decision making will lead to the best possible decision for the actor based on his or her interests.

The classical rational model and variations of it form the basis of much of the economic analysis and forecasting used by corporations and government. Its assumption that every decision maker employs similar processes makes it possible to estimate how very large groups of people – for example, the millions of consumers and companies in modern nations – will act in response to various conditions (for example, when employment goes up and they are less certain they will have jobs and income). This forms the basis for the economic planning that has guided governments and corporations since the Great Depression of the 1930s.

The classical model assumes that decision makers adopt a rational and calculative frame of mind and that they are not influenced by "irrational" factors like wishful thinking or biases. This approach encourages decision makers to avoid alternative approaches to decision making such as "short cuts" like relying on what worked in the past or intuition. Instead it exhorts decision makers to apply the ideal model to every significant decision.

There are, however, some issues with the classical rational model of decision making. First, the model requires a lot of the decision maker, and there is some question whether ordinary human beings (that is 99.9999 percent of us) can carry out the required operations. Second, there is the question of whether ordinary people can remain unbiased and objective. Finally, the rational model itself fails in some critical situations. These issues cause many to question whether the classical rational model really should be the "ideal" model for organizational decision making.

Challenges to the Classical Rational Model Studies of individuals' actions during decision-making situations indicate both that humans cannot act in accordance with the classical rational model and that they do not do so (Sutcliffe, 2000; Nutt, 2002). The classical rational model, however, has been presented as *the* best way to make decisions in the media and taught as such for so long that it remains widely accepted, one of myths we discussed in Chapter 2. Not only do most people expect important decisions to be made according to the model, but also, when decision makers explain their decisions, they often present them so that they appear to conform to the model. We will explore why this is so later in the chapter, but first we must consider some challenges to the rational model.

People cannot be rational actors as defined by the classical model because they have limited analytical skills and because their decision making is handicapped by a variety of situational factors (Gigerenzer, Todd, and the ABC Research Group, 1999; Connolly, Arkes, and Hammond, 2003). For one thing, people rarely have accurate and complete information to base their decisions on. Obtaining information is costly in terms of time, money, and other resources. With limited resources, decision makers are forced to settle for the information that it is feasible to obtain. Even with the increased access to information provided by the internet, search is still generally limited. Think of the last time you did research on some topic on the internet. Did you spend several hours looking everywhere you could possibly find information and trying different search strategies? Or did you settle for the first couple of websites that provided you information that was "good enough"? If you are like most people, you took the second route. Only when a decision is exceptionally important and resources are plentiful do people conduct the comprehensive search for information about the problem, consider solution alternatives, and weigh the probability that different alternatives will satisfy criteria that are presumed by the rational model.

Second, several cognitive biases tend to hamper human information processing (Tversky and Kahnemann, 2003; Bazerman and Watkins, 2004).

- There is a tendency to overestimate the likelihood of "good" outcomes and underestimate the probability of "bad" ones. For example, no matter how much information students are given about past patterns of grading in a course and about their own academic records, they invariably seem to overestimate their chances of receiving A's and B's and underestimate their chances of getting C's, D's, or F's.
- There is a bias toward emphasizing short-term, immediate outcomes over long-term outcomes. In part this is because it is more difficult to project long-term consequences of our actions. It can also be traced to the desire to obtain "quick wins" and immediate gains. In the run-up to the Iraq intervention, for instance, US public opinion was overwhelmingly in favor of the invasion as a means of punishing terrorists immediately and forestalling what were presented as imminent attacks with weapons of mass destruction. The possibility that the United States would be involved in a multiyear war that would cost thousands of lives and billions of dollars was not in the forefront of public thinking at the time.
- There is also a tendency to assume that the examples one can call immediately to mind are the most likely to occur (this is called the **availability bias**). For instance, a manager trying to decide whether employees will adopt an innovation may call to mind a recent event in which several administrative assistants sabotaged a new word-processing program because they wanted to stick with their old word-processing application. With this example in mind, the manager is likely to conclude that resistance is very likely. However, the manager's judgment is based on one example; it may well be the case that in making the judgment based on the one example, the manager has overlooked ten other cases in which employees embraced innovations.
- Another bias involves overestimating the degree of control one has over the situation. Individuals have a self-serving tendency to presume they can control events because it reassures them and reinforces their feelings of competence and power. Many individuals who took on risky mortgages or other types of loans prior to the 2008 financial crisis, presumed that they would keep their jobs and that their property would continue to appreciate in value, enabling them to repay these loans (in part because so-called experts

kept telling them these assumptions were true). They did not consider the possibility of a broad economic collapse that would cost millions – including them – their jobs or listen to warnings that many parts of the United States were in the midst of housing price "bubbles" that inevitably would deflate.

These are examples of biases in individual thinking.[2] Other biases arise when people make decisions in groups and still others due to the organizational context. We will consider these later in this chapter.

Third, circumstances can sometimes limit rationality. When a decision must be made quickly, for example, there is not time to gather or fully process the relevant information. In organizations with cultures that place a high value on quick and decisive action, taking a rational approach can make one look bad. Decision makers are also confronted with multiple demands on their time. The classical rational model assumes that the decision maker can focus his or her attention solely on the decision at hand. This is, however, rarely the case in practice. Decision makers must "multitask" and therefore cannot devote themselves "heart and soul" to the painstaking analysis that the classical model requires.

Due to limitations in the available information, deficiencies in human information processing, and the demands of the situations decision makers face, the requirements of the classical rational model are more often violated than met. Instead, human rationality is bounded by these processes and conditions, and decision makers must "make do" with a more limited approach to decision making.

Bounded Rationality: A More Realistic Model of Decision Making Herbert Simon and James March advanced a model of **bounded rationality** as an alternative to the classical rational model (Simon, 1956; March, 1970; March and Simon, 1965). While it has not attained the mythical status of the classical model, research and practitioner's reflections suggest that bounded rationality offers a more accurate picture of how most decisions are made by individuals, groups, and organizations (Connolly *et al.*, 2003; Nutt, 2002)

According to the bounded rationality model, people make decisions not through optimizing, but through a process that Simon called **satisficing**. In satisficing people consider a limited number of options on a few criteria that are particularly important to them, and they stop searching for options when they find one that satisfies their criteria (hence the name "satisficing"). In satisficing we look for a decision that is "good enough," and meets current needs rather than one that is the best possible option. Satisficing allows decision makers to function within the bounds of real world situations. It can operate within the constraints of limited information about the situation, the needs of the decision maker, and the available options. Satisficing is also a much faster decision-making method than optimizing. So it is well suited for situations when decisions must be made quickly or when the decision maker must handle many decisions and has limited time and resources for any single decision.

Let's return to our earlier example of the job decision. In that discussion we assumed that our job candidate had complete information about stock options, flexibility, salary, and bonus for all three companies, as well as a large amount of other types of information that indicate that the firms do not differ in other important respects. We also assumed that the candidate has a very clear idea of the relative importance of the criteria. Finally, we assumed that the candidate has information that enables him or her to make accurate estimates of the probability that he or she is to obtain each benefit from the three jobs.

In most real situations, however, decision makers do not enjoy the luxury of full information or the ability to process it. For example, the candidate may be able to get accurate information about stock options about one company, but discover that policies are changing in another and therefore there is uncertainty about its stock options. "Flexibility" is a notoriously ambiguous term, as we will see in Chapter 10, so any information about this will have a great deal of uncertainty associated with it. Some information might require considerable expenditure of time and effort to collect and so be judged not worth going after. The candidate may also have deadlines by which decisions must be made for the different firms that will impede information gathering and force the candidate to "shortcut" weighing the pros and cons of the job

When it is impossible to apply the classical rational model, the decision maker usually does one of two things (Reimer, Kuendig, Hoffrage, Park, and Hinsz, 2007). She or he may limit information processing by focusing on the subset of criteria on which there is relatively trustworthy information on all three jobs. For instance, the focus may be on salary and bonuses, dropping the other two criteria from consideration. Alternatively, he or she may try to make an overall assessment of each of the three jobs based on whatever information he or she has about each option, regardless of whether he or she has comparable information. For instance, he or she may make an overall assessment of Job A based on information about salary, bonus, and flexibility and an overall assessment of Job B based on salary and stock options. Assessments of the two jobs are made on the basis of non-equivalent information, whatever the decision maker has at hand. Selection will be based on satisficing rather than optimizing: the decision maker will choose the option that is "good enough" in terms of meeting the criteria or in terms of overall assessment. If any of the three jobs meets minimum standards of acceptability, it will be chosen and there will be no further search for a different job that might be even better. The decision discussed in Box 8.1 offers another example of decision making according to bounded rationality and underscores the centrality of communication in this process.

Box 8.1
Making a Green Decision

While we may not be able to be rational, we still have to make choices. To do so, we must simplify the complicated situations that we face. We can do so largely because we are able to communicate. Once two of Charley Conrad's students (an engaged couple) sought advice about purchasing a new automobile. Their goal was noble – to shift from their old gas guzzler to a fuel-efficient model to do their part to forestall a worldwide energy crisis. He suggested that this goal would be best achieved if they kept their old car. The amount of fuel they would save during the lifetime of their new car would be far less than the amount of energy and nonrenewable materials that would be used in the manufacture of their new car. Besides, there was no guarantee that the person who purchased their old car would use it to replace an even less fuel-efficient vehicle. Thus the net effect of their buying a new car, regardless of how fuel efficient it might be, would be to increase the depletion of nonrenewable resources, bringing the world even closer to eco-catastrophe.

Now, the classical rational model does not predict that the students would discover that Dr. Conrad was correct. But it does suggest that they should respond to his argument by seeking out information about the resources used in fabricating new automobiles, the means of controlling the energy use of potential purchasers of their old car, and the relative scarcity of petroleum compared to the scarcity of the other resources used in the fabrication of cars. The model predicts that they would use their communicative and intellectual skills to obtain the information needed to find out whether he was right. However, the model fails to recognize that some of the needed information may either not exist or be so difficult to locate that it would not be worth the effort, that the decision makers could not care less about the effects that their actions might have on other people's actions, that their friends are committed to energy conservation and have encouraged them to buy a more fuel-efficient car, or that a host of other intangible factors may influence their decision making.

Eventually the students chose a course of action that did incorporate some of these considerations. They returned after a lengthy discussion and produced the following changes in their position: They were going to be concerned only about gasoline (because it is too much work to determine what the net effect of our purchase will have on other resources), they were going to ignore the effects that their decision had on anyone else's energy use, and they were going to buy a new fuel-efficient car, because doing so would symbolize their commitment to conservation whether it hasthat effect or not. So, in retrospect their interchange (and their private discussion) did not lead to a strictly rational decision, at least not as the classical rational model defines that term. But their communication with one another did allow them to (1) simplify their decision situation and make it more manageable, (2) provide mutual validation of their new view of the situation, and (3) provide social and emotional support for one another's decision-making processes. They were, in the end, able to make a decision and to make it with conviction. Communicating usually helps people make decisions, but not make strictly "rational" decisions as described in the classical rational model.

Compared to the clean and rigorous classical model, the bounded rationality model seems somewhat haphazard. With its emphasis on gathering complete and accurate information, generating a large pool of options, and systematic comparison of alternatives according to a specific formula, the classical model is able to offer one "single best way" to make decisions. Bounded rationality, by comparison, seems less systematic and offers no single best way to make decisions.

Does this mean that bounded rationality leads to inferior decisions to those made following the classical rational model? Not at all. Research has shown that decisions and judgments made according to bounded rationality can be as good as or better than those following the classical rational model (Gigerenzer and Goldstein, 2003; Salas and Klein, 2001; Zsambok and Klein, 1997). When a decision maker is highly trained, has great experience and extensive knowledge about the subject, he or she knows which criteria are really important, which deserve less attention, and which options are more likely to work than others. In these cases, bounded rationality is likely to lead to quite effective decisions. The decision maker is able to ignore irrelevant and distracting information and focus on the essentials, resulting in a more efficient decision process.

Ironically, a comprehensive rational process may encourage decision makers to consider information, criteria, and options that are not particularly valuable or valid and "swamp" more valid information, resulting in suboptimal choices. Vodosek and Sutcliffe (2000) summarize succinctly: "Although in some cases extensive [rational] analyses may lead to better decision making . . . it consumes valuable time and resources, decreases the speed with which decisions can be made, and creates a false sense of security" (161).

It has been argued that many managers make decisions by **intuition** (Vodosek and Sutcliffe, 2000; Miller, 2009). Faced with complex information and a demand for fast decision making, managers are said to "go with their guts" or "play hunches." It is more likely, however, that they are acting according to bounded rationality and making decisions on the basis of the few key factors they know are critical or through "recognition primed decision-making," in which a few critical cues suggest a tried and true course of action (Zsambok and Klein, 1997). This process often happens so quickly that it seems as though it is simple intuition.

It is important to underscore, however, that bounded rationality does not always lead to good decisions. There are better and worse ways to make decisions under bounded rationality. If the decision maker does not have the required training, experience, and knowledge (but thinks he or she does), then the resulting decisions are very likely to be ineffective and have negative results. A sad and amusing book, *Imperial Life in the Emerald City* (Chandrasekaran, 2006), recounts how the George W. Bush administration sent hundreds of young administrators who had very little experience to run the provisional government in Iraq – people with little or no direct experience who had nothing to base intuitive judgments on. These novices made disastrous decisions that set back US efforts and had very negative consequences for Iraqis based on bounded rationality.

Bounded rationality also leads to bad decisions when the decision maker falls prey to the various biases discussed above. They distort the decision maker's interpretation of information and judgmental processes, resulting in inferior deliberations. It is important that decision makers be aware of possible biases to avoid decision debacles.

The classical rational decision model provides a useful normative framework for individual decision making. However, in the rough-and-tumble of real-world decision making, it is difficult if not impossible to apply. Instead, individuals most often make decisions following the bounded rationality model. Employed properly, with valid information and careful information processing, bounded rationality can lead to effective, prompt decision making. However, it is easy for an individual to delude him or herself into thinking that he or she is making careful, prudent choices when in fact, there are deficiencies in knowledge and experience or biases. One way to counteract this problem is to have several parties make the decision together, in the hope they will check one another's errors and excesses.

Group Decision Making: Are Several Heads Better Than One?

One way to overcome the liabilities of individual decision makers is to have a group make the decision.[3] Groups have several potential advantages over individuals. Members of a group generally have a broader knowledge base than any individual. They can check one another's ideas by exposing flaws in reasoning, mistaken assumptions, and misinformation. Properly composed groups also have a broader range of interests and perspectives, and therefore their decisions may be more politically acceptable to different interest groups in the organization. Finally, groups can sometimes achieve synergy, where the performance of the group as a whole is greater than the performance of the members' efforts combined. In this case, the group is more competent and creative than any individual could be.

Traditional models of group decision making are based on rational models of individual decision making. Early twentieth-century philosopher John Dewey argued that people confront problems through a five-step process: (1) a problem or general feeling of uneasiness is recognized, (2) the problem is located and defined, (3) the person sets standards by which to test a solution, (4) several response options are identified and tested, and (5) a solution is selected and implemented. From this individual model, a **standard agenda** model of group decision making developed. To make an effective decision, it was reasoned, groups should follow steps that are somewhat parallel to those in the classical rational model:

1. Define the task facing the group, making sure each member understands why the task is important, what its final product will look like, and what that product will be used for; then
2. Reach agreement on group and individual responsibilities (who is to do what about what); then
3. Seek out all the information needed by the group, arrange it for easy access, and evaluate its accuracy; then
4. Establish criteria for evaluating possible courses of action, including recognizing what options and outcomes are realistic; then
5. Discover and evaluate options; and finally
6. Prepare to present persuasively and defend its choice to people who will be involved in implementing it.

Each phase has characteristic goals, tasks that must be performed, and obligations for members and leaders. It is also important to define and understand the problem and establish criteria *prior* to considering options or solutions. Premature consideration of options or solutions may lead decision makers to attend to only those aspects of the situation or problem that pertain to the solution. This procedure is designed to promote open-minded and full exploration of the situation, and creative generation of appropriate solutions.

It is important to register a qualification at this point. While the model of effective group decision making resembles the classical rational model, it does not embrace its restrictive assumptions concerning the need for full information and exhaustive analysis. John Dewey and the scholars who built on his work believed that people always operate with incomplete information and that decision making was a process of inquiry that uncovered additional information and assumptions (though never everything) (Keith, 2007).

Traditional models of group decision making are based on the assumption that groups should and do follow this agenda. This implies that the group's decision process should evolve in a simple, consistent, and straightforward manner. Contemporary research indicates that these assumptions are only partly correct. Groups are constantly dealing with pressures from their subsystems and suprasystems. Some of these pressures are constant throughout the decision-making process. For instance, the group's assigned task is a continual pressure. Other pressures are intermittent. They occur only at certain points during the process and pressure the group to change its direction, at least temporarily. Some are external, as when members discover and introduce new information from outside of the group. In organizational groups, external pressures are often political, and they often slow, sidetrack, or reverse decision-making processes (Poole and Dobosh, 2009; Poole and Baldwin, 1996). Other pressures are internal, developing out of the group discussion. Groups seem to participate in "reach testing," where they propose, develop, modify, drop, and then restart testing of ideas.

As a result, the linear, step-by-step standard agenda rarely is implemented in the way that the traditional model envisioned. Instead, group processes are idiosyncratic and cyclical. Different phases overlap: Members move from one phase to another and back again, and roles change with the flow of the conversation. The key to effective participation is not adapting to the "phase" of group development, but adapting to the specific situations that emerge as the process continues. Participation is "strategic," in the sense that this book uses the term. Participation involves monitoring and interpreting the communication of the group, choosing productive ways of responding to that situation, and communicating effective strategic responses, while recognizing that each member's actions transform the situation and communication of the other members.

Each of the tasks envisioned in the traditional model – establishing criteria, evaluating alternatives, seeking and presenting information, and so on – must still be fulfilled properly to make an effective decision. However, groups may make a number of missteps as they attempt to make decisions. Five errors can contribute to poor group decisions (Gouran and Hirokawa, 1996; Hirokawa and Salazar, 1999):

1. The improper assessment of the situation
2. The establishment of inappropriate goals and objectives
3. The improper assessment of the strengths and weaknesses of various alternatives
4. The establishment of a flawed information base
5. Faulty reasoning based on the group's information base

Improper uses of information sometimes results from errors in information gathering. In complicated and ambiguous situations – the kind in which groups often promise to be better decision makers than individuals – members often do not know what kinds of information are useful or when they have sufficient information to make the choice. Thus, they often unknowingly collect too little information, the wrong information, or so much information that they cannot process it adequately. In other cases, they may not evaluate the information they obtain accurately. Organizational power relationships and political considerations may also lead members to withhold or distort the information they provide the group. In still other cases, groups may have to make a decision quickly, without sufficient time to properly understand the problem or the situation. This was the case for President Gerald Ford's response to the swine flu epidemic of the mid-1970s. Feeling intense pressure from what seemed to be an impending disaster, the Ford administration set up an inoculation program on an emergency basis. However, not only did it turn out that the inoculation program was unnecessary, because the epidemic was overstated and did not materialize, but also the vaccine led to illnesses among some of those who were inoculated.

In addition, the communication processes that occur within the group may create distortions. Groups collaborate in creating realities based on the information they have gathered (recall Chapter 1). Once these realities begin to be shared, they influence subsequent interpretations of information. Citing Irving Janis, Dennis Gouran and Randy Hirokawa (1996) noted that this kind of process seemed to influence US policy during the Korean War:

> The Chinese were seen by President Truman and his advisors as weak puppets of the Soviet Union. . . . The puppet like image created in presidential discussions, coupled with the belief that the Soviets were reluctant to become involved in a ground war, laid the foundation for predicting success in the contemplated action (crossing the border into North Korea). In reality, the decision proved to be one of the president's most costly. Something of the same mentality has been attributed to those in the Johnson administration who recommended increased military involvement (in Vietnam). (105)

Emotional connections among group members both help and hurt group decision making. **Group cohesion** refers to the degree to which members are attracted and committed to the group (Thompson, 2008; Gastil, 2010). There are at least three sources of group cohesion: *task cohesion*, which is due to members' beliefs that the group's work is valuable and significant; *attraction-based cohesion*, which is due to liking for other members of the group; and *status cohesion*, which is due to the rewards that members receive based on the reputation and status of the group. Research suggests that task cohesion is positively related to group effectiveness; the other two forms of cohesion are unrelated to group performance but are positively related to member satisfaction. Overall, the value of cohesion is curvilinear; that is, it is valuable most of the time, but if it a group is very highly cohesive, it reduces group performance. In an important way "cohesion" is similar to "identification" as explained in Chapter 5. When people identify fully with their organizations, they make decisions through the processes and based on the accepted premises of their organizations. If those processes are inappropriate or if the premises are incorrect or irrelevant in specific situations, people make choices that are inappropriate. When group members identify fully with one another, that is, when the group is highly cohesive, they may make the same kinds of errors.

In all groups, but especially in highly cohesive groups, pressures develop that may reduce the range and quality of information presented and thus eliminate the advantage of having decisions made by groups rather than by individuals. Often these pressures are not deliberate. Groups may develop *norms of concurrence*, which pressure members into agreeing with other members rather than seeking the best solutions. If an individual member dissents from the group's position or questions the assumptions the other members seem to share, others respond by arguing with, ignoring, or in extreme cases (or if the deviant persists) expelling the dissenter from the group. As the discussion continues, the group shifts to the position initially taken by the majority or by its most vocal members. These "choice shifts" depend not on the information available to the group, but on in-group communicative pressures. As a result, groups may make "extreme" decisions – ones that unquestioningly continue precedents and existing policies or that are inordinately risky (Thompson, 2008).

Since cohesion generates high levels of commitment to decisions and the high levels of motivation necessary to implement them, excessive cohesion may also lead groups to do everything they can to implement foolish decisions and to ignore or distort feedback indicating that their decision was unwise. The communicative processes that *should* lead to the generation of creative ideas, sharing of accurate and relevant information, and the critical analysis of options begin to support what often may be unwarranted and unwise decisions (Nutt, 2002; Thompson, 2008).

Irving Janis coined the term **groupthink** to refer to cases in which groups place consensus above all other priorities (Janis, 1982; Turner and Pratkanis, 1998). Examples of groupthink leading to decision-making debacles are common in politics and the corporate world. They include the 1941 decision by the commanders at Pearl Harbor to ignore warnings and other evidence that Japan might attack, the Committee to Re-elect the President's 1974 decision to break into the Democratic Party's headquarters in the Watergate Hotel, the 2003 decision to invade Iraq, and the decision by Beech-Nut baby food company to continue to distribute tainted apple juice for over a year after it was discovered (Janis, 1982; Nutt, 2002). In each case, extensive group deliberations preceded the decision, and ample information was available that suggested that the outcome was unwise. But concurrence seeking became the driving impulse and group members discounted negative information, went along with the prevailing opinion even when they privately disagreed, and browbeat members who disagreed with the majority. The intelligence, extensive experience, and power of these groups did little to compensate for the communicative pressures that prevented constructive dissent.

Another symptom of groupthink is an illusion of invulnerability. Not only does this illusion hamper decision making but also, in organizational settings, it leads members to see themselves as separate from and better than other work groups. The competitive orientation that develops increases intergroup conflict. In time, the errors that highly cohesive groups make and the conflicts they have with other groups may create dissension. Members may respond by even more intensely suppressing disagreement, which increases cohesion and its disadvantages. In a continuing cycle, highly cohesive permanent groups may become less and less capable of making good choices.

There is evidence, for example, that these dynamics short-circuited the decision-making process at Merrill-Lynch and led to its disastrous performance during the 2008 financial crisis (Morgensen, 2008). Prior to the crisis, analysts who disagreed with Merrill-Lynch's CEO Stanley O'Neal were replaced by "yes men" who reinforced the firm's investments in risky securities. Current employees who witnessed these replacements learned to hold their tongues and go along with the prevailing currents of thought. This reaped huge profits, which seemed to bear out the wisdom of prior decision, but eventually the investments turned out to be worthless, leading to Merrill's demise.

To counteract the negative impacts of group cohesion, groups should seek diverse points of view and cultivate disagreements and conflict (provided it is managed properly). In fact, a group's search for a mutually acceptable decision requires conflict if it is to succeed. Comparing and evaluating ideas – classifying, narrowing, refocusing, selecting, eliminating, and synthesizing – depend on the expression of divergent points of view. Properly managed, *substantive* conflict focused on the issues aids group decision-making processes (Thompson, 2008; Gastil, 2010, chaps. 3–5).

Group decision making can also be distorted by a member's need to control or impose his or her agenda on the group. Gouran and Hirokawa (1996) illustrate this **egocentric influence**:

> As more than one observer has noted, former President Richard Nixon was ultimately responsible for his own political undoing in the Watergate case because of his inability to permit normal investigative processes to move forward in regard to the break-in at Democratic National Headquarters. Instead his need for control dominated discussions among members of his inner circle and culminated in the fateful decision to engage in a cover-up.

Signs of egocentric influences on group decision making include (1) one or more members adopting a win-lose orientation and appearing to be preoccupied with getting the group to adopt their particular solutions; (2) highly defensive members; and (3) statements such as "Please, don't question me, I know what I'm talking about," "I have been dealing with this kind of problem for over ten years," or "It's the principle of the thing."

To counteract egocentric influences, a group should adopt procedures that force it to approach the problem systematically and that do not give one member's viewpoint too much weight. It is also important that other members clearly indicate to the egocentric member that they are not going to knuckle under to him or her. Working out creative decisions that meet the member's needs but also guard against problems in the hidden agenda is another way of handling egocentric influences without creating serious fractures in the group.

A Brief Reflection on Rationality in Individual and Group Decision Making

The argument that individuals and groups cannot be strictly rational in the classical sense does not necessarily mean they cannot make good, reasoned decisions. An individual who conducts a reasonable search for information, takes his or her biases into account, and tries to be as systematic and thorough as is feasible can do quite well. For complex decisions or decisions that impact a wide range of people and units, groups can be effective if they are aware of the processes that can hinder decision making and find ways to counteract them and ensure that they cover all the bases in the problem-solving model outlined in the previous section.

It is important to realize, however, that the tidy classical rational model of decision making is only a standard – an ideal that can be approached but not attained – and only one standard at that. In addition to rationality, individual and group decisions should also take into account (1) the impact of the decision on other people, both those immediately affected by the decision and those who might be over the longer run; (2) the importance of democracy and inclusion of all points of view; and (3) ethical concerns (Keith, 2007; Poole and Dobosh, 2009; Gastil, 2010). Each of these three standards may require the decision maker to forgo a decision that would be rational according to the classical model.

These issues add to the complexity of an already complex discussion of decision making. As we move into the organizational arena, additional factors influence decision making.

Organizational Decision Making

When applied to organizations, the classical rational model depicts decision making as a systematic process through which the following occurs:

1. An employee recognizes that a problem or opportunity exists and that it is caused by some unexpected, or as yet, unaddressed change in the organization's environment or by the actions of some of its members.
2. Each member of the organization who, because of his or her formal position, expertise, or available information, has an interest in the problem or opportunity is told about it and invited to help solve it.

3. Extensive and exhaustive research is conducted to understand the problem or opportunity, involving organizational members and outside experts.
4. Extensive and exhaustive search for solution options is conducted by members and outside experts.
5. Alternative courses of action are compared through open, problem-solving communication.
6. The optimal solution is chosen and implemented.
7. The impact of the solution is monitored and information about its affects is gathered and stored for use in similar situations in the future.

Through the feedback process in step 7, the rational decision process is able to correct itself.

As with individual and group decision making, in some cases organizations can and do make decisions in this way, but more often than not the decision process deviates from this model. As we will see, this is because making an effective decision is only one of several motivations that drive organizational decision making.

Making Decisions in the Face of Organizational Complexity To this point we have dealt with decision making as a singular, separate process in which an in dividual or clearly defined group makes a single decision. If what you have read in previous chapters of this book tells you anything, however, it is that organizations are exceptionally complex. The complexity of organizations places constraints on the degree to which an organization can hue to bounded rationality, to the steps necessary for effective group decision making, and to the steps of the ideal model of organizational decision making just outlined. Here we will focus on two types of complexity that affect decision making, the complexity of activities that occur in most organizations and environmental complexity.

Decision Making as Part of a Complex Action System An organizational decision is usually not just an isolated action.[4] It is shaped by the precedents of previous decisions and has implications for future decisions. It is only one of a number of decisions being made at many levels of the organization at any given time and goes on in parallel with many other organizational activities. Different members of the organization may be responsible for those other decisions and activities, and while they may sometimes coordinate their efforts, in many cases they either are not aware of one another or simply do not have the time or desire to coordinate.

A decision thus competes for the attention, time, and resources in the organization. To be able to carry out the seven steps outlined in the previous section takes considerable time and resources and these are in limited supply. Hence, it may simply not be feasible to undertake a thorough decision process.

One factor that influences the amount of time and resources devoted to a decision is the level at which the decision is made and its potential impact on the organization. Organizational decisions range from routine operating decisions made by workers, to more consequential decisions about coordination of organizational activities and exceptions by middle managers and staff, to extremely important strategic decisions by top management that set high-level policies and general directions of the organization for the long term. Obviously, decisions at higher levels affect those at lower levels. A strategic decision by a government agency to stop offering a certain service affects the decisions and actions in the middle and at the bottom of the organization. But it is also the other way around: Decisions made at the bottom – even seemingly simple operating decisions – may affect higher levels and trigger higher-level decision making.

The organizational decision-making process can be described as a set of "flows" involving a mix of the decision types that move through the organization to the various involved units and parties (Mintzberg, 1979; McPhee and Zaug, 2009). For instance, an employee might decide to provide an extra service to one customer at the operational level. When other customers find out about it and complain that they want the same service, this then triggers an exception decision by a middle manager that this was a "one-time" case. The middle manager might on reflection decide that the additional service was a pretty good idea and forward it as a suggestion to top management who then make the decision to offer the service to all customers. Middle management must then decide on policies that govern providing the service and convey them to operators at the bottom. Both formal and informal communication channels route information around the organization to support the decision and various members at different levels and from different departments will attempt to influence the decision (for example, the employee who first thought of the service might enlist colleagues to mention it to their superiors and increase support for the decision).

The Complexity of Organizational Environments The environment is a critical reference point for most consequential organizational decisions. Our earlier discussion of environment did not consider how organizations discover the nature of their environment. It takes a lot of time and effort on the part of the organization to do this, especially for complex, turbulent environments. The environment usually does not just announce itself to the organization; instead the organization must gather information and this takes time and money. For instance, organizations often don't know who all their competitors are. To take a simple example, a boutique clothing store, for instance, knows who its competitors are in its local area (via information gathered through scanning the phone book and driving around the area and going to local malls), but it may have no idea what competitors are thinking of moving into the area and what all its competition on the internet is. The owner may know some of the new fashion trends, but this knowledge is "hard won" since it comes from reading lots of publications and surfing the internet, but by no means does he or she know enough to predict these trends with certainty, and certainly she or he does not know what competitors know about trends. As with competitors, so it is with much other information about things like novel technology, how likely government regulators are to enforce rules the organization is violating, whether clients are satisfied with service, and scores of other potentially important issues. In short, most organizations live with a great deal of uncertainty about their environments. This uncertainty tends to increase with the size of the organization and with the degree to which it operates in many different geographical areas or markets.

The situation is made even more complex when we realize that actions the organization takes affect its environment. To continue our example, if the boutique owner brings a "hot" new line of Parisian garments in, she or he may be so successful at attracting new business that several local competitors go out of business, rendering the boutique's environment less complex and turbulent. The increased income, however, might also attract the attention of tax authorities who, unbeknownst to the owner, begin an investigation of the owner's finances. Actions taken by organizations change their environments in ways they are aware of as well as ways they are unaware of. This interdependence between organization and environment turns environment into a "moving target" that is even more difficult to understand and to predict.

While this section focuses on the organization's external environment, many internal features and processes are also difficult for decision makers to understand. Gathering information within an organization, especially a large one, can require considerable resources. For example, the Honeywell Corporation, with 80,000 employees in several hundred facilities around the world, conducted a yearly survey of employees to ascertain their needs and issues. This survey was conducted by a team of six employees and required a significant budget. Even then, only a limited amount of information could be gathered. Organizations are often as uncertain (sometimes even more uncertain) about internal issues than they are about their external environments.

The Pressure to be Rational (Classically) The complexity of the decision process and of the environment makes it unlikely that organizations will be able to make decisions according to the classical rational model. If individuals and small groups have trouble conforming to this model, it is little wonder that organizations do, considering all the added layers, actors, and uncertainty.

The institutional pressures to make decisions according to the classical rational model are strong. This model is so widely accepted as "the" best way to make decisions that organizations must live up to the myth. If they do not, they run the risk of being regarded as ineffective or illegitimate by other organizations they depend upon, by government regulators, and by the public in general. As the "nonrational" decision making behind the British Petroleum (BP) Deepwater Horizon oil spill came out, it became a nightmare for BP (Barstow, 2010). Government officials, other energy companies, the press, and the public questioned the very legitimacy of the company, sales fell, boycotts were organized, and investigations commenced. As a result, organizations engage in a combination of actually trying to carry out decision making according to the classical rational model and of doing things that make it appear they are acting according to this model. This leads to some interesting and sometimes amusing behavior as decision are made, which we will explore later in this section.

Nonrational Processes in Organizational Decision Making

Organizational Learning, Sense Making, and Decision Making The models of individual decision making – both the classical rational model and bounded rationality – assume that when organizations have to make decisions they first gather information, either exhaustively (in the case of the classical model) or until they get enough information to decide (in the case of bounded rationality). In this instance, information seeking is an action in its own right.

Influential organizational scholar Karl Weick (1979, 1995, 2000), however, argues that information seeking for its own sake is fairly rare in organizations. Instead, he proposes that organizations and their members learn incrementally through repeated interactions with the organization's external and internal environments. This process of **sense making** occurs through a three-stage cycle in which members first take what information is at hand

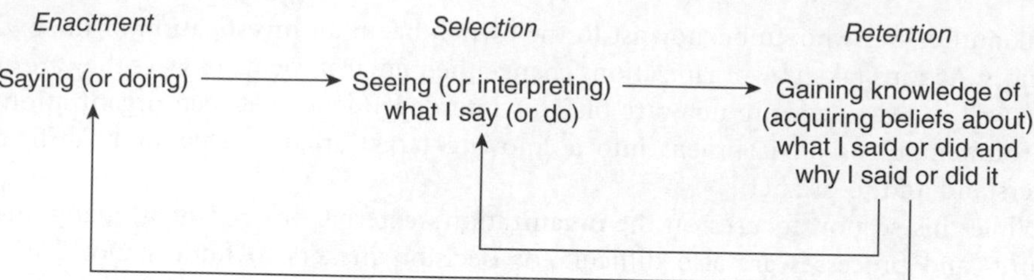

Figure 8.1 Weick's model of organizational "learning."

and simply take action based on it (a phase Weick terms **enactment**). Then, based on the effects that result from the action, members (and the organization) learn about their environment and develop explanations for why their actions had the effects they did (a phase he calls **selection**). Those actions that are interpreted as effective are repeated and incorporated into the organization's procedures and processes (in the **retention** phase). Later, organizational decision makers remember the solutions (actions) that succeeded in the past, and a rough outline of the situations in which they seemed to work. This list gives them guidelines about when not to act and how and when to act. In fact, organizational learning and sense making are largely processes of constructing a link between the present and the past. This entire process is repeated constantly as the organization acts and adjusts its actions. The social workers in the "Managing the Ambiguity" case in this chapter provide a good example of this cycling process in making sense of their situation.

Weick treats decision making as a by-product of acting. In many situations that confront organizations, he argues, it is more important simply to *act* than to take the *best* action; accurate perceptions and decisions are nice, but often they are simply unnecessary. Acting also generates new information and encourages employees to communicate with one another in ways that correct misconceptions. As a result, organizations that prefer acting over rational decision making tend to understand the environmental pressures they face better. Through continued cycling through the sense-making phases, they are able to update their information more rapidly and build up a picture of the situation that enables them to adapt quickly.

In some cases acting may be the only way to solve a problem. Karl Weick tells a story about a small Hungarian military unit that became lost during maneuvers in the Swiss Alps. Snowbound for two days, one soldier finally found a map in his pocket, and using it, they found their way back to camp. Eventually, they discovered to their astonishment that the map was of the Pyrenees Mountains, not the Alps. Weick (2000) concludes,

> This incident raises the intriguing possibility that when you are lost, any old map will do. . . . [Maps and plans] animate and orient people. Once people begin to act (enactment), they generate tangible outcomes (cues) in some context (social), and this helps them discover (retrospect) what is occurring (ongoing), what needs to be explained (plausibility), and what should be done next (identity enhancement). (60)

In short, simply acting or making a quick decisions often generate effective solutions and may be the only forms of decision making possible under intense time pressure or when other limiting factors are present. Even though it is "nonrational" in the strict sense, this approach is compatible with the bounded rationality model of decision making, which we noted can produce very good decisions provided the decision maker has the proper training and experience.

Another way in which members make sense of situations in order to justify decisions is to construct stories (Oliver and Roos, 2005). From childhood, we are all told stories that teach us how things work, what is right and wrong, and what to expect from various situations. Story narratives are an important form of explanation in almost all societies (Polkinghorne, 1988). Because of this, plausible narratives are persuasive. A well-told narrative makes the result of the narrative seem natural. Narratives that recount the sequence of events leading up to the decision give decision makers a sense that the decision emerged as it should have.

Oliver and Roos (2005), for example, recount the Lego corporation's decision to create its robotic toy division, Lego Mindstorms. The Mindstorms division operated largely independently of the rest of the company. and the decision emerged during discussions in which it was portrayed as a "satellite" that emerged from a small group and began to "orbit" Lego. The story implies a relationship in which the two are dependent on one another, but the Mindstorms division is subordinate.

The desired end product of sense making and learning is understanding of the situation facing the decision maker and the organization. This understanding can then guide decision making and action. However, the involvement of multiple people in any decision process and wide array of activities occurring in organizations at any given point in time make it difficult to achieve any sort of stable understanding of the situation.

Managing Uncertainty: The Myth of Understanding The classical rational model depicts communication as a process through which people obtain information to reduce uncertainty and ambiguity. According to the sense-making model, communication is a process through which people *manage* confusion and ambiguity during decision making. Members encounter situations, act in response to them, and make sense of them through processing the effects of their actions. But in acting, members change those very situations (Nutt, 2002; Weick, 2000; O'Reilly, 1982).

These changes create confusion and ambiguity for other members, and perhaps even for themselves as well. Other employees act in response and take actions on related issues, which also change the situation. In time, these cycles of acting and interacting transform the situation, creating new ambiguities and confusion and so on in a continuous cycle of acting, confusing, and coping (see Figure 8.2). The situation never really becomes clear; ambiguity is never completely eliminated, nor is full understanding achieved. But ambiguity is managed; people are able to make choices and take actions that satisfy their needs and the needs of their organizations.

Due to imperfect understanding, in many cases the underlying causes of the problems are not addressed, and their negative impacts crop up over and over again. But for people who are paid to make decisions, having a never-ending supply of problems to be solved may not be all that bad.

Nonrational Uses of Information: The Myth of "Being Informed" Careful and thorough collection and analysis of information is a hallmark of both the classical and bounded rationality models. However, in the complex and protracted processes of organizational

Case Study 8.1

Managing the Ambiguity[1]

One of the key assumptions of nonrational models of organizational decision making is that while ambiguity and uncertainty can rarely be eliminated, they can be managed. One of the most ambiguous roles played in a hospital is that of the social worker. Usually hospital social workers work with terminally ill patients and their families. But what they do with their clients is multidimensional and ambiguous. Some social workers say they "get families to communicate better when someone is dying"; others "help people live better when they are under stress"; still others "prepare people to leave the hospital as quickly as possible." Although almost all say that their primary concern is with providing the best possible care for their patients, the meaning of "quality care" depends on a number of factors. Sometimes "quality care" means playing the role of a bureaucrat – getting people out of the hospital as quickly as possible (or at least before their insurance or HMO coverage ends) or dealing with the mountains of paperwork that are part of helping a family move their loved one to a nursing home. Sometimes quality care involves providing psychotherapy, either for the family members or for the dying patient. Sometimes it involves helping people work through religious issues regarding death and afterlife. But always, there is a great deal of ambiguity about what a hospital social worker "does."

A social worker's role in the medical organization also creates ambiguity. Most hospitals operate on the basis of a "medical model," the view that medicine is "about" curing people – fixing what's broken, treating a disease through objective, emotionally detached, scientific methods, sending the patient home when she or he is "cured." In this view of medical care everyone with the same condition should receive the same treatment, and only outcomes – getting the patient well – matter. But social workers often have been trained to operate on the basis of a very different view of reality, a "psychosocial" model that calls for treating each individual patient as a whole person who has psychological, medical, social, and economic needs. This model values empowering the patient, giving him or her as much control over what happens as possible. It treats emotions and emotional responses as central to the healing process. It tells social workers to be empathic and focus on the treatment process as well as its outcomes. But since hospital social workers practice in organizations that are dominated by the medical model, they often are "caught in the middle" between two different views of patient care and must find ways to manage the ambiguities and tensions that result.

Finally, authority relationships create ambiguities. Social workers are taught to value egalitarian relationships, but hospital social workers work in bureaucratic, authoritarian organizations. An egalitarian supervisor might be more comfortable to work with, but may not have sufficient credibility with the hospital administration to get the resources necessary for improving patient care. None of these ambiguities and tensions can be eliminated, because they are inherent in the nature of social work as a discipline and in hospitals as bureaucratic organizations. But managing them adds stress to an already stressful occupation. This does not mean that they cannot be managed. But the ways in which the tensions and ambiguities are managed have important implications, both for patients and for the social workers themselves.

One way of managing the ambiguity is through controlled chaos. In some social work units people all talk at the same time, come and go as they please, communicate as if no one else is in the room, and hold meetings that are unstructured free-for-alls. Social workers in these units describe life at work as "like you're trying to find a place to stand in the middle of a kaleidoscope"; others said that "life is gray, not black and white. If you want black and white go to Macy's, not to a social work unit." Not only did their confusing, chaotic "madness" allow them to manage incongruities, but it even contributed to their satisfaction with work and with their careers.

Another way of coping was less chaotic, but still not traditional. In these units the social workers accepted the fact that they were part of a bureaucracy, but felt that their role was to keep "an elbow in the system's side," to constantly advocate for individual patients and their unique needs in a context that was designed to treat everyone alike. They lacked the formal authority necessary to change the hospital's rules, so they had to affect change by working within the rules. For them, life involved constantly looking for opportunities to change the system from the inside, to rebel against the system while accepting their role in it. They coped with this contradiction by developing a "healthy cynicism," by using humor to diffuse the most frustrating situations, or by expressing the group's shared emotions about unjustifiable policies that they knew could never be changed. Neither chaos nor cynicism eliminated the ambiguities or resolved the contradictions that hospital social workers faced, but they did allow them to manage their situations.

Social workers also seem to adopt one of two approaches to making sense out of their own experiences. Social work is a stressful occupation; stress that is sustained over long periods of time often leads to *burnout*, feelings of emotional exhaustion and psychological withdrawal from one's job. Stress and burnout also are ambiguous experiences. They can be interpreted as either an individual employee's problem or as a symptom of the organizational situation. In most hospitals, social workers seem to use the medical model to make sense out of their own stress and burnout – they are abnormal responses, caused by individuals' inability to manage stress properly, that need to be treated and controlled. One social worker said, "I think that they [people that burn out] will have the same problem wherever they go. They probably had the problem before they came here. I see it as an internal problem. I don't see it as job-situated at all." Another concluded, "Yeah that's my professional job [to fight off burnout]. See, I would consider that if somebody said to me, 'I'm burned out' then I would call them a very nonprofessional person. I wouldn't deal with them anymore because they should quit" (Meyerson, 1994, 643). Stress and burnout are understandable during times of crisis, organizational change, or when someone is new to a job. But it is something that can and should be cured. In the words of The Eagles, "get over it." Viewing stress as an individual weakness has a number of advantages for the organization – it means that the organization is not responsible for changing the conditions that create stress and gives supervisors permission to intervene in their subordinates' lives to "fix" their stress (Barley and Knight, 1992).

But stress and burnout can be interpreted through a socio-psychological model: stress is a normal condition, a healthy response to stressful situations: "there is no way not to have occasional bouts of burnout when you do this kind of work. . . . Burnout is the need to detach and I think that there's something healthy about needing to detach sometimes. . . . And just like stress, it's not a bad thing when you start to feel the signs and symptoms of stress, it's a warning signal to take care of yourself, and it can be a positive thing." It is an organizational and situational problem, not an individual pathology. It should be addressed by the organization, by providing time off for people who are burned out, by offering retreats that provide training in stress management, and so on. One social worker noted that "I read something somewhere that hospice has the lowest turnover rate in social work because it's a place that honors that [stress and burnout]. If you get really depressed you can honor that, take a few days off for mental health days. That saves you in the long run" (Meyerson, 1994, 648).[2]

Although Meyerson does not indicate that any of the social workers in her study interpreted their experiences in this way, stress also can be viewed from a broad, social and political perspective (Mattson *et al.*, 2000). Social work is a predominantly female profession. Like other "helping professions," it has relatively low social status and correspondingly low rates of pay. Because many of hospital social workers' activities are not directly related to the profit streams of their organizations, they are relegated to marginal positions in the organizational hierarchy and their problems are not treated as legitimate organizational concerns. Their clients – elderly, poor, chronically ill, or addicted people – are similarly relegated to the fringes of society. Treating social worker stress as either an individual pathology tends to "lump together" social workers and their clients as "sick" people. Treating stress as evidence of how much they care about their careers and clients or as something that they should be allowed to quickly "get over" so that they can return to work, defines them as means to organizational ends (profits). Both interpretations allow society and its organizations (hospitals) to keep social workers and their clients in marginalized positions. Their experiences can be treated as "normal" and "natural" elements of their career choices; their voices can easily be quieted or ignored (recall Chapter 7).

Applying What You Have Learned

1. In Chapter 1, we argued that organizations and organizational communication is "contextualized" within the broader society. What assumptions must a society take-for-granted for the first interpretation of stress to make sense? The second interpretation? The final one?
2. How are the social workers employing the sense-making model in Figure 8.1 to construct their situation in their organizations?
3. Many scholars argue that organizational decision making can be better understood if it is treated as a ritual or ceremony rather than as an effort to solve problems. What kind of ceremony is stress management in these hospitals (recall Chapter 4)?What functions does that ritual play?

To Think About and Discuss

1. Try to recall the most ambiguous or confusing experience you have ever had in an organization. Briefly describe the actions taken by members of the organization that caused your confusion. How did you manage the frustrations that you experienced? How did the other members of the organization manage the confusion that you caused them?
2. Now try to recall the most confusing experience that you have had with an organization in which you were not a member. How did members of that organization deal with you (and thus with the confusion, ambiguity, and frustration that you caused them)? Why might they have chosen those ways of dealing with you instead of others?

Notes

1 This case is based on Meyerson (1994, 199).

2 See Miller (2009, chap. 11) for a good discussion of stress, burnout, and its management.

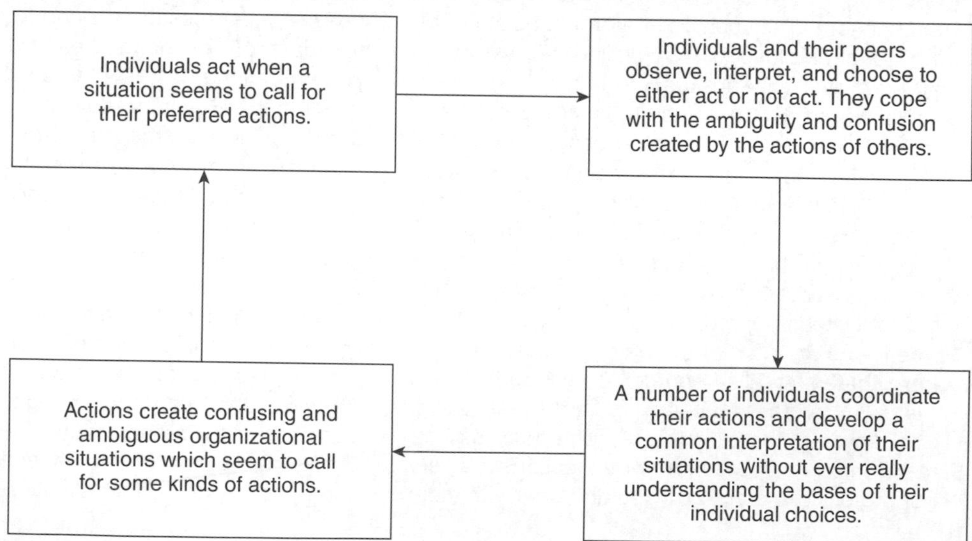

Figure 8.2 Acting, coping with, and managing ambiguity.

decision-making members often manage information nonrationally. After all, organizational decision makers are people who are often acting in groups and thus are subject to all the pressures and nonrational processes described in the first parts of this chapter. They rationalize decisions already made, engage in groupthink, and persist in failing policies long after the available evidence makes it clear that they should be abandoned.

Members have different and sometimes competing goals for a decision that may change during the process, are frequently inconsistent, and often not clear. The "intelligence" of an organization is more a loose and transient collection of impressions than a systematic and logical group of tightly interlocked preferences and procedures. Each employee has a set of preferred "solutions" when looking for problems; each person is a decision maker looking for work (Poole and Ahmed, 2008). Following the nonrational approach of "act first, make sense later," members make choices and then begin to construct, share, and publicize seemingly rational explanations and rationalizations of their choices.

This turns the situation on its head: instead of using information to guide decision making, decision makers often use it to *rationalize* actions made without reference to the information in question. Even when their information searches precede decisions, decision makers may use information as much because it is readily available as because it is accurate or relevant. Not only does it take time and effort to obtain information, seeking information usually involves admitting one's ignorance. In organizations in which appearing to be uninformed is punished, it may be wiser to rely on information that is easily accessible than to search for better information that cannot be obtained without publicly admitting one's ignorance (Weick, 2000).

In a classic article, Feldman and March (1981) argued that information often plays more of a symbolic than substantive role in organizational decision making. A key aspect of the job of management (and, by extension, any decision maker) is to gather and process information so that they are prepared to respond to problems and opportunities and to make effective decisions. Recall that the term "bureaucracy," the epitome of the classical strategy of organization, derives from "bureau," a desk which is presumably stuffed with information-rich documents. Hence, when confronted with the need to make a decision, managers often engage in extensive information search, delegating subordinates to conduct research and appointing committees to gather data and investigate the matter. However, when the time comes to make the decision, only a small subset of this information is consulted.

What, then, is the reason for all this information gathering and processing when the information is barely consulted? Mainly this activity serves symbolic purposes. It demonstrates that the manager is doing his or her job, gathering and processing information. It suggests that the decision makers exhibited "due diligence," that is, that they put a great deal of time, effort, and care in researching all avenues before finally making a prudent decision. Finally, the piles of information can be used as evidence that the decision maker is not to blame if the decision goes wrong. After all, they did a thorough job of research and had the best and most relevant information available. If something unforeseen occurred, then they cannot be to blame.

One of the authors witnessed this early in his career. Scott Poole was employed by a consulting firm that had been hired to conduct an assessment of needs of older citizens of a medium-sized city. The firm planned a large public event at which a complex procedure was used to collect ideas and priorities from older citizens. The information was compiled in a large report, which the firm duly submitted to the city planners. The report was filed in a bottom drawer and apparently never consulted as the city developed a "master plan" for services to "elderly" citizens.

Ritualistic Decision Making: The Myth of Solving Problems The classical rational model (and common sense) also presumes that the purpose of decision making is to solve problems. Decision processes, however, can also be viewed as political rituals in which members of organizations demonstrate their competence, power, and commitment to the organization by participating. To an observer who believes that decision making should lead to choices, it might seem that nothing ever gets done in these decision-making events. If the observer is an anthropologist or sociologist, he or she soon will realize that what gets done is the doing, the act of participating. If the observer is a recently hired college graduate who has been trained in strategic decision making, he or she is likely to be surprised and bit taken aback to realize that what goes on in meetings is meeting (Schwartzmann, 1989). When former students return to their alma maters and complain to their mentors, "I'm always going to meetings where nothing ever gets decided" (as they invariably seem to do), they provide testimony to the ritualized nature of organizational decision making.

Viewing decision-making events as rituals also helps explain the otherwise mystifying processes through which employees decide when and how to become involved in decision-making events. Employees have a variety of personal goals, favored actions, and pet plans. They move along during the day-to-day activities of their organizations until they discover a decision-making event relevant to one of their concerns. They then choose to participate in that event. Other members participate in the same event for different reasons. If they eventually do agree on a course of action, their consensus may be based on a long list of individual and often inconsistent goals. One supervisor may support a building plan, because it gives his subordinates more overtime. A department head may support it, because it gives her an opportunity to transfer two troublesome workers to another section. Other employees may agree because it diverts upper management's attention away from the large equipment purchases that they plan to make during the next week. They use the decision episode like a garbage can, dumping into the discussion a plethora of concerns, only some of which are logically related to the problem being discussed (Cohen, March, and Olsen, 1972; O'Connor, 1997; Poole and Ahmed, 2008).

Of course, it is not likely that the participants will admit their real motives in public. Instead, they search for a rationale for the building project that is acceptable to everyone and that can be stated in public. In this way, communication obscures the participants' real motivations rather than reveals them; but in the process, it also allows the participants to make what seems to be a rational decision. When an agreement is reached in organizations, it sometimes is an agreement over decisions and public justifications of them, not over the reasons or goals that lie behind the choice (see Figure 8.3).[5]

In fact, political considerations and power relationships may influence the decision-making process far more than does the goal of making the best decision (Hickson, Butler, Cray, Mallory, and Wilson, 1986; recall the hidden face of power discussed in Chapter 7). Powerful employees can push an issue through the process rapidly or can interrupt the process by pressuring for a longer information search, demanding that other interested parties be involved in the process, tabling the issue, or referring it to a subcommittee. For example, the president of a subsidiary of a large multinational corporation chairs an 11-person committee that includes the vice presidents and department heads (remember, organizational groups tend to be larger than the optimal five to seven members because of

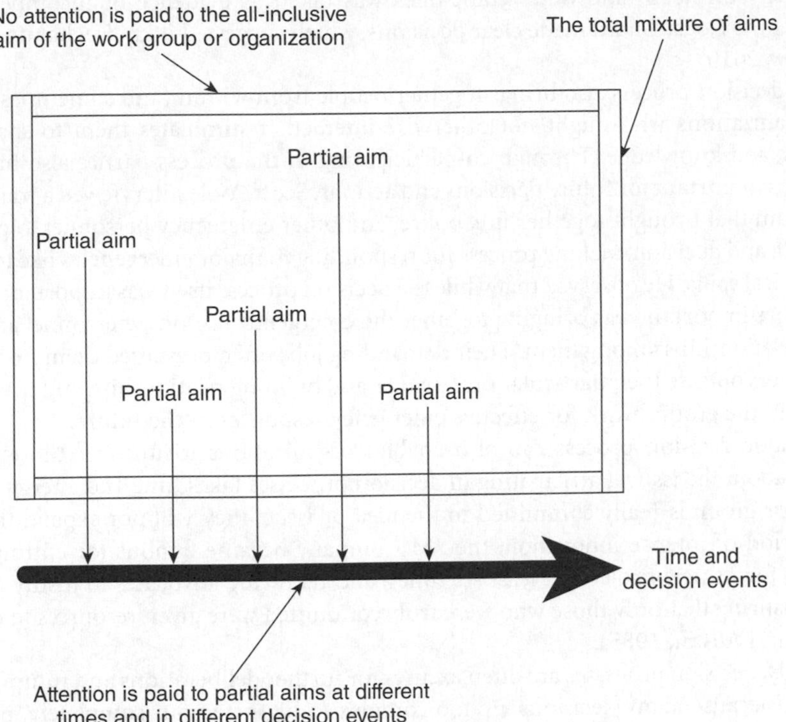

Figure 8.3 Coping with multiple aims and multiple decision events.
Source: Adapted from Gunnar Westerlund and Sven-Erik Sjostrand, *Organizational Myths* (Harper and Row, 1979).

political considerations). The group must decide between the terms of an existing contract and a new pricing system. After a half an hour, it becomes clear that the president and executive vice president disagree on the proposal. One senior vice president adds information about international market conditions, but no other members speak up, because they realize that doing so may alienate one of the two top-ranking people in the organization. No action is taken, but another meeting is scheduled to discuss the issue further (and then another, and another . . .).[6] In many organizations, employees attend meeting after meeting, year after year, where the same issues are discussed and the same arguments and information are presented. This repetitiveness is irritating primarily to employees who believe our cultural myths that problem-solving rituals should solve problems once and for all. For employees who realize that the purpose of meeting is meeting, repetitive problem solving is easy to understand.

Other Functions of Decision Making Major decisions serve a number of additional functions than simply making choices that lay the groundwork for action. Major decisions also serve as symbols, suggesting to outsiders that the organization really does know what it is doing. During the Gulf of Mexico oil spill in the summer of 2010, the indecisiveness of British Petroleum and other companies was taken as evidence of incompetence. In contrast, the Coast Guard made clear decisions, which suggested it knew what it was doing (Barstow, 2010).

The decision process also brings together people from within (and sometimes outside) the organizations who might not otherwise interact. It stimulates them to share ideas, insights, and knowledge. Through co-participating in the process parties also build relationships important for future decisions and actions. Scott Poole interviewed a trainer from a program that brought together fire, police, and other emergency personnel to practice a planning and decision-making process for responding to major emergencies like tornadoes or chemical spills. He observed that while the decision process itself was important, perhaps even more important was bringing together the emergency response personnel and developing relationships among them. Their demanding jobs often prevented them from talking with others outside their particular professions, and building relationships and trust among them laid the groundwork for effective emergency responses in the future.

A major decision process can also enables organizations to uncover those who are serious about the issue. Participating in decision processes takes time and energy. Unless a person or group is really committed to the idea or issue, they will not expend the effort. In a period of intense innovation, the 3M Company became famous for cutting off the funding for its new projects at least six times, and requiring advocates to justify getting it back, ensuring that only those who were truly committed were given resources to continue (Peters and Austin, 1985).

Finally, decision processes are often excuses for further deliberations and future decision making. Because many decisions are too complex to be sorted out completely in a single episode, they must be managed incrementally (Lindblom, 1959; Mintzberg and McHugh, 1985). Decision makers "muddle through" complex problems by making a series of small decisions. Eventually, the minor actions that they take provide new information and help them make sense out of complicated problems. In the process they act, and by doing so, they convince others that they really do understand those problems.

A Contingency Model of Organizational Rationality The goal of the preceding sections has been to suggest that people often do not act in ways that conform to the classical rational model, either in everyday decision making or in their organizations. We do not intend to disparage employees. Nor do we mean to reject wholesale models of rational decision making, either the classical rational model or bounded rationality. On the contrary, as we have pointed out, we want readers to understand that people violate societal myths of strict rationality for a number of good, understandable reasons.

Some of these reasons involve the nature of the decision itself. It is possible to array organizational decision situations along a continuum. At one pole of the continuum are simple problems for which the effects of different courses of action can be quantified; where the information needed to make the decision is finite, well defined, and readily available; where only a limited number of options are possible; and where the relevant communication networks are simple. At the other pole are decision situations that are so ambiguous, problems so complex, and information so inaccessible that rational decision making is impossible (see Table 8.2). Using the classical rational decision-making model is both possible and preferable at the simple extreme; it is either inappropriate or impossible at the other, and it is often not appropriate in the middle.

Table 8.2 A Continuum of Forms of Decision Making

"Classical rational model" – both possible and preferable	*"Bounded rationality and nonrational decision making" – either impossible or inappropriate*
Quantifiable outcomes	Ambiguous outcomes
Clear decision–effect links	Ambiguous decision–effect links
"Finite" communication	Unknown or ill-defined parameters
Redundant available sources	A very large number of sources
Defined information needs	Unknown or indefinite information needs
Limited communication networks	Diverse or undefined communication networks
Minimal organizational and environmental change	Constant organizational and/or environmental change
Precedented and/or simple problems	Unprecedented and/or complex problems or issues

A second continuum reflects the need to implement organizational decisions once they are made. It *is* important for organizational decision makers to make decisions of at least satisfactory quality. But it often is just as important to arrive at decisions that people will support actively. For example, in a six-year study of how hospitals make decisions about purchasing CAT scanners and other equipment costing millions of dollars, Alan Meyer (1984) uncovered a recurring decision-making process that combined rational and ritual processes in a complicated maze.[7] In general, the decision-making episodes started with careful consideration of program needs, equipment costs, projected payoff periods, and other objective factors. Necessary information was gathered before the decisions were made, important people were involved in the process, and so on. In short, the early phase of the decision-making process approximated the classical rational model.

But eventually the process deviated from the rational model in most of the episodes. Communication among participants became vaguer and focused on abstract topics like the parties' shared beliefs, values, goals for the hospital, and vision of its future. Later the decision makers started to restructure and redefine what actually had taken place during the deliberations so that the events seemed to fit the myth of rational decision making. The later, nonrational (ritual) phase of the process served two important purposes for the hospitals' personnel. It allowed them to emerge from what often had been highly competitive, heated discussions with a revised image of themselves as tough but cooperative members of a functioning team. In addition, their symbolic strategies allowed them to gain a sense of psychological closure on the process – to feel that the decision had been made, the battle was over, and their attention could now turn toward using the new equipment effectively. In effect these groups had used the communication strategies that bind cultures together – myths, rituals, and ceremonies – to reunify themselves into a cohesive mini-society.

In hospitals where the decision makers used rational communication strategies throughout the process, the groups seldom reunified. Dissension continued, debates proliferated, and in some cases, key staff members resigned and expensive new equipment was left sitting in the basement. Meyer's research suggests that rational communication strategies are neither always superior to nor always inferior to less rational processes. Making rational

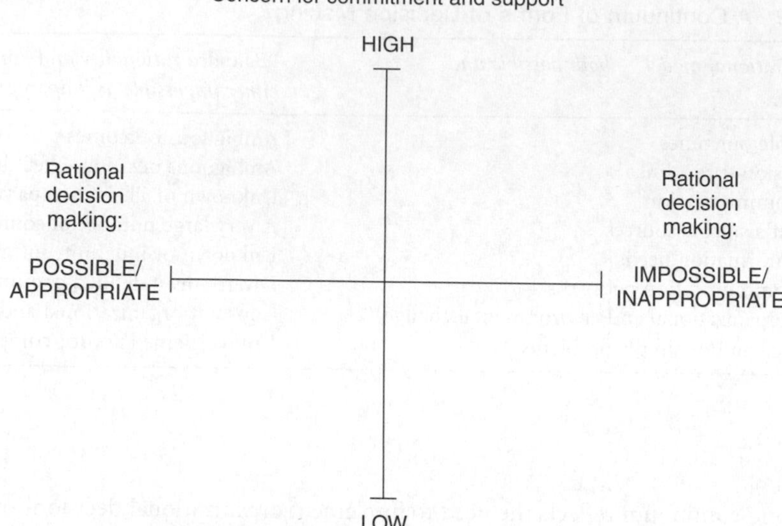

Figure 8.4 Continua of organizational decision contexts.

decisions and making decisions that people will support are separate but interrelated elements of decision making processes.

Thus, as Figure 8.4 suggests, organizational decision situations can be described by two interrelated continua. One continuum reflects the extent to which rational decision making is possible and appropriate. The second involves the extent to which gaining commitment to and support for a decision is important. Different combinations of concern for rationality and concern for commitment call for different combinations of communication processes (we will also find this and discuss different processes in Chapter 9, which is concerned with organizational change). What is important is that the mixture of these two factors be appropriate to a particular context, not that decision makers try to conform to social myths about how people ought to act or how organizational decisions ought to be made.

Rationalizing Organizational Nonrationality Nonrational aspects of organizational decision making are difficult to accept because they violate many of the taken-for-granted assumptions of modern Western societies. The notion that good decisions need not be strictly rational decisions may seem counter to common sense. But, as we have suggested throughout this book, the commonsense notions of a society are strategic, symbolic creations. And the notion that decision makers must be as rational as possible is a core assumption in Western societies. In a provocative article aptly entitled "The Technology of Foolishness," James March (1970) explained that Western societies embrace three primary articles of faith:

1. *The preexistence of purpose:* People begin with goals, make choices based on these goals, and can offer adequate explanations of their actions only in terms of their goals.

Case Study 8.2

Koalas and Roos Flying Through Chaos[1]

We're overrun with information, but we're dying for lack of knowledge.

Allan Moore, Qantas' strategic planning director (quoted in Baumard, 1999, 133)

There probably is no industry that faces as chaotic an environment as airlines. The industry has faced a series of major, rapid, abrupt changes since the United States deregulated its airlines in 1979. By 1992 only three of the world's airlines (British Airways, Singapore Air, and Cathay Pacific) were profitable. Eastern Airlines, the largest carrier in the free world only ten years earlier, no longer existed. Worldwide deregulation of the industry was only one factor. Airport congestion, declining values of "pre-owned" airplanes, overcapacity created by the birth of a plethora of new airlines that were interested only in short-term profits, constant price wars (usually stimulated by the "start-ups" who could undercut established airlines because they did not have to invest in the future), and a patchwork of government policies that gave preference to some airlines combined to create a situation that no airline decision maker had ever before encountered. To make matters worse, customers also were changing. Business travelers had started using new communication technologies to reduce overseas travel, had started to combine multiple destinations into one long trip instead of a number of small ones, and had started to demand low fares and enforce those demands by shopping around.

In response to this confusing situation, competitors had started to behave in ways that seemed irrational, or at least nonrational. For example, previously the Qantas management had been able to predict what the management of Continental Airlines and Canadian Air would do. But, now these and other companies were going in and out of bankruptcy, announcing aircraft purchases and then changing their minds, and generally behaving irrationally, and thus unpredictably. Qantas's motto had become "Make sense, and quickly" (Baumard, 1999, 122).

Qantas faced its own sources of chaos. Because Australia is located at the end of international routes rather than in the middle, Qantas was affected more by the global chaos than other airlines. They also recently had merged with Australia Airlines and were coping with trying to integrate two very different organizational cultures. The "Australia Airlines people" were a mystery to the "Qantas people." They feared that the newcomers would "take over their territory," leaving them landing rights only at Hong Kong and Los Angeles. They thought the bushman's hats worn by AA's stewards were "stupid," and felt that "they're keeping them just to be different." In short, they felt that "we're different from them. We don't have the same history."

Qantas management tried to deal with the culture clash by redistributing the workers so that all teams had members from both airlines. It seemed to be working, but the adjustment was slow, and the returns on the merger so small that the airline had to seek outside funding.

A bigger problem was a breakdown in the circulation of knowledge through the organization. Things had become so chaotic that employees had started to protect themselves by focusing inward, on their own, individual tasks and work groups. The communication networks that once extended throughout the organization had become fragmented; the organization's knowledge had become compartmentalized. Communication had become more formal, with all of the problems that accompany formalization (recall Chapter 3). Information, especially information that could be quantified, began to dominate decision making because it *seemed* to be stable. A new computer information system was installed to facilitate information flow, but it was so expensive that only a small percent of the workforce had access to it. As a result it became more of a status symbol than a decision-making tool. One employee confided, "When you don't know where you're going any more, you want to hear someone's voice, you don't want to read about it. And when nothing is going right you want to be face to face, not looking at a screen" (Baumard, 1999, 132).

But, knowledge was something that Qantas desperately needed. It faced one of the most important decisions it had ever made: deciding between merging with Singapore Airlines or British Airways. British Airways was easier to understand. Its strategy was to globalize, and to do so as quickly as possible. Its first step was to form an alliance with US Airways. Its second would be a merger with Qantas. Singapore Airlines' strategy was more ambiguous, even though it had made moves to globalize through alliances with Swissair and Delta Airlines. The key question for Qantas was "How would the airline we don't merge with respond?"

Time was short: Qantas's "knowledge team" had to make a recommendation to upper management soon. But, how could they sort through the piles of data they had and make sense out of it – how could they transform "information" into "knowledge?" After consulting with two outside advisors, the knowledge team decided to use a "decision tree" model: "we decided, I can't remember exactly when, to adopt the technique of decision trees. We were finally convinced that this was the direction to take" (Roger Robertson, strategic planning manager). The decision was made in favor of British Airways, but Robertson admitted that "it is not easy to think strategically at difficult moments. Something occurs in the environment, and one has a tendency to use it as an excuse" (Baumard, 1999, 132).

Applying What You've Learned

1. To what extent was Qantas' decision to merge with BA "rational"? Why? Does it conform more to the classical rational model or to the bounded rationality model?
2. What aspects of nonrational decision making were present in the situation they faced? How did they influence the decision process?

Questions to Think About and Discuss

1. How could Qantas' management have responded differently to the decision situations they faced?
2. What does your response imply about the possibility of "rational" organizational decision making?

Note

1 This case is based on Baumard (1999).

2. *The necessity of consistency:* People choose to act in ways that are consistent with their beliefs and with their roles in their social groups (families, organizations, communities, and so on).
3. *The primacy of rationality:* People make decisions by carefully projecting the probable effects of different courses of action, *not by intuition* (in which they act without fully understanding why they do what they do) or by tradition or faith (in which they do things because they always have been done that way).[8]

A major part of acculturation in Western societies (and increasingly the world, as Western models spread) involves learning these three "commandments." People learn that children act impulsively, irrationally, and playfully. Adults act calmly and rationally, making decisions by carefully considering a number of complicated factors, and are spontaneous only when they have calmly and rationally decided to be spontaneous. Because people are products of their societies, their individual identities and self-esteem are linked to the belief that they are rational people. And, as we noted at the outset, organizations must present themselves as rational and emphasize rational elements of their decision process in order to respond to institutional pressures to conform to the "correct" rational mode of operation. Otherwise, they may lose legitimacy and their identity as *bona fide* organizations.

As a result, when people and organizations do behave in ways that are not strictly rational, they feel pressure to pretend that they have not. People and other organizations usually cooperate in maintaining the myth that everything is rational, even if they sometimes doubt that they, their peers, and their organizations really are. People persist in pretending that they are rational actors, because doing so allows them to gain comfort from the knowledge that they live in a stable, predictable, rational world. But, like all taken-for-granted assumptions, rationalizing human nonrationality has the effect of perpetuating social and organizational power relationships.

Chapter 7 introduced social theorist Jürgen Habermas's distinction between practical and technical reasoning. All societies can be defined by the kind of balance they maintain between technical and practical reason. In traditional societies (some people use the more pejorative term "primitive"), practical reason dominates technical reason. The experience of living is valued in itself; the meaning of an act lies more in the act itself than in what it might allow people to obtain. In industrial societies, technical reason dominates practical reason.

For example, when Charley Conrad teaches time management skills, he begins by asking people to play a simple "priority clarification" game: "Pretend that you just learned that you will live only one more year. Your situation will not change markedly – you will not become richer or poorer, smarter or dumber, and so on. What would you begin to do that you now do not do and what would you quit doing that you now are doing?" When he asks students this question, at least 80 percent say, "I'd quit school and start to travel or spend time with my family." Now, it is possible that they could be in college primarily for practical reasons, for what school gives them in and of itself – because college piques and fulfills their curiosity about life or because it meets their natural craving for knowledge (remember, Habermas's definition of "practical" is *not* the usual definition). His students tell him, however, that they *really* are going to school for technical reasons – because getting a degree is a means for obtaining other goals like getting a real job (recall Chapter 1), increasing their social status, or buying an expensive sports car. School is merely a means of obtaining something (knowledge or a diploma) that is merely a means of obtaining something else. When these technical goals become irrelevant because of their impending death, they have no reason to stay in school. In Habermas's terms, technical reason dominates practical reason in their lives, just as it does in the lives of everyone in "modern" societies.

But like other societal assumptions, the particular balance of technical and practical reason that exists in a society privileges some people and groups of people over others. In "traditional" societies those people who control symbolism – priests or shamans – are granted more power than other members of the culture. In technical societies people who control "rational" decision making are granted a privileged position. In the organizations of modern societies, the bias in favor of rational decision making favors managers. Upper-level male managers are in especially privileged positions. Men usually are assumed to be more rational than women. People in upper-level positions (usually men in US organizations) have superior access to information. Their background and training give them greater facility with the language of rational decision making. So, they *seem* to have a superior ability to decide what should be done, when, where, and by whom. As long as modern societies privilege technical reason (rationality, efficiency, effectiveness, and so on) and as long as decision-making rituals allow managers to *appear* to be rational actors, their superior power positions will be protected. Low-power people will tend to perceive that they have less power because they are "naturally" and "normally" less rational (recall the discussion of "hegemony" in Chapter 2). Rationalizing nonrationality helps preserve the deep structure of power in modern organizations and modern societies. We will explore this theme further in Chapter 10, which is concerned with diversity and difference in organizations.

Summary: Communication and Decision Making

Contemporary models of decision making teach two important lessons about the functions of communication in organizations. They indicate that both the *processes* of communicating and the *products* of communication (decisions, plans, deals, and so on) allow members of organizations to *manage* ambiguous and confusing situations. If one embraces the assumptions of the classical rational model uncritically, the ambiguity management function of communication will seem inefficient and perhaps a little bit perverse. But blending rational and nonrational elements of decision making together in the same decision-making episodes may be neither strange nor ineffective. Doing so allows employees to *act*, and acting is often more important than reaching *optimal* decisions.

The danger facing organizational decision makers is not that they will make decisions that are not strictly rational. Incorporating the ethical, political, personal, and interpersonal considerations that are excluded from the rational actor model often – perhaps usually – leads to more productive outcomes than blindly following the dictates of rationality. The danger is that decision makers may become trapped in their patterns of communicating and making decisions. Patterns of acting provide people with a degree of stability. But, as Karl Weick has noted, the stability and predictability that come from tried and true ways of acting may themselves keep people from adapting to new needs and demands. Adaptation to past needs may prevent adaptability to future ones.

To avoid both of these problems – inappropriately imposing the classical rational model of decision making and becoming trapped in patterns of acting – members must constantly monitor their communication and the communication patterns of their organizations, searching for strategies that can improve their ability to adapt. They must ask themselves, "Does strategy X work? Should I do it?" rather than asserting, "I know X works; it always has. We should use it." They must be able to obtain and accurately process information that casts doubts on their perceptions, beliefs, and interpretations. And they must be able to suspend their views of the "realities" of their organizations to understand how they can best respond to the situations they face.

COMMUNICATION AND THE MANAGEMENT OF ORGANIZATIONAL CONFLICT

This section examines another practical reality of organizational life: Disagreement and conflict are inevitable aspects of working relationships, and the need to manage conflicts is always with us. For many years, researchers and managers focused on the negative aspects of organizational conflict. Conflicts were assumed to reveal a weakness in the organization, a flaw in its design, operation, or communication. Conflicts needed to be resolved. Their sources had to be discovered and eliminated, and peace and stability had to be returned to the organization.[9]

However, contemporary views regard organizational conflicts as inevitable and potentially valuable, both for individuals and for organizations. Conflicts give employees opportunities to publicize, test, and refine their ideas and to demonstrate their competence and value to the organization. Conflicts also can help organizations adapt to changes, foster innovation, and integrate their diverse constituent groups into a functioning whole. Conflicts are neither inherently good nor intrinsically bad, although they do vary in the degree to which they are *productive.* Conflicts that are relatively productive for the organization as a whole may be destructive for some of the participants. Similarly, episodes that are disruptive and damaging to the organization may be productive for many of the participants.

When people think about organizational conflict, they may conjure images of executives shouting at one another in a boardroom, giant oligopolies bidding for a majority share of a competitor's stock, or, for the more fanciful of us, secret meetings on foggy nights when technological secrets are exchanged for chalets on the Riviera. Although overt and sometimes hostile confrontations are part of organizational conflict, they are only one part. We will define **conflict** more broadly, as communication between people who depend on one another and who perceive that the others stand between them and the realization of their goals, aims, or values. This definition encompasses each of the examples listed earlier, as well as everyday discussions of organizational policies and projects, negotiations between employees or groups of employees (for instance, labor–management negotiations), and cooperative attempts to find mutually acceptable solutions to problems. In short, conflicts are communicative interactions among people who are interdependent and who perceive that their interests are incompatible, inconsistent, or in tension (Folger, Poole, and Stutman, 2011).

The Organizational Conflict Process

Organizational scholar Louis Pondy (1967; see also Folger *et al.*, 2011, chap. 4) developed an influential model of the *bases* and *phases* of organizational conflict, and our discussion will be loosely based on his model. Pondy observed that conflicts move through phases from being latent in the organization to being perceived by members to being overtly enacted and finally leading to an aftermath. Our discussion will be organized along these terms.

Latent Conflict In **latent conflict**, there is the potential for conflict, but the parties have not yet framed the situation as a conflict. Grounds for conflict stem from at least three different sources. The most important ground for conflict is a real conflict of interests between parties. The divergence of interests between management and their subordinates is a good example. Management is motivated to keep the organization going in the most efficient possible manner, often no matter what, reducing costs and maintaining high quality. The interests of employees, on the other hand, more often center on personal concerns, such as compensation levels, amount of work required, working conditions, and quality of work life.

Any time different interest groups are created in an organization, latent conflicts arise. The particular set of groups that arise differs across organizations and over time in the same organizations. Possible oppositional groups include employees from two previously separate organizations in a newly merged organization; employees of different genders, ethnicities, or backgrounds; recently hired and experienced employees; and white-collar, blue-collar, and pink-collar employees. Depending on the organizational culture, the particular history of the organization, and trends in the surrounding society, any of these or dozens of other oppositions could create latent conflict in an organization.

It is often said that most conflicts are due to communication problems and if we could just communicate more effectively, we would not have conflicts. While miscommunication plays a vital role in conflicts and is the source of some conflicts, it is a mistake to assume that most conflicts are due to a lack of communication. In fact, organizations are shot through with conflicts of interest that may develop into open conflict. Acknowledging this is often the first step toward managing conflicts effectively.

A third source of latent conflicts is the legacy of previous conflicts. Parties usually have both a history of interacting with one another in the past and the expectation that they will encounter one another in the future. Pondy noted that many latent conflicts are actually products of the aftermath of prior conflicts. A resolution in favor of one party may create resentment on the part of others that blooms into conflict at a later time. A mishandled conflict may sow seeds of discord at a later time. Unresolved grievances may suddenly reappear in the guise of issues completely unrelated to the original complaint.

Conflicts are most likely to develop among those employees who are interdependent. A high level of interdependence creates multiple issues over which conflicts can arise – tangible objects, such as rewards and resources, or intangible factors, such as status and power. When people rarely interact with one another, they have few reasons or opportunities to fight. In organizational settings, the vast majority of conflicts arise in what theorists call **mixed-motive situations**. This means that the parties have incentives both to cooperate and to compete. Even if employees have little incentive to cooperate during the discussion of a single issue, the fact that they will have to depend on one another in the future means that they always have incentives to reach a cooperative outcome to conflicts.

Several factors influence or shape the emergence of latent conflicts. One factor is the culture and climate of the organization (Folger *et al.*, 2011, chap. 7). Some strategies of organizing simply tend to generate more conflicts than others. Organizations dominated by traditional strategies are often rife with conflicts, because they exaggerate distinctions among employees and interest groups; they also on a slow and balky communication system that creates misunderstandings and rely on a structure that creates tensions among the different positions in the hierarchy. In contrast, using a relational strategy that is legitimately empowering is less likely to promote conflicts. No organizational strategy eliminates conflict situations altogether, however. Conflicts always emerge.

Relationships among parties also influence the development of latent conflict. Trust developed during past interactions decreases the number of latent conflicts, because parties assume that they will be able to work through issues effectively. The opposite is true of distrustful relationships, which tend to breed conflict (Roloff and Miller, 2006; Thomas and Pondy, 1977).

Ironically, attempts to improve communication can sometimes crystallize conflicts by surfacing or defining opposing interests. While still in graduate school, Charley Conrad was asked to mediate between a university administration (not his university) and the school's African American Students' Association. The more he talked with both sides, the clearer it became that they had almost no objective reason to cooperate and many reasons to compete with each other. They still were talking largely because they did not know how they really felt about each other. The situation was exceptionally volatile, because "getting them to talk to one another" – the task he had been called in to perform – almost certainly would have made it clear to everyone that a latent conflict actually did exist. If continued, "improving communication" easily could have transformed a latent conflict into a perceived one.

Another function of communication in organizations runs counter to open expression; communication often functions to hide and downplay latent conflicts, particularly conflicts of interest (Kolb and Bartunek, 1992). Almost all organizations experience the conflicts of interest discussed earlier in this section. Dealing with them usually requires significant time and resources, resulting in a decrease in resources devoted to organizational effectiveness and efficiency. As a result, management has incentives to paper over or to obscure conflicts of interest. It may do this through messages that deny conflict and differences: Company newsletters, for example, may carry the theme "We're all in this together." Other messages may highlight different interests that draw attention away from oppositions between groups. One tactic is to define an outside threat that serves to unite people within the organization and focuses their attention on differences in interests between the organization and outside groups. For example, a school administration might inform teachers that the legislature is going to cut appropriations to public schools in order to forestall teacher–administration conflicts.

Perceived Conflict **Perceived conflict** occurs when one or more parties come to believe that someone stands between them and achieving their goals. This perception can be created in a number of ways. Sometimes an outsider explicitly tells one party that his or her interests are incompatible with someone else's. More often, the perception stems from a "precipitating event." One party criticizes another or makes a demand that the second perceives as illegitimate. Or one party makes what she or he perceives is a legitimate request and is rebuffed. Or a long period of annoyance builds up until a party realizes that a conflict exists.

Perceived conflict can exist when latent conflict does not, as when siblings fight over a serving of rapidly melting ice cream so large that they cannot possibly eat all of it. There is no objective reason for conflict in this situation, although the children *believe* that their interests are incompatible. Also, latent conflict can exist without perceived conflict, as when siblings are given a mound of ice cream that seems to be, but is not actually sufficient for both.

In organizations perceived conflict exists without latent conflict if members believe that someone else is their enemy even when their interests really do coincide. Conflicts between "line" and "staff" personnel are quite common in all kinds of organizations. Often they exist because both groups ignore or deemphasize their need to cooperate and instead focus their attention on their incentives to compete. Latent conflict also exists without perceived conflict if people overlook minor day-to-day frictions, or if they concentrate so completely on routine or easily resolved disagreements that they suppress major problems.

Parties' perceptions exert strong influence over what happens during conflicts and what effects conflicts have on organizations. Table 8.3 summarizes a number of ways in which employees may perceive a conflict. If they define the situation as all-or-nothing, or see only a small range of alternatives as acceptable solutions, or believe that they can win only if the other parties lose, or believe that the difference of opinion has a strong moral or ethical dimension, they tend to try to impose their wills on others. In such cases, they also tend to perceive others as hostile and untrustworthy and adopt a narrow and inflexible course of action during overt conflicts (Neale and Bazerman, 1991).

Table 8.3 Defining Conflict

Definitions that make conflicts easier to manage productively	*Definitions that make conflicts difficult to manage productively*
1. "Mixed motive" (or non-zero-sum) definition: Each party perceives that it can obtain desired outcomes without the others losing the same amount of reward.	1. Zero-sum definition: Parties perceive that whatever one gains, the other loses. The outcome will either grant them complete success or complete failure.
2. Empathic definition of the issue: Parties perceive the issue from both their own and the other parties' perspectives.	2. Egocentric definition of the issue: Parties perceive the issue only from their own frame of reference.
3. Broad contextualization of the issue: Parties search for underlying concerns that place the overt issue in a broad, organizational context.	3. Narrow focus on a single issue and its immediate effects.
4. "Commercial" issue: The issue is defined as problem centered.	4. "Ideological" issue: The conflict is defined as a moral struggle between forces of good and evil.
5. A large number of possible solutions is available.	5. A small number of alternatives is available.

An important influence on perceived conflict is the frames of reference that parties bring into conflict situations (Rogan, 2006). Through past experiences, both in their organizations and in their outside lives, people develop assumptions about conflicts (Roloff and Miller, 2006). **Conflict frames** include assumptions about what a conflict or issue is about, predictions about the costs and rewards associated with different outcomes, definitions of one's position on a particular issue or group of issues, and preferences about how the conflict should be managed. When people "frame" a conflict as an opportunity to achieve some kind of gain, they tend to use more open communicative strategies; when they "frame" it as an event that may lead to losses, their communicative strategies tend to be less flexible and the likelihood of the conflict reaching an impasse is increased (Neale and Bazerman, 1983).

Frames also involve a complex set of expectations – about how the parties in a conflict will and should act, what kinds of persuasive strategies can legitimately be used to influence the outcome of the conflict, and how the conflict episode will unfold (Roloff and Miller, 2006). For example, employees' perceptions of how well they handled past conflicts seem to influence the way they handle future conflicts. People who expect to handle a conflict well tend to employ more open and cooperative orientations and communication strategies; people who expect that they will not handle conflicts well tend to avoid conflicts or adopt competitive orientations and strategies.

Conflict Interaction The parties' response to a perceived conflict constitutes **conflict interaction.** Conflicts are made up of communication, of interactive cycles of messages, responses, and counterresponses (Folger *et al.*, 2011, chap. 3). Once these cycles commence, their development and outcomes are not within the control of any single participant. A conflict tends to have a momentum all its own; it is a co-creation of the parties, their interpretations, arguments, definitions, and strategies. Parties make choices about how they respond (communicate) based in part on their interpretations of the communicative strategies used by the other parties. They look to the other parties' communication for clues about how they are likely to respond to available communicative strategies. In a real sense, neither party controls interaction during conflict. The interaction often seems to take on a life of its own.

For example, after much delay and the gathering of a great deal of evidence, Elias decided to confront one of his subordinates about his use of illegal drugs. Elias's orientation was collaborative; he wanted to help the man get professional help for what seemed to be a serious addiction and was willing to go to great lengths to see that he could keep his job during and after the treatment. Elias called the worker in and explained his concerns. The worker denied using drugs, which made Elias a little angry; but Elias's emotions were tempered by his knowledge that drug and alcohol addicts almost always deny their dependence. He presented all the evidence that he had collected, assuming that doing so would help facilitate an open and honest discussion of the problem. Suddenly the worker blew up, shouting about Elias's dual standard. Everyone knew, he said, that Elias had taken a three-month leave of absence several years ago to enter a treatment program for alcoholism after the company had tolerated his tardiness, absenteeism, and excuses for three years.

Elias, he said, had a "lot of gall" confronting him. As suddenly, Elias lost his temper. He had been promised that the referral would be kept secret and thought that it had been. He felt betrayed and projected his quite justifiable anger on the employee. He started screaming too and ended the episode by firing the worker and throwing him out of the office. His intention to be cooperative and collaborative had dissolved during a communicative interaction that he could never have predicted.

In conflicts that have productive outcomes, communication is both flexible and strategic. Parties begin with a wide range of acceptable outcomes and believe that everyone will be able to get something out of the episode (a "win–win" orientation). Initially, all parties generally do (and should) make lengthy statements that clearly state their positions on the key issues and the reasons for those positions (in the jargon of conflict research they "differentiate" their positions from those of the other parties). The parties engage in short cycles of different kinds of communication. Periods of coercion, cooperation, joking, relaxation, threats, and promises are mixed together as the parties move toward a solution that will be mutually acceptable. Of course, the movement is rarely smooth or easy. Tension between the parties' incentives to cooperate and to compete lasts throughout the interaction. As a result, the balance shifts back and forth, and the parties' communication also shifts from cooperative strategies to competitive strategies and back again. As long as it seems that progress is being made, a positive interchange will continue. When the interaction turns in a positive direction, parties respond with supportive statements or tension-reducing strategies, such as jokes, which in turn move the interaction in productive directions.

If, however, one party seems to be excessively stubborn or noncompliant, the other party is likely to shift to more competitive communication strategies, especially if he or she has more power in the organization. If the other parties reciprocate, they all may suddenly become trapped in escalating cycles of competitive communication, transforming a productive interaction into a destructive one (Caughlin and Vangelisti, 2006; Messman and Canary, 1998). It is this fear of uncontrolled escalation that encourages people to try to avoid conflicts. Ironically, avoiding conflicts often tends to make uncontrolled escalation likely, because it allows people to develop a deeply held anger that may explode once a conflict does occur. The same thing may happen if two parties have accommodative orientations and real differences. They tend to repeatedly ignore their problems and over time build up a large reservoir of unexpressed hostility.

Table 8.4 Communication Strategies in Conflicts

Confrontive strategies	*Avoidant strategies*
1. Coercion: overt displays of power	1. Delay and procrastination
Formal rank	Manipulating procedures
Coalitions	"Putting off" communication
Expertise	Focusing on rules of interaction
2. Coercion: threats or promises	2. Regression
3. Personalization	3. Commitments to revenge
Moral accusations	4. Refusing to admit existence of conflict
Ad hominem attacks	5. Accommodation
Revelation of secrets	
4. Toughness	
Pure form	
Reformed sinner	
5. Compromise	
6. Problem solving	
Superordinate goal	

In contrast, in destructive conflicts, the parties usually begin with a win–lose orientation and view only a small number of outcomes as acceptable. Their communication is rigid and *reflexive* (mirroring the other parties' communication) rather than flexible and strategic (Folger *et al.*, 2011). Long periods of competitive strategies dominate the interaction, with little or no periods of joking, relaxation, or cooperation. For example, a labor union that used *Robert's Rules of Order* called a meeting to decide whether to stop work in support of a grievance against the plant's management. Although most of the members favored the proposal, a minority used parliamentary tactics long past the point where the outcome was in any doubt. The longer they argued against the proposal, the more polarized the group became and the more committed the majority became to winning the battle. The dispute left such a bitter legacy that the minority group eventually left the organization. Although the parties' orientations to the conflict set the stage for a destructive escalation, it was their way of communicating that led to a negative outcome.

Avoidance Strategies Table 8.4 summarizes the communicative strategies that have most often been observed in organizational conflicts (Nicotera and Dorsey, 2006; Folger *et al.*, 2011). One group of strategies allows parties to avoid a threatening issue. **Avoidance** can take several more specific forms. Delaying or procrastinating can be overt ("I don't have time to talk about it now") or subtle. Employees can manipulate procedural rules to delay or avoid sustained confrontations. For instance, they can refer an issue to a committee or manipulate agendas so that it is either excluded from the discussion or discussed too late in a session to be taken seriously. Or they can focus the discussion so completely on establishing proper rules of interaction that the issue itself is never addressed. For example, when peace talks started during the Vietnam War, the two sides argued for months about the shape of the bargaining table, proper display of flags, and rules for speaking times and turns. Although these topics were important for symbolic reasons (round tables symbolize that the participants are of equal status; rectangular tables do not), their discussion delayed the start of real negotiations.

Sometimes parties regress to childlike tactics or quietly make commitments to "let this one go by but get revenge later on." Commitments to get revenge, silently obsessing about felt conflicts, running away, unproductive worrying, begging, and pouting all are far too common among adults and children alike. Often one or more parties avoid conflicts by refusing to admit that there is an issue between them, either through statements like "I really think we basically are in agreement on this" or transcend to a level at which agreement does exist: "I know we both have the welfare of the students at heart" (Bush, 1983). A final avoidant strategy is **accommodation**, in which one party avoids the conflict simply by giving in to the other.[10]

Southern High School is a rural school led by a principal who makes virtually every decision and watches teachers and students like a hawk. Like many small, service-oriented organizations, it had a family atmosphere. However, an issue arose over a failing grade given an all-state fullback in a required history course. The principal, who was also the football coach, asked the teacher to let the student do some remedial work. When she refused, he quietly changed the student's grade in the main office. Eventually the faculty member discovered the change (on Friday night, when she saw the fullback start an important game) and confronted the principal in private. The principal minimized the event, arguing that the fullback would drop out of school if he could not play, and that his dropping out would weaken the teachers' negotiating position in upcoming contract talks. He apologized but argued that for the good of the student, and for the good of the family, he had little choice.

Unconvinced, the teacher brought the issue up at the next meeting of the history department. Many of them agreed with the teacher, feeling that all had been insulted when the principal went over the teacher's head. They also were concerned about the contract talks, however, and encouraged her to forget the matter. But the anger didn't go away. Eventually the history teachers started to take sides over the issue and fight among themselves over what really were trivial issues. Others became quietly dissatisfied and started to disengage from their work. Morale dropped, as did the quality of teaching. But their school did win the state football championship.

The moral of this story is really quite simple. There are cases in which avoidant strategies are productive. Avoidance may be the best response if issues really are trivial, if organizational power relationships make successful resistance impossible, if the parties lack the communication skills necessary to prevent destructive escalation, if the circumstances surrounding the issue are likely to change in ways that will eliminate the bases of the conflict, or if there is insufficient time to work through the issue adequately. But, avoidant strategies usually only delay confrontations; they do not manage or resolve differences. When people use avoidant strategies, the people who raised the issue are frustrated. They have taken risks without having an opportunity to realize any gains. Consequently, avoidant strategies may only generate hostilities that will come out in conflicts over other issues, making it more difficult to manage them productively.

Confrontive Strategies Another approach is to confront the conflict directly. Though confrontation sounds competitive, it refers to directly addressing the issues at hand. It can be done in a competitive manner or in an integrative, problem-solving manner (Folger *et al.*, 2011). Both competitive and integrative confrontation can work hand in hand: in some cases, for example, to motivate another party to cooperate in an integrative solution, one must show them that one is willing to compete and will extract considerable costs unless they cooperate.

First, consider the more competitive approaches to confrontation. **Personalization** and **coercion** probably are best known, more because they are so often used than because they are most productive. Personalization, attacking the person of one's opponent(s), especially when the attack impugns morals, reveals secrets, or makes accusations of assorted "-isms" (racism, sexism, fascism, communism, and so on), denies that person any defense except counterattacking or acquiescing. Coercion comes in two forms, overt displays of power and **threats** or **promises**. Threats and promises, surprisingly, function in essentially the same way; they depend on the same conditions for their success and are, in effect, two sides of the same coin. Three conditions must be present for threats or promises to succeed. First, the source must be perceived to have sufficient organizational power to be able to carry out the threat or promise. The threat or promise must also be communicated in a way that makes the desired responses clear and specific and the consequences of compliance or noncompliance vivid. Both "I'm gonna cover you with honey and tie you to a hill of biting red ants in a glaring Arizona sun" and "I'm gonna cover you with whipped cream and . . . " are vivid threats or promises. Finally, the consequence must be perceived as being fair, equitable, and appropriate to the magnitude of the action that is requested. Consequences that are either trivial or horrendous compared to the request will not be taken seriously. In some cases a combination of threats and promises is used – "If you go along with me, I'll give you X, but if you don't, I'll lower the boom" – an effective strategy quaintly labeled as a "thromise."

Threats are risky because they insult the other party. They help the other party understand the threatener's priorities and thus may increase the potential to avoid misunderstandings. The problem with threats and promises is that people's perceptions about what is credible, equitable, fair, and appropriate differ widely. In addition, the very act of threatening or promising may influence those perceptions in unpredictable ways. Threats and promises tend to provoke counterthreats and promises, creating a sometimes comical response ("My mommy will beat up your daddy"). They often lead to destructive cycles of escalation.

A final competitive strategy is **toughness**, in which the party takes a firm stance and refuses to make concessions at the outset. In cases when all parties adopt the tough approach, it can lead to productive results. Because no party appears to be willing to acquiesce or be intimidated, all parties are forced to take one another seriously and search for a mutually acceptable resolution of their differences. Eventually concessions are made, and if they are handled properly, the parties converge on a mutually acceptable solution. The key is knowing when to make an initial concession. If it is made too early the other parties will see it as a sign of weakness and become more intransigent. If too late, the conflict already may have escalated to a destructive level. If the parties are careful not to fall into a cycle of escalation, for example, by pausing and thinking strategically for a while before matching the other party's offer, matching can allow both parties to appear simultaneously both tough and reasonable (Axelrod, 1984).

A more integrative, but related, strategy has been called playing the **reformed sinner**. In the reformed sinner strategy, one party takes a tough stance until the negotiation reaches an impasse and then makes a significant concession. This signals that the party could compete, but is willing to cooperate. Generally the issue on which the concession is made is important, but not vital to the party. In societies with strong norms of reciprocity, the act of conceding creates strong psychological pressures for the other parties to concede something in response.

During a bad housing market, Charley Conrad's wife's career led the Conrads to decide to move. Fortunately, BJ (Charley's wife) had purchased a nice, middle-priced, brick ranch house that had appreciated a bit, thanks primarily to her renovation work. She also had negotiated a great interest rate on their mortgage that was assumable by any buyer. In short, as long as they asked a somewhat reasonable price, they had a strong negotiating position. Their first potential buyer was a newly hired assistant professor in the psychology department of a major private southeastern university whose primary research area was conflict management. This situation created a wonderful opportunity to watch conflict strategies in action.

He and his wife said they were delighted with the house, but somewhat concerned with the deterioration of an exterior brick staircase into the basement. But they would go home and talk about it and call the next day. Because this concern was over what could be perceived as a major problem, but actually was not, it provided an excellent opportunity for the new professor to use the reformed sinner strategy – taking a tough stance and then conceding on the staircase to force a reciprocal concession on a more important issue, like price. The next day Charley Conrad had two contractors come by and give him written estimates for repairing the stairs ($200 and $800, which should tell you something about why you should always get multiple bids on construction and home repair projects). That night the assistant professor called, explained that they were excited about the house but very concerned about the stairs and what they might suggest about the structural integrity of the foundation. They had talked about the problem with his father-in-law, who "knew a lot about construction," and learned that it could cost $4,000 or $5,000 to repair it. So, they would be happy to buy the house for $3,000 below the asking price. After the Conrads told the buyer about their written estimates, the buyers quickly agreed that they would love to move in next week (after paying the asking price, of course).

We provide this example for two reasons. One is to explain the reformed sinner strategy. In studies of conflict and negotiation, it has proven to be a useful strategy for motivating others to shift from competitive to cooperative (integrative) approaches. This example also shows that being able to identify the communication strategies employed by other parties is often as important as being able to use those strategies oneself. There is substantial evidence that conflicts become destructive when there is a major power imbalance between the parties (Folger *et al.*, 2011, chap. 5). Understanding communication strategies in conflicts provides a potent source of power, which can lead to unfair domination of the less powerful parties (i.e., those who do not grasp the other party's strategies). One path to empowerment – the creation of the power balances that lead to productive outcomes in conflicts – begins with training all parties in the use of strategic communication.

There are also more cooperative confrontive strategies. One of these is **compromise**. When we compromise, the parties work together to find a resolution that partly satisfies both parties. One common formula for compromise is splitting the difference 50–50. Each party gives up some of what he or she wants in exchange for getting some of what he or she wants. Compromise requires some degree of willingness to sacrifice individual goals, but it also involves some assertiveness in that parties will not settle for a compromise that gives them nothing. It involves more open communication than toughness or the more competitive strategies, but it does not require that parties exchange information fully, because compromises can be reached just by trading offers and with degree of assertiveness. Compromise is a useful way to resolve conflicts when differences in parties' interests are substantial, but there is a balance of power such than neither party can force the other to comply. However, because neither party fully satisfies their interests, problems may still remain and over the long run parties may become dissatisfied with the resolution.

The most open confrontive strategy is **problem solving**, in which the parties utilize one of the decision-making models defined earlier in this chapter to work jointly through the conflict issues and identify options that meet both parties' needs. Problem solving requires open communication in which parties work to understand one another and conduct an honest search for mutually acceptable solutions. This often requires parties to put aside their initial interpretations of the conflict and to reframe the conflict by "thinking outside the box," to use a worn phrase.

Two counselors in a halfway house, Jeff and Lois, repeatedly engaged in tense confrontations in which each challenged the other's professional competency and blamed the other for problems with residents. When their supervisor sat down to discuss this with Jeff and Lois, it came out that Jeff felt stressed from overwork and wanted a more flexible schedule so he could be with his newborn daughter more. He believed that Lois was being inflexible in drawing up their work schedule. Lois, on the other hand, believed that Jeff was trying to take advantage of her and wanted her to take on some of his patients for no extra compensation. These differences were framed in professional terms through questions about handling of patients, which were regarded as legitimate in this organization, rather than in terms of meeting personal needs, which were not regarded as legitimate issues in the halfway house. Once the supervisor had helped Jeff and Lois cut through the "acceptable" framing of the issue and better understand the grounds of their differences, the two developed a solution: Jeff would take a pay cut and work five hours a week less, and Lois would take on some of his patients and work five more paid hours, which she was glad to do.

Problem solving is a constructive mode of conflict resolution. Successful attempts at problem solving build trust among parties and pave the way for future collaboration. Problem solving also, however, requires a great deal of time and energy, both of which may be in short supply. It is also not very effective when parties' interests are mutually inconsistent.

A common strategy for problem solving is to identify a superordinate goal in which parties find a common goal significant to both that gives them some common ground. A classic experiment by Sherif was one of the first studies of this technique (Sherif, Harvey, White, Hood, and Sherif, 1961). Sherif and his colleagues first created two opposing groups in a summer camp, the "Bulldogs" and the "Red Devils." These groups engaged in a number of competitions, and members developed a strong sense of the value of their own group, while devaluing the competing group. Sherif and colleagues then created several emergencies that required both groups to work together to overcome problems at the camp. For example, they had to work together to get a truck unstuck from the mud. This common activity in service of a valued shared goal significantly reduced competition between the groups, as well as undermining the strong boundaries between them. The superordinate goal approach works only if the goal is truly desired by both parties and if accomplishing it is beyond the capacities of any single party or group. Moreover, it is not a foolproof integrator: If the parties fail to achieve the superordinate goal, they may go back to blaming one another for the failure, polarizing even more (Folger *et al.*, 2011).

In some cultures, confrontive strategies are not as highly valued as they are in the United States. In some non-Western cultures saving face, preserving the honor and self-esteem associated with one's position in the social order, is a primary concern in conflict management. Stella Ting-Toomey (1985) described the complicated face-saving system that characterizes Japanese approaches to conflict management. One principle of this system is the concept of *Nemawashi*, the subtle process of achieving consensus and support for a proposal. Extensive informal communication eventually involves every relevant member of the organization, but never includes a "group confrontation" in which everyone meets in a formal negotiating session. The second principle is the *Ringi* system, a way of preventing open conflicts by circulating a document widely and getting everyone's seals of approval. This system diffuses responsibility and saves face for those people who initially may oppose the proposal, and it saves face for everyone should the proposal fail. The third principle is the go-between system, in which people with different opinions seek out a third party to mediate. This complex, time-consuming, indirect system of conflict management is appropriate for Japanese organizations, because the demands and constraints of Japanese culture make it more important to prevent conflicts than to manage them in the open.

Summary: Productive and Destructive Conflict Interaction Conflicts are not made up of one party using one strategy. They are made of interactions, of patterns of communication, response, and counterresponse. In productive conflicts these patterns consist of a number of brief episodes during which the parties adopt a wide range of strategies. Coercion, threats, promises, redefinition, relational comments, digressions, joking, and relaxing are intermixed in a variety of proportions. No single strategy takes over; no sustained cycle of threat and counterthreat, coercion and regression distorts parties' perceptions or clouds their analysis of the situation.

In destructive conflicts a narrow range of communicative strategies is used. Escalating cycles of threat, coercion, expansion of issues, and personalization lock parties into competitive, zero-sum patterns of interaction. Sometimes – perhaps often – destructive cycles are accidentally initiated by more powerful employees. They misperceive less powerful people as jealous, resentful, or hostile and overreact, adopting competitive strategies when other approaches would have been more appropriate. Or they inadvertently place weaker people in positions where they feel they must either fight or be humiliated. But conflict cycles are never under any one member's control. It is the participants' ability to manage and control tendencies for escalation that determines whether a conflict will be productive or destructive.

Case Study 8.3
The Bargaining Case

Bargaining is a special kind of conflict management. It looks like compromise, but involves negotiating shared rules and cooperation within these rules to gain a competitive advantage. It focuses on the exchange of formal offers; but making offers is only one kind of communicative interaction in bargaining sessions. As Chapter 1 explains, a major function of communication is the creation of "realities" that guide and constrain further communication. But "realities" are constantly changing throughout processes of communicative interaction. These processes – and the way in which "history" is defined and redefined through communication – are illustrated in the following case study of bargaining between teachers and the school board in a small rural, Midwestern district. It is based on the research of Linda Putnam and her associates, and is one of the few studies that provides a detailed account of the negotiations and the interactions that occurred during and around them.[1]

The state teachers association provided the 133 teachers with a professional bargainer, Doug. The school board hired its own professional negotiator. Usually teacher bargaining (and most formal labor–management negotiation) is limited to an exchange of offers related to money (salaries and fringe benefits) versus teacher control over working conditions. The teachers' "reality–creation" process involved three stories (see Chapter 5). One story was about "the bad old days" of bargaining. For years, the two sides had engaged in hostile bargaining: long and heated arguments over rules of negotiation, threats, fist pounding, name calling, and refusals to settle had dominated yearly discussions. One year, the two sides' initial offers were thinly veiled insults: The board offered a $1 raise, and the teachers demanded a 25 percent increase. Four years ago, the hostility erupted into a strike. This story affected how they viewed the current negotiations.

The townspeople supported the teachers – telephoning board members at home and insulting and haranguing them as they walked down the streets. But the story the teachers told one another was about the immaturity that they had shown during the strike. They prided themselves in their newfound maturity, which essentially meant that they would cooperate with the board and do everything possible to avoid another strike. Their reasoning was simple and self-fulfilling: We must avoid antagonistic bargaining because it could result in a strike, which is unacceptable because it would show that we are immature bargainers. Because we have matured we will not strike. Of course, accepting this story and forgoing a strike in the present eliminated the only threat the teachers had; but it created a comfortable reality that would guide and constrain their communication.

The second story was about Doug. He had started working with the teachers during the strike, and although no one remembered exactly what he did to achieve it, he negotiated an acceptable settlement. Telling this story reinforced the teachers' trust for Doug and led them to accept his goals, strategies, and decisions throughout the negotiation. Doug told the third story. He had faced Jim, the board's pro, many times in the past and found him to be "a bear" on power issues – he just would not give in on these issues. The teachers adapted the story and applied it to their board. One said, "It'll be a cold day in hell before that board will give us any policy issues (control)." The fact that Doug failed to tell them that their district was far behind the other districts in the state in terms of teacher control of working conditions added to the power of the story. So the teachers decided to introduce issues related to control of work, but to drop them early during the bargaining. Unfortunately, the "reality" they had created was inaccurate. Jim had advised the board to be ready to give up some policy issues to minimize financial costs in the new contract. In fact, the board was surprised when Doug dropped these items; but of course it had no reason to say so.

The teachers told and retold these three stories throughout the bargaining session. They asked for, and thus received, less than they could have gotten. But they communicated in a way that maintained the reality that they had created – they behaved maturely, reached an acceptable settlement (70–75 percent of the teachers supported the final contract), and avoided a strike. Of course, if you consider only the offers they made and accepted, they took a very soft bargaining position. But they compensated for that kind of softness through a ritual that proved they were tough negotiators. Negotiations regularly continued night after night, extending into the early morning hours. The bargaining team even enjoyed going to breakfast together after a long night of negotiations, arriving at school just in time to go to class. This ritual, repeated every year, proved to the negotiators and the other teachers that their representatives were tough bargainers.

(Sometimes late-night negotiations are more than ritual. Charley Conrad once was on a teacher bargaining committee that stayed late to exhaust the opposition. The teachers enlarged the committee so that no single member had to attend more than one late-night meeting, knowing that the school board did not have this flexibility. After five weeks of negotiating, when rumor had it that four board members were on the verge of divorce, the teachers obtained what they wanted: the transfer of a much-hated principal, and the largest salary increase in the district's history. But that was a different situation, and a very different "reality.")

Applying What You've Learned

1. What conflict strategies did the parties apply in this negotiation? How did they work out?
2. How did the parties' definitions of "reality" influence communication? The relative power of the bargainers?
3. In this situation, could an individual teacher or member have argued successfully for taking a tougher negotiating position?

Questions to Think About and Discuss

1. What functions did the "staying-all-night" ritual play in addition to demonstrating toughness?
2. What long-term effects is this negotiation likely to have on the teachers' perceptions of reality? Doug's image and role? the board's negotiating strategies? the outcomes of subsequent negotiations?

Note

1 This case draws on results reported in Putnam and Van Hoeven (1986, 1987); Putnam, Van Hoeven, and Bullis (1991); and Putnam (1987).

The Aftermath The final phase is the **aftermath** of the conflict. Two criteria are appropriate for evaluating the short-term effects of conflicts: the quality of the final decision and the effect of the conflict on relationships among parties. If a sensible solution emerges that meets the needs of every party or is supported by a legitimate consensus, the short-term effects will be positive. However, such integrative solutions are difficult to attain, and consensus is often elusive. In fact, in many cases a conflict will move from issue to issue with no real resolution. When new issues arise, the same patterns of communicative interaction recur.

The more common modes of managing conflicts in organizational settings – compromise, majority vote (when it involves coercion of the minority by procedure), or accommodation – leave residual frustrations that may prompt future conflicts and complicate their management. Similarly, the dynamics of conflict episodes may leave behind changed perceptions of each party, unmanaged emotions, and thoughts of revenge, all of which influence relationships. Repeated, escalating conflicts may lead employees to view their relationships with one another as competitive rather than cooperative. Because their tasks are interdependent, competitive relationships may undermine the participants' performance and the organization's success (Roloff and Miller, 2006).

This potential for long-term negative effects on relationships has led many organizations to use formal procedures and make structural changes to minimize the impact of unproductive conflicts. Some have tried to reduce unit or employee interdependence, both to minimize the number of issues over which differences might occur and to decrease the adverse effects of long-term relational problems. But interdependence cannot be reduced beyond a certain point, and when it is reduced, the parties' incentives to cooperate with one another are also reduced. Other organizations create formal conflict managers or formal procedures for handling even minor disagreements. Third-party interventions *can* prevent escalation, as long as the third party is skilled in conflict management and has sufficient formal power (Bush and Folger, 1994; Putnam and

Kolb, 2000). Formal rules and procedures can structure conflicts in ways that reduce ambiguity and prevent the use of the communication strategies that prompt escalation. Although there are limits to the effectiveness of structural changes, their use accents the need to evaluate the productiveness of each episode within the long-term perspective of the organization's operation.

Conflicts can be valuable and productive for organizations and employees alike. For organizations, conflict can stimulate creative problem solving; it can generate or publicize superior ideas and adjust perceived power relationships to better fit the skills and abilities of employees. For individual employees, conflict can provide opportunities to test, expand, and demonstrate their skills; better understand their organizations; and develop their self-esteem and confidence. If conflicts are kept within civil bounds and if satisfactory solutions to problems can be found, the total impact of each conflict can be positive.

Two implications emerge from the preceding discussion. First, organizational conflicts must be evaluated in terms of many considerations. Open conflicts are invariably disruptive and leave behind negative legacies. But their impact on the long-term effectiveness of the organization may on balance be favorable. Attempting to suppress or repress conflicts often damages organizations more than allowing them to surface and be managed. Second, controlling processes of escalation is the key to productive conflict management. The aftermath of organizational conflicts depends on maintaining patterns of communication that simultaneously allow people to demonstrate their competencies and solve problems. Escalation robs the participants of these opportunities and establishes the bases of non-productive legacies. The strategic use of communication is the key to productive conflict management.

Organizational Dispute Resolution Systems

Conflict is so common in organizations that they often develop characteristic procedures or structures for handling it (Cooper, Nolan, and Bales, 2005; Lipsky, Seeber, and Fincher, 2003). Ury, Brett, and Goldberg (1988) argue that the structure and culture of organizations influence the development of their **dispute resolution systems**, their preferred ways of managing conflicts.[11] Some organizations have formally established dispute resolution systems, such as a grievance procedure or a mediation program. For example, the Farm Service Agency of the US Department of Agriculture has had a dispute resolution system in place since 1999.[12] Other organizations rely on informal dispute management systems, such as letting it fall to managers to handle conflicts. Some dispute resolution systems, such as the courts or community mediation services, are provided by the government or the larger community.

Three types of dispute management systems can be distinguished in US organizations. Interest-based dispute resolution systems attempt to help parties find a resolution that satisfies their needs or interests. One example of a formal interest based system is the dispute mediation services that are increasingly being implemented in large organizations. For example, the University of Michigan has an Office of Dispute Mediation where parties can file formal cases that go through a multistep conflict management procedure. Interest-based systems tend to favor the problem-solving and compromising styles.

Rights-based dispute resolution systems attempt to establish which party's position is more valid based on independent standards that parties accept as legitimate and fair. The legal code is one such standard. Another type of standard is a socially accepted norm, such as seniority or equity. The most familiar rights-based dispute resolution system is the courts of law, in which a judge or jury determines the correct outcome based on arguments and evidence from the parties. Participating in this system requires the assistance of an attorney, because its procedures are so technical and complex. However, a manager who stops an argument over a new computer between two employees by giving it to the more senior employee is also engaged in rights-based dispute resolution. Rights-based dispute resolution systems tend to promote competitive and compromise conflict strategies. Parties make their best cases to the adjudicator – whether judge, parent, or manager – and rely on him or her to make the call. And if parties are fearful that the decision will not go their way, they may reach a side agreement before the rights-based adjudication is final.

In power-based dispute resolution systems parties attempt to coerce the other into doing what they want. Examples of power-based dispute resolution are strikes by workers and lockouts by employers, a manager ordering an employee to do a task the employee finds unpleasant, and one employee browbeating another into doing what he wants. Power-based dispute resolution tends to occur in the absence of interest- and rights-based systems. It is the "default" mode of dispute resolution in most organizations. In power-based systems competing, avoiding, and accommodating styles are most common.

The three dispute resolution systems are not necessarily independent of one another. Rights-based systems often evolve to correct for the problems and abuses of power-based systems. For example, the labor mediation system evolved because of the damage caused by strikes and labor–management conflict. Interest-based dispute resolution systems are often established as alternatives or supplements to rights-based systems. Today mediation is commonly offered as an alternative to trial in divorce courts, on the grounds that it offers both parties a chance to satisfy their interests, while a judge's or jury's decision may favor the interests of one side over the other.

Ury, Brett, and Goldberg's (1988) research suggested that in most organizations the majority of conflicts are handled through power-based approaches, a goodly portion through rights-based approaches, and the least number through interest-based approaches. In organizations that do not have formal interest-based systems or organizational cultures that encourage interest-based approaches, power-based and rights-based conflict management will prevail. Even in organizations with formal dispute resolution systems, power-based approaches are common. Parties may fear being labeled as a troublemaker if they formally complain or as incompetent for not being able to manage their own affairs. Those with power may avoid formal systems because they believe they can get their way in any case and that the formal system may not decide in their favor.

Most dispute resolution scholars recommend that organizations try to change organizations so that they manage most of their conflicts using interest based approaches. This may require not only establishing a formal dispute resolution system based on problem solving, but also changing the organization's culture and employee attitudes. Organizational dispute resolution practices generally develop gradually over the years and are grounded in deep-seated habits of thought and action.

For example, Bryant High School in Oakland, California, implemented a mediation program to help students manage conflicts more constructively. Tension and violence among students and between students and teachers were growing increasingly common at Bryant, and its administration decided to implement the mediation program to defuse a potentially dangerous situation. A major barrier to the success of the mediation program was lack of communication, negotiation, and problem-solving skills among students. One student put it this way, "All I ever wanted to do was fight. If some said something to me I didn't like, I didn't think about talking, I just thought about fighting" (Ury *et al.*, 1988, 34). To change the situation, the school undertook a major training effort, providing workshops and classes in problem-solving and nonviolence techniques to more than 3000 students and staff. The workshops were designed to develop attitudes and skills that promoted nonviolent dispute resolution. After several years of training and demonstration projects, the mediation program was successfully implemented. It is used to manage a significant number of conflicts, and violence has been reduced at Bryant.

A Feminist View of Communication and Conflict

Linda Putnam and Deborah M. Kolb (2000) articulated a view of conflict and negotiation that represents a significant departure from the approach to conflict taken so far in this chapter. Traditional perspectives on negotiation and conflict management rest on a limited set of taken-for-granted assumptions about the nature of conflict, negotiation, and conflict management. This set of assumptions and related understandings reflects the predominant perspective in the United States and Western Europe. It underlies almost all the hundreds of studies and books that have been published on conflict in the past 40 years. Those assumptions are as follows:

1. The goals of parties in conflict is mutual gain that helps them achieve their interests.
2. Conflicts are best managed through setting up conditions whereby parties can make tradeoffs that enable them to realize their goals. The ultimate outcomes of conflicts should be assessed in terms of winning and losing, with the preferred outcome being win–win results (i.e. all parties gain).
3. Relationships between parties in conflicts are seen in terms of one party related to another with different interests. Parties view each other instrumentally, in terms of how they are either a barrier against or means for achieving their goals. Trust, which refers to the degree to which parties uphold their agreed upon bargains, is a critical dimension of relationships.
4. Conflict management and negotiation occurs in the form of proposals and counter-proposals, with each side suggesting courses of action that benefit their own interests. The conflict is regarded as a problem that must be solved by parties or third parties brought in to help them reach an acceptable resolution.
5. Communication in conflicts functions largely to exchange information about parties' positions and interests that can be used to develop a final solution. Communication should play a largely informational role in effective conflict management and should not inflame the situation by injecting counterproductive emotions.

However, like all accepted assumptions, this frame automatically excludes other legitimate perspectives. Based on feminist perspectives, Putnam and Kolb argue that the goal of conflict management and negotiation can be more than achieving a mutually beneficial outcome in the short term. It also can transform a situation so that parties understand themselves and their world better and develop stronger relationships for the long term. This alternative view criticizes the traditional perspective on conflict for its short-sighted and overly narrow focus on satisfying immediate interests. Instead, the alternative view would advocate that the entire point of engaging in conflict and negotiation is not simply to fulfill immediate needs, but to work toward a better life. Focus on immediate needs may in fact detract from bettering oneself.

For example, in the "bargaining case" introduced previously, the negotiators took a traditional approach to their conflict, assuming that it had to be settled in terms of a contract that addressed the issues that the parties thought important. Doug and Jim worked out a contract that resulted in a mutually acceptable solution. However, as the case shows, the stories the teachers told themselves led them finally to obtain less than they might have. Consider what might have happened if the parties had taken the alternative view offered here: They would not have focused on immediate, concrete issues, but rather on the nature of the relationship between teachers and the board. Both parties would have entered the negotiation interested in improving their relationship and in understanding the best ways to educate children. This would have eventually led the discussion to the degree of control teachers should have over working conditions. Teachers would likely have argued that they needed more control over their work to have the flexibility needed to meet student needs. The board would have had to face the hard fact that though keeping control was comfortable for them, the degree of control they had was probably too great. The end result might have been that the board granted the teachers more control, and that the teachers in turn would have increased respect for the board for giving up something that gave it a clear advantage. This admittedly hypothetical discussion could not have occurred if the parties had restricted themselves to talking about issues only, because control over work would be reduced to an issue – recall that this is exactly how Doug had treated it – and therefore as something to trade away or win rather than discuss.

The longer-term, more general goals of the alternative perspective imply that the ultimate end of negotiation is not a settlement of immediate issues, but instead transformation of the situation and the people in it. Conflict and negotiation aim to transform the situation by creating new understandings and new ways for members to work together. It aims to transform the parties by giving them insights into themselves, into how they are contributing to the conflict and how they might change to improve the situation and also deeper insights that help them live their lives better. The emphasis shifts from winning and losing to how to develop actions that parties can undertake together to a new level of collaboration. It also assumes that there may be no fundamentally opposed interests, in the sense that novel, transforming actions may allow seemingly different interests to be reconciled. In our hypothetical extension of the bargaining case, this is exactly what would happen. Through open discussion, parties come to understand each other better and see the situation differently. The result was that the board of its own accord would give up some of its power, thus fundamentally transforming how education occurred in the district. It would also fundamentally transform and build the relationship between teachers and board.

In the bargaining case, the board and teachers – through their intermediary bargainers Doug and Jim – viewed each other in instrumental terms. Each viewed the other as someone who could be convinced or enticed to give in on one or more issues of interest, or, if the worst happened, as a barrier to achieving their ends. Trust had been achieved between Doug and Jim, but it was not a trust based on appreciation of each other and on the importance of the relationship between board and teachers; instead, trust was based on living up to prior commitments on issues and on a contract hammered out in the negotiations. On the alternative view of conflict, the board and teachers would try to understand each other's motivations and needs, not with an aim of finding out what sort of offer to make, but with true concern for the other as someone each had a long-term relationship with. Their communication would not aim at finding points of agreement, but of understanding the other and with figuring out how to improve the current situation and relationship. This could then be the basis for future cooperation that went well beyond the immediate contract negotiations.

Conflict management and negotiation are viewed as problem-solving processes in the traditional perspective: Each side has to define the requirements for a good solution, and these then constitute a problem that the sides have to solve by finding a course of action that meets the requirements. The alternative perspective would not give problem solving primacy, but rather dialogue between the parties whereby they communicate with the goal of achieving understanding and transformation. This communication might take the form of a deep "I and thou" discussion in which parties bare their souls, but it could also be more restrained as parties regard their counterpart as other and try to appreciate this other from their own point of view. Once effective communication has been established, the best course of joint action might simply suggest itself in the flow of discussion. Problem solving would be reserved for jointly defined issues that did not have readily apparent solutions.

In the bargaining case, the teachers and the board might have promoted communication by demoting (in a sense) their professional bargainers to one of a team of people who met in an open communication forum to simply discuss their points of view. The goal of this forum would be to understand, not to solve things or define problems, or any other instrumental goal. Simple understanding is the goal, and it is expected that this understanding will lead to sympathetic interactions that generate joint actions endorsed by all parties.

The alternative, **feminist view of conflict** is fundamentally different from the confrontive, problem-oriented "Let's-make-a-deal" traditional approach. In fact, it is so different that it may seem Utopian in a world full of hard bargainers. However, traditional strategies often fail. Instead of leading to mutually acceptable outcomes, they often produce conflict situations that are increasingly difficult to resolve. The intransigence and polarization that results often has disastrous consequences for organizations and for their employees. Perhaps a different perspective is needed, one that would not make it more difficult to manage conflicts by restricting the flexibility of negotiators. Unfortunately, the traditional perspective is so deeply imbedded in the political, societal, and legal context surrounding organizations that it is difficult to implement or even to imagine any alternative. But in an era of globalization, where alternative forms of organizing are rapidly emerging, alternative forms of conflict management may be viable. For example, the alternative perspective seems particularly well suited for the network strategies of organizing described in Chapter 6. In these organizations, open communication and the establishment of long-term relationships is of fundamental importance. In view of the complexity of their structures and how often they must change them, network organizations are best coordinated in exactly the sort of communicative exchanges that the alternative model envisions. This enables them to continuously improve and address the actual, often ill-defined problems the network encounters, rather than simply react to well-defined issues handed down from previous groups and leaders.

Summary: Communication and Conflict

Conflicts are inevitable parts of organizational life. Whenever people depend on one another and interact with one another, grounds for cooperation and competition exist.

Although there is substantial evidence that it is counterproductive to try to avoid or suppress conflicts, especially in the long term, our fear of conflict escalation and the accepted assumptions of some organizational cultures make it difficult to deal with conflicts openly and productively. Fortunately, a wide variety of communicative strategies are available to employees before and during overt conflicts. Understanding those strategies and using them *strategically* determines whether a particular conflict will be productive or destructive.

CONCLUSION

Organizational decision making and conflict management involve the pursuit of impossible dreams. The longstanding ideal of decision making – perfect rationality – is extremely difficult to attain. Individual, group, and organizational limitations set up powerful barriers to rational decision making. The ideal goal of conflict management – a resolution that meets the needs of all parties – is equally difficult. Individual tendencies, unfortunate framings, preexisting power relations, and lack of imagination work against problem solving. In both cases, our organizations rarely live up to expectations.

What then, should we do? Some would argue that we should be realistic and set our sights on other goals – to make decisions that are good enough and make adjustments later on, or to resolve conflicts in ways that enable us to go on with our work and lives. Others would argue that, despite the fact that these goals are rarely realized, they still represent worthy targets we should strive for.

What do you think?

NOTES

1 The first two quotations are drawn from Tripp (1970, 141). The third is from Coser (1956).

2 There is debate concerning whether these biases represent errors or, instead, simply tendencies that sometimes benefit people and sometimes lead to problems. For example, focusing on immediate gain can be beneficial because it helps people meet urgent needs. It is only if negative long-term consequences emerge (and they do not always result) that this "bias" is harmful. Adherents of the classical rational model tend to regard biases as errors, while other analysts challenge this (Jungermann, 2003).

3 This survey is based on Hirokawa and Poole (1996), Hirokawa and Salazar (1999), and Poole and Dobosh (2009).

4 The description of decision making in this section draws on Mintzberg's (1979) classic description of organizational decision making and Weick's (2000) analysis of organizational sense making. Both these sources recognize the complexity of the decision process. Some major points from both works are discussed in Poole and Ahmed (2008).

5 For a revision of the original garbage can model, see Masuch and LaPotin (1989).

6 This example is based on George Farris (1981).

7 Of course, our brief summary oversimplifies Meyer's research. See Meyer (1984). Karl Weick takes an even more explicit position, concluding that a search for "accurate" conclusions sacrifices commitment and motivation (1995, 60).

8 Also see Cohen and March (1974). Harrison Trice and Janice Beyer (1993) take an even more direct position, arguing that rationality is *the* core assumption of organizations in Western societies, including the United States. See especially Trice and Beyer (1993, chap. 2).

9 This section is based primarily on four sources: Pondy (1967), Putnam and Kolb (2000), Oetzel and Ting-Toomey (2006), and Folger, Poole, and Stutman (2011).

10 See Folger *et al.* (2011, chap. 4) for discussions of variants of avoidant and confrontive strategies and tactics.

11 Alternative dispute resolution (ADR) is a growing field as evidenced by numerous websites on the subject and professional associations devoted to ADR. An internet search on this topic will yield hundreds of organizations and programs devoted to ADR.

12 See US Department of Agriculture (2008).

REFERENCES

Axelrod, R. (1984). *The Evolution of Cooperation*. New York: Basic Books.

Barley, S. and Knight, D. B. (1992). "Towards a Cultural Theory of Stress Complaints." *Research in Organizational Behavior* 14: 1–48.

Barstow, D. (2010). "Deepwater Horizon's Final Hours: Missed Signals. Indecision. Failed Defenses. Acts of Valor." *New York Times*, December 26, sec. A: 1, 26–29.

Baumard, P. (1999). *Tacit Knowledge in Organizations*. London: Sage.

Bazerman, M.H. and Watkins, M.D. (2004). *Predictable Surprises: The Disasters You Should Have Seen Coming and How to Prevent Them*. Cambridge, MA: Harvard Business School Press.

Bush, D. F. (1983). "Passive-aggressive Behavior in the Business Setting," in Parsons and Wicks, eds., *Passive-Aggressiveness*. New York: Brunner-Mazel.

Bush, R.B. and Folger, J.P. (1994). *The Promise of Mediation: Responding to Conflict Through Empowerment and Recognition*. San Francisco: Jossey-Bass.

Canary, D. and Spitzberg, B. (1990). "A Model of the Perceived Competence of Conflict Strategies." *Human Communication Research* 15: 630–649.

Caughlin, J.P. and Vangelisti, A.L. (2006). "Conflict in Dating and Marital Relationships," in Oetzel and Ting-Toomey, eds., *The Sage Handbook of Conflict Communication: Integrating Theory, Research, and Practice*. Thousand Oaks, CA: Sage.

Chandrasekaran, R. (2006). *Imperial Life in the Emerald City: Inside Iraq's Green Zone*. New York: Vintage Books.

Cohen, M. and March, J.G. (1974). *Leadership and Ambiguity*, 2nd ed. Boston: Harvard Business School Press.

Cohen, M., March, J. and Olson, J. (1972). "A Garbage-can Model of Organizational Choice." *Administrative Science Quarterly* 17: 1–25.

Connolly, T. Arkes, H.R. and Hammond, K.R. (2003). *Judgment and Decision Making*, 2nd ed. Cambridge: Cambridge University Press.

Cooper, L.J., Nolan, D.R. and Bales, R.A. (2005). *ADR in the Workplace*. St. Paul, MN: West.

Coser, L.A. (1956). *The Functions of Social Conflict*. Glencoe, IL: Free Press.

Donohue, W. and Kolt, R. (1992). *Managing Interpersonal Conflict*. Newbury Park, CA: Sage.

Farris, G. (1981). "Groups and the Informal Organization," in Payne and Cooper, eds., *Groups at Work*. New York: John Wiley.

Feldman, M.S. and March, J.G. (1981). "Information in Organizations as Signal and Symbol." *Administrative Science Quarterly* 26: 171–186.

Folger, J.P., Poole, M.S. and Stutman R. (2011). *Working Through Conflict*, 7th ed. New York: Longman.

Gastil, J. (2010). *The Group in Society*. Los Angeles: Sage.

Gigerenzer, G., Todd, P.M. and the ABC Group. (1999). *Simple Heuristics That Make Us Smart*. New York: Oxford University Press.

Gouran, D. and Hirokawa, R. (1996). "Functional Theory and Communication in Decision-Making and Problem-Solving Groups: An Expanded Perspective," in Hirokawa and Poole, eds., *Communication and Group Decision Making*, 2nd ed. Thousand Oaks, CA: Sage.

Hickson, D.J., Butler, R.J., Cray, D., Mallory, G.R. and Wilson, D.C. (1986). *Top Decisions: Strategic Decision-Making in Organizations*. San Francisco: Jossey-Bass.

Hirokawa, R.Y. and Poole, M.S., eds. (1996). *Communication and Group Decision Making*, 2nd ed. Thousand Oaks, CA: Sage.

Hirokawa, R.Y. and Salazar, A.J. (1999). "Task-Group Communication and Decision-Making Performance," in Frey, Gouran and Poole, eds., *Handbook of Group Communication Theory and Research*. Newbury Park, CA: Sage.

Janis, I.L. (1982). *Groupthink: Psychological Studies of Policy Decisions and Fiascoes*, 2nd ed. New York: Houghton Mifflin

Jungermann, H. (2003). "The Two Camps on Rationality," in Connolly, Arkes and Hammond, eds., *Judgment and Decision Making*, 2nd ed. Cambridge: Cambridge University Press.

Keith, W.M. (2007). *Democracy as Discussion: Civic Education and the American Forum Movement*. Lanham, MA: Lexington.

Kolb, D. and Bartunek, J., eds. (1992). *Hidden Conflict in Organizations*. Newbury Park, CA: Sage.

Lindblom, C. (1959). "The Science of Muddling Through." *Public Administration Review* 19: 412–421.

Lipksy, D.B., Seeber, R.L. and Fincher, R.D. (2003). *Emerging Systems for Managing Workplace Conflict: Lessons From American Corporations for Managers and Dispute Resolution Professionals*. San Francisco: Jossey-Bass.

March, J. (1970). "The Technology of Foolishness," in March and Olson, eds., *Ambiguity and Choice in Organizations*. Bergen, Norway: Universitetsforlaget.

March, J. and Olson, J. (1970). *Ambiguity and Choice in Organizations*. Bergen, Norway: Universitetsforlaget.

March, J. and Simon, H. (1965). "The Concept of Rationality," in Singer, ed., *Human Behavior and International Politics*. Chicago: Rand-McNally.

Masuch, M. and LaPotin, P. (1989). "Beyond Garbage Cans." *Administrative Science Quarterly* 34: 38–68.

Mattson, M., Clair, R.P., Chapman Sanger, P.S. and Kunkel, A.D. (2000). "A Feminist Reframing of Stress," in Buzzanell, ed., *Rethinking Managerial and Organizational Communication From Feminist Perspectives*. Thousand Oaks, CA: Sage.

McPhee, R.D. and Zaug, P. (2009). "The Communicative Constitution of Organizations: A Framework for Explanation," in Putnam and Nicotera, eds., *Building Theories of Organization: The Constitutive Role of Communication*. New York: Routledge.

Messman, S.J. and Canary, D.J. (1998). "Patterns of Conflict in Personal Relationships," in Spitzberg and Cupach, eds., *The Dark Side of Interpersonal Relationships*. Mahwah, NJ: Lawrence Erlbaum.

Meyer, A. (1984). "Mingling Decision-Making Metaphors." *Academy of Management Review* 9: 231–246.

Meyerson, D. (1991). "'Normal' Ambiguity?" in Frost *et al.*, eds., *Reframing Organizational Culture*. Newbury Park, CA: Sage.

Meyerson, D. (1994). "Interpretations of Stress in Institutions." *Administrative Science Quarterly* 39: 628–653.

Miller, K. (2009). *Organizational Communication: Approaches and Processes*, 5th ed. Belmont, CA: Wadsworth.

Mintzberg, H. (1979). *The Structuring of Organizations: A Synthesis of the Research*. Englewood Cliffs, NJ: Prentice Hall.

Mintzberg, H. and McHugh, A. (1985). "Strategy Formation in an Adhocracy." *Administrative Science Quarterly* 30: 160–197.

Morgensen, G. (2008). "How the Thundering Herd Faltered and Fell: Merrill Lynch Couldn't Escape the Housing Crash." *New York Times*, November 9, bus. sec., 1, 9.

Neale, M.A. and Bazerman, M.H. (1983). "The Role of Perspective Taking Ability in Negotiating Under Different Forms of Arbitration." *Journal of Applied Social Psychology* 13: 45–65.

Neale, M. and Bazerman, M. (1991). *Cognition and Rationality in Negotiations*. New York: Free Press.

Nutt, P.C. (2002). *Why Decisions Fail: Avoiding the Blunders and Traps That Lead to Debacles*. San Francisco: Berrett-Koehler.

O'Connor, E. (1997). "Discourse at Our Disposal." *Management Communication Quarterly* 10: 395–432.

Oetzel, J.G. and Ting-Toomey, S., eds. (2006). *The Sage Handbook of Conflict Communication: Integrating Theory, Research, and Practice*. Thousand Oaks, CA: Sage.

Oliver, D. and Roos, J. (2005). "Decision Making in High Velocity Environments: The Importance of Guiding Principles." *Organization Studies* 26(6): 889–913.

O'Reilly, C. (1982). "Variations in Decision makers' Use of Information Sources." *Academy of Management Journal* 25: 756–771.

Peters, T. and Austin, N. (1985). *A Passion for Excellence*. New York: Random House.

Polkinghorne, D.E. (1988). *Narrative Knowing and the Human Sciences*. Albany, NY: State University of New York Press.

Pondy, L. (1967). "Organizational Conflict: Concepts and Models." *Administrative Science Quarterly* 12: 296–320.

Poole, M.S. and Ahmed, I. (2008). "Organizational Decision Making." In Donsbach, ed., *Blackwell Encyclopedia of Communication*, vol. 3. Oxford: Blackwell.

Poole, M.S. and Baldwin, C. (1996). "Developmental Processes in Group Decision-Making," in Hirokawa and Poole, eds., *Communication and Group Decision Making*, 2nd ed. Thousand Oaks, CA: Sage.

Poole, M.S. and Dobosh, M. (2009). "Group Decision-Making," in Berger, Roloff and Roskos-Ewaldsen, eds., *Handbook of Communication Science*, 2nd ed. Thousand Oaks, CA: Sage.

Putnam, L.L. (1987). "Negotiation of Intergroup Conflict in Organizations." Hallie Mande Neff Wilcox Published Lecture. Waco, TX: Baylor University.

Putnam, L.L. (1990). "Reframing Integrative and Distributive Bargaining," in Lewicki, Sheppard and Bazerman, eds., *Research on Negotiation in Organizations*, vol. 2. Greenwich, CT: JAI Press.

Putnam, L.L. and Kolb, D.M. (2000). "Rethinking Negotiation: Feminist View of Communication and Exchange," in Buzzanell, ed., *Rethinking Organizational and Managerial Communication From Feminist Perspectives*. Thousand Oaks, CA: Sage.

Putnam, L.L. and Van Hoeven, S. (1986). "Teacher Bargaining as a Cultural Rite of Conflict Reduction." Paper presented at the Central States Speech Association Convention, Cincinnati, OH, October.

Putnam, L.L. and Van Hoeven, S. (1987). "The Role of Narrative in Teachers' Bargaining." Paper presented at the Temple University Discourse Conference on Conflict Intervention, Philadelphia, PA.

Putnam, L.L. Van Hoeven, S. and Bullis, C. (1991). "The Role of Rituals and Fantasy Themes in Teachers' Bargaining." *Western Journal of Speech Communication* 55: 85–103.

Reimer, T., Kuendig, S., Hoffrage, U., Park, E. and Hinsz, V. (2007). "Effects of Information Environment on Group Discussions and Decisions in the Hidden-Profile Paradigm." *Communication Monographs* 74: 1–28.

Rogan, R.G. (2006). "Conflict Framing Categories." *Communication Quarterly* 54: 157–173.

Rogers, E. (1995). *Diffusion of Innovation*. New York: Free Press.

Roloff, M.E. and Miller, C.W. (2006). "Social Cognition Approaches to Understanding Interpersonal Conflict and Communication," in Oetzel and Ting-Toomey, eds., *The Sage Handbook of Conflict Communication: Integrating Theory, Research, and Practice*. Thousand Oaks, CA: Sage.

Salas, E. and Klein, G. (2001). *Linking Expertise and Naturalistic Decision Making*. Mahwah, NJ: Lawrence Erlbaum.

Schwartzman, H.B. (1989). *The Meeting: Gatherings in Organizations and Communities*. New York: Plenum Press.

Sherif, M., Harvey, O.J., White, B.J., Hood, W.R. and Sherif, C.W. (1961). *Intergroup Conflict and Cooperation: The Robber's Cave Experiment*. Norman, OK: University Book Exchange.

Simon, H.A. (1956). "Rational Choice and the Structure of the Environment." *Psychological Review* 63: 129–138.

Sutcliffe, K. (2000). "Organizational Environments and Organizational Information Processing," in Jablin and Putnam, eds., *The New Handbook of Organizational Communication*. Thousand Oaks, CA: Sage.

Thomas, K.W. and Pondy, L.R. (1977). "Toward an 'Intent' Model of Conflict Management Among Principle Parties." *Human Relations* 30: 1089–1102.

Thompson, L.L. (2008). *Making the Team: A Guide for Managers*, 3rd ed. Upper Saddle River, NJ: Pearson/Prentice Hall.

Ting-Toomey, S. (1985). "Toward a Theory of Conflict and Culture," in Gudykunst, ed., *Communication and Culture*. Beverly Hills, CA: Sage.

Trice, H. and Beyer, J. (1993). *The Cultures of Work Organizations*. Englewood Cliffs, NJ: Prentice Hall.

Tripp, R.T. (1970). *The International Thesaurus of Quotations*. New York: Harper & Row.

Turner, M.E. and Pratkanis, A.R. (1998). "Twenty-Five Years of Groupthink Theory and Research: Lessons From Evaluation of a Theory." *Organizational Behavior and Human Decision Processes* 73: 105–115.

Tversky, A. and Kahneman, D. (2003). "Judgement Under Uncertainty: Heuristics and Biases," in Connolly, Arkes and Hammond, eds., *Judgment and Decision Making*, 2nd ed. Cambridge: Cambridge University Press.

Ury, W.L., Brett, J.M. and Goldberg, S.B. (1988). *Getting Disputes Resolved: Designing Systems to Cut the Costs of Conflict*. San Francisco: Jossey-Bass.

US Department of Agriculture (2008). "Alternative Dispute Resolution." www.apfo.usda.gov/FSA/hrdapp?area=home&subject=labr&topic=adr.

Vodosek, M. and Sutcliffe, K. (2000). "Overemphasis on Analysis," in Quinn *et al.*, eds., *Pressing Problems in Modern Organizations (That Keep Us up at Night)*. New York: AMACOM.

Weick, K. (1979). *The Social Psychology of Organizing*, 2nd ed. Reading, MA: Addison-Wesley.

Weick, K. (1995). *Sense-Making in Organizations*. Thousand Oaks, CA: Sage.

Weick, K. (2000). *Making Sense of the Organization*. New York: Wiley.

Westerlund, G. and Sjostrand, S-E. (1979). *Organizational Myths*. New York: HarperCollins.

Zsambok, C. and Klein, G. (1997). *Naturalistic Decision Making*. New York: Psychology Press.

CHAPTER 9
ORGANIZATIONAL CHANGE

Nothing is permanent save change
Heraclitus

One of the greatest pains to human nature is the pain of a new idea. It . . . makes you think that after all, your favorite notions may be wrong, your firmest beliefs ill-founded. . . . Naturally, therefore, common men hate a new idea, and are disposed more or less to ill-treat the original man [sic] *who brings it.*

Walter Bagehot[1]

CENTRAL THEMES

- Organizational change comes about when an innovation, developed within or outside the organization, is implemented and becomes a routine part of the organization and its operations.
- Innovations diffuse through organizations and society in a gradual process that starts slowly with adoption of the innovation by a few "cutting-edge" individuals or organizations, then slowly gathers momentum as more respected and credible individuals and organizations adopt it and are followed by the greater mass of adopters, which rapidly accelerates adoption.
- An individual's decision to adopt an innovation occurs in a series of five stages that starts with awareness and knowledge about the innovation and concludes with confirmation and continued use.

Strategic Organizational Communication: In a Global Economy, Seventh Edition.
Charles Conrad and Marshall Scott Poole.

- Adoption of an innovation by an organization is more complex than individual decisions to adopt and also includes the need to adapt the innovation to the organization and to build coalitions in support of the change.
- Whether an innovation will be adopted depends on characteristics of the innovation itself, the organization's external communication system, institutional pressures, and the actions taken by change agents.
- Effective implementation of organizational change requires change agents to involve stakeholders, those with a stake in the change.
- Stakeholders can be involved in at least four ways, by participating in the core change team, by participating in task forces focused on specific issues related to the change, through input and feedback meetings, and through information dissemination.
- There are a number of different general strategies for implementing change and those that emphasize participation and control by stakeholders tend to be most effective.
- Sense making and storytelling are two communication processes that influence implementation of organizational change.
- The strategies chosen for communicating with stakeholders during organizational change will differ depending on the need for efficiency and need to build consensus perceived by change agents.
- Change has come to be valued for its own sake and it is important to deliberate about substantive reasons for change before setting forth on a change campaign.

KEY TERMS

innovation
diffusion
adoption
implementation
discontinuation
routinization
reinvention
relative advantage
compatibility
complexity
trialability
observability
two step flow model
change agent
champion
uniformity
fidelity
stakeholders
edict implementation strategy
persuasion implementation strategy
intervention implementation strategy
participation implementation strategy
uncertainty
equivocality
sense making
storytelling
equal dissemination
equal participation
quid pro quo
need to know
marketing
reactionary strategy

In Chapter 2 we noted that the situation facing today's organizations is more complex, more dynamic, and more uncertain than ever. Globalization, diversification, and acceleration of technological change have intensified the pressure on organizations to change and to adapt in order to meet ever-changing demands. Modern organizations often hear the echo of words spoken by Greek philosopher Heraclitus 2500 years ago that head this chapter.

Ralph Katz (2004), longtime scholar of organizational change, observed that today's organizations "are faced with the challenges of 'dualism,' that is, operating efficiently in the present while innovating effectively for the future" (xiii). Managing this dualism makes organizational change difficult. The need to remain efficient and effective in the present (not to mention vested interests that benefit from the status quo) creates resistance to change. The future is always uncertain and the prospect of change raises questions and doubts. Yet not to change often brings disaster to organizations and to society. The British Petroleum (BP) Deepwater Horizon disaster in the summer of 2010 can be traced in part by the unwillingness of those who managed and maintained the oil rig to change existing approaches that were profitable for them and to adopt more expensive (in the short run) state-of-the-art safety standards.

Addressing the tensions involved in organizational change requires us to be innovative and steadfast simultaneously. Creativity and innovation are vital in order to craft an effective response to demands for change. Steadfastness is essential because change takes time. Changing an organization requires lengthy design and implementation processes, it often arouses opposition, and it causes dislocations that may be painful for members of the organization and for the communities it affects. As this chapter will show a steady and inclusive approach is the hallmark of effective change efforts.

At the outset, we should sort out some terminology. The terms innovation, adoption, implementation, and diffusion of changes are often used interchangeably. However, we will distinguish them based upon a model of organizational change devised by Laurie Lewis (2011) and shown in Figure 9.1. Organizational change occurs through the adoption of innovations which are then implemented in the organization.

Innovation refers to the creative process of generating ideas for practice. It may sometimes occur within the organization, but the vast majority of innovations that organizations adopt and implement come from outside. For example, the quality improvement processes that revolutionized manufacturing during the late twentieth century were developed in Japan as that country rebuilt its industries after World War II. During the 1950s, Japanese manufacturers were known for producing cheap, but shoddy goods.[2] The label "Made in Japan" was a term of derision during the early 1960s, used to refer to anything cheap and easily breakable. In the late 1950s and the 1960s, Japanese companies like Toyota brought in quality control engineers like William Deming from the United States to advise them on how their manufacturing could become competitive with the rest of the world (Cole and Scott, 2000). Deming and his colleagues had had little success persuading US firms to adopt their techniques. However, the Japanese companies embraced them and adapted them to everyday manufacturing practices. When high-quality Japanese cars, electronics, and appliances burst upon the world market in the 1970s, it was because of Japanese manufacturers' emphasis on continuous quality improvement.

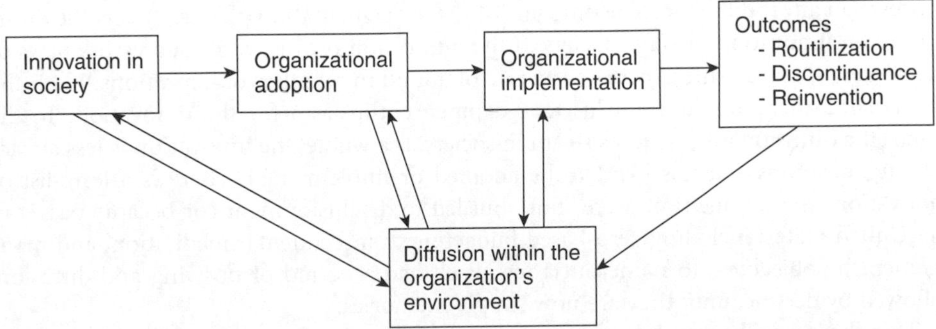

Figure 9.1 Relationships among concepts associated with innovation.

Innovations spread through societies through **diffusion**, "the process involved in sharing new ideas with others to the point that they 'catch on'" (Lewis, 2011, chap. 1). As new ideas diffuse, the organization encounters them and may decide to try them out, that is, to begin the process of **adoption**. Toyota and a few other manufacturers were the innovators of quality improvement practices, and then they diffused to other Japanese firms. As US and European firms perceived the competitive advantage that quality gave Japanese goods, they began to embrace and adapt them to their contexts as well. Today continuous quality improvement in various forms has diffused around the globe.

Once adopted an innovation must be put into practice, or implemented by the organization. **Implementation** is "the translation of any tool or technique, process, or method of doing from knowledge to practice" (Tornatsky and Johnson, 1982, 194). Every organization is different, and so implementation involves adapting the innovation to the specific context of the organization. Chastened by their experience competing against the Japanese in the 1980s, US carmakers and other manufacturers tried to implement Japanese quality improvement methods. Toyota even agreed to set up a joint venture with General Motors, NUMMI, to implement quality manufacturing techniques such as just-in-time inventory and continuous improvement with a US workforce (Adler, 1992). While some aspects of quality manufacturing transferred easily, others did not. Japanese techniques had to be adapted to the US context. Moreover, continuous improvement had to be adapted to different industries. It took one form in the auto industry and another in the health care sector (Blumenthal, 1995).

Successful implementation of an innovation is by no means certain. If the implementation process goes badly, the innovation may be rejected, an outcome termed **discontinuance**. If the implementation process goes well, then the innovation may be incorporated into the everyday working of the organization, that is, it undergoes **routinization**. The checkered history of quality improvement efforts in the United States in the 1980s and 1990s had its share of discontinuances as well as routinizations. Sometimes, however, the innovation must be adjusted in some major ways in order to work or, alternatively, the innovation is used in ways unanticipated by its original developers. When this occurs there has been **reinvention** of the innovation. In the health care sector quality methods imported from industrial contexts often had to be reinvented because of differences in practices and personnel in the two sectors. Doctors and nurses, unlike auto workers, are professionals with their own professional training and codes of conduct, and this necessitated the need to rework quality techniques to fit both the demands of the immediate work and the demands of professional codes (Blumenthal and Scheck, 1995).

Lewis's model also incorporates feedback loops whereby the organizational change process can affect diffusion. The outcome of the implementation process affects the diffusion of an innovation through society. If the innovation proves wildly successful, news of the success spreads, which increases its rate of adoption by other organizations. If, on the other hand, there are failures, this may dampen enthusiasm for the innovation. To the extent the diffusion process loses steam in society as a whole, the innovation is less attractive organizations and less likely to be adopted or implemented. There is a long list of innovations that at one time were "hot," but led to disillusionment (or became passé) in the United States, including zero-based budgeting, transcendental meditation, and management by objectives, to name but a few. Each had a period of upswing and diffusion, followed by decline, until they are now simply memories.

This chapter will cover the elements of organizational change in the order in which the process unfolds. We will start with the sources of innovation and invention. Then we will turn to the adoption process and consider what factors encourage organizations to adopt innovations. Following this we will discuss the implementation process, including how it generally tends to unfold and measures that can be taken to encourage effective implementation of organizational changes.

INNOVATION

The sources of innovation are many. Rogers (2003, chap. 4) argues that most innovations are created because of some recognized need. An agricultural scientist, for example, foresaw a severe shortage of tomatoes in the early 1960s due to suspension of the Mexican visiting farmworkers' program in California. He set out to breed a tomato that could be picked by machine rather than by hand. This led to the square-round and somewhat hard tomatoes that are now common in US stores. (Whether this is a good innovation or a bad one, we will leave to your judgment). In some cases innovation is spurred not by individual recognition, but by statewide or national agendas. The development of safer child car seats and regulations requiring their use was stimulated by such an agenda-setting campaign.

But not all inventions are so deliberate. Some discoveries come from "pure science." Hertz, for example, discovered radio waves based on predictions from earlier scientific theories, and at the time of his discovery there were no practical uses (Nelson and Rosenberg, 1993). We have all experienced firsthand the many practical innovations that have flowed from this discovery. Other innovations are due to serendipity. The famous story of the discovery of penicillin by Alexander Fleming, who was curious as to why his bacteria cultures kept dying unexpectedly, is one example of this. Serendipitous inventions are also developed by ordinary people, not just scientists. As Rogers notes, "SMS (short message service), which transmits short text messages by cellular phones, is thought to have been discovered by Japanese teenagers in the mid-1990s" (Rogers, 2003, 194).

There is evidence that there are "hot spots" for innovation, geographical areas where large number of innovative firms and people are collocated (Kao, 2009). Examples include Silicon Valley for electronics, Southern California for entertainment, Israel for software, Singapore and Boston for biotechnology, and Southern Finland for telecommunications and design. In these hot spots, firms and people interact and stimulate creative thinking and idea development. Some, like Silicon Valley, develop due to the interaction of universities and private industry, while others, like Finland, are driven by strong governmental stewardship.

We tend to think of innovations as "inspirations," and images of inventors like Thomas Edison as a lone genius are common. Edison, however, worked in a laboratory with dozens of assistants, and could not have developed his inventions without a team. Edison tried hundreds of materials as filaments for the light bulb, something that was only possible because of his assistants. Creativity is very often grounded in groups, not a single individual (Sawyer, 2007).

Nor is genius a prerequisite for inspiration. Studies of innovation show that 80 percent of new ideas came from users or customers (von Hippel, 1988). It is a truism among designers that effective innovators are not just close to their customers and users, but to their most demanding customers and users. An effective way to get new ideas is to interact with users and come directly into contact with problems they face and modifications they make in the product or service so it works better for them (the von Hippel study also showed that between 10 and 40 percent of users modify the products that they buy). When the Lego Corporation decided to update their "Lego Mindstorms" robot construction kit, they went to fans of the product and identified four users who were particularly respected in online forums about the kit. They asked these users for advice and had them test prototypes. Eventually Lego increased the size of the test group to 100 users. Since 2006 IBM has invited customers to join their yearly "Innovation Jam," which develops and discusses ideas for new products and services.[3] Box 9.1 summarizes some practices that can enable organizations to promote innovation.

Box 9.1
Organizing for Creativity

Research has generated a number of insights regarding how organizations can encourage creativity and innovation. These guidelines are based on Kanter (1988), Poole and Van de Ven (2004), Sawyer (2007), Schroeder et al. (1986), and Van de Ven, Angle, and Poole (2000).

1. **Give employees time to innovate:** Encourage people to try new projects and support their efforts. 3M, Gore Industries, and Google, for instance, give employees 10–20 percent of their time to work on new ideas and projects that have nothing to do with their regular projects or day-to-day work.
2. **Create a "Department of Surprise":** To take advantage of the ideas that come from keeping many irons in the fire, have one or more units that comb the organization for the best new ideas or projects and choose them to develop further (generally with the collaboration of the originator of the new idea or project). Royal Dutch Shell, for example, has six "GameChanger" teams of six members each that go through the organization and find ideas to commercialize. They have the authority to allocate up to $20 million to develop ideas. Other employees email their ideas to the teams, and the teams meet once per week to sift through the innovations.
3. **Expect failures:** Most new ideas do not pan out, but if one in ten does, you have a success, provided you have enough ideas in the pipeline. It is important not to penalize people who try to innovate and fail. Penalties will discourage them from trying again. Then, too, we learn from failures. Many successful innovations are the product of a series of failed experiments that helped innovators learn what would work.
4. **Build spaces for creative conversation:** These should be designed to attract people, with coffee bars and maybe food.
5. **Allow time for ideas to emerge:** There need to be open spaces in people's time so they can let ideas percolate, daydream, and the like. Creativity studies have shown that open time is essential for the creative process. People are not very creative under pressure.
6. **Manage the risks of improvisation:** There are at least three that have to be taken care of the following: (1) When people are improvising, they must take

time away from planned projects so there must be a balance; (2) improvisation can make it impossible to sustain a central vision and long-term strategy; and (3) too many new ideas may bubble up, so it is important to settle on a few key ones to pursue at any point in time.

7. **Innovation is controversial:** There are often competing ideas, and this competition can spark innovation. There should be arenas for competition in which people know they are competing and on what basis.
8. **Idea generation is encouraged by several factors:** These include (1) close connection to need sources, including customers and stakeholders; (2) cross-fertilization of ideas; (3) broadly defined rather than narrowly specialized jobs; (4) organizational expectations for innovation; (5) gathering together of people rather than isolation; and (6) outreach by units.
9. **Set up structures that encourage creativity and improvisation:** In such structures, there are well-defined departments for key functions such as engineering and security, but then there are project teams with people assigned from these department and the teams and departments constantly communicate with each other. Kanter (1988) found that innovation was enhanced by structural integration in matrix organizations that brought together experts from diverse backgrounds and departments around temporary project teams.
10. **Manage knowledge for innovation:** Transfer knowledge among groups, build knowledge and expertise directories so people know who to turn to for help, and circulate ideas throughout the organization.
11. **Build dense networks:** Members of the organization should engage in intensive interaction (this is encouraged by spaces for interaction). Some examples include the toy company Hasbro, which frequently schedules open meetings to exchange ideas among workers and top management, and Pixar University, in which employees are trained to share ideas. This promotes creative conversations. Characteristics of creative conversations include (a) people practice "deep listening" in which they really listen to others and appreciate others' points of view, (b) they build on one another's ideas, (c) they recognize that only after some time does the meaning of an idea emerge, (d) they ask questions, and (e) there is "psychological safety" where people feel safe to take risks and express themselves
12. **Measure the right things:** This means not measuring inputs or hours spent on projects, but results such as patents, articles, and the achievements of projects. If rewards are based on the right measures – those that assess creativity and innovation – then people have incentives to innovate.

Innovation is only rarely due to one lone person's inspiration. Instead good ideas tend to evolve gradually over time and to build on previous, often unrecognized work. In his book, *Where Good Ideas Come From*, Steven Johnson notes, "We like to think of our ideas as . . . shipped fresh from the factory. In reality they've been cobbled together with spare parts that happened to be sitting in the garage" (Johnson, 2010).

Once an innovation is developed it diffuses through society. Innovations – both genuinely useful ones and "fads and fashions" – spread through a population over time by following a series of stages that represent adoption by different types of people, as shown in Table 9.1. Early in the process there are relatively few adopters, and as time passes the number of adoptions increases steadily and then gradually decreases until only a few people do not adopt. If we think of this in terms of the cumulative number of adopters, we see that the percentage of adopters increases very slowly at first (as shown by the relatively level slope of the S-curve from time 0 to time 1), then it takes off and the proportion of users who adopt the innovation increases rapidly (from time 1 to time 2), and at a certain point, the population is saturated and the rate of increase levels off (past time 2). (See Table 9.1 and Figure 9.2.)

Table 9.1 Categories of Adopters

Adopter category	*Description*	*Total number of adopters (%)*
Innovators	Very early adopters; tend to be different from general populations.	2.5
Early adopters	Innovative individuals who are respected in the community; they have widespread networks and learn about the innovation from the innovators; they are opinion leaders who influence later adopters.	13.5
Early majority	Somewhat more innovative than average; influenced through connections with early adopters.	34
Late majority	Slower on the uptake than early majority members; they require more evidence of effectiveness than earlier adopters; they tend to be conservative.	34
Laggards	Very slow in picking up of the value of the innovation; more conservative than others; may be locked in to earlier arrangements and therefore be reluctant to adopt the innovation.	16

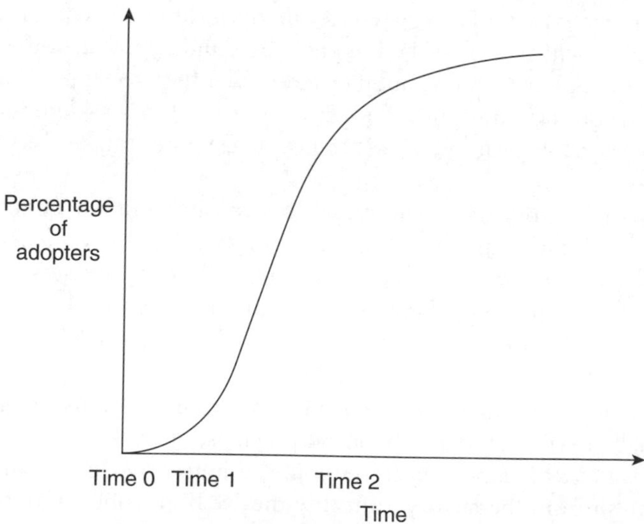

Figure 9.2 The diffusion curve.

Innovation scholars have divided adopters into five groups depending on how long it takes them to adopt an innovation, innovators, early adopters, early majority, the late majority, and laggards.[4] The "innovators" are the earliest 2.5 percent of adopters. They tend to be venturesome types, with a great interest in new ideas. They also tend to have connections to a lot of other people (so they come into contact with a lot of new ideas and things), financial stability (so they can afford new things), and the ability "to understand and apply new technical knowledge."

The next 13.5 percent of adopters are the "early adopters." They tend to be respected by their peers for being "on the ball" when it comes to useful new ideas. They are strongly connected into communities of other potential users and are respected "opinion leaders." They serve as role models for other potential adopters. Following the early adopters is the next 34 percent, the early majority. These people tend to wait to see how an innovation works out before committing themselves. They interact with the early adopters and get reports on how the innovation is working, as well as advice about using it properly.

The "late majority," makes up the next 34 percent of adopters. They tend to be skeptical of new ideas and things and only adopt them when it becomes evident that others are getting an advantage over them by adopting. They tend to give a great deal of weight to the norms in the social system, and once an innovation becomes the norm, they follow it. Finally come the "laggards." They are very traditional and tend to be suspicious of innovations and those who bring them. They tend to value the past and changing to new ways takes a great deal of deliberation.

One might think that innovators would make a great deal of difference in the diffusion of an innovation. However, innovators tend to be different from the rest of those in a social system. So the early majority, late majority, and laggards tend to view them with some skepticism. They are not particularly good models. Instead, the early adopters, who are respected and connected to others in the social system, are the real leaders in the innovation process. Change agents, those who want an innovation to spread, often target early adopters for this reason. If they can persuade the opinion leaders, change agents have their best chance of having an impact on a social system.

The term "laggards" carries negative connotations, and one might think they are a drag on innovation. Marketing scholars Jacob Goldenberg and Saul Oreg (2007) argue otherwise. In areas in which there is rapid technological change, such as portable audio players or computers, laggards may wait so long that several generations of devices come out before they adopt. When they do they tend to adopt the newest, most advanced innovations. In 2007 Goldenberg and Oreg surveyed laggards who purchased new audio players and found that a sizable percentage had jumped from cassette audio players to MP3 players, the newest technology at the time. They conclude that laggards "leapfrog" to novel technologies because they are convinced that the innovations will work by watching others use older-generation technologies of the same type. Hence, laggards can create demand for new devices beyond that of innovators and early adopters.

This typology of adopters gives us some idea of how innovations spread through a population. But each adoption and its ultimate success or failure depends upon a complex process occurring within the organization and among its members. The next section will explore the adoption process in greater detail.

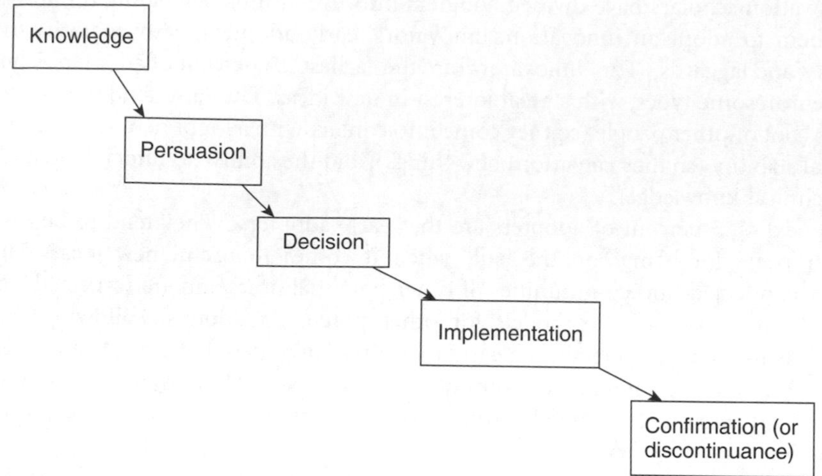

Figure 9.3 **The innovation decision process.**

ADOPTION

The Innovation Decision

Rogers (2003) portrays the "innovation-decision process" as a more or less rational process that occurs in five stages, shown in Figure 9.3. The process begins with the knowledge stage, during which the potential adopter becomes aware of the innovation and its functions and also needs that it may meet. In the persuasion stage the potential adopter forms an attitude toward the innovation based on what he or she learns about it. In this stage the potential adopter becomes more psychologically involved with the innovation and evaluates its characteristics in terms of whether it will meet her or his needs. If a positive attitude toward the innovation forms and it is feasible to acquire the innovation (e.g., if it is within the adopter's budget), then a decision is made to adopt the innovation. On the other hand, if the potential adopter forms a negative attitude toward the innovation or if acquiring the innovation is not feasible, a decision to reject the innovation occurs.

Once the decision is made to adopt, a phase of implementation ensues in which the adopter begins to use the innovation and gains experience with it. If the innovation delivers on its promise and meets the adopter's needs, then it is confirmed for the adopter and use is likely to continue. On the other, if it does not work out as expected, it is likely to be discontinued, especially if discontinuing it does not entail costs to the adopter. As implementation occurs, those who decided not to adopt the innovation often continue to be exposed to it, especially if they can witness others' use of the innovation. They may make a later adoption decision or confirm their rejection, depending on what they learn through exposure.

Rogers's model lays out a logical set of steps for decision making on whether to adopt and implement an innovation. However, what we know about power, decision making, and the various strategies for organizing suggest that this model may need to be expanded to fit many organizational changes (as discussed in Chapters 7 and 8).

Rogers's model is designed for cases where an individual is in a position to make an adoption decision for him or herself. The original studies that supported this model, for example, pertain to farmers deciding to adopt a new type of seed for planting, doctors making decisions about whether to prescribe a new drug, and women deciding whether to adopt a new method of contraception (Rogers, 2003, chap. 2). In each case there is a single decision maker and the innovation represents a single choice. This model clearly applies to innovations such as a new word processing program that the organization has purchased, but left it to individuals to decide whether they will actually use it (or not).[5] For instance, many organizations which are implementing Web 2.0 applications such as blogs or social networks leave the choice of whether to adopt such tools to their employees, on the grounds that only if the employee is comfortable with these applications will they yield expected benefits.[6] The innovation decision may also apply to innovations that an employee can bring into the workplace whether the organization wants it or not. Early use of instant messaging in many organizations was by employees who communicated with one another other outside the organization's officially sanctioned phone and email systems.

Many innovations, however, are more complicated. Quality improvement, for example, will only succeed if adopted at the unit level (indeed, some quality improvement advocates argue that it will only work if adopted by the *entire* organization, top to bottom). In some cases, management decides to adopt an innovation and to mandate its use, whether lower level employees want to use it or not. In others, an individual decides that the innovation is important and decides to become a change agent who promotes it to the organization, building support for it among management and coworkers. In still other cases, competing factions or units advocate different versions of the same innovation as a means of building their power base. In each of these instances, adoption and implementation of an innovation requires more than a single user's decision.[7]

Who – or what – is the "adopter" in the case of organizational change? While we may refer to the organization as a whole, it is clear that it is people within the organization who do the actual adopting. One important group of adopters is the organization's top managers and resource controllers, who often make the decision to adopt and implement an innovation. They are making this decision for others in the organization who may be the ones who ultimately have to make the innovation work. These users of the innovation comprise a second group of adopters. In some cases, they are expected to comply with the innovation decision without much choice in the matter. How well they cooperate during the implementation process influences how well the innovation works out. In other cases, adoption and use is optional. For example, a company may decide to implement an employee assistance program to provide mental health care to employees with problems, but leave it up to individual employees whether to use the program or not.

Thus, organizational change often involves multiple decision processes that occur over a fairly long period of time in several units and levels of the organization. The initial authoritative decision to adopt an innovation may be taken by top management, but successful implementation of the change may hinge on additional decision processes that users work through at varying rates. Various other actors, including change agents who advocate for the innovation and middle managers, peers, and subordinates who have to provide support for users, also make their own innovation decisions.

Due to the complex nature of organizational innovation processes, organizational change requires more than adoption of an innovation through individual user commitment. It also requires (1) the development of the innovation idea into a model, plan, or prototype suitable for the organization; (2) the construction of coalitions to support the innovation; and (3) an extended period of routinization that embeds the innovation into the organization's structure and practices (Kanter, 1988; Lewis, 2011). We will discuss these in more depth in the next section on implementation, but it is important to note that coalition building and idea development usually occur during several earlier stages of the change process in addition to the implementation stage.

Influences on Adoption

Several factors influence the rate of adoption of an innovation by organizations and by their members, including attributes of the innovation itself, communication channels, institutional pressures, and change agents' promotion efforts.

Attributes of the Innovation Rogers (2003) discusses five attributes of innovations that have been shown to influence the rate with which they are adopted:

1. **Relative advantage** of the innovation over the products, processes, or ideas which it succeeds. This is often measured in terms of economic advantage, but it may also be gauged in terms of status enhancement, easier use, or greater effectiveness. The greater the relative advantage and the more types of advantage there are, the higher the rate of adoption.
2. **Compatibility** of the innovation with values, experiences, and needs of potential adopters. The more compatible the innovation is, the higher the rate of adoption.
3. **Complexity**, the degree to which the innovation is "relatively difficult to understand and use" (Rogers, 2003, 257). The greater the complexity of an innovation, the lower the rate of adoption.
4. **Trialability**, the degree to which users may experiment with the innovation before making a commitment to adopt. Higher degrees of trialability make adopting the innovation reversible. The greater the trialability of an innovation, the higher the rate of adoption.
5. **Observability**, the degree to which the innovation and its results are observable to others. Provided the innovation gives a solid relative advantage and it is positively socially regarded, the greater the observability, the higher the rate of adoption. However, for an innovation with some degree of stigma, observability may decrease the rate of adoption (for example, safe sex programs that distribute condoms are often slow to take off, because of the stigma associated with sex).

Consider the example of cell phones when they were first introduced.[8] The relative advantage of a cell phone compared to traditional phone systems is that it enables one to be in touch with others almost anywhere there is reception. This can result in several benefits for cell phone adopters, including economic advantages, safety, and the ability to keep in touch with loved ones or the home office, not to mention that status boost that early cell phones gave their users (who felt technologically advanced). Since the cell phone connects with the traditional phone system and uses the same dialing–talking–listening protocols as the regular phone system it has a high degree of compatibility. Additional features added as cell phone technology matured, such as connectivity with email, an electronic address book, date and time, and the ability to connect with the internet provided additional advantages relative to the "plain old telephone system" (POTS).

In terms of complexity the cell phone is a mixed bag. Its basic function – making and receiving calls – was rather simple, since it resembled what the POTS provided. However, additional features and unfamiliar keyboard layouts sometimes rendered cell phones too complex for users. The "jitterbug" phones in the United States, which have no additional features beyond a phone, electronic address book, and date and time, have become popular with some users, particularly older ones who do not want to learn new technologies. Trialability is possible with the cell phone, because an individual can try out a friend's while an organization can purchase just a few on a trial basis without having to commit itself to wholesale use. Finally, in terms of observability, potential adopters could see the potential advantages and flexibility cell phones afforded.

This example illustrates an important point about characteristics of innovations and adoption. What matters is not the attributes of the innovation per se, but these attributes *as they are perceived by potential adopters*. Complexity, for example, is not an objective characteristic; the degree of complexity depends on how the potential adopter perceives the technology. Someone who focused mainly on phone calls would find cell phones relatively simple, while someone else who focused on all the extra features would perceive cell phones as complex.

Change campaigns designed to promote adoption of innovations are therefore often designed to shape the perceptions of the innovation. For example, early cell phone campaigns stressed the safety aspects of cell phones, which would allow teenagers to call their parents if they were in trouble, as a means of convincing parents that cell phones had a relative advantage over the pay phones that the POTS provided.

In most advocacy campaigns, compatibility, manageable levels of complexity, trialability, and observability are presented as virtues of an innovation. When advocates are urging radical changes, however, they may also be presented as vices. If an organization is being urged to totally redefine how it operates, for example, the incompatibility of the change with the status quo might be emphasized, rather than its compatibility. Quality management has often been presented in this light, as a fundamental shift in operating philosophy. In a similar vein, a radical change may be presented as something so major and so new that it is neither trialable nor observable. Instead a commitment that breaks with the past and sets the organization on an unprecedented course is required.

The External Communication System The nature of the communication system that links the organization to its environment also influences adoption. Television, print, and radio media, along with the internet and other new media, provide massive amounts of information on new ideas and innovations. Research suggests that this type of diffuse information is most influential in the knowledge stage, while direct communication with other people is more influential in the persuasion stage (Rogers, 2003, 202–213).

The media, including specialized publications such as *Computerworld* and *Forbes* and more general outlets like the *New York Times*, regularly report on innovations. These reports circulate widely due to the tendency of media competitors to mirror one another's stories. The internet has become a great aggregator of information on innovations, and those interested in them can find multiple stories of success and failures in the results of careful searches. The internet is a truly global medium, and so innovations are likely to spread more rapidly and broadly than they have in the past. Innovators and influential early adopters tend to be more active in their media consumption and hence are exposed to promising new ideas that they then bring back to their organizations.

Innovations tend to spread via a **two-step flow** process first identified over 50 years ago (Lazarsfeld, Berelson, and Gaudet, 1944; Rogers, 2003, 304–305). In step 1, opinion leaders, a subset of the early adopters discussed in the previous section, learn about the innovation via media reports. In step 2, opinion leaders influence others in their networks to adopt the innovation via processes of interpersonal influence, and the innovation spreads through communication networks throughout the society. Through interpersonal communication between opinion leaders and others in the network, positive attitudes form and influence adoption decisions. Once some others in the network have adopted, they tend to influence still others and the innovation diffuses until it runs its course.

The original study that discovered the two-step flow model (Lazarsfeld, Berelson and Gaudet, 1944) focused on physicians and their prescribing habits and provides a good example of process. Opinion leader physicians tended to learn about new pharmaceuticals through reading medical journals and their advertisements, attending medical conferences, and conversing with pharmaceutical salespeople. They served as early adopters of new drugs and spread the word about them through networks of other physicians they talked with during golf games, over meals, and in passing. This second group of physicians tended to look up to the opinion leaders, and they were thus motivated to tell others about the new drugs, who spread the word further, and so on. Use of the new drug eventually diffused throughout the community of physicians.

Opinion leaders are important to the diffusion of innovations. They are admired and used as a reference point by others in a social system. They tend to make greater use of mass media than the typical member of a social system and have more contact with those outside the system, and so are more likely to know about promising innovations. They also tend to engage in higher levels of social participation than their neighbors, and this enables them to spread word of the innovation and exert influence on others.

Frances Hesselbein, the CEO of the Girl Scouts of America discussed in Chapter 6, is a good example of an opinion leader. Identified by Peter Drucker, eminent management scholar, as the best CEO in the United States, she is the recipient of numerous awards and speaker at dozens of meetings a year. At these meetings and through personal contact, Hesselbein is in a good position to spread the word about innovations and her credibility among top managers of other firms allows her to influence them.

Organizations can also be opinion leaders. There are numerous lists of "most admired" organizations in every sector, and other organizations look to them for examples of "best practices," many of which are innovations. In the late 1980s, for example, the influential book *In Search of Excellence* (Peters and Waterman, 1982) identified common characteristics of high-performing US corporations, and set off a wave of emulation among organizations that wanted to be "excellent" too.[9] In a classic study of state governments in the United States, Walker (1966) found that states looked to certain exemplar states for new practices. States like California, Massachusetts, and New York served as models for innovations that, once proven, spread to other states.

Opinion leaders are not, however, always agents of change. They tend to follow the overall norms of their social system. If the social system is generally conservative, then opinion leaders are less likely to advocate innovation than if it is more open to change. The industry or sector an organization belongs to is a particularly influential social system for innovation. Organizations tend to pay attention to other organizations that are like themselves and to attend to what they do. In industries in which change is common, such as the telecommunications industry, norms are likely to foster change, whereas in industries which are quite stable, such as the baked goods industry, conservative norms are likely to prevail.

The discussion of opinion leaders reminds us of the importance of communication networks in innovation. As we noted in Chapter 4, weak ties in communication networks are important to the spread of innovative ideas. Weak ties, recall, are connections between people or organizations that reflect occasional and infrequent contact. Weak ties serve as bridges among more strongly tied local networks and are thus important in the transmission of new ideas and innovations from one network to another.

Institutional Pressures In Chapter 1 we discussed the importance of institutions in shaping organizations. Institutional forces – coercive, normative, and mimetic – often influence the adoption of innovations.

To continue with our example of quality improvement programs, in the health care industry several organizations pioneered large scale quality improvement with impressive outcomes in the 1970s and 1980s. Their story spread through the industry and in order to keep up, other large health care organizations experimented with quality improvement due to these mimetic pressures. Health care organizations sought to replicate quality improvement processes and programs developed in exemplary organizations like the Intermountain Health Care System in Salt Lake City, Utah.

The Institute for Healthcare Improvement (IHI) was founded to serve as a research incubator and clearinghouse for quality improvement methods and approaches.[10] Its stated goals were to "energize a profound movement in health care" and to "spread improvement knowledge across the globe." It advocated six improvement aims for health care: Safety, Effectiveness, Patient-Centeredness, Timeliness, Efficiency, and Equity.[11] The vision of the IHI was to have "no needless deaths, no needless pain or suffering, no helplessness in those served or serving, no unwanted waiting, no waste, no one left out."

The IHI became one of the centers for research on quality improvement in health care, and as such was another exemplary organization imitated by health care organizations. But IHI was more than this. It had a collection of "best practices" and proven quality improvement processes, and so served as a source of normative pressure. Its longtime director, David Berwick, became a widely consulted authority on quality in health care, projecting the norms of IHI nationally and internationally.

Pressure to adopt and implement quality improvement practices became coercive when the agency that licenses hospitals, the Joint Commission for the Accreditation of Hospitals (originally JCAH, now the Joint Commission),[12] incorporated a requirement that hospitals must have quality programs in place in order to receive the certification necessary to participate in the Medicare program. The combination of mimetic, normative, and coercive pressures exerted by important health care institutions led to widespread adoption of quality management by hospitals, clinics, and group practices. Quality management has been routinized in health care to such an extent that it is no longer regarded as an innovation, but has become part of standard operating procedure.

Does this mean that every health care institution adopted and implemented quality management? Yes and no. Institutional pressures led to widespread diffusion of quality practices and processes, but many institutions resisted by adopting quality "in name only," They set up quality programs, but did the bare minimum to be certified; they devoted relatively few resources to their quality programs and did not internalize the vision or values behind quality management, largely because they viewed it more as a PR stunt than a meaningful organizational change.

The role of institutional pressures in the adoption of organizational innovations has been documented in a number of other areas, including civil service reforms in the US cities and towns during the late 1800s and early 1900s (Tolbert and Zucker, 1983) and of the spread of radio show formats and radio station management structures (Leblibici, Salancick, Copay, and King, 1988). These studies have established that generally the greater the institutional pressure and the more types of pressure there are, the faster and more thorough the diffusion process (Scott, 2008). For example, Tolbert and Zucker's study showed that civil service spread through cities more rapidly when states passed laws mandating civil service (thus adding coercive pressure to the normative pressure behind civil service reform and the elimination of corruption) than when states merely encouraged adoption (normative pressure only).

Change Agents Adoption of innovations is also influenced by the people who want to bring the change about, **change agents**. At least five critical roles that change agents may play in the change process have been identified:[13]

- **Idea generator:** This involves finding or creating a new idea, product, process, or procedure. It often requires intense analysis of complex information and problems solving. It also may involve synthesis of seemingly unrelated concepts or ideas to create a novel approach. People who fit this role tend to be experts on one or two fields and are comfortable with abstract, conceptual thinking. They are usually individualists and may work alone.
- **Champion:** Champions recognize the merit of an innovation, turn it into a proposal, push it and advocate for it until it is adopted and implemented. Those who fit this role generally have a wide range of interests and can see "the big picture" in which the innovation fits. They typically have interests in application and are energetic and persistent. Champions have also been called "intrapreneurs" (Pinchot, 2004).
- **Project leader:** There is also a need for planning and coordination of the actual work involved in developing the new idea, adapting it to the organization, and implementing it. Project leaders put ideas into action. People who fit this role are good at working with others and leading teams (projects usually are organized around teams). They know the ins and outs of the organization and are willing to serve as the central coordinator of decision making, information, and practical problem solving. Effective project managers have been described as "generalists with a specialty," that is, they have some acquaintance with a wide range of subjects involved in implementing an innovation (in the case of a new technical product, a project manager might need to have some knowledge of engineering, marketing, finance, and manufacturing), but they are expert in at least one area that members of the project team respect (our project manager might have been a brilliant engineer in a previous role).
- **Gatekeeper:** This role involves collecting and channeling information about important changes in the organization and external environment as the innovation and change process proceeds. A person with a good fit to this role will have extensive networks and is personable and approachable. They will be interested in helping others and making the change process succeed. They also generally possess a high level of competence in one or two fields, which helps them recognize important information and also potential problems looming on the horizon.

- **Sponsor:** Also sometimes called a "coach," this role provides "behind-the-scenes" support in the form of political support, resources, and advice. A person who fits this role is usually a senior member of the organization who has good connections within the organization and, sometimes, outside the organization. He or she provides access to the power base of the organization. A sponsor is also "outside" the actual project and is able to develop a more or less objective view of how things are proceeding.

While there may be a single person for each role, in other cases, the same person may play more than one role. There are also cases in which several people or a team may be necessary to fulfill a particular role. This is particularly true for complex and/or highly technical innovations, because there may be a need for "hard" technical as well as "soft" relational skills.

Most change agents come from within the organization, and this is advantageous in some respects. Insiders speak the language of the organization and understand its traditions and norms. Their personal stake in the organization often gives insiders a special motivation to accomplish change and a perspective that enables them to effectively adapt the innovation to the organization. There is also a downside to inside change agents, however. They may lack objectivity and use the change process to advance their own goals or to settle scores. They may also have inadequate skills to manage the change process.

For this reason, organizations sometimes bring in outside change agents to complement internal agents. Outsiders have the advantage of bringing a more objective perspective to the organization. They also often bring in fresh ideas. Outsiders, particularly those from consulting organizations that specialize in facilitating organizational change, also often possess superior skills in the change process. For example, the Joint Commission, which promotes quality improvement in hospitals, has a nonprofit subsidiary, Quality Healthcare Resources, that provides consulting services to help hospitals design and implement quality programs. The downside of outsiders is that they do not understand the organization as well as insiders and so may make missteps. And although outsiders tend to be more objective, they also do not identify with organizational problems as much as insiders. For this reason, change is often most effective when a combination of internal and external change agents works together.

A particularly important role is the **champion** of change, the person (sometimes a small group) who takes an idea and advocates it in the organization. In a widely cited study, Howell and Higgins (1990) interviewed a number of champions of technological changes and painted a detailed picture of how they successfully advocated change. Howell and Higgins found that the most common champions are middle managers with a good deal of experience and technical expertise. They tend to have good communication skills and to be able to articulate a compelling vision of the change. They are also committed to the organization and what to help improve it. Finally, champions are comfortable with ambiguity and a degree of risk taking.

IMPLEMENTATION

Implementation is concerned with successful routinization and reinvention of the innovation. The steps leading up to adoption usually build some support for the change that lends it momentum as implementation begins As we noted above, two key processes during implementation include continuing development of the innovation and coalition building.

Innovations win the approval of management and other key constituencies because they present a promising vision of the future. Making this vision a reality, however, requires working "in the trenches" with users, adjusting the innovation to specific contexts, and addressing problems and setbacks. Hence, the innovation idea is never fully realized until implementation is complete; idea development continues throughout the process. The final product is often quite different from the idea that was originally adopted. Hospitals adopted quality improvement programs because of visions like IHI's. As they implemented them, however, the hospitals had to experiment with and adapt the programs to their own situations, as Case 9.1 illustrates.

Case Study 9.1

Implementing a Moving Target: Quality Improvement at TopHill Hospital System[1]

TopHill Hospital System set out to implement a quality improvement program in the early 1990s. Hospital administrators were confident that they could put a program into place in three to four years. Over the six years the program actually took to implement, however, the administrators, physicians, nurses, and other employees of TopHill saw it change from a seemingly simple and straightforward program into an organizational transformation.

The TopHill System was founded in 1902 by a pair of physicians who wanted to provide unique and high quality care for their patients. Their practice grew into a large group which by 1990 numbered over 400 physicians, with 20 clinics spread around a 2000 square mile area. TopHill Hospital served this physician group exclusively, with 500 beds and numerous specialty treatment clinics for cancer, drug addiction, and so on. The System developed its own health plan, with about 200,000 enrollees as of 1990. The TopHill System was affiliated with a major university medical school and served about 200 medical interns per year. TopHill was consistently rated among the best health systems in the country.

Quality care was the hallmark of TopHill. The System was very conscientious in its review of cases and moved quickly to correct problems. TopHill followed the approach to quality typical in the 1980s and early 1990s, "quality assurance" (QA). The central focus of QA was the identification and elimination of problems, which were defined as deviations from accepted state of the art medical practice. Quality Assurance was enforced by the Joint Commission for Hospital Accreditation (the Joint Commission, introduced in this chapter), which certified that hospitals met standards set for adequate QA. A hospital that failed to be certified by JCAH could not receive payment from various government programs, including Medicare. Failing the Joint Commission certification process also hurt a hospitals' reputation.

The two main components of QA at TopHill were physician review of cases and the Quality Assurance Department. Committees of senior physicians in each specialization at TopHill (e.g., surgery and neurology) regularly reviewed medical records to ensure that the care provided was consistent with prevailing state of the art practice and to identify medical errors. These committees introduced new practices and in the case of serious errors sanctioned physicians, who could lose their right to practice in the hospital for repeated violations. The QA Department compiled information about medical errors and other care-related statistics and prepared the documents for the Joint Commission certification. It coordinated a network of Quality Assurance Committees for each major hospital function (physicians, nurses, food service, etc.). The focus of both the physician committees and the QA Department was identification and elimination of medical errors.

The quality improvement program was initiated by a transformational leader, Martin Macy, president of the TopHill System. Widely regarded as a visionary within TopHill, Macy was convinced to pursue quality by the fact that several health care systems that he regarded as TopHill's peers had initiated quality programs Macy sent one of the system's leading physicians, Jack Silver, to a training course in quality improvement offered by the Institute for Healthcare Improvement. Discussions with Silver convinced Macy to strongly back a quality improvement program at TopHill. They convened a meeting of important physicians from the system to explain quality improvement and to advocate implementing it at TopHill.

Quality improvement (QI) is based on a fundamentally different approach than the traditional QA process. Due to its focus on errors, QA tends to assume that the quality of current care is just fine and that individuals who make the errors are the problem. QA assigns blame to these individuals, who are then expected to change (and sometimes punished or fired for committing the error). The problem with QA is that because it singled out individuals, there was no recognition that larger systems of procedures led to errors. Moreover, it encouraged those who made errors to hide them so they would not be blamed.

Quality improvement, in contrast, focuses not only on errors, but also on finding ways to improve and to make the health care processes more efficient. It focuses on processes, not simply on individuals who carry them out, on the assumption that if the process can be made safe and effective and individuals carry it out faithfully, then quality and efficiency of care will be enhanced. QI is not done in order to satisfy outside regulators (though in time the Joint Commission and other regulators did require it), but to give those delivering health care – doctors, nurses, orderlies, everyone – control over the process and the satisfaction of delivering great care. Most people, after all, go into health care not only for the money, but because they care. QI motivates them because they truly want to help their patients and it enables them to deliver the best possible care.

Having won the support of leading physicians, Knudson assigned Silver to implement QI in TopHill. Silver hired an assistant, Sylvia Tear, and they set up a core team of composed of two physicians, two nurses, an assistant hospital administrator, and two service personnel. After some research the team brought in a consulting firm to set up a quality improvement program based on the Juran model of quality improvement (there are several different approaches to QI which operate quite differently). The Juran approach stresses training employees in quality methods and in a specific problem solving process similar to the group problem-solving process discussed in Chapter 8. Employees are then assembled into QI teams composed of members from several different departments and functions who did not previously know one another very well. The rationale for these "cross-functional" teams is that members who are not friends and who come from different units are likely to bring a useful set of diverse perspectives, skills and approaches to the team that will spark creative ideas and facilitate problem solving.

Juran QI teams are encouraged to identify "big" critical problems, collect data about these problems, devise a diverse set of solutions, and then test these solutions for workability. The teams report to a Quality Council that is comprised of representatives of the various units in the organization. The Quality Council must approve the problems the QI teams propose to tackle and then decide whether their solution to these problems should be put into action.

More than ten Juran QI teams started work in the first two years of the QI program in TopHill. They usually included at least two physicians, two nurses, two administrative personnel, and two service personnel from different departments to ensure a representative and varied group of perspectives. The program was launched with great fanfare. However, by the end of the second year only two had finished work, due to multiple problems. Teams took a good deal of time to get started, because members did not know one another and had to build the team from scratch. The different perspectives members brought to the teams did encourage "out-of-the-box" thinking, but they also made it difficult for teams to reach agreement on their problems. The problems the teams took on were so big and complex that they had trouble diagnosing them and finding workable solutions. Physicians were so busy they did not attend team meetings. The results from the Juran QI teams were not particularly impressive. The main accomplishment of the first two years was that more than half the employees of TopHill had been trained in quality methods.

The QI implementation team decided to let the Juran QI process continue for a third year, but added a second process, Unit Quality. Unit Quality operated on different premises from the Juran QI approach. Unit Quality projects were defined and carried out by members from existing units of TopHill, and the problems they addressed were from that unit. For example, a nursing floor would set up a Unit Quality team and they would identify problems, ways to improve quality, and make plans to implement these plans. The unit would have complete control over the change process. Many types of projects could be undertaken by Unit Quality teams; they ranged from small improvements to large projects. The point of Unit Quality was to give unit employees control over the process. For example, one unit had consistent problems with tubing used to administer intravenous fluids. It experimented with several other types of tubing and finally found tubes that eliminated the problems. This change was implemented immediately and the unit monitored the results for six months to document that the new tubing actually solved their problems.

Unit Quality worked so well that TopHill redefined QI in terms of "continuous improvement," which emphasized continuous pursuit of quality, relatively small changes, and experimentation and adjustment of practices in light of the results they yielded. Unit Quality represented a move in TopHill's thinking away from the Juran approach, which set up special project groups that tackled big problems and took a long time to deliver results. While large-scale quality improvement efforts were still occasionally undertaken, by the fourth year, the Juran approach had been superseded by Unit Quality.

A side effect of Unit Quality and the training of the majority of TopHill employees in quality methods was that "quality thinking" began to pervade most activities. Instead of simply following traditional practices, employees began to question how they could improve care. They gathered data to evaluate current practices and kept their eyes open for new opportunities constantly. As a result, quality was permeating the organizational culture at TopHill.

To support this less formal quality improvement work, TopHill founded the Clinical Practice Program. This program gave physicians budgets to fund improvement programs and provided consultants to help gather data and assess results.

After a six-year journey toward quality improvement, TopHill Director of Quality Francine Bermini commented, "Quality is not a program any more, it's part of everything we do at TopHill." The system had undergone a wholesale transformation on its quality journey.

Using What You Have Learned

1. Identify the key change agent roles that appear in the case. How did the people in these roles move the implementation of quality improvement forward?
2. What institutional pressures drove change at TopHill? Were some more powerful than others? If so, which ones?
3. Characterize the Juran QI process, unit quality, and Clinical Practice Program in terms of the innovation characteristics each displayed. Are there differences in innovation characteristics across the three quality improvement processes? Do these make a difference in how successful they were?

Questions to Think About and Discuss

1. The quality program at TopHill changed considerably over the six years in which it was implemented and so did TopHill's view of quality. Should this be expected for any change of this size? What are the benefits of the change for TopHill?Are there any disadvantages or downsides to these changes?
2. Implementing quality at TopHill took twice as long as its champions originally projected. Why? Is this inevitable with any large-scale change program? What might have been done to speed the change up?

Note

1 This case is a composite based upon interviews conducted by Scott Poole and his research team with a number of hospital quality improvement experts and participants in quality improvement programs. Special thanks to Kevin Real and Jessica Wunsch for assistance in conducting the interviews.

In addition to idea development, coalition building is important to maintain support throughout what is sometimes a long, drawn-out implementation process. Supportive coalitions help to maintain commitment for the change process and help to navigate through rocky spots. As Case 9.1 illustrates, a strong coalition greatly strengthened the TopHill Hospital System's ability to experiment with quality projects that often resulted in dead ends until they finally arrived at a workable program.

The implementation process differs depending on the outcomes that change agents are aiming for. Lewis (2011) distinguishes two dimensions of change outcomes: uniformity and fidelity. **Uniformity** refers to the degree to which all adopters use the change in the same way and to the same degree. An organization implementing an ethics program would have high uniformity if it required all employees to participate by completing the same online ethics course. In a low-uniformity change process, adopters are allowed to use the innovation in different ways and also to implement some. A low-uniformity ethics program might provide a variety of options to enhance employees' ethical standards, including the online course, books on ethics, discussion groups, and credit for completing an ethics class at a local community college. Employees would be allowed to select which of these to participate in and even to opt out if they chose to. It is usually easier to implement changes that are low uniformity, but in some cases high uniformity is important. A new policy requiring employees to file a new type of form in order to use their vacation time will work best if every employee is required to file the form, rather than making exceptions for some employees. Once exceptions are made, motivation to file the form is likely to go down and employees are likely to request the same exemption.

Fidelity refers to the degree to which the intended design of the innovation is maintained during implementation. A high-fidelity implementation of an online ethics program would take care that the program was not changed during implementation. A low-fidelity implementation would experiment with the program and change it to adapt to the organization's situation. Although it is generally easier to implement innovations when they can be changed and adapted, it is sometimes important to maintain high fidelity. Medical checklists, which require health care personnel to follow the exact same set of steps when performing procedures such as inserting catheters or stitching up a wound, have been shown to greatly reduce infections and associated hospitalizations and deaths. They only work, however, if everyone follows the steps in the list exactly the same way every time. In this case, adaptation is not a good thing.

The degree of uniformity and fidelity that change agents are aiming for shapes the nature of the implementation process. High uniformity requires change agents to find or to develop a design for the innovation that works throughout the organization. To achieve high uniformity they may also have to provide training and support to overcome problems that may arise for individual users or units. Finally, the change may have to be mandatory with penalties for not participating. In the case of one online ethics program, for example, implementers found and purchased an ethics training package that was meaningful for all of the varied units in the university, which included academic departments, administrators, and grounds crews. They also provided support for those who did not know how to use a computer or who had problems taking the online course. They were assisted in their task by an order from the university president that every employee had to take the course or they would be laid off.

Maintaining high fidelity often requires changes to other aspects of the organization and its members. Many innovations – particularly those brought in from outside the organization – run against the grain of current organizational structures and practices. If the innovation is implemented without changing them, structures and practices inconsistent with the innovation are likely to undermine it and prevent the organization from reaping its advantages. Medical checklists, for example, run counter to traditional physician authority over medical decisions, because they require physicians to adopt practices developed by others. To implement checklists with high fidelity requires that physicians give up some of their autonomy. Getting them to do this may require a good deal of time and effort on the part of change agents. Among other things, physicians may worry that their agreement to utilize checklists will set a precedent and that they will be asked to give up other aspects of their authority. This may encourage them to resist the change effort. Obtaining physician cooperation requires altering how physicians make decisions.

As in the case of uniformity, maintaining high fidelity may also require the organization to design training programs and support services. Penalties for altering the innovation may also help to achieve fidelity.

Engaging Stakeholders

Our discussion to this point has focused on change agents and users. There are, however, other parties to change processes. A more comprehensive view considers **stakeholders**, all those who have a significant stake in the change (Lewis, 2011). Stakeholders include change agents and adopters, but also may include other groups, including people who must give service or support to adopters, those who are displaced by the innovation, customers and clients of the organization, stockholders and owners in the case of private organizations, concerned citizens in the case of public organizations, and resource controllers, among others.

In the case of hospital quality improvement programs, for example, stakeholders would likely include not only health care personnel and top management, but also patients, government agencies that regulate hospitals and health care, local governmental agencies involved with health care and licensing, stockholders or owners of the hospital, affiliated hospitals and health care organizations, and relevant medical and nursing associations, among others. Each of these has different concerns and some are likely to support the change, while others may be inclined to resist it (and there may be differences of opinion within each stakeholder group as well). For change to be implemented effectively, significant concerns must be identified and addressed.

How do we identify relevant stakeholders? Straus (2002) argues that at least four types of stakeholders should be considered in any change effort:

- Those with the formal power to make decisions and the resources necessary to carry out the change
- Those with the power to block the change
- Those who are affected by the change
- Those with relevant information or expertise to facilitate and carry out the change

In the previous paragraph we identified possible stakeholders for the hospital quality improvement program by brainstorming our way down this list. For any significant change this will result in quite a lengthy list, so it is important to narrow down the set of stakeholders who will be considered in planning and implementing change.

Table 9.2 Four Types of Stakeholders

Stakeholder type	*Support for change*	*Importance of stakeholder*
Low priority	Moderate to high	Moderately low to low
Advocate	Moderate to high	Moderately high to high
Problematic	Neutral to low	Moderately low to low
Antagonistic	Moderately low to low	Moderately high to high

As a first step, the concerns the various stakeholders have about the change and their position on the change should be ascertained. This is generally done by talking to representative stakeholders, or through more formal methods like focus groups. The concerns of stakeholders are important information that can assist in planning the change effort. Nutt (2002) suggests that stakeholders should then be prioritized in terms of their importance. Importance should be considered broadly, not just in terms of degree of relative power of the stakeholders, but also in terms of degree to which the change affects them, the degree to which their cooperation is required, and the degree to which they should be considered for ethical reasons.

Based on this analysis, stakeholders can be divided into four rough categories, shown in Table 9.2:

1. Low-priority stakeholders are those who generally support the change and are of relatively low importance compared to other stakeholders. These stakeholders should not be ignored, but they require less attention than other categories.
2. Problematic stakeholders are those who are opposed to the change, but are of relatively low importance. They should definitely not be ignored, because they can potentially be recruited as allies against the change by those opposed to it. However, relatively less effort should be spent on them than on the next two categories.
3. Advocate stakeholders are those who are in favor of the change and are important. They should be enlisted as allies in the change effort if possible. They may provide active support or behind the scenes advocacy, depending on their level of involvement.
4. Antagonistic stakeholders are those who oppose the change and are important. They should be engaged as much as possible and attempts to win them over should be made.

The numbers and nature of the stakeholders in each category suggest the amount of effort that will be required to carry out the change. If there are a lot of antagonistic stakeholders and not many advocates, the odds are stacked against success for the change effort. In this case, it is sometimes advisable to put the change "on hold" until the political climate improves.

How should stakeholders be involved in the change process? Straus (2002) defines four levels of involvement for stakeholders in the change process. First, they can become members of the core team and work closely on the change effort (Straus, 2002). A project to implement a quality improvement program in a hospital, for example, is typically managed by a small team of change agents who do much of the work and coordinate the involvement of other parties (recall the discussion of project and development teams in

Chapter 4). Members of the core team are often key stakeholders who have the knowledge, skills, and contacts necessary to make the project a success. The team in our example might include a physician, a nurse, a hospital administrator, and a quality expert, among other members, so that key stakeholder constituencies are represented. This level of involvement requires a significant commitment of time and effort on the part of team members. In some cases, members of the core team may be formally assigned to the project and devote 100 percent of their working hours to it.

At a second level of involvement, stakeholders can serve on task forces, short-term groups that convene to address a specific problem or issue related to the change. The quality management implementation might convene task forces around issues such as patient safety and relation of the quality program to the nurses' union. These task forces would be specifically formed to include concerned stakeholders who have the insights, knowledge, and contacts to develop workable solutions to the problem at hand. A patient safety task force, for example, might focus on how to ensure that quality improvement projects did not endanger patients and preserved the highest standards of care. This task force should include a member from or consult closely with the hospital's Patient Safety Review Board, a formal committee that investigates adverse incidents in which a patient suffers harm due to caregiver errors. The task force might also include a health care consumer advocate to represent the patient's point of view. It might be formed about one month into the implementation and meet for a couple of months, preparing a report and recommendations concerning how to maintain patient safety and also improve quality of care. At the conclusion of its work, the task force would disband.

The third level of involvement is through input and feedback meetings. These meetings are scheduled during the implementation process in order to obtain input from stakeholders who are not at one of the first two levels of involvement and also to disseminate information about the change. In the quality improvement implementation, for example, the core team might schedule regular informational meetings and invite any interested persons from the hospital or community to attend. This would give stakeholders who are not actually working on the implementation an opportunity to learn more about it and to express their concerns.

Fourth, the core team may involve stakeholders through communication and outreach. This is a broad-based activity that may use newsletters, email lists, or mass media to get a message out to a large audience. There may also be feedback opportunities for stakeholders through a survey or poll. Outreach keeps a broad range of stakeholders "in the loop," of the change effort. It also invites those with concerns or objections to become more involved.

The four levels of involvement are arranged in order of decreasing amount of time and effort they require of the stakeholder. Each offers opportunities for change agents to include stakeholders' opinions, to honor stakeholder viewpoints, and to draws on their talents and knowledge.[14] Stakeholders serve as a valuable extension of the change agents' network that can provide important information about problems and unanticipated consequences, as well as new ideas and suggestions for enhancing the innovation.

A sense of inclusion is critical to building coalitions supporting the change process. Straus (2002) comments that

> a stakeholder can do more damage to a process by being left out than by being included. Often, if you extend an invitation to someone with an explanation of the time commitments required,

> the individual will feel acknowledged but opt for a less-intense [level of] involvement. If you exclude that person, however, he or she may come pounding at the door. (50)

Change agents should attempt to engage all significant stakeholders at some level, even those opposed to the change. Although it is tempting to regard opposing stakeholders as enemies who must be neutralized or cut out of the process, involving them often improves the chances that the change effort will succeed. In some cases their opposition may be due to misunderstanding of the change and its benefits. Engagement is an opportunity to communicate the change and to win over opponents by clearing up misunderstandings. For example, a group of physicians may believe that the quality improvement program will force them to adopt new practices that run counter to their professional norms. Clarifying that this is not the case in an outreach meeting has a good chance of converting resistance to support (or at least to passive acceptance).

In other cases, stakeholders may be opposed to a change effort for legitimate reasons.[15] Introducing change into any complex system may lead to consequences unanticipated by the change agents, and resistance and opposition are often signals of experienced or anticipated problems. Understanding potential problems enables change agents to address them, either by adjusting the innovation or by taking steps to minimize negative impacts. For example, a group of nurses might oppose the quality improvement program because they have heard from colleagues at other hospitals that its approval process is cumbersome and slow. Their resistance suggests a useful amendment to the local hospital's program so that getting approval is less taxing. In this case, attending to opponents has not only led to a more workable program, it has likely added supporters to the cause.

Most challenging are stakeholders who are opposed to a change because it threatens their privileged position or power in the organization. For example, there may be a group of physicians who believe their control over the hospital is threatened by the quality program, because it would enable lower-power participants, such as nurses and orderlies, to have some say over how care is given. Fearing loss of their power, and other privileges it gives them, the physicians are likely to resist the new program and attempt to undermine it. Their opposition may be open – they might, for instance, wage a campaign to discredit quality improvement. Alternatively, they might appear to go along with the change, but attempt to water down participation – they might, for example, try to add a "physicians' council" that had approval authority over all quality ideas, effectively giving them a veto over suggestions from low-power participants (see the discussion of problems with participation in Chapter 4).

This last type of opponent is not likely to be won over by changes or amendments that preserve the fidelity of the innovation. As discussed in Chapter 7, power expresses itself in a number of ways, many of them hidden, and sorting out legitimate from illegitimate issues that groups such as these physicians raise is difficult. It is important to engage these stakeholders to the degree possible to ascertain whether they will cooperate if their legitimate issues are addressed. Straus (2002) comments that

> it's human nature to want to exclude those people who disagree with your ideas or who are hard to work with. . . . But, truly, the process would be the weaker for it. Excluding a powerful blocker can only make him or her more powerful – more able to claim with justification that the process was closed and unfair. (39, 42)

At some point, change agents may decide to proceed without certain opponents' support and attempt to build a coalition sufficiently strong to overcome change. However, it is important to have made the effort to include opponents.

As this discussion indicates, involvement of stakeholders in change efforts is both important and complicated. It is also, to a great degree, a matter of symbolism. Recall the point made earlier that it is not the objective characteristics of an innovation that lead to its adoption so much as potential adopters' perceptions of the innovation's characteristics. The same is true of the change effort itself. The degree to which a change effort engages stakeholders shapes outside parties' perceptions of the change agents' intentions and attitudes. If there is little engagement of those outside the "inner circle," then the innovation may appear to be a special agenda of the change agents. This is likely to harden the opposition and arouse suspicions in those who are on the fence. Conversely, opening up the process to stakeholder influence invites ownership by the larger group of stakeholders. Doing so is likely to take extra time and energy on the part of change agents, and it requires the change agents to give up some control of the process. But giving up a measure of control is precisely what allows others to buy into the change. Involving stakeholders and addressing their concerns and problems legitimizes the change process.

Implementation Strategies

As might be expected, strategies for implementing change have received a lot of attention by scholars and practitioners. Numerous formulas for successful change line the bookshelves of popular bookstores and crowd online booksellers' websites. For most of these there is little hard evidence of effectiveness beyond the authors' experience and a few case applications. One exception is the work of Paul Nutt (2002), who has studied the subject for more than 20 years and collected in-depth case studies of over 400 significant decisions and their implementation.[16]

Nutt found that implementation strategies fall into four categories. The **edict** strategy involves issuing a directive to implement the innovation without consulting with stakeholders. It is a top-down strategy in which top management orders those below to adopt and implement an innovation. It relies on the power to drive the implementation process, on the assumption that those below will follow orders. Edicts are often used when a change agent wants to implement the change rapidly, sometimes in the face of a perceived emergency or threat to the organization. To continue our example, hospital administration and the hospital's board of directors might issue an edict that a quality improvement program offered by a particular consulting group would be implemented and order lower-level personnel – physicians, nurses, support staff, everyone – to use it or face penalties.

Change agents using the **persuasion** strategy gather arguments and support for the change, including endorsement and advice from experts. They then use this information and arguments to sell the change to the organization. Persuasion, too, is a top-down strategy, because it relies on management support for success, but it is less heavy-handed than the edict approach. It gives stakeholders some role in the process as it tries to win their support through persuasion. If stakeholders do not respond positively to the persuasive arguments, then change agents may tailor or adjust the innovation, and in this way stakeholders have some influence. However, this influence is filtered through the change agents. If the change agents do not wish to alter the innovation, then they may also simply change their persuasive strategy. Persuasion is often used when change agents want to maintain high fidelity and are concerned that wider involvement by stakeholders might change the innovation in ways that make it less effective.

Persuasion has been a fairly common strategy in health care quality improvement. Studies by organizations like the IHI are passed around to convince physicians and others that quality improvement efforts will yield significant benefits for the hospital; special emphasis is placed on physicians in this case because they tend to be the "movers and shakers" in hospitals. Following this, consulting organizations like Quality Healthcare Resources (mentioned previously) and champion hospital physicians hospital physicians who champion the change bring their expertise to bear to convince members that quality improvement is not only a good idea, but that it works. Often, one or more pilot projects are launched to demonstrate how the improvement process works and to show its benefits (which change agents fervently hope will result, rather than an embarrassing failure). Based on organizational context and suggestions from stakeholders, the program will be adjusted in minor ways. If persuasion works, then there will be a convinced and committed cadre of members ready to implement quality improvement.

The **intervention** strategy starts with the problem or performance gap that motivates the change effort rather than with the solution (i.e., the innovation). Change agents try to convince stakeholders of the need to act by providing evidence of current problems or failures. Change agents network broadly to persuade stakeholders there is a problem and to point out actions other organizations have taken to address the same problem. In addition, change agents solicit and listen to suggestions from stakeholders about how to address the problem. These suggestions may result in a shift from the innovation originally favored by change agents to the new idea or in a blending of the two. As implementation proceeds, change agents continue to network with stakeholders, assessing whether the innovation is addressing the problem and making adjustments in response. Before and after measurements of the problem or gap are compared in order to assess the degree to which the change effort has addressed it.

In hospital quality improvement the intervention strategy hinges on establishing a problem or gap between desired and actual performance. Change agents can cite findings of studies conducted by organizations like the IHI and the JCAH that show significant shortfalls in quality in large samples of hospitals, pointing particularly to findings for hospitals similar to the one they work in. General statistics, however, are often insufficient to motivate change. More specific studies of problems such as medication errors or operating room infections in the hospital itself are often more effective. Change agents circulate both general and specific results throughout the hospital via presentations at meetings, newsletter articles, word of mouth, and posters, among other things. Once the problem is understood and accepted by a significant portion of stakeholders, a task force or other representative body is charged with formulating a plan for change. Once the plan has been approved by top management, a core team with change agents as key members coordinates the implementation of the quality program. The program may be brought in by outside consultants or "home grown." One or more pilot projects are generally set up to demonstrate the quality program and adapt it to the hospital, and then the program is rolled out through the organization. Stakeholders are involved at all levels in every step of the process along with the change agents, who facilitate and channel stakeholder input and energy.

Change agents delegate various aspects of the change effort to stakeholders when using the **participation** strategy. As Nutt (2002) comments, "Problematic stakeholders and people with important points of view, vested interests, and knowledge" are included in the participatory process. Change agents work with the parties to develop the change and share control of the process and final product with participants. One or more change agents often propose the initial plan for participation, which is subject to amendment by participants, and facilitate the process (see Straus, 2002, for an excellent discussion of facilitation).

There are two types of participation strategies. *Complete participation* involves all of the stakeholders in specific roles. For example, a stakeholder with financial acumen might focus on this aspect of quality improvement, another with a pathology specialization might focus on improvements in this area, while a nurse might focus on workload and role implications for nurses and orderlies. In the case of *delegated participation* representatives of the stakeholder groups work on the change. In some cases the representatives are formally selected by the groups, while in others the change agents invite a credible representative of a stakeholder group to join the process. One example of delegated participation in hospital quality improvement is the quality council, a representative body in which delegates of each stakeholder group make key decisions.[17] The key for both types of participation is that change agents hand over elements of the change process to stakeholders and position the stakeholders as primary drivers of change.

Nutt calculated the frequency of use of each of the four strategies, their success rates, and the average "installation time" from the beginning of the change effort to adoption or rejection of the change. Table 9.3 summarizes his findings.

Nutt's results are telling. Edict was the most commonly employed strategy, with persuasion following close behind. Much less common were participation and intervention, used in only about a quarter of the time. This suggests that top management and change agents felt a need to control most change processes. However, *feeling* a need to control change is not the same as *being able* to control it. Nutt assessed how many of the changes were sustained for at least two years and fully implemented. Intervention and participation are much more effective in terms of these criteria than are persuasion and edict.

In terms of time for implementation, none of the approaches took less than about a year to succeed – significant change takes time. But of the four approaches, intervention and delegated participation took the least time, clearly besting the other approaches. Persuasion fared most poorly of the approaches in terms of punctuality, taking 26 months on average.

It may seem easy to simply order people to change or to ask them to trust the experts and follow along. Conversely, involving people, particularly those who may disagree with you and "make waves," may seem to require too much trouble and effort. Nutt's research – and the testimony of many other change agents and scholars – suggests precisely the opposite conclusion, however. The greatest chance for successful change comes when

Table 9.3 **Implementation Strategies, Frequency of Use, Success Rate, and Time Required**

Strategy	*Frequency of use*	*Success rate*	*Average time required*
Edict	40%	38–50%	17 months
Persuasion	36%	49–58%	26 months
Intervention	6%	90–100%	11 months
Participation: complete	6%	90–100%	16 months
Participation: delegated	10%	79–84%	10 months

key stakeholders are engaged and involved. Putting in the extra effort to plan and to involve stakeholders pays dividends, leading to a greater chance of successful change and shorter time to implement. In short, a more intense, involved change effort at the outset increases chances of success.

Nutt's study focuses primarily on major changes. What about smaller changes within a department or in one aspect of an organization that affect only a small number of stakeholders? Provided that stakeholders care about the change and are required to implement it, engaging and involving them is most likely to lead to success. In cases in which no one is particularly concerned or in which stakeholders can be compelled, less participative strategies are likely to work just as well.

Nutt's study also implies that organizations employ only a single strategy when implementing changes. It is, however, possible that different strategies will be employed at different stages of the implementation. An involvement strategy might, for example be employed to get a change rolling, and then once momentum had built, edicts could be used to force the relatively smaller group of employees who do not want to cooperate to comply with the change.

Communication and Implementation

Communication plays an important role in implementation. It is the primary means by which the nature and merit of the change is conveyed. Communication enrolls and engages stakeholders, and each of the modes of stakeholder involvement has a significant communication component. Campaigns for change are in large part communication campaigns.

Sense Making and Storytelling So far we have discussed the role of communication in shaping innovation decision making, influencing the development of the innovation idea, building coalitions, and involving stakeholders. This section will focus on two related communication processes that are particularly important during implementation, sense making and storytelling (Lewis, 2011).

Uncertainty (too little knowledge to enable clear interpretations of the situation and events) and **equivocality** (ambiguity that leads to too many possible interpretations of the situation and events) are commonplace during organizational change. Members of the organization face a future that is difficult to anticipate and the tension that goes with it. While some people are quite comfortable with uncertainty and/or equivocality, most desire to reduce them.

As we discussed in Chapter 8, Karl Weick (1995) has observed that people engage in **sense-making** processes in order to reduce uncertainty and equivocality. As we also noted in Chapter 8, while we often think of interpretation as something that goes on in our heads, Weick observes that we often create interpretations by interacting with others. For example, a group of employees might engage in a discussion to work out how an innovation will change their jobs and, perhaps, whether it will render their jobs redundant.

One of the reasons that the more participatory strategies tend to be more effective in bringing about change may be that the high level of contact among change agents and stakeholders promotes sense making. Change agents are able to share information with stakeholders that reduces their uncertainty and equivocality about the change. Through mutual interaction, stakeholders and change agents construct compatible interpretations of the change. In some cases, these interactions enable change agents to influence stakeholder perceptions of the change and in others stakeholders and change agents both contribute to sense making. Change agents are not always clear on the nature of change themselves. One change agent involved in implementing a quality improvement program in a hospital commented to Poole that she did not realize the extent to which the program would change the patient experience in the hospital. It was only after talking with several nurses that she grasped the potential of the program to speed the recovery process and shorten hospital stays. This was self-evident to the nurses (who were great supporters of the program), and they had to explain it to the change agent.

Storytelling is a second important communication process in organizational change. Psychologist Jerome Bruner (1986) observed that human understanding comes in two forms, logical understanding that comprehends the world by clearly defining its parts and showing how they interrelate, and narrative understanding that shows how one event led to another and that to another and so on in story form. Narrative understanding underpins academic fields such as history, but it is also a key ingredient of everyday life. As children we learn from stories and throughout life we account for our own and others' behavior with stories. Stories also have deep emotional appeal, which adds to their impact. There are common story lines that all members of a culture are familiar with, such as the rags-to-riches story common in the United States and also more general stories common throughout many cultures, such as the heroic quest storyline (Bormann, 1996; Campbell, 1949; Cawelti, 1974).

Bartel and Garud (2009) identified two ways in which stories help to sustain organizational change. First, they help people translate ideas into their own context and project the change will impact them. A narrative that tells what change is needed and what it will require of them helps members picture themselves changing. Second, stories help the sense making process that reduces uncertainty and equivocality. A story's plotline offers an interpretation of the situation, how the change will unfold, and what consequences it will have. Case 9.2 illustrates the role of stories and sense making in organizational change efforts.

Case Study 9.2

Storytelling Journeys Into Change

In the 1990s, New Zealand undertook a major shift from a regulated economy to one that resembled the United States free market economy. Often such changes happen gradually, but in New Zealand they were undertaken in a systematic and holistic manner. In the financial markets, interest rates were no longer controlled but were allowed to freely vary, and many regulations on banks and investments were relaxed or eliminated. Subsidies for agriculture and industry and financial support for exports of goods were cut or eliminated. Government was downsized and, as in the United States, many services previously provided by the government were "privatized," that is private companies were contracted by the government to provide them. This was a period of change (and some turmoil) for New Zealand's government and economy.

Infotech, a New Zealand-based subsidiary of the large US information technology company HugeInfo, experienced a period of change and turmoil in the 1990s, though not for the same reasons as New Zealand as a whole. The US parent company of Infotech was mired in a terrible slump in sales and loss of profitability. The attention of HugeInfo's management was largely on its major divisions in the United States, Europe, and Asia, and units in smaller countries like New

Zealand were left adrift. Infotech management was ordered to downsize considerably, laying off more than half its staff. Infotech was also told that it had to find ways to turn a profit or it might be closed, but it had to do so without resources of its parent company. In short, Infotech was being told it had to operate more independently and be more entrepreneurial.

As Infotech undertook these changes, its management wove stories about them. These stories circulated among Infotech employees and became touchstones for managers and employees alike as they enacted the changes demanded of Infotech. The company succeeded in transforming itself over a period of a couple of years, and stories played a part in this success.

Managers described the first few months of independence as "rebel days," in which they felt free to rebel against the culture of HugeInfo and develop their own approach. One manager commented that they would "overturn the sacred cows of the past" and "rebuild the mindset and behavior of the company" (Dunford and Jones, 2000, 1212).

To do this, these "rebels" would set out on a "1000-day journey" in which they would transform Infotech. The journey was framed as a round-the-world yacht race, a type of competitive sport that New Zealanders had excelled in. The goal of this race was to "recover faster than our competitors" (Dunford and Jones, 2000, 1212). And they would do it in "the Kiwi way," referring to the unique bird symbolic of New Zealand. This 1000-day journey would help the company reinvent itself, develop a new culture, revitalize sales, and perhaps even turn out new products. "Kiwi ingenuity" would be used to overcome problems and surmount obstacles blocking their progress.

One important goal of this journey was for Infotech to "learn to stand on its own two feet," independent of HugeInfo. Cast adrift as it was, the managers of Infotech took as a prerogative that they should operate more independently and entrepreneurially. As one put it, "The world does not owe us a living." So the journey was cast as a quest for independence. This theme of the Infotech change story reflected the changes taking place in New Zealand at the time. As described previously, the entire nation was moving from a social security model to a more individualistic free enterprise model. The need for Infotech to learn to "stand on its own two feet" resonated with these larger changes.

The story was further elaborated after a few months to reflect a major issue. The downsizing signaled a major shift as well in the employment contract between workers and the parent company: whereas before they assumed they would have lifetime employment, now they knew they were expendable. So, standing on their own two feet was further elaborated with a theme of "the end of the welfare state," which signaled that they were independent and had to make their own way. The story helped members make sense of the change and set a new course for the future. Interestingly, two versions of the story were spun out after this. In one, members declared that some members would do better than others in this new order. In the other, members said that it was important to find "the right place" in the organization so everyone could prosper.

This narrative was not created from scratch. It developed over time and was elaborated with each retelling. It was also dependent on members' prior knowledge of Infotech and previous stories about the branch and on events occurring in the larger society of New Zealand. Whereas previously Infotech drew its identity from HugeInfo, now they were "rebels" on a "1000 day journey." The journey plotline, in which one is traversing new lands, discovering new things, and dealing with problems along the way to the final (successful) destination, is common in literature and myth. As such, it gives members of Infotech a degree of certainty and familiarity, rather than positioning them as adrift in the unknown. The narrative also drew on themes from the media and other sources that were popular at the time, such as "the end of the welfare state.

The story and the changes it described were so compelling to Infotech managers and employees that they resisted when their parent company began a "reglobalization" effort the next year. This effort consisted of an attempt to reassert control over the same subsidiaries that had been tossed adrift. It was difficult for the members of Infotech to reconcile their journey toward independence with reglobalization, and another difficult process of change ensued. They saw the reimposition of control by HugeInfo as a "bureaucratization" of the company they had worked for two years to transform, something that threatened to bring an unwelcome end to their journey.

Using What You Have Learned

1. How do the stories help managers and members make sense of the change that Infotech was undergoing? How did they assist in getting the employees of Infotech to accept and contribute to the change process?
2. Infotech's change story incorporated themes similar to those circulating around New Zealand society regarding the social changes occurring during the late 1980s and 1990s toward a more open, market-oriented economy. Why did this enhance the effectiveness of the story among Infotech employees?

Questions to Think About and Discuss

1. One characteristic of an effective story is its coherency, the degree to which it is unified and presents a sensible account of events. Is the Infotech story coherent? Why or why not?
2. The Infotech story developed naturally, as managers talked to one another and to their employees about the changes that were taking place. Would the story have been as effective if managers had consciously planned and written it in an effort to "sell" the change to employees? Some organizational culture consultants advocate the creation of stories like Infotech's as a way to change culture. Is this strategy likely to work? Why or why not?
3. Did the Infotech story take stakeholders to the changes in Infotech into account, and if so, how? Was it likely to be equally effective with all groups of stakeholders?

Change agents can attempt to shape the change process by participating actively in sense making and storytelling. They can shape these processes to foster positive attitudes toward the change and to encourage implementation. Like all symbolic and communicative processes, however, neither sense making nor storytelling can be scripted or fully controlled. Once commenced, these processes take on a life of their own as multiple parties participate and contribute to them. A storyline that a manager might promote to encourage change can easily be diverted to resist it (for example, a counterstory to the one above might be "a 1000 day journey into nowhere"). Sense making and stories are most likely to follow routes marked out by the organization's existing culture and trying to propose interpretations or stories that run counter to it like swimming against the current – it can be done, but it takes a great deal of effort.

Strategies for Communication During Implementation Previously we discussed various ways in which stakeholders can be involved in organizational change and criteria for deciding who should be included and how to involve them. But it would be useful to consider in more detail how change agents might communicate with stakeholders. Lewis, Hamel, and Richardson (1991) derived a useful typology of six strategies for communicating with stakeholders during implementation processes, based on a study of nonprofit organizations.[18] They also defined two variables that seem to guide strategy selection.

In the **equal dissemination** strategy, change agents communicate to all stakeholders. This strategy emphasizes information sharing about the change, and information is shared readily and often. All types of communication media – including, but not limited to interpersonal contacts, meetings, press releases, email lists, and social media pages – are utilized. One change agent described this approach as follows:

> We're talking about nearly every day, using almost every mode possible. We made a conscious effort to communicate until we were blue in the face, because we didn't want the agencies to say, "we didn't know this change was coming." (Lewis *et al.*, 1991, 18)

Involvement is the change effort is selective under the equal dissemination strategy: different stakeholders will be involved in different ways. This strategy can be used with the edict, persuasion, and intervention strategies identified by Nutt.

The benefits of the equal dissemination strategy are that it is very open and projects an image of fairness, because change agents are communicating freely about the change. One cost of this strategy is that it requires a lot of effort on the part of change agents. Communication campaigns take time and resources, and it is often a good idea to dedicate one or more positions to this function.

A more serious potential cost is that, while this strategy projects openness, the underlying change strategy is that of selective involvement and control by the change agents. Disseminating information widely informs potential foes of the change and they may choose to raise objections. When such objections are broached, it is important to find ways to respond to them and, possibly, to involve the objectors. It is important to plan ahead how to involve potential or real opponents who "come out of the blue," or they may seize center stage and reroute discourse about the change in a negative direction. When this occurs, change agents must often spend an inordinate amount of time to mollify and win over opponents. In some cases, this will prove to be difficult if not impossible, because not involving them earlier in the process has alienated them.

The **equal participation** strategy employs interactive, two-way communication that invites stakeholders to contribute ideas, advice, and concerns. One change effort that employed this approach was described as follows:

> One thing we did was use town meetings to communicate internally. Externally, teams of volunteers from our regional office went to local city officials, community elite, and talked about [the change]. Then press releases were sent out. . . . We engaged in a lot of consensus building. . . . It helps to retain trust. (Nutt, 2002, 19)

Involvement in the equal participation strategy is broad, with important stakeholders or all types actively engaged in the various forms of involvement. This communication strategy is consistent with the intervention and participation implementation strategies described by Nutt.

One benefit of this communication strategy is that it is truly open. It offers an opportunity to build a community around the change in which disagreements and problems can be surfaced and dealt with. It also requires a great deal of time and effort on the part of all involved, especially the change agents. The main potential drawback is that this openness may surface stakeholders no one anticipated who object to the project. Again, planning ahead regarding how to deal with this eventuality will make the change effort much more likely to succeed.

A third communication strategy, **quid pro quo**, involves concentrating communication efforts on stakeholders who have valuable resources that the organization needs, such as its key sources of funding and individuals with important contacts. Those who are most valuable are given privileged access to information and to the change agents, enabling them to have greater influence over the change. This strategy assumes that there are limited resources to devote to communication and that they should be committed where they will do the most good for the organization in the long term. This also means that some stakeholders who might otherwise be included will receive less communication and may be cut out of the process altogether. One change agent described the attitude behind this strategy as follows:

> I try to give the board, especially the executive committee, the most information. Because they own this organization. They are the public trustees. . . . If we can get key stakeholders to accept change, then it happens. (Nutt, 2002, 22)

Quid pro quo, by definition, hinges on restricted involvement. It is most consistent with the edict and persuasion implementation strategies, but could also be employed in a limited form of intervention.

The quid pro quo communication strategy is more efficient than the first two. It reduces the time and effort that must be devoted to communication, though it is critical to communicate effectively and sufficiently with the chosen stakeholders. If word of the change can be kept within a limited network, it is also possible that quid pro quo can enable the change to "sneak in under the radar," and keep objections to a minimum. This is most likely to be feasible when the change is relatively small and its impacts limited. If, however, word gets out about the change effort, those left "out of the loop" are likely to be angry and alienated. The change agents may find, ironically, that some of those it originally left out are more valuable to the organization than they originally thought they were. If there is serious underestimation of stakeholder value, then the quid pro quo strategy could have negative long-term consequences.

In a fourth strategy, **need to know**, change agents do not communicate about the change except with those who really have to know or who express a desire to be informed. As with quid pro quo, there is an emphasis on efficiency of communication. Whereas in the case of quid pro quo the motivation was to ensure that key stakeholders would continue to support the organization after the change, in the case of need to know the motivation is to avoid arousing opposition and/or to avoid overburdening others with unnecessary information. As one change agent commented about this strategy,

> One of our programs is... partially funded by the state. Because we've had so many management changes in that program, we're going to be monitored by the state. And the CEO told us not to tell the board that we're monitored because they don't want them to try to micromanage [us]. (23)

The need to know strategy is premised on limited stakeholder involvement and so is most consistent with the edict and persuasion implementation strategies. It could also be used with a limited intervention approach.

The need-to-know strategy has the benefit of being efficient. If information about the change can be controlled and contained within a limited network, then potential opponents may not become aware of the change until it is sufficiently implemented that it cannot be dislodged. But, if concerned stakeholders learn of the change, they may react at being left out of the process, just as with previous communication strategies.

Marketing, the fifth communication strategy, hinges on tailoring messages to the variety of stakeholders involved. Each stakeholder is likely to be concerned with different elements and effects of the change. Marketing requires change agents to adapt the communications to the concerns of various stakeholders. For example, advisory board members might receive messages focusing on the economic and budgetary aspects of the change, whereas clients might be informed about improvements in service or product. A practitioner of this strategy commented,

> Depending on what group you're talking to, your strategies are going to be different. When you talk to staff, you can depend on their direct experience. When you talk to the board, somehow, you have to make it illustrative. . . . The staff knows how important [change] is. The board has to be led to it. (25)

This communication strategy casts a broader net than the quid pro quo or need to know strategies, but the change agents keep control of the message. They decide what information to share and frame how it is presented to particular stakeholder audiences. It can be used with any of the implementation strategies. However, to use it properly with the intervention and participatory strategies, care must be taken to present the full range of information relevant to stakeholders and to avoid strategic omissions. There should also be the opportunity for two way interaction if the strategy is to be used with intervention and participatory strategies.

Tailoring messages to the intended audience is a staple of effective communication. It reduces the information load so that audiences are provided with what they need and do not have to deal with extraneous topics. The research involved in defining, understanding, and adapting to audiences also helps change agents understand their concerns and may enable them to adapt the change so that it more suitable for those who must support it and are affected by it. The major cost of this strategy is the significant commitment of time and effort that marketing requires.

The final strategy for communicating change is the **reactionary** approach, in which change agents do not engage in planned communication with stakeholders and communicate only when required to do so. This approach is characteristic of change efforts in which change agents do not recognize the importance of communication. In this case, little in the way of time and resources is devoted to communication. The downside of the reactive approach is that change agents lose control of the communication agenda, which tends to be set by demands from stakeholders for responses from the change agents. (See Table 9.4.)

Lewis *et al.* proposed that change agents' selection of strategies was related to their perception of two needs in the implementation process: the need for communicative efficiency and the need for consensus building. Communicative efficiency refers to the accomplishment of the communication task with "a minimum expenditure of time, effort, and resources" (28). Consensus building refers to building joint agreement around the course of action in the change effort. They posited that depending on the specific needs perceived by change agents, different communication strategies would be utilized, as shown in Table 9.5.

As the table shows, if the need for communicative efficiency and consensus building are both perceived to be low, the equal dissemination model, which assumes one-way communication is likely to be used. When there is low need for consensus and high need for efficiency, then the need to know model is predicted to be most effective.

When the need for efficiency is low but the need for consensus building is high, then the equal participation and marketing models are expected to have the best fit. The equal participation model emphasizes reaching out and interacting with a range of stakeholders,

Table 9.4 Communication Strategies During Implementation

Strategy	*Definition*	*Openness*	*Time and resources required*	*Nature of stakeholder involvement*	*Qualifications*
Equal dissemination	One-way communication with all stakeholders	High	High	Selective	May surface opposition
Equal participation	Two-way communication with all stakeholders	High	High	Broad and inclusive	May surface opposition
Quid pro quo	Two-way communication with key stakeholders	Low	Low	Selective	May omit parties who will object because they are left out
Need to know	Limit communication and interaction to those who are directly involved	Low	Low	Selective	May omit parties who will object because they are left out
Marketing	Adapt message to specific stakeholder interests and values	Moderate	High	Selective	Messages must be properly adapted to the intended audiences
Reactive	Do not plan communication strategy; react to events that arise	Low	Low	Low	Opponents of change may set agenda

Table 9.5 Best Communication Strategies Depending on Need for Efficiency and Need for Consensus Building

	Low need for communication efficiency	*High need for communication efficiency*
Low need for consensus building	Equal dissemination	Need to know
High need for consensus building	Equal participation and marketing	Quid pro quo and marketing

which as we noted is likely to build consensus. The marketing model tailors messages to stakeholders and is likely to persuade them to go along since it focuses on their particular concerns and values.

When the need for both efficiency and consensus building is high, Lewis *et al.* recommend the quid pro quo and marketing models. They argued that quid pro quo would be the most likely strategy to be applied in this case, as it represents a case where there are limited resources for communicating and to expend them most effectively, they should be devoted to the most significant stakeholders. Since only a few stakeholders are involved in this case, the marketing approach could be used to adapt to these stakeholders while sustaining the efficiency required for this case.

Although we have discussed the six strategies as though they were either-or choices, many implementation efforts combine some of them. Marketing is a strategy that is particularly easy to combine with other strategies. Quid pro quo can also be combined with other strategies when efficiency is important, because it stresses focusing on a limited number of critical stakeholders.

To what extent does the Lewis typology extend to other types of organizations? Nonprofit organizations face the most complex environments and taxing problems of any type of organization. They must balance the needs of multiple stakeholders, including clients, government agencies, the public, donors, and private companies they work with. We would argue that the most complete typology of strategies will emerge from considering such organizations.

Reflections on Organizational Change

Throughout this chapter we have discussed the importance of including stakeholders in organizational change efforts. But, as we noted in Chapter 4, participation can be hollow if those in positions of power do not really open the process up. Either knowingly or unaware, powerful parties may orchestrate change efforts in ways that benefit them and preserve privileged positions that ought to be altered by a sincere change process.

Zorn, Page, and Cheney (2000) argue that change became a central organizing principle during the last decades of the twentieth century. The assumption of the need for continuous change organized around quality improvement, customer service, and teamwork has become so established, they argue, that it operates largely unquestioned. An organization's ability to change is taken as a sign of its effectiveness, and more meaningful metrics such as quality of its products or services or its contribution to the economy and society, receive less emphasis as a result. For example, a change leading to an improvement in quality measured in relationship to the quality of similar or competing organizations might actually still result in substandard products or services, if the prevailing standards of quality are low (as they were, for example, in the US auto industry in the 1970s). However, because of the emphasis on change, *that the organization changed to become a leader among its peers* is likely to be taken as an indicator of effectiveness.

Change for change's sake is a waste of time and energy. Organizational change always involves some pain, even when it is necessary. It may, for example, result in layoffs, reorganizations that cause as many problems as they solve, and alterations in previously satisfying jobs so that they are no longer as enjoyable. Unless there is a tangible gain from the change – or at least the potential of such even if it is not realized – then a good case can be made that the organization is *not* effective merely because it undertakes a change program.

Valuing change for the sake of change keeps the organization from confronting important questions like "Why are we changing?" "What purpose does the change serve?" "Who does this change really benefit?" and "Is this change really workable for stakeholders?" It is critical to ask and to revisit these questions throughout the change process. In any prolonged change effort, there are many points at which key decisions and choices must be made, and at any of these sectional interests may prevail at the expense of the larger good of the broad set of stakeholders. For example, if a change involves reducing positions, is this necessary for enhanced efficiency and quality or is it rather driven by an agenda of reinforcing management control or of settling scores?

Organizations like the Institute for Healthcare Improvement, which has been mentioned often in this chapter, emphasize the importance of changing toward quality, service, and empowerment of stakeholders against well-defined benchmarks, rather than in a relative sense. It is important for change agents to keep concrete goals as reference points and not to assume that simply bringing about change means they have improved the organization.

It is also important to recognize that a high quality change process is also important. Change communication practices should be evaluated in terms of their inclusiveness, transparency and emancipating qualities. This is important for two reasons. First, an inclusive, transparent change process enables stakeholders to participate effectively and to "keep each other honest" throughout the process. An open change process fosters discussion of the key questions outlined above and other concerns. Second, an open change process can literally transform the organization. Change processes should not only bring about organization change, they should build members' capacity to innovate, to develop ideas, and to work together for the greater good. Change should not simply improve what the organization does; it should improve its members as well.

CONCLUSION

As this chapter shows, organizational change may seem relatively straightforward – you just order people to change! As we have seen, things are hardly this simple. First, change agents must understand the problem or opportunity confronting the organization, and then they must build a constituency supporting change to counteract the problem or to take advantage of the opportunity. This constituency consists of stakeholders who are needed to carry out the change, who are affected by the change, who have necessary resources, or who could mount significant resistance that could torpedo the change.

Innovations must be invented or discovered, a complex process in its own right. Most new ideas come from outside the organization, and so must be adapted to fit it. Adaptation takes time and experimentation, and this necessitates continuous work by change agents to maintain a coalition in favor of the change.

Members' decision to adopt also follows a protracted process much akin to the process of persuasion. Adoption depends on characteristics of the adopters, such as their innovativeness, characteristics of the innovation itself, institutional pressures, and the actions of change agents. Diffusion of an innovation through an organization begins slowly and gradually gains momentum until it suddenly "takes off" and spreads more rapidly, eventually slowing down as a few resistors refuse to make the change.

Change agents utilize a variety of strategies to press implementation of organizational change, including edict, persuasion, intervention, and participation. Ironically the most commonly used strategies, edict and persuasion, are less effective in bringing about change than the lesser used intervention and participation strategies. The latter two strategies rest on involving stakeholders to a greater degree than do edict and persuasion strategies.

To help carry out these implementation strategies, appropriate strategies for communicating with stakeholders must be developed. As we have seen, the relative importance of the need for efficiency and the need to build consensus are likely to influence change agents' choices among strategies.

Scholars have likened organizational change to a journey (Van de Ven, Polley, Garud, and Venkatraman, 1999). We set out with a clear destination in mind, but unexpected events, twists and turns, and setbacks require us to change course and adjust throughout.

Sometimes the journey ends where we intended. In other cases, the journey ends in a completely unexpected place. Missteps and setbacks help us learn. In some cases, learning helps us move forward with the change; in other cases, it may lead us to blunder and result in setbacks (not all learning is valid). Sometimes we must discontinue the journey, return to the beginning, and bide our time until conditions are more favorable to restart. Making this journey helps us learn about the organization and about ourselves. This may make us more effective in the long run. But it is always important to ask and repeat the question: What is the purpose of this change, and is it for the greater good?

NOTES

1 Tripp (1970, 147).

2 This was not the case for certain items, such as porcelain and pottery. However, Japanese companies flooded the US and European markets with cheap toys and novelties, and the wide exposure of these products contributed to the poor reputation of Japanese goods.

3 Both of these examples are described in Sawyer (2007).

4 Everett M. Rogers has written the authoritative description of adopter types in Chapter 7 of *Diffusion of Innovations* (2003). The descriptions of adopters draw largely on this chapter. The categories are defined based on standard deviations for the mean adoption time for the population of adopters. The innovators are two standard deviations earlier than the mean, which means they are *really* early on the curve; the early adopters are one standard deviation earlier than the mean; the early majority is between the mean and one standard deviation above the mean; the late majority is between the mean and one standard deviation below the mean; and the laggards are more than one standard deviation below the mean adoption time.

5 This is the case at the universities where we work, for example. Each university stocks several different types of computers, office software suites, and statistical programs, and each faculty member has the options of choosing those that he or she prefers, or even of purchasing a different one if it is not too much more expensive than those offered by the university. However, in many organizations there is much less choice.

6 For example, see Gaudin (2010), which recounts how the telecommunications company Alcatel-Lucent is encouraging the use of social-networking applications.

7 Rogers is aware of this and discusses the differences between organizational adoption and individual adoption of innovations.

8 This example is adapted from Rogers (2003, 262–265).

9 It is interesting to note that many of these "excellent" corporations had severe problems within ten years of the publication of *In Search of Excellence* (Peters and Waterman, 1982). Several of them went out of business, and many would not be recognizable to today's readers. Evidently, excellence in the immediate term does not mean survival over the long term.

10 The Institute for Healthcare Improvement (IHI) was founded specifically to enhance quality in medical care. More information can be found at www.ihi.org.

11 These goals were originally set by the Institute of Medicine.

12 The Joint Commission for the Accreditation of Hospitals (JCAH) was founded by the American College of Physicians (ACP), the American Hospital Association (AHA), the American Medical Association (AMA), the Canadian Medical Association (CMA), and the American College of Surgeons in the 1950s. It is an independent, not-for-profit organization whose primary purpose is to provide voluntary accreditation for hospitals. In the 1980s Congress tied Medicare funding to certification by the JCAH (now known as the Joint Commission). The Joint Commission has long been interested in quality. It founded Quality Healthcare Resources (QHR) as a consulting subsidiary in the 1960s. Like IHI, QHR was another of the organizations that constituted the normative pressure to adopt quality management in health care. See Joint Commission (2011).

13 Roberts and Fusfield (2004); see also Pinchot (2004) and Rogers (2003, chap. 9).

14 Paul Nutt's (1984) book on methods for planning has encyclopedic coverage of numerous methods for involving stakeholders in change.

15 In a classic article, Donald Klein (1976) points out that resistance may cue the change agent to real problems in the innovation and to unanticipated consequences of the change for the organizational system.

16 A classic treatment of the planning and implementation of change can be found in Gerald Zaltman and Robert Duncan (1977). They divide implementation strategies along lines similar to those found by Nutt (2002) in his empirical investigation. Their book has a wealth of useful detail on how to carry out and combine their four classes of strategies: facilitative strategies, reeducative strategies, persuasive strategies, and power strategies.

17 Quality councils are common in hospital quality programs, and not all of them represent true delegated participation. In some cases, they are established after or alongside edict and persuasion strategies in an effort to legitimize the change. In this case the quality council might be mere window dressing, with top management, change agents, and experts making the consequential decisions and choices and the council merely "rubber stamping" their decisions. Nutt (2002) calls this type of participation "token participation," and we have discussed its problems in Chapter 4. Quality councils may also be established for change efforts using the intervention strategy as one means of soliciting stakeholder input.

18 Nonprofit organizations are nongovernmental organizations that provide goods and services for purposes other than making a profit. Examples include churches, charities, the Red Cross, the Girl Scouts, Doctors Without Borders, and Oxfam.

REFERENCES

Adler, P.S. (1992). "The 'Learning Bureaucracy': New United Motor Manufacturing, Inc." *Research in Organizational Behavior* 15: 111–194.

Bartel, C.A. and Garud, R. (2009). "The Role of Narratives in Sustaining Organizational Innovation." *Organization Science* 20: 107–117.

Blumenthal, D. (1995). "Applying Industrial Quality Management Science to Physicians' Clinical Decisions," in Blumenthal and Scheck, eds., *Improving Clinical Practice: TQM and the Physician*. San Francisco: Jossey-Bass.

Blumenthal, D. and Scheck, A.C. (1995). *Improving Clinical Practice: TQM and the Physician*. San Francisco: Jossey-Bass.

Bormann, E.G. (1996). "Symbolic Convergence Theory and Communication in Group Decision Making," in R.Y. Hirokawa and M.S. Poole, eds., *Communication and Group Decision Making*, 2nd ed. Thousand Oaks: Sage.

Bruner, J. (1986). *Actual Minds, Possible Worlds*. Cambridge, MA: Harvard University Press.

Campbell, J. (1949). *The Hero With a Thousand Faces*. New York: MJF Books.

Cawelti, J. (1974). *Apostles of the Self-Made Man*. Cambridge, MA: Harvard University Press.

Cole, R.E. and Scott, W.R. (2000). *The Quality Movement and Organization Theory*. Thousand Oaks, CA: Sage.

Dunford, R. and Jones, D. (2000). "Narrative in Strategic Change." *Human Relations* 53: 1207–1226.

Gaudin, S. (2010). "Telecom Giant Takes to Web 2.0." *Computerworld*, July 26, 5.

Goldenberg, J. and Oreg, S. (2007). "Laggards in Disguise: Resistance and Adoption and 'The Leapfrog Effect.'" *Technological Forecasting and Social Change* 74: 1272–1281.

Howell, J.M. and Higgins, C.A. (1990). "Champions of Change: Identifying, Understanding, and Supporting Champions of Technological Innovations." *Organizational Dynamics* 19: 40–55.

Johnson, S. (2010). *Where Good Ideas Come From: The Natural History of Innovation*. New York: Riverhead Books.

Joint Commission (2011). "History of the Joint Commission." www.jointcommission.org/AboutUs/joint_commission_history.htm.

Juran, J.M. (1992). *Juran on Quality by Design: The New Steps for Planning Quality Into Goods and Services*. New York: Free Press.

Kanter, R.M. (1988). "When a Thousand Flowers Bloom: Structural, Collective, and Social Conditions for Innovations in Organization." *Research in Organizational Behavior* 10: 169–211.

Kao, J. (2009). "Tapping the World's Innovation Hot Spots." *Harvard Business Review*, March, 109–116.

Katz, R., ed. (2004). *The Human Side of Managing Technological Innovation*, 2nd ed. New York: Oxford.

Klein, D. (1976). "Some Notes on the Dynamics of Resistance to Change: The Defender Role," in Bennis, Benne,

Chin and Corey, *The Planning of Change*, 3rd ed. New York: Holt, Rinehart and Winston.

Lazarsfeld, P.F., Berelson, B. and Gaudet, H. (1944). *The People's Choice: How the Voter Makes up His Mind in a Presidential Campaign*. New York: Duell Sloan.

Leblibici, H., Salancik, G.R., Copay, A. and King, T. (1988). Institutional Change and the Transformation of Interorganizational Fields: An Organizational History of the U.S. Radio Broadcasting Industry." *Administrative Science Quarterly* 36: 333–363.

Lewis, L. (2011). *Organizational Change: Creating Change Through Strategic Communication*. Malden, MA: Wiley-Blackwell.

Lewis, L., Hamel, S.A. and Richardson, B.K. (1991). "Communicating Change to Nonprofit Stakeholders: Models and Predictors of Implementers' Approaches." *Management Communication Quarterly* 15: 5–41.

Nelson, R.R. and Rosenberg, N. (1993). "Technical Innovation and National Systems," in Nelson and Rosenberg, ed., *National Innovation Systems: A Comparative Analysis*. New York: Oxford.

Nutt, P.C. (1984). *Planning Methods for Health and Related Organizations*. New York: Wiley.

Nutt, P.C. (2002). *Why Decisions Fail: Avoiding the Traps and Blunders That Lead to Debacles*. San Francisco: Barrett-Koehler.

Peters, T. and Waterman, R. (1982). *In Search of Excellence*. New York: Harper & Row.

Pinchot, G. (2004). "Innovation Through Intrapreneuring," in Katz, ed., *The Human Side of Managing Technological Innovation*, 2nd ed. New York: Oxford.

Poole, M.S. and Van de Ven, A.H. (2004). "Theories of Organizational Change and Innovation Processes," in Poole and Van de Ven, eds., *Handbook of Organizational Change and Innovation*. New York: Oxford University Press.

Roberts, E.B. and Fusfield, A.R. (2004) "Critical Functions: Needed Roles in the Innovation Process," in Katz, ed., *The Human Side of Managing Technological Innovation*, 2nd ed. New York: Oxford.

Rogers, E.M. (2003). *Diffusion of Innovations*, 5th ed. New York: Free Press.

Sawyer, K. (2007). *Group Genius: The Creative Power of Collaboration*. New York: Basic Books.

Schroeder, R., Van de Ven, A. Scudder, G. and Polley, D. (1986). "Managing Innovation and Change Processes: Findings from the Minnesota Innovation Research Program." *Agribusiness* 2: 501–523.

Scott, W.R. (2008). *Institutions and Organizations: Ideas and Interests*. Thousand Oaks, CA: Sage.

Straus, D. (2002). *How to Make Collaboration Work*. San Francisco: Barrett-Koehler.

Tolbert, P.S. and Zucker, L.G. (1983). "Institutional Sources of Change in the Formal Structure of Organizations: The Diffusion of Civil Service Reform 1880–1935." *Administrative Science Quarterly* 30: 22–39.

Tornatsky, L.G. and Johnson, E.C. (1982). "Research on Implementation: Implications for Evaluation Practice and Evaluation Policy." *Evaluation and Program Planning* 5:193–198.

Tripp, R.T. (1970). *The International Thesaurus of Quotations*. New York: Harper & Row.

Van de Ven, A. H., Angle, H. and Poole, M.S., eds. (2000). *Research on the Management of Innovation*. New York: Oxford University Press.

Van de Ven, A., Polley, D., Garud, R. and Venkatraman, V. (1999). *The Innovation Journey*. New York: Oxford.

Von Hippel, E. (1988). *The Sources of Innovation*. New York: Oxford University Press.

Walker, J.L. (1966). "The Diffusion of Innovations Among the American States." *American Political Science Review* 63: 880–899.

Weick, K.E. (1995). *Sensemaking in Organizations*. Thousand Oaks, CA: Sage.

Zaltman, G. and Duncan, R. (1977). *Strategies for Planned Change*. New York: John Wiley and Sons.

Zorn, T.E., Page, D.J. and Cheney, G. (2000). "Nuts About Change: Multiple Perspectives on Change-Oriented Communication in a Public Sector Organization." *Management Communication Quarterly* 13, 515–566.

CHAPTER 10

COMMUNICATION AND DIVERSE WORKPLACES

Diversity is the one true thing we all have in common; celebrate it every day.
Anonymous

We should all know that diversity makes for a rich tapestry, and we must understand that the threads of this tapestry are all equal in value, no matter what their color.
Maya Angelou

By the end of the 1980s, over two thirds of the American [US] workforce was employed in organizations with international connections. . . . Indeed, it is now virtually impossible to conceive of a completely domestic, unicultural organization or organizational communication practices that do not have intercultural dimensions. The Hudson report, Workforce 2000, highlights the increasing racial, gender, ethnic, cultural, lifestyle, and age mix of American organizations; the open borders of the European Union have diversified their workforces; the political upheavals across Europe, Asia, and Africa have increased immigration, and communication technologies have minimized the saliency of geographical boundaries and national borders.
Cynthia Stohl[1]

CENTRAL THEMES

- The dominant perspective on organizations focuses on homogeneity and separation. Managers are separated from workers, organizations are separated from their environments, and employees are separated from their families and from members of other organizations.

Strategic Organizational Communication: In a Global Economy, Seventh Edition.
Charles Conrad and Marshall Scott Poole.

- Two processes – diversification and globalization – have challenged the dominant perspective by collapsing time and space. Organizations are increasingly heterogeneous, and "different" peoples are working in closer and closer proximity with one another.
- Organizational responses to increased diversification can be arrayed along a continuum from *denying* that it has occurred, to reducing its impact by attempting to *homogenize* the "others," to accepting their presence but *marginalizing* them, to *confronting* it as a positive development.
- In the long term, strategies of balanced innovation may affect significant change. They are sufficiently subtle to generate little resistance; although they make small changes, they can have major unintended consequences. Eventually, these small wins may actually change the dominant perspective and the power structure of organizations.
- Societal expectations and organizational processes combine to limit the organizational power and upward mobility of *other* employees.
- Confronting the dominant perspective begins in legitimate efforts to value "others" ways of acting and leading and by treating flexibility as more important than consistency.
- A number of factors have combined to make it increasingly difficult to balance home and work. Both organizations and individuals can take steps to enhance that balance.

KEY TERMS

essentializing
role encapsulation
quid pro quo sexual harassment
hostile environment sexual harassment
glass ceilings
flextime
flexplace
glass walls
mentors
familialism
machismo
simpatía

In Chapter 2 we introduced the concept of *hegemony*, the idea that the hierarchical relationships that exist within a society come to be treated as if they are *natural* (that is, inevitable) and *normal* (that is, expected and morally correct). Within each society, a set of taken-for-granted assumptions develops about organizations and organizational life. At least since the Industrial Revolution, and especially since traditional strategies of organizing were first articulated and spread throughout the world, organizations have been regarded as sites where managers control workers in an effort to maximize performance through rational decision making and the efficient use of resources. In these organizations, thinking is separated from doing, and the people responsible for one activity are assumed to be very different from the people charged with the other.

Along with separation comes homogeneity. In the nineteenth and twentieth centuries, most societies were built around segregation along gender, educational, class, and racial lines and there was a hierarchy among social groups. Those higher in the hierarchy tended to become the thinkers in the traditional organization and those lower down tended to become the doers. So in much of the world, men supervised women, upper classes supervised lower, those with more education were the thinkers, while those with less were the doers. Organizations also homogenized along occupations. Nurturing occupations tended to favor women and more "active" occupations – manufacturing, for example – favored men. There was also homogenization. And in some cases organizations homogenized along social divisions. Prior to World War II in the United States, whites and African Americans were often segregated into separate organizations.

Preconceived notions embedded in social representations of gender, race, and class often shape how work is organized and how organizations are structured (Ashcraft, 2001; Mumby, 1998; Nicotera, Clinkscales, Dorsey, and Niles, 2009). In a society where women are viewed as docile and easily molded, and men as naturally dominant, an organization may structure itself as a hierarchy in which women work on the production line and men in management positions (as is the case within Mexican *maquiladoras*). These hegemonic assumptions make the structure of the organization seem completely natural and inevitable – everyone *seems* to be playing organizational roles that are natural and normal.

Separation and homogeneity tends to build strong relations and enhanced communication within each group. This in turn increases the likelihood that a member of one group will find it difficult to occupy a position within divisions of the organization that are dominated by people with other attributes. When combined with taken-for-granted assumptions, homogeneity simplifies and stabilizes organizations, making organizational life more comfortable and predictable.

However, this dominant perspective has not gone unchallenged (Hafen, 2005). One does not have to observe organizations closely to realize that the doers possess a great deal of task-related expertise and that the thinkers often act in nonrational ways. Personal interests and political considerations often lead them to sacrifice efficiency and organizational performance. Organizational power and managerial control are resisted in many different ways. Instead of being the smoothly oiled machines depicted in the dominant perspective, organizations are sites where contradictions, fissures, and tensions constantly play out.

During the past two decades, homogenization has been challenged further by two processes – *diversification* and *globalization*. As people from different backgrounds and experiences enter organizations, and especially as they move into powerful positions in those organizations, and as Western organizations move into societies with different taken-for-granted assumptions, tensions are very difficult to ignore. The most important effect is that the heterogeneity that results can lead people to recognize that dominant organizational strategies are neither natural nor normal. They reflect a group of *choices* that societies and their members have made and reinforced through their everyday activities. They suggest that other forms of organizing are possible. Relational, cultural, and networking strategies of organizing make it clear that other options are available, and successful alternative forms of organizing indicate that prevailing assumptions themselves may be inaccurate. With change comes resistance, and strategic responses to that resistance.

RESISTING "OTHERS"

During the 1960s, women started to move into professional and managerial roles throughout northern Europe. During the 1970s and 1980s these trends reached the United States, United Kingdom, former Commonwealth countries (Canada, Australia, and New Zealand), and Korea, among others. During this same period, members of racial and ethnic minority groups increasingly entered the workforce. Today virtually every economy in the world is experiencing some degree of workforce diversification (Lerman and Schmidt, 2010).

Organizational responses can be arrayed along a continuum from denying that this has occurred, to trying to reduce its impact by attempting to homogenize the "others," to accepting their presence but attempting to marginalize them, to confronting it as a positive development. Different organizations and different societies respond in their own unique ways to the presence of different "others," just as different employees have unique experiences with diversification and develop distinctive strategies for dealing with resistance to the process. When discussing diversification, it is important not to **essentialize** the widely varying experiences and responses of individual members of different organizations, genders, classes, races, or individuals. Broad generalizations invariably obscure important differences in the experiences of the members of different societal groups (Ashcraft, 2004; Nicotera, Clinkscales, Dorsey, and Niles, 2009). Employees' perceptions and actions are influenced by their culture, gender, race, and economic class; but they also are influenced by family values, personality characteristics, life history and a host of other individual attributes. Conversely, it is also important to recognize that there are similarities in the strategic options that are available to employees in different organizations and different societies. Consequently, their strategic choices also may be quite similar (Hege, 1998; Oetzel and Bolton-Oetzel, 1997; Mohamed and Lloyd, 1990; van Dijk, 1993).[2]

Denying "Others" a Legitimate Place in the Organization

The simplest response to diversification, and the one that seems to be most common when an organization or economy is just beginning the process, is to deny "others" a legitimate place in organizations. In some cases, denial is not intentional. People interact with one another based on the whole person, which includes race and gender as well as organizational position, task assignments and professional expertise. Because managers and professional personnel in US organizations still are disproportionately white and middle-class, they often have not had much experience communicating with people who are different than they are and feel uncomfortable doing so. Or, they may fear that if they do offer advice or help, the newcomer will view their efforts as patronizing, sexist, or racist. So, they withdraw from him or her, and it takes longer for newcomers who are not white males to form effective interpersonal relationships, if they ever do. In highly paternalistic societies such as Latin America or traditionally Confucian cultures, young women often find that their suggestions are ignored by their superiors and they are ostracized by their peers (Kwong, 1994).

Current employees also may expect "others" to occupy low-power positions in their organizations, and as a result are less accommodating about providing inside information to newcomers who are in positions outside of those stereotypical roles. In spite of narrowing educational gaps in the United States between genders and races, women still tend to be concentrated in nurturing careers, such as nursing sales, and teaching among college-educated employees and clerical or service occupations for women without college degrees (Armas, 2003; US Department of Labor, 2005). These occupations are incredibly important to the society but typically carry limited power. Similarly, nonwhite college-educated men in the United States tend to be in staff positions, while those without degrees are disproportionately in lower-level production positions (Valdivia, 2003; US Department of Labor, 2010).

In ambiguous situations, people rely on stereotypes to guide their interactions – stereotypes that may be very inaccurate and misleading (Abrams and Hogg, 2003; Allen, 2000; Orbe and Everett, 2006). The newcomer experiences ***role encapsulation***, processes through which individual employees are perceived through racial or gender stereotypes. For example, some women simply are not warm, supportive, nurturing people and do not want to be, in spite of what dominant stereotypes suggest. Nurturance, like any other behavior, is learned, not innate. But, the stereotype is so powerful that supervisors, and peers, often assume women are nurturing "by nature" and try to negotiate them into support-oriented organizational roles (both formal and informal). Alternatively, they may attempt to train women to behave in more stereotypical ways, frequently without realizing that they are doing so. Similarly, some male engineers negotiate roles that allow them to focus on their families and avoid burnout, even in organizations where burnout and devaluing family life is both normal and a sign of masculinity (Eyer, 1992; Kunda, 1992; Mumby, 1998). Indeed, 75 percent of male employees in the United States say that they would exchange promotion opportunities and raises for more time to spend with their families. They are often unable to do so, because of the negative impact on their careers, status, and job security (Wood, 2009; DeHaven, 2002). As the "Childless/Childfree" case later in this chapter indicates, it may be even more difficult for men to escape encapsulated masculine roles than it is for women to escape traditional feminine roles.

Denial also may be conscious and intentional. In these cases it is accomplished through exclusion, overt discrimination, and/or through harassment. Its goal is to keep "others" out of the organization, to persuade them to leave it prematurely, or to force them to submit completely to the demands of dominant employees. In the West, discrimination usually is thought of in terms of overt bias in hiring and promotion decisions. First in northern Europe, then in Canada, the United States, and later in Australia, New Zealand, and southern Europe, a number of laws have been passed that make this kind of discrimination illegal. However, organizations often devise complicated strategies to circumvent or ignore these laws. Major corporations worldwide are regularly convicted of discriminating on the basis of race, sex, age, religion, or disability, or choose to settle cases out of court. For example, the Coca-Cola corporation in the United States accepted a record $192.5 million out-of-court settlement of a case in which 2000 current and former employees alleged that they were "systematically bypassed for raises and promotions" because of their race (the previous US record was $176 million in the Texaco case discussed in Chapter 12). The plaintiffs complained of a closed promotion system in which job openings were filled by less qualified and experienced white employees without ever being announced in public. Plaintiffs also complained of Coca-Cola's strategy of refusing promotions for minority employees on the grounds of budget constraints while finding ways to circumvent those constraints to promote whites. Plaintiff Elvenyia Barton-Gibson noted that "it's so unfortunate that in the year 2000, we are still fighting this kind of case. These should be dead issues" (quoted in Ivanovich, 2000, 20A; also see Prasso, 1996; Adame, 2011).[3]

Most instances like the Coca-Cola case only surface years after they occur, because they take so long to litigate (a more recent, less egregious example than the Coca-Cola case is a Wisconsin firm that paid a $1.65 million settlement for discriminating against women in its hiring practices [Ramde, 2011]). However, another measure of the prevalence of discrimination is the number of discrimination cases filed. In the United States, a record number of discrimination cases were filed in 2010 (Volk, 2011; Adame, 2011). This seems to be due to the fact that the recession of 2008 led to massive layoffs in 2009 and 2010. One attorney who represents those filing such cases commented, "When the economy goes bad more people get laid off. They start to look back" (Adame, 2011). An important implication of this comment is that many instances of discrimination are never reported, especially by those who continue in their jobs or just do not think it is worth the trouble.

However, discrimination often goes far beyond formal hiring and promotion decisions, and in many countries, employees have little legal recourse when they are discriminated against. For example, during the 1980s and 1990s many governments in Asia (for example, Hong Kong, Taiwan, South Korea, and Singapore) and Latin America acted to weaken labor movements and legal protections afforded workers, sometimes in the guise of anticommunism. Their goal was to create the "industrial peace" necessary to attract investment by Western organizations. In turn, Western corporations who were moving their production operations to Latin America and Asia sought out a labor force of young, single women, who they believed would be easy to control. For example, a manager of a *maquiladora* said that he preferred young and inexperienced female workers because they are "easier to shape to our requirements" and have a higher capacity for "eating bitterness."[4] Supervisors and labor contractors, almost all of whom were men, referred to women workers as "daughters," and treated them as "children" who should always "obey their parents (supervisors)." In societies where daughters are viewed as poor long-term investments, families and organizations sometimes collude to have workers work long hours at low pay because a substantial proportion of their income is returned to the family. These payments help compensate for the expenses of raising a "low-worth" (female) child. A Taiwanese worker reported that the system left her feeling trapped, like a "frog beneath a coconut shell" (Ong, 1987).

However, control systems also spawn resistance. Workers often view their jobs and income as a means of gaining independence, a measure of self-esteem, and as a way to improve their technical skills and obtain better jobs. Outside of work, they reject traditional mores regarding dress; they form friendships with coworkers from communities with very different societal standards and demand the right to select their own husbands and begin to act like Western consumers. For example, in Malaysia sales of cosmetics quadrupled in only two years, in spite of a traditional link between cosmetics and prostitution. (Asia is now by far the fastest growing market for Avon products). Of course, with this increased independence has come an increase in economic and personal insecurity, and increased efforts by their local societies to control their behavior more tightly. In Asia and Latin America, the creation of a large, single, female labor force has led to increased public pressure for women to behave "properly." Malay women, as well as women workers in West Java and Thailand, are perceived as invading male (public) places, and their social activities are closely monitored and controlled. Transnational companies in Islamic countries hold religious classes in the workplace in an effort to enhance "moral discipline," including working hard and obeying orders without question. In both Latin American and Asian countries, multinational corporations control workers by appealing to feminine sex roles through beauty pageants and cooking classes.[5]

In industrialized economies, denial is more frequently expressed in various forms of harassment than in overt discrimination. Racial harassment and ***quid pro quo* sexual harassment** (where a person is promised rewards in exchange for sexual activity or threatened with punishment or job loss if they reject sexual proposals) have been illegal for some time. In 1994, Australia, following Europe, Canada, and the United States also made "hostile environment" harassment illegal. Two landmark cases from Australia help explain this concept (Grace and Cohen, 1995). In 1989, a woman who was employed by Effective

Cleaning Services to clean the Brisbane K-Mart store was harassed by K-Mart manager Brian Drysdale, who told her she was a "naughty little girl." He touched her in inappropriate places, lifted her off the ground, chased her around the room, and made comments about her anatomy. When she complained to upper management, they believed Drysdale's denials. The worker took her case to the Human Rights and Equal Opportunity Commission and won her case. Since Drysdale never demanded sexual activity, her case was not covered under laws regarding *quid pro quo* harassment. But his behavior clearly created a hostile work environment based on her sex.

In virtually all Western countries, hostile environment laws were eventually expanded to encompass actions by coworkers that are known to management.[6] Again, Australia provides a typical case. Heather Horne and Gail McIntosh received compensation after being subjected to two years of verbal abuse, graffiti, and the display of softcore and hardcore pornography in their workplace, some of which the Western Australian Equal Opportunity Tribunal found to be grossly offensive and degrading. The worker's union sided with the organization, but the Tribunal did not. Damien Grace and Stephen Cohen (1995) explain the basis of the decision and why harassment often should be interpreted as a denial strategy:

> The display of pornography was anything but innocent. The two workers were bullied because they were different. This difference happened to be one of sex. It might as easily have been one of religion. . . . [T]he harassment is a particularly nasty display of sexism; the women were attacked as *women*. There was a clear assumption that women did not qualify for equal esteem with men . . . that they were powerless, and that they could be degraded through ridicule of their sex. (42, 148, emphasis in original)

As in similar cases in other industrialized countries, episodes such as these helped establish the illegality of **hostile environment sexual harassment**. Unfortunately, as the following case study indicates, harassment is still prevalent in organizations in the industrialized world, and the legal system is still emerging. In the United States, same-sex harassment was not ruled illegal until 1999, and educational institutions were not held liable for harassment of students until 2000. Even today, the legal requirements that must be met for a successful sexual harassment suit are more restrictive than in cases involving racial harassment, and maximum penalties are much smaller. Laws regarding religious- and age-based harassment are only now emerging in the United States and Canada as workforces become more diverse. Many societies – in Scandinavia, Southern Europe, Africa, and Asia – attempt to create conditions in which the distinctive contributions made by both male and female contributions can be combined and rewarded. But, in the United States, United Kingdom, and British Commonwealth countries, treating members of different groups in similar ways is valued, and those values are enforced through antidiscrimination law. Consequently, legal gaps and inequities create greater disadvantages than they might in more communitarian societies.

In addition, there is some evidence that harassment – in both nonviolent and violent forms – is increasing or holding steady in Europe, the United States, and Russia, among other nations. Overt hostility in the workplace – racist, sexist, and homophobic slurs in conversations, hate mail/graffiti/faxes, sabotage of work projects and computer files, and physical assaults – may be increasing, suggesting that attitudinal barriers to diversity may be on the upswing.[7]

Case Study 10.1

Sequestering Sexual Harassment[1]

Our media deliver repeated evidence of how pervasive sexual and racial harassment are in US organizations. In the 1990s Professor Anita Hill's testimony during the US Senate confirmation hearings for Supreme Court Justice Clarence Thomas brought the problem into the living rooms of everyone who owns a television set and the US Navy's Tailhook scandal, in which a number of female officers were shoved down a crowded Las Vegas hotel hallway and molested by a large group of Navy aviators, provided compelling evidence of the extent of the problem for those people who had doubted the veracity of Professor Hill's testimony.

Nor have things improved in the twenty-first century. Ninety percent of US high school women (and over 30 percent of men) report being sexually harassed at some point during their time in school. In previous editions of this book we recounted substantial settlements for sexual harassment cases, such as the 1996 lawsuit against Mitsubishi Motors Corporation for allowing sexual harassment to continue at its Normal, Illinois, assembly plants, which was settled for $34 million to the plaintiffs in 1998. Unfortunately, such cases are still common news. In 2009 Lowes home improvement company paid $1.72 million to three employees for sexual harassment, one of them a woman who was sexually assaulted by her supervisor and the other two men who were repeated taunted as "gay" by coworkers. When the men reported this behavior to their supervisor, he told them they should not spend so much time together and did nothing else.

When the subject of sexual harassment comes up, it is most common to focus on physical or direct verbal abuse. A common form of open harassment is *quid pro quo* harassment, in which a superior offers something of value such as a promotion or favorable job evaluation for sexual favors. Another type of harassment, *hostile environment* harassment, is more difficult to define and prevent. During the late 1990s, US courts have consistently ruled that repeated physical affronts – touching, groping, or pinching – are illegal. Symbolic actions – written or oral comments including sexual jokes or lewd comments, or displays like nude pinups or obscene or pornographic displays in electronic media – are, however, especially difficult to interpret and so are ambiguous. The US courts have ruled that these activities are illegal only if they are sufficiently extreme and pervasive that a reasonable person would conclude that they create a *hostile and intimidating work environment*, they were unwanted, and they were known by the plaintiff's supervisors, or reasonably could be expected to have been known by them. Consequently, what constitutes a hostile environment varies across different courts and different cases. Some courts still use a reasonable person standard – would a reasonable person interpret the behaviors in question as constituting a hostile work or educational environment. Other courts have substituted a "reasonable woman" standard, because there is clear research evidence indicating that women generally perceive a wider range of symbols and behaviors to be unwanted, hostile, or intimidating than do men.

The Mitsubishi Motors case provides an excellent example of the range of activities that may be illegal. The suit alleged that male workers called their female peers "sluts, whores and bitches"; they placed drawing of genitals and breasts and various sexual acts labeled with female employees' names on car fenders and cardboard signs along the assembly lines; explicit sexual graffiti such as "Kill the slut Mary" were scrawled on rest area and bathroom walls and one supervisor declared, "I don't want any bitches on my line. Women don't belong in the plant;" anonymous callers made threats like "You better watch your back, bitch" or "Die bitch, you'll be sorry." Women were subjected to groping, forced sex play, and male flashing; one complainant found her car defaced; another was forced off the road as she drove home from work; and in another case, a worker put an air gun between a woman worker's legs and pulled the trigger. However, only one of these actions – the supervisor's comment – is *in itself* illegal. Peer harassment is illegal only if supervisors are directly involved or know about, or could be expected to know about, the harassment. The allegations at Mitsubishi also claimed that plant management was repeatedly told of the actions and failed to take corrective measures.

Because of the threat of retaliation and intimidation if they complain, and because of the low likelihood of winning harassment cases (it is *very* difficult to produce sufficient evidence to meet the legal requirements), only about 10 percent of targets of harassment actually report the incidents. Fewer still file formal complaints. However, these open attempts to suppress harassment complaints are not the only things that keep them from coming out. Organizations and their employees exert more subtle pressures, pressures that are often neither obvious nor acknowledged.

In all kinds of organizations, harassment is most likely when the organization accepts and reinforces what we have called the "dominant perspective" – that the "normal" employee is white and male and that the number of "other" employees is relatively small. It is also likely in organizations in which power relationships between supervisors and their subordinates are highly unequal.

In a classic study that illuminated the hidden dimensions of response (or nonresponse) to sexual harassment, Robin Clair (1993) interviewed 50 working women concerning incidents they had experienced. The sample was designed so it was representative in terms of occupational status, race, whether the women were married or single, and whether they worked full- or part-time. Clair found that responses to sexual harassment reflected the operation of hegemony, as discussed in Chapter 2.

Organizations typically tried to frame harassment so that it did not represent a problem for them. For example, one woman said that her manager told her that to bring a sexual harassment lawsuit was not in the best interests of the company, attempting to take advantage of her identification with and loyalty toward the organization to prevail on her to let things pass. This attempt to represent the specific interests of the organization as identical with those of all employees is typical of the operation of hegemony.

Managers also attempted to deny or disguise the problem. For example, one manager swore that he would never let someone sexually harass anyone else. As a result, the complaining woman must have misunderstood the incident. Weaving a fog of uncertainty and doubt, the manager leads the victim to question her judgment, potentially weakening her resolve to pursue punishment for her harassment.

Some managers pursued "classic" hegemonic tactics, portraying the interests of the dominant male group as natural and "just part of things." The old "boys will be boys" excuse serves this function nicely. By portraying men as creatures whose natural desires must simply come out, a choice by the harasser to victimize the woman is converted into something that "just happens" as a natural course of things. So no one is to blame.

Hegemony operates through convincing the dominated group (women, in this case) to adopt the perspective of the dominant group as its own. The result is that the dominated group thinks along the same lines that the dominant group does, and therefore accepts and goes along with the dominant group's explanations, serving its interests. Clair found that a number of the women seemed voice interpretations of the harassment that served the interests of the organization. One woman, Abby, reporting on a case of harassment in a bar that started as joking but became more serious said, "I felt that I was jeopardizing my job, and [the harasser's] job. And I saw that there was no reason for that so I had to leave" (quoted in Clair, 1993, 124). By law and by right, the harasser should lose his job, but the victim instead gives up hers to keep from causing a difficult situation for the organization. That men have "natural urges" that lead them to engage in harassing behavior is not taken as a problem for the organization, but as something that must be taken as a given part of organizational behavior. Abby, in effect, took the blame for the incident on herself by taking the punishment for the incident.

Another common frame put on harassment by the victims was that it was just a misunderstanding. Perhaps the harasser was just flirting and should be forgiven for doing what men just naturally do. That the behavior of the harasser likely went well beyond flirtation in some cases is masked by this interpretation. As we observed in Chapter 8, the idea that conflicts are primarily due to communication problems is commonly expressed. More often, however, conflicts are rooted in real differences – in this case, the differences in interests between the victim, who simply wants to be left alone to do her job, and the harasser, who is pursuing another goal entirely – and to label them "communication problems' is to trivialize a serious situation. One victim commented that she just ignored harassment, that it was really not that important compared to other aspects of the job, trivializing things. Lisa indicated that she felt that "'he was just being touchy feely' and after some time she 'made a joke of it'" (quoted in Clair, 1993, 127).

Clair termed another common response "denotative hesitancy," referring to the fact that victims described what to an outsider was clearly harassment, but then refused to label it as such. One victim described harassment and interpreted it as a friendly, not sexual, gesture. Another described an incident in which one of her male coworkers cornered her and nearly touched her chest, but when asked if it was harassment, she replied, "Uh, kind of" (quoted in Clair, 1993, 129). This uncertainty does not offer much competition to the certainty that management offers in the examples discussed above. Harassment tends to be dismissed or trivialized in such cases.

Of course, not all women bought into the hegemonic viewpoint. Several indicated that they complained to managers or coworkers who took their stories seriously and moved to stop the harassment. Still others took more informal routes – "When my husband hears about this, he is not going to be happy" – that shut down the harasser. Still others pursued legal recourse.

Bringing legal charges of harassment, however, often proved to be unsatisfactory. An issue of the *Journal of Applied Communication* (Eadie & Wood, 1992) on sexual harassment in academic settings, contained many accounts that indicated the difficulty of making harassment charges "stick." Coworkers would often waffle or even refuse to provide evidence supporting the charges. Superiors would explain the harassment in ways that trivialized or naturalized them. In short, while instances of harassment are often against the law, it is something of an uphill battle to prove that they are, in fact, illegal.

The studies of harassment in academe showed that even to lodge a charge of harassment often endangers one's career. A Latina university employee explained that nonfaculty and nonstudent women have similar experiences:

> Everyone likes to pretend it doesn't happen. When you go from one position to the next in this university it's so small that bosses know each other and say, "Hey, this woman – watch out for her." So, you get blackmailed that way.

This self-sealing pressure against lodging harassment charges, suggests that prosecuting harassment is problematic.

Applying What You've Learned

1. What is *quid pro quo* harassment? *Hostile environment* harassment?
2. Why is harassment considered to be an issue of power or coercion?
3. What role does hegemony play in responses to harassment by the organization and by the victims?

Questions to Think About and Discuss

1. At a number of points in this book we have suggested that bureaucratic organizations typically suppress dissent, avoid conflicts, and restrict the flow of negative information. To what extent is the silence surrounding sexual or racial harassment simply another example of communication breakdowns in organizations? To what extent is it a function of racist or sexist attitudes? How might the two be interrelated?
2. Why isn't there more resistance to harassment? In other words, why do the women described by Clair fall victim to hegemony, being in effect victimized a second time?
3. What can be done to break this cycle of sequestering sexual harassment, which in turn leads to more silence and so on?

Note

1 This case is based on Clair (1993), Eadie and Wood (1992), and Keyton and Rhodes (1999). While these are rather old sources, unfortunately, the problem they depict has not changed very much.

Homogenizing "Others"

A second possible form of resistance to diversification is to accept it while trying minimize its impact. If "other" employees can be persuaded (or forced) to mimic the beliefs, values, and actions of organizational power holders, their entry into organization will lead to little or no change. "Old timers" in organizations have a number of reasons for wanting newcomers to change to "fit in" to existing organizational roles and practices instead of them having to change to accommodate newcomers. These incentives are especially strong when the newcomer is "different."

The Discourse of Accommodation Regardless of the country, one of the most common responses to "different" employees is to encourage them to minimize their "differentness," to accommodate themselves to the norms of their organizations, to learn and use the communicative strategies of the dominant group. But people who are all find it difficult to fit in. For example, lower class Latinos/as clearly *are* different than the educated, middle- to upper-class, white males who dominate "organization XYZ." In many cases, their lack of familiarity of "others" with the communication style of bureaucratic discourse makes fitting in all the more difficult (Ashcraft, 2001; Buzzanell, Meisenbach, Remke, Sterk and Turner, 2009; Nicotera *et al.*, 2009).

One means of doing so is always to *appear to be rational.* Because societal myths depict women, African American men, and Latinos as emotional (nonrational), using highly rational (that is, unemotional) forms of communication is especially important. A key part of the language of rationality is justifying decisions or proposals in data-based terms (recall Chapter 9) or in terms of the dominant values of the organizational culture. A second way of fitting in is to create an image of loyalty to the organization. In an era of rapid job turnover (recall the Generations case study in Chapter 1), perceived loyalty is an even more powerful image. The most common way of creating perceptions of loyalty is to repeatedly signal that the organization is one's highest priority. Although the symbols of loyalty differ in various organizations, there seems to be one common component: sublimating all other activities and relationships to one's career and one's working relationships. Consistently taking work home, seeking and accepting promotions or transfers even when they would be disadvantageous to one's family and limiting social ties to business contacts all seem to be widely accepted indices of loyalty. Of course, there is little evidence that these activities are either a reliable sign of loyalty or necessary to the successful operation of organizations. But they are part of the symbolic reality that guides perceptions. In traditionally structured middle- and upper-class families (Ward and June Cleaver of *Leave It to Beaver*, Reverend and Mrs. Camden of *7th Heaven*, or almost every family in the *Mad Men* television series), creating these impressions is possible. The professional's wife is available to serve as hostess, secretary, child care specialist, and therapist. But for unmarried professionals or married women professionals, there often is no one available to play this "wifely" role.

Presumably the husbands of women professionals could assist in home activities. However, studies of time allocation have found that they often spend no more time doing home-related work than husbands whose wives do not work outside of the home. Surveys have shown since the 1970s that husbands do less housework than wives, though the gap has narrowed somewhat from 1970 to 2008 (National Science Foundation, 2008). This narrowing suggests that in some families, women are able to negotiate more equitable distributions of household work.

For example, in separate studies Denise Segura (1997) and Beatri'z Pesquera (1997) examined how Latinas negotiated workload arrangements at home. Since Latin cultures strongly support traditional sex role arrangements, they expected that Latinas would find these negotiations to be especially difficult. They did find that it was a struggle for Latinas to negotiate more equitable arrangements, just as it is a struggle for non-Latin women to do so. The title to Pesquera's study is taken from a comment made by one of the women she interviewed: "In The Beginning He Wouldn't Even Lift a Spoon," or, as they say in Spanish, *no levanta ni una cuchara*. But, both researchers found that over time, couples often do negotiate more equitable task sharing, and that the dominant factors in their being able to do so are income and task requirements as much as culture.

White-collar Latinas bring a great deal of work home and have frequent evening meetings. Blue-collar Latinas often work evening or night shifts, or work more than one job. In both cases, the visible evidence of work spillover into family life makes it easier for them to negotiate more equitable arrangements with their husbands. Similarly, the closer a wife's income is to her husband's, the more bargaining power she has. But, they still have to negotiate. Pesquera observed that "women also utilize a variety of strategies in their daily struggle: they retrain, coach, and praise husbands for a job well done. At times they resort to slowdowns or work stoppages, so that eventually men are forced to contribute more to household labor." Husbands respond by stalling, doing slipshod work, or discrediting their wives by comparing about them to women who do even more household work (Pesquera, 1997). Many women find it easier to give up the struggle and do the work themselves. In fact, the total number of nonleisure hours worked by women employed full time is almost double the total for traditional housewives (Hochschild and Machung, 1997; Hochschild, 1997; Carter, 1995; Potuchek, 1997; National Science Foundation, 2008).

Of course, discourse that advises women and minority employees to strive to fit in often fails to recognize how complicated it is to do so. Employees are told to actively seek promotions that involve relocation and assignments that involve travel, to stay with the same firm for long periods of time, and to make decisions about their non-organizational life that put their careers and organizations first – choosing not to marry, to delay marriage, or to wait to begin a family until after they are well established in their careers (Reuther and Fairhurst, 2000; Morrison, White, and Van Velsor, 1992). If they do marry or form long-term partnerships, they are advised to negotiate a lifestyle with their partners which allows them to pursue their careers and simultaneously participate in a fulfilling family life.

Given the very real difficulties involved in following this advice, it is somewhat surprising that so many women in US firms have been able to do so. Executive women change jobs for career, not family, reasons and are as likely, or more likely, to relocate to further their careers than are male executives; and they take the same number of vacation days. But ironically, in spite of this evidence, upper managers still *perceive* that women put family before career and *believe* they will turn down assignments involving travel or relocation, and so on. So, when women *do* experience career interruptions, they have a disproportionately negative effect on their careers. Studies in the United States and Europe indicate that women lose seniority, opportunities for training, and salary, and the impacts are more severe, the longer the leave.[8] Women who take time off lose an average of 18 percent of their earning power, and the longer they spend out of the workforce, the greater the penalty – across sectors of the work world, women who take three or more years out of the workforce lose an average of 37 percent of their earning power (Hewlett, Sherbin, and Forster, 2005, 2010).

A final strategy that women and minority employees are told will help them fit in is to develop an exceptional performance record. Virtually all studies of the upward mobility of successful women and African Americans and Latinos in US firms have found that their performance had to be better and more consistent than the performance of Anglo men. A Latina white-collar worker told Denise Segura (1997),

> I've seen it! In interviews with a white candidate, they see it written on the paper and they say, "Isn't this great!" But, when you bring a Latina in, it's almost like they're drilled: "Tell us;" "Give us examples;" "How long did you do it?" . . . You always have to prove yourself. . . . You almost have to fight harder to demonstrate that you can do a job just as well. (301)

This pattern is explained in part by overt discrimination. But it also is related to the weak link between performance and rewards that exists in most organizations. Excellent performance is rewarded only if it also is *visible* to the organization's power holders and only if they *perceive* that it provides evidence of exceptional competence. How, then, does one make his or her performance visible? The simplest way is to tell others about it. Even simple strategies are complicated by societal assumptions. In many societies, openly talking about one's successes is unacceptable, because it taken to be bragging or an attempt to advance individual over collective. An employee must rely on communication through informal networks. But, "other" employees often are excluded from those networks. In Western societies, men typically learn to be more comfortable talking about their exploits than most women do. In fact, they tend to exaggerate their successes ("I caught a fish/made a sale/won a case that was *this* big") and to express them in comparative and competitive terms. Women brag less frequently; they tend to understate their accomplishments and attribute their successes to other members of their team. As a result, males' bragging creates impressions of competence, confidence, pride, and success (all positively valued in managerial settings) while females' bragging makes people like them more and praise them for being sensitive, not for being successful (Miller, Cooke, Tsang, and Morgan, 1992).

For women and members of minority groups, visibility is paradoxical in other ways. In organizations or units that have small numbers of women, African Americans, or Latinos/as (Rosabeth Moss Kanter, 1977, has suggested that 15 percent is a crucial level), the ones who are there often live in "glass houses". As one woman executive explained, "There is an element of derailment built into the system for women – the pressure created by having to be a role model and a 'first' along with personal competency. Men don't have to deal with this added pressure." Another admitted, "I feel that if I fail, it will be a long time before they hire another woman for the job. . . . Carrying that burden can lead women to play it safe, to be ultraconservative, to opt out if a situation looks chancy." Everyone makes mistakes. If power holders focus on an employee's mistakes instead of successes, or if they attribute an occasional error to a person's race or sex, visibility becomes a barrier, not an advantage (Morrison, White, and Van Velsor, 1992; Morrison and Von Glinow, 1990).

Differential Perceptions and Attributions The visibility paradox is further complicated by perceptual and attributional processes. Societal myths about race, gender, and ethnicity create perceptual sets through which people *interpret* events and actions. Researchers have long recognized that, in general, subordinates receive significantly higher ratings from persons of their own race and sex, even when objective performance standards are used

(Davidson and Swigert-Ruderman, 2000; Kraiger and Ford, 1985). This results in part from the continuation of overtly racist attitudes and behaviors, as the Texaco, Coca-Cola, and other cases so clearly indicate. But differential evaluation also seems to occur even when overt racial biases are not evident. Societal assumptions also influence attributions. Even when excellent performance by women, African American men, or Latinos is made visible, it may be attributed to factors outside of the employee's control – luck, special advantages, the help of other employees, the effectiveness of the organization as a whole, or high motivation and effort (which cannot be sustained over the long term) – rather than to skill and expertise. Even when performance is attributed to the same factors, it may have different effects. If a white male's success is attributed to hard work, it usually helps his career because evaluators assume that he is also competent. But when a woman's or minority employee's success is attributed to hard work, evaluators tend to assume that it disguises limits to her or his competence, so it may do little to help him or her advance in the organization (Nadler and Nadler, 1993; Nkomo, 1992). In addition, supervisors also seem to feel and express less confidence in their evaluations of women and minority subordinates than of their white male subordinates. When evaluators express a lack of confidence in their judgments about an employee's performance, it creates less positive perceptions than the performance merits. In organizations, as in the rest of life, perceptual "realities" are more important than actual performance.

Finally, Anglo male supervisors tend to base their evaluations of African American and Latino/a subordinates more on the extent to which they *conform* to the organization's norms of behavior than on their performance (the reverse is true for Anglo subordinates). As a result, "fitting in" is transformed from a means to an end. In general, Anglo male supervisors and employers feel more comfortable with people who they perceive as similar to them and tend to promote similar people. Because Latinas and African American women are most dissimilar, they are least likely to be promoted. To complicate matters further, Anglo male supervisors are often unaware of their perceptions or the role that those perceptions play in their actions toward and evaluations of women and African Americans and Latinos (Dovidio *et al.*, 1992; Segura, 1997). "Different" employees experience a complex web of double binds as they try to fit in to organizations in which being a white male is perceived to be "normal" and "natural."

Dealing With Homogenization There is substantial evidence that women all over the world are beginning to successfully test the **glass ceiling**, an invisible barrier beyond which "other" employees are not promoted (Rosin, 2010). Worldwide 24 percent of senior management positions are held by women, with the Philippines, Russia, and Thailand topping the list with 46, 42, and 38 percent of senior management positions held by women, respectively (Zahidi *et al.*, 2010). The Netherlands, India, Denmark, Belgium, and Japan are at the bottom of the list, with women holding less than 15 percent of senior management positions. In the United States, only 16 percent of CEOs and board seats in Fortune 500 firms were held by women as of 2008 (Bureau of Labor Statistics, 2010; Catalyst, 2010a). However, in 2009, for the first time ever, more than 50 percent of managers at all levels in the United States were women (Catalyst, 2010b), in part because males bore the brunt of the 2008 downturn than women. Occupations that were traditionally dominated by men, such as heavy manufacturing, were also hardest hit by the downturn in the United States. With more women in management positions, it is likely that the glass ceiling will come under increasing pressure in the next few decades as these women move up the ladder. In terms of change, Mexico, Turkey, Canada, and Russia have seen the fastest growth in number of female managers from 2007 to 2009 (Grant Thornton, 2009).

Although the concept of the glass ceiling is most often associated with women, it also applies to members of ethnic and religious minority groups and to people with disabilities. And it is a worldwide phenomenon. Progress for Latino, African American, and Asian American men has been slower, but still is substantial (Department of Labor, 2010).

Members of all groups seem to have found ways to balance the conformity demands of organizations while maintaining their own distinctive styles of leading and managing, although the leadership and management strategies used by people at the very top of organizations seems to vary little by race, gender, or ethnicity (Buzzanell *et al.*, 2009; Kuitenbrouwer, 2003). They may accept the overall constraints imposed by their organizations but find ways to create cohesive, high-performing work groups within those constraints. For example, they may maintain a highly structured, unemotional mode of communicating with people outside of their units, but encourage openness and honest communication with their subordinates while providing them with support for creative risk taking.[9] Educated Muslim immigrants in US firms seem to adopt the attitudes and behaviors of their organizations while at work, but retain their original culture outside of work, especially if they are highly committed to their faith (Alkhazraji, Gardner, Martin, and Paolillo, 1997). However since the attacks of September 11, the number of hate crimes and harassment against Muslims has increased substantially.

African American and Asian American women, as well as Latinas, have experienced less progress, in part because they are doubly (or triply, if socioeconomic class is included) "different" from the white male norm. The glass ceiling once was assumed to be located at the level of middle management. Above that point in an organization's hierarchy, the number of openings falls rapidly, and performance evaluation becomes much more subjective. However, recent research has found that the ceiling is even lower than middle management for Anglo women, and lower still for African Americans and Latinos/as (Buzzanell, 1995; Reuther and Fairhurst, 2000). This does not mean that the ceiling cannot be penetrated – there are a number of noted successes – but it does suggest that the combination of differences in opportunity and societal attitudes make it difficult to do so. And "the barriers to the upper rungs of the corporate ladder for minority women appear to be nearly impenetrable;" the percent of Latinas, African American and Asian women in the corporate offices of Fortune 500 firms (1.3 percent) has not changed in recent years (Kilborn, 1995; Kim and Lewis, 1994; Page, 1994).

In the long term, these strategies of balanced innovation have the potential for effecting significant change. They are sufficiently subtle to generate little resistance, while making small changes that over the long term will have major unintended consequences. Eventually, these small wins may actually change the power structure of bureaucratic organizations. For example, if the supervisor of one division of an organization successfully implements structural changes, such as **flextime** (allowing employees to work schedules that fit their needs) or **flexplace** (allowing people to work at home whenever possible), it may serve as a model for other divisions and eventually for the organization as a whole. When significant numbers of "different" employees enter organizations they *will* truly be different, and they eventually and *inevitably will* have to make fundamental changes. When the upper levels of organizational hierarchies begin to include some people who are not Anglo men, new perspectives, values, and ideas will become part of the discourse of upper management.

When substantial numbers of Anglo men have worked successfully with women and persons of color as peers below the glass ceiling, they will bring more positive attitudes with them when *they* move into upper management (Dezso and Ross, 2008).

Marginalizing "Others"

A third possible organizational response to increased diversification is to accept the presence of "different" others in the organization, but to isolate them in "spaces" that have relatively low levels of power. In some societies these spaces often are literal – in Mongolia, South America, India, the Philippines, and North Africa, women workers tend to be segregated in homes or "out-of-the-way" places. In US organizations, they are more likely to be placed in relatively powerless departments (Spain, 1992). Obtaining power is crucial to upward mobility. It also is necessary to achieve a number of other personal and career goals, such as effectively serving one's customers and clients, successfully obtaining and completing challenging and meaningful projects, and so on. As Chapter 8 explained, power is closely related to one's place in the formal structure of one's organization.

Manipulating Opportunity Structures Latinos, African Americans, and Anglo women often are in industries that provide little opportunity for advancement and divisions of organizations that have low levels of power (Zahidi, Ibarra, Tesfachew, Bekhouche, Cuenod, Farrell, and Niforos, 2010). As indicated earlier in this chapter, this location results in part from broad socialization processes which encourage non-white-male employees to enter fields with limited organizational power – "nurturing" or "people-oriented" fields for women, and "applied" or "practical" (as opposed to theoretical or managerial) careers for African Americans and Latinos (Bureau of Labor Statistics, 2010). Even when African American men, Latinos, and women do not "choose" staff-related careers, organizations tend to shunt them in those directions anyway. For example, in 2000 only 7.3 percent of *line* divisions (those that contribute directly to the profitability of the firm) in the Fortune 500 (the largest 500 firms in the United States) had women managers, although this represents a significant increase over the 5.3 percent in 1997. Because virtually all organizations require upper managers to have experience in "mission-critical jobs," being limited to staff positions reduces one's organizational power and may preclude one being promoted. In a survey of the 100 largest employers in the 30 nations belonging to the Organization for Economic Cooperation and Development, on average women held 16 percent of mission-critical jobs, ranging from 25 percent in Finland, France, Greece, and the United States to 10 percent or less in Mexico, Germany, Japan, and the United Kingdom (Zahidi *et al.*, 2010). Staff positions seem to be surrounded by **glass walls**, and these walls may be the greatest barrier to upward mobility for women and minority managers (Amparano, 1992; Powell, 1993).

Not only does creating racially and gender-segregated sectors of an organization harm individual employees, but also it also reduces organizational effectiveness. People who have the same backgrounds and experiences are more prone to problems of "trained incapacity," "groupthink," and communication breakdowns. Organizations with one unit or subculture composed of all upper-class Anglo males and other units or subcultures made up of people with widely differing attributes and experiences tend to have low levels of cross-sector cooperation and high levels of cross-unit communication breakdowns (Ospina, 1996). But upper managers' preferences for coworkers with whom they are comfortable seem to be more important in promotion decisions than concerns about efficient communication or "objective" decision making.

Dealing With Marginalization To compensate for "glass walls" and "glass ceilings," women and members of racial or ethnic minority groups adopt a number of strategies. Two of them involve obtaining information about the organization, its culture, and its practices through mentors and by cultivating informal communication networks. There is widespread agreement that newcomers who successfully navigate the entry experience do so largely because they are able to establish close, personal mentoring relationships with one or more senior employees early in their careers (Dickens and Dickens, 1991; Knouse, 1992; Ragins, 1995; Knoke, 2001; McLean, 2006). From these **mentors**, newcomers obtain all the different kinds of information discussed in this chapter. Organizations are aware of the importance of mentoring. In the United States and Britain, almost all large companies offer employees access to internal mentoring and networking opportunities (Zahidi *et al.*, 2010).

However, like all interpersonal relationships, mentor–mentoree relationships are difficult to form and maintain, especially when mentorees are of a different gender, race, or ethnic background than their mentors (Knoke, 2001). Informal mentoring systems tend to exclude African Americans and Latinos/as, and to a somewhat lesser degree, white women. A study by Catalyst, a New York-based research organization, found that half of African American women had been unable to establish a mentoring relationship compared with a third of white women.[10]

Both mentor and protégé may feel awkward, especially at first. Once the relationship is established it may be difficult to avoid creating an actual or perceived dependency relationship. In US firms, women or members of minority groups occupy fewer positions near the top of organizations and as a result the majority of mentors will be European American men (Knoke, 2001). In general, these supervisors seem to be willing to mentor or assist male subordinates if they are sufficiently competent. However, they seem to be willing to mentor European American women, Latinos, and African American men only if they are near the bottom of the organizational hierarchy. Once they are promoted and begin to become potential threats to the European American male supervisors, they withdraw their help, even if they espouse egalitarian attitudes (Bullis and Rohrbauck Stout, 2000; Dovidio *et al.*, 1992).

Traditional sex role stereotypes also complicate mentoring relationships by making it difficult for the parties to know how to act toward one another or interpret one another's actions. The relationship may be strained and communication may be less open and spontaneous than in same sex relationships. Cross-sex (or cross-race/ethnicity) mentoring relationships also seem to be weaker, less stable, and more limited to discussions of task issues than are same-sex (and same-race/ethnicity) relationships. European American male mentorees also seem to obtain access to other relationships through their mentors, while this is much less true for women, African American men, and Latinos. As a result, establishing and maintaining positive mentoring relationships is more difficult for women, African American men, and Latinos than it is for Anglo men, and the mentoring relationships that they do establish seem to be less beneficial to their career advancement. The complicated nature of mentoring is one reason why women and minority men often do not become fully integrated into their organizations and eventually move on (Knoke, 2001).

Another mechanism for helping newcomers make sense of their organization is to encourage them to join informal communication networks (Zahidi *et al.*, 2010; Hewlett, Sherbin, and Forster, 2005; Knoke, 2001). For the reasons described in the previous paragraphs, "different" employees often find it difficult to become integrated into the informal networks that exist within their firms. An alternative is external networks. Most major cities and many smaller ones now have active networks for women, African American, and Latino managers and professionals. External networks have proven to be valuable to all three groups. Contacts made in networks provide a wide variety of information about how organizations work as well as social and emotional support. Employees who have experienced overt discrimination or racial or sexual harassment are supported by people who have had similar experiences and have learned how to deal with those problems. Networks share information about which firms have good (and poor) records of advancing women and minority employees. They provide advice about handling everyday work-related problems and exchange information about when and where vacancies are anticipated. At times, networks can become elitist, shifting their focus from aiding all their members to assisting a selected few. But, when they work effectively, they can provide members with all the information that European American men traditionally have gained through informal good-old-boy networks. In short, external networks help compensate for the fact that Latinos/as, European American women, and African Americans are often excluded from the internal networks of their organizations (Ibarra, 1993, 1995; Marshall, 1995; Edwards and Polite, 1992).

"Different" employees also can deal with marginalization by adopting particular career strategies. They can actively prepare for, seek out and accept assignments in traditionally Anglo male occupations, industries, and specializations. Although doing so often means that they will suffer temporary financial losses or personal dislocation and will have to deal with more extensive sexism and racism and sexual and racial harassment than they would experience in service or staff positions, their long-term career prospects will increase.

Interestingly, many women seem to have recognized that these barriers continue to exist and have responded by starting organizations of their own (Lerman and Schmidt, 2010). Starting in the 1980s a much larger number of women – one of three MBAs in one study – have left large organizations to start their own businesses. These decisions were motivated in part by anticipation of the freedom, excitement, and feelings of achievement that accompany succeeding in running one's own business in a highly competitive environment. But they also stemmed from frustration with gender-related barriers in their old firms that kept them from being rewarded adequately and equitably for their contributions, and from moving into positions of greater challenge and creativity.

The growth has been remarkable. In 1980, there were 2 million women-owned businesses with $25 billion in sales or receipts in the United States; in 2008 there were 10.1 million firms majority owned by women (38 percent of US firms) and $1.9 trillion in sales or receipts (Center for Women's Business Research, 2009). Women of color in the United States owned 1.9 million firms that employed 1.2 million people in 2008. In Australia about one half of small businesses are owned by women, and their growth rate is double that of small businesses owned by men. Women entrepreneurs are just as successful as male entrepreneurs; they provide better benefits packages for their employees (especially in the United States and Mexico) and play an increasing role in traditionally male sectors of the economy such as construction, transportation, agriculture, and manufacturing. Consequently, as a result of their inability or unwillingness to meet the personal and career needs of professional women, large, complex organizations have lost a great deal of talent and expertise and in the process have created a large number of effective competitors.

CONFRONTING THE DOMINANT PERSPECTIVE

Organizations have a variety of strategies available to resist workforce diversification. Each of these strategies sacrifices the potential benefits of diversity, but allows the organization to avoid making changes. "Other" employees use an equally varied group of strategies to overcome organizational resistance. An alternative approach is for organizations to recognize the potential benefits of diversity, and devise strategies for confronting the dominant perspective.

Valuing Others' Ways

A number of researchers have noted that the people who make up the workforce of today's organizations in the developed world have a different set of core values than those that are included in the dominant perspective. No longer are an unquestioning loyalty to the organization and pursuit of money the main concerns. Instead, today's workers value recognition, feelings of accomplishment, being treated with respect and dignity, psychological involvement and pride in meaningful work (recall Chapter 3), and quality of life, including opportunities for self-development, health, and wellness. These values are inconsistent with traditional, bureaucratic strategies of organizing and are consistent with the more flexible, relationship-, culture-, and network-oriented strategies that were described in Unit I. They underlie a pattern of acting and a set of leadership strategies that are especially appropriate to the turbulent and globally competitive environments faced by modern organizations.

Others' Ways of Leading In a now-classic study, Sally Helgessen (1990) compared the day-by-day work activities of (primarily Anglo) male managers to those of (primarily Anglo) female managers. She found that males tend to work at an unrelenting pace, with no scheduled breaks during the day. Their days are characterized by interruptions, discontinuity, and fragmentation. They spend little time in long-term planning or reflecting on their goals or the effectiveness of the strategies they use. They prefer face-to-face communication to written messages, but have difficulty sharing information with coworkers and subordinates. Anglo women, Helgessen observed, tend to prefer more open face-to-face interactions. They work at a steady pace and schedule small breaks during the day; they take a broader and long-term perspective instead of focusing solely on day-to-day activities; they actively share information with others and gain satisfaction from *both* the process of working *and* its results. They define power as the ability to *act with* others to accomplish goals that could not be achieved by individuals acting alone, rather than as *power over* others (recall Chapter 8). For these women, leadership involves empowering others, being at the *center* of a group rather than in front of it (Fine and Buzzanell, 2000). Leaders' claims to expertise and authority must be justified continually and be explained to other employees in terms they can readily understand. Diane Kay Sloan and Kathleen Krone's (2000) study of 30 women managers in multiple sectors of the US economy found similar results – feminine leadership styles that focused on openness and support in contrast to a much more widespread masculine style that focused on closedness and intimidation.

Box 10.1
Feminist Strategies for Organizing

Although there are a number of different versions of feminism, both in the United States and in the rest of the world, feminists agree that masculine conceptions of reality, modes of organizing, and ways of communicating dominate the public realm in Western societies. Masculine organizations are dominated by metaphors suggesting hierarchy, rely on "power over" views of interpersonal influence, define effectiveness as achieving goals in spite of resistance by others, and privilege centralized expertise and decision making. In contrast, feminine (as well as feminist) organizations are defined by metaphors that describe webs of interconnected interpersonal relationships, define effectiveness in terms of achieving consensus among organizational members, and focus on systems of shared leadership and diffuse expertise. The distinction between feminine and feminist organizations is important because many alternative organizations, while composed primarily or exclusively of women, are not based on feminist goals regarding social change and their members may not espouse feminist values at all.

For example, Nancy Wyatt (1988) described a women's organization composed primarily of middle-class, conservative women who were unified by their common interest in sewing and weaving but never expressed an interest in feminist politics. But they created and sustained a "Weaver's Guild" that was fundamentally different from any of the strategies of organizing discussed in this book. The women provided one another with mutual support and opportunities to learn new skills from one another; they saw failure as an equally important part of learning as success; they were avidly noncompetitive and maintained diffuse and nonhierarchical power relationships and modes of decision making. Leadership was shared by eight members of the weavers' guild, some of whom were leaders because they were uniquely able to articulate a shared vision for the organization, and some of whom were leaders because of their ability to organize the group's activities. But all eight were very much concerned that they not dominate the others – they provided advice and direction only when asked, for example. This was in part because of the history of the group. At one time it had a strong, centralized leader, and when that woman left the guild it almost fell apart. But it also was because of their focus on maintaining a supportive community within the group. So, formal roles rotated among the group's members so that a variety of talents and interests were represented in decision making, and the guild's activities were orchestrated so that each member's goals were met.

There were tensions within the Weavers Guild, usually over the organization's unique form of organizing. One member once had been a weaver by profession and tended to withhold her expertise from the other members, because doing so had been a successful political strategy in her previous organizations. Members who wished to use the guild as a stepping-stone for a future career in "typical" weaving organizations were frustrated by the shared responsibility and shared credit characteristic of the guild. In spite of these tensions, the weavers' guild was able to create and sustain a fundamentally different kind of organization – one that was able to simultaneously be a community and address the needs and desires of its individual members.

Other feminist organizations have found it more difficult to maintain that kind of balance. Frequently, feminist organizations begin with an emphasis on consensus, equality, collectivity, and legitimate participatory decision making; but they emerge toward more traditional, hierarchical strategies of organizing in which representative democracy replaces participation. This shift seems to stem from environmental pressures on the organization. Feminist organizations face an important dilemma: How can an alternative organization maintain a collective, nonhierarchical, participatory, egalitarian strategy of organizing while simultaneously pursuing other goals like profitability? Some external pressures are overt and direct. In Western societies, organizations need funds to survive and especially to grow. A major donation or grassroots political campaign may provide sufficient funding for an organization to be created and even to succeed at a relatively small size. But if it is to grow, other sources of funds become necessary, and significant funds are usually available only from traditional, bureaucratic organizations – government agencies, banks, and the financial markets. Decision makers in traditional bureaucracies are comfortable with organizations that operate on the basis of similar strategies of organizing. So they pressure alternative organizations to be less alternative or at least to appear to be. Alternative strategies of organizing become less alternative, and, if the organization is involved in social change efforts, those efforts are moderated or made less visible.

For example, *MS* magazine faced a central tension from the day it was created: it drew its content from feminist publications but designed its format and marketing to be like mainline women's magazines. Its funding came from readers who were attracted to the magazine because of its feminist ideology, and from advertisers who saw it as an opportunity to reach women readers. Advertisers pressured the editorship to focus content on career feminists, who had the disposable income that they coveted. But career feminists were only part of the *MS* readership, and many of them were attracted mainly because of *MS*'s feminist ideology. As competition and costs increased during the 1980s, advertising revenues became more necessary, and the advertisers' influence over content increased. Readers found many of the ads offensive and resisted the shift. The opposition crystallized around a 1987 issue on women and addiction, which included none of the tobacco and alcohol company ads that had become common. Readers were irate about what they saw as blatant hypocrisy, and the editors' argument that the *MS* policies had led to improvements in advertising directed toward women fell on deaf ears. Although the magazine's content had become progressively less political as the advertisers exerted increased control, advertisers abandoned the magazine during the highly conservative political climate of the late 1980s. In 1989 the magazine folded, only to be reborn the following year with no advertising (Farrell, 1995).

People, regardless of their gender and regardless of the strategy of organizing that is in place, bring the dominant assumptions of their societies with them into their organizations. Thus, people in Western societies tend to value efficiency, expertise, and experience. Consensus decision making and participation consume a great deal of time and energy (recall Chapter 4) and thus seem to be inefficient, especially in the short term; differences in expertise and experience seem to warrant hierarchical power relationships. Members of alternative organizations are pressured by the many different traditional organizations in which they also are involved – churches, schools, clubs, and so on. These competing organizations work on a schedule and through a process that contradicts the flexibility and adaptability of the alternative organization. Consequently, it is difficult for members to continue to support forms of organizing that seem to be so non-normal, so unnatural. A number of factors may help offset these pressures – small organizational size, common goals, relatively equal knowledge and experience, and a benign environment. As noted in Chapter 6, there are a number of flourishing cooperatives and collectives that operate on the basis of alternative strategies; but sustaining them involves a constant process of managing tensions (Cheney, 1995; Acker, 1995; Whitt and Rothschild-Whitt, 1986).

Feminist organizational strategies face a second dilemma: Can these strategies expand to successfully include people from diverse racial, ethnic, class, and gender groups (Buzzanell, 2000)? Alternative organizations tend to begin with local, grassroots organizing. These groups tend to have common interests and homogeneous backgrounds and experiences. For example, in the United States, feminist groups have primarily involved educated middle- and upper-middle-class Anglo women. Unless they actively reach out to men and to people of other classes, races, and ethnic origins, they tend to remain homogeneous. Since an alternative form of organizing does not in itself bridge racial, class, or ethnic differences, and since the concerns that bring middle-class Anglo women together in alternative organizations may not be salient to anyone else (and vice versa), diversifying alternative organizations is quite difficult. Doing so is more likely when the organization emerges from a multiclass, multiethnic community; but even then it takes a great deal of time and energy to sustain a truly diverse organization. Consequently, pressures for efficiency may be especially acute for these organizations, making factors like small size and common goals even more important (Pardo, 1995).

The different ways of leading that women bring also seem to benefit the bottom line. Firms with female members on their top management team outperform those with all-male management teams (Dezso and Ross, 2010). This "female participation effect" did not extend to female CEOs – there was no difference in performance between firms with female CEOs and male CEOs – but rather was related to the percentage of females below the CEO level in top management. The female participation effect also ran both ways: females on top management teams improved the performance of their firms and higher performing firms were better able "at identifying, attracting, and developing female managers" (Dezso and Ross, 2010, 7). The benefits of the female participation effect were strongest in firms that adopted innovation intensive strategies, which would benefit from participatory, collaborative approaches characteristic of women's leadership styles.

Research with Latinos and Latinas also suggests a preference for a particular form of leadership. Latin cultures are grounded in the concepts of familialism, *machismo*, and *simpatía* (Ramirez, 2005–2006). ***Familialism*** involves strong values attached to family and community, and a commitment to hard work and achievement as a way of honoring one's

Case Study 10.2
Trying to Stay Balanced[1]

All organizations must deal with tensions and inconsistencies. In alternative organizations like feminist organizations those tensions often are more visible because they are not obscured by taken-for-granted assumptions. In these two case studies, separated by more than 20 years, feminist organizations confront and manage the tensions that they face.

Redwood Records began as a "mom and pop" (literally) operation designed to produce and market records by Holly Near. Although she had a sizable and stable following, major record companies refused to contract with Near because her anti-Vietnam War message was controversial and because her music was not as "submissive" as women's music was "supposed" to be. By the mid-1970s, Near's parents tired of running the company, creating a need for a new organization. Near restructured Redwood Records into a feminist alternative organization: an all-woman, worker-run, nonhierarchical, social change-oriented organization. All employees performed all of the necessary tasks – from licking stamps to making strategic decisions. Their ideology was explicitly anti-profit, and their goals focused on helping create a women's music industry designed to foster social change. Communication among members was excellent, information flow was good, and power really was shared among members, creating high levels of morale, effort, and commitment. But, like many alternative feminist organizations founded during the 1970s, Redwood's combination of participatory, consensus decision-making and lack of formal structure created problems: Service was inconsistent, salaries and job security were low, burnout and turnover among staff members was high, and the organization constantly faced financial problems. In short, Redwood Records was a social movement that happened to be a business.

After 1980, Redwood evolved to become a business that had an alternative strategy of organizing and a vision of social change. It signed a number of other women artists, and as Near's role in the organization declined, it began to rely more and more on profits to sustain itself. Redwood maintained an atmosphere of informality and support as well as its commitment to consensual decision making and open confrontation as a primary mode of conflict management. But it began to focus more on efficiency in order to keep up with growing demand for its products. Eventually a management team was formed, and day-to-day communication became more formal and bureaucratic – meetings involved the minimum number of people necessary rather than all employees and meeting times were set in advance instead of being spontaneous, for example. After 1985, Redwood decided to quit limiting its selections to music designed for a women's audience, but continued to have an all-woman staff.

Throughout its existence, Redwood has had to manage a tension between economic demands and its political change ideology and commitment to an alternative strategy of organizing. It maintains a balance by being very strategic about the projects it takes on. Money and profits were redefined to be means to a social change end. Profits gained from some products allow Redwood to support social change activities that do not in themselves make money. Some members focus more on profits than politics; others more on politics than profits; and most are in the middle, trying to simultaneously maintain both. Its continued openness and commitment to consensus policy making allow it to manage this central tension successfully. It has found a middle ground between bureaucratic structures and modes of operating and a fluid and structureless mode of operating.

Haven is a feminist organization that provides emergency help to survivors of domestic violence and tries to prevent future cases through education and counseling.[2] It has 25 paid staff members and 125 volunteers, some of whom answer the organization's crisis hotline, others work with children stayi ng at the shelter, and others serve as victims' advocates who respond to police calls and counsel victims at the scene. The paid staff emphatically says that what makes Haven different from other domestic violence organizations is its commitment to *ethical communication*. The key to ethical communication is empowerment that transcends the formal hierarchy of the organization. In training sessions, meetings, and everyday interactions among staff members, members learn to express emotions, deal openly with conflicts, and promote equality. However, there are important differences in how the two groups – staff members and volunteers – interpret and enact ethical communication.

Volunteers think of Haven as something unique, different from both "home" and "work" (where they obtain their livelihood). In a sense, it is a place where they can escape the responsibilities and decision-making challenges that they experience in the other parts of their life. It is a place where the volunteers do make decisions, where they do feel autonomous and strong as persons, and where they can feel good about their contributions to others. But, they also felt that their connections to Haven were temporary, and that their tasks were unique – ambiguous, fluctuating, supportive, relationally oriented, part-time, and unpaid. For them, "empowerment" meant being able to (a) choose the level of involvement and responsibility that they want, (b) have access to the information and skills they need to do their jobs, (c) have an opportunity for personal and professional growth and a sense that they are making a contribution to others, and (d) have the freedom that comes from someone else being ultimately responsible for things. The final aspect means that they are not offended by the level of hierarchy that exists at Haven, in fact they find it to be comforting, especially since it seemed to be based on the degree of involvement and responsibility that different people had. They realized that the staff members were ideologically opposed to hierarchy – they talked about it almost every day – and some were a little disillusioned about the inconsistency between the staff's expressions of their ideology and the fact that there really was a hierarchy in place. But, the volunteers were much more concerned about not getting the kind of emotional support that they needed, and about their feelings that the support they did receive sometimes seemed forced and inauthentic. They also were frustrated that they rarely were told what happened to their clients once they left the shelter. They provided support to one another, but all in all they still felt isolated, and felt guilty that they did not work as many hours as others did. For them, doing their jobs and feeling good about what they were doing was more important than enacting an ideology.

The staff members interpreted ethical communication and empowerment very differently. They talked about being anti-hierarchy, and encouraged the volunteers to undercut the hierarchy by taking care of themselves, challenging supervisory authority, and even poking fun at the supervisors. Ironically, one of the reasons that they were so committed to fighting hierarchy was their belief that it could not be eliminated – the battle would never actually be won. A second irony was that they were committed to persuading the staff to practice empowerment and ethical communication, almost "whether they wanted to or not." Volunteers wished that staff members would spend more time and energy preparing them to perform their tasks, supervise them and provide feedback on their work, and give them more guidance when they asked questions – in short, to act more like supervisors and less like equally empowered peers. (For similar cases of managing tensions in feminist organizations, see Edley, 2000; Ashcraft, 2001.)

Applying What You Have Learned

1. What tensions existed at Redwood Records and at Haven? What were the source(s) of those tensions? How were they managed?

Questions to Think About and Discuss

1. Some critics of feminist organizations complain that they eventually "sell out" their political commitments in order to be economically successful? Evaluate this criticism, and explain how members of an alternative organization can "know" when they have tipped the balance too far toward ideology or too far toward success?
2. Other critics argue that feminist forms of organizations inevitably will fail if they maintain their alternative mode of operating. Others note that alternative forms of organizing are becoming so common, there no longer is any marketing advantage in being "different." Evaluate these criticisms.

Notes

1 This case is based on Lott (1988).
2 This case is based on Ashcraft and Kedrowicz (2002).

family (Diaz-Saenz and Witherspoon, 2005). It also involves aiding others who are in need. It is for this reason that having a job that pays low wages is even more stressful for Latinos than for other males. ***Machismo***, a concept that is widely misunderstood by non-Latinos/as, embraces a strong sense of loyalty and duty to other members of the community and a sense of honor and duty, not to an impersonal organization, but to other people. ***Simpatía*** is a complex concept that involves engaging in positive, agreeing behaviors whenever possible, showing respect for one's superiors by conforming to their wishes, and avoiding conflict and confrontation *in public settings.* But it does not mean conformity and blind obedience, because it also requires superiors to show respect to their subordinates, especially in public. These values lead to a high level of concern for interpersonal relationships and the feelings of other people, emphasis on community building, a participatory, open-door leadership style, and a preference for face-to-face communication (Ramirez, 2005–2006). They also generate a desire for fair treatment and high levels of freedom and autonomy. Latino and Latina supervisors tend to feel a responsibility for developing their subordinates' skills and abilities. Latin culture also encourages a high level of flexibility in leadership strategies, including a willingness to ignore the formal chain of command when it is inefficient. In sum, Anglo men tend to use what Chapter 4 called "transactional leadership." Women and Latinos prefer what Chapter 5 called "transformational leadership," an approach that is particularly well suited to the turbulent environment of a competitive, global economy (recall Chapter 2). Of course, individual employees have had their own distinctive developmental experiences and may have developed leadership styles that deviate from both their general cultural backgrounds and the norms of their organizations. However, if organizations pressure "others" to adopt transactional leadership styles, as they seem to do much more frequently in US firms than in European organizations, they sacrifice the strengths that can come with diversity (Powell, 1993; Bullis and Rohrbauck Stout, 2000; Hafen, 2005).

Challenging the Underlying Attitudes of the Dominant Perspective

Instead of resisting diversification, organizations can confront the dominant perspective directly by valuing attitudes that are appropriate to a diverse workforce in a global environment. A key assumption of the dominant perspective is that thinking and doing should be separated; the thinking function should be treated as superior and should be conducted by a group of people who were similar to one another in every possible respect, and actions should be guided by stable policies and procedures that are arrived at through rational decision making. Employees should be chosen based largely on how well they fit into the existing organization, and once they arrive, they should be encouraged to adapt to an existing organizational role. Of course, attempting to assimilate employees into existing organizational practices and valuing diversity are contradictory ideas (Blanchette, 1994; Hafen, 2005).

The most important attitudinal change in confronting the dominant perspective is to celebrate *flexibility*. This has two components: *recognizing* that achieving goals of equity and effectiveness does not mean treating everyone in the same way, but means treating them all fairly; and *believing* that organizations should be adapted to fit the needs and develop the talents of every *individual* employee, instead of *demanding* that every employee adapt to the organization. An organization needs to make very different adjustments to utilize fully the talents of a single mother of two preschoolers, a computer programmer who is confined to a wheelchair, a deaf investment counselor, a group of Latina production workers, or a middle-aged Anglo male who has "plateaued" (reached the highest level in the organization that he will ever reach). For example, the Aluminum Company of America (ALCOA) hired Kevin Kennedy, an operations engineer who had a degenerative eye condition that restricted his peripheral vision and would eventually lead to blindness. Instead of declaring that Kevin inevitably would be incapable of doing his job, ALCOA's management asked how the organization could enable Kevin to continue to contribute. They assigned an assistant to help him when his job involved operating large industrial machinery or visiting plants with which he was unfamiliar. When his vision deteriorated further, the organization responded by redefining his duties so that they focused on computer modeling; they provided special lighting for his workspace and a large magnifying glass to help him read and purchased a large-screen computer and software for converting written texts to Braille. In this way the company was able to retain a highly competent employee at a cost far below what it would take to hire and train a replacement (Jamieson and O'Mara, 1991). In the process, they discovered what researchers have known for some time – meeting the needs of disabled workers is far less expensive than managers tend to believe that it will be.

The Hallmark Corporation no longer encourages members of its artistic staff to specialize. Instead, it rotates new employees through a number of different assignments to give them a wide range of actual job experiences. If potential candidates for a promotion lack a specific set of skills, the organization may assign them to a different department for six months or so to give them a chance to develop the skills necessary to move up. In some cases, the employees may discover that they are better suited for the division to which they are temporarily assigned, and the organization does everything possible to facilitate a move to that division. Traditionally, promotion has meant abandoning one's technical specialty and becoming a manager. But many people who have exceptional technical skills do not have the interests or abilities necessary for them to be successful managers. So, they are forced to either remain in the same unchallenging positions or move into a role with which they are uncomfortable. Diversity management proposes that organizations create alternative career paths, in which people stay within their specialties but receive promotions and increasingly complex technical assignments, or which allow people to cycle in and out of management positions.

Another attitudinal change involves focusing on *outcomes* instead of constraints. Different employees produce the best outcomes if they are enabled to do their jobs in their own ways. Jim James, a research engineer, had promised his wife that he would retire in two months. He knew he would not be able to finish the project that he was working on in that amount of time. His supervisor decided that his expertise on the project was too valuable to lose, so he arranged to have James spend 20 hours a week as a consultant to the firm and to be assigned a co-op student from the local university as a research assistant. James was able to arrange his own working schedule, keep his commitment to his wife, and offer his firm expertise on specified projects that only he could provide.

Developing Supportive Policies

The single most important step that an organization can take to challenge the dominant perspective is to change its reward system. Rewarding employees for conforming to organizational norms merely serves to perpetuate dominant attitudes and behaviors. Rewarding them for performance not only generates change, it adds credibility to change efforts. Performance-based systems involve collecting data on the number and proportion of people who are promoted, breaking that data down by gender, race, and ethnicity, and *publicizing* that data throughout the firm. This is because upper managers tend to *overestimate* the success of diversity programs, leading to complacency, and Anglo males who are competing with newcomers tend to *underestimate* their own opportunities, leading to unnecessary resistance and backlash. Like all organizational change efforts, diversity will succeed only if it is strongly, honestly, and openly supported by upper management. *They* must establish policies and procedures that target women, African American men, and Latinos for recruitment, professional development, and advancement. *They* must support the development of internal advocacy groups and task forces to provide emotional support for diverse groups of employees and *they* must keep the organization's diversification goals at the forefront of everyday activities. Policies and programs alone are meaningless. After all, Texaco and Coca-Cola had a number of diversity management and fair employment practices, policies, and procedures on the books, and had even won a number of awards for them. So did San Diego Gas and Electric Company when, in 1994, the courts ordered it to pay $3 million to a former worker who had been repeatedly called "nigger," "coon," or "boy," and subjected to threats and racial and sexual graffiti about him. So did Walmart when it lost a $50 million sexual harassment suit (later reduced to $5 million on appeal) in spite of the company's "strong" commitments, policies, and procedures. In all of these cases, there was no evidence that the commitments and policies had ever been translated into action – no one had been disciplined for any of the activities included in the cases (Morrison, 1992).

Case Study 10.3

Is That Term "Childless" or "Childfree"?

On the surface it seems pretty simple to adapt organizational policies and practices to meet the needs of today's workers, rather than those of the 1950s. But, diversity means differences, and with difference comes the potential for conflict.

A number of polls and surveys conducted in the United States during that past two decades have found that one of the greatest concerns that employees have is balancing work and family. This tension results in part from the "downsizing" of US organizations that started in the 1980s and is continuing in the 2000s, in part due to jobs moving overseas and in part due to technology. Downsizing has meant that a smaller number of workers must do the same amount of work that was previously done by a larger workforce. The result is longer hours and less time to take off for family purposes. The ubiquity of cell phones, email, and other mobile communication devices also cuts into family time because the organization can contact employees for emergencies, questions, and other matters that ordinarily would have waited until they were back in the workplace.

Challenges to work and family balance also result from US public policy. While 178 countries have paid maternity leave, the United States is one of the few who do not. Fifty countries, including most of those in the West, guarantee paid paternity leave as well.[1] Only two states in the United States, California and New Jersey, currently mandate paid maternity leave. The 1993 national-level Family and Medical Leave Act does not cover businesses with fewer than 50 employees (who employ almost half of the US workforce), and does not require maternity or paternity leave (or sick leave or care for a sick relative) to be paid. Consequently, it tends to be used by upper-middle-class to upper-class workers, because lower-income workers simply cannot afford to forego a paycheck for an extended period of time. The lack of legal mandate also leaves it up to organizations to establish their own policies on these matters.

We have discussed that family friendly" policies like flexwork (which can involve either flexible work times or flexible places of work – telecommuting, for example) or dependent care are becoming more common. There is, however, great variability in which organizations offer these options. These programs are most common in industries in which the workforce is largely composed of women *and* they have relatively strong bargaining positions with management, either because they have hard-to-find skills or because they are in tight labor markets, which give workers a stronger bargaining position on all issues.

However, even when companies have favorable policies, it may be difficult to use them. Managers may not tell their subordinates about the policies or may pressure them into not using them. People who use these policies tend to be perceived as less ambitious, committed, and professional than those who forego them. The penalty that women who interrupt their careers to have children pay when they return to work that was discussed in the main text is an example of the disadvantages that can accompany taking advantage of family friendly policies.

Men may be at a particular disadvantage when they try to take advantage of family-friendly policies. *Chicago Tribune* columnist Carol Kleiman (2000) summarizes the available evidence rather bluntly: "The workplace gives a lot of lip service to family-friendly policies, but when it comes to crunch time and a male employee isn't there, he's considered disloyal. In fact, if he puts his family first, he's considered a wimp." For example, attorney Ariel Ayanna sued his law firm for withholding work from him and firing him after he took time off under the Family and Medical Leave Act. In his complaint, he noted that "partners at his firm bragged about how little time they spent on family obligations."[2]

Sometimes being involved in one's family requires creative resistance (Kleiman, 2000). One new father parks his car at the far corner of the parking lot so that he can disappear (to home) at 5:00 P.M.; another leaves his desk lamp and computer on when he takes his child to the physician; many cobble together vacation and sick leave time so that they can spend time with their children without admitting it. One noted, "I know other men who are doing the same thing" and compared their group to Alcoholics Anonymous: "We know who we are and why we're doing this, but we don't give our names."

Choosing to have family as a top priority is a difficult decision because it often requires people to violate powerful social norms. For example, while Japanese workers are officially allotted 18 paid vacation days each year; on average, they only take nine. They have learned to see vacation time as a burden on their coworkers, not as an entitlement they have earned. When holidays are institutionalized – meaning that everyone takes them off – Japanese workers actually take them. Even in northern Europe, where lengthy paid vacations have been mandated by law for decades, people hesitate to take them for fear that they will be viewed as disloyal. But, in the United States, a trend toward maintaining a greater balance between work and family seems to be taking hold. The post-baby boom generational groups consistently list work–family balance as a high priority, suggesting that there will be increasing pressure for organizations to change. But, it also is clear that many organizations will strongly resist those changes, so choosing an organization with similar values will continue to be important.

Because long-term career advancement (and lifetime income) is reduced by taking leaves, these policies tend to be underused. In fact, in organizations that offer paid paternity leave (about 13 percent do), and take steps to ensure that employees are not penalized for taking it, a surprising number do so (58 percent of men take advantage of these policies).[2]

Taken-for-granted assumptions about the "proper" economic roles that women and men should play, and about government non-interference in the free market contribute to these public policies, and to managerial choices about organizational policies and practices. But, those assumptions go even deeper, into the ways in which people communicate with one another at work. Erika Kirby and Kathleen Krone (2001) studied an organization that had adopted rather liberal "family-friendly" policies, at least by US standards. They found a very complicated pattern of communication surrounding the use of those policies. Regulatory Alliance (a pseudonym for the organization they studied) is a government agency charged with making sure that banks follow legal requirements. Employees' jobs require a great deal of travel and they are sufficiently technical that it is impossible to hire and train replacement personnel to cover for an employee which she or he is out on leave, unless everyone knows that the leave will be for an extended period of time. As a result, when people take leave other employees have to pick up the workload.

Kirby and Krone found that two themes dominated talk about leave policies. The dominant theme involved perceptions of preferential treatment of employees who had children and resentment by employees who did not. The resentment focused on women who took maternity leave, primarily because very few men did so. But, when they did, people perceived that new mothers "have got it a little bit easier" than new fathers: new fathers "may have had two hours of sleep the night before and yet soon after the birth they're expected to go into work the next day and perform like nothing ever happened" (Kirby and Krone, 2001, 61).

The perceptions of unequal treatment went beyond leave itself. Employees perceived that single workers were assigned a disproportionate amount of travel, especially long trips: "if we've got a big complicated bank coming up, I can pretty well guarantee it's not going to be a new mother in charge of it" (Kirby and Krone, 2001, 61). Similarly, people working part-time (all of them were mothers) were regarded as not as dedicated as those who worked full-time. And, again, there were gender differences in the perceptions: "If a man went part-time, the 'question would be, "Well, why is he only working part-time?" as opposed to if it's a mother there's kind of a reason.' A male examiner agreed that 'realistically, I think it's much more difficult for probably the male to go part-time. . . . I think it just kind of goes against the norm.' This perception that part-time was just a program for women could be problematic. A female ERC member illustrated that 'if the only really good [reason] is women having children, that fosters that resentment. . . . "She wants to go part-time and I am going to have to pick up more work" and then you get that backlash' " (62). Interestingly, the part-timers worked very hard in order to counter this perception, but it was pervasive enough that it reduced the likelihood that employees would request part-time status. There really was an "us versus them" attitude about the issues.

The second theme that Kirby and Krone discovered involved a distinction between using the policies and abusing them. People who were perceived as abusing the policies were targeted for a great deal of peer pressure. As often is the case (see Chapter 5), it was the work team, more than supervisors, that exerted control on its members. Workers told one another stories about people who had abused the system, and about the reactions they received. One story was about a female manager who recently had a baby and went to her supervisor "horrified that people were going to think that she was getting preferential treatment in staying in town longer, when in fact it was a mere coincidence. She didn't want anybody to think that she was asking for special accommodations" (65). This made it difficult for managers to approach employees about the policies that were in place, and for workers to know when and to what extent they should use the policies. They often resorted to "testing the waters" to see how coworkers would respond to the idea of their using the policies.

Using What You Have Learned

1. What taken-for-granted assumptions are played out at Regulatory Alliance? Be sure you go deeper than the obvious issues. For example, some organizations have the same leave policies for adopting a baby and for giving birth to one. Some do not. Others treat

"elder care" leave the same way that they treat maternity and paternity leave. Others do not. What are the differing assumptions underlying each of these policy options?

2. How are those assumptions related to one another? For example, if a policy reduces organizational efficiency but enhances worker job satisfaction, which should take priority? Why?
3. Devise a communication campaign to reduce the prejudices among Regulatory Alliance employees against taking parental leave. What chance would you give such a program of succeeding in changing employee attitudes?

Questions to Think About and Discuss

One of the clearest demographic trends of the past twenty years has been the falling reproduction rate around the world, but especially in northern Europe (which has had negative population growth rates for some time) and among whites in the United States and Canada (both of which will have negative population growth rates within a very few years if current trends continue). Of US women aged 40–44, 19 percent are childless, twice as high a percentage as 20 years earlier (Livingston and Cohn, 2010). Some of this shift results from increasing infertility rates, and some of it results from a reduction in the percentage of adult women who are married. But, nearly 7 million US women defined themselves as voluntarily childless (or "childfree" to use a popular term), up from 2.4 million in 1982. The rates are substantially higher among educated, professional workers. In part because of a general feeling of being discriminated against, and in part because it is more difficult for childless or childfree employees to locate one another, support groups for "childfree" workers have mushroomed (for example, "No Kidding," which now has 40 active chapters).

1. Who should take responsibility (individual employees, organizations, government, etc.) for encouraging and enabling workers to have and care for children? Why? What groups of people will be treated unfairly if your answer becomes social policy? What groups will be given preferential treatment? Can you justify those differences? How?
2. Design an organizational benefits package that is likely to *maximize* the potential tensions and conflicts among the various employee groups at Regulatory Alliance. Be sure to include the indirect effects of policies (for example, if the company's health care policy is designed to minimize costs of "family" coverage, it is likely to reduce the scope of coverage for workers themselves; if it covers pregnancy care as a medical condition instead of an elective condition, health care costs borne by the company and employees who participate in the program will be higher, etc.). Design one that is likely to *minimize* those tensions.

Notes

1 This information was taken from a summary of a Human Rights Watch study of international family leave policies by the Huffington Post. See www.huffingtonpost.com/2011/02/23/paid-parental-leave_n_826996.html.

2 www.parenting.com/blogs/show-and-tell/kim-babytalk/paternity-leave-front-line-new-daddy-wars.

TAKING A HOLISTIC PERSPECTIVE

As we have noted, a key assumption of the dominant perspective is the notion that organizations are "containers," places that are separated by time and space from the places where employees live their nonwork lives. Of course, this notion has never been accurate for professional and managerial employees. Taking work home, being on call, and spending sleepless nights thinking about work-related problems have all been normal parts of white-collar employees' lives in the industrialized world. However, the advent of many new technologies – laptop computers, the internet, cell phones, paging systems, and so on – mean that many people never actually leave work. It is ironic that historically technologies that promised people more control over their time – from the telephone to the personal computer – usually have not provided the promised control. Instead they often have increased organizations' ability to limit or invade employees' private time.

Organizational downsizing has created a situation in which a smaller number of workers are available to complete the same amount of work. Increased organizational demands to work overtime during the past decade have created a situation in which balancing work and family is one of the greatest problems faced by modern employees. For example, in 2001, fully employed US workers in private industry worked an average of 1978 hours per year (about 40 hours per week allowing for a two-week vacation), over 100 hours a year more than workers in Australia, France, Mexico, and Germany (Anderson, 2001; in fact, the only country whose citizens worked more than the United States was South Korea).

If you look at the overall average hours per week worked in the United States, it is generally around 35. This is because the statistics include those who are underemployed and working less than full time. For example, the average workweek in the United States in March, 2011 was 34 hours per week[11], but this includes hours worked by part-time workers and the underemployed. As a result, as the new century started the US workforce was divided into two disparate groups: those who are unable to work full-time because the jobs are not there, and those whose workload has skyrocketed. For the latter group the experience of Elizabeth Oaks, a lawyer who works in the oil and gas industry, is typical: "We come home, we barely get something to eat, and we're exhausted. . . . I can't imagine what people do who have children."[12]

For example, in the United States, 40 percent of adults average seven or fewer hours of sleep a night, even though most people need eight or nine hours (National Sleep Foundation, 2005). In 2011 the average US citizen worked more hours (8.7) than they slept (7.7) and much more than spent in leisure or sports (2.6) (Bureau of Labor Statistics, 2011). Bureau of Labor Statistics figures for 2009 show that the average number of paid vacation days in US firms is 14. These figures are comparable to those of the Philippines, Hong Kong, and Mexico, but substantially below those of German (18), Italian (28–42), or British (35) workers (Bureau of Labor Statistics, 2009). On many measures of quality of life, US workers do not fare well. And conditions are eroding in other nations as well.

The rapid movement of women into the professional labor force during the past 20 years has significantly increased the number of people who experience work–home spillover. More than half of new mothers return to the workforce within a year of giving birth. Two-thirds of women with some college qualification do so, as do three-quarters of women with graduate or professional degrees. In general, mothers with higher incomes are more likely to return (two-thirds of those making $75,000 or more do so compared to half of those earning less than $20,000). These differences result in part from personal goals; educated, upper-income mothers have usually postponed having children until they have completed their education, become established in their careers, and moved up through their organizational hierarchies. The high level of career commitment that results gives them extra incentives to return to work. But it also results from their greater ability to afford high-quality child care and their enhanced bargaining power with their employers.

"Family-friendly" policies are rarely made available to all members of an organization. Instead they are offered to employees who are difficult to replace and/or who have other sources of organizational power. Lower-level, lower-income workers, those who need benefits the most, often are not eligible for them, or are pressured not to use what benefits are available (Kirby and Krone, 2001). It is for this reason that *Working Mother* magazine (see www.workingmother.com), whose annual list of the "100 Best Companies for Mothers to Work For," is the most comprehensive survey of "family-friendly" policies, entitled its 2000 study "Nice Perks, If You Can Get 'Em." In short, employees have multidimensional lives, each part of which demands their time, energy, and commitment. Unfortunately, some organizations refuse to take a holistic perspective, one that recognizes these multiple responsibilities. Fortunately, some do.

Organizational Choices and Family–Work Balance One of the easiest ways to get a sense of the kinds of programs and policies that can be valuable to a diverse workforce is to peruse *Working Mother*'s "100 Best" list, updated each year. Firms are evaluated in part on the fairness of their salary schedules and their record of promoting women. But they also gain points for having programs, such as child care assistance (including back up day care for children who are ill, out of school for a holiday, vacation, or snow day), flextime, flexplace, and flexible benefits plans. But *Working Mother* also warns readers about surveys that look *only* at a company's policies, because policies are often either not implemented or implemented in a way that penalizes employees who use them.

As Kirby and Krone (2001) observed, the pressure to remain productive, while at the same time addressing family needs creates a tension for managers. As a result, they sometimes send mixed messages about policies like family leave and flextime that lead people to be informally penalized for doing anything that takes away from a 100 percent effort. As the Childless/Childfree case indicates, even if upper management supports the policies – and a growing percentage do because it is very clear that these policies really do increase productivity and reduce costs related to absenteeism and turnover – middle- or lower-level managers and peers may not.

In spite of these challenges, there are many examples of programs and policies that seem to have been implemented successfully. Ben and Jerry's Homemade (Ice Cream), Inc., pays health club fees and reimburses parents for adoption fees (up to the cost of a hospital delivery of a baby); Beth Israel Hospital in Boston provides breast-pumping stations for returning mothers who are nursing their babies; Arthur Andersen and Company provides onsite day care for employees during the peak tax preparation season; Barnett Bank in Florida provides round-trip transportation for employees' children to summer day camp at the local YMCA; Lincoln National Insurance has trained 300 family day care providers to be employed by their workers; and Colgate-Palmolive pays the full cost of in-home emergency care for ill children for its employees. At the Bureau of National Affairs, Inc., employees with ten years of service are eligible for six-month sabbaticals at half-pay, and Consolidated Edison of New York has a new training program to attract women to higher-paying jobs traditionally held by men (such as utility repair work).[13] The list could be extended almost endlessly.

Even small and medium-sized businesses can help. They often lack the funds to establish expensive benefits, such as onsite day care or scholarships for employees' children. But, they can provide flexibility. Abbott Labs made the *Working Mothers* top 100 list in 2010 by allowing 89 percent of their employees to utilize flextime and two-thirds to telecommute. Abbott and other companies on this list demonstrate that any organization can consult with employees about what *their* needs are and design flexible programs that *individualize* policies, procedures, and benefits, while staying within the constraints imposed by budgets and concerns for fairness.

CONCLUSION

On the one hand, in the United Stated and many other countries, substantial progress has been made in changing organizations to meet the challenges of a diverse workforce. Today there are far more women, African Americans, and Latinos in entry-level professional and managerial positions than there were 20 years ago. Between 1970 and 2010 the proportion of female managers in the US economy as a whole increased from 15 percent to more than 50 percent. In 2010, 60 percent of the people earning bachelor's degrees were women, as were more than 50 percent of advanced degree earners, suggesting that in the future the number of women in influential positions in organizations will continue to grow. A majority of students in US medical and law schools are women.

However, people who are not Anglo males are still concentrated at the lower levels of organizations and in sectors with lower salaries and mobility opportunities. Upper management still is almost exclusively the province of Anglo males – 90 percent of *Fortune* 500 firms do not have a woman among the five most compensated officers.

Salaries for all women in the labor force have reached around 78 percent of men's salaries as of 2010. In 2003 surveys by the National (US) Association for Female Executives and the General Accounting Office found that "no matter how much you try to explain it away there is somewhere between a 12 percent to 20 percent wage can that can only be attributed to discrimination."[14] Among professional occupations, the gap varies, and changes with different economic conditions. In contrast, African American men still earn approximately 50 percent of Anglo men's salaries; African American women earn approximately 30 percent of Anglo men's incomes and approximately 60 percent of the income of Anglo women. Overall, Latinos earned two-thirds of the salaries of Anglo men. Of course, many of these gaps are still significant, even if the data are corrected for education, experience, or seniority within the firm.

Attitudes about a diverse workforce also have improved but still serve as barriers to change. And, as the US workforce becomes more diverse, other groups of employees have started to confront the dominant perspective. For example, age discrimination has become an increasing problem during the 2000s and is likely to grow in importance as the baby boomers age. Like other forms of differential treatment, ageism is both pervasive and subtle. It is grounded in the cultural assumption that older people are inherently less capable than younger workers, as reflected in implicit attitudes that people hold but are not aware of (Nelson, 2004). For example, when managers described 30-year-old and 60-year-old workers, they used the terms "more productive, capable of working under pressure, flexible, able to learn, and decisive" for the younger workers and "reliable, honest, committed to quality, have good attendance records, and use good judgment" for the older ones in spite of consistent research evidence indicating that intellectual skills do not decline substantially with age. They also tend to assume that younger workers will stay with the company for 25 to 30 years, in spite of substantial evidence that long-term connections to a single organization no longer can be assumed of *any* group of employees (recall the Generation X case study in Chapter 1).

So, at least in the United States, Europe, and the Commonwealth countries, there is evidence that some organizations have started to confront the dominant perspective while others engage in resistance. The barriers that traditionally have separated different groups of employees have started to dissolve. But, it is not yet clear whether the vestiges of those barriers will continue to exist, new barriers will be created, or the dominant perspective will disappear.

NOTES

1 Cynthia Stohl (2001, 234).

2 Sullivan and Taylor's study of Korean and Japanese employees illustrates the combined influence of cultural and individual characteristics.

3 As is typical in out-of-court settlements, Coca-Cola's management denied that discrimination was systematic or consistent with the values of the organization. See also Adame (2011).

4 This hiring preference came as a surprise to local governments, who had hoped that the new factories would provide jobs for a potentially much more troublesome group – young males who recently had migrated from rural areas to the cities in search of employment.

5 Some sophisticated studies of these changes are by Aihwa Ong. See Ong (1987, 1991; Ong and Nonini, 1997). Also see Stohl (2001).

6 And, in some countries, coworker actions that could reasonably have been expected to be known by management.

7 Excellent sources on harassment and its meaning include Susan Faludi (1991) and Reardon (1995). For recent statistics documenting harassment and attacks, see, for example, Townsend (2009), France 24 (2008), and Human Rights First (2008).

8 For a summary of studies supportive of this claim, see the first part of Lequien (2010).

9 Dickens and Dickens (1991) argue that eventually all African American employees will need to confront their supervisors over issues of racism and provide extended advice about when, how, and over what specific issues to do so. Many of the other sources cited in this chapter provide similar advice. Interestingly, self-help books oriented toward white women rarely provide advice about how subordinates should confront their supervisors over issues of sexism, except perhaps in cases of overt sexual harassment, perhaps because they are written from a more completely accommodationist perspective. For analyses of how African American women implement the balancing act, see Bell (1990) and Allen (2000).

10 See "Little Upward Help for Minority Females: Executive Women Say Mentors Needed" (1999, C3), Maynard, (1994), and Scherer (1994).

11 See Bureau of Labor Statistics (2001).

12 Daniel Creson, cited in Kever (2000); also see "Overworked America?" (1999).

13 Many of these policies have been mandated by law for decades outside of the United States. In Ecuador, for example, firms must provide women with three months of paid maternity leave and schedule them for only six hours of work at a time during the next three months so that they can nurse their babies. Most European and Canadian firms have on-site day care and provide special breaks for nursing mothers.

14 Betty Spence, president of the National Association for Female Executives, cited in "Women's Pay Gap Widens in Some Fields" (2003, B4).

REFERENCES

Abrams, D. and Hogg, M. (2003). "Collective Identity: Group Membership and Self-Conception," in Hogg and Tindale, eds., *The Blackwell Handbook of Social Psychology: Group Processes*. Malden, MA: Blackwell.

Acker, J. (1995). "Feminist Goals and Organizing Processes," in Ferree and Martin, eds., *Feminist Organizations*. Philadelphia: Temple University Press.

Adame, J. (2011). "Workplace Discrimination Complaints Up in Abilene." *Abilene Reporter News*, February 6. www.reporternews.com/news/2011/feb/06/workplace-discrimination-complaints-up/.

Alkhazraji, K.M., Gardner, W., Martin, J. and Paolillo, J. (1997). "The Acculturation of Immigrants to U.S. Organizations." *Management Communication Quarterly* 11: 217–265.

Allen, B. (2000). "A Black Feminist Standpoint Analysis," in Buzzanell, ed., *Rethinking Organizational and Managerial Communication From Feminist Perspectives*. Thousand Oaks, CA: Sage.

American Association of University Women. (2003). "'Pink Collar' Jobs Still Lure Most Women, Study Finds." *Houston Chronicle*, May 5, 5A.

Amparano, J.L. (1992). "Study Says Women Face Glass Walls as Well as Glass Ceilings." *Wall Street Journal*, March 3: 1, 13.

Anderson, P. (2001). "U.S. Employees Put in Most Hours." *CNN Archives*, August 30. http://archives.cnn.com/2001/CAREER/trends/08/30/ilo.study/.

Armas, G. (2003). "Educational Gaps Between Genders, Races Diminish." *Houston Chronicle*, March 21, 27A.

Ashcraft, K.L. (2001). "Organized Dissonance: Feminist Bureaucracy as Hybrid Form." *Academy of Management Journal*, 44: 1301–1322.

Ashcraft, K. and Kedrowicz, A. (2002) "Self-Direction or Social Support?" *Communication Monographs* 69: 88–110.

Bell, E.L. (1990). "The Bicultural Life Experience of Career-Oriented Black Women." *Journal of Organizational Behavior* 11: 459–477.

Blanchette, D.P. (1994). "Technology Transfer in a Culturally Diverse Workforce (Part I)." *Industrial Management*, July–August, 31–32.

Bullis, C. and Rohrbauck Stout, K. (2000). "Organizational Socialization: A Feminist Standpoint Approach," in Cheney and Barnett, eds., *International and Multicultural Organizational Communication*. Creskill, NJ: Hampton Press.

Bureau of Labor Statistics. (2001). "Economic News Release: Employment Situation Summary." August 5. www.bls.gov/news.release/empsit.nr0.htm.

Bureau of Labor Statistics. (2010). *Current Population Survey*. Washington, DC: Bureau of Labor Statistics.

Buzzanell, P. (1995). "Reframing the Glass Ceiling as a Socially Constructed Process." *Communication Monographs* 62: 327–354.

Buzzanell, P., ed. (2000). *Rethinking Organizational and Managerial Communication From Feminist Perspectives*. Thousand Oaks, CA: Sage.

Buzzanell, P.M., Meisenbach, R.J., Remke, R., Sterk, H. and Turner, L.H. (2009). "Positioning Gender as Fundamental in Applied Communication Research: Taking a Feminist Turn," in Frey and Cissna, eds., *Routledge Handbook of Applied Communication Research*. New York: Routledge.

Carter, J. (1995). *He Works, She Works*. New York: AMACOM.

Catalyst. (2010a). "Women in Management in the United States, 1950–Present." www.catalyst.org.

Catalyst. (2010b). "Women in U.S. Management." www.catalyst.org.

Center for Women's Business Research. (2009). *The Impact of Women-Owned Businesses in the United States*. www.womensbusinessresearch.org.

Cheney, G. (1995). "Democracy in the Workplace." *Journal of Applied Communication Research* 23: 167–200.

Clair, R. (1993). "The Use of Framing Devices to Sequester Organizational Narratives." *Communication Monographs* 60: 113–136.

Davidson, M. and Swigert-Ruderman, S. (2000). "A Matter of Perspective: The Effect of Race of Rater and Ratee on Managerial Performance Feedback." *Social Science Research Network Electronic Paper Collection*. http://ssrn.com/abstract=392422.

DeHaven, J. (2002). "Aggressive Women Get Help." *Houston Chronicle*, September 22, 5D.

Dezso, C.L. and Ross, C.G. (2008). *"Girl Power": Female Participation in Top Management and Firm Performance*. College Park: Robert H. Smith School of Business, University of Maryland.

Diaz-Saenz, H.R. and Witherspoon, P. (2005). "Possessing a 'Sense of Community': A Study of Employee Perceptions in Selected Organizations in Mexico," in Cheney and Barnett, eds., *International and Multicultural Organizational Communication*. Creskill, NJ: Hampton Press.

Dickens, F. and Dickens, J. (1991). *The Black Manager*. New York: AMACOM.

Dovidio, J.S., Gaertner, S., Anastasio, P. and Sanitioso, R. (1992). "Cognitive and Motivational Bases of Bias," in Knouse, Rosenfeld and Culbertson, eds., *Hispanics in the Workplace*. Newbury Park, CA: Sage.

Eadie, W. and Wood, J. eds. (1992). *Journal of Applied Communication Research* 20: v–418.

Edley, P. (2000). "Discursive Essentializing in a Woman-Owned Business." *Management Communication Quarterly* 14: 271–306.

Edwards, A. and Polite, C. (1992). *Children of the Dream: The Psychology of Black Success*. New York: Doubleday.

Eyer, D.E. (1992). *Mother-Infant Bonding: A Scientific Fiction*. New Haven, CT: Yale University Press.

Faludi, S. (1991). *Backlash: The Undeclared War Against American Women*. New York: Crown.

Farrell, A. (1995). "Like a Tarantula on a Banana Boat," in Ferree and Martin, eds., *Feminist Organizations*. Philadelphia: Temple University Press.

Ferree, M.M. and Martin, P.Y. (1995). *Feminist Organizations*. Philadelphia: Temple University Press.

Fine, M. and Buzzanell, P. (2000). "Walking the High Wire," in Buzzanell, ed., *Rethinking Organizational and Managerial Communication From Feminist Perspectives*. Thousand Oaks, CA: Sage.

France 24. (2008). "Racist Attacks Surge After Obama's Victory." www.france24.com/en/20081119-usa-barack-obama-racist-attacks-surge-after-victory-race.

Grace, D. and Cohen, S. (1995). *Business Ethics*. Melbourne: Oxford.

Grant Thornton (2009). "Women Still Hold Less Than a Quarter of Senior Management Positions in Privately Held Business." www.gti.org.

Hafen, S. (2005). "Cultural Diversity Training: A Critical (Ironic) Cartography of Advocacy and Organizational Silence," in Cheney and Barnett, eds., *International and Multicultural Organizational Communication*. Creskill, NJ: Hampton Press.

Hege, R.S. (1998). "A View From Elsewhere." *Communication Theory*: 271–297.

Helgessen, S. (1990). *The Female Advantage: Women's Ways of Leadership*. New York: Doubleday.

Hewlett, S.A. and Luce, C.B. (2005). "Off-Ramps and On-Ramps: Keeping Talented Women on the Road to Success." *Harvard Business Review*, March, 43–54.

Hewlett, S.A., Sherbin, L. and Forster, D. (2010). "Offramps and Onramps Revisited." *Harvard Business Review* 84: 30.

Hochschild, A. (1997). *The Time Bind*. New York: Metropolitan Books.

Hochschild, A. and Machung, A. (1997). *The Second Shift*. New York: Avon Books.

Human Rights First. (2008). "Racist Violence: What Available Data Reveals." www.humanrightsfirst.org/our-work/fighting-discrimination/2008-hate-crime-survey/racism-and-xenophobia/i-racist-violence-what-available-data-reveals/.

Ibarra, H. (1993). "Personal Networks of Women and Minorities in Management." *Academy of Management Review* 18: 56–87.

Ibarra, H. (1995). "Race, Opportunity, and Diversity of Social Circles in Managerial Settings." *Academy of Management Journal* 38: 673–703.

Ivanovich, D. (2000). "$192.5 Million Settles Coca-Cola Race Suit." *Houston Chronicle*, November 17, 1A, 20A.

Jamieson, D. and O'Mara, J. (1991). *Managing Workforce 2000*. San Francisco: Jossey-Bass.

Kantor, R.M. (1977). *Men and Women of the Corporation*.

Kever, J. (2000). "Life in the Tired Lane." *Texas Magazine*, August 13, 8.

Keyton, J. and Rhodes, S. (1999). "Organizational Sexual Harassment." *Journal of Applied Communication Research* 27: 158–173.

Kilborn, P.T. (1995). "For Many in Work Force, Glass Ceiling Still Exists." *New York Times*, March 16.

Kim, P.S. and Lewis, G. (1994). "Asian Americans in the Public Service." *Public Administration Review* 54: 285–290.

Kirby, E. and Krone, K. (2001). "The Policy Exists but You Can't Really Use It." *Journal of Applied Communication Research* 30: 50–77.

Kleiman, C. (2000). "Men Still Suspect if Priority Is Family." *Houston Chronicle*, April 9, 2D.

Knoke, D. (2001). *Changing Organizations: Business Networks in the New Political Economy*. Boulder, CO: Westview.

Knouse, S. (1992). "The Mentoring Process for Hispanics," in Knouse, Rosenfeld, and Culberson, eds., *Hispanics in the Workplace*. Newbury Park, CA: Sage.

Kraiger, K. and Ford, J.K. (1985). "A Meta-analysis of Ratee Race Effects in Performance Ratings." *Journal of Applied Psychology* 70: 56–65.

Kuitenbrouwer, P. (2003). "Female Executives Not So Different: Study." *Calgary Financial Post*, August 11, FP8.

Kunda, G. (1992). *Engineering Culture*. Philadelphia: Temple University Press.

Kwong, J. (1994). "Ideological Crisis Among China's Youths: Values and Official Ideology." *British Journal of Sociology* 45: 247–264.

Lequien, L. (2010). "The Impact of Parental Leave Duration on Later Career." www.crest.fr/ckfinder/userfiles/files/Pageperso/llequien/Leguien_ape_2010.pdf.

Lerman, R.I. and Schmidt, S.F. (2010). "An Overview of Economic, Social, and Demographic Trends Affecting the U.S. Labor Market," in *FutureWork: Trends and Challenges for Work in the 21st Century*. Washington, DC: US Department of Labor.

"Little Upward Help for Minority Females: Executive Women Say Mentors Needed." (1999). *Houston Chronicle*, July 14, C3.

Livingston, G. and Cohn, D. (2010). "More Women Without Children," *Pew Research Center Publications*. www.parenting.com/blogs/show-and-tell/kim-babytalk/paternity-leave-front-line-new-daddy-wars.

Lott, C. (1988). "Redwood Records: Principles and Profit in Women's Music," in Bate and Taylor, eds., *Women Communicating*. Norwood, NJ: Ablex.

Marshall, J. (1995). *Women Managers Moving On*. London: Routledge.

Maynard, M. (1994). "Diversity Programs Work, Where They Exist." *USA Today*, September, 5.

McLean, G.N. (2006). *Organization Development: Principles, Processes, Performance*. San Francisco: Berrett-Koehler.

Miller, L., Cooke, L., Tsang, J. and Morgan, F. (1992). "Should I Brag." *Human Communication Research* 18: 364–399.

Mohamed, A.R.J. and Lloyd, J., eds. (1990). *The Nature and Context of Minority Discourse*. Oxford: Oxford University Press.

Morrison, A. (1992). *The New Leaders*. San Francisco: Jossey-Bass.

Morrison, A., White, R. and Van Velsor, E. (1992). *Breaking the Glass Ceiling*. Greensboro, NC: Center for Creative Leadership.

Morrison, A.M. and Von Glinow, M.A. (1990). "Women and Minorities in Management." *American Psychologist* 45: 200–208.

Mumby, D. (1998). "Organizing Men." *Communication Theory* 8: 164–183.

Nadler, M. and Nadler, L. (1993). "Feminization of Public Relations," in Berryman-Fink, Ballard-Reich, and Newman, eds., *Communication and Sex-Role Socialization*. New York: Garland.

National Science Foundation. (2008). "Chore Wars: Men, Women, and Housework." www.nsf.gov/discoveries/disc_summ.jsp?cntn_id=111458.

National Sleep Foundation. (2005). "National Sleep Survey." www.sleepfoundation.org/article/sleep-america-polls/2005-adult-sleep-habits-and-styles.

Nelson, T., ed. (2004). *Ageism: Stereotyping and Prejudice Against Older Persons*. Cambridge, MA: MIT Press.

Nicotera, A.M., Clinkscales, M.J., Dorsey, L.K. and Niles, M.N. (2009). *Routledge Handbook of Applied Communication Research*. New York: Routledge.

Nkomo, S. (1992). "The Emperor Has No Clothes: Rewriting Race in Organizations." *Academy of Management Review* 17: 487–512.

Oetzel, J. and Bolton-Oetzel, K. (1997). "Exploring the Relationship Between Self-Construal and Dimensions of Group Effectiveness." *Management Communication Quarterly* 10: 289–315.

Ong, A. (1987). *Spirits of Resistance and Capitalist Discipline: Factory Women in Malaysia*. Albany, NY: SUNY Press.

Ong, A. (1991). "The Gender and Labor Politics of Postmodernity." *Annual Review of Anthropology* 20: 196–214.

Ong, A. and Nonini, D., eds. (1997). *Underground Empires: The Cultural Politics of Modern Chinese Transnationalism*. Durham, NC: Duke University Press.

Orbe, M. and Everett, M. (2006). "Interracial and Interethnic Conflict in the United States," in Oetzel and Ting-Toomey, eds., *The Sage Handbook of Conflict Communication*. Thousand Oaks, CA: Sage.

Ospina, S. (1996). *Illusions of Opportunity*. Ithaca, NY: ILR/Cornell University Press.

"Overworked America?" (1999). PBS Newshour online, September 6. www.pbs.org/newshour/bb/business/july-dec99/overwork_9-6a.html.

Page, P. (1994). "African Americans in Executive Branch Agencies." *Review of Public Personnel Administration* 14: 24–51.

Pardo, M. (1995). "Doing It for the Kids," in Ferree and Martin, eds., *Feminist Organizations*. Philadelphia: Temple University Press.

Pesquera, B. (1997). "In the Beginning He Wouldn't Even Lift a Spoon," in Lamphere, Razone and Zavella, eds., *Situated Lives*. New York: Routledge.

Potuchek, J. (1997). *Who Supports the Family?* Palo Alto, CA: Stanford University Press.

Powell, G. (1993). *Women and Men in Management*. Newbury Park, CA: Sage.

Powell, G. and Butterfield, D.A. (1994). "Investigating the 'Glass Ceiling' Phenomenon." *Academy of Management Journal* 37: 68–86.

Prasso, S. (1996). "Study: Stereotypes Hinder Female Executives." *Houston Chronicle*, February 29.

Ramde, D. (2011). "Wisconsin Plant Settles Discrimination Case for $1.65 Million." *Business Week*, February 4. www.businessweek.com/ap/financialnews/D9L60CP00.htm.

Ramirez, A. (2005–2006). "Hispanic Leadership Development and Its Policy Impact." *Harvard Journal of Hispanic Policy Studies* 18: 85–89.

Reardon, K. (1995). *They Don't Get It, Do They?* Boston: Little, Brown.

Reuther, C. and Fairhurst, G. (2000). "Chaos Theory and the Glass Ceiling," in Buzzanell, ed., *Rethinking Organizational and Managerial Communication From Feminist Perspectives*, Thousand Oaks, CA: Sage.

Rosin, H. (2010). "The End of Men." *Atlantic Magazine*, July–August. www.theatlantic.com/magazine/archive/2010/07/the-end-of-men/8135/.

Rothschild-Whitt, J. and Whitt, J.A. (1986). *The Cooperative Workplace*. Cambridge: Cambridge University Press.

Scherer, R. (1994). "First National Survey of Minority Views Shows Deep Racial Polarization." *Christian Science Monitor*, March, 4.

Segura, D. (1997). "Chicanas in White-Collar Jobs," in Lamphere, Razone and Zavella, eds., *Situated Lives*. New York: Routledge.

Sloan, D. and Krone, K. (2000). "Women Managers and Gendered Values." *Women's Studies in Communication* 23: 111–130.

Spain, D. (1992). *Gendered Spaces*. Chapel Hill: University of North Carolina Press.

Stohl, C. (2001). "Globalizing Organizational Communication," in Jablin and Putnam, eds., *The New Handbook of Organizational Communication*. Thousand Oaks, CA: Sage.

Sullivan, J. and Taylor, S. (1991). "A Cross-Cultural Test of Compliance-Gaining Theory." *Management Communication Quarterly* 5: 220–239.

Townsend, M. (2009). "Police Alarm as Anti-Gay Attacks Rise." *The Guardian*, May 31. www.guardian.co.uk/world/2009/may/31/homophobic-attacks-increase-police-statistics.

US Department of Labor. (2010). *Occupational Outlook Handbook, 2010–2011 Edition*. Washington, DC: US Department of Labor.

Valdivia, L. (2003). "A Burgeoning Hispanic Middle Class? Doubtful." *Houston Chronicle*, September 5, 25A.

van Dijk, T. (1993). "Principles of Critical Discourse Analysis." *Discourse and Society* 4: 249–283.

Volk, J. (2011). "Discrimination Charges Soar in Down Economy." *Philadelphia Post-Gazette*, February 7. www.post-gazette.com/pg/11038/1123012-499.stm.

"Women's Pay Gap Widens in Some Fields." (2003). *Houston Chronicle*, December 10, B4.

Wood, J. (2009). *Gendered Lives*, 9th ed. Belmont, CA: Wadsworth.

Wyatt, N. (1988). "Shared Leadership in a Weavers' Guild," in Bate and Taylor, eds., *Women Communicating*. Norwood, NJ: Ablex.

Zahidi, S., Ibarra, H., Tesfachew, T., Bekhouche, Y., Cuenod, M., Farrell, E. and Niforos, M. (2010). *The Global Gender Gap Report*. Geneva: World Economic Forum.

CHAPTER 11

COMMUNICATION, ORGANIZATIONS, AND GLOBALIZATION

All of this [globalization] creates a problem for democracies. Democracy and capitalists have very different core values. Democracy is founded on equality – one vote per citizen regardless of his [sic] intelligence or work ethic. Capitalism, however, is motivated by inequality: differences in economic returns create the incentive structure which encourages hard work and wise investment. . . . The economically fit are expected to drive the economically unfit out of existence; there are no equalizing feedback mechanisms in capitalism.

Lester Thurow

[D]uring the next decade [the global labor pool] will absorb nearly 2 billion workers from emerging markets, a pool that currently includes close to 1 billion unemployed and underemployed workers. . . . These people will be earning a fraction of what their counterparts in developed countries earn and will be only marginally less productive. You are either someone who is threatened by this change or someone who will profit from it, but it is almost impossible to conceive of a significant group that will be untouched by it.

David Rothkopf

[In a globalized economy] Security of employment for an Australian sheep shearer, for example, might be affected by trends in Japanese fashions . . . the cost of synthetic fibers which is in turn determined by the price of oil which might in turn be determined by American military intervention in the Persian Gulf, and the extent to which the Australian government accepts prevailing global ideologies of marketization and privatization

Malcolm Waters

How we learn to strike the right balance between globalization's inherently empowering and humanizing aspects and its inherently disempowering and dehumanizing aspects will determine

Strategic Organizational Communication: In a Global Economy, Seventh Edition.
Charles Conrad and Marshall Scott Poole.

whether it is reversible or irreversible, a passing phase or a fundamental revolution in the evolution of human society.

Thomas Friedman[1]

CENTRAL THEMES

- There is little question that since early 1990s the world economy has become increasingly globalized, creating new challenges and new opportunities for organizations, workers, and governments.
- A key to dealing with globalization is understanding cultural differences, and understanding that differences are not deficiencies.
- Free trade is based on the "theory of comparative advantage," a concept that has become increasingly politicized during the past decade.
- As the theory of comparative advantage predicts, globalization has led to massive increases in economic inequality, both within and between nations.
- Globalization forces organizations to become *responsive,* not just reactive.

KEY TERMS

culture
fatwa
power distance
uncertainty avoidance
masculinity–femininity
individualism–collectivism
utilitarian individualism
expressionistic individualism
Confucian dynamism
universalism–particularism
neutral-affective
specific-diffuse
low-context cultures
high-context cultures
glocalized
theory of comparative advantage
responsive organizations

One of the dominant themes of this book is that there is an important and complex relationship between organizations and the societies from which they draw their members. To this point we have focused on one side of that relationship – the ways in which societal assumptions, structures, and processes influence organizations and organizational communication. For millennia, those processes encouraged homogeneity, separation, and often antagonism – workers versus managers; men versus women; racial and ethnic majorities versus minorities; Europeans versus Americans versus Africans versus Asians; and upper versus middle versus lower classes. Homogeneity and separation were sustained through a number of human-made social barriers and through the seemingly natural realities of time and space.

However, at least since the time of the industrial revolution and the democratization of Europe and North American, there also have been pressures toward heterogeneity. During the past 20 years, those pressures have become progressively more potent. Workforces have become more diverse and the barriers that exist within organizations to separate "different" groups of "others" have started to break down. As a result, new assumptions, structures, and processes are beginning to emerge. As Chapter 10 explained, this increased proximity *within* organizations demands the development of new systems and communicative strategies.

At least since the beginning of the 1980s, organizations and their members have been challenged to deal with a second kind of proximity, an unprecedented collapsing of the barriers of time and space. Of course, the late twentieth and early twenty-first centuries are not the first time that economic activity has taken on a global dimension. Extensive trade networks extending from the Persian Gulf to North Africa flourished thousands of years before the Christian era (BCE); even larger systems existed among Asia, Africa, and Europe at the time of Alexander the Great (around 300 BCE) and were expanded during the Roman Empire. Extensive systems developed in Meso-America soon after. The mercantile system of the fifteenth through the nineteenth centuries established a worldwide economic system dominated by Europe – the trade in African slaves was globalized by the 1440s and silver mined in the Spanish colony of Manila during the 1570s went to China to pay for products that in turn were shipped to Europe. In fact, the key characteristics of today's globalization – declining transportation costs, increased economic inequality in the developed countries and declining inequality in poor countries, volatile and destabilizing flow of capital across national boundaries, and cross-border migration – all were greater between 1840 and 1914 than they are today.[2] Even some of today's controversial issues give a sense of *déjà vu*. During the 1990s and early twenty-first century, US economists, politicians, and CEOs seem obsessed with reducing barriers to the burgeoning Chinese market – US and European luxury auto makers are expanding their operations in and near Shanghai as fast as they can – just as their counterparts during the 1890s and early twentieth century were obsessed with the opportunity to make "shoes for the Chinese" (Varg, 1968).

However, today's globalization does seem to be historically unique. In earlier eras, international trade involved a small number of hardy risk takers whose efforts served a small number of economically elite consumers. Today's globalization influences the daily lives of many people through complex networks. New electronic technologies have given people from multiple economic strata access to information and expertise that once was only available to the wealthy and educated. In an effort to benefit from this change, governments around the world have significantly increased the level of education provided to their citizens. Between 1980s and 1997 male illiteracy rates in the 13 poorest countries fell from 19 percent to 12 percent; for women they fell even more, from 36 percent to 22 percent. In China and Indonesia, illiteracy declined by more than 75 percent. Similar increases in school enrollment suggest that the trends will continue. Thus, even in the developing world, populations are increasingly capable of using new technologies and the information and expertise that they provide.[3]

As a result, today it is almost impossible to predict where a given organization (or its many divisions) will be located. People who log on to AOL's help desk to straighten out a bill or correct a technical glitch will be talking to a Filipino techie working at what used to be Clark Air Force Base in the shadow of Mount Pinatubo. People who dial the Mexico tourism hotline may talk with someone who is located in Bend, Oregon, and employed by Destination Ventures. The odds are less than 50–50 that she or he is from Mexico. McDonald's Restaurants of Canada and the Moscow (Russia) City Council have established joint ventures. Swissair moved its entire accounting division to India to take advantage of lower labor costs for secretaries, accountants, and programmers; British Air's office that corrects reservation errors and keeps track of frequent flyer miles is located in Mumbai, India.

Within a decade, the barriers to global production and economic activity that existed during the Cold War have largely disappeared, to be replaced by international economic bodies (largely controlled by the United States and Europe) such as the World Trade Organization (WTO) and the International Monetary Fund (IMF). Both critics and defenders of globalization have noted that these changes have significantly shifted power away from individual citizens and governments and toward large multinational organizations. Massachusetts Institute of Technology (MIT) economist Lester Thurow is explicit:

> Because countries need corporations more than corporations need countries, the relative bargaining power of governments and multinational corporations is shifting. High profile multinational companies . . . no longer pay taxes to governments. Governments pay taxes to them.

For example, Israel paid $600 million (in grants, facility construction, and tax rebates) to land an Intel plant, and Brazil committed $700 million to attract a Ford plant. Worldwide, the ratio of taxes collected to a country's Gross Domestic Product (GDP) has stayed relatively stable since the fall of the Berlin Wall. But, as political power has shifted to large, multinational corporations, "the taxes on capital and employment have come down while other forms of taxation, particularly on consumption, have been increasing. In other words, the burden of taxation has shifted from capital to citizens."[4]

The effects of these changes have been decidedly mixed – some people, countries, and societies have benefited in many ways; others have suffered. As we have noted throughout this book, the unintended consequences of choices and actions often are more important than the intended ones. No advocate of globalization intended that the expansion of modern, Western culture would lead to the growth of fundamentalist strains of Islam or the decline of the US automobile industry; few even anticipated these changes. Some of the effects of globalization *have* been intentional, but the mixture of unintended and intended consequences and local conditions has produced a complex, fragmented system (Waters, 1995). Whatever the specific results of globalization may become, it is clear that organizations now have a significantly increased ability to influence the societies from which they draw their members. It is too early to make any firm predictions about the outcomes of globalization. Instead, our goal in this chapter is to outline the changes that have taken place and to explore the ongoing debate about their consequences. We begin by examining the challenges faced by organizations because of the multicultural nature of the global economy. Then we examine its economic and organizational dimensions.

CULTURE, DIFFERENCE, AND ORGANIZATIONAL COMMUNICATION

A decade ago, organizational communication scholar Cynthia Stohl chided her colleagues for being parochial in their research and writing, working almost completely from a Western, and usually from a US, perspective. Even in those rare occasions when scholars take an international or intercultural focus, she argued, they are oriented toward helping people from predominantly white, Western, industrialized societies better manage people and/or organizations from "other" societies. The goal is to get everyone, regardless of their backgrounds, values, or interests, to sing together in a harmonious chorus, with everyone singing predetermined notes, rather than as a "letting all voices, on and (arguably) off key, into the choir."[5] This orientation is not especially surprising because US citizens and US organizations have long been noted for their cultural parochialism, and US organizations for their preoccupation with control. For example, in 1979 the first major US government report that advised academic organizations to increase training in foreign (non-English) language and international cultures was published. A decade later only 23,000 US college students were studying Japanese, while 20 million Japanese were studying English. Today the figures are not significantly different, although the number of Anglos learning Spanish has increased in the five states with large Latino populations (New York, California, Texas, Florida, and Arizona). Change has been almost as slow in non-educational organizations. US firms spend a small percent of their training budgets on international or intercultural education (10–15 percent). Only 30 percent of firms in one study offered formal intercultural communication training, and the ones that were offered lasted only three days. Even though American employees are critical of their international colleagues' errors when speaking English and believe that these breakdowns hurt productivity, they often make no attempt to learn even the simplest foreign phrases (Parker, 2005). In contrast, international firms take language learning much more seriously. In fact, the two major Japanese banks spend 50 percent of their training funds on international training.

However, increasing cross-cultural understanding is a worldwide challenge. A survey of 1300 Japanese managers and their Southeast Asian subordinates found that the managers thought their local colleagues were illogical, indecisive, and inflexible, and the local managers perceived that their Japanese supervisors were secretive, intolerant, and inflexible. As the "Going South" case study (chapter 4) showed, major cultural differences also exist within countries.[6] Important linguistic and cultural differences have existed between northern and southern China for centuries, and between rural and urban China for decades. Rice University in Houston, Texas, conducts popular training programs that are designed to explain Texas and Texan culture to "expatriates" who have been transferred to the "Republic" from the rest of the United States. And, as the "Can You Trust Anyone Under Thirty" case studies (in Chapter 1 and later in this chapter) indicate, cultures are constantly changing, both because of globalization and because of other factors. An alternative view is expressed in the concept of "celebrating" diversity, of recognizing that multiple backgrounds and perspectives can enrich organizations and organizational life, far beyond the financial advantages that may come from diversification. The first step in celebrating diversity involves understanding the concept of culture and cross-cultural differences.

Defining Culture

In previous chapters we described the concept of **culture** as a learned system of beliefs, values, and meanings that guide, usually nonconsciously, the ways in which people make sense of their surroundings, and choose how to act in those surroundings. Cultures are learned by their members, so they presumably can be learned by outsiders. While this is most true of the artifacts of a culture – it is easy to teach outsiders how to present one's business card to Japanese associates, or under what circumstances one should entertain Korean colleagues in one's home instead of taking them to a restaurant – it is much more difficult to explain the deeper levels of culture, especially when some there simply is no word in one language that captures the meaning of a core concept in another culture. In fact, it is very difficult to accurately assess deeper levels of culture from artifacts alone. For example, wearing the traditional Muslim *hijab* (veil and head cover), or not wearing it, has become an issue in many countries. But, women make their decisions about the *hijab* for a variety of reasons. Some refuse to wear it because it symbolizes patriarchal subjection of women; others, including converts to Islam from the United States and Japan, wear it for the same reasons – it allows women to minimize the likelihood that they will be viewed (literally) as sex objects. In other situations it symbolizes class differences. Indeed, in 2010 when France was about to enact legislation banning the wearing of Islamic veils (and Belgium and Spain were debating similar acts), popular Saudi cleric Sheik Aedh al-Garni issued a **fatwa** (religious advice that is not legally binding) permitting Muslim women to reveal their faces in countries where garments are banned so that they could avoid being harassed or involved in legal action. Most Saudi clerics agreed that wearing a head scarf is strictly required; some argued that wearing a face veil is a tradition, not a requirement; some encouraged Muslim women to not travel to countries with restrictive laws; and others took a more traditional position. Social theorist Anthony Giddens concludes that "the *hijab* has no unitary meaning. It reflects the diversity of women's experience and aspirations around the world."[7] As a result, trying to draw conclusions about the values and beliefs underlying this very important artifact is virtually impossible, especially given the influences of globalization. Indeed, because so much of a person's culture is taken-for-granted, it is even difficult to teach people to be sensitive to their own cultural biases. For example, few white people in US organizations think of themselves as members of a "white" culture, although nonwhite members of those same organizations have very clear views of the distinctive values, communication styles, and behavior that they associate with "whiteness" (Ashcraft and Allen, 2003; Drzewiecka and Wong, 1999; Grimes, 2001). In some ways it is easier to learn to accurately interpret "other" employees' actions – a white male supervisor can quickly learn that he may misinterpret an Asian Americans' (or Latino/Latinas') respect for modesty and deference to authority as evidence of lack of leadership skills or managerial competence.[8]

The most influential model of cultural differences is Geert Hofstede's study of IBM employees in 53 different nations during the 1970s and 1980s. His model differentiates cultures based on their **power distance** (the amount of power that supervisors can acceptably exercise over their subordinates – high in China, low in Israel or Austria), **uncertainty avoidance** (the degree to which people are uncomfortable with ambiguity and risk and therefore prefer to work with long-term acquaintances or friends rather than with strangers – high in Japan, low in the United States), **masculinity–femininity** (the extent to which the culture values the stereotypically masculine traits of assertiveness and competitiveness or the stereotypically feminine attributes of cooperativeness and interdependence – high in Latin America and Japan, low in Scandinavia), and **individualism–collectivism**. Asian, Latin, Middle-Eastern, and African cultures also tend to be collectivist, which means that people in those societies learn to place a high value on solidarity, cooperation, and concern for others. In the Confucian tradition, individualism is portrayed as the cause of selfishness and anarchy, a barrier to the achievement of the rightful goals of a community or state. Confucian communication styles are guided and constrained by concerns about hurting the other person's feelings, minimizing impositions placed on the other person, and avoiding negative evaluations of the other person. A persons' identity is closely tied to his or her membership in important referent groups, especially family. In contrast, Western European and North American societies tend to be individualistic, and people learn to value competition and independence from other people or groups. They learn to value communication that is clear, efficient, and effective and adapt their own communication to correspond to those guidelines or constraints. It is not surprising that organizations in collectivist societies (and organizations located in individualist societies but dominated by people from collectivist societies) tend to operate according to collectivist principles, while organizations in individualistic societies operate in accord with the core values of those societies.[9]

A number of criticisms were offered for Hofstede's model. One was that it overgeneralized cultural characteristics. For example, both Hofstede and other researchers eventually concluded that the most important distinction was between individualism and collectivism. But, research by Robert Bellah and his colleagues found that there are at least two different strains of individualism in the most individualistic society, the United States (Bellah, Madsen, Sullivan, Swidler, and Tipton, 1985, 1991). One is utilitarian – a person's individual identity is tied up in his or her work and her or his life satisfaction is grounded in the material trappings of financial success. The other form of individualism is expressionistic – in which a person views public, income-related work as a necessary evil or a means of supporting a private realm of interpersonal relationships, hobbies, and service to others. **Utilitarian individualism** and collectivism are inherently in tension, if not contradictory, with one another; **expressionistic individualism** is very much compatible with communitarian cultural assumptions. Critics of Hofstede's original research also noted that it was limited to employees of IBM, and thus excluded countries in which the company had no operations. It also ignored individual and subcultural differences within each culture. For example, people from industrialized parts of a country tend to be more individualistic than rural residents, even if they are part of collectivist societies. Another was that it was dated – his initial surveys were collected between 1967 and 1973, before the advent of the internet, for example. Cultures change over time, and that the leaders may overtly, even blatantly, try to mold popular values and assumptions. For example, during the Maoist era in China, the government attempted to replace Confucian ideas with Marxist-Leninist doctrine. Both are "collectivist," although the most important referent "group" in Confucianism is one's family, while the most important referent group for Maoists is the party and state. Under the leadership of Deng Xiaoping, the government rejected Maoist collectivism and encouraged Confucian values and individualism. Both were seen as necessary for opening the Chinese economy to the West. Similarly, Saudi Arabia's leaders have been trying to persuade its young men to engage in work now largely performed by immigrants, although with only limited success. Perhaps the most important criticism is research indicating that individualism and collectivism are separate dimensions, so that cultures can be both highly individualistic and highly collectivist, and so on (see the "Under Thirty" case study later in this chapter).[10] A final criticism was that the model included too few dimensions of culture, and in the process overemphasized those that were salient in Western societies while slighting Asian cultures. Hofstede responded to these criticisms by replicating his study in a larger sample of societies, and added a fifth concept, **Confucian dynamism**, which differentiated cultures in which people learn to take a short-term time orientation (low Confucianism, as in the United States) instead of a long-term one (as in China). For example, in some cultures (e.g., Germany) violations of "normal" schedules are viewed as serious affronts. Other cultures accept a more flexible time orientation (e.g., Latin societies, although the influx of multinational employees is rapidly changing this norm in urban areas). In still other cultures, obeying "promptness" rules depends on one's rank, age, or status; in others, everyone is expected to use the same clock.

Subsequent research, including Trompenaars and Hampden-Turner's analysis of data collected from 15,000 managers in 23 nations, both confirmed and modified Hofstede's conclusions. Two of the factors they identified were similar (both models included an individualism-collectivism dimension, and Hofstede's "power-distance" dimension was equivalent to Trompenaars and Hampden-Turner's achievement–ascription dimension). But, Trompenaars and Hampden-Turner's research included three new dimensions, all of which were directed related to communication: **universalism–particularism** (the belief that core principles apply equally in all situations contrasted to the belief that leadership and communicative strategies should be adapted to particular situations and cultural contexts), **neutral-affective** (the belief that feelings should be masked compared to ones that value the expression of emotion as a core component of authentic communication), and **specific-diffuse** (a belief that most interactions should be public, with only small amounts of private space versus a more guarded view of public and private space). The latter concepts seem to be consistent with Edward Hall's distinction between **low-context** cultures in which people focus their attention on the explicit content of a message when they try to make sense out of it; and **high-context** cultures, in which much of the meaning is extracted from the context in which a message is uttered, and messages themselves are considered to be ambiguous. As a result, the messages constructed by people from "low-context" cultures seem to be blunt and excessively detailed to people from high-context cultures; messages from "high-context" cultures seem to be excessively vague, confusing, and/or noncommittal to people from "low-context" cultures. When New York's Corning Corporation began collaborating with Mexican firm Vitro, Mexican employees sometimes felt that Corning moved too fast to integrate the two operations. (They also found the Americans to be too blunt and direct.) Conversely, the Americans felt that Vitro was moving too slowly (and that their dogged pursuit of politeness kept them from acknowledging problems that needed to be dealt with; Trompenaars and Hampden-Turner, 1998; also see DePalma, 1994).

In addition, there are many culture-related differences in expected behaviors. In some cultures, relationships are defined solely by organizational rank and expertise; in others they are influenced by non-organizational considerations, such as age, kinship, sex, and wealth. In some societies, intimate relationships are expected to be monogamous; in others, forms of polygamy such as polygyny (multiple wives) and polyandry (multiple husbands) are normal. In some, providing alcohol and prostitutes (for example, Thailand and some parts of Nevada) is a normal part of business entertaining; in others, it is a capital offense. For example, in Chapter 3 we introduced the concept of piece-rate reward systems – each employee is paid a certain amount for each unit she or he produces. It is easy to legitimize these systems in highly individualistic cultures such as the United States, especially if they are used with all employees (universality) in a given work group or employment category. However, in highly communitarian cultures, individualistic and universalistic reward systems are viewed as unethical and unfair because they do not take relational considerations into account. For example, Trompenaars and Hayden-Turner described a US computer company, MCC (a pseudonym), which tried its pay-for-performance system in a much more collectivist Middle Eastern country. At first it succeeded because workers enjoyed seeing their coworkers receive rewards. But, once they realized that a few workers profited from the system while most suffered, morale and unit performance declined. When they discovered that some subordinates were making more money than their supervisors, something that simply does not happen in high power-distance cultures, they were incensed. Eventually they learned to game the system to make it more appropriate to their cultures. They determined appropriate rewards for each employee, based on the traditional practices of their culture. Then they created performance measures that justified their predetermined rewards. In effect, they **glocalized** the company's reward system, that is, adapted it to local cultures, much as McDonald's and Coca-Cola have adapted their marketing strategies, the ingredients in their products, and even their mode of providing service to Asian cultures.[11]

In sum, people in different cultures are pleased, worried, annoyed, and embarrassed by different things; seemingly identical conventions and rituals mean very different things to different peoples, and showing respect and deference vary in importance across different societies. Different societies *normalize* and *naturalize* different attitudes about work, tasks, the division of labor, and various practices, including punishments, and rewards. But adapting to cross cultural differences creates its own paradox. On the one hand, they benefit from borrowing the best practices and ideas from the many cultures in which they operate, and adapting their operations to local cultures. But, on the other hand, they need to create internal cultures that are coherent enough to create unity and predictability (Hoecklin, 1995).

INCREASING CULTURAL UNDERSTANDING

Well-designed intercultural training programs focus on communication itself. For example, the Canadian International Development Agency's pre-departure program for its expatriates provides training in seven core communication skills:

- Communicating respect (in the language or behavior of the host society)
- Being nonjudgmental (of others' attitudes, beliefs, and behaviors)
- Recognizing the influence of one's own perceptions and knowledge
- Being empathic (trying to understand the others' point of view and life situation)
- Being flexible (being able to accomplish a task in a manner and time that is appropriate to the host culture and the other's needs)
- Demonstrating reciprocal concern (actually listening and promoting shared communication)
- Tolerating ambiguity, especially about cultural differences

The goal of these programs is to convince managers not to define "differences" as "deficiencies." All organizational change efforts are difficult to implement; diversification training is even more difficult. After years of designing and conducting such programs Carnavale and Stone warn,

> In most organizations, valuing and managing diversity requires nothing less than cultural transformation. This is a prodigious task, for it requires people – especially those in the dominant culture – to let go of the assumptions about the universal rightness of their own values and customary ways of doing things in order to become receptive to other cultures. (1994, 24)

And even well-designed and conducted training can have negative, unintended consequences. If they focus solely on *differences* among employees, the values, beliefs, and experiences that they have *in common* may be obscured. The result is to perpetuate stereotypes and polarize the workforce. Ellen Castro became a successful consultant after she left her job as a manager of 500 employees in a $90 million retail profit center because of her boss's continual use of ethnic slurs. She explains how her experience led to her current approach to consulting:

> [So, you have to value differences. But] what you [often] do with these programs is emphasize how we're different, that people can get their feelings hurt. But what about how we're alike? All employees want respect. We all want to be involved in decision making. By emphasizing "diversity" we've created a chasm. Instead, let's look at people for who they are, what's their best skill? What can she bring to the table as a female? Diversity is not going to work until you have a culture where everyone is given respect and dignity.[12]

Of course, none of what we said suggests that everyone from a particular society has the same core beliefs and values. Gender, age, economic background, educational level, and individual experiences all influence the way in which people interpret the messages that they receive and incorporate them into their own views of the world and ways of communicating. The complete package of beliefs and values that people bring with them into their organizations exert a powerful influence on their communication. Since they are grounded in a lifetime of experience, they are very difficult to change. As a result, members of organizations must find ways to manage what often are complex webs of differences in beliefs, values, and modes of communicating.

Case Study 11.1

Can You Trust Anyone Under Thirty, Part 2?[1]

China always has been an economic giant. For most of human history it was the world's largest economy and most advanced civilization. It started to decline after 1450, but even as late as the early 1800s it accounted for one-third of the world's Gross Domestic Product (GDP). During the late twentieth century, it revived – its GDP grew at an astounding 10 percent per year from 1978 until 2000, and tripled between 2000 and 2010. Almost all projections suggest that it will continue to be one of the world's fastest growing economies in the near term. During the summer of 2010, China overtook Japan as the second-largest consumer economy in the world. Still, only 36 percent of its GDP comes from consumer spending (compared to more than 70 percent in the United States and more than 60 percent in the European Union [EU] and Japan), in part because 16 percent of its population still makes less than US$1.00 per day (down from 36 percent in 1999). Although Western organizations have flocked to China, their managers constantly complain about how difficult it is to deal with Chinese culture and the Chinese economic system. They should not have been surprised – after all, China invented bureaucracy more than 4000 years before Max Weber argued that it was the most appropriate organizational form for the Protestant nations of Europe. But, Chinese society has repeatedly undergone profound social changes. If one's attitudes, values, interpretative frames, and ways of acting are a function of one's experiences at key times in one's life (as we suggest in the Generations case study in Chapter 1), then generational differences, and the potential for cross-generational conflict, should be even greater in China than it is in the United States. If members of non-Chinese organizations hope to deal successfully with China, they must understand these changes and the differences they have spawned.

Of course, China has been a Confucian society for more than 2000 years and Confucian ideas were encouraged by the government during the Nationalist era (1911–1948) Although Western interpretations of Confucianism focus on its long-term time orientation, it has a number of other important dimensions. Its fundamental principle is that society is made stable by unequal and complementary relationships – ruler–subject, father–son, older brother–younger brother, husband–wife, and senior friend–junior friend – and each role contains a characteristic ethical property: father, kindness; son, filial piety; elder brother, goodness; younger brother, respect; husband, righteousness; wife, compliance; the sovereign, benevolence; and officials, loyalty. The family is the prototype of all social organizations. All people are responsible for "virtuous behavior" (which includes being benevolent, charitable, and humane *toward other members of one's referent group* – family and friends, but *not* outsiders – and treating other members of that referent group as one would like to be treated), and the pursuit of virtue through acquiring skills and education, working hard, living a frugal life, being patient, and persevering in the face of adversity. But Confucius also was concerned with good government: one that rules through moral, not physical, force (that is, through hegemony as the term was defined in Unit I). It requires a good ruler and good officials to implement his will, people who embody the individual virtues and whose rule is characterized by the "unfailingly benevolent treatment of the people.

Confucian principles lead to a distinctive concept of authority, *li*, and a distinctive mode of organizing, labeled *Guanxi*. *Li* dictates that people must follow proper social obligations, including especially toward people higher in the social hierarchy, during their social interactions – a "harmony through hierarchy." *Guanxi* focuses on traditional Confucian role relationships, and focuses on mutual, reciprocal exchanges as the basis for business interactions. Unlike the Western approach of regulating business through legal contracts – which is inherently offensive from a Confucian perspective – *guanxi* is grounded in developing trust through time-consuming, long-term relationships, and legitimizes "pulling strings" in order to help people with whom one has those relationships. Although it is more flexible than Western legalism, it also is more cumbersome because it creates a complex and ever-changing maze of obligations. As important, it also creates secret spaces within which nepotism, favoritism, and even corruption, can flourish.

During the Maoist era (1949–1965) and Great Cultural Revolution (1966–1976), the government attempted to discredit everything Western and to replace Confucian loyalty to the family with the doctrines of communist collectivism, which focused on loyalty to the state and society as a whole. Mao vilified Confucius' "stinking corpse" and Maoists attacked it as one of the "four olds" (old and discredited ideas) which stood in the way of achieving a truly communist society. To replace Confucianism, Maoism advocated an austere lifestyle defined by self-sacrifice and simple living. After Deng Xiaoping came to power in 1978, the official interpretation of Mao's ideas was revised and government policy has started to celebrate Western individualism under the notion that "being rich is glorious." Because Mao's legacy is an important support for the ruling party's legitimacy, it cannot be discarded completely or attacked too directly. Instead, anticapitalist aspects of Mao's thought are defined as "ultra-left" distortions. Within this revised ideology, the Maoist concept of equal distribution of wealth can be criticized for retarding economic progress. Comfort and material rewards now can be celebrated, and efficiency, nationalism, and pride in country can be stressed. For some Chinese, these changes have led to incredible accumulation of wealth – every Western luxury car maker, from BMW and Mercedes-Benz to Cadillac, views China as a key market for the present and future. But for the millions of Chinese who work in sweatshops and are paid the local minimum wage (which is far lower than the living wage), life is very different. For example, at Foxconn Technology, an electronics maker that employs 800,000 people to assemble parts for Apple, Dell, and HP, suicide has become a serious problem. At the Pingdingshan Cotton Textile Company, workers make 65 cents an hour, working grueling two-day shifts, often in 100-degree heat. As Daniel Gardner, director of the Program in East Asian Studies at Smith College, notes,

> [U]nbridled economic growth has spawned a host of problems: a widening gulf between rich and poor, urban and rural; heightened social tensions; increasing unemployment; rising crime; rampant corruption, especially among government officials and local business leaders; environmental degradation; healthcare and elderly care that is out of the reach of vast numbers of people; and a skyrocketing incidence of public protests (tens of thousands annually). The Communist Party is neither unaware of nor insensitive to these problems. But it is determined to confront them without surrendering any of its political control or authority. (2010)

One of the government's strategies for dealing with these tensions is to revive *some* of Confucius ideas. For example, during the opening ceremonies of the 2008 Olympics, the world was greeted with warm homilies about social harmony, empathy, and treating ones fellow human beings with respect. Evidently, the government now hopes to create a society in which people will place trust in their government and be obedient to it, with minimal dissent (the concept of "hegemony" that we introduced in Unit I). The obligations of leaders are included in this revised rhetoric, but the obligations of citizens are foremost. As a result, today's Chinese culture is a complex mixture of Confucianism, collectivism, and individualism.

Although a number of nongenerational factors almost certainly influence the relative importance of the three cultural assumptions for individual Chinese people – gender, geographic location during one's formative years, company size, industry, and current geographical location – generational differences are likely to be important. There now seem to be three (or four) distinct but overlapping generational groups. People who now are older than 60 grew up under Maoism and under communist and collectivist cultural assumptions. A second group, often labeled the "Lost Generation" (currently in their fifties), came of age during the turmoil and social instability of the Cultural Revolution, and thus largely lost the benefits of a real education. The "post-Tiananmen" or "New" generation has primarily experienced the rising expectations and China's return to economic and political power. Some of them witnessed the Tiananmen Square Demonstrations of 1989, which saw huge numbers of Chinese students protest against the government. The subsequent military crackdown greatly disappointed the generation of students and workers, and has largely weakened the political consciousness of the students who have grown up since that time. Other members of this age group, particularly those who lived in rural areas, were less influenced by the events of 1989.

There are definitely differences between the older generation and those who grew up in the 1960s and 1970s, but the primary contrast seems to be between those who were born before the end of the Cultural Revolution, who strongly hold to values of social duty and responsibility, and the individualistic post-Tiananmen Generation, particularly young men who were raised in urban and/or industrialized parts of the country. Traditional thought continues to influence Chinese attitudes and organizations, especially outside of the major industrial centers, but surveys have found that as many young people listed a "good job, good careers, and comfortable lives" as their highest priority (37 percent) as listed "to make our motherland rich and powerful" (36 percent). By the end of the 1990s only 21 percent put national interests at the top of their priority list, while almost two-thirds focused on personal gain. Almost half admitted that they would take time and energy helping someone else only if it did not interfere with their own, individual success.

This generation is sometimes known as the "Little Emperor" (or "Chinese Brat," "Chinese Me," or "Chuppie" [Chinese yuppie]) generation, children who, due to the government's "One Child Policy", grew up as only children, and in the second generation, with few if any cousins. Thus, they were usually doted on by multiple grandparents and parents who were often afraid to discipline the children, lest they lose their affection. Some have estimated that a typical family dedicated almost 50 percent of their disposable income on these "little emperors," for extra education, computers, toys, tutoring, or other luxuries, compared to a comparable rate of approximately 20 percent in the United States.

Although empirical evidence has not shown strong differences in attitudes among these youth, anecdotal evidence abounds of youth with a strong sense of entitlement and a correspondingly weaker sense of self-control or the humility that was valued by the traditional Confucian value system.

Members of the older generations see the younger generation as hedonistic, and interested only in designer goods, luxury, and comfort. They tend to believe that, instead of creating a New Generation with "one foot in the new economy" and "one foot in Confucianism," China has created a generation which focuses on conspicuous consumption and self-indulgence. Stanley Lau, deputy chairman of the Hong Kong Federation of Industries, whose 3000 firms employ more than 3 million workers in mainland China, complained that "this young generation thinks differently than their parents, they have been well-protected by their families, and they don't like to 'chi ku' [eat bitterness]" (Jacobs, 2010). Zhang Jinfang, a 28 year old, seems typical of his generation. He has cycled through a number of jobs since leaving high school, and explains that "sometimes I'll quit after a few weeks because the work is too hard or too boring. Money is important, but it's also important to have less pressure in your life" (Jacobs, 2010). He saves almost none of his salary, another deviation from more traditional ideals.

Although Chinese workers still support China's political system, they are cynical about their leaders, in part because corruption has been a serious problem as China has moved toward capitalism, and politically connected families have been the primary beneficiaries of that corruption.

However, others note that outside of cities and towns the effects of the one-child policy and Westernization have had less impact. Ethnic minorities are legally entitled to have two children, and some rural families have been able to have two children because local officials recognize that incomes are much lower in rural areas (perhaps as low as 20 percent of national norms), so one child is not likely to be able to support his or her parents. Consequently, rural societies have retained more traditional values and family arrangements. As a result, both the older generations and the rural New Generation may provide a continuing challenge to individualism. Even in the cities, Chinese students try to stay near family if it is at all possible to do so, and connections with cousins, nieces, and nephews in extended families reproduce traditional relationships even among only children. Chinese schools retain traditional hierarchical relationships, so there are many Confucian and collectivist influences still in place to counter the pressures of individualism.

Applying What You've Learned

1. What expectations does each of these generational groups have about life and about organizations?
2. What messages and experiences have contributed to those expectations?
3. Over what issues are the three groups likely to have conflicts? Why?

Questions to Think About and Discuss

1. To which, if any, of the three generational groups do you belong? (Remember, it's the experiences you've had more than your age that influences generational membership). How do your expectations and experiences correspond to theirs? Over what issues are you likely to have conflicts with members of the three groups? Why?
2. Which of the (US) generational groups described in the "Under Thirty" case in Chapter 1 are most like the New Generation in China? Which ones are most unlike the New Generation?
3. There is an alternative explanation of both the US (Chapter 1) and Chinese "generations" case studies – when people age their values change because of a complex set of psychological, sociological, and economic factors. This is why there is evidence of an older generation despairing the lost values of their children and grandchildren, going back as far as ancient Egypt, Assyria, India, and China. For example, there is a 2000-year old Chinese expression, "The newer generation is always not as good as the older one," that is used

even by college sophomores in response to foolish actions by freshmen and -women. We have presented both case studies as if the economic and sociological-political factors are dominant. Could the changes we have outlined be primarily a function of psychological changes that accompany aging? Why or why not? What implications does your answer have for organizational interpersonal relationships across generations?

Note

1 We would like to thank Randy Kluver, director of the Texas A&M Confucius Institute, for his input on this case study. Sources: Bajaj (2010); Boumphrey (2007); Chen (2000); Child (1996); Ching (1982); Crowell and Hsieh (1995); Gardner (2010); Hassard, Sheehan, and Morris (1999); Hong and Engstrom (2004); Jacobs (2010); Kristof (2002b); Kwong (1994); Lin and Clair (2007); *New York Times* Editorial Board (2010); Ralston, Egri, Stewart, Terpstra, and Kaicheng (1999); Varg (1968); Whalen (2007); and Wong (2010).

ECONOMICS, GLOBALIZATION, AND ORGANIZATIONAL COMMUNICATION

The theoretical justification of globalization is free market (*laissez-faire*) capitalism, introduced in Chapter 2. Although these concepts were developed for a nation's internal economic system, they are easily applied to international economics.

Globalization and the Discourse of Free Trade

The key link is a concept called the **theory of comparative advantage.** This theory starts with the observation that different areas of the globe have different *natural* economic advantages. Some areas have abundant natural resources; some have an especially productive labor force; some are strategically located on trade routes, and so on. If the economy of an area relies on its natural advantages, it will be more efficient than if it tries to develop industries in which it does not have an advantage. With increased efficiency comes increased profits, incomes, and wealth. If every area focuses on its advantages and refuses to develop industries in which it does not have a comparative advantage, the entire global economy benefits – market forces *alone* will ensure the greatest welfare for all people. Conversely, if governments interfere with these natural processes by adopting tariffs, quotas, or currency values that artificially support industries in which their country does not have an advantage, or if they create artificial barriers to the free flow of trade, finance, and labor, they reduce the wages and wealth of their own people and make the whole world's economy less efficient than it otherwise would be.[13]

Even the strongest advocates of free trade recognize that it may be socially disruptive and create serious economic inequities for short periods of time. Industries in which an area does not have a competitive advantage will be unable to compete. Companies in non-advantaged industries will go bankrupt, and workers will either have to shift to advantaged industries or move to areas where their old companies have a comparative advantage. These areas are likely to have lower standards of living and incomes than workers enjoyed when their companies were being artificially supported. Within each country, inequities in income and wealth are likely to grow as groups with ready access to the basis of each country's "advantage" benefit, and other groups are disadvantaged. Industries that are inappropriate to a particular area's "advantages" will move elsewhere or go out of business. Capital will flow to advantaged industries and/or to countries that are effectively exploiting their advantages. But, the theory argues, eventually each area will be dominated by organizations that produce the products or provide the services in which it has a comparative advantage, and all of the employees of those organizations will benefit (Otis, 2003; Schaefer, Conrad, Cheney, May, and Ganesh, 2010).

In free market theory, each economy will begin to grow as long as the wealth that is created by exploiting its advantages is invested wisely. Over the long term, the system will self-correct, and wage rates will rise (as noted in the case study you just read). Eventually the world and each area will arrive at an equilibrium point. For example, there is evidence that many counties are investing more in their educational systems to compete more effectively in a global market. In the industrialized countries, this means increasing the percentage and number of residents who go to college and to encourage college students to focus on technologically oriented careers, processes that have been much more successful in Europe and Asia than in the United States. Doing so gives them and their countries a comparative advantage in the high-tech sectors of the world economy. In developing countries, it means taking the actions described at the beginning of this chapter – increasing literacy rates and the number and percent of their residents who are in school, especially among women and girls. Unfortunately, in some cases the international organizations charged with implementing free trade make decisions that short-circuit these processes. For example, the World Bank and International Monetary Fund traditionally have imposed strict austerity plans on most of the countries to which they provide assistance, and have engaged in economic policies that place controlling inflation above maintaining low levels of unemployment. The resulting cuts in government spending make it difficult for developing countries to adjust adequately to global competition, and slower growth exacerbates these problems. For example, the benefits of globalization in Latin America have been very unequally distributed, in large part because their governments have not had the funds necessary to improve public education in ways that give the bulk of their citizens the skills needed for them to compete in the global economy. In parts of both the developed and developing world, these strategies already seem to be increasing incomes and wealth. However, the correction occurs only if the newly acquired capital stays in the home country. Since investors can now easily shift their funds to any country in the world at the touch of a button, much of the wealth created by exploiting a country's comparative advantage leaves the country. As a result, national economies are vulnerable to events about which they may not even be aware. This interdependency was demonstrated with a vengeance during the financial market meltdown of 2008 and 2009. Freer flows of capital allowed Icelandic financial institutions to invest heavily in UK banks, which had been free to invest heavily in undercapitalized and underregulated US financial organizations, which had been free to write millions of high-risk, "subprime" mortgage loans in Nevada, California, and Florida. Once the bottom fell out of the Las Vegas housing market, Iceland's bankruptcy was virtually inevitable, short of a "bailout" by its trading partners.[14]

Of course, even the strongest advocates of free trade admit that in some cases there may be good non-economic reasons for violating the tenets of the theory. For example, a government may wish to support its own computer or steel industry as a matter of national defense, or it may want to protect a fledgling industry from foreign competition until it is sufficiently well established to compete successfully, or it may wish to restrict migration across its borders for political reasons. But, the theory argues, any artificial barrier reduces the efficiency of the national (and world) economy, and reduces wealth, wages, profits, and employment in the long run. They should be continued only as long as the non-economic advantages clearly outweigh the economic disadvantages. Too many barriers to the free movement of trade, capital, and labor – whether imposed by government, labor organizations, or cultural norms – upset the global free market and reduce the total amount of wealth that is created. It is for this reason that some proponents of free trade, such as American philosopher-educator John Stuart Mill, advocated having governments pay compensation to workers and industries that lose out to global competition. Doing so reduces social costs and potential social unrest, but does not interfere with market processes. The modern version of this argument comes when governments invest funds for retraining of employees who have lost their jobs due to globalization (Irwin, 1996). But, such programs are controversial because they deviate from the tenets of free market theory.

The debate over "exceptions" and compensation make a very important point about free trade and globalization – although it is discussed in economic terms, its implementation is a highly political process and can only be understood fully from that perspective. An important issue, especially to developing countries, is US agriculture policy. In 1997 the US government adopted the "Freedom to Farm" act, which reversed many subsidies and protections that farmers and ranchers had received for decades. The primary rationale for the change was free market theory and the concept of "comparative advantage – subsidies and tariff protection encouraged the continuation of industries in which the United States did not have a natural advantage. The shift in policy had a devastating effect on many sectors of US agriculture, and led to a bipartisan effort to repeal the act. The result was the $180 billion Farm Security Act, passed in the fall of 2002. It revived and even expanded many of the protective provisions, and was wildly popular in heavily agricultural states even though approximately 80 percent of the benefits go to giant agribusinesses and wealthy farmers (Ted Turner and Arthur Schwab often are singled out as examples) rather than struggling rural families. The bill immediately encountered threats of litigation and retaliation by US trading partners, criticism by free trade purists, and ridicule at home. Humorist Dave Barry focused on a rather small part of the bill, a subsidy to encourage the domestic production of mohair. Initiated during World War II to provide warm coats for soldiers, the subsidy primarily helps ranchers in the Texas hill country. In 1997 it was eliminated because the reason for its creation no longer was relevant (modern military coats are made with synthetic fibers). However, it was reinstated in 2002: "if you're like most American taxpayers, you often wake up in the middle of the night in a cold sweat asking yourself, 'Am I doing enough to support mohair producers?'" The new bill even subsidizes US firms to buy subsidized US agricultural products. Other developed countries have similar programs. As of 2002, the richest countries spent $311 billion per year in agricultural subsidies. In Europe and Japan, farmers receive 31–59 percent of their income from subsidies (20 percent in the United States). Since subsidies guarantee a particular price regardless of supply and demand, they encourage overproduction, which drives down world prices and the incomes of farmers in countries without subsidies. Eventually they go out of business, making their countries even more dependent on agriculture in other countries.[15]

The US position on immigration has oscillated in much the same way. At times the owners and managers of US organizations actively seek immigrants – for example, supposedly "docile" laborers from continental Europe during the 1880s and 1890s, computer experts from Asia during the "dot com" boom of the 1990s, or unskilled laborers from Mexico since 2000. For owner and managers, a ready supply of workers who are willing to work for low wages and are unlikely to complain about working conditions because they fear being deported is enticing. Historically, they have been joined by politicians who covet immigrants' votes. Restrictions on immigration have historically been supported by various citizen groups, whose limited resources and lack of political organization give them less influence than the pro-immigration coalition.[16] The shifts in immigration policy, and to an extent owner and managers' positions on the issue, have largely resulted from a shifting balance between these two political pressure groups. Immigration currently is a highly contentious political issue throughout the world, as is its counterpart – outsourcing jobs. Once limited to manufacturing (e.g., automobile assembly and textiles), since the turn of the century the outsourcing industry has focused on white-collar jobs. Financial analysis, medical transcription, interpretations of X-rays, and computed tomography (CT) scans all are increasingly being done for Western firms by professionals in Asia. The number of Indian law firms conducting business that has been outsourced from the United States mushroomed from 40 in 2005 to more than 140 at the end of 2009; revenue is expected to grow by $440 million during 2010 and exceed $1 billion by 2014. To meet this growing demand, Indian outsourcing firms are actively courting attorneys in US firms and law schools. One in ten high-tech US jobs moved overseas between 2000 and 2004, and at least 3.3 million white-collar jobs, paying $136 billion in wages, will have shifted from the United States to developing countries between 2000 and 2015. Backlash to outsourcing in the developed world became so intense that it led to a 2004 summit of 30 Asian countries held in Hyderabad, India, and blocked President George W. Bush's 2008 proposal for immigration reform. Anti-outsourcing websites like OutsourceCongress.org and professional organizations like The Information Technology Professionals Association of America have institutionalized these political trends.[17] Worldwide, the rhetoric of policy makers still is strongly in favor of free trade and unrestricted immigration, public policy is much more guarded. Economic policies are made for political reasons, but justified on economic grounds. However, the lesson for managers is clear – there are two ways to deal with the dislocations of globalization, become more competitive, or become more politically active (see Chapter 12 for more detail). But, even that lesson is complicated because some companies benefit and some companies suffer from any trade-related policy.[18]

Organizations, Discourse, and the Effects of Globalization

In many ways, globalization has worked precisely as the theory of comparative advantage predicts. Areas with competitive advantages have been experiencing unparalleled economic growth. The economies of Taiwan and parts of India – Bangalore and Hyderabad – are booming. The Malaysian economy continues to expand, as does China's and much of southeast Asia. International firms have moved to the United States for the same reasons that US firms outsourced jobs offshore. Mercedes-Benz, Toyota/Lexus, and BMW have decided to build vehicles in the southern United States in order to be closer to the US market, but also because of lower wage rates and weaker worker and environmental protection laws. Chinese appliance manufacturer Haier Group moved to South Carolina in order to reduce transportation costs and in order to gain status among China's growing economic elite. An increasing number of immigrants to the United States, especially from Asia and Latin America, now are returning home because their economic prospects are better there, a process that accelerated during the "Great Recession" that started in 2007–2008. This reversal is not unique to the United States in the twenty-first century – almost half of the immigrants to the United States during the nineteenth century either died or returned home when they found that life was not as good as they had expected, and Polish immigrants who moved to Germany looking for work after the fall of the Berlin Wall now are returning home, even though wages in Poland are one-third of those in Germany. The rural poverty rate in Vietnam has been slashed from 70 percent to 30 percent. One of its great success stories was the catfish industry, which benefits from its warm climate, abundant water, and cheap labor. It quickly captured 20 percent of the US frozen catfish market, and drove prices down, at least until US catfish farmers persuaded Congress to place tariffs of 37 to 64 percent on Vietnamese fish imports. The Philippines, Poland, and much of southern Europe also have been caught in the middle of shifts toward free trade, and then away from it, by more industrialized countries.[19]

However, areas and industries which do not enjoy a "natural" advantage have been devastated. Mining towns in New Mexico and Arizona cannot compete with offshore operations, often owned and managed by US firms. Cotton farmers from Arizona to Georgia no longer were able to compete with African and Latin American producers. The giant Lifesavers Candy plant in Holland, Michigan, closed because its managers could save at least $90 million over the next 15 years by moving to Canada, where sugar is cheaper as a result of the North American Free Trade Agreement (NAFTA). The Domino sugar plant in Sugarland, Texas, moved its operations out of the United States. The heavy industries in Monterrey, Mexico, can no longer compete with foreign imports, including steel, and are slowly disappearing. News reports of additional US blue-collar and lately white-collar jobs being moved overseas appear weekly. At least the "destruction" aspect of "creative destruction" is clearly in evidence, although its impact sometimes is exaggerated – about 30 percent of recent US manufacturing job losses can be attributed to foreign competition (the rest resulted from new technologies and recurring recession since 1980).[20]

Over time, companies that shifted production to low-wage countries have been able to shift production to even lower-wage countries. This movement erased any of the gains of developing countries, and short-circuited the corrective effects of free trade. South Korea's economy became strong enough to sustain its growth when foreign countries shifted to lower-wage countries; the economies of Mexico and other Latin American countries were not. In five years, almost 20 million additional poor people were added to the region. But, soon, wage rates rose in Asia, so the multinational corporations (MNCs) shifted their production back to Latin American countries whose standard of living had fallen. It is clear that in the process of shifting jobs from country to country, the managers of MNCs have been able to increase the incomes of their nonproduction workers and their investors.[21]

In short, globalization has had major effects on the power relationships that exist among nations, and between groups within nations. As we have indicated throughout this book, with the exercise of power or with changes in power relationships comes resistance. Some countries are attempting to cushion or offset the adverse effects of globalization. The European Economic Union and European Trade Union Confederation are implementing a number of strategies designed to increase productivity (and thus support wages) and attract investment capital while adjusting their social support programs. At the same time, they have passed new environmental, worker protection, and tax laws that target US firms operating on the continent. China has been slow to devalue its currency relative to the US dollar, making their products more attractive to US consumers and their workforce more attractive to US companies. Developing countries, primarily in Latin America, are discussing ways to pool their resources to insulate themselves against currency fluctuations and the capital markets, much as Europe has done with the Euro. Developed nations in Asia are taking similar steps. Anti-free trade politicians have been elected throughout the world – Ecuador, Brazil, and Venezuela – even in countries like Chile, which is in the process of negotiating new trade agreements. Recent trade negotiations, which invariably are met with protests in the streets of the host countries, have ended when developing countries decided to go home. Even some of the strongest economies in some areas, and protests occur almost daily throughout the world, even in closed societies like China. But, at this point no region has devised strategies that promise to protect their economies from the pressures of globalization successfully over the long term, and no region has fully embraced the concept of "creative destruction" that underlies the theory of comparative advantage.[22]

Organizational Practices and Strategies of Organizing Globalization has also had a major impact on organizations themselves. Throughout this book, we have noted that some strategies of organizing are better suited for turbulent, highly competitive environments than others. Relational, cultural, and networking strategies all increase the speed of information flow and the quality of organizational decisions. Each strategy creates a communication system that allows an organization to rapidly respond to environmental pressures. But, in a global economy, being able to *react* quickly and decisively may not be enough. Globalization "requires that an organization *anticipate* change and move *proactively.* In a **responsive organization** (in contrast to a reactive one), structures and procedures must enhance the organization's ability to take advantage of changes in the environment to increase its competitive advantage" (St. Clair, Quinn, and O'Neill, 2000, 45). One of the realities of globalization is that minor differences in an organization's ability to exploit its environment have major effects on its performance. The most effective firm in a given sector of the economy can completely dominate the market; being second best may not mean having a smaller share of the market, it can mean having no share at all (Frank and Cook, 1998). Global organizations have two options – to become *the* dominant force in their field, or to become a highly selective niche player. Organizational size has a number of advantages – it allows an organization to dominate governments, suppliers, and workers. This is why corporate mergers, both within the core countries and between them, today occur on almost a daily basis.

But, historically, size also has meant bureaucratization, and as we have seen in earlier chapters bureaucratization has meant inflexibility. So, the optimal strategy for global organizations is to be both large and nimble, a combination that requires new and different strategies of organizing. It means that some activities need to be centralized while others need to be decentralized. There are various ways to accomplish this. As we pointed out in Chapter 3, an organization that wishes to maintain a traditional strategy can use information and communication technologies to monitor employees in decentralized units. However, this strategy is ultimately limited in its flexibility. Eventually organizations will be pressured to move to networked structures (Chapter 6) that incorporate centralized and decentralized components. Dell Computer Corporation, now the world's largest PC manufacturer, centralized the billing, inventory management, and distribution networks for its European operations in a single site in Ireland. But, it decentralized decision making to its individual sales and service centers in each European country. A large European food corporation requires all its European branches to interact with the Italian branch for their own ice cream marketing because the Italian market is so complex. But, the Italian director of manufacturing must interact with his or her French colleague who is responsible for European manufacturing. Every national manager has several bosses worldwide, and also is a worldwide supervisor for some specific practices.

Monsanto still is searching for the optimal mix of centralization and decentralization, specialization and "global vision." Monsanto CEO Robert Shapiro realizes that any strategy that denies information to its employees, or encourages the firm to hire people because they take orders well, will not survive. He also realizes that the final strategy will reduce his control over the organization and even reduce his awareness of "what's going on." Monsanto has not yet settled on a final strategy, but it is clear that it cannot be a traditional bureaucracy. It will involve a form of "radical decentralization," one that focuses on enhancing internal and external communication. Globalization does not mean that every organization will develop radically new strategies of organizing. For example, the family business model that long has dominated Asia seems to be especially well suited to globalization – their members are highly motivated, more committed, more flexible, and less bureaucratic than the state-owned businesses with which they compete. As the "Under Thirty" case study earlier in this chapter illustrated, China's government still is struggling to find ways of combining Maoist and Confucian models in ways that balance "the modern and the traditional while remaining competitive in the global economy."[23] Alternative forms of organization may also be useful. The heterarchy will be effective in environments that are rapidly changing. The cooperative and feminist forms are useful because they shelter their employees from some of the negative effects of hostile and changing environments. However, whatever strategy a given organization develops, it must deal effectively with the pressures of globalization.

In sum, the economic theories underlying *laissez-faire* capitalism and free trade predict many of the observed effects of globalization. While these theories predict that the resulting economic dislocations will eventually be corrected, there is reason to doubt those predictions. Neither theory adequately anticipates the effects of a free market in capital, and both assume that multinational organizations will be less monopolistic than they are becoming. Both factors may undermine the corrective mechanisms noted in economic theory. If these mechanisms do fail, economic inequality is likely to increase further; social tensions are likely to continue to grow, and the democratizing pressures of globalization will be undermined. Organizations and their members could find themselves in a world that is both chaotic and increasingly hostile and divided. (For an extended illustration of the concepts presented in this section, see Case Study 11.2 on page 438.)

Globalization, Ethics, and Organizational Democracy Although we will discuss ethics at length in Chapter 12, it is important to realize that globalization has created and/or highlighted a number of ethical issues. Historically, US organizations have been decidedly undemocratic institutions. And throughout US history formal organizations have exerted strong influences on political decision making, increasingly out of sight of the public eye. When combined with widespread acceptance of the assumptions underlying *laissez-faire* capitalism, these realities have created a social situation in which powerful organizations can operate freely, without being held responsible to the larger society. For example, Stanley Deetz concludes that in the contemporary United States "commercial corporations function as public institutions but without public accountability." Given US residents'

Case Study 11.2

Small Companies, Global Approaches[1]

Organizations internationalize in different ways. The most familiar cases are those we mentioned earlier in this chapter – large multinational firms such as McDonald's and Coca-Cola discover international opportunities and adapt their products, marketing, and delivery systems to different cultures. Ironically given their visibility, examples of large organizations successfully globalizing their operations are really quite rare. It is much more common for a company to be "born global" or for a small company to "go global." This case study describes two small organizations. The first was born global; the other has involves multinational manufacturing and supply chains, but focuses on a specific US market.[2]

In 1990, US citizen Gayle Warwick found herself in London, where her husband had relocated as part of a new job. An art history major with some coursework in law school and some experience in corporate public relations, she had no experience running a business. That is not to say that she had no experience – she had run a family on two continents and was from an entrepreneurial family. She knew that "going global" is all the rage among US small businesses these days, but she really hadn't thought much about creating a global business. Then, at a social engagement hosted by one of her husband's business associates, she admired a hand-embroidered tablecloth from Vietnam, and was invited to visit the couple's home country. Ms. Warwick accepted the invitation, and while in Vietnam had some samples made and shipped home to sell at charity Christmas fairs. They were quickly snapped up, and after conducting more research and spending $16,000 of her savings to travel to Italy, Ireland, and Switzerland to talk with linen and organic-cotton spinners, weavers, and finishers; to France and Germany to attend textile trade fairs; and to Vietnam to find embroiderers, she decided to become an entrepreneur.

Her new expertise and contacts quickly started to pay off. Executives of a French quality control company she met while in Ho Chi Minh City put her in touch with exporters in Hanoi, who helped her find the skilled craftspeople in rural Vietnam who would work on her designs. She hired a French company to handle shipping, an accountant to handle taxes, a consulting firm to market her table linens, and an artist to help design them. Together they spent hours studying textiles in London museums. She incorporated the business in 1998, and began selling from a converted dining room in her London home. A set of organic-cotton sheets and pillow shams sells for more that US$600; napkins and place mats start at $75 each. Thanks to favorable reviews in the *Times of London* and *The Financial Times*, she began to receive orders from internationally known interior designers. She also started selling to upscale stores on the US east coast. As a result, she has overcome one of the biggest problems facing any small company – the lack of name recognition. Sales increased from $40,000 in 1998 to an estimated $300,000 in 2004, which allowed her to make a profit for the first time. The firm continues to grow, and Ms. Warwick is planning a new range of products, including children's pajamas, women's silk loungewear made in Vietnam, and cashmere bed throws made in Italy. She also is contemplating a product line to be sold in target stores.

Advocates of globalization cite Ms. Warwick's record as an example of the virtues of world trade; Ms. Warwick attributes it to hard work and tenacity. Donna Sharp, executive director of the World Trade Institute of New York's Pace University, said that "with a little know-how, creativity and confidence, even the smallest business can find opportunities around the globe. Almost everyone can take advantage of trade-lead Web sites, or go to global conferences or trade shows. The small businesses of today are the multinationals of tomorrow" (Levere, 2004, 4).

Gayle Warwick Fine Linens are designed to be sold to an international economic elite – people in multiple countries who are becoming increasingly wealthy due to globalization and increasingly connected with one another as a result of new technologies. Knights Apparel was born out of CEO Joseph Bozich's concern for the opposite end of the globalization spectrum – impoverished workers in the Dominican Republic, one of the New World's poorest countries – and an opportunity created by student anti-sweatshop activists. Encouraged by Reagan administration tax breaks and other policies, US textile and shoe manufacturers shifted their production to Asia. Nike opened seven factories in China and South Korea by 1984, later shifting much of their production to Indonesia and other Southeast Asian countries in the search for even lower wages and even more favorable labor and environmental laws. Almost immediately, an anti-sweatshop movement began in the United States and Europe which criticized these organizations for paying poverty-level wages, often in violation of local minimum wage laws, or not paying workers at all, demanding excessive overtime, allowing sexual harassment of women workers, showing little or no regard for workplace safety, and so on. For a number of reasons, the movement quickly focused on the biggest player in the industry, Nike. Labor groups sent investigators to Nike's Asian factories, whose reports were combined with those of religious and human rights groups to create an appalling picture of Nike's treatment (through its subsidiaries) of its workers, including women and children.

In 1993, CBS' newsmagazine *Street Stories* featured a story on Nike that focused on the gap between the poverty-level wages paid to its workers and the lucrative contracts offered celebrities such as Michael Jordan. The publicity began a drumbeat of pressure on the company. Nike's initial responses – attacking its critics, denial, blame-shifting, using internal "audits" to counter critics' claims, and creating a workplace Code of Conduct which did not contain a single reference to worker rights and was not implemented – weakened Nike's credibility and focused attention on its hypocrisy. A generally favorable report by GoodWorks International was quickly discredited and contradicted by an internal Ernst and Young audit that was leaked to the press by a Nike employee. It found serious threats to worker health and safety in Vietnamese plants contracted to Nike. Essays by *New York Times* columnist Bob Herbert; a series of *Doonesbury* comics; and a Michael Moore film, *The Big One*, in which CEO Phil Knight "found himself saying unbelievably callous, stupid, and uniformed things," made the situation worse. Even individual customers joined the battle. When Nike offered customers the chance to personalize their new sneakers, Jonah Peretti ordered a pair with the term "sweatshop" printed on them. Nike refused, and the ensuing email exchange was circulated widely on the internet, eventually reaching an audience of more than 10 million people. Nike was quickly becoming better known for its hypocrisy than for its products. Eventually a student anti-sweatshop movement began at Duke University, whose licensed products generate more than $25 million per year for the university, and spread to more than 100 other universities. Students used a wide variety of strategies to pressure administrations into ensuring that licensed goods are not produced in sweatshops, including sit-ins (at Georgetown, Wisconsin, Michigan, and Arizona).[3]

After learning that the entire industry was guilty of many of the workers abuses uncovered at Nike contractors' factories, Bozich (who was director of Gold's Gym's apparel division) decided to do something about it, and founded Knights Apparel. He was most concerned that, while the anti-sweatshop movement had led most firms to start paying at least the local minimum wage, in many countries the minimum wage is not large enough to lift families out of poverty (15 cents an hour in Bangladesh and 85 cents a day in the Dominican Republic.) Bozich worked closely with the Worker Rights Consortium, one of two university-related groups working to eliminate sweatshop abuses (the other is the United Students Against Sweatshops), to eliminate abuses in the 30 plants with which Knights has contracts. Thanks to Knights' reputation and favorable publicity from organized labor and anti-sweatshop groups, the company moved past Nike as the No. 1 supplier of apparel featuring college logos. Then, he decided to go farther, and build an exemplary plant. He spent $500,000 to renovate an abandoned baseball cap plant in Villa Altagracia, complete with state-of-the-art lighting, equipment, and ergonomic chairs for workers. The plant pays a living wage, three times the average pay in the country's apparel industry, and allows workers to unionize without management opposition if they wish to do so. He plans to sell T-shirts for $8 wholesale, with most retailers selling them for $18, a price comparable to that charged by other manufacturers. With an extensive advertising campaign by retailers – Duke University placed a $250,000 order and will put postcards advertising the goods in student mailboxes and place flyers on campus lamp poles, Barnes and Noble plans to heavily market them in their campus bookstores, and United Students Against Sweatshops will do the same – and higher quality materials and workmanship, Bozich hopes that the plant will be profitable over the long term. In the end, its success will depend on students, alumni, and their values.

Applying What You Have Learned

1. What characteristics of globalization allowed Gail Warwick and Joseph Bozich to build their companies?
2. What barriers to success have they (and will they continue) had to overcome? What strategies have they employed to do so?

Questions to Think About and Discuss

1. What are the long-term prospects for the two firms? Warwick Linens growth will be limited unless globalization continues to create a growing number of wealthy customers; Knights Sportswear will continue to grow only if it catches the attention and conscience of relatively wealthy customers (college students and alumni).
2. Devise a strategy for competing with these two organizations. What can you do to overcome their current advantages? What will they have to do in the future to successfully compete with you?

Notes

1 This case study is based on Levere (2004) and Greenhouse (2010a).

2 See Douglas and Wind (1987), Ger (1999), and Onkvisit and Shaw (1987). For analyses of "born global" firms, see Rennie (1993); Madsen, Rasmussen, and Servais (2000); and Madsen, Rasmussen, and Evangelista (2001).

3 For analyses of the student anti-sweatshop movement, see Featherstone (2002) and Mandle (1999). For the Nike story, see Boje (1999); for an explanation of why Nike was such a good target for the movement, see Knight and Greenberg (2002). Robert Kuttner (1996) analyzes the Moore film. Student groups continue to successfully pressure Nike, for example forcing it to pay Honduran workers legally required severance pay that two of its contractors had denied them when they closed two factories (see Greenhouse, 2010b).

commitments to openness and democracy, this is somewhat surprising. The tension between democracy and autonomous, nondemocratic organizations is the basis of a distinctive view of corporations' responsibilities to the larger society.[24]

One clear result of globalization is that worker power worldwide has declined substantially. This results in part from structural factors. First, labor organizations are highly bureaucratic and thus are unable to respond rapidly to changes in global power relationships. In addition, they have traditionally relied on political action. As governments have become progressively less powerful relative to multinational organizations, workers' ability to influence corporate practices through political action has declined. The policy decisions that are most important to workers now are made by international organizations, not national governments. Corporations have shifted their operations to areas in which labor's influence is weak, for example, the developing world and the southern US International trade; economist Dani Rodrik concludes,

> Employers are less willing to provide the benefits of job security and stability, partly because of increased competition but also because their enhanced global mobility makes them less dependent on the good-will of their local work force. Governments are less able to sustain

> social safety nets, because an important part of their tax base has become footloose because of increased mobility of capital. . . . Globalization creates an inequality in bargaining power that 60 years of labor legislation in the U.S. has tried to prevent. (1997, 17, 19; also see Brown, 2002)

As a result, a two-tiered labor force has emerged throughout the developed and developing world. One tier is composed of highly educated workers in stable, high-paying jobs that provide substantial benefits and job security. Their skills and their ability to move from company to company provide them with relatively strong bargaining positions, as long as the economy is strong. The other tier is composed of workers who typically (but not always) have less education or education that is not relevant to high-tier jobs. Bridging these two tiers are workers who hold various kinds of contingent positions that may (but often do not) provide high salaries, but no benefits or job security (Conrad and Poole, 1997; also see Barley and Kunda, 2004, 2006; Rifkin, 2004; Smith, 2001). Of course, there have been notable instances of successful resistance to the creation of a two-tiered system, especially in Europe and British Commonwealth countries, and even in the United States. But, the global trend toward a two-tiered workforce seems to be quite clear. Although different groups of stakeholders are increasingly affected by the actions of MNCs, they are increasingly powerless to affect those actions.

NOTES

1 See Thurow (1997/1998, 42), Rothkopf (1997, 117), Waters (1995: 50), and Friedman (1999, 47).

2 See Parry (1967), O'Rourke and Williamson (2000), Robertson (1990, 1992), Uchitelle (1998), and Flynn and Giraldez (2002).

3 See Heston and Weiner (2000), and Keohane and Nye (2000). However, substantially less progress has been made in sub-Saharan Africa.

4 See Thurow (2000, 21, 22); also see Soros (1998; 2000, 112), Thurow (1997/1998), Browning (2004), Rodrik (1998), Burless *et al.* (1998), Friedman (1999), and Ganesh (2007).

5 See Stohl (2001, 326). David Rooney, Bernard McKenna, and Jim Barker (in press) examined the decade since Stohl's article and found that, while researchers in the former British Commonwealth countries have taken a larger role, Stohl's conclusions still are apt. Also see Hafen (2003) and Munshi (2003).

6 See Harris and Moran (2000). For an excellent case study of cross-cultural conflict between Japanese managers and Anglo-US engineers and human resource officers, see Banks and Riley (1992).

7 See "'Hijab' Debate" (2004) and Al-Shihri (2010). We recognize that there are a number of different types of face and body coverings worn by Muslim women, including the abaya and the burqa. We have chosen the term "hijab" because it seems to be the most common generalized term.

8 An interesting exception is Gannon (2000), which does a wonderful job of showing how a key ritual of a culture reveals a great deal about deeper levels of culture – such as American football, the Mexican fiesta, and the German symphony. Unfortunately, there is little evidence that education itself will overcome racism or sexism (Kraiger and Ford, 1985).

9 See Alkhazraji, Gardner, Martin, and Paolillo (1997); Cox, Lobel, and McLeod (1991); Kim, Hunter, Miyahara, Horvath, Bresnahan, and Yoon (1996); and Adler (1991).

10 See Krone, Chen, and Xia (1997); Lin and Clair (2007); Triandis, Bontempor, Villareal, Asai, and Lucca (1988); Ralston, Holt, Terpstra, and Kaicheng (1997); and Marti (2002).

11 The term "glocalization" was coined by Roland Robertson (1997). The McDonalds example is taken from Watson (1998). For additional examples, see Acosta, Leon, Conrad, and Malave (2010).

12 See Cantu (1999). Also see Paskoff (1996); Gonzalez, Willis, and Young (1977); Rizzo and Mendez (1990); and Reskin and Padavic (1994).

13 The theory of comparative advantage was first proposed in 1817 by David Ricardo in *Principles of*

Political Economy and Taxation. It is summarized at length in any good economics textbook and is examined at length in Irwin (1996). For an application to environmental issues, see Williams (1996) and Jilne, Kearins, and Walton (2006).

14 Johnson (2010). The 2008–2009 meltdown started in the United States because of a combination of deregulatory policies pursued by multiple administrations since 1979 and creative financiers' ability to capitalize (personally and to some extent on behalf of their organizations). When combined with multitrillion-dollar bailouts using taxpayer money, the US economy was so weak by the middle of 2009 that it was not eligible for loans from the International Monetary Fund (IMF) and World Bank, at least using the debt-to-income requirements that those institutions had long imposed on developing countries. But, the dominant economic rhetoric claimed that punishing the United States for its irresponsibility would have destroyed the entire world economy. In short, like the financial institutions that were bailed out in the United States and United Kingdom, the US economy was considered to be "too big to fail." Iceland's was not, although it eventually did receive a US$6 billion bailout package from the IMF. For a longer historical view, see Freeman and Katz (1994), Hoagland (2000), and Soros (2000).

15 Barry (2002), Kristof (2002a, 2002b), "Welfare Reform for Farmers" (2003), Becker (2003), "The Hypocrisy of Farm Subsidies" (2002), Magnusson (2002), and Thurow and Windstock (2002).

16 Owners' and managers' positions also vary with economic conditions (less labor is needed during recessions) and new information. For example, those who supported the immigration of workers from central, southern, and eastern Europe during the 1890s quickly found that these workers were not nearly as "docile" as they had expected them to be. Organized labor's position has varied depending on specific economic situations. For overall analyses, see Higham (2002), Skerry (2009), US Senator John Cornyn (2004), Navattette (2004), and Buckley (2004).

17 See Timmons (2004, 2010). For an overall analysis, see Bowe (2007).

18 For an expanded analysis, see Conrad (in press). Also see Cowell (2003), Rosenbaum (2003), and Andrews (2002).

19 Friedman (2002), Engardio (2003), "Tech Leaders Urge Congress Not to Act to Keep Jobs in U.S." (2004), O'Brien (2004), Zhao (2003), Egan (2003), Beauprez (2003), Fisher (2003), "The Rigged Trade Game" (2003), and "The Great Catfish War" (2003).

20 Josepheson (2005), Andrews (2003), and Uchitelle (2003a). Summaries of the effects on the candy industry are available in Moreno (2002) and Reynolds (2002). Excellent summaries of the economic effects of NAFTA are available in Stiglitz (2004); a November 11, 2002, broadcast of Bill Moyer's *N.O.W.* television show (a transcript is available on the PBS website, www.pbs.org); and a multipart investigation published in the *Houston Chronicle* in November and December 2002, available on the newspaper's website, www.chron.com.

21 See Barboza (2010), Black and Rodriguez (2010), Bussey (2002), Mocada (2002), Moreno (2002), Rampersad (2000), Sachs (1998), and Soros (1998).

22 See Chua (2003), Loewenberg (2003), Althus (2002), Leonhardt (2003), Becker and Rohter (2002), Rosenthal (2003), and Uchitelle (2003b).

23 See Sheehan (2003) and Chen (2000). The other examples in this paragraph are from Cesaria (2000) and Friedman (1999).

24 See Deetz (1995), Greider (1992, 1997), Bakan (2004), Schaefer et al. (2010), and Conrad (2011).

REFERENCES

Acosta, C., Leon, V.J., Conrad, C. and Malave, C. (2010). *Global Engineering*. New York: Taylor and Francis.

Adler, N. (1991). *International Dimensions of Organizational Behavior*, 2nd ed. Boston: Kent.

Alkhazraji, K., Gardner, W., Martin, J. and Paolillo, J. (1997). "The Acculturation of Immigrants to U.S. Organizations." *Management Communication Quarterly* 11: 217–265.

Al-Shihri, A. (2010). "Saudi: OK to Uncover Face in Anti-Burqa Countries." Associated Press, July 24. http://pewforum.org/Religion-News/Saudi-cleric-says-its-OK-to-uncover-face-in-antiburqa-countries.aspx.

Althus, D. (2002). "Voters Rejecting Free-Trade Model." *Houston Chronicle*, November 24, 1D.

Andrews, E.L. (2002). "A Civil War Within a Trade Dispute." *New York Times* online, September 20. www.nytimes.com.

Andrews, E. (2003). "Imports Don't Deserve All That Blame." *New York Times* online, December 7. www.nytimes.com.

Ashcraft, K.L. and Allen, B.J. (2003). "The Racial Foundation of Organizational Communication." *Communication Theory* 13: 5–38.

Bajaj, V. (2010). "Bangladesh, With Low Pay, Moves in on China." *New York Times* online, July 16. www.nytimes.com/2010/07/17/business/global/17textile.html.

Bakan, J. (2004). *The Corporation*. Boston: Free Press.

Banks, S. and Riley, P. (1992). "Structuration Theory as an Ontology for Communication Research," in Deetz, ed., *Communication Yearbook 16*. Newbury Park, CA: Sage.

Barboza, D. (2010). "China Shifts Away from Low-Cost Factories." *New York Times* online, September 15. www.nytimes.com/2010/09/16/business/global/16factory.html.

Barley, S. and Kunda, G. (2004). *Gurus, Hired Guns, and Warm Bodies*. Princeton, NJ: Princeton University Press.

Barley, S. and Kunda, G. (2006). "Contracting." *Academy of Management Perspectives* 20: 45–66.

Barry, D. (2002). "Rest Easy Knowing the Mohair Business Is Thriving." *Bryan/College Station (TX) Eagle*, June 23, D3.

Beauprez, J. (2003). "A Better Life, but Not in the U.S." *Houston Chronicle*, August 17, D2.

Becker, E. (2003). "U.S. Subsidizes Companies to Buy Subsidized Cotton." *New York Times* online, November 4. www.nytimes.com.

Becker, E. and Rohter, L. (2002). "U.S. and Chile Reach Free Trade Accord." *New York Times* online, December 12. www.nytimes.com.

Bellah, R., Madsen, R., Sullivan, W.M., Swidler, A. and Tipton, S.M. (1985). *Habits of the Heart*. Berkeley: University of California Press.

Bellah, R., Madsen, R., Sullivan, W.M., Swidler, A. and Tipton, S.M. (1991). *The Good Society*. New York: Vintage.

Black, T. and Rodriguez, C.M. (2010). "Mexico Is Taking Back Manufacturing Work." *Houston Chronicle*, September 12, D4.

Boje, D. (1999). "Is Nike Roadrunner or Wile E. Coyote?" *Journal of Business & Entrepreneurship* 2: 77–109.

Boumphrey, S. (2007). "China's Little Emperors Control the Purse Strings." *Euromonitor*, August 21. www.euromonitor.com/Chinas_little_emperors_control_the_purse_strings.

Bowe, J. (2007). *Nobodies: Modern American Slave Labor and the Dark Side of the New Global Economy*. New York: Random House.

Brown, R.H. (2002). "Global Capitalism, National Sovereignty, and the Decline of Democratic Space." *Rhetoric and Public Affairs* 5: 347–357.

Browning, L. (2004). "Study Finds Accelerating Decline in Corporate Taxes." *New York Times* online, September 23. www.nytimes.com.

Buckley, W.F. (2004). "Face It, We Surrendered on Immigration." *Houston Chronicle*, January 10, A36.

Burless, G., Lawrence, R. and Shapiro, R. (1998). *Globaphobia*. Washington, DC: Brookings Institution Press.

Bussey, J. (2002). "Reduction in Poverty Stalls in Latin America." *Houston Chronicle*, December 1, D6.

Cantu, H. (1999). "Racial Slur Helped Form New Career." *Houston Chronicle*, March 21, 3D.

Carnavale, A.P. and Stone, S.C. (1994). "Diversity: Beyond the Golden Rule." *Training and Development*, October, 21–26.

Cesaria, R. (2000). "Organizational Communication Issues in Italian Multinational Corporations." *Management Communication Quarterly* 14: 161–172.

Chen, L. (2000). "Connecting to the World Economy." *Management Communication Quarterly* 14: 152–160.

Child, J. (1996). *Management in China During the Age of Reform*. Cambridge: Cambridge University Press.

Ching, C.C. (1982). "The One-Child Family in China." *Studies in Family Planning* 13: 208–212.

Chua, A. (2003). "Power to the Privileged." *New York Times* online, January 7. www.nytimes.com.

Conrad, C. (2011). *Organizational Rhetoric*. London: Polity Press.

Conrad, C. and Poole, M.S. (1997). "Introduction [to the special issue 'Communication in the Age of the Displaced Worker']." *Communication Research* 6: 581–592.

Cornyn, J. (2004). "Pragmatic Reasons for the Guest-Worker Proposal." *Houston Chronicle*, January 8, A29.

Cowell, A. (2003). "Europeans Plan to Press for Tariffs Against U.S." *New York Times* online, December 6. www.nytimes.com.

Cox, T., Lobel, S. and McLeod, P. (1991). "Effects of Ethnic Cultural Differences on Cooperative and Competitive Behavior on a Group Task." *Academy of Management Journal* 34: 827–847.

Crowell, T. and Hsieh, D. (1995). "Little Emperors or Brats?" Asiaweek, December 1, 44–50.

Deetz, S. (1995). *Transforming Communication, Transforming Business*. Creskill, NJ: Hampton Press.

DePalma, A. (1994). "It Takes More Than a Visa to Do Business in Mexico." *New York Times*, June 26, 16–17A. www.nytimes.com.

Dolfang, H. (2010). "China's Workers Are Stirring." *New York Times* online, June 17. www.nytimes.com/2010/06/17/opinion/17iht-edhan.html.

Douglas, S. and Wind, Y. (1987). "The Myth of Globalization." *Columbia Journal of World Business* 22: 19–29.

Drzewiecka, J. and Wong (Lau), K. (1999). "The Dynamic Construction of White Ethnicity in the Context of Transnational Cultural Formations," in Nakayama and Martin, eds., *Whiteness: The Communication of Social Identity*. Thousand Oaks, CA: Sage.

Egan, T. (2003). "Amid Dying Towns of Rural Plains, One Makes a Stand." *New York Times* online, December 1. www.nytimes.com.

Engardio, P. (2003). "Corporate America's Silent Partner." *Business Week* online, December 15. www.businessweek.com/bwdaily/dnflash/dec2003/nf20031215_8942_db046.htm.

Featherstone, L. (2002). *Students Against Sweatshops*. New York: Verso.

Fisher, I. (2003). "As Poland Endures Hard Times, Capitalism Comes Under Attack." *New York Times* online, June 12. www.nytimes.com.

Flynn, D. and Giraldez, A. (2002). "Cycles of Silver." *Journal of World History* 13: 391–427.

Frank, R. and Cook, P. (1998). *The Winner Take All Society*. Reading, MA: Addison-Wesley.

Freeman, R. and Katz, L. (1994). "Rising Wage Inequality," in Freeman, ed., *Working Under Different Rules*. New York: Russell Sage Foundation.

Friedman, T. (1999). *The Lexus and the Olive Tree*. New York: Farrar, Straus & Giroux.

Friedman, T. (2000). "You've Got Mail – from the Philippines." *Houston Chronicle*, September 30, 36A.

Friedman, T. (2002). "Globalization Movement Alive and Well." *Houston Chronicle*, September 22, C3.

Fuat Firat, A. (1997). "Educator Insights." *Journal of International Marketing* 5: 77–86.

Ganesh, S. (2007). "Sustainable Development Discourse and the Global Economy," in May, Cheney, and Roper, eds., *The Debate Over Corporate Social Responsibility*. New York: Oxford University Press.

Gannon, M. (2000). *Understanding Global Cultures*, 2nd ed. Thousand Oaks, CA: Sage.

Gardner, D. (2010). "What Confucius Says Is Useful to China's Rulers." *Los Angeles Times* online, October 1. http://articles.latimes.com/2010/oct/01/opinion/la-oe-gardner-confucius-20101001.

Ger, G. (1999). "Localizing in the Global Village." *California Management Review* 41: 64–83.

Gonzalez, A., Willis, J. and Young, C. (1997). "Cultural Diversity and Organizations," in Byers, ed., *Organizational Communication*. Boston: Allyn & Bacon.

"The Great Catfish War." (2003). *New York Times* online, July 22. www.nytimes.com.

Greenhouse, S. (2010a). "A Factory Defies Stereotypes, but Can It Thrive?" *New York Times* online, July 18. www.nytimes.com.

Greenhouse, S. (2010b). "Pressured, Nike to Help Workers in Honduras." *New York Times* online, July 26. www.nytimes.com/2010/07/27/business/global/27nike.html.

Greider, W. (1992). *Who Will Tell the People?* New York: Simon & Schuster.

Greider, W. (1997). *One World, Ready or Not*. New York: Simon & Schuster.

Grimes, D. (2001). "Putting Our Own House in Order." *Journal of Organizational Change Management* 14: 132–149.

Hafen, S. (2003). "Cultural Diversity Training," in Cheney and Barnett, eds., *Organization: Communication*, vol. 7. Creskill, NJ: Hampton Press.

Harris, P. and Moran, R. (2000). *Managing Cultural Differences*, 5th ed. Houston, TX: Gulf Publishing.

Hassard, J., Sheehan, J. and Morris, J. (1999). "Enterprise Reform in Post-Deng China." *International Studies of Management and Organization* 29: 107–136.

Heston, A. and Weiner, N. (2000). "Dimensions of Globalization." *Annals of the American Academy of Political and Social Science* 570: 8–18.

Higham, J. (2002). *Strangers in the Land*. New Brunswick. NJ: Rutgers University Press.

"'Hijab' Debate Isn't Just a French Affair." (2004). *Houston Chronicle*, January 11, C4.

Hoagland, J. (2000). "Can't Leave Backyard Politics Out of Globalization." *Houston Chronicle*, October 22, 3C.

Hoecklin, L. (1995). *Managing Cultural Differences*. Reading, MA: Addison-Wesley.

Hong, J. and Engstrom, Y. (2004). "Changing Principles of Communication Between Chinese Managers and Workers." *Management Communication Quarterly* 17: 552–585.

"The Hypocrisy of Farm Subsidies." (2002). *New York Times* online, December 1. www.nytimes.com.

Irwin, D. (1996). *Against the Tide*. Princeton, NJ: Princeton University Press.

Jacobs, A. (2010). "Chinese Factories Now Compete to Woo Laborers." *New York Times* online, July 12. www.nytimes.com/2010/07/13/world/asia/13factory.html.

Jilne, M., Kearins, K. and Walton, S. (2006). "Creating Adventures in Wonderland." *Organization* 13: 801–839.

Johnson, S. (2010). *13 Bankers*. New York: Pantheon.

Josepheson, P. (2005). *Resources Under Regimes*. Cambridge, MA: Harvard University Press.

Keohane, R. and Nye, J., Jr. (2000). *Governance in a Global World*. Washington, DC: Brookings Institution Press.

Kim, M., Hunter, J.E., Miyahara, A., Horvath, A., Bresnahan, M. and Yoon, H. (1996). "Individual vs. Culture-Level

Dimensions of Individualism and Collectivism." *Communication Monographs* 63: 29–49.

Knight, G. and Greenberg, J. (2002). "Promotionalism and Subpolitics." *Management Communication Quarterly* 15: 541–570.

Kraiger, K. and Ford, J. (1985). "A Meta-Analysis of Ratee Race Effects in Performance Ratings." *Journal of Applied Psychology* 70: 56–65.

Kristof, N. (2002a). "America's Failed Frontier." *New York Times* online, September 3. www.nytimes.com.

Kristof, N. (2002b). "Will China Blindside the West?" *New York Times* online, December 3. www.nytimes.com.

Krone, K., Chen, L. and Xia, H. (1997). "Approaches to Managerial Influence in the People's Republic of China." *Journal of Business Communication* 34: 289–315.

Kuttner, R. (1996). *Everything for Sale?* New York: Random House.

Kwong, J. (1994). "Ideological Crisis Among China's Youths." *British Journal of Sociology* 45: 247–264.

Leonhardt, D. (2003). "Globalization Hits a Political Speed Bump." *New York Times* online, June 1. www.nytimes.com.

Levere, J.L. (2004). "A Small Company, a Global Approach." *New York Times* online, January 1. www.nytimes.com.

Lin, C. and Clair, R.P. (2007). "Measuring Mao Zedong Thought and Interpreting Organizational Communication in China." *Management Communication Quarterly* 20: 395–429.

Loewenberg, S. (2003). "Europe Gets Tougher on U.S. Companies." *New York Times* online, April 20. www.nytimes.com.

Madsen, T.K., Rasmussen, E. and Evangelista, F. (2001). "The Founding of the Born Global Company in Denmark and Australia." *Asia Pacific Journal of Marketing and Logistics* 13: 75–107.

Madsen, T.K., Rasmussen, E. and Servais, P. (2000). "Differences and Similarities Between Born Globals and Other Types of Exporters." *Advances in International Marketing* 10: 247–265.

Magnusson, P. (2002). "Farm Subsidies." *Business Week*, September 9, 50.

Mandle, J. (1999). "The Student Anti-Sweatshop Movement." *Annals of the American Academy of Political and Social Science* 570: 92–103

Marti, M. (2002). *China and the Legacy of Deng Xiaoping*. Washington, DC: Brassey's.

Mocada, E. (2002). "Made in China." *Houston Chronicle*, November 18, A23.

Moreno, J. (2002). "China Replaces Mexico as Land of Cheap Labor." *Houston Chronicle*, October 25, C1.

Moreno, J. (2003). "Mexico Takes a Bite Out of the Market." *Houston Chronicle*, November 25, B1.

Munshi, D. (2003). "Through the Subject's Eye," in Cheney and Barnett, eds., *Organization: Communication*, vol. 7. Creskill, NJ: Hampton Press.

Navattette, R., Jr. (2004). "Grandson of Immigrant Now to the Right of Rove." *Houston Chronicle*, January 8, A29.

New York Times Editorial Board. (2010). "China, the Sweatshop." *New York Times* online, July 5. www.nytimes.com/2010/07/06/opinion/06tue2.html.

O'Brien, K. (2004). "Unusual Pattern on Polish Border." *Houston Chronicle*, January 11, D6.

Onkvisit, S. and Shaw, J. (1987). "Standardized International Advertising." *Columbia Journal of World Business* 22: 43–55.

O'Rourke, K. and Williamson, J. (2000). *Globalization and History*. Cambridge, MA: MIT Press.

Otis, J. (2003). "Ailing Schools Can't Set Free Peru's Youth." *Houston Chronicle*, December 22, A1.

Parker, B. (2005). *Introduction to Globalization & Business*. London: Sage.

Parry, J., ed. (1967). *The Establishment of the European Hegemony, 1415–1715*. New York: HarperCollins.

Paskoff, S. (1996). "Ending the Workplace Diversity Wars." *Training: The Human Side of Business*, August, 2–8.

Ralston, D., Egri, C., Stewart, S., Terpstra, R. and Kaicheng, Y. (1999). "Doing Business in the 21st Century with the New Generation of Chinese Managers." *Journal of International Business Studies* 30: 415–428.

Ralston, D., Holt, D., Terpstra, R. and Kaicheng, Y. (1997). "The Impact of National Culture and Economic Ideology on Managerial Work Values." *Journal of International Business Studies* 28: 177–208.

Rampersad, F. (2000). "Coping With Globalization." *Annals of the American Association of Political and Social Science* 570: 115–125.

Rennie, M. (1993). "Born Global." *The McKinsey Quarterly* 4: 45–52.

Reskin, B. and Padavic, I. (1994). *Women and Men at Work*. Thousand Oaks, CA: Pine Forge Press.

Reynolds, D. (2002). "Sticky Situation." *ABC News* online, March 25. www.abcnews.com.

Ricardo, D. (1817/1996). *Principles of Political Economy and Taxation*. Buffalo, NY: Prometheus Books.

Rifkin, J. (2004). *The European Dream*. New York: Penguin.

"The Rigged Trade Game." (2003). *New York Times* online, July 20. www.nytimes.com.

Rizzo, A. and Mendez, C. (1990). *The Integration of Women in Management*. New York: Quorum.

Robertson, R. (1992). *Glozalization*. London: Sage.

Robertson, R. (1997). "Glocalization," in Featherstone, Lash and Robertson, eds., *Global Modernities*. Thousand Oaks, CA: Sage.

Rodrik, D. (1997). "Sense and Nonsense in the Globalization Debate." *Foreign Policy* 107: 17, 19.

Rodrik, D. (1998). "Has Globalization Gone Too Far?" *Challenge* 41: 81–94.

Rooney, R., McKenna, B. and Barker, J. (In press). "History of Ideas in *Management Communication Quarterly*." *Management Communication Quarterly*.

Rosenbaum, D. (2003). "They Support Free Trade, Except in the Case of . . . " *New York Times* online, November 16. www.nytimes.com.

Rosenthal, E. (2003). "Workers' Plight Brings New Militancy in China." *New York Times* online, March 10. www.nytimes.com.

Rothkopf, D. (1997). "In Praise of Cultural Imperialism?" *Foreign Policy* 107: 38–53.

Rozman, G. (1991). *The East Asian Region*. Princeton, NJ: Princeton University Press.

Sachs, J. (1998). "Making It Work." *Economist*, September 12. www.economist.com.

Schaefer, Z., Conrad, C., Cheney, G., May, S. and Ganesh, S. (2010). "Economic Justice and Communication Ethics," in Cheney, ed., *The ICA Handbook of Communication and Ethics*. London: Sage.

Shattuck, H. (2000). "Mexico Offers Better Assistance." *Houston Chronicle*, November 12, 1G.

Sheehan, C. (2003). "Steelworkers Roll with the Changes." *Houston Chronicle*, November 12, D8.

Skerry, P. (2009). "The Real Immigration Crisis," in Faulkner and Shell, eds., *America at Risk*. Ann Arbor: University of Michigan Press.

Smith, V. (2001). *Crossing the Great Divide*. Ithaca, NY: Cornell University Press.

Soros, G. (1998). *The Crisis of Global Capitalism*. New York: Public Affairs.

Soros, G. (2000). *The Open Society*. New York: Public Affairs.

St. Clair, L, Quinn, R. and O'Neill, R. (2000). "The Perils of Responsiveness in Modern Organizations," in St. Clair, Quinn and O'Neill, eds., *Pressing Problems in Organizations (That Keep Us up at Night)*. New York: AMACOM.

Stiglitz, J. (2004). "The Broken Promise of NAFTA." *New York Times* online, January 6. www.nytimes.com.

Stohl, C. (2001). "Globalizing Organizational Communication," in Jablin and Putnam, eds., *The New Handbook of Organizational Communication*. Thousand Oaks, CA: Sage.

"Tech Leaders Urge Congress Not to Act to Keep Jobs in U.S." (2004). *Houston Chronicle*, January 8, 204.

Thurow, L. (1997/1998). "New Rules." *Harvard International Review* 19: 7–42.

Thurow, L. (2000). "Globalization." *Annals of the American Academy of Political and Social Science* 570: 21–24, esp. 22.

Thurow, R. and Windstock, G. (2002). "How an Addiction to Sugar Subsidies Hurts Development." *Wall Street Journal*, September 16, A1, A10.

Timmons, H. (2004). "Critics of Outsourcing Hope to Start Movement." *Houston Chronicle*, January 20, B4.

Timmons, H. (2010). "Legal Outsourcing in India Draws Western Talent" *New York Times* online, August 4. www.nytimes.com/2010/08/05/business/global/05legal.html.

Triandis, H., Bontempor, R., Villareal, M., Asai, M. and Lucca, N. (1988). "Individualism and Collectivism." *Journal of Personality and Social Psychology* 21: 323–338.

Trompenaars, F. and Hampden-Turner, C. (1998). *Riding the Waves of Culture*. New York: McGraw-Hill.

Uchitelle, L. (1998). "Some Economic Interplay Comes Nearly Full Circle." *New York Times* online, April 30. www.nytimes.com.

Uchitelle, L. (2003a). "A Missing Statistic." *New York Times* online, October 5. www.nytimes.com.

Uchitelle, L. (2003b). "When the Chinese Consumer Is King." *New York Times* online, December 14. www.nytimes.com.

Varg, P. (1968). "The Myth of the China Market, 1890–1914." *American Historical Review* 73: 72–758.

Waters, M. (1995). *Globalization*. London: Routledge.

Watson, J., ed. (1998). *Golden Arches East*. Cambridge, UK, and Palo Alto, CA: Cambridge University Press and Stanford University Press.

"Welfare Reform for Farmers." (2003). *New York Times* online, November 10. www.nytimes.com.

Whalen, G. (2007). "Corporate Social Responsibility in Asia," in May, Cheney and Roper, eds., *The Debate Over Corporate Social Responsibility*. New York: Oxford University Press.

Williams, M. (1996). "International Political Economy and Global Environmental Change," in Vogler and Imber, eds., *The Environment and International Relations*. London: Routledge.

Wong, E. (2010). "As China Aids Labor, Unrest is Still Rising." *New York Times* online, June 20. www.nytimes.com/2010/06/21/world/asig/21chinalabor.html.

Zhang, W.B. (1999). *Confucianism and Modernization*. London: Macmillan Press.

Zhao, Y. (2003). "When Jobs Move Overseas (to South Carolina)." *New York Times* online, October 25. www.nytimes.com.

CHAPTER 12

COMMUNICATION, ETHICS, AND ORGANIZATIONAL RHETORIC

What I found was really disappointing. Before undertaking this research I believed that people's personal values made a big difference in how they behave (ethically) in the workplace. But now I'm convinced they don't.

Arthur Brief

We may compartmentalize ethics in our work lives and our professional interactions, holding ourselves to different ethical standards in other spheres of our lives. Second, we may essentialize ethics and morality in the embodiment of a person, particular institution, or country, thereby missing the point about how individuals, organizations, or a nation come to be as they are and to act in particular ways. Third . . . we may abstract ethical considerations and lose sight of their relation to our situation and life. What these actions share . . . is that they all place strict limitations on ethics' potential, diminishing the range of questions that actions can ask us.

George Cheney, Dan Lair, Dean Ritz, and Brenden Kendell

Many conservative economists . . . strongly committed to an austerely rational model of human behavior, have exaggerated the degree to which businessmen and consumers make decisions based on sufficiently complete information, accurately processed, to avoid making huge mistakes. This exaggeration has prevented them from understanding the causes and course of the depression.

Judge Richard Posner[1]

Strategic Organizational Communication: In a Global Economy, Seventh Edition.
Charles Conrad and Marshall Scott Poole.

CENTRAL THEMES

- Unethical and illegal behavior by members of organizations has become a recurring theme in US economic history. Organizational ethics should be viewed through a systems or institutional theory frame of reference. Organizational actors make choices within complex webs of guidelines (incentives) and constraints, and draw upon cultural assumptions to legitimize their actions and create preferred social and organizational structures.
- At least since the time of Adam Smith, societies with capitalist economies have struggled with the need to constrain greed while not undermining the economic advantages of free market systems. This tension is reflected in the three major models of organization–society relationships: corporate social responsibility, corporate social responsiveness, and multiple stakeholder perspectives.
- Organizational rhetors have many strategies available that can be used to protect their organizations from external pressures, including forming alliances with policy makers.
- The first decade of the twenty-first century witnessed a series of corporate scandals. The best known of these involved the Enron corporation at the beginning of the century, and the financial industry meltdown at the end of its first decade. The history of those scandals provides informative case studies involving many of the concepts discussed in this chapter and this book.

KEY TERMS

subprime mortgages
creative destruction
charity principle
stewardship principle
corporate social responsibility
corporate social responsiveness
multiple-stakeholder model
derivatives
business case for ethics
defeasibility
proactive image management
ethical segregationists
organizational imperative
bubbles
paradox of thrift
deflationary psychology
moral hazards
regulatory arbitrage
leverage
ratings agencies
credit default swaps

Throughout the first decade of the twenty-first century, one of the "hottest" topics in US society has been fraud, corruption, and ethical malfeasance in major corporations. The decade started with the largest bankruptcies in US history – Enron and Worldcom – and ended with even larger bankruptcies and near bankruptcies that were prevented by massive taxpayer bailouts, especially in the United States and United Kingdom. Academics, journalists, and even the politicians who helped create the conditions that allowed and/or encouraged these events claim to have been surprised and shocked by the machinations of corporate executives who benefited so handsomely from the economic ruin they created. Of course, the most recent era of corruption clearly is not unique. The "robber baron" era of the late 1800s, which led to Theodore Roosevelt's short-lived "trust-busting" crusade; revelations of profiteering by US munitions companies during World War I, which culminated in jail sentences for some of the worst offenders; the corruption of politics by organizational money during the 1920s, which in part led to the Great Depression and the reforms of the "New Deal;" the investment scandals and Savings and Loan crisis and bailout of the 1980s; and the financial crisis and bailouts of 2007 and beyond all indicated that unethical behavior by corporations and their leaders are a recurring, if not continuous, aspect of US history.

Between 1975 and 1990, two-thirds of the *Fortune* 500 firms were *convicted* of serious crimes ranging from price fixing to illegal dumping of hazardous wastes. Between 1990 and 2010 the percentage fell somewhat, largely because a series of Congresses weakened regulations and a series of administrations significantly reduced enforcement of the regulations that did exist. When actions were taken, they were economically insignificant when compared to associated financial gains. For example, in late 1996, Archer Daniels Midland was fined $100 million by the US Justice Department for illegally fixing the prices of citric acid and lysine (an additive in animal feeds). To that point it was the largest fine ever levied against a US corporation, but it paled in comparison to profits of $200–600 million that ADM made by engaging in the illegal activities. A decade later, Pfizer Inc. delete , was slapped with a $2.3 billion fine for illegally marketing four of its prescription drugs, again the largest fine in US history. But, that "total stands small compared to the $44.2 billion in pharmaceutical sales the world's largest drugmaker made last year." Indeed, income from only one of the drugs, Lyrica, exceeded the fine by $300 million. Four years later, in 2010, Toyota USA paid the largest fine in the history of the US Department of Transportation (also the maximum penalty allowed by federal law) for hiding defects related to uncontrolled acceleration of its vehicles, $16.4 million. The fine equaled almost $2.50 for each vehicle Toyota eventually recalled. Later that year, Citigroup, whose irresponsible risk taking, encouraged by former US Treasury Secretary Robert Rubin, was instrumental to the financial crash of 2007–2008, was fined $75 million by the Securities and Exchange Commission (SEC) for lying to investors about the value of **subprime** (highly risky) mortgages that it held. The fine equaled less than one-third of one percent of the company's *second-quarter* revenue; as Judge Ellen Huvelle commented when she approved the fine, "seventy-five million dollars will not deter anyone from doing anything." Many other organizations reached out-of-court settlements or were convicted of misdemeanors; in many others, improper and/or illegal behavior was successfully covered up. Indeed, in some sectors of the economy, pressures to engage in illegal or unethical actions are so intense and the actions are so frequent that they have come to be seen as the normal way of doing business (for example, financial fraud in defense contracting, sexism in the military, and racism and homophobia in the petroleum and petrochemical industry).[2] For many observers, it seems that in many US organizations, ethics is something that simply is not done.

On first glance, it may seem strange that we have decided to discuss organizational ethics and organizational rhetoric in the same chapter. But, for anyone familiar with the history of rhetorical studies, the link will not seem strange at all. At least since the time of Plato, ethics, politics, rhetoric, and economic institutions have been linked to one another. Plato's student Aristotle told his students that they must consider politics and rhetoric as two sides of the same coin – literally, rhetoric is the "ethical branch of politics" – because it is through rhetoric that the taken-for-granted values (ethics) of a society are linked to political decision making. In fact, the treatise on ethics that Aristotle wrote for his own son is filled with links between these concepts. Contemporary organizational communication scholars and rhetorical theorists have continued the link.[3]

Organizational ethics and organizational rhetoric are intertwined in two ways. First, leaders of organizations do not merely adapt to the environmental pressures they face, they also attempt to mold those pressures.[4] (Note: as in earlier chapters, we define "environment" in very broad terms, as the totality of external pressures experienced by members of an organization, including the effects that its actions have on the physical environment.) One way that managers mold environmental pressures is to establish favorable images of themselves and their organizations in the minds of their audiences. A second means of managing environmental pressures, one that has become increasingly important as a result of globalization, is to persuade politicians to pass favorable regulations and laws. As we explained in Chapter 11, competing in the global marketplace is an incredibly difficult undertaking. It is much easier, and much less risky, to persuade governments to enact laws that insulate one's company from competition, or require their citizens to pay some of costs of competing globally. For example, at the height of the US ethical scandals at the beginning of the twenty-first century, Vanguard Mutual Funds founder John Bogle explained that it is much more rational for corporate executives to spend their money influencing politicians than it is for them to use it to build new plants or purchase new equipment. A new plant will return between ten and twenty percent of the money invested in it each year during its lifetime. But, political donations and related lobbying activities return 300–500 percent, and do so with much less risk. For example, contributing to the political campaigns of candidates who promise to weaken environmental standards is often much less expensive than conforming to them. Creating and/or exploiting weaknesses in government regulations and monitoring are more cost-effective than acting in legal and ethical ways, as the examples at the beginning of this chapter illustrate. However, many voters are very suspicious of corporate influence on public policy makers, so the link between the two must be legitimized, and advocates of increased government involvement in the market must be discredited. Consequently, organizational rhetoric has two primary functions: (1) to strategically mold popular opinions, attitudes, and values in ways that create support for organizational practices and/or undermine opposition to them; and (2) to strategically influence and legitimize public policies. Both are inherently ethical activities, and both serve as the basis for ethical judgments about organizational policies and practices.[5]

ETHICS, ORGANIZATIONS, AND SOCIAL CONTROL

Over time, capitalists and scholars alike have struggled to deal with the moral and ethical dilemmas created by *laissez-faire* capitalism. For example, free market purists (financier George Soros calls them "free market fundamentalists" because of their steadfast commitment to their faith in spite of abundant disconfirming evidence) almost always trace their views back to Adam Smith's concept of the "invisible hand." In *The Wealth of Nations* Smith (which does not include the term *laissez-faire* and uses the phrase "invisible hand" only once) argues that people are motivated by the desire for maximizing their individual economic gains. In the best of worlds, a free, open, and informed competition among potential buyers and sellers will lead everyone to make the best possible deals with one another, and by doing so eventually establish a society that balances economic needs in the most efficient way possible. In the interim, societies may undergo a great deal of dislocation and their members may experience a great deal of pain. In the famous phrase of American economist Joseph Schumpeter, the invisible hand operates through processes of **creative destruction**, of increasing overall economic efficiency by eliminating less productive people, companies, and social systems. In the short term creative destruction is devastating, but in the long run the economy will reach an equilibrium point at which everyone will benefit, and at that point the end will justify the means (recall Jürgen Habermas's distinction between technical and practical rationality from Chapter 8). But Smith also realized that the primary challenge for market societies is to appropriately guide and constrain those individual motivations. Greed is a highly effective motivator, but if left unchecked it can destroy societies and economies. It does so in two ways. First, it encourages people to act in ways that undermine key elements of market economies. Greed encourages economic actors to avoid or short-circuit competition by creating monopolies, not to celebrate its virtues. Greed encourages managers to hide or distort information available to consumers about the quality of the products being sold, the production processes being used to make them, or the financial health of the companies. Furthermore, the mantra that "greed is good" also encourages a populace to celebrate and sympathize with the rich and powerful while denigrating the poor, lowly, or wise.

Second, unrestrained greed leads to the "tragedy of the commons." The phrase harkens back to the Middle Ages, when communities held an area in common where every citizen could graze his or her livestock. The "tragedy" is that the incentives lead everyone to use the commons as much as possible in order to save his or her own pastureland. Eventually the commons will become overgrazed, and useless to everyone. This concern is the basis of much contemporary concern about the environmental effects of market economies – that eventually unbridled use of natural resources will exhaust them, especially since organizations rarely pay for the resources themselves. Economists call the costs like public education, transportation systems, military security and cleaning up environmental damage "externalities" because they normally are not included in the costs of a transaction between a buyer and seller, and thus are "external" to the value of the exchange. Of course, both parties in an economic exchange have absolute incentives to treat as many of their costs of doing business as possible as "externalities" because doing so means that they are not responsible for bearing those costs. In short, "what's good for General Motors" (and any other organization) is to get taxpayers, suppliers, and competitors to pay for as much of its "external" costs as possible, and to minimize the amount that it has to pay through taxes and other fees.[6]

In addition, Smith realized that free market economies face inevitable ethical challenges, but economics does not provide a basis for making ethical decisions. He discussed these issues in a companion book to *The Wealth of Nations*, entitled *The Theory of Moral Sentiments*. Through its multiple editions, Smith struggled with how a society can constrain greed without undermining the economic growth that is stimulated by the free market. In early editions he argued that informal constraints are adequate. As people mature within stable communities, they develop a sense of right and wrong, as well as a commitment to the welfare of their neighbors. They also learn the traditional Protestant values of prudence and self-control, which encourages them to sacrifice short-term profits and pleasures for long-term security and peace. Some people learn these lessons so completely that they become saints (although Smith noted that this is "a select, though, I am afraid, a small party"). The "average" person is constrained by his or her own conscience, but needs the additional constraint of public opinion and pressure – the potential shame that would come from being seen as excessively greedy or treating ones neighbors in unfair ways would be sufficient. This is why Smith believed that factory owners should live in the same town in which their factories operated. Doing so creates interpersonal relationships, which fosters feelings of shared responsibility, which encourages all parties to act in ways that respect their relationships with others. Having to breathe the same air, walk the same streets, and drink the same water as one's workers and customers, also has tangible effects on how one operates one's business.

Unfortunately, Smith continued, some people have neither a conscience nor a capacity to feel disgraced. Freed of these restraints, they engage in vicious economic behavior that is destructive to their communities and societies (and ultimately to themselves because one cannot have a full and meaningful life without a connection to one's community, the lesson that Ebenezer Scrooge learned one cold winter night). Smith concluded that those people and the organizations they ran would have to be constrained by the power of the state through regulations and laws. The corrupting influence of unrestrained greed is greatest for people working in the capital markets – banking, international finance, and trade – so government would have to be most active in that sector of the economy. During Smith's lifetime, England became more and more industrialized and more and more urban. Smith realized that with these trends came increased mobility and decreased opportunities for surveillance by members of a person's community. These changes reduced the likelihood that "average" people would internalize the values of prudence and self-control. Society was changing in ways that made informal processes of social control less effective and government intervention in markets increasingly necessary. Unlike Smith's economic theory, which stayed virtually the same throughout various editions of *The Wealth of Nations*, Smith's social theory adapted to these new realities. It is interesting that similar processes seem to be taking place today. In Asia (recall the "Under Thirty" case in Chapter 11), Confucian values and informal social ties through family networks historically have served as instruments of social control. But, the rapid growth of capitalist organizations has undermined centuries-old informal social controls, thereby increasing problems of exploitation and corruption.[7] Although today's free market fundamentalists ignore *The Theory of Moral Sentiments* almost completely, it establishes the fundamental ethical issue facing societies with free market economies – how can a free society simultaneously obtain the economic advantages of the "invisible hand" while avoiding the excesses of human greed?[8]

SOCIETAL ASSUMPTIONS AND ORGANIZATIONAL RHETORIC

The proper relationship between organizations and society has been a highly contested concept since the creation of the corporation in the 1800s. By the end of the century widespread anger about the excesses of large corporations eventually led to the creation of a new industry – public relations – and a new ideology about the proper relationship between organizations and society. One of the most visible organizational rhetors during the "gilded age" was Andrew Carnegie, the founder of US Steel. Carnegie argued that two principles needed to be accepted if *laissez-faire* capitalism was to succeed over the long term. One was the **charity principle,** which required more fortunate members of the society to assist its less fortunate members, either directly through philanthropy or indirectly through corporate support of social service organizations. Carnegie roundly criticized other "captains of industry" (the term "robber barons" was an equally popular adjective at the time) for ignoring broader social concerns in their narrow pursuit of wealth and power. Somewhat ironically, Carnegie seemed to be less concerned about the wealthy industrialists' treatment of their employees, but his commitment to the society as a whole was clear. Carnegie was also committed to the **stewardship principle,** which suggested that businesses and wealthy people had an obligation to try to increase the wealth of the society as a whole by wisely investing the resources they controlled. For the following 50 years, Carnegie's assumptions were accepted and codified into a concept of **corporate social responsibility**, a belief that organizations had a responsibility to assist in the solution of social problems in addition to making money, especially if they had helped to create those problems. But, by the 1960s this model of corporate social responsibility was being challenged (Marchand, 1998).

A group of conservative theorists, led by economist Milton Friedman of the University of Chicago, argued that the only responsibility corporations have is to pursue their own economic self-interest. Managers have no particular expertise in defining social problems, no incentives for trying to solve them, and capitalism provides no means of holding them accountable for the effects of their purportedly "socially responsible" activities. To the extent that they *do* invest the organization's capital in such activities, they make it vulnerable to competitors who invest all their resources in enhancing their firm's economic position. Thus, in the long run, they threaten the jobs of their employees and violate the trust of their investors. In short, Friedman argued, Carnegie's two principles are contradictory – in an economy defined by competitive, *laissez-faire* capitalism, corporate *charity* reduces the economic viability of a firm, thus violating the *stewardship* principle. In a democratic society, only government is responsible for dealing with social problems, because only government can be held accountable for doing or not doing so. Organizations should be concerned with *generating* wealth and government should not interfere in that process (recall the discussion of the futility, jeopardy, and perversity theses in Chapter 2). Governments should concern themselves with *distributing* wealth and not ask the leaders of corporations to make those difficult political decisions for them (Friedman, 1962; also see Friedman and Friedman, 1980; Friedman, 1999).

Debates over the social responsibility doctrine continued until the late 1970s, eventually leading to a new doctrine of **corporate social responsiveness** based on a **multiple-stakeholder model** of organizational relationships. In theory, advocates of multiple-stakeholder perspectives argue, there are a great many groups that have legitimate stakes in the decisions made by managers and the actions taken by the organizations they control. Management should be held responsible for finding ways to meet the needs and interests of all legitimate stakeholders. Workers, suppliers, consumers, host communities, stockholders, and the society as a whole often have taken more risks and made greater long-term investments in their organizations than upper management has. Through their taxes, *they* have paid to educate the workers hired by the organization, built the infrastructure needed for the organization to function (roads, airports, electric systems, etc.), and invested *their* labor and capital in the organization. And *they* are harmed most when the organization downsizes, despoils the environment, engages in discriminatory actions, and so on. Consequently, management should be responsive to the needs of all stakeholders, regardless of their political or economic power. However, when applied corporate responsiveness models moved in a very different direction. Faced with multiple, often incongruent demands, managers have to *strategically* choose among stakeholders. They should obey existing laws and regulations (all the while trying to weaken them), satisfy the demands of powerful external interest groups, and placate or ignore others. In many cases, it is easier to circumvent or overpower external pressures than to be responsive to them (Freeman and Gilbert, 1988).

The social responsiveness doctrine is problematic in a number of ways. First, it establishes an adversarial relationship between managers and stakeholders, both government agencies and interest groups. Instead of fostering a cooperative effort to deal with social and economic problems, it encourages secrecy, distortion, and hostility. Moreover, it encourages managers to play one stakeholder group off against others. This usually privileging the interests of economically powerful stakeholders over others, thus defeating the goals of fairness and equity that underlie the perspective (Freeman and Gilbert, 1988). Second, it encourages managers to be narrowly utilitarian. Legitimacy is reduced to power – organizations are responsive to global financial institutions because they have the power to enforce their demands, but not to indigenous peoples because they do not. Interests are taken seriously if they are quantifiable and concrete, which elevates economic gains and losses over all others. For example, on what basis should an organization distribute donations to victims of the 2001 attacks on the World Trade Center? The standard approach, regularly used by insurance company actuaries and legal scholars, is lifetime earnings potential. But, this criterion would mean that a 30-year old custodian would receive a much smaller share of the donations than a 30-year old **derivatives** (a complex and risky form of investment) trader who has no dependents but a much larger salary.[9] An elderly minister would receive only a pittance in comparison to a young corporate raider. Similarly, British Petroleum (BP) would be expected to compensate Gulf Coast fishermen and fisherwomen for a certain number of years of lost income – a tangible and quantifiable loss – but not for having destroyed a culture, way of life, and network of interpersonal relationships. In short, the social responsiveness doctrine would eliminate organizational responsibility for precisely the kinds of losses that most people see as most important.

Consequently, by the turn of the twenty-first century, and faced with increasing evidence of corporate irresponsibility, noncorporate stakeholders (consumer, labor, and environmental advocacy groups) sought to revive the corporate social *responsibility* (CSR) doctrine. However, they recognized from the outset that the perspective could be distorted by managers and owners who treat CSR as "merely a branch of PR" instead of a meaningful shift in values, one that

- Recognizes that actions by corporations influence the societies within which they operate which in turn contributed significantly to the success of a business;
- Involves actively managing corporations in ways that conform to international values and benefit all stakeholders; and
- Works cooperatively with other groups and organizations – local communities, civil society, other business, and multiple governments.[10]

Many owners and managers did accept the underlying assumptions of the revised CSR perspective, although some did so as much because they believed doing so would be profitable (eventually labeled the **business case for ethics**) as because they accepted its underlying ethic.[11] Others found the notion of being socially responsible to be excessively burdensome, and sought a rhetorically advantageous alternative. They found it in a distortion of the concept of "sustainability" that had become popular among environmental groups. From a purely rhetorical perspective, this concept has a number of advantages. First, it shifts the ethical analysis of a corporation's policies and practices from the present to an undefined future. In an important way, this rhetorical move parallels free market theory. It asserts that the "invisible hand" of the market eventually will lead to an "equilibrium point" in which economies operate as efficiently as possible, presumably to everyone's benefit. Similarly, the promise of a "sustainable" future can be used to justify activities that would be deemed unethical if evaluated in the present. Second, the concept of sustainability can be strategically redefined in ways that privilege economic growth over other social values. The usual rhetoric asserts that without economic growth, societies will lack the resources necessary to sustain themselves and meet other needs. Thus, growth must take precedence. Since free markets are depicted as necessary for sustained economic growth, any government action is objectionable if it interferes with market processes, including processes of creative destruction. As a result of these distortions of the original concept of sustainability, many advocates of sustainable development discarded the phrase once it became a "code for perpetual growth . . . force-fed to the world community by the global corporate-political-media network."[12]

RHETORIC AND ORGANIZATIONAL CRISIS AND IMAGE MANAGEMENT

As we explained at the beginning of this chapter, organizations can protect themselves from external pressures by developing images that are consistent with the core values of the cultures within which they operate, and by persuading policy makers to enact legislation that gives them advantages in a globally competitive marketplace. Like the components of all systems (recall Chapter 2), image management and political influence are interrelated. Politicians find it difficult to support organizations – even in private – if they have developed images as unethical, and corrupt. Conversely, political influence allows corporations to keep unethical actions secret, successfully manage popular indignation, and obtain financial subsidies and legal protections that make it easier to compete. The two key dimensions of organizational image management also are tightly interrelated. Moreover, an organization's image in the minds of its stakeholders will influence the likelihood that an unfortunate event will turn into a reputational crisis and will limit the rhetorical strategies that are available to organizational rhetors when crises do occur. Conversely, how well an organization's rhetors manage reputational crises will have long-term effects on its image(s), and on their ability to manage future crises. All of these interrelationships make it difficult to organize a discussion of organizational image management and political influence. But, authors have to start somewhere and we have chosen to begin with image management, and with the role that crisis management plays in it.

Reactive Image Management: Managing Organizational Crises

Managing organizational images is most complicated during crises.[13] Events themselves provide *opportunities* for image management; but they do not automatically become crises. For example, when hurricanes Katrina and Rita hit the US Gulf Coast every organization involved in disaster response was overwhelmed by the magnitude of the storm. Some organizations responded competently and engaged in rhetoric that enhanced their image – notably the Salvation Army and NOAA (weather bureau) – while others responded ineptly and produced rhetoric that further weakened their public image – for example, the US Red Cross and the Federal Emergency Management Agency (FEMA). Others, for example the US Corps of Engineers initially were able to maintain a positive image by deflecting responsibility to other organizations. But, over time new information became public indicating that the Corps had made decisions that exacerbated the damage, and that many of their initial claims were inaccurate. So, the first challenge for organizational rhetors is to keep events from becoming a crisis.

When a negative event occurs *within* an organization, the transformation from event to crisis is almost automatic. For example, sexual abuse of children by adult leaders of organizations, whether secular (the US Boy Scouts) or religious (the Roman Catholic Church), is perceived as significant, indeed horrendous, by almost all stakeholders. In extreme events such as these, the established protocol for managing crises is the only realistic option: Disclose the event(s) immediately so that the organization will not later have to backtrack and "retract" or "clarify" its previous statements and in the process destroy its trustworthiness; offer a full and heartfelt apology, including an acceptance of responsibility; offer restitution to victims; and describe steps that already have been taken to ensure that the error will not recur. The goal of this strategy is to control rhetoric about the crisis, and get it off of the media agenda and out of stakeholders' minds as soon as possible; the underlying assumption is that the two things that organizational rhetors must avoid are ridicule and claims of hypocrisy.

However, full apologies are quite rare, perhaps one case in a hundred. It is clear that organizations which fail to adequately manage reputational crises are likely to suffer significant economic losses over the long term (Baucus and Baucus, 1997; Marcus and Goodman, 1991). It also is clear that full apologies can minimize this long-term damage. But, in the short term (less than five years), full apologies open the organization up to litigation and/or increased regulation. As a result, legal staffs typically advise management to do almost anything *but* confess, *especially* if the organization actually is guilty. Since today's CEOs rarely stay with the same organization for long periods of time, the short-term economic costs of lawsuits are much more salient to them that the potential long-term economic costs of a weakened organizational image.[14] Consequently, it is much more likely that organizational rhetors will offer some form of "nuanced regret," including an admission that the event(s) did take place, and expression of its willingness to compensate victims out of its goodwill and social responsibility, and a commitment to invest whatever is necessary to ensure that similar events do not happen in the future.

Usually, nuanced regret is combined with some effort to shift responsibility, by claiming that the event was unintentional or accidental (an "act of God"), could not possibly have been anticipated given the information available to the organization (a strategy generally labeled **defeasibility**), or was someone else's fault.[15] If the event(s) took place within the organization, rhetors may try to shift responsibility from the *organization* to individual employees, a "bad apple" strategy. Although the latter claim can succeed in highly individualistic societies such as the United States, rhetors must successfully argue that upper management was unaware of unethical or illegal activities going on in the organization. As we pointed out in Chapter 3, management can "plan ahead" to use this strategy by actively discouraging employees from talking about ethical issues, especially when possible illegal activities are involved (the concept of "plausible deniability" established by the Reagan administration). In fact, there is substantial evidence that in most organizations upper management is more likely to fire employees for *talking about* ethical issues than for committing unethical actions. Then, if employees *do* act in unethical or illegal ways, management can plead ignorance and escape responsibility, even if organizational rules and reward systems encouraged workers to act unethically. Although more and more companies are stating publicly their commitment to ethics in management, few employees find it comfortable to raise such concerns in public or even in the privacy of their offices. Toffler concluded that "there seems to be a sense among managers that talking about ethics is 'just not done here.' And, unfortunately, they are usually right." Of course, the strategy will fail if upper management can be shown to have been actively involved in the event(s), and/or if there is evidence that they engaged in a "cover up."[16]

Organizational rhetors also can attempt to shift responsibility to outsiders, a "scapegoating" strategy. Not just any outsider will do. To be a good scapegoat, a target must be seen as sufficiently powerful to actually be responsible for an event. They also must be suspect in terms of some legitimized cultural values. Given the ambivalence that many stakeholders have about government "interference" in the economy, regulatory agencies fulfill these requirements quite nicely. Events can attributed to regulatory failure and organizations can shift responsibility by claiming that they did everything that regulators demand of them. In this sense, there are rhetorical advantages to being in a lightly regulated industry. Weak regulators cannot significantly impinge on an organization's operations, but they are ready scapegoats when things go wrong.[17] Organizational rhetors also may offer a *quasi-theory* to explain away errors. In our culture commonly used quasi-theories include "Boys will be boys," "We had a falling out," or "Organizations *have* to make a profit." One may *justify* one's actions by blaming them on some socially accepted rule or conduct. Organizational actors also can offer *counterclaims*, in which they deny intentions to influence or hurt anyone or asserts that they really had the other person's interests at heart ("I really wasn't trying to sell you more life insurance, I was just telling you what I do for a living," or "this policy is such a wonderful deal that I really had to share it with you"). When it was revealed that Toshiba of the United States sold advanced submarine technology to the Soviet Union during the late stages of the Cold War, the organization claimed that it never had any intent to undermine US security, but instead was trying to help the United States by providing good jobs for American workers. Another common strategy is *bolstering*, in which the accused person (or company) accepts the charges but attempts to overcome them by linking himself or herself to relationships, concepts, or objects that the audience values.[18]

Crisis management is especially difficult when events are extended over long periods of time (for example, BP's Deepwater Horizon oil spill of 2010, which lasted for months). In those cases, crisis managers adopt strategies that resemble extended political campaigns. But, the longer an event lasts, the greater the possibility of additional revelations and of rhetorical errors. For example, earlier in this book we mentioned a highly publicized case of racial discrimination at the Texaco Oil Company. What started as an expose' of incredibly offensive corporate practices became a case study in effective crisis management. Initially, Texaco *denied* that any discrimination had taken place. Federal law requires plaintiffs to produce hard evidence that their treatment was both discriminatory and that the discrimination was because of their race. There are many ways for a company to hide evidence of discrimination – obscuring discriminatory decisions in larger downsizing moves, changing job descriptions to make a qualified minority applicant seem unqualified, or (as Texaco did) simply keeping one set of records for private use and another for government agencies, courts, and the public. As a result, it is almost impossible to obtain direct evidence of discrimination, so denial is a very effective strategy. Without direct evidence, the 1994 suit had languished, although in early 1996 the Equal Employment Opportunity Commission issued a preliminary decision in favor of the plaintiffs. This decision triggered what was to become a fateful meeting among Texaco executives.

The meeting was a frank and wide-ranging discussion of issues related to Texaco's affirmative action programs. Worried about the suit, David Keough (senior assistant treasurer) discussed ways to *carefully* destroy company documents so that evidence of discrimination was eliminated but evidence supporting Texaco's case was retained. The secret appraisal documents and minutes of meetings during which they were discussed were the biggest concern. Robert Ulrich, the company treasurer, concluded that "you know, there is no point in even keeping the restricted version anymore. All it could do is get us in trouble." After reviewing Texaco's promotion history, Ulrich noted that "all the black jelly beans seem to be glued to the bottom of the bag." Eventually the executives discussed their feelings about the suit and the employees who had filed it. Ulrich complained that those "niggers" were causing difficulties for them. None of this would ever have been known except for two events. Richard Lundwall, the coordinator of personnel in Texaco's finance department, had been assigned to keep minutes on the meeting and had tape-recorded it to have an accurate record. In August 1996 Texaco fired Lundwall in a downsizing move, and he turned his tapes over to the plaintiffs' attorneys, who released them to the *New York Times*.

Denial was no longer a viable response; and there simply were no quasi-theories, excuses, or justifications readily available. Texaco immediately shifted strategies to a barrage of *bolstering*. Texaco attorney Andrea Christiansen was "shocked and dismayed" by the tapes; CEO Peter Bijur announced that "the rank insensitivity demonstrated in the taped remarks . . . offends me deeply. . . . This alleged behavior does not represent the way the company feels about any of our employees. This alleged behavior violates our code of conduct, our core values, and the law. . . . Wherever the truth leads, we'll go." He also announced that Texaco would hire an outside attorney to assist the authorities with the investigation, would spend $35 million on outside evaluations and enhancement of Texaco's affirmative action and diversity management programs, and had hired an outside expert to evaluate the tape. On November 14, Texaco announced a new scholarship program for minority students, but said that "the program has nothing to do with recent negative publicity concerning published reports of racial slurs used by company executives." Faced with a boycott of its products by civil rights groups, Texaco settled the two-year-old suit within two months and accepted external oversight of hiring and promotion programs as part of the settlement. Virtually everything that a company and its spokespersons can say or do to bolster its image as a nondiscriminatory employer was done between November 1996 and January 1997.

In addition, the company briefly offered a *counterclaim*. The independent specialist hired and paid by Texaco to analyze the tape reported that the word that had initially been translated as "nigger" really was "St. Nicholas." But this strategy was short-lived, because, as CEO Bijur admitted when the finding was announced, "these preliminary findings merely set the record straight as to the exact words spoken in the conversations; but they do not change the categorically unacceptable context and tone of these conversations."[19] Eventually the crisis subsided, boycotts ended, and stakeholder attention shifted to other issues. More than a decade later, Texaco seems to have rebuilt its image as a nondiscrimintory employer, at least in comparison to the petrochemical industry as a whole. When organizations handle crises well, they end quickly and in a whisper, leaving little or no long-term memory. In some cases, events may be handled so well that they may even improve the organization's image in the eyes of key stakeholders. In others, the damage may eventually decline.

Proactive Image Management

All people and all organizations have images. The question is not whether or not an image exists, the question is whether it is developed carefully over time through strategic communication, or whether it is developed haphazardly in response crises. **Proactive image management** advocates the former. We already have discussed most of the key concepts underlying the perspective – organizations must legitimize themselves and their activities by linking themselves to the core values of the societies in which they operate. For example, mainstream US society seems to composed of people who are **ethical segregationists**, applying very different standards to the operations of organizations, politicians, and "regular" people, and/or "compartmentalizing" ethical codes – one ethic for the Sabbath, a different one for Saturday nights, and another for the week at work.[20] Organizational image management also is made easier by a widespread belief in an **organizational imperative**, an assumption that everything good in life comes through private sector organizations. When combined, these processes mean that organizations are evaluated almost completely on economic terms – if they persuasively argue that they produce jobs and tax revenues for a community, they generally are allowed to engage in activities that would discredit politicians or individuals.

Finally, image management is simplified by the incoherent nature of societal values. As we explained in earlier chapters, the taken-for-granted assumptions of cultures are full of tensions and contradictions. These incongruities provide organizational rhetors with socially legitimized appeals and arguments for virtually any situation. For example, health care organizations have historically been able to manipulate a "trilemma" (a dilemma with three poles instead of two) created by inconsistent popular demands. US citizens want quick and easy access to providers of their choice, high-quality care, and low prices. Unfortunately, for economic and structural reasons these desires conflict with one another. Increasing quality drives up prices because current patients (and their insurers and employers) must pay for the research necessary to develop improved technologies and procedures, speedy access requires the creation of expensive treatment capacity that goes unused most of the time, controlling costs (which is a synonym for controlling incomes and profits) reduces access and quality, and so on. When stakeholders (politicians, patients, or the corporations that purchase health insurance for their employees) try to improve one part of the trilemma, rhetors from threatened organizations can (accurately) argue that the other two values are threatened (Conrad and McIntush, 2003). Similarly, efforts to increase national security can be criticized for undermining individual freedoms (and vice versa), rules and regulations designed to provide consistency and fairness can be attacked because of their inflexibility (and vice versa), and so on.

Organizational image management also is complicated by a number of factors. Chief among these is the need to simultaneously address the concerns of multiple stakeholders. Doing so is especially complicated for companies that operate internationally because the core values of one society in which they operate may be very different than the core values held by stakeholders in other societies. The simplest solution to this problem is for organizational rhetors to adapt their image-messages to the demands of each group. At one time, organizational rhetors could be comfortable that messages designed for one stakeholder audience would not be communicated to others. But, modern communication technology allows messages that are carefully crafted for one stakeholder group to be instantly disseminated among other stakeholders.[21] Consequently, managers (or the corporate communication specialists to which image management activities often are delegated) often must prioritize stakeholder groups, focusing their efforts on those whose concerns are most urgent, whose power over the organization is greatest (recall Chapter 8), and/or who are viewed as most legitimate by other stakeholders (Agle, Mitchell, and Sonnenfeld, 1999). To complicate things further, the relative importance of different stakeholders changes. Even the best-laid plans for proactive image management can be undermined by those changes.

For example, the paradigm case of proactive image management was the Malden Mills Corporation and its CEO Aaron Feuerstein. For literally decades, Malden Mills had been the best possible corporate citizen. It contributed to its community in every possible way, and its CEO was known worldwide for his personal and professional ethics. In an industry that long has been known for abruptly closing plants and shifting jobs out of the United States, Malden Mills innovated so that it could continue operating in Massachusetts. When it faced bankruptcy in the mid-1980s, Feuerstein was forced to lay off many of his workers, but rehired them as soon as possible. When a fire devastated the plant in the mid-1990s, he tapped his personal fortune to pay a full salary to his out-of-work employees. Because of the high level of trust developed over time, his customers (companies like Land's End and L.L. Bean) honored their contracts while the factory was being rebuilt. When the plant reopened, the ceremony was covered by almost every national news organization. In short, Malden Mills had the best possible relationship with virtually every stakeholder group, except one. When the recession of 1999–2003 hit, Malden Mills again faced bankruptcy. Feuerstein, whose personal reserves had not been rebuilt since the fire, could not support the company and was forced into bankruptcy. The court gave him extra time to seek funds to pay off his creditors, but G.E. Capital, which had taken over the firm, refused to allow him an extra month. Malden's heroic CEO was replaced, and the company's new owners immediately shipped its operations to Southeast Asia, with the exception of a contract with the US Department of Defense, which requires production to take place within the United States. When bankruptcy hit, the most important stakeholders were Malden's creditors, and no amount of goodwill with other stakeholders could overcame their power (Milne, 1995; Ulmer, 2000; and Seeger and Ulmer, 2002).

In sum, proactive image management draws upon the taken-for-granted assumptions of societies and significant stakeholders to legitimize an organization. But, it also functions to reproduce and support the societal values underlying organizational rhetoric. In the United States, no industry has been more successful in doing this than the petroleum industry. For decades the industry largely had been reactive to a string of crises, from Standard Oil's abuses at the turn of the twentieth century to the Teapot Dome scandal of the 1920s to energy crisis and charges of price gouging during the 1970s and early 2000s. But, by the end of the 1970s the industry realized that consumer and environmental groups had become strong enough to present a continuing challenge. So, the industry embarked on a campaign to create an image as the irreplaceable "engine" that drives the American economy.[22] By depicting themselves as primarily concerned with balancing economic and environmental needs, they drew on cultural values regarding managerial and scientific expertise. By casting themselves as calm and rational in the face of extremism they increased their credibility. By focusing attention on the economic necessity of energy, they elevated those concerns in the popular mind, and they continue to do so. Cultural assumptions must be reinforced if they are to be available when needed in the future. Organizational rhetoric serves that function.

Case Study 12.1

Lanxess Cleans Up Its Act[1]

The state of Ohio does not have the kind of notoriety among environmentalists and public health activists that Love Canal, New York, or Cancer Alley, Louisiana (the stretch of the Mississippi River between Baton Rouge and New Orleans), have, but it comes close. The ignition of the Cuyahoga River in 1969 was not especially newsworthy, since the river had burned at least 13 times in the past, beginning in 1868, but it coincided with a burgeoning environmental movement in the USA and helped galvanize support for the Clean Water Act. The other "bookend" in Ohio's environmental record probably was the EPA's 2002 announcement that airborne carcinogens between Portsmouth and just west of New Boston made it 20 times more likely that residents would contract cancer than in the United States as a whole, a contrast to Ohio's below-average cancer rates. In addition to airborne and waterborne toxins, the petrochemical industry along the Ohio River valley provides thousands of high-paying jobs, which creates local support for the industry, tax revenues for the state and local governments, and campaign contributions for Ohio's policy makers. It also generates grassroots activism, which creates pressure on corporations and policy makers.

Addyston, Ohio, is about 120 miles downriver from Portsmouth. In 2004 an environmental advocacy group (OCA) initiated a Good Neighbor Campaign (GNC) designed to reduce or eliminate the release of toxins by Lanxess Corporation's (a division of Swiss pharmaceutical giant Bayer) plant. With OCA's help, the West Side Action Group (WAG) was formed. Most of the group's members were from working- and middle-class backgrounds, and the most active members were women, something that is typical of environmental and public health advocacy groups. The leader was Sara, an English/humanities major who had learned a great deal about chemistry and plant operations from county environmental regulators and from engineers who were friendly with the OCA. Good Neighbor Campaigns encourage the development of cooperative relationships between target corporations and advocate open negotiation among various stakeholders. However, leaders recognize that they face significant challenges. They have vastly fewer resources than corporate targets, and know that they will face resistance from community members and organizations that benefit from the presence of the target organization in their area. They also know from experience that corporations will not enter into meaningful negotiations unless they are persuaded that refusing to do so will negatively affect their productivity, profitability, and/or reputation/image. Because of this power imbalance, leaders of GNCs seek optimal times to exert pressure on an organization – just before a plant is re-licensed or after events that promise litigation, for example. OCA started its GNC by canvassing the community to assess the nature and intensity of citizens' concerns. The results were not surprising – residents were concerned about toxins in the air, ground and drinking water, and river, as well as foul odors coming from the plant.

Because petrochemical operations are so often involved in reputational crises, the industry's lobbying group encourages its member companies to engage in proactive image management through the creation of Community Advisory Panels, groups comprised of community leaders – elected officials, emergency responders, and local businessmen – who can serve as pro-industry spokespersons in the event of a crisis. The CAPs produce newsletters about the "wonders of chemistry" and the socially responsible activities of the plant, company, and industry to be distributed to the local communities. They also sponsor community dialogue sessions where citizens can ask questions about the organization and its operations. CAPs also spearhead events such as park clean-ups, fundraising events for local charities and schools, and so on. CAP meetings also allow the company's PR department to identify local activists and invite them to join the group, an age-old strategy of "co-opting" opposition. Of course, many residents recognized that the company was more interested in using the CAP to get its message out than to seek citizen input, and the group's members were not representative of the community as a whole – more white, more educated, and wealthier. But, the CAP provided a structure that would be available to the company in the event of a crisis.

Good Neighbor Campaigns encourage citizen advocates to communicate directly with company managers. When Sara approached them directly and was granted access, her neighbors were surprised. They had long believed that management viewed them as "a bunch of dumb hillbillies" who didn't deserve to be listened to. Sara encouraged management to commit to reduced emissions because "emissions are a waste. Keep your chemicals in your products and out of our lawns. Save money that way and not by cutting jobs." Management agreed, but said that they simply could not afford to make the necessary changes. But, the meetings continued. Management used all of the tactics that are available to those who dominate communicative structures – control the agenda of the meetings so that core issues were not discussed, overload the group members with technical data and scientific terms while providing no (or ambiguous) information about odors and toxic releases. Then, during the community's annual Oktoberfest, the company released a cloud of toxins – acrylonitrile, butadine, and styrene, something that the WAG did not learn about until much later. (Note: this level of secrecy is not all that uncommon. For example, for 40 days during the spring of 2010 BP burned a half million pounds of toxic chemicals, including 17,000 pounds of cancer- and birth defect-causing benzene over its Texas City, Texas, refinery without the public knowing about it. State law only requires companies to tell the state EPA that they plan to release chemicals into the air or water, and to report and summarize the event on the day it concludes. There is no requirement to notify the surrounding communities.) At the first meeting after the release became public information, WAG members demanded an explanation. But the mediator the company had hired to run their meetings refused to change the published agenda, leaving only minutes to discuss the release. This created a strategic opportunity for WAG and OCA, who exploited the community's anger about the release through increased press and TV coverage to create an expanded letter writing campaign. The release had undermined management's credibility and their assertions that there was little risk of toxic releases.

Sara encouraged neighbors to keep logs of odors, and to call state and county regulators when they happened. Residents from Louisiana's cancer alley taught them to take "bucket samples" of air and water quality. These tactics provided scientific evidence to counter management's rhetoric, and increased neighbor confidence in their ability to confront plant management. When management claimed that the releases were benign, residents told about headaches and nosebleeds that accompanied the odors, and spoke about elevated cancer rates. At a meeting when the regional environmental regulator parroted the company's position, one neighbor asked if he knew that there was an elementary school across the street from the plant. He said he didn't; neither did he know the ages of the children who went there or the safe exposure levels for small children. A new plant manager was appointed, although the company said the change was not related to the environmental controversy.

In December there was another release and more public outcry. In February, the company reported that they now had the funds to increase safety, although they continued their usual rhetorical strategies of denying that the releases took place, claiming that they presented no serious threats to public health, overloading citizens with technical information, avoiding discussion of the issues that were important to community members, and stalling. After yet *another* release, WAG started demanding zero emissions, and OCA began a petition calling on the German CEO of Bayer to replace the plant manager. A neighbor delivered it personally. WAG also started scheduling community meetings in which they could control the agenda. Community members who supported the plant, including the principal of the elementary school, started a counterattack. WAG continued its efforts, and started to raise questions about the county regulator's inactivity.

Bayer replaced the plant manager and its head of North American Operations, and allocated $1.5 million to improve production processes, while actively denying that their decision had anything to do with the campaign.

The new manager, who told the WAG that he was "annoyed by the releases, they make for bad PR," apologized for past problems and announced that the organization would become more transparent and proactive in notifying the mayor and PAG (but not the citizen groups) about future releases. Citizens responded that these moves were positive, but demanded that the company start focusing on prevention as well. Little was done during the next few months, although residents friendly to plant management increased their attacks on the advocacy groups and their leaders. The citizen groups continued their pressure on the company, and increased their pressure on regulatory agencies who had for years done very little to deal with the issue. Eventually, Lanxess (which by now had been sold to a British company) announced that it would spend an additional $1 million on pollution and process controls at the plant. The OCA and WAG announced that they would end the public phase of their advocacy campaign.

Applying What You Have Learned

1. Who were the "players" on both sides of the Lanxess issue? What were their incentives and motivations?
2. What rhetorical strategies did the various parties use? What effects did those strategies have on the rhetoric of the other parties?

Questions to Think About and Discuss

1. Late in the Lanxess campaign, the company's rhetors claimed that its "proactive" approach to communication with the community, including the creation and operations of its CAP, was proof of its goodwill and commitment to social responsibility. Sara responded that being proactive was meaningless unless it involved changes in the plant's operations as well as its rhetoric – a legitimately "proactive" firm would constantly focus on *preventing* releases and accidents in addition to focusing on image management and communication. Which position is most persuasive? Why?
2. One of the tenets of Good Neighbor Campaigns is that outcomes are the only thing that matter; how battles were won and who deserved credit for success is unimportant. When Lanxess made the changes that the WAG had advocated for more than two years, the company claimed that they had done so voluntarily and pro-plant officials commended them for their "voluntary and proactive" actions. It used the same arguments when it appealed the fines levied against it by the EPA. Consistent with the assumptions underlying GNCs, the WAG never challenged these claims. Evaluate this GNC strategy.

Note

1 This case study is based on Zoller (2009), and Zoller and Tener (2010). The BP/Texas City release is profiled in Hatcher (2010). For an analysis of Community Advisory Panels, see Sim and Seewald (2003).

PUBLIC POLICY MAKING AND ORGANIZATIONAL RHETORIC

Organizations influence public policies in two ways, by persuading policy makers to enact favorable legislation, and by blocking unfavorable laws. Some legislation assists organizations directly by providing government subsidies, granting preferential tax treatment, or constructing barriers for competitors. Import quotas and tariffs disadvantage foreign competitors. Regulatory processes often do the same for domestic competition. Most US citizens believe that government regulations and regulatory agencies were created to protect citizens from misdeeds by corporations or other actors. In a few cases this assumption has been accurate: popular pressure focused legislative attention on a moral "evil," personified by a corporation or industry, and illustrated by "horror stories" that stressed the virtue of victims and the venality of perpetrators. However, throughout US history it has been much more common for regulation to be enacted in response to pressure from industries themselves. Existing organizations or professions wish to obtain regulatory protection and/or to impose legal burdens on potential competitors. They justify these pro-corporation regulations through a rhetoric of "reining in excessive competition" or rescuing their industry or the overall economy from "chaos." Regulation is designed to achieve what market processes cannot, and regulation is enacted because "the imperfections of government action are [viewed as] preferable to the imperfections of the market."[23] Recent revelations of safety problems with virtually everything imported from China by US firms – from children's toys with lead-based paint to vegetables treated with toxic pesticides – have even led industries to seek additional regulation of Chinese imports, in order to protect themselves from themselves. No company wants to import tainted food or products, but none can afford to be the first to stop doing so because it would give their competitors an advantage. If regulators ban such imports, all of the involved organizations can escape from this dilemma. Other legislation has an indirect effect. If legislators declare that a company's or industry's ethically questionable practices are legal, those practices are much easier to defend. If stakeholders complain about the practices, organizational rhetors can shift attention and responsibility to the policy makers.

Organizations, Elites, and Public Policy Making

Political scientists long have recognized that elite groups, including executives in organizations, have clear advantages in influencing public policy. Corporations stay in contact with policy makers through lobbyists who create and maintain communication networks that can be activated at a moment's notice. In spite of the public perception that lobbyists are constantly wining and dining policy makers in an orgy of influence, research indicates that their lives are much less exciting than the stereotype suggests. Sometimes organizations do actively seek change, but that advocacy takes place in private, through constant, quiet lobbying of regulators and policy makers, especially the chairpersons of legislative committees who control political agendas. In those venues they advocate, sometimes for years, waiting for opportunities to argue that their pet proposal is appropriate to a particular problem. If they fail, they merely wait for the next opportunity. However, the primary function of lobbying, and related campaign contributions, is to block change, not to help create it. In general, corporations are satisfied with the status quo, largely because they have been so successful in influencing past policies. They spend most of their time and energy in "watchful waiting," husbanding their resources for those rare cases in which change seems imminent. Sometimes lobbyists provide policy makers with research that supports their employers' positions on key issues. Most of the time they engage in rhetoric designed to make policy makers and the public fear change. This private rhetoric usually deals with abstractions – the sanctity of the free market, the superiority of the "American way," the evils of government "interference" in corporate activities, and so on. When lobbyists do discuss specific policy proposals, they do so in pretty mundane terms – the feasibility and costs of proposed policies, the ways in which the current system achieves desirable goals, and so on. Their primary objective is to create doubts and fear about change and the risks it involves, which establishes the groundwork needed to block change when it threatens.[24]

However, it is important to realize that the relationships that lobbyists form with policy makers are, like any other interpersonal relationship, *mutually* beneficial. Politicians usually need the help of lobbyists in pursuing their own agendas, which is necessary for getting re-elected. Lobbyists provide them with the contacts, expertise, and good will that they need in order to do so.

Privatizing Public Policy Making In general, members of elite groups, including corporate executives, prefer to influence public policies in private.[25] Making policy in public is risky. It gives opponents an opportunity to get organized, and form coalitions with other interested stakeholders. It also can undermine coalitions that organizations have formed with one another, as some members decide that their interests are best served by abandoning their peers. Making policy in public also forces elites to justify their positions on key issues. Although they have a number of influential rhetorical strategies available, they may fail to persuade key audiences, who actively interpret messages in terms of their own perceived interests. Fortunately for corporations, there are many means of privatizing public policy making. The simplest strategy is to press for laws that allow them to hide information about their operations. This can be done directly, as when the petrochemical industry persuaded the US Environmental Protection Agency (EPA) to allow firms to release up to 5000 pounds of toxic chemicals – DDT, PCBs, and so on – into the environment (a tenfold increase over the previous limit) without disclosing their actions (recall the Lanxess case study earlier in this chapter). The EPA also allowed BP to use chemical dispersants to fight its 2010 Gulf of Mexico oil spill, which had the effect of keeping a large proportion of the oil underwater where it could not be seen, and to do so without revealing their chemical composition. The Bush administration persuaded Congress to fund a $700 billion bailout of the US financial industry without requiring firms to reveal what they used the money for; and when the bailout created a firestorm of protest, the new Obama administration's treasury secretary quietly provided at least $2 trillion more without going through the public venue of Congress (Posner, 2009, xiv). Policy making also can be privatized indirectly, as when companies arrive at out-of-court settlements that seal information gathered during legal proceedings from public view, or when they reach negotiated settlements with regulators whose terms are not divulged.

Organizations Going Public However, events sometimes overwhelm these processes, and an issue that interests organizations does reach the public agenda. Again, organizations have a number of advantages. Pro-business groups are more tightly organized than groups that represent other stakeholders. As a result, they are better able to quickly mobilize resources to remove threatening proposals from the policy-making agenda or block their enactment. Mobilization depends on advocates' rhetorical skills, on their ability to define a particular proposal as beneficial to a sufficiently large group of people to gain policy makers' attention and respect, and to energize that coalition. Another advantage for organizational rhetors is time. If they can delay policy making until public attention shifts and the emotional fervor underlying calls for reform subside, they can maintain the status quo. This is especially true of issues like corporate unethical behavior because it is newsworthy for only a brief period of time, and it is usually too complex to be explained in 30-second sound bites or 3-minute news reports. Media, and thus popular, attention quickly shifts to other issues. For example, at both the beginning and end of the first decade of the new century, US residents learned that financial industry managers had engaged in questionable and/or illegal activities that cost small investors billions of dollars. But, within a few months most of those investors were no longer concerned about the scandal. The stock market went up, investors' retirement plans were showing gains, and their outrage had dissipated.[26] Similarly, during early 2010 a mining disaster in West Virginia and the explosion of BP's Deepwater Horizon rig in the Gulf of Mexico created popular outcry to tighten regulation of the two industries. After multiple hearings and strong industry opposition, Congress adjourned for its August recess, returned to Washington, and once again adjourned, all without taking any action on either set of issues.

In those rare cases in which pressure is sustained over time, organizational rhetors may have to engage in public rhetoric. Fortunately, they can define socioeconomic "problems" as "private sector" concerns, not matters for government policy. The credibility of this argument is grounded in the cultural assumption that free-market capitalism is inherently superior to any other economic system, and that government "interference" in the free-market system is inherently futile and perverse (recall Chapter 2). This strategy has long been successful in blunting pressure for increased government regulation after periods of business corruption and malpractice. In most cases, corporate rhetoric is creative, sophisticated, and effective. For example, during the late 1990s the US Congress debated the McCain-Feingold bill, which would have severely restricted advertising by the tobacco industry. The bill's sponsors used recently released evidence to argue that the industry had long hidden the addictive nature of its product and had even used that research to maximize the addictive power of cigarettes. However, the industry was able to use that argument to their advantage. Since the funding mechanisms in the bill relied on increased tobacco taxes, opponents were able to define the proposal as a tax bill in disguise, one that unfairly penalized precisely those poor and middle-class victims that the bill's proponents had demonstrated were incapable of shaking their addiction.

If public rhetoric fails, organizational rhetors can quietly advocate for the passage of "hollow laws" that *seem* to solve problems but do not make substantive changes. Because bills almost always pass the US Senate and House of Representatives in different forms, they are referred to "conference committees" that iron out differences between the bills in private, where organizational rhetors have a great advantage. For example, when the 2010 Financial Reform package emerged from conference committee, auto dealers had been omitted completely from its restrictions (in spite of clear evidence that some dealers use tactics such as tacking on unapproved charges in "fine print," and jacking up interest rates to as much as 17 percent without customer knowledge); the enforcement mechanisms that applied consumer protections to small banks had been eliminated; and restrictions on the financial industry practices that had led to the Great Recession had largely been eliminated. Finally, in the unlikely event that substantive laws are enacted, organizational rhetors can shift their attention to the implementation process, which largely takes place in private. For example, the Bayh-Dole Act is a provision of US patent law that requires pharmaceutical firms that receive federal research grants (which help fund about 80 percent of the drugs developed in the United States) to make those drugs available at a reasonable price. However, the law has never been enforced. More often, organizations quietly negotiate arrangements with regulators that minimize the impact of laws, a process that political scientists have labeled "regulatory capture."[27]

Summary Throughout Unit I, we discussed the challenges created for organizations by pressures in the environments surrounding them, a discussion that culminated in our summary of systems theory and institutional theory. In this chapter, we have argued that organizations are able to proactively mold and manage environmental pressures, by influencing popular attitudes and public policies. We also have argued that it is impossible to fully understand organizational ethics unless one takes a systemic perspective to understand the complex matrix of forces and processes that influence employees' ethical choices. We conclude this chapter with an extended case study that applies these concepts further – the most visible example of corporate illegality in US history.

Case Study 12.2
Ike the Prophet?

On January 17, 1961, after a half-century of serving his country and two terms as president, Dwight David Eisenhower said farewell. Like the first US general-turned-president, George Washington, his address was part celebration and part warning. Ike first noted that the world had changed in ways that made it imprudent for the United States to radically downsize its military and fully convert its armaments industry to peacetime pursuits.

> [We now (i.e., in 1961) spend] on military security alone more than the net income of all United States corporations. Now this conjunction of an immense military establishment and a large armaments industry is new in the American experience. The total influence – economic, political, even spiritual – is felt in every city, every Statehouse, every office of the federal government. We recognize the imperative need for this development. Yet, we must not fail to comprehend its grave implications. Our toil, resources, and livelihood are all involved. So is the very structure of our society. In the councils of government, we must guard against the acquisition of unwarranted influence, whether sought or unsought, by the military-industrial-complex. The potential for the disastrous rise of misplaced power exists and will persist. We must never let the weight of this combination endanger our liberties or democratic processes. We should take nothing for granted. Only an alert and knowledgeable citizenry can compel the proper meshing of the huge industrial and military machinery of defense with our peaceful methods and goals, so that security and liberty may prosper together. (Eisenhower, 1961, 3)

Increasing the formal, structural power of the military-industrial-complex, Eisenhower continued, was a new conception of time, a taken-for-granted cultural assumption that substituted short-term impulses for long-term planning:

> We – you and I, and our government – must avoid the impulse to live only for today, plundering for our own ease and convenience the precious resources of tomorrow. We cannot mortgage the material assets of our grandchildren without risking the loss of their political and spiritual heritage. We want democracy to survive for all generations to come, not to become the insolvent phantom of tomorrow. (Eisenhower, 1961, 4)

Two score and ten years later, Eisenhower's warning seems prophetic. After the collapse of the Soviet Union in 1991, leaders of the military-industrial complex faced a crisis. The end of the Cold War and the virtual elimination of a direct military threat from Russia led many politicians and interest groups to demand that defense spending be decreased and the "peace dividend" be spent on social needs. The defense industry responded in three ways, which combined to ensure that there would be little or no peace dividend. First, armaments firms merged, and justified the creation of an oligopoly by arguing that budgetary realities required them to be more streamlined and efficient, even if the mergers reduced competition in the industry and thus potentially drove up costs. Second, they geographically dispersed their operations and increased the number of suppliers with whom they had contracts. Finally, they significantly increased their campaign donations and lobbying activities. As a result, by the turn of the twenty-first century, two companies dominated the industry, and almost every congressperson and senator had constituents and campaign war chests which depended on the continuation of defense contracts. The Department of Defense budget exceeded $700 billion per year, almost one-third of total federal spending.

Since 1990, every US president has tried to reduce defense spending and shift monies from weapons systems designed to meet the Soviet threat to more relevant, contemporary equipment. Every one of them has failed. In 2009, highly respected Secretary of Defense Robert Gates (originally appointed by Republican President George W. Bush but retained by Democratic President Barack Obama) proposed to eliminate a number of archaic weapons systems, including the F-22 fighter plane and the C-17 transport. The F-22 had gone wildly over budget, was designed for a war in Europe against the Soviet Union, and had never been used in combat. After an intense battle, Congress did cancel the F-22 project, but

> Despite objections and veto threats from the White House, a $636 billion Pentagon spending bill passed [the House of Representatives] by a 400–30 vote Thursday, although it contains money for a much-criticized new presidential helicopter fleet, cargo jets that Gates said aren't needed, and an alternative engine for the next-generation F-35 Joint Strike Fighter [which received much of the F-22's funding] that the Pentagon says is a waste of money. (Shanker, 2010, 1)

As *ABC News* reporters Matthew Mosk and Lee Ferran noted in "The Boondoggle That Wouldn't Die" (2011), funding for the alternative engine program was extended through March 2011, in spite of President Obama's veto threat. The $9 million advertising and lobbying campaign by engine manufacturer General Electric paid off handsomely, at least for a time. However, in spite of appointing GE's CEO as chair of the President's Council on Jobs and Competitiveness, Secretary Gates stuck to his guns and the second engine was removed from the DoD budget. GE vowed to "fight like hell [to get the engine included in] the 2012 budget" (Schouten, 2011, 5A). In the meantime, the F-35's cost, once estimated as $40 million per plane, has risen to $133 million each.

The C-17 transport story ends a little differently. *Los Angeles Times* military correspondent Michael Hiltzik explained the situation:

> If you're interested in contemplating the harvest of this country's decades of failed economic policies, failed military policies and just plain failed politics. . . . I know just where to send you. It's a Boeing aircraft factory on the outskirts of Long Beach Airport. . . . This is the last factory in America capable of building large military aircraft, and it's headed for extinction. In approving a $626-billion military budget for fiscal 2010 this week, the Senate threw in $2.5 billion for 10 more C-17s. . . . The Air Force didn't actually request the planes. Defense Secretary. . . . Gates wants to kill the program. (Hiltzik, 2009, B1)

But, it is virtually impossible to kill a program that involves contractors – and jobs – in 44 states and is supported by legislators from both parties and all political ideologies – from liberal Senator Barbara Boxer (D-CA) to moderate Senator Dianne Feinstein (D-CA) to conservative Representative Dana Rohrabacher (R-CA), who voted against both the financial industry and automobile bailouts and President Obama's economic stimulus package because they would increase the federal debt. Interestingly, defenders of the C-17 have not employed the usual "national security" rhetoric to defend the spending. Senator Boxer argued that the planes could be used for humanitarian missions in the future, but most supporters focused on the jobs it created. However, Robert Pollin, a University of Massachusetts economist who specializes in military spending, concluded that the same amount of money would create more jobs if it were spent on education, health, or clean energy, "not just next year, but in the next 10 years." This is especially true since the average age of the plant's workers is 56, which means that spending money on them now is not likely to have long-term positive economic effects (cited in Hiltzik, 2009). In spite of the decision to fund more C-17s, Lockheed continued the process of reducing its US workforce that started during the early 1990s. Nine hundred jobs were eliminated at the Long Beach plant in January 2011. More layoffs will follow unless Congress extends the C-17 contract further.

In sum, the politics of the "peace dividend" are simple. Even with a Congress dominated by Obama loyalists,

> the draw of defense industry jobs for weapons systems is strong even among the most liberal members. Typically, contractors and subcontractors are spread across the country to maximize support. The items Gates seeks to kill mean jobs in such [key political] states as Georgia, Texas, California, Connecticut, New York, Indiana, and Ohio. (Shanker, 2010, 3)

Questions to Think About and Discuss

On August 8, 2010, Secretary Gates announced a new round of Department of Defense budget cuts, including a proposal to close the Joint Forces Command in Norfolk, Virginia, a hiring freeze for most of the Pentagon, and a 10 percent reduction in the use of civilian contractors. He also would reduce the number of generals by 50 and the number of civilian upper-management positions by 150. *New York Times* correspondent Thom Shaker noted that these rather modest cuts "are certain to earn strong opposition" because "members of Congress tend to fight to protect jobs and spending in their districts." Gates justified his proposals as a necessary step to reduce the burgeoning federal budget deficit and as a way to shift money away from the DoD bureaucracy and toward soldiers' needs.

1. Given what you know about the military-industrial-complex and the dynamics of public policymaking, what would you predict will be the outcome of Secretary Gates's proposal? Why?
2. Note: a month after announcing his proposal, Secretary Gates announced that he would resign during 2011. What effects will his announcement have on the outcome of his proposal? Why?

SYSTEMS, ACTIONS, AND ETHICS

Throughout this book we have explained that there is a complicated relationship between communication and the social and organizational systems in which it takes place (recall Unit I). Through communication, structures – meaning systems, patterns of acting, and institutions – are created and institutionalized. Through communication, societies develop complex sets of taken-for-granted assumptions that define certain structures and actions as normal and natural. Members teach newcomers those assumptions, and by learning their lessons well, newcomers become qualified to participate in those societies and organizations. Included in those assumptions and structures are guidelines and constraints that tell members what actions are required, allowed, and proscribed – including what is ethical and what is not. By acting in appropriate ways, members reproduce the structures and assumptions, thereby providing everyone with stable and predictable social situations and strategies that they can use to pursue their goals. This does not mean that the dimensions of social and organizational systems are always coherent and mutually supportive. Indeed, in all societies and organizations there are tensions and contradictions that provide space within which people can act strategically. Nor does it mean that social and organizational systems never change – through strategic communication people exploit tensions and contradictions, and in the process create pressure for change. But it does mean that fundamental changes are rare, emerge over long periods of time in response to sustained communicative acts, and often have very different effects than change agents intended or anticipated.

In the concluding section of this book, we will illustrate these processes by examining the two economic crises that served as "bookends" for the first decade of the twenty-first century – the explosion of the "dot.com" bubble in 1999, which led to the largest corporate bankruptcies in American history, and the financial crisis of 2007–2008, that led to the Great Recession and taxpayer bailouts of 2007 and beyond. There is a widespread consensus that each of these events involved unethical and/or illegal actions by the leaders of a number of major corporations. But, this consensus tends to oversimplify the context within which the events took place, and in the process oversimplifies organizational ethics. Those systems allow people to make choices that may be judged to be improper (illegal and/or unethical) and they include complex incentive systems that guide those choices. Organizational ethics is the outcome of individual choices made *within* social and organizational systems.

Bubbles and Bailouts

In important ways, the events of the early twenty-first century are nothing new. During the 1800s, the US economy experienced repeated cycles of massive economic expansion ("booms") followed by deep depressions ("busts"). These cycles typically resulted from the development of investment **bubbles**, that is, steep increases in the value of some kind of asset that cannot be explained by "rational" factors such as a growing population, increased organizational efficiency, or new technologies. Instead, bubbles expand because people are *persuaded* that some fundamental change has taken place, a change that heralds a new age. Although speculators pursuing "get rich schemes" are present during the expansion of every bubble, most of the people who buy into a bubble are not being irrational. People see others purchase an asset whose value is increasing, and are exposed to rhetoric that extols the virtues of the asset and confidently predicts that the surge in value will continue (Posner, 2010, 28, 37). As the bubble expands, people whose incomes depend on increasing stock prices or other symbolic measures of economic health exaggerate the positives and obscure the negatives. For example, in both of the cases we will examine in the rest of this chapter – Enron in 2001 and the housing and banking industry in 2007 – the business press *and* government officials whose jobs involve setting economic policy touted the growth potential of these organizations *even after* they declared bankruptcy.

Since a certain type of investment is gaining value, it attracts more new investors. But, if it begins to lose value, people are slow to abandon it (recall the concept of "too much invested to quit" from Chapter 10). This *asymmetry* blinds people – even professional economists who should know better – to the level of risk that an investment involves. Investors become "irrationally exuberant," to use former Federal Reserve Chairman Alan Greenspan's now infamous term, and begin to take on far more debt and risk than they should. As stock prices and real estate values soar, people begin to feel secure and optimistic, even though their new-found wealth is only "on paper." They begin to purchase other assets, and to take on additional debt, and invest in riskier ventures that offer even greater returns because they assume that the good times will continue to roll. Eventually, calmer voices point out that there is a significant and growing gap between the market value of an asset and tangible measures of its value, but their cautionary statements are dismissed as the rantings of "alarmists, prophets of doom, naysayers, sourpuses, attention-seekers."[28] In theory, government regulations and other constraints on investments (for example, down payment requirements for obtaining a mortgage) will prevent bubbles from forming and government agencies such as the Treasury Department will alter monetary policy to slow or stop the downward cycle. But, regulators also can fall prey to irrational exuberance during times of rapid growth, and politicians tend to pressure them into forgoing actions that might suppress the boom – no one wants to touch the geese that are laying what seem to be golden eggs, even if they are rotten. At some point, the bubble bursts – because of external events, or because the number of new investors has fallen to such a level that the bubble collapses under its own weight, or for any number of other reasons – and the economy begins to slow. The value of investments falls, especially those that made up the bubble. People start to feel poorer and/or begin to fear the future and stop consuming. This reduces the demand on which the economy relies, initiating a vicious downward cycle. As the layers of the economy start peeling off, people begin to default on their debts, which reveals the excessive risk levels that exist in the economy, and uncovers ethically or legally questionable actions that were overlooked during the boom. Suddenly, the system seems to be corrupt, trust plummets, and the downturn accelerates.

After the bubble bursts, it becomes clear that the naysayers were correct. Government agencies may attempt to stop the decline by reducing interest rates and using other strategies to free up money needed for economic growth. But frightened consumers are unlikely to increase their spending, and bankers whose institutions are on the verge of bankruptcy because they have taken on too much risk are unlikely to make loans, since doing so would increase that risk. Ironically, everyone acts in ways that are *individually* (albeit boundedly) rational. Savings rates skyrocket, which further reduces economic demand, and perpetuates the downward cycle (economists call these processes the **paradox of thrift**). In some declines, people who still have jobs and/or sufficient savings to feel secure notice that prices are falling, so they delay purchases until prices seem to have reached the lowest possible level (**deflationary psychology**). The downward cycle continues. The recession pushes some organizations to the edge of bankruptcy, something that would hasten the decline and/or deepen the depression. If the bubble is in a peripheral part of the economy (e.g., the dot.com stock crash of 1999), the damage may be contained and monetary policy may stem the decline. In these cases the recession may be mild and brief. But, if it is in the core sector of an economy, for example banking and finance, the decline can be protracted and deep. Under those circumstances, government officials may be faced with an unenviable choice between letting the decline continue until the economy corrects itself or "bail out" failing or threatened institutions. Allowing the decline to continue would be consistent with the "creative destruction" aspect of free market fundamentalism, but the economic pain that would ensue would be politically disastrous. Bailouts are politically unpalatable, and risk creating **moral hazards** (situations "in which one person makes the decision about how much risk to take, while someone else bears the cost if things go badly").[29] But bailouts may be seen as the lesser to two very bad evils, which explains why politicians rail against them in their public rhetoric, but enact them anyway. If the organizations that are on the brink are so large that their bankruptcy would seriously damage the overall economy, or so interconnected that their loss would initiate a chain of other bankruptcies (like a row of dominoes falling down), or are so politically powerful that they can dictate policy, decision makers may conclude that a bailout is their only viable option.[30]

Creating a Fraud-Inducing System, I: Incentives

In the United States, managers and executives long have had a privileged position. Beginning with scientific management (recall Chapter 3), managers have commanded high levels of power and compensation based on their presumed superior expertise. The assumptions that "What's good for corporations is good for the United States" and "What's good for managers is good for everyone else" have long been taken for granted by members of Western cultures, especially the United States. As a result, US firms have a far larger number of managers relative to nonmanagers, and a much bigger gap between managerial compensation and worker compensation, than other industrialized nations. But, during the 1980s and 1990s, CEOs were elevated to the status of cultural icons (Deetz, 1992; Gordon, 1996; Seeger, 1986). According to the leadership theories dominant during those decades, managers monitor environmental pressures and changes and adapt their firms, and they do so in spite of imperfect information, political constraints, organizational inertia, "heavy opposition and seemingly bleak odds." It is for that reason that "top executives matter"; indeed, they are heroic if not divine:

> These illusions are furthered by organizational folklore. . . . [O]rganizations actively foster beliefs in the control exercised by managers. . . . Efforts associated with successful outcomes tend to be more popular stories. These stories focus on the successful outcome as if it were an inevitable outcome of individual and organizational actions, ignoring many likely (but not experienced) paths toward failure.[31]

While the ideology of managerial heroism was being solidified, two changes were made in the structures that influenced their power and compensation. First, a new industry of "compensation consultants" was created, whose income was based on a percentage of the income granted their clients by boards of directors. Until the 1980s, boards compared executive salaries to the incomes of other employees within their companies. Although the gap between executive salaries and those of non-executive employees was much greater in the United States than in other countries (a ratio of around 150:1 compared to ratios one-tenth as large in the other major economies), internal comparisons served as a constraint. But, during the 1980s, compensation consultants persuaded boards to compare their executives' salaries with those of other executives. Bidding wars began, much like those that take place among media stars and professional athletes, but with no salary caps or revenue sharing rules. Since compensation consultants are paid on a percentage basis, and since boards of directors tend to be composed of executives from other firms, whose incomes would rise as the incomes of other executives rose, the sky quickly became the limit. By 2010, the ratio of executive compensation to non-executive workers increased to more than 500:1 in general and more than 1000:1 in Fortune 100 firms.

It soon became clear that there was little relationship between corporate performance and executive compensation. As a result, there was a great deal of pressure to tie compensation to the value of a company's stock, on the somewhat erroneous assumption that stock prices provided an accurate estimate of a company's net worth.[32] As a result, by 1999, more than 60 percent of CEOs' compensation came from stock and stock options. However, basing executive compensation on stock values has three unintended consequences – it encourages managers to ignore or deemphasize the interests of stakeholders other than stockholders (employees, the communities within which a corporation operates, and so on); it gives them incentives to sacrifice long-term organizational stability and growth for short-term stock appreciation; and it encourages them to exaggerate the value of a company's assets and underestimate or hide the size of its liabilities and debts. The Shell Oil scandal of 2004, in which executives knowingly overestimated the company's proven reserves by 4 *billion* barrels provided the paradigm case of the former; the machinations of Citibank and Bank of America leading up to the Great Recession illustrated the latter.[33] The system that emerged encouraged executives to take inordinate risks and, in extreme cases, engage in unethical and illegal conduct. Honest managers were swept up by the need to produce rising profits and stock values just to keep their jobs, and by the fortunes they could amass through what came to be called "creative accounting." Dishonest managers had an almost unlimited opportunity to create an illusion of value (Johnson & Kwak. 2010; also see Cadette, 2002; Madrick, 2003). As a result, Harvard economist Michael Jensen concluded that "when a company's stock is overvalued it sets in motion a set of organizational pressures that can destroy rather than create shareholder value."

Creating a Fraud-Inducing System, II: Relaxing Constraints

Changes in incentive systems encouraged the wave of unethical and/or illegal executive activities that engulfed the United States at the beginning of the twenty-first century. But, incentive systems did not allow them to happen. Understanding the economic events of the 2000s should start where this book started, with an analysis of the rhetoric of *laissez-faire* capitalism. By the end of the 1970s federal policy was controlled by people who believed in free market fundamentalism. During the next 30 years, power shifted to advocates of an extreme version of the theory, one that saw government action as inherently objectionable. One effect of this shift was a wave of deregulation that started with the airlines in 1978 under President Jimmy Carter. More and more of the US economy was removed from federal regulation, and in those sectors that still were regulated, government oversight and control was scaled back. Proponents of deregulation justified it in familiar terms – markets automatically correct themselves through the "invisible hand," and government intervention in markets is inevitably harmful.

In addition, they claimed that globalization, technological development, and "high-speed management" had combined to create a fundamentally "new" economy, one that cannot function effectively if saddled with the constraints that were imposed on organizations of the "old economy." Government regulation makes little sense when capital flows across political boundaries at the speed of light, production facilities can readily be moved from country to country as multinational firms search for the most profitable environmental laws, regulatory environments, and labor arrangements, and corporations are organized in forms that were not even imagined when regulatory schemes were created. Indeed, it is *futile* for governments to try to resist the power of the international markets, and their efforts to do so *inevitably* reduce the competitiveness of their firms, thereby disadvantaging their own citizens. One might expect that the insider trading scandals of the mid-1980s, the Savings and Loan (S&L) crisis and bailout of the late 1980s, and the bankruptcies at the start of the new century would have tempered this move toward wholesale deregulation. But, these events were stressful and complex. This combination creates high levels of uncertainty, and in uncertain times the simplicity and certainty of ideology is comforting. Instead of moderating the shift, these events seem to have generated a caricature of *laissez-faire* theory, one that ignored the complications suggested by behavioral economics, the paradox of thrift, and other complications. The Great Recession, Judge Posner concludes, has shown "how ideology can distort economic policy" (2009: 17).

Deregulation rhetoric allowed Congress to legitimize actions that had been advocated by corporate lobbyists and supported by extensive campaign contributions. By the time the economic boom of the 1990s started, there was a patchwork quilt of policies and practices in place that allowed organizations to exploit deregulation in some sectors, avoid sectors that still were regulated, and pressure regulators, legislators, and local, state, and federal executives to create favorable rules and regulations in others. Indeed, the genius of management at Enron, and later Citigroup, Bank of America, Washington Mutual, and a host of other firms which contributed to the economic crises of the new century involved the ability to engage in **regulatory arbitrage**, the strategic maneuver around and among regulatory agencies until the weakest regulator is located.[34] After 2000, politicians weakened almost all regulations and/or regulatory agencies to such an extent that arbitrage was no longer necessary. For example, during 2000 and 2001, the SEC, which regulates the investment industry, proposed banning accounting firms which audit a company's books from signing consulting contracts with those same firms. Critics had long argued that the potential income from consulting contracts, granted by upper management with little or no oversight, would discourage accounting firms from revealing questionable accounting practices in their audits. Enron CEO Ken Lay wrote to then-SEC Chairman Arthur Levitt in opposition to the proposed limits, basing his position on standard claims of efficiency: "Enron has found that its 'integrated audit' arrangement to be more efficient and cost-effective than the more traditional roles of separate internal and external auditing function."

Congresspersons, most of whom had received major campaign funding from the accounting and investment industries, forced the SEC to back down by threatening to cut its already inadequate funding. The public rationale for each of these changes was the argument that markets are efficiently self-regulating and that government interference in managerial prerogatives would reduce organizational efficiency, increase costs, and stifle creativity.[35] Chairman Levitt, realizing that the SEC's situation was impossible, resigned. He was replaced by Christopher Cox, who was so convinced that markets could be self-regulating that the "Securities and Exchange Commission could go to sleep. And go to sleep it did. . . . Cox has been roundly criticized for shrinking, undermining, and demoralizing the commission's enforcement staff."

While regulators were falling asleep, corporations used litigation and political influence to weaken other forms of external control. The *Lampf* (1991) decision denied private investors the right to bring lawsuits against employees and executives who aid and abet a fraud, even if they do so knowingly; *Reves v. Ernst & Young* (1993) declared that external advisors (primarily accounting firms that audit company books and law firms that provide legal advice to them) could not be held liable in fraud cases; *Raab v. General Physics* (1993) created highly specific evidence requirements that made it virtually impossible for outside stakeholders to demonstrate that fraud had taken place; and *Central Bank of Denver, N.A. v. First Interstate Bank of Denver, N.A.* (1994), which ruled that private plaintiffs could not sue under the Securities and Exchange Act.[36] Each of these restrictions was written into law in the 1995 Private Securities and Litigation Reform Act. This legislation was passed over President Clinton's veto after an intense campaign led by Democratic National

Chairman and Senator Christopher Dodd (CT), who received almost a quarter of a million dollars in donations from the accounting industry during the 1995–1996 election cycle, even though he was not up for reelection. The primary justifications offered for these changes was that litigation had gotten out of hand and was destroying necessary capital formation; companies were routinely being sued for stock declines even if no fraud or malfeasance was involved; frivolous lawsuits were rampant and expensive in spite of recent reforms; and companies were being forced to settle groundless suits in order to avoid the costs of litigation. Although there was little or no empirical evidence to support any of these claims, they were persuasive because they are consistent with the free market, fundamentalist view that no outside forces should be allowed to interfere with managerial prerogatives.

Four years later, Congress passed the Gramm-Leach-Bailey Act, which further weakened regulation of financial institutions and repealed the Glass-Steagal Act. During the Great Depression of the 1930s, Congress concluded that one of the key factors in turning a serious recession into a depression were a series of "runs" on banks, during which customers attempted to withdraw more cash than the banks had on hand. In response it passed laws that provided a government guarantee for deposits in certain accounts. The rationale was partly economic – without such a guarantee people would not deposit funds in banks, so there would be no money available to be loaned to businesses and thus no way of getting out of the depression – and partly philosophical – small depositors had done nothing to create the depression and should not be punished for decisions made by others. But, such a government guarantee would be foolish unless banks were tightly regulated in ways that minimized the risks involved in their use of guaranteed deposits. In particular, they could not be involved in the stock market and could not trade mortgages and mortgage-based securities. The repeal of Glass-Steagal eliminated the regulations but not the deposit insurance program – "deposits that were insured by the Federal Deposit Insurance Corporation could be invested in risky assets, with the assurance that losses would be made up by the FDIC." In short, moral hazard was written into law. This was only one of many regulatory battles fought during the 1990s and 2000s, all with the same outcome. In the fundamentalist climate of the 1990s they were easily rationalized.[37]

The Enron Saga

Enron was born in the 1984 merger of two traditional, rather boring, energy companies, Houston Natural Gas and Internorth. In order to complete the merger and gain control of the company Kenneth Lay, a Horatio Alger story from rural Missouri, had to defeat a competing bid by Irwin Jacobs. To do so he used funds in his company's employee pension funds to purchase the necessary stock. Although perfectly legal, the maneuver was a harbinger of things to come. Lay knew that the deregulation mania of the 1980s created an opportunity for Enron to move into a much more exciting, and potentially much more lucrative arena of energy trading. In order to do so he hired Jeffrey Skilling, who knew that the first thing Enron needed was capital, and in order to get capital he needed to improve the company's apparent strength.

One way to do this was to persuade regulators to change existing accounting rules. Accounting is a rhetorical act. Manipulating accounting results is an especially powerful form of rhetoric because they *seem* to be objective, scientific, and reliable (Roslender, 1992; also see Powers and Laughlin, 1992). Executives can get by with constructing a favorable-but-misleading image of their firms as long as their internal accountants, external auditors, the investment community, and regulatory agencies accept their estimates. In 1993, after extensive lobbying by Enron and its auditor, Arthur Andersen, the SEC officially allowed the company to shift to a form of accounting that previously had been limited to tightly regulated financial organizations. Called "mark-to-market," the system allows companies to creatively adjust the value that is claimed for different years of multiyear contracts. The rationale offered by Enron and Andersen was a simple application of the ideology of the "new economy." Because no energy trading company had ever used the system, no outsiders really knew how to evaluate the contracts made with it. But, Enron insiders knew, and profited handsomely from that knowledge. For example, on a single transaction, a $1.3 billion contract with the New York Power Authority, Skilling received a $65 million bonus because mark-to-market accounting allowed him to book most of the gain on a 23-year-long deal in one quarter. Under the previous accounting system, his bonus would have been less than 1/23 that amount (Bryce, 2002).

The second strategy used by Enron's management involved derivatives, financial contracts between two or more parties that managers are able to keep off of their companies' official books. Before 1992 derivatives were limited to quasi-public agencies like the New York Mercantile Exchange and the Chicago Board of Trade, which were closely regulated by state agencies and the Commodity Futures Trading Commission (CFTC). In 1992 Enron asked the CFTC's chair, Wendy Gramm, to grant it an exemption that would allow it to operate its own unregulated energy trading market using its own standards and without CFTC oversight. During her last days as CFTC chair, Gramm granted the exemption, and included a clause that eliminated CFTC oversight of energy traders even when contracts were designed to defraud or mislead buyers. The exception was written into law in the Commodity Futures Modernization Act of 2000, sponsored by Senator Phil Gramm, Wendy's husband. The legislation passed the Senate on a unanimous vote after virtually no debate and was signed into law by President Clinton on December 13, 2002. The rationale for both actions was the argument that regulatory structures needed to be adapted to the new global economy. After her resignation from the CFTC, Ms. Gramm joined Enron's board of directors at a salary of $300,000 per year.

Changes were made within Enron as well. At Harvard Business School and McKinsey & Co. Consulting, Skilling had been trained to use a reward system originally developed by General Electric. Each year the various divisions of the company are labeled as "stars," "dogs," or "cash cows," based on their reported earnings for the year. Their budgets for the next year are adjusted accordingly, and if the "dogs" do not show improvement they are eliminated. The system forces each division to be accountable to upper management, and each employee to be accountable to his or her supervisor, but it also encourages short-term thinking and fraud. Labeled "rank and yank," the new reward system treated short-term on-paper profits as the only basis for evaluating employees, and it also demanded complete conformity: "because the rank-and-yank system was both arbitrary and subjective, it was easily used by managers to reward blind loyalty and quash brewing dissent."[38] Of course, there was dissent, but dissenters soon resigned or were removed (recall Chapter 8). Once "old-style" managers like Rich Kinder and J. Clifford Baxter, who valued positive manager–employee relationships and opposed questionable accounting practices, left the firm, there were no internal limits to fraud. In 1998 Enron discovered the internet and internet trading, a sector of the economy where there also were no controls.

After 1998, Enron's management was spectacularly successful at creating an illusion of success. In spite of failing projects on four continents, Enron was the darling of the investment community and became a symbol of the new economy. Even after its losses started to mount, investment analysts remained loyal. There were a few doubters in the investment community, but Enron management dealt as forcefully with them as it dealt with internal dissenters. Its artificially elevated stock prices became the primary form of collateral used in its deals. For a year or so after the dot.com stock bubble burst in 1999 and 2000, Enron's management was able to maintain the illusion. But, by late 2000 its stock price started to decline, and the house of cards started to collapse. In August, 2001 Skilling resigned, taking his multimillion dollar stock options with him. Kenneth Lay immediately deluged Enron's employees with emails telling them that he thought the company's stock was still an "incredible value," although he had been systematically selling his for some time. In January, 2002, Sherron Watkins sent an anonymous memo to Kenneth Lay expressing her fear that Skilling's departure would lead to a full-scale investigation of the company's accounting practices. Fastow attempted to have Watkins fired for her prophetic dissent, but failed. By mid-October Enron's stock had lost 80 percent of its value, but 10 of the 17 investment analysts who were experts on the firm still rated it as a "strong buy." In fact, only Carol Coale of Prudential Securities advised her investors to sell the stock. On October 22 the SEC announced that it was starting to investigate some of the deals made by Andrew Fastow; two days later, he was fired. Lay desperately sought a bailout, but neither his old friends in the Bush administration, nor the investment community would help. On December 2, Enron filed for bankruptcy protection under Chapter 11 of the federal bankruptcy code. It immediately fired 4000 workers; other firings soon followed. Heavily invested in Enron stock, almost all lost their life savings, and their retirement plans. Outside investors also sustained heavy losses. Enron's management had brilliantly manipulated gaps in the US regulatory system to build a house of cards. Their political connections allowed them to quietly weaken the regulatory system that had been seriously undermined during the 1990s. Their public rhetoric also was compelling. It drew on the faith in "progress" and in managerial saviors that long has characterized mainstream US culture, while articulating the tenets of free market fundamentalism and the promises of the "new economy." Ironically, its political connections eventually became its undoing, because once those connections became public knowledge, its allies could not justify bailing Enron out.

Bankruptcies at other large firms soon followed, including the largest in US history (Worldcom). With polls indicating that upwards of 80 percent of Americans supported reform, upcoming elections at the state and congressional levels, and a plethora of proposed "solutions" to issues of corporate malfeasance, 2002 would seem to have all of the ingredients needed for a major change in US regulatory policies (*New York Times*, Editorial Board, February 2, 2002). However, many business leaders argued that no new laws were necessary. For example, Tom Donohue, president of the US Chamber of Commerce, claimed,

> The issue facing Congress and the administration is simple: Will government actions and rhetoric make things more certain or more uncertain? Will business reforms be given a chance to work, or will there be more beating up and piling on? Will government policies make business leaders so risk-averse that we lose our creativity, innovation, and competitiveness?

Grady Rosier, chairman of the National Association of Wholesale Distributors, echoed Donohue's comments, warning policy makers to "resist throwing the baby out with the bath water" through excessive regulation.[39] In short, increased government regulation would inevitably have perverse economic consequences.

Some legal reforms were enacted, but attention soon shifted away from Congress to the criminal justice system. Because US society is so highly individualistic, social problems usually are viewed as the results of individual failings. From welfare reform to motorcycle helmet laws to health policy, individuals rather than systems are held responsible for social ills. During the debate over corporate governance at Enron, systemic problems were individualized through the metaphor of "a few bad apples." Everyone involved vowed to see that wrongdoers would serve hard time. Prosecutors arranged to arrest criminals in front of television cameras, timed to coincide with morning television news shows. Seeing executives being led away in handcuffs is a powerful form of political-legal theater, but it also serves to assuage popular anger and undermine pressure for reform. Perhaps most important, it ignores the simple fact that all but a small fraction of the actions leading to the "corporate meltdown" were perfectly legal, as Kenneth Lay, Jeffrey Skilling, and Andrew Fastow consistently argued in their defense. For politicians, the crisis soon passed. Poll data indicated that the issue of corporate corruption had no impact on the 2002 elections, even in Houston, Texas, where the largest number of people lost their jobs. Enron disappeared from the television screens, except for an occasional indictment, plea bargain, or conviction. The 2002 Corporate Accountability Act (nicknamed Sarbanes-Oxley after its sponsors) plugged a number of loopholes in US accounting law, and increased the enforcement budget of the SEC, but not to pre-1990 levels. Individuals did go to jail. But, the system that generated the crisis changed little. The key structural changes that allowed the management of Enron and other firms to hide their debts and exaggerate their value – strategic selection of accounting systems and the use of derivatives – were not changed.[40] Policy makers *should* have learned that the combination of an asset bubble and deregulation invites risk taking and allows fraud, just as policy makers *should* have learned from the Savings and Loan crisis of the 1980s that the combination of deposit insurance and deregulation creates serious moral hazards.[41] But, with the rapidly growing political influence of the financial industry, policy makers had a great deal of incentive to not learn.

Creating the Great Recession

The modest regulatory reform after the corporate meltdown of 2000–2001 did nothing to deal with the recession that had resulted from the bursting of the dot.com bubble. To deal with it, the Federal Reserve used its control over the money supply to drive interest rates down in hope of stimulating lending and economic activity. With falling interest rates, US consumers, who already were saving very little, had even less reason to save. As the economy recovered, they had even more reason to spend. Much of this spending focused on housing, traditionally a safe investment, and long touted as the key symbol of the "American dream." The now largely unregulated banking industry developed creative ways for people to purchase homes, people who previously would not have qualified for mortgages. In the process, they took on additional debt, both in absolute terms and relative to their other assets. With rapidly increasing home values, especially in California, Nevada, and Florida, mortgagees felt wealthy and secure, and increased their spending on other things (including furniture, appliances, and so on to outfit their new homes). But **leverage** (the ratio of debt to assets) is dangerous, both for banks and for consumers.

During the mid-2000s some creative accountants figured out that a bank could reduce its risk by bundling its mortgages together and issue stock that used the mortgages as collateral. If all of the mortgages had been high quality, this would not have created serious problems. But, some banks started packaging subprime mortgages (the ones made to people who should never have been allowed, much less encouraged, to take on long-term debt in order to buy a house) with good ones, much like unscrupulous butchers who put beautiful pieces of meat on top of some really unattractive ones and wrap them together in order to fool the customer. Since some of these packages were worth a billion dollars or more, a lot of very risky mortgages could be included in the packages without anyone noticing. Since the financial institutions that purchased these packages planned to sell them to other institutions, making massive profits through the transaction, they had little incentive to look closely at the packages of mortgages. In theory, **ratings agencies** are supposed to protect buyers by labeling bundles of financial assets as A++, B+, and so on, but in this case they failed to do their jobs. To make matters worse, bankers decided they could reduce the risk in their portfolios even more if they could persuade insurance companies, which are even more loosely regulated than banks, to offer policies that guaranteed the value of these bundles of mortgages. The insurance companies (the biggest one was AIG) acted as if the bundles were safe, both because they had been fooled and because they were going to make so much money from the policies that *they* had little incentive to look at the bundles very closely. Since these insurance policies (which were called **credit default swaps**) protected the bankers, they were able to take on even greater risks which paid even greater returns. In the process, the value of bank stocks skyrocketed, and since executive compensation was tightly linked to stock value, the risk takers made millions, sometimes billions. Eventually even they did not even know how much risk they had taken on. Nobel Prize-winning economist Paul Krugman concludes,

> [W]hy did the bankers take on so much risk? Because it was in their self-interest to do so. By increasing leverage – that is, by making risky investments with borrowed money – banks could increase their short-term profits. And these short-term profits, in turn, were reflected in immense personal bonuses. If the concentration of risk in the banking sector increased the danger of a systemwide financial crisis, well, that wasn't the bankers' problem. (2010)

In the meantime, the largest banks grew even larger, and more tightly interconnected, both within the United States and internationally. In 1995 the six largest US banks were worth an amount equal to less than twenty percent of the Gross Domestic Product; in 2009 their value exceeded 60 percent of the GDP. Economists disagree about whether it is the size of the banks or their interconnectedness that makes them "too big to fail" (TBTF), but they agree that if one of these behemoths ever goes under, it could take the world economy with it. Being TBTF is a wonderful thing for banks and their executives, but it creates three major problems for society – it (1) virtually guarantees that government (that is, taxpayers) will bail them out when they do fail, which (2) creates even more severe *moral hazards*, thereby leading to increased risk-taking and increased likelihood of future bailouts, regardless of politicians' "never again" rhetoric claims, which (3) is bad for competition and thus bad for the economy. Giant, bailed-out banks are less risky than other institutions, so they are able to borrow money at lower interest rates than smaller, risk-aversive banks. And, ironically, they often use that money to buy the smaller, well-managed banks because doing so makes the big, bailed-out ones look more secure to investors. Stock values and executive compensation increase, and so on. Today, even the government officials whose actions and inaction helped create the crisis recognize the problem. Federal Reserve's Ben Bernanke told the Financial Crisis Inquiry Commission that "if the crisis has a single lesson, it is that the too-big-to-fail problem must be solved." Ironically, Bernanke's comments came a week after President Obama signed a financial reform act that did nothing to solve the TGTF problem. Neither did it impose interest rate caps on credit cards, which restrain risk taking, or reverse the excessive deregulation passed by Congress in 1999 and 2000, or limit executive bonuses (even for bailed-out banks) as some European countries have done.[42] The system, with its incentives and (weak) constraints, continues.

CONCLUSIONS AND IMPLICATIONS FOR ETHICS

At the beginning of this section, we suggested that one of our goals was to highlight the complexity of organizational ethics. The primary complication involves the nature of human action in organizational settings. One perspective *individualizes* actions and ethics. Especially attractive to members of individualistic cultures such as the United States, this view locates ethics in the motivations, self-discipline, and personal morality of actors.[43] Good people do good things, even in situations in which it would be economically rational not to; "bad apples" do evil, self-serving things even in situations that encourage them to act rightly. But, this perspective is problematic in (at least) two ways. First, it raises perhaps unanswerable questions about *what* and *how much* an individual should be expected to sacrifice in situations that allow and/or encourage unethical action. Are individuals required to act ethically when doing so almost certainly will cost them their jobs or careers (recall the discussion of whistleblowers in Chapter 8), making it less likely that other employees will act ethically? Second, by focusing attention away from systems, individualizing ethics allows systems that encourage unethical actions to continue unchanged, as in the case of policy makers' tepid response to the scandals of 2000–2002.

The opposite perspective *systematizes* ethics by focusing on the incentives and constraints that are included in organizational and societal systems. But doing so treats human beings as automatons whose actions are determined by situational factors, thereby robbing them of the opportunity to make meaningful choices, and the responsibility for the choices they make. Moreover, members of politically powerful organizations often strategically act in ways that create systemic constraints – the regulatory changes that allowed Enron's management to create a highly profitable house of cards, or those that led to the Great Recession resulted from conscious, sustained, strategic action that was intended to allow people to stretch the laws in ways that promised massive personal and organizational gains. In saying this, we do not want to minimize the costs of these actions – the end of the dot.com bubble cost US households more than $5 trillion in lost incomes and investments, and the Great Recession will cost innocent people many times that amount. But, surely, judgments of a person's or organization's or an industry's ethics must focus both on systems and individuals.

A second complication involves the concept of multiple stakeholders. Even Milton Friedman's (in)famous dictum that the only obligation a manager has is to maximize returns to his or her company's owners (individuals or shareholders), recognizes that doing so will have different effects of other stakeholders, and on the society within which the organization operates. For example, during the 1980s regulatory changes allowed banks to take on more financial risk than they previously could. As a result, they were able to offer various products that paid more interest than still-tightly regulated savings and loans, which quickly started losing customers who moved their funds to bank money market accounts and other products. In the process, the S&Ls' reserves shrank because they had made long-term commitments in the form of 15-year or 30-year mortgages. Federal deposit insurance (through the FSLIC) protected the savings still in the S&Ls, but many of the companies themselves faced bankruptcy, which would have been devastating to employees, managers, their families, and the communities, including small businesses, which relied on them. Many S&L managers responded by taking on greater risks in hopes of reviving their organizations. Some succeeded, and made themselves rich in the process; some didn't, especially in California, where a housing bubble was about to burst, and in Texas, whose economy was about to suffer from a massive drop in oil prices. Some stakeholders, primarily the taxpayers who funded the S&L bailout, suffered. We do not mean to minimize these costs – the bailout cost around $700 billion in 2008 dollars, ironically the exact figure of the TARP bank bailout enacted in the waning months of the Bush administration – but every action taken by organizational decision makers affects multiple stakeholders, and does so in different, and often unanticipated ways. S&L officers did little to foster the globalization of finance after the fall of the Iron Curtain, and little to foster deregulation of banks. Each of these steps was largely outside of their control, but they significantly increased the competition and risks they faced, and did so at the worst possible point in the economic cycle. Surely, ethical judgments must recognize that every action influences different stakeholders in different ways.

NOTES

1 This paraphrase of Professor Brief's comments appeared in Blalock (1996, D3). Also see Cheney, Lair, Ritz, and Kendell (2010); Fox (2009); and Posner (2009, 2010).

2 See Menn (1996), Murphy (2009), and "Toyota Pays" (2010). For overall analyses, see Amatai Etzioni, cited in Gorman (1989); Hosmer (1987); and Wyatt (2010).

3 See Barker (1976). For an updated analysis of the role that rhetoric plays in politics, see Stone (1997). For a detailed application of Aristotle's ethical perspective to contemporary organizational life, see Rowland and Womack (1985), and Cheney, Lair, Ritz, and Kendall (2010).

4 For applications to both organizational and political leadership, see Grint (2001, 2005).

5 See Bogle (2002, 1) and Moyers (2002). A transcript of this interview is available on the PBS website (www.pbs.org). Former US Senator William Proxmire estimated the payoff from political donations at a much higher level, 1000 percent. See his introduction to Stern (1992); also see Palast (2001). Although these figures seem fanciful, and neither Bogle nor Proxmire explained how they developed them, the 2008–2009 financial industry bailout makes them seem credible. The ratio of six months of lobbying and one year of campaign contributions to the size of the bailout (assuming that the *lowest* estimate – $2.1 trillion – is used) is 4000:1; the ratio of campaign contributions alone to the bailout is 1000:1, precisely as Senator Proxmire predicted. Of course, these figures do not include subsidies and tax breaks granted to the financial services industry by the federal government through normal legislative procedures. For an extended analysis, see Conrad (in press).

6 For a thoughtful analysis of the paradox of externalized costs for corporations, see Leonhardt (2011).

7 See Whalen (2007), Backman (1999), and La Porta, Lopez-de-Silanes, and Vishny (2003). George Soros (2000) makes a similar argument about Russia.

8 This very, very brief summary of Smith's very complex ideas is based on our reading of Smith's work and on six secondary sources: Cropsey (2001), Farrell (2002), Gore (2001), Muller (1993), Peters (1995), and Werhane (1991). For an analysis of the tragedy of the commons, see Hardin (1968).

9 For an analysis of how the US Red Cross dealt with this issue, see Williams (2001).

10 See Peterson and Norton (2007). For an analysis of the role and importance of civil society, see Lewis (2005).

11 More than 100 studies have examined this relationship. The results have been mixed, but as a group they suggest that socially responsible firms perform no worse than non-socially responsible firms, especially over time (Gagne, Gavin, and Tully, 2005; Simpson and Kohers, 2002; Steiner and Steiner, 2005; Zadek, 2004). However, it is clear that a large (around 80 percent) and increasing percentage of corporate leaders believe in the business case for CSR (PriceWaterhouseCoopers, 2003; Rochlin, Witter, Monaghan, and Murray, 2005).

12 The two quotations are from Ganesh (2007, 385) and Willers (1994, 1146). Also see Peterson and Norton (2007), and Cheney *et al.* (2010, esp. chap. 5).

13 Marcus and Goodman (1998). For general treatments of crisis management, see Barton (2001), Benoit (1995), Coombs (2007), and Herit (2007).

14 Sydney Finkelstein, management professor at Dartmouth University, could find only one instance in which the CEO of a Fortune 500 firm offered a full apology in more than 100 cases he studied (cited in Martin and Maynard, 2010). For extended analyses of the tension between image management and litigation, see Cohen (2002), Herit (2007), Llewellyn (2007), Seeger and Hipfel (2007), and Kellerman (2006).

15 See Benoit (1995). This section is based on Conrad (in press).

16 See Toffler (1986). When managers *do* talk about ethics, it usually is to avoid taking responsibility for ethical choices (Seeger, 1992). Gary Weaver, Linda Klebe Trevino, and Philip Cochran (1999) analyze this "decoupling" process as a managerial strategy that is used to avoid responsibility. Excellent examples of these processes are available in Christiansen and Hanson (1996), Elsbach and Sutton (1992), and Patterson and Allen (1997). For analyses of general processes that make people feel that ethics "is someone else's job," see Scott and Hart (1979, 1989). See Cheney *et al.* (2010, esp. chap. 5). For an analysis of the metaphor's use in Germany, see Hartz and Steger (2010).

17 There are, however, two risks involved in using regulators as scapegoats. The first is that some audiences may realize that organizations exercise substantial influence over regulations and regulatory agencies, something that we will discuss later in this chapter. Trying to shift blame to regulators can remind audiences of this cozy relationship, and in some cases may force the regulators to attack the company's credibility or begin to actively regulate the industry in order to protect their legitimacy. The second risk is that their rhetoric may inadvertently encourage policy makers to increase regulation of the industry. Corporations usually are able to block increased regulation (recall Chapter 4), but doing so may become expensive, in terms of both lobbying costs and an image of social responsibility (see Baker, Conrad, Cudahy, and Willyard, 2009; Conrad, Baker, Cudahy, and Willyard, 2010; Posner, 2009, 2010; Dunham and Powell, 2010; Johnson and Kwak, 2010; Martin and Maynard, 2010).

18 See Hobbs (1995). For an extended analysis of bolstering and other apologia that do not actually involve apologies, see Rowland and Jerome (2004). For additional case studies in the strategies that organizational rhetors use to maintain the images of their firms, see Toth and Heath (1992), and Toth, Heath, and Waymer (2010). For an extended summary of available strategies, see Charles Conrad (in press, esp. chap. 5).

19 See Eichenwald (1996), Walsh (1996), Sixel (1996), and Bryant (1996). For an extended analysis, see Brinson and Benoit (1999). For many similar examples, see Benoit (1995), Coombs (2007), Herit (2007), and May (2006).

20 See Cheney *et al.* (2010), Sims (1992), and Jackall (1983). For overviews of organizational image management, see Botan and Taylor (2004), and Leeper (2001).

21 For excellent case studies of organizations dealing with multiple audiences, see Allen and Caillouet (1994), Benoit (1995), and Kostova and Zaheer (1999). Two multiple-stakeholder models have been developed by Stan Deetz (1995) and by Freeman (1984). For an extension of Freeman's model, see Frooman (1999).

22 See Diosonopolous and Goldzwig (1992), Farrell and Goodnight (1981), Crable and Vibbert (1983), Potter (1992), Stutts and Barker (1999, 209–244), and Diosonopolous and Crable (1988).

23 See Wilson (1974, 137). The "classic" case studies in this debate involve the creation of the Interstate Commerce Commission and the Federal Aviation

Administration/Civil Aeronautics Board (see Kuttner, 1996). Also see Baker, Conrad, Cudahy, and Willyard (2009); and Llewellyn (2007). The Food and Drug Administration (FDA) emerged through a combination of these two processes. Regulation of drugs was motivated by pressure from physicians who were finding it difficult to compete with purveyors of "patent medicines." Today, one of the FDA's primary functions is to restrict procedures that typically are called "alternative medicine." Conversely, early regulations regarding food safety and preparation stemmed from popular outcry, originally encouraged by Upton Sinclair's book *The Jungle*. These included the Pure Food and Drug Act and the Meat Inspection Act of 1906; the Food, Drug, and Cosmetic Act of 1938; and the Kefauver drug probe of 1962.

24 See Baumgartner and Leech (1998), and Baumgartner, Berry, Jojracki, Kimball, and Leech (2009). A brief summary (with a somewhat inaccurate title) of the latter book is available in Burns (2010).

25 This section is based on Conrad and McIntush (2003), and Conrad (2011). Also see Baumgartner and Jones (1983), Baumgartner and Leech (1998), Baumgartner *et al.* (2009), and Stone (1997).

26 See "As Funds Gain, Scandal Concerns Fade" (2004, D3).

27 See Hall and Jones (1997), Mahon and McGowan (1997), and "Who Won Big in the Financial Bill," (2010).

28 See Posner (2009, 29). Excellent historical treatments of boom–bust cycles are available in Roy (1997) and in Kindleberger, Aliber, and Solow (2009).

29 See Krugman (2008, 63). Bank bailouts became federal policy in 1907, when the US Treasury bailed out J.P. Morgan, and have continued to the present. The most expensive were the Savings and Loan bailout of the late 1980s (by the Reagan and George H.W. Bush administrations), which cost approximately $700 billion in 2008 dollars (Krugman, 2008); the TARP bailout (by the George W. Bush administration); and multiple bailouts by the Obama administration, whose exact size is currently unknown. For analyses of the history of bailouts, see Bruner and Carr (2009), and Kindleberger, Aliber, and Solow (2009). By 2010, conservative judge and economist Richard Posner admitted that moral hazards are built into the corporate form – the concept of limited liability insulates managers from losses that might result from excessively risky actions, especially if they have constructed protective incentive systems (e.g., "golden parachutes"), and it limits the losses of stockholders (Posner, 2010: 93, 347).

30 Observers of the Great Recession have argued that all three factors led to the banking bailouts, although their focus differs. Liberal Nobel Prize-winning economist Paul Krugman and (somewhat surprising) conservative economist Richard Posner focus on size and interconnectednes (see Krugman, 2008; Posner, 2009, 2010), while former chief economist at the International Monetary Fund, Simon Johnson, attributes the bailouts by the Bush and Obama administrations to the political power of big banks (Johnson and Kwak, 2010).

31 See Levinthal and March (1993). For an extended analysis, see Conrad (2011), Child (1974), Thompson (1967), Hambrick (1994), Hambrick and Mason (1984), and Staw and Ross (1980).

32 See Leonhardt (2002). The interests of other stakeholders had been defined out of the equation by free market fundamentalism.

33 Excellent treatments of executive actions leading up to the 2000–2001 corporate meltdown include Altman (2002), Bogle (2002), Buffett (2002), and Blasi and Kruse (2002). The Shell Oil case is examined in Cummins and Beaserit (2005). Key sources for the origins of the Great Recession will be provided later in this chapter.

34 See Bryce (2002), Fusaro and Miller (2002), and Chan (2010). For a more general analysis, see Soros (1998) and Nobel Prize-winning economist George Stiglitz (2002).

35 See "Bigger than Enron" (2001) and Levitt (2002). The Center for Responsive Politics found that the accounting industry gave more than $50 million to candidates for federal offices during the 1990s, with 56 percent going to Republicans and 43 percent going to Democrats. However, these data are a bit misleading: At the beginning of the decade, these contributions were almost identical across party lines, but by 1999 Republican candidates were receiving about twice as much accounting industry money as Democratic candidates.

36 See "Bigger than Enron" (2001) and Levitt (2002). For an excellent summary of the Enron saga, see McMillan (2007).

37 The quotation is from Johnson and Kwak (2010, 134). Also see Lerach (1995) and Seligman (1994). It is important to not view these processes as limited only to the 1990s. Bryan Hall and Bryan Jones (1997) have shown that the business lobby has long been effective in blunting calls for increased regulation after periods of business malpractice. In addition, by arguing that the private sector and free market have a built-in

self-corrective mechanism, the SEC has repeatedly been able to avoid taking a more active regulatory role. Similarly, J.F. Mahon and Richard McGowan (1997) have demonstrated that the accounting industry has long been able to avoid increased government regulation and/or oversight by claiming that accounting practice is too complex and individualized for government to be able to effectively intervene in the industry.

38 See Fusaro and Miller (2002, 51–52). For an assessment of the GE system, see Conrad (1993). The best summary of Enron's lobbying activities is Bryce (2002).

39 Both comments are available in transcripts of the Panel on Economic Recovery and Job Creation (2002). For an extended analysis of the use of "bad apples" rhetoric to undermine systemic reform, see Cheney, Lair, Ritz, and Kendall (2010); for an analysis of its use in post-Enron reform efforts, see Conrad (2003, 2004).

40 See Oppel (2003), Thomas (2003), "Calpers Sues" (2003), *Wall Street Journal* (2003), Labaton (2004), McGeehan (2003a, 2003b), "Get Independents to Chair Boards" (2004), Eichenwald (2003), "Spitzer Threatens to Sue" (2003), and Kaplan (2004). For an assessment of business school ethics programs, see the "Forum: Teaching Business Ethically" (2003). Harvard's program is examined in Weisman (2004).

41 Even the S&L industry admitted this (see Strunk and Case, 1988). For broader analyses, see Black (2005), and Cottrell, Lawlor, and Wood (1995).

42 For a summary of the reforms and what they did not do, see Goodman (2010). Johnson and Kwak (2010) explain the bailout cycle clearly and persuasively. Alessandri and Haldane of the Bank of England have demonstrated that with each bailout (remember, the first bank bailout in the United States was in 1907), the "never again" rhetoric becomes less credible (2009). Baker and McArthur (2009) calculated the interest rate advantage that TBTF banks had after the Bush administration bailout at 0.78 percent, for a total advantage of $34 billion, accounting for roughly half of their profits during 2009. Summers's comments are available at Summers (2000); Bernanke's comments are available at Bernanke (2010). Also see Floyd Norris (2010).

43 For an excellent summary–analysis of ethical systems and their complexities, see Steve May (2012).

REFERENCES

Agle, B., Mitchell, R. and Sonnenfeld, J. (1999). "Who Matters to CEOs?" *Academy of Management Journal* 42: 507–525.

Alessandri, P. and Haldane, J. (2009). "Banking on the State." BIS Review 139. www.bis.org/review/r091111e.pdf.

Allen, M.W. and Caillouet, R. (1994). "Legitimation Endeavors." *Communication Monographs* 61: 44–62

Altman, D. (2002). "How to Tie Pay to Goals, Instead of the Stock Price." *New York Times* online, September 8. www.nytimes.com.

"As Funds Gain, Scandal Concerns Fade." (2004). *Houston Chronicle*, January 26, D3.

Backman, M. (1999). *Asian Eclipse*. Singapore: John Wiley & Sons.

Baker, D. and McArthur, T. (2009). "The Value of the 'Too Big to Fail' Bank Subsidy." Center for Economic and Policy Research Issue Brief. September www.cepr.net/documents/publications/too-big-to-fail-2009-09.pdf.

Baker, J., Conrad, C., Cudahy, C. and Willyard, J. (2009). "The Devil in Disguise: Merck, the FDA, and the VIOXX Recall," in Heath, Toth, and Waymer, eds., *Rhetorical and Critical Perspectives on Public Relations II*. New York: Routledge.

Barker, E., ed. and trans. (1976). *The Politics of Aristotle*. London: Oxford University Press.

Barton, L. (2001). *Crisis in Organizations, II*. Cincinnati, OH: South-Western.

Baucus, M. and Baucus, D. (1997). "Paying the Piper." *Academy of Management Journal* 40: 129–151.

Baumgartner, F. and Jones, B. (1983). *Agendas and Instability in American Politics*. Chicago: University of Chicago Press.

Baumgartner, F. and Leech, B. (1998). *Basic Interests*. Princeton, NJ: Princeton University Press.

Baumgartner, F., Berry, J., Jojracki, M., Kimball, D. and Leech, B. (2009). *Lobbying and Policy Change*. Chicago: University of Chicago Press.

Benoit, W.L. (1995). *Accounts, Excuses, and Apologies*. Albany, NY: SUNY Press.

Bernanke, B. (2010). "Bernanke: 'Too-Big-to-Fail' Must Be Fixed." *CBS News* online, September 2. www.cbsnews.com/stories/2010/09/02/business/main6829076.shtml.

"Bigger Than Enron." (2001). *Frontline* [Television broadcast]. June 28. Boston: WGBH. www.pbs.org.

Black, W. (2005). *The Best Way to Rob a Bank Is to Own One*. Austin: University of Texas Press.

Blalock, D. (1996). "Workplace Ethics Take a Vacation," *Houston Chronicle*, March 31, D3.

Blasi, J.R. and Kruse, D.L. (2002). *In the Company of Owners*. New York: Basic Books.

Bogle, J. (2002). "Interview with Bill Moyers." *NOW*, July 19. www.pbs.org.

Botan, C. and Taylor, M. (2004). "Public Relations." *Journal of Communication* 54: 645–661.

Brinson, S. and Benoit, W. (1999). "The Tarnished Star." *Management Communication Quarterly* 12: 483–510.

Bruner, R. and Carr, S. (2009). *The Panic of 1907*. New York: John Wiley.

Bryant, S. (1996). "Texaco Initiates Scholarship Program to Help Minorities." *Houston Chronicle*, November 12, 17A.

Bryce, R. (2002). *Pipe Dreams*. New York: Public Affairs Press.

Buffett, W.E. (2002). "Who Really Cooks the Books?" *New York Times* online, July 24. www.nytimes.com.

Burns, M. (2010). "An Unprecedented 10-Year Study's Surprising Verdict." *Miller-McCune*, September–October, 62-67.

Cadette, W. (2002). "How Stock Options Lead to Scandal." *New York Times* online, July 12. www.nytimes.com.

"Calpers Sues the Big Board." (2003). *New York Times* online, December 17. www.nytimes.com.

Chan, J. (2010). "U.S. Faults Regulators Over a Bank." *New York Times* online, April 11. www.nytimes.com/2010/04/12/business/12wamu.html.

Cheney, G., Lair, D., Ritz, D. and Kendall, B. (2010). *Just a Job?* New York: Oxford University Press.

Child, J. (1974). "Managerial and Organizational Factors Associated With Company Performance." *Journal of Management Studies* 11: 13–27.

Christiansen, A. and Hanson, J. (1996). "Comedy as Cure for Tragedy." *Quarterly Journal of Speech* 82: 157–170.

Cohen, J.R. (2002). "Legislating Apology." *University of Cincinnati Law Review* 70: 101–122.

Conrad, C. (1993). "The Ethical Nexus," in Conrad, ed., *The Ethical Nexus*. Norwood, NJ: Ablex.

Conrad, C. (2003). "Stemming the Tide." *Organization* 10: 549–560.

Conrad, C. (2004). "The Illusion of Reform." *Rhetoric and Public Affairs* 7: 311–338.

Conrad, C. (2011). *Organizational Rhetoric*. London: Polity Press.

Conrad, C. and McIntush, H.G. (2003). "Communication, Structure and Health Care Policymaking," in Thompson, Dorsey, Miller and Parrott, eds., *Handbook of Health Communication*. Hillsdale, NJ: Lawrence Erlbaum.

Coombs, W.T. (2007). *Ongoing Crisis Communication*. Los Angeles. CA: Sage.

Cottrell, A., Lawlor, M. and Wood, J., eds. (1995). *The Causes and Costs of Depository Institution Failures*. Boston: Kluwer Academic Publshers.

Crable, R. and Vibbert, S. (1983). "Mobil's Epideictic Advocacy." *Communication Monographs* 50: 380–396.

Cropsey, J. (2001). *Polity and Economy*. South Bend, IN: St. Augustine's Press.

Cummins, I. and Beaserit, J. (2005). *Shell Shock*. London: Mainstream.

Deetz, S. (1992). *Communication in the Age of Corporate Colonization*. Albany, NY: SUNY Press.

Deetz, S. (1995). *Transforming Communication, Transforming Business*. Cresskill, NJ: Hampton Press.

Diosonopolous, G. and Crable, R. (1988). "Definitional Hegemony as a Public Relations Strategy." *Central States Speech Journal* 39: 134–145.

Diosonopolous, G. and Goldzwig, S. (1992). "The Atomic Power Industry and the NEW Woman," in Toth and Heath, eds., *Rhetorical and Critical Approaches to Public Relations*. Hillsdale, NJ: Lawrence Erlbaum.

Eichenwald, K. (1996). "Texaco Reeling From Racial Scandal." *Houston Chronicle*, November 5, 1C.

Eichenwald, K. (2003). "In String of Corporate Troubles, Critics Focus on Boards' Failings." *New York Times* online, September 21. www.nytimes.com.

Eisenhower, D.D. (1961). "Farewell Address." www.americanrhetoric.com.

Elsbach, K. and Sutton, R. (1992). "Acquiring Organizational Legitimacy Through Illegitimate Actions." *Administrative Science Quarterly* 35: 699–738.

Farrell, C. (2002). "The Other Side of Adam Smith." *Business Week*, November 15. www.businessweek.com/bwdaily/dnflash/nov2002/nf20021115_2141.htm.

Farrell, R. and Goodnight, G.T. (1981). "Accidental Rhetoric." *Communication Monographs* 48: 271–300.

"Forum: Teaching Business Ethically" (2003). [Special issue]. *Management Communication Quarterly* 17: 126–164.

Fox, J. (2009). *The Myth of the Rational Market*. New York: Harper Business/HarperCollins.

Freeman, R. (1984). *Strategic Management*. Boston: Pitman.

Freeman, R.E. and Gilbert, D. (1988). *Corporate Strategy and the Search for Ethics*. Englewood Cliffs, NJ: Prentice Hall.

Friedman, M. (1962). *Capitalism and Freedom*. Chicago: University of Chicago Press.

Friedman, M. (1970). "The Social Responsibility of Business Is to Increase Profits." *New York Times Magazine*, September 13, 122–126.

Friedman, M. and Friedman, R. (1980). *Free to Choose*. San Diego, CA: Harcourt Brace and Company.

Friedman, T. (1999). *The Lexus and the Olive Tree.* New York: Farrar, Straus and Giroux.

Frooman, J. (1999). "Stakeholder Influence Strategies." *Academy of Management Review* 24: 191–205.

Fusaro, P. and Miller, R. (2002). *What Went Wrong at Enron.* New York: Wiley.

Gagne, M.L., Gavin, J.J. and Tully, G.J. (2005). "Assessing the Costs and Benefits of Ethics." *Business and Society Review* 11: 181–190.

Ganesh, S. (2007). "Sustainable Development Discourse and the Global Economy," in May, Cheney and Roper, eds., *The Debate Over Corporate Social Responsibility.* New York: Oxford University Press.

"Get Independents to Chair Boards of Funds, SEC Says." (2004). *Houston Chronicle*, January 15, B4.

Goodman, P. (2010). "Rule No. 1: Make Money by Avoiding Rules." *New York Times* online, May 21. www.nytimes.com/2010/05/23/weekinreview/23goodman.html.

Gordon, D. (1996). *Fat and Mean.* Ithaca, NY: Cornell University Press.

Gore, D. (2001). *Adam Smith's Rhetorical Sympathy.* Master's thesis, Texas A&M University.

Gorman, C. (1989). "Listen Here, Mr. Big!" *Time*, July 3, 40–45.

Grint, K. (2001). *The Arts of Leadership.* Oxford: Oxford University Press.

Grint, K. (2005). "Problems, Problems, Problems." *Human Relations* 58: 1467–1494.

Hall, B. and Jones, B. (1997). "Agenda Denial and Issue Containment in the Regulation of Financial Securities," in Cobb and Ross, eds., *Cultural Strategies of Agenda Denial.* Lawrence: University of Kansas Press.

Hambrick, D. (1994). "Top Management Groups," in Staw and Cummings, eds., *Research in Organizational Behavior*, vol. 15. Greenwich, CT: JAI Press.

Hambrick, D. and Mason, P. (1984). "Upper Echelons." *Academy of Management Review* 9: 193–206.

Hardin, G. (1968). "The Tragedy of the Commons." *Science*, December 13, 1243–1248.

Hartz, R. and Steger, T. (2010). "Heroes, Villains and 'Honourable Merchants': Narrative Change in the German Media Discourse on Corporate Governance." *Organization* 17: 767–785.

Hatcher, M. (2010). "40 Days of Emissions – but Who Knew?" *Houston Chronicle*, August 19, 1A.

Heath, R., Toth, E. and Waymer, D. (2009). *Rhetorical and Critical Approaches to Public Relations II.* New York: Routledge.

Herit, K.M. (2007). "Corporate Deception and Fraud," in May, Cheney and Roper, eds., *The Debate Over Corporate Social Responsibility.* New York: Oxford University Press.

Hiltzik, M. (2009). "Billions Are Spent to Defend 5,000 Jobs at Boeing C-17 Plant." *Los Angeles Times* online, October 8. www.latimes.com/hiltzik.

Hobbs, J. (1995). "Treachery by Any Other Name." *Management Communication Quarterly* 8: 323–346.

Hosmer, L. (1987). "The Institutionalization of Unethical Behavior." *Journal of Business Ethics* 6: 439–447.

Hwee Sim, P. and Seewald, N. (2003). "Reminder: CAPs Are for Listening." *Chemical Week* 165: 35–36.

Jackall, R. (1983). "Moral Mazes." *Harvard Business Review* 61 (September–October): 99–123.

Johnson, S. and Kwak, J. (2010). *13 Bankers.* New York: Pantheon.

Kaplan, D. (2004). "Fighting for Workers' Rights." *Houston Chronicle*, January 15, 1D.

Kellerman, B. (2006). "When Should a Leader Apologize and When Not?" *Harvard Business Review* 84: 72–81.

Kindleberger, C., Aliber, R. and Solow, R. (2009). *Maniacs, Panics, and Crashes*, 5th ed. New York: John Willey.

Kostova, T. and Zaheer, S. (1999). "Organizational Legitimacy Under Conditions of Complexity." *Academy of Management Review* 24: 64–81.

Krugman, P. (2008). *The Return of Depression Economics and the Crisis of 2008.* New York: W.W. Norton.

Krugman, P. (2010). "Bubbles and the Banks." *New York Times* online, January 8. www.nytimes.com/2010/01/08/opinion/08krugman.html.

Kuttner, R. (1996). *Everything for Sale?* New York: Random House.

Labaton, S. (2004). "Defying Election-Year Tradition, S.E.C. Draws Up a Busy Agenda." *New York Times* online, January 2. www.nytimes.com.

La Porta, R., Lopez-de-Silanes, F., Shleifer, A. and Vishny, R. (2003). "Investor Protection and Corporate Governance." *Journal of Financial Economics* 58: 3–27.

Leeper, R. (2001). "In Search of a Metatheory for Public Relations," in Heath, ed., *Handbook of Public Relations.* Thousand Oaks. CA: Sage.

Leonhardt, D. (2002). "Options Do Not Raise Performance, Study Finds." *New York Times* online, August 11. www.nytimes.com.

Leonhardt, D. (2011). "The Paradox of Corporate Taxes." *New York Times* online, February 1. www.nytimes.com/2011/02/02/business/economy/02leonhardt.

Lerach, W.S. (1995). "Testimony Before the Subcommittee on Telecommunications and Finance, House Committee on Commerce, Legislation on Securities Fraud Litigation (H.R. 10)." January 19. Washington, DC: Government Printing Office.

Levinthal, D. and March, J. (1993). "The Myopia of Learning." *Strategic Management Journal* 14: 95–112.

Levitt, A. (2002). *Take on the Street.* New York: Pantheon.

Lewis, L. (2005). "The Civil Society Sector." *Management Communication Quarterly* 19: 238–267.

Llewellyn, J. (2007). "Regulation," in May, Cheney and Roper, eds., *The Debate Over Corporate Social Responsibility*. New York: Oxford University Press.

Madrick, J. (2003). "A Theory on Corporate Greed." *New York Times* online, February 20. www.nytimes.com.

Mahon, J.F. and McGowan, R.A. (1997). "Making Professional Accounting Accountable," in Cobb and Ross, eds., *Cultural Strategies of Agenda Denial*. Lawrence: University of Kansas Press.

Marchand, R. (1998). *Creating the Corporate Soul*. Berkeley: University of California Press.

Marcus, A.A. and Goodman, R.S. (1991). "Victims and Shareholders." *Academy of Management Journal* 34: 284–305.

Marcus, A. and Goodman, R. (1998). "Victims and Shareholders." *Academy of Management Journal* 42: 479–485.

Martin, A. and Maynard, M. (2010). "For Bankers, Saying 'Sorry' Has Its Perils." *New York Times* online, January 13. www.nytimes.com/2010/01/13/business/13blame.html.

May, S., ed. (2006). *Case Studies in Organizational Communication: Ethical Perspectives and Practices*. Thousand Oaks, CA: Sage.

May, S. (2012). *Case Studies in Organizational Communication: Ethical Perspectives and Practices*, 2nd ed. Thousand Oaks, CA: Sage.

McGeehan, P. (2003a). "Top Executives' Lucrative Deals Tie the Hands That Pay Them." *New York Times* online, June 28. www.nytimes.com.

McGeehan, P. (2003b). "Quick, What's the Boss Making?" *New York Times* online, September 21. www.nytimes.com.

McMillan, J. (2007). "Why Corporate Social Responsibility? Why Now? How?" In May, Cheney and Roper, eds., *The Debate Over Corporate Social Responsibility*. New York: Oxford University Press.

Menn, J. (1996). "ADM Fine Criticized as Too Low." *Houston Chronicle*, December 1, C13.

Milne, R. (1995). "Mill Owner Says He'll Pay Workers." *Boston Globe*, December 15, B50.

Mosk, M. and Ferran, L. (2011). "The Boondoggle That Wouldn't Die." *ABC News* online, January 21. http://abcnews.go.com/Blotter/joint-strike-fighter-engine-boondoggle-die/story?id=12724248.

Muller, J. (1993). *Adam Smith in His Time and Ours*. Princeton, NJ: Princeton University Press.

Murphy, T. (2009). "Fine Unlikely to End Bogus Drug Marketing." *Houston Chronicle*, September 5, A20.

Norris, F. (2010). "A Baby Step Toward Rules on Bank Risk." *New York Times* online, September 16. www.nytimes.com/2010/09/17/business/17norris.html.

Oppel, R., Jr. (2003). "Senate Votes to Strengthen S.E.C.'s Hand." *New York Times* online, April 10. www.nytimes.com.

Palast, G. (2001). *The Best Democracy Money Can Buy*. New York: Plume.

"Panel on Economic Recovery and Job Creation" [Video]. (2002). Panel discussion at the President's Economic Forum, moderated by US Treasury Secretary Paul O'Neill, Baylor University, Waco, TX, August 13. www.c-spanvideo.org/program/171918-2.

Patterson, J., II and Allen, M.W. (1997). "Accounting for Your Actions." *Journal of Applied Communication Research* 25: 293–316.

Peters, J. (1995). "Publicity and Pain: Self-Abstraction in Adam Smith's Theory of Moral Sentiments." *Public Culture* 7: 657–684.

Peterson, T.R. and Norton, T. (2007). "Discourses of Sustainability in Today's Public Sphere," in May, Cheney and Roper, eds., *The Debate Over Corporate Social Responsibility*. New York: Oxford University Press.

Posner, R. (2009). *A Failure of Capitalism*. Cambridge, MA: Harvard University Press.

Posner, R. (2010). *The Crisis of Capitalist Democracy*. Cambridge, MA: Harvard University Press.

Potter, W.M. (1992). "The Environment of the Oil Company," in Toth and Heath, eds., *Rhetorical and Critical Approaches to Public Relations*. Hillsdale, NJ: Lawrence Erlbaum.

Powers, M. and Laughlin, R. (1992). "Critical Theory and Accounting," in Alvesson and Willmott, eds., *Critical Management Studies*. London: Sage.

PriceWaterhouseCoopers. (2003). *6th Annual Global CEO Survey*. www.pwc.com/extweb/service.nsf/docid/d0c36bf56dbfd3ba8526d890080e377.

Rochlin, S., Witter, K., Monaghan, P. and Murray, V. (2005). "Putting the Corporate into Corporate Responsibility." *Accountability Forum* 5: 5–13.

Roslender, R. (1992). *Sociological Perspectives on Modern Accountancy*. London: Routledge.

Rowland, R. and Jerome, A. (2004). "On Organizational Apologia." *Communication Theory* 14: 191–211.

Rowland, R. and Womack, D. (1985). "Aristotle's View of Ethical Rhetoric." *Rhetoric Society Quarterly* 15: 13–31.

Roy, W. (1997). *Socializing Capital*. Princeton, NJ: Princeton University Press.

Schouten, F. (2011). "Budget Concessions Under Fire." *USA Today*, April 13, 5A.

Scott, W.G. and Hart, D.K. (1979). *Organizational America*. Boston: Houghton Mifflin.

Scott, W.G. and Hart, D.K. (1989). *Organizational Values in America*. New Brunswick, NJ: Transaction.

"SEC Turned Timid as Corruption Became More Complex." (2003). *Houston Chronicle*, December 26, D4.

Seeger, M. (1986). "C.E.O. Performances." *Southern Speech Communication Journal* 52: 52–68.

Seeger, M. (1992). "Responsibility in Organizational Communication," in Jaska, ed., *Proceedings of the National Communication Association Ethics Conference*. Annandale, VA: National Communication Association.

Seeger, M. and Hipfel, S. (2007). "Legal versus Ethical Arguments," in May, Cheney and Roper, eds., *The Debate Over Corporate Social Responsibility*. New York: Oxford University Press.

Seeger, M. and Ulmer, R. (2002). "A Post-Crisis Discourse of Renewal." *Journal of Applied Communication Research* 30: 126–142.

Seligman, J. (1994). "The Merits Do Matter." *Harvard Law Review* 108: 438–457.

Shanker, T. (2010). "Pentagon Plans Steps to Reduce Budget and Jobs." *New York Times* online, August 9. www.nytimes.com/2010/08/10/us/10gates.html.

Simpson, W.G. and Kohers, T. (2002). "The Link Between Corporate Social and Financial Performance." *Journal of Business Ethics* 35: 97–109.

Sims, R. (1992). "The Challenge of Ethical Behavior in Organizations." *Journal of Business Ethics* 11: 501–513.

Sixel, L.M. (1996). "Workplace Racism Cases Hard to Win." Houston *Chronicle*, November 13, 1C.

Soros, G. (1998). *The Crisis of Global Capitalism*. New York: Public Affairs Press.

Soros, G. (2000). *The Open Society*. New York: Public Affairs.

"Spitzer Threatens to Sue U.S. Regulator Over Loan Exemption." (2003). *New York Times* online, December 11. www.nytimes.com.

Staw, B. and Ross, J. (1980). "Commitment in an Experimenting Society." *Journal of Applied Psychology* 65: 249–260.

Steiner, G.A. and Steiner, J.F. (2005). *Business, Government, and Society*, 11th ed. New York: McGraw-Hill.

Stern, P. (1992). *Still the Best Congress Money Can Buy*. Chicago, IL: Regnery.

Stiglitz, G. (2002). *Globalization and Its Discontents*. New York: W.W. Norton.

Stone, D. (1997). *Policy Paradox*. New York: W.W. Norton.

Strunk, N. and Case, F. (1988). *Where Deregulation Went Wrong*. New York: United States League of Savings Associations.

Stutts, N. and Barker, R. (1999). "The Use of Narrative Paradigm Theory in Assessing Audience Value Conflict in Image Advertising." *Management Communication Quarterly* 13: 209–244.

Summers, L. (2000). "International Financial Crises." *American Economic Review Papers and Proceedings* 90: 1–16.

Thomas, L. (2003). "Memo Shows MFS Funds Let Favored Clients Trade When Others Couldn't." *New York Times* online, December 9. www.nytimes.com.

Thompson, J. (1967). *Organizations in Action*. New York: McGraw-Hill.

Toffler, B.E. (1986). *Tough Choices*. New York: John Wiley.

Toth, E.L. and Heath, R., eds. (1992). *Rhetorical and Critical Approaches to Public Relations*. New York: Praeger.

"Toyota Pays Fine Over Recall." (2010). *Houston Chronicle*, May 19, D1.

Ulmer, R. (2000). "Effective Crisis Management Through Established Stakeholder Relationships." *Management Communication Quarterly* 14: 590–615.

Walsh, S. (1996). "Plaintiffs Say Texaco Tough in Bias Cases." *Houston Chronicle*, November 14, 1C.

Weaver, G., Trevino, L.K. and Cochran, P. (1999). "Integrated and Decoupled Corporate Social Performance." *Academy of Management Journal* 42: 539–552.

Weisman, R. (2004). "Harvard Digs Deeper on Ethics." *Houston Chronicle*, January 4, 3D.

Werhane, P. (1991). *Adam Smith and his Legacy for Modern Capitalism*. New York: Oxford University Press.

Whalen, G. (2007). "Corporate Social Responsibility in Asia," in May, Cheney and Roper, eds., *The Debate Over Corporate Social Responsibility*. New York: Oxford University Press.

"Who Won Big in the Financial Bill." (2010). *New York Times* online, July 15. www.nytimes.com/2010/7/15/who-won-big-in-the-financial-bill.html.

Willers, B. (1994). "Sustainable Development." *Conservation Biology* 8: 1146.

Williams, G. (2001). "Turmoil at the Red Cross." *Chronicle of Philanthropy*, November 1.

Wilson, J.Q. (1974). "The Politics of Regulation," in McKie, ed., *Social Responsibility and the Business Predicament*. Washington, DC: Brookings Institution.

Wyatt, E. (2010). "Judge Accepts Citigroup's Settlement with the S.E.C." *New York Times* online, September 24. www.nytimes.com.

Zadek, S. (2004). "The Path to Corporate Social Responsibilty." *Harvard Business Review* 82: 124–134.

Zoller, H. (2009). "Narratives of Corporate Change," in Dutta and Harter, eds., *Communicating for Social Impact*. Cresskill, NJ: Hampton Press.

Zoller, H. and Tener, M. (2010). "Corporate Proactivity as a Discursive Fiction." *Management Communication Quarterly* 24: 391–418.

POSTSCRIPT TO UNIT III

EPILOGUE

The past 20 years have been dominated by a realization that our current times are both very different than they were a generation ago and even less like they will be a generation from now. As in all times of social and cultural change, the 1990s and early 2000s have witnessed a great deal of anxiety and controversy about the directions that societies, economies, and organizations will take. It is clear that people now work in closer proximity to one another than ever before. Increased proximity comes in the forms of a diverse workforce and a global economy. Some of the strategies of organizing that were discussed in Unit II may soon become obsolete; others may experience a resurgence. Alternative forms of organizing have emerged and will continue to do so. They will dominate some sectors of the global economy for a time and then be eclipsed by others. Each of the challenges described in Unit III will become more relevant and more pronounced. Technological change will continue, organizational power and politics will become more complex, decision making will be more difficult, conflict management will be more important, and diversity and corporate ethics will be increasingly important issues.

It also is clear that social and organizational power relationships continue to privilege the interests of some groups while failing to meet even the minimal, basic needs of others. Indeed, with globalization and worldwide deregulation, these gaps seem to be growing rapidly. None of this is especially surprising, because it results from the fundamental tensions described in Chapters 1 and 2. The problem – and the challenge – is that societies and their organizations can deal with these fundamental tensions in one of two ways. They can focus on *individuality*, domination, and control, and become more competitive and divided, with one group of members turning against another and magnifying long-held antagonisms based on organizational rank, nationality, class, race, ethnicity, and gender.

Strategic Organizational Communication: In a Global Economy, Seventh Edition.
Charles Conrad and Marshall Scott Poole.

Or they can focus on creating a meaningful *global community* that represents the interests of multiple stakeholders and meets the needs of all of its members. But "societies" and "organizations" do not make choices – people do. Human beings are, after all, choice-making beings. It is *our* choices that will determine the road our society and our organizations take. The strategies that *all of us* choose will determine the kind of organizations that *we* live in for the rest of our lives, and the kind of society that *we* will create for ourselves and for our children. Make good choices.

INDEX

Strategic Organizational Communication: In a Global Economy, Seventh Edition.
Charles Conrad and Marshall Scott Poole.